THE MACROECONOMY OF IRELAND

Fourth Edition

Anthony J. Leddin
University of Limerick

Brendan M. Walsh
University College, Dublin

Gill & Macmillan

Gill & Macmillan Ltd

Goldenbridge

Dublin 8

with associated companies throughout the world

© Anthony J. Leddin and Brendan M. Walsh, 1990, 1992, 1995, 1998

0 7171 2671 4

Index compiled by Helen Litton

www.gillmacmillan.ie

Technical note

The text of this book was composed by the authors using Windows 97. The drawings
were generated on Micrografx software and the graphs on Excel and Prism. The final
document was brought to camera ready copy using the facilities of the University of
Limerick.

Contents

Chapter 3   **Introduction to the**

                Theory of Income Determination

Chapter 6   Fiscal Policy and the National Debt

Chapter 7   The Public Finances

Chapter 8   Fiscal Policy in Ireland

Chapter 9   Money and Banking and the History of the Irish Monetary System

Chapter 16   Fixed Exchange Rate Systems: Theory and History

Chapter 17   EMS and the Push for a

Single European Currency

Chapter 18   Inflation and Interest Rates

in Open Economies

Chapter 19   Some Aspects of International Financial Markets

Chapter 20   The Open Economy Monetary Model

Chapter 21 The Adjustment of the Open Economy in the Short Run

Chapter 22 Irish Exchange Rate Policy from the Sterling Link to EMU

**Chapter 23   The European Central Bank
and Economic Policy in EMU**

Chapter 24   Will Membership of EMU be Good for Ireland ?

Chapter 1

Introduction to Macroeconomics

1.1   Introduction

*Macro*economics is concerned with the study of the economy as a whole. It deals with topics such as the growth of national output and income, the level of unemployment, the rate of inflation, interest and exchange rates. *Micro*economics, on the other hand, is concerned with the behaviour of individual firms and households, and relative prices. The two branches of economics are not rigidly segregated. In many areas, macroeconomics draws on the analytical techniques developed by microeconomics. The main goals of macroeconomic policy are to achieve:

- An improvement in the *standard of living* of the population;
- A low *unemployment rate*;
- A low *inflation rate* is also desirable in itself and because it may help promote the other two objectives.

These three objectives have to be achieved subject to two important constraints:

- Maintaining a long-run balance in the *public finances* and the *balance of payments*.

In this chapter we discuss these objectives and the associated constraints and the relationship between them.

1.2   A Rising Standard of Living

Economics is above all concerned with the factors that contribute to improving people's well-being over the long run. In order to track the performance of an economy over time and to compare it with other economies, we have to measure the output of all the goods and services being produced. This is no easy feat. Imagine that you have a bird's eye view of Ireland. Think of the hundreds of thousands of different goods and services produced in the country. If we add together the value of all the goods and services produced in the country over the course of a year, we obtain the value of the total output of the economy. One measure of this is known as *Gross National Product* (GNP).[1]

---

1. The CSO publishes two measures of GNP, which we discuss in detail in Chapter 4. We have used the average of the two series. Our data was obtained from the Department of Finance's *Databank of Economic*

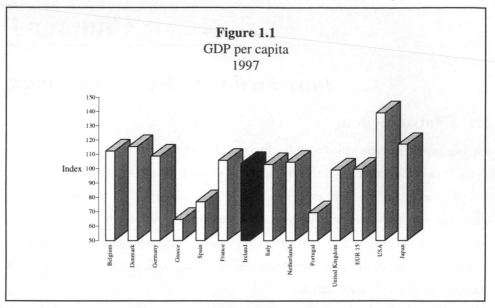

Figure 1.1
GDP per capita
1997

The Central Statistics Office (CSO) estimates that GNP in Ireland in 1998 was IR£43,960 million or IR£12,211 per person (per capita GNP). Closely related to GNP is the concept of *National Income*. This is the total amount of income received by residents in the country. The nation's output is closely linked to the nation's income. If a person works harder at her job and produces more goods, then she would expect her income to rise accordingly. The same is true at national level: the more the nation produces, the more income is generated. We stated that a principal objective of macroeconomics is to find ways of increasing GNP and national income.

If this objective is achieved, then the standard of living of the population is raised. There is more income for the country as a whole to use, and in principle this means that everyone could be made better off.

Figure 1.1 shows per capita Gross Domestic Product (GDP)[2] for selected countries in 1997. The US, Japan and Denmark are among the richest countries in the world. The standard of living in Ireland is slightly above the average of the European Union 15 (EU15) and is well ahead of Spain, Portugal and Greece.[3]

Time Series (1987) and *National Income and Expenditure*, published by the CSO. A major revision to the data for the years since 1986 affects the continuity of the series.

2. We shall discuss the concept of GDP, which is closely related to GNP, in Chapter 4.

3. In making international comparisons, it is necessary to convert domestic currencies into a common currency (usually the US dollar). However, exchange rates fluctuate widely and the data from different countries will vary according to what exchange rate is used. For example, at the beginning of 1995 an Irish pound was worth

Table 1.1

Calculating nominal and real GNP

Hypothetical example where the only good produced is bicycles.

	Real GNP	*×*	*Price level (£)*	*=*	*Nominal GNP (£)*
	Quantity of bicycles produced	*×*	*Price of bicycles*	*=*	*Value of bicycles produced*
1961	3,000	×	10	=	30,000
1998	5,000	×	120	=	600,000

It is important to emphasise at the outset that there are some serious problems encountered in calculating the nation's output and there are major limitations in using it as a measure of welfare or the standard of living. These issues are examined in some detail in Chapter 4.

1.3   Real Growth and Inflation

GNP measures the level of output for a given year. We are also interested in how GNP changes from year to year. In this context, it is important to distinguish between changes in nominal and real GNP. Nominal GNP is equal to real GNP multiplied by the price level. An increase in real GNP means that a greater volume or quantity of goods has been produced. In terms of improving the country's standard of living, it is the change in the volume or real GNP that matters. Also, as explained in section 1.5 below, changes in real GNP are closely associated with changes in both employment and unemployment.

Consider the hypothetical data in Table 1.1. Suppose that bicycles are the only good produced in the economy. In 1961, 3,000 bicycles were produced at a price of £10 each. Hence nominal GNP was £30,000. By 1998, production has increased to 5,000 bicycles at a price of £120 each. Nominal output in 1998 has increased to £600,000.

$1.62, but by February 1998 it had fallen to $1.37. If these exchange rates were used to calculate the level of Irish GDP in dollars, it would be implied that we were 15 per cent worse off in 1998 than in 1995. In order to avoid misleading comparisons of this type, the OECD has calculated what are called *purchasing power parity* (PPP) exchange rates. The idea behind PPP is that exchange rates should reflect the relative cost of a bundle of goods and services in the different countries. We shall discuss this topic in greater detail in later chapters.

3

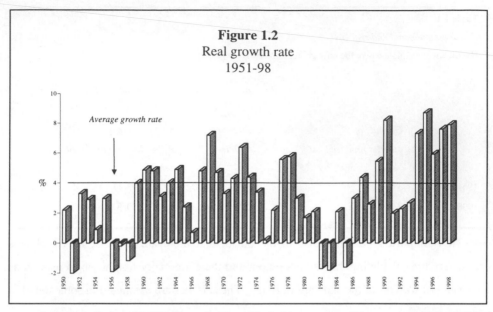

Figure 1.2
Real growth rate
1951-98

In calculating real GNP, the price level is held constant. Hence, real GNP in 1998 (based on 1961 prices) is £50,000 (5,000 × £10). Real output has increased by 66 per cent over the period 1961 to 1998. The important point is that improvements in a country's standard of living only come about through changes in real GNP. If increases in nominal GNP are due to price increases only, people are not becoming any better off.

The real growth rate measures the percentage change in real GNP from one year to the next. A high and stable rate of economic growth is one of the principal goals of macroeconomic policy.

1.4 The Business Cycle

Figure 1.2 maps out the real growth rate in Irish GNP for each year from 1950 to 1998. The variability of the real growth rate over time is referred to as the *business cycle*. It can be seen that the Irish growth rate has fluctuated widely from year to year. The real growth rate was very high in the 1960s, early 1970s and the 1990s but was low or even negative in the mid-1980s. In fact, the Irish economy has gone through much wider swings from boom to bust than most other countries since the post-war years. However, the upward trend in the growth rate is clear, as is the fact that since 1993 the Irish economy has been growing considerably faster that its trend growth rate.

The following terms are useful when describing the business cycle. A *peak* describes the upper turning point, and a *trough* is the lower turning point. A downturn in the business cycle is referred to as a *contraction* in output, and an increase in the growth rate is referred to as an *expansion*. In the US, if a contraction lasts for two or more consecutive calendar quarters, the economy is said to be in a *recession*. If a recession is prolonged and deep, it may be called a *depression*. The distinction between recession and depression is not always clear cut. President Harry S. Truman remarked that a recession was when your neighbour was out of work and a depression was when you were out of work!

Importance of the business cycle The business cycle is crucially important as it acts as a barometer of business activity. During periods of rapid growth, firms find that sales rise and order books fill up. In periods of slow growth or decline, sales fall and unsold stocks accumulate. Because of their importance for business, firms are willing to pay a lot of money for economic forecasts. If slow growth is predicted, firms will "tighten the belt" and adopt policies to weather the storm. They will postpone investment plans, cut back production and reduce the size of their workforce. If, on the other hand, a high growth rate is expected, they will contemplate investing in new machinery and hire additional workers so as to be able to meet the demand for their product as the economy expands.

Note that if the economy were to grow at a steady 3.5 per cent per annum, real output would double every twenty years. Each successive generation would be more than twice as well off as the preceding one. In fact, real income per person in Ireland is now more than double what it was at the beginning of the 1960s. Such is the power of compound interest!

Potential GNP

One of the main goals of macroeconomics is to increase real GNP and raise the standard of living in the country. In terms of the business cycle, the objective is to smooth out booms and recessions and maintain a stable level of economic activity. In this regard it is helpful to introduce the concept of potential GNP. Potential GNP is that level of output that could be produced given the state of technology and the size of the labour force, without increasing prices in the economy.[4] It is sometimes referred to as full employment GNP. As the size and average educational level of the labour force increases, and new

4. For a discussion of Irish potential GNP, see Geoff Kenny, "Economic Growth in Ireland: Sources, Potential and Inflation", Central Bank of Ireland, *Quarterly Bulletin*, Autumn 1996.

technology is introduced, potential GNP grows over time. It is reasonable to assume that the growth rate of potential GNP in Ireland is about 4 per cent per annum.

A line representing the growth rate of potential GNP 4 per cent is included in Figure 1.2. When the actual growth rate exceeds the potential (long-run average) growth rate, the economy is booming. There is upward pressure on wages and prices. Overheating encourages firms to raise prices. The distance from the actual GNP line to the potential GNP line is referred to as the inflation gap. One of the remarkable achievements of the Irish economy in recent years has been its ability to sustain a growth rate that is almost double its long-run average while containing inflation to a very low rate.

If the actual growth rate falls below potential GNP, unemployment will tend to rise. The economy is operating below capacity and, as stocks build up, firms cut production and lay off workers. The distance from the actual GNP line to the potential GNP line is known as the *output* (or *unemployment) gap*. Good macroeconomic management avoids increasing prices on the one hand and excessive unemployment on the other, by keeping the actual growth rate as close as possible to the potential GNP line.

1.5 Unemployment

Although unemployment is a topic of grave public concern, its definition and measurement are fraught with difficulties. The general principle is that a person is regarded as being unemployed if *he or she is looking for work and willing to accept a job at the going wage rate for the type of work that he or she is qualified to do*. If someone is only casually looking for a job or holding out until a suitable position with a high wage becomes available, then they may not be classified as unemployed.

The *labour force* is defined as the sum of the numbers employed and unemployed:

Labour force = employed + unemployed

The unemployment *rate* is defined as the number unemployed as a percentage of the labour force:

Unemployment rate = unemployed/labour force

In 1997 the Irish labour force totalled 1,539,000, of whom 1,379,900 were employed and 159,000 unemployed. The unemployment rate was therefore 10.3 per cent.

Note:

There are two principal measures of unemployment in Ireland. The first is a survey of households called the *Labour Force Survey*. The second is the *Live Register*, which records the number of people registered for

6

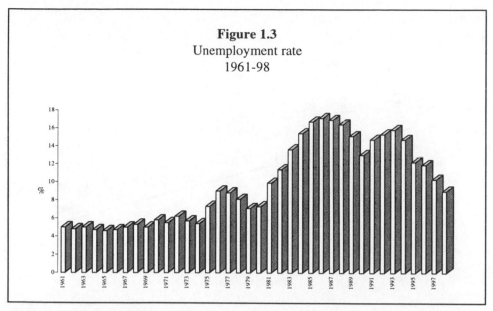

Figure 1.3
Unemployment rate
1961-98

unemployment benefits and assistance. In January 1997 the number registered as unemployed was 262,400, compared to 159,000 unemployed in the Labour Force Survey. The data in this chapter are based on International Labour Office (ILO) definitions used in the Labour Force Survey. We discuss the differences between these two sources in Chapter 14.

Figure 1.3 shows the unemployment rate in Ireland from 1961 to 1998. Until the mid-1970s it remained between 4 and 6 per cent. However, it rose to 9 per cent in 1976 and to 17.5 per cent in 1987 as the rate of economic growth slowed. However, due to rapid growth in the 1990s, the unemployment rate declined to 10.3 per cent in 1997. The unemployment rate in Japan is only 3.5 per cent compared to 22.5 per cent in Spain. The Irish rate is only slightly above the average for the 15 countries of the European Community (EUR 15).

The natural rate of unemployment

Earlier in this chapter we introduced the concept of potential GNP or full employment GNP. The unemployment rate associated with potential GNP may be referred to as the *natural rate of unemployment*. The natural rate is that level of unemployment that reflects the friction in the labour market. If the economy is at the natural rate of unemployment, the labour market may be said to be in equilibrium. In the 1970s the natural rate of unemployment could be taken to be approximately 5 per cent. However, since then the natural rate has undoubtedly increased. Economists now disagree on what constitutes

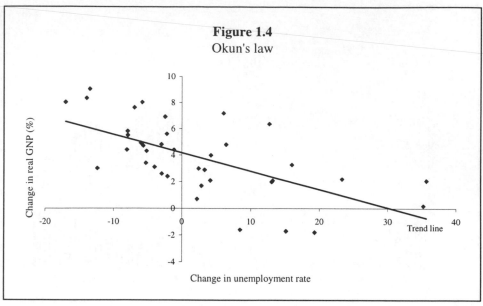

Figure 1.4
Okun's law

Change in real GNP (%)

Change in unemployment rate

Trend line

"equilibrium" or natural rate of unemployment. The task is complicated by the openness of the Irish labour market and the importance of emigration, as well as by the persistence of higher unemployment after each successive recession. This makes it difficult to identify a precise policy target for unemployment.

Okun's law

Economic growth is not an end in itself, but a means towards improving the well-being of the population. We have already emphasised how the growth of real GNP raises real living standards. But it is important also to consider how the fruits of this economic growth are distributed. A high unemployment rate combined with rapid growth of GNP would not be a very satisfactory situation. Fortunately, however, a growing GNP tends to reduce unemployment. The link between the two variables may be seen from a comparison of Figures 1.2 and 1.3, which suggests that there has been a relationship between cyclical swings in the level of output and the rate of unemployment in Ireland. During periods of rapid growth, the 1960s, 1977-79 and the 1990s, for example, more jobs were created and this led to a fall in unemployment. Conversely, during periods when output is falling, such as the mid-1980s, employment falls and unemployment rises.

The relationship between growth and unemployment can be examined more formally by plotting the percentage change in real GNP against the change in the unemployment rate. Figure 1.4 shows the relationship between these two variables from

1961 to 1997. Each point shows the growth/unemployment combination for that year. The line running through the scatter, the regression line, summarises this relationship. The line slopes downwards, indicating that as the growth rate increases, the unemployment rate falls, and vice versa. The American economist Arthur Okun first investigated this relationship between growth and unemployment. He estimated that in the United States for every 4 per cent increase in real GNP, the unemployment rate fell by one percentage point. This relationship has become known as Okun's law.

Because of emigration and other factors, the association between the growth of GNP and changes in the rate of unemployment is not as close in Ireland as it is in the US. Nevertheless it is important to note that the macroeconomic objectives of growth and unemployment are closely associated. If the policy maker is successful in maintaining actual GNP close to potential GNP, then over time the unemployment rate should converge to its natural rate.

Costs of unemployment

The costs of unemployment to individuals and society are very serious.

- Most unemployed people feel a low level of self-esteem and this can lead to personal stress and suffering.[5]
- The unemployed suffer a loss of income.[6] In developed countries this loss is shared between the employed and unemployed through transfer payments such as unemployment benefits, which are paid for by taxes levied on the working population. However, these transfers do not make up all of the income lost through unemployment, and as a result there is a close relationship between the rate of unemployment and the incidence of poverty in a country.
- The budgetary implications of high unemployment are very serious. In 1997 social welfare spending on unemployment support amounted to just over £1 billion, equal to

5. A study found that the unemployed were five times more likely to suffer high levels of psychological distress than people at work, and that this distress increased with the duration of unemployment: see Christopher Whelan, Damien Hannan and Sean Creighton, *Unemployment, Poverty and Psychological Distress*, Economic and Social Research Institute, General Research Paper, No. 150, January 1991.

6. For data on the Irish situation, see T. Callen, B. Knolling, B. W. Whelan, D. F. Hannan with S. Creighton, *Poverty, Income and Welfare in Ireland*, Economic and Social Research Institute, General Research Series, Paper No. 146, September 1989, and the collection of papers published in *The Economic and Social Review*, Vol. 20, No. 4, July 1989.

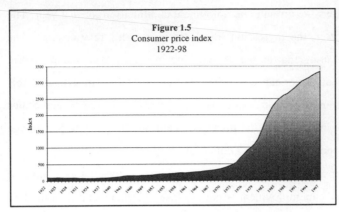

Figure 1.5
Consumer price index
1922-98

25 per cent of all social welfare spending, or 8.6 per cent of current government expenditure. In addition, high unemployment results in a loss of tax revenue. A country with a high rate of unemployment therefore faces the unpalatable prospect of having to impose a heavy tax burden on the employed population. As we shall see, a heavy burden of taxation makes it harder to alleviate the unemployment problem.

- The national economy loses the output and income that would be produced if the unemployed could find work. The extra output that could be produced by those looking for work in Ireland today would increase GNP by several billion pounds.

Types of unemployment

It is customary to talk about different types of unemployment, even though it is never possible to identify who falls into each category.

Frictional unemployment   In a dynamic economy people's preferences or tastes are ever changing, new technologies are constantly being introduced and relative prices vary. As a consequence, some firms go out of business, while others open up. There are always people losing their jobs, switching between one job and another, and entering and leaving the labour force. Unemployment that arises because of changes or friction in particular markets is referred to as frictional unemployment. A particular type of frictional unemployment is seasonal unemployment. Some industries, such as tourism and fishing, are seasonal in nature. During the off-season, people engaged in these industries become temporarily unemployed.

Cyclical unemployment   During the contractionary phase of the business cycle, firms lay off workers and unemployment rises. In principle, many of these workers should be hired back during the recovery phase of the business cycle. This is by far the most serious form of unemployment.

10

Structural unemployment Structural unemployment arises when there is a permanent decline in employment in the industries located in a particular region or country. If enough people do not migrate between regions there will be growing disparities between rates of unemployment. Jobs may be available in one region while there is a high level of unemployment in another region. Similarly, job vacancies may not match the skills or the occupations of the unemployed. There may be job vacancies for carpenters, but this will do little to alleviate unemployment among coal-miners. Cyclical unemployment can turn into structural unemployment if the recession is prolonged or the recovery weak.

1.6   Inflation

Microeconomics is concerned with the relative prices of goods and services. Macroeconomics, on the other hand, is concerned with the *aggregate* price level. This is measured using a price index, which is a weighted average of the individual prices included in it. The most widely used price index in Ireland is the Consumer Price Index (CPI). To construct the CPI, the CSO collects the prices of 807 different goods and services every three months and averages them on the basis of their relative importance in the typical household budget.

Note:
The CSO uses the *Household Budget Survey* to ascertain consumers' expenditure patterns. Based on a sample of 7,705 private households around the country, the CSO calculates expenditure (the weight) on categories such as food, drink, clothing, fuel, housing and so on.

These expenditure shares are known as the weights of the price index. The value of the index in the base year is set equal to 100. Changes in the index are then monitored relative to the base year. Figure 1.5 shows the CPI for Ireland for the period 1922 to 1998. The index increased significantly after the first oil crisis in 1974. Overall the index rose from 100 to 3,357, or by 3,257 per cent, over this 75 year period.

The annual *inflation rate* is defined as being equal to the percentage change in the price index over a year:

$$\text{Inflation rate} = [(P_t - P_{t-1})/P_{t-1}] \times 100$$

where P_t and P_{t-1} are the price indices in the current and previous years, respectively. Figure 1.6 displays the annual rate of inflation (measured by the CPI) since the formation of the state. There were periods of *deflation* or falling prices in the 1920s and 1930s, but

11

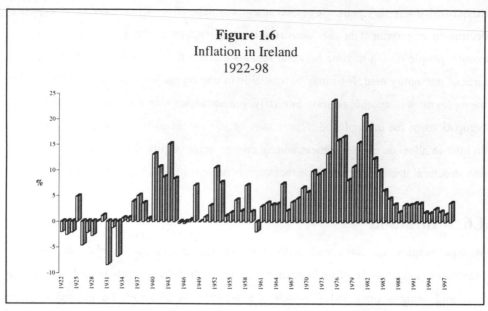

Figure 1.6
Inflation in Ireland
1922-98

since 1951 there was only one year (1959) when there was no inflation. High rates of inflation were recorded in the late 1930s, and there was a massive rise in prices between the late 1960s and the mid-1980s. Between 1970 and 1985 the annual average rate of inflation was over 13 per cent. After entry into the European Monetary System (EMS) in 1979, however, inflation subsided.

Effects of inflation

Should we worry about inflation? Should we be willing to squeeze inflation out of the economy if this entails high unemployment and slow growth? To answer these questions we need to consider the costs of inflation.

Value of money Inflation lowers the purchasing power of money and people living on fixed incomes (such as pensioners) suffer a decline in their living standards as a result. The long-run decline in the purchasing power of money as a result of inflation is illustrated by the fact that one pound (£1) in 1998 is only worth the equivalent of about three pence (£0.03) in 1922 money. In other words, prices have risen more than thirty-fold over this period. A wage of £3 a week in 1922 was the equivalent of £100 a week in today's money.

Note:

James Joyce's *Ulysses* takes place in Dublin on 16 June 1904. Readers will find numerous references to the cost of living at that time in the book. For example, a pint of milk and a pint of stout both cost 2*d*. The morning newspaper cost 1*d*. A domestic servant was paid £12 a year. (Remember that *d*. was the symbol for a penny and there were 240 pence in the pound in pre-decimal currency.) It is clear from these examples that in addition to the overall inflation since 1904, relative prices have also changed: a pint of beer now costs more than twice the cost of a pint of milk!

Over the longer run, people will tend to anticipate inflation and make appropriate adjustments. Interest rates will rise to reflect the loss of purchasing power of borrowed money. Incomes, including pensions, will be indexed to allow for future inflation. However, all of these adjustments take time and are rarely perfect, so that the unfair effects of inflation persist.

International competitiveness Inflation can have very serious implications for an economy's international competitive position, that is, the ability of domestic firms to compete with their international rivals. If, for example, Ireland has an inflation rate of 10 per cent while foreign inflation is only 5 per cent, Irish goods and services will be progressively priced out of both the domestic and export markets, unless the currency is allowed to depreciate. As a result, the real growth rate and employment will fall and unemployment will rise. The cost of excess inflation will be a loss of output and increased unemployment. It is therefore desirable that a country keeps its rate of inflation lower than that of its main trading partners. We shall return to this issue in the context of exchange rate policy in later chapters.

Dollarisation Once inflation becomes entrenched, the risk is that the rate of inflation will increase. This can lead to astronomical rates of inflation or hyperinflation, as experienced in Germany after World War I, in several Latin American countries during the 1980s and, most recently, in some of the former communist economies of Europe. Serbia probably holds the record, where inflation reached 100,000 per cent *a month* towards the end of 1993! The national currency, the Serbian dinar, became worthless. Faced with this situation, people will try to spend their money as fast as they can before rising prices further reduce its value. They will also seek to be paid in a stable currency, such as US dollars or German marks, while trying to use the local currency to pay their debts, especially their taxes! This response to inflation is known as "dollarisation". It is easy to see that hyperinflation undermines the economic life of a country and can destabilise it both socially and politically.

Menu and shoe leather costs Price increases impose costs on firms and shops, which have to reprint price lists etc. to convey the new prices to their customers. Customers have to go to some trouble to find out about price changes in order to keep up to date. Economists call these the "menu cost" of inflation. Also during periods of high inflation people will hold less currency. As a result they will make more trips to the bank to withdraw cash. This is referred to as the "shoe leather" costs of inflation. While these effects may not be very large, they are a nuisance.   It is also likely that if the rate of inflation varies over time, consumers may get confused by the way prices are changing. This reduces the efficiency of the price system.

Effects on income distribution   Inflation can result in a redistribution of income between different groups in society. Consider, for example, a person who saved and put money in a bank in Ireland in the 1970s. The interest received on the bank deposit (8 per cent in interest (before tax)) was less than the inflation rate (15 per cent). Savers were therefore penalised by inflation. Conversely, borrowers paid an interest rate that was lower than the inflation rate and benefited by going into debt and repaying the loan in money whose value had declined. Thus one effect of inflation has been to transfer real wealth from savers to borrowers. In general, inflation (when it is not fully anticipated) acts like a tax on the weaker groups in society – the elderly living on fixed incomes, people with small savings receiving only fixed-interest payments, and others who are not able to act to offset the effects of rising prices on their income and wealth.

Summary A low rate of inflation is considered desirable because it implies certainty and stability and facilitates economic growth. In the short run, there may be some trade-off between the objectives of high growth and low inflation. (An increase in growth may be achieved at the cost of higher inflation.) However, it is generally agreed that low, or even zero, inflation provides the best environment for promoting economic growth.

1.7 Macroeconomic Policy

Policy makers would like to raise incomes and achieve more rapid growth, but they are constrained in how effective they can be in this area. The constraints they face are two-fold, real and financial.

Real constraints A nation's income depends on what its population can produce and sell. The key *factors of production* are labour and capital. The labour force and its skills is by far the most important determinant of what a country produces. This labour force works with the country's capital stock. The more capital equipment available to each worker, and the more technically advanced this capital, the higher the value of what is produced.

Labour and capital act as constraints on the value of what an economy can produce. Put another way, the rate of growth of the economy's GNP depends on the rate at which these inputs are growing. Ireland has achieved a very rapid rate of growth of GNP in recent years because we have been able to increase employment by over 3 per cent a year – much higher than would be possible in other European countries. Moreover, the rising educational standard of the Irish workforce is also a key factor in maintaining a high growth rate. Finally, our stock of capital has been rising and its quality improving. There has been a large inflow of foreign investment, much of it in very high tech sectors. All these factors have combined to bring about a record growth in real GNP.

Financial constraints All too often policy makers are impatient with the achievements of their country in regard to economic growth. In order to increase their popularity they would like to see the economy growing faster. But they should be aware that they face important financial constraints when pursuing the goals of high growth and low unemployment. The first is the country's *fiscal deficit*, the second is its *balance of payments*. These can act as constraints on the authorities' freedom of action in trying to achieve growth and employment objectives.

The fiscal deficit From time immemorial governments have found it hard to live within their means and have been tempted to run fiscal deficits. This is particularly true in times of recession when output is stagnant and unemployment is rising. Governments come under pressure to increase spending in order to stimulate the economy.

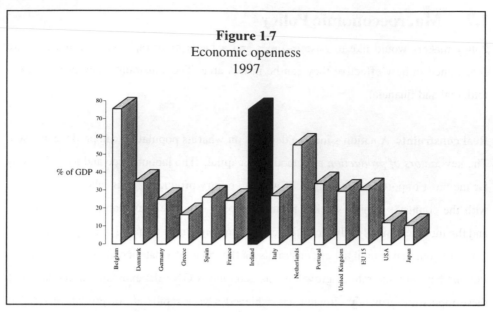

Figure 1.7
Economic openness
1997

% of GDP

Belgium, Denmark, Germany, Greece, Spain, France, Ireland, Italy, Netherlands, Portugal, United Kingdom, EU 15, USA, Japan

The fiscal deficit is the balance between government revenue (mainly from taxation) and government expenditure. Cumulative borrowings to finance the fiscal deficit lead to an increase in the *national debt.* The problem with the national debt is that it has to be serviced. Interest must be paid on the outstanding balances. Furthermore, with so much money committed to debt service, the burden of taxation is heavy and the government's ability to spend in other areas, such as education or job creation, is severely constrained. If the national debt does increase significantly then this will undermine the government's ability to intervene in the economy. A government may end up introducing policies to cut the fiscal deficit, regardless of the consequences for growth and unemployment, if the debt grows at an unsustainable rate. In a sense, a policy instrument (government expenditure) becomes a policy objective which ends up taking priority over the growth, unemployment and inflation objectives.

As we shall see in more detail in Chapter 7, this is essentially what happened in Ireland in the 1980s. In 1997 Ireland's national debt stood at IR£30,704 million. Of this, IR£8,531 million is *external* debt owed to foreigners or non-residents. In 1997 interest payments on the national debt amounted to £2,275 million or 46 per cent of the yield of income tax.

The balance of payments Another constraint arises due to the economy's relations with the rest of the world. Ireland is a classic example of a *small open economy* (SOE). In this context, "small" relates to the very small size of Irish firms in relation to the overall world

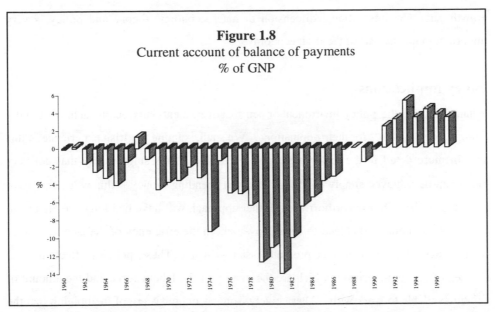

Figure 1.8
Current account of balance of payments
% of GNP

market, and "open" refers to the importance of international trade to the economy. One measure of "openness" is exports as a percentage of GDP. Figure 1.7 shows that using this yardstick, Ireland is considerably more open than Germany, the UK, the US and, perhaps surprisingly, Japan.

Because of the openness of the Irish economy we must pay particular attention to the country's balance of payments. The balance of payments is a record of a country's transactions with the rest of the world. Figure 1.8 shows the current account of the balance of payments (as a percentage of GDP) over the period 1960-98. Throughout the 1970s and 1980s, a very sizeable deficit (an excess of imports over exports) was recorded. However, in recent years the balance of payments has moved into a surplus (an excess of exports over imports) position.

In terms of macroeconomic objectives, a balance of payments deficit could lead to a depreciation of the exchange rate. Conversely, a balance of payments surplus can lead to an appreciation of the exchange rate. Without getting into details at this early stage, changes in the exchange rate can have far-reaching implications for the economy and in particular for the inflation rate.

This consideration imposes a constraint on the policy makers' ability to achieve the macroeconomic objectives. For example, a policy which increases the real growth rate could result in a rapid increase in imports and a balance of payments deficit. An associated depreciation of the exchange rate could increase inflation and undermine the growth rate. The international dimension of macroeconomic theory and policy is very important in an analysis of the Irish economy.

Policy implications

What, then, are the policy instruments open to governments anxious to achieve rapidly rising living standards for their populations? We shall examine the Irish experience in this area in more detail in the following chapter. Suffice at this stage to say that not very much can be achieved simply by the government spending money – this will either have to be raised through taxes or borrowed. Either approach will have bad long-run effects on the economy. Policies that lead to an improvement in the efficiency of the labour force or higher rates of investment can promote faster growth. These policies affect the real sources of economic growth, which are the quality of the labour force and the amount of capital available to work with. Alternatively, some economists are of the opinion that the best results will be achieved if the economy is left to itself. Market economies have proved remarkably capable of raising living standards and reducing poverty around the world. Centrally planned or socialistic economies have failed dismally to deliver remotely comparable results.

1.8 Summary

Looking back over the various charts in this chapter it can be seen that the Irish economy is currently in a very favourable position. The economy is experiencing fast growth, unemployment is falling and inflation remains subdued. In the background, there is a surplus on both the fiscal budget and the balance of payments. We have been one of the best performing economies in the OECD in the 1990s. Things were not always so good in Ireland. A glance at Figures 1.2 and 1.3 will show that during the depression of the mid-1980s unemployment reached unprecedented levels. A central issue in this book is to determine how best to avoid a recurrence of such a recession.

1.9   Conclusion

In this chapter we

- Introduced the main topics to be dealt with in a course on macroeconomics
- Outlined the concepts of gross national product (GNP), national income, unemployment and inflation

- Provided data on Irish national output, unemployment and inflation, and some international comparisons
- Discussed the principal goals of macroeconomic policy, which are to maintain over the long run a high rate of growth of real output and income and low rates of unemployment and inflation
- Discussed the costs associated with unemployment and inflation
- Discussed the manner in which the fiscal deficit and the balance of payments act as constraints on policy makers in a small open economy such as Ireland.

Data appendix

Year	Real GNP growth rate %	Unemployment rate %	Inflation rate %
1961	4.8	5.0	2.8
1962	3.1	4.8	4.3
1963	4.0	5.0	2.5
1964	4.9	4.7	6.7
1965	2.4	4.6	5.0
1966	0.7	4.7	3.0
1967	4.8	5.0	4.8
1969	4.7	5.0	7.4
1970	3.3	5.8	8.2
1971	4.3	5.5	9.0
1972	6.4	6.2	8.6
1973	4.4	5.7	11.4
1974	3.4	5.4	17.0
1975	0.2	7.3	20.9
1976	2.2	9.0	18.0
1977	5.6	8.8	13.6
1978	5.8	8.1	7.6
1979	3.0	7.1	13.2
1980	1.7	7.3	18.2
1981	2.1	9.9	20.4
1982	-1.7	11.4	17.1
1983	-1.8	13.6	10.5
1984	2.1	15.4	8.6
1985	-1.6	16.7	5.4
1986	3.0	17.1	3.8
1987	4.4	16.9	3.1
1988	2.6	16.4	2.1
1989	5.5	15.1	4.1
1990	8.3	13.0	3.3
1991	2.0	14.7	3.2
1992	2.3	15.3	3.1
1993	2.7	15.8	1.4
1994	7.4	14.7	2.4
1995	8.8	12.2	2.5
1996	6.0	11.9	1.7
1997	7.7	10.3	1.5
1998[f]	8.0	9.0	3.75

Sources:

Real GNP: Department of Finance, *Databank of Economic Time Series* (1987) and *National Income and Expenditure*, various issues. There is a discontinuity in the series in 1986.

Unemployment rate: *The Trend of Employment and Unemployment* and *Labour Force Survey*, various issues.

Inflation: *Statistical Bulletin*, October 1997, Consumer Price Index, Table 4.

Chapter 2

The Performance of the Irish Economy in the Long Run

"Little else is requisite to carry a state to the highest degree of opulence from the lowest barbarism, but peace, easy taxes, and tolerable administration of justice." Adam Smith.[1]

2.1 Introduction

Until recently economists and historians generally gave Ireland's economic performance since Independence low marks. One influential study stated:

"It is difficult to avoid the impression that Irish economic performance has been the least impressive in Western Europe, perhaps in all Europe, in the twentieth century."[2]

This pessimistic view was strongly influenced by the Irish economy's dismal performance between the 1920s and 1960. In the 1960s and 1970s Ireland's growth rate accelerated but the change was not sufficient to close the gap in living standards with the richer European countries. Since the mid-1980s, however, and especially in the 1990s, Ireland's rate of economic growth has been markedly above the European and OECD averages and this has led to a convergence of Irish living standards on those of the richer nations.

---

1. This is quoted in Paul Kennedy, *The Rise and Fall of Great Powers*, New York, Random House, 1987, p. 20. The exact source in Adam Smith's work is not given, but it captures the spirit of his discussion of the development of the New World in Book IV, Chapter VII of *The Wealth of Nations* ("Causes of Prosperity of New Colonies"). See also Smith's *Lectures on Jurisprudence*.

2. J. J. Lee, *Ireland 1912-1985: Politics and Society,* Cambridge, Cambridge University Press, 1989, p. 521. See also Kieran A. Kennedy, Thomas Giblin and Deirdre McHugh, *The Economic Development of Ireland in the Twentieth Century*, London: Routledge, 1988, p. 121.

In this chapter we look at Ireland's economic record and at the factors that have influenced our growth rate in the longer term. Particular attention is given to the explanations that have been offered for the poor performance up to 1960 and the exceptional performance in the 1990s.

2.2 The Record

"[In a] free Ireland, gracious and useful industries will supplement an improved agriculture, the population will expand in a century to 20 million and it may even in time go up to 30 million." (Padraic Pearse 1916)[3]

The most striking symbol of the long-run failure of the Irish economy is the decline of the population. While the mass exodus from the country after the famines of the 1840s could be blamed on British misrule, emigration and the population decline of the 1950s were due to shortcomings of domestic policy. Not until the 1960s, forty years after Independence, was sustained population growth recorded.

We begin this review of the long-run performance of the economy by briefly summarising the migration and population record before turning to a discussion of the rate of growth of output and other indicators.

Net migration

The level of net migration has been the dominant influence on the level of the population. Figure 2.1 shows the net migration rate (immigration *minus* emigration) from 1871 to 1996. With brief interruptions, large-scale emigration continued from the 1850s up to 1971. It was particularly high during the late nineteenth century and again during the 1950s. The net emigration rate reached almost 3 per cent a year in the mid-1950s – a dismal record surpassed only by Communist East Germany. Only for a brief period in the late 1970s and since 1991 has there been a net inflow of population into Ireland. Even in the current boom, the immigration rate has remained modest compared with the rate of emigration recorded in the past. For example, the net immigration rate was only 0.2 per cent in 1996 and 0.4 per cent in 1997.

3. Cited in J. F. Meenan, *The Irish Economy since 1922*, Liverpool University Press, 1970.

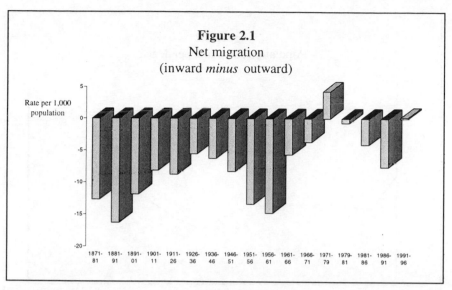

Figure 2.1
Net migration
(inward *minus* outward)

Population

The first census after Independence showed that the population had fallen from 3,139,688 in 1911 to 2,971,992 in 1926.[4] The population stabilised close to this level until the 1950s when the high rate of emigration led to a renewed decline. The population fell by 5 per cent between 1951 and 1961, when the low point of 2,818,000 was reached.

In the 1960s as emigration tapered off a modest rate of population growth was recorded. This accelerated in the 1970s, especially towards the end of the decade when there was significant net immigration. However, the return of large-scale emigration in the 1980s halted the increase. Population growth resumed in the 1990s and is now estimated to be running at one per cent a year. If this is maintained, the population will reach four million by the year 2010. Between 1961 and 1997 the population of the Republic increased by 30 per cent, proportionately the largest increase recorded in a European country over this period. These trends are shown in Figure 2.2.

---

4. The population of the twenty-six counties was 6,529,000 in 1841.

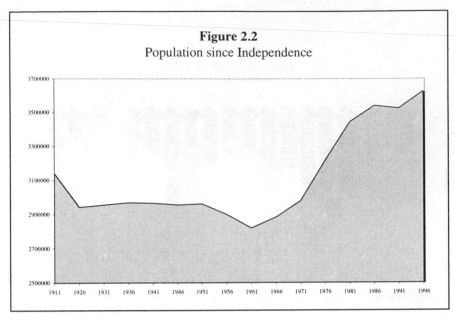

Figure 2.2
Population since Independence

Living standards

Between 1920 and 1945 the Irish economy suffered the effects of Partition, Civil War, the Great Depression, the Anglo-Irish Economic War, and World War II. In addition, the country turned its back on the world economy in the 1930s, embracing indiscriminate protectionism. Policy remained inward looking until the 1960s. As a consequence it is hardly surprising that the average standard of living was little higher in 1945, or even 1961, than it had been in 1914.[5]

The post-war experience was also disappointing. After a spurt of growth in the late 1940s, the 1950s were disastrous. Employment fell, emigration soared and the population dipped to a new low. The annual average growth of income *per capita* in the 1950s was only 2.2 per cent, compared with 2.5 per cent in Britain and 4.75 per cent in Western Europe. While Ireland's performance might not seem too bad in comparison, it has to be borne in mind that the declining population was the main reason any gains were made in income *per capita*. With people streaming out of the country and the standard of living of those that remained improving only

---

5. For an account of Ireland's economic history from Independence to the outbreak of World War II, see Cormac Ó Gráda, *Ireland: A New Economic History 1780-1939,* Oxford University Press, 1994. For the post-war period, see the same author's *A Rocky Road: The Irish Economy since the 1920s,* Manchester University Press, 1997.

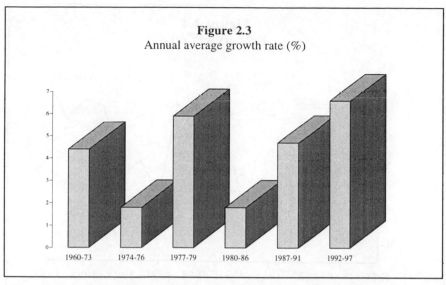

Figure 2.3
Annual average growth rate (%)

slowly, serious concerns were voiced about the viability of an independent Irish economy.

The country's economic fortunes changed markedly after 1960. Between 1960 and 1997 the annual average growth rate of GDP was 4.2 per cent – well above the average of the OECD countries and higher than had been recorded over any lengthy period since Independence. Even if allowance is made for the fact – discussed in Chapter 4 – that GDP tends to overstate the rise in living standards in Ireland, there is no questioning the rapid improvement in living standards that occurred. As we shall document below, the traditional gap between average real incomes in Ireland and Britain closed. It was particularly gratifying to combine rising levels of real *per capita* income with a rapid population growth. Figure 2.3 shows the growth rate of real GDP averaged over selected sub-periods defined to reflect the major changes in economic performance since 1960.

1960-73 Between 1960 and 1973 the Irish economy grew at an annual average rate of just over 4 per cent. Initially this growth was due to an almost inevitable recovery from the prolonged recession of the 1950s. Subsequently the benefits of the gradual reintegration of Ireland into the world economy began to be felt. This was a period of optimism when the phrase "a rising tide lifts all boats" was applied to the way in which most sectors of society shared in the fruits of economic growth. The only recession was a short-lived one in 1966.

25

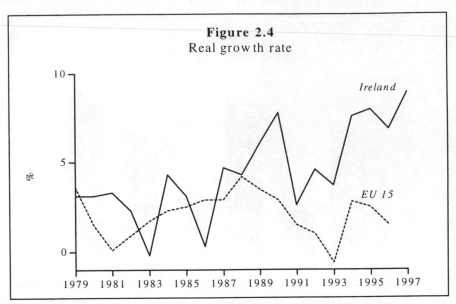

Figure 2.4
Real growth rate

1974-77 This golden era came to an end not just in Ireland but throughout the world when the oil price increase of 1973 plunged the global economy into recession. In Ireland there was no improvement in living standards over the years 1974 to 1977.

1977-79 The economy recovered towards the end of the decade and rapid growth was fuelled by a major fiscal stimulus in 1978. (We discuss this episode in more detail in Chapter 8.) The rate of growth attained in the closing years of the 1970s proved unsustainable.

1980-86 When the world was once again plunged into recession by the second oil crisis of 1979-80, Ireland was particularly vulnerable. The combined effects of the global recession and the attempts to restore order to the public finances after the excesses of the late 1970s caused the most severe recession since the 1950s. Living standards declined over the first half of the 1980s. Unemployment rose inexorably and emigration was held in check only by the severity of the recession in Britain and America. The extraordinary fiscal and current account deficits prompted talk once again of the failure of the country as an economic entity.

1987-91 A recovery in output and a dramatic improvement in the key macroeconomic indicators were evident after 1986. However, Irish unemployment

26

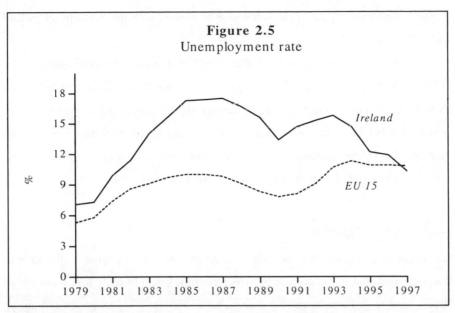

Figure 2.5
Unemployment rate

remained at crisis levels and emigration rose when the British economy boomed in the late 1980s. There was much scepticism about the genuineness of the recovery, but accelerating output growth eventually reversed the rise in unemployment and halted emigration.[6] In the 1990s there was an unprecedented expansion in employment: between 1986 and 1997 the numbers at work in Ireland rose by 26 per cent. This contrasts with the stagnation of employment over the previous sixty years and the declining level of employment in Europe in the 1990s.

Figure 2.4 and Figure 2.5 show dramatically how the behaviour of output growth and unemployment improved. The image of Ireland abroad changed radically as our economic performance improved. Kevin Gardner, an economist with Morgan Stanley Dean Whitter (London-based stockbrokers), coined the phrase "Celtic Tiger" in 1996, comparing Ireland's growth with that of the successful economies of East Asia. The idea was publicised by *The Street Journal* (5/12/1996) and *Newsweek* (23/12/1996). It is interesting to note that in January 1988 *The Economist* magazine had carried a survey of Ireland called "Poorest of the Rich", the cover showing children begging on O'Connell Street. In May 1997 the same magazine published another survey of Ireland entitled "Europe's Shining

---

6. The unemployment rate peaked at 17.1 per cent in 1986 and the net emigration rate at 1.25 per cent in 1989.

Light". This time the cover showed a map of Europe with the Republic of Ireland surrounded by a halo.

We have drawn attention to the exceptional growth in employment after 1986. The rate of growth of *output per worker* has therefore been significantly below that of total output.[7] Judged by this standard Ireland's performance remains impressive but by no means as exceptional as is suggested from the figures on the growth of GDP. Furthermore, the data for output per person employed show less clear-cut evidence of a break with the past during the mid-1980s.

2.3 Convergence

In recent years economists have devoted a great deal of attention to the idea of *convergence*, that is, the process by which countries with initially low standards of living tend to grow more rapidly than richer countries. This leads to catching up and a narrowing of the gap between rich and poor. For example, formerly poor countries like Hong Kong, Singapore and South Korea achieved spectacular growth in the 1950s and 1960s, while since the economic reforms of the 1980s real GDP in China has been growing at almost 10 per cent a year.

There are several reasons why poor countries might be expected to grow more rapidly than rich countries. These include:

Trade Standard economic theory suggests that poor countries benefit by exporting the goods and services in which they have a comparative advantage. The Heckscher-Ohlin theorem goes further and suggests that this trade will lead to an equalisation of factor prices (wages and rents) across countries. Provided a country remains open to international trade, market forces should therefore tend to raise incomes in poor countries relative to rich countries.

Migration The flow of people from poor countries to rich countries will also tend to equalise incomes. In the nineteenth century there was a massive flow of population westwards across the Atlantic from overpopulated European countries like Ireland to the land-rich New World. This lowered rents in Europe and raised

---

7. The rate of growth of total factor productivity (TFP), that is, output adjusted for both labour and capital inputs, has been even lower.

them in the New World, while simultaneously raising wages in Europe and holding them in check in the New World. This mechanism was very important for Ireland from the 1840s to the 1980s.[8]

Foreign direct investment (FDI) and technology transfer A large stock of modern technologies is available to poor countries once they embark on the path of development. Because their wages and other costs are low, underdeveloped countries can attract foreign investment in plant and equipment. This foreign direct investment (FDI) results in a transfer of technology that allows poor countries to move rapidly from very simple to the most advanced technologies. To benefit in full from this process a country must have political stability, an environment that is friendly to business, and a well-educated labour force. Ireland in the 1990s fulfilled most of these preconditions.

Diminishing returns to physical and human capital In rich countries each worker already has a lot of capital to work with, whereas in poor countries workers have very little. As a consequence the marginal productivity of an extra £1 of capital in a poor country tends to be much higher than in a country that is already well endowed with capital. This is the logic of the diminishing marginal productivity of capital. It tends to work in favour of poor countries provided they can equip their labour force with capital from domestic savings or attract a significant inflow of FDI. Diminishing returns also applies to human capital or the educational level of the population. In many poor countries most of the labour force is illiterate. Investing in basic education has a high pay-off. In rich countries, on the other hand, most school leavers go on to third level education. The marginal product of an additional £1 spent on education in these countries is low.

However, the tendency towards convergence is not absolute. It is possible for advanced countries to preserve their leadership through the cumulative nature of growth – success breeds success. External economies, such as the availability of a pool of common knowledge and skills, a large trained labour force and specialist

---

8. For an account of how this mechanism operated, see Kevin O'Rourke and Jeffrey Williamson, "Late Nineteenth-Century Anglo-American Factor-Price Convergence: Were Heckscher and Ohlin Right?", *Journal of Economic History*, 54 (4), December 1994, pp 892-916.

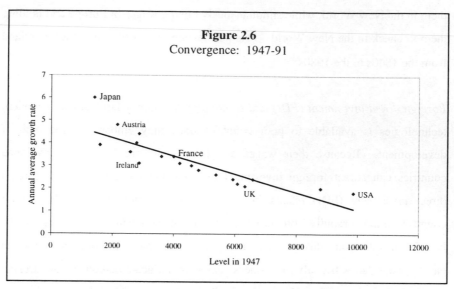

Figure 2.6
Convergence: 1947-91

suppliers, allow advanced regions to continue to attract new investment. As a result certain industries remain concentrated in established centres, to the detriment of peripheral areas.

It is difficult to assess the relative importance of the theoretical arguments for and against convergence. The empirical evidence is mixed too. There is a well documented tendency for living standards to converge across regions and countries with similar levels of human and physical capital formation, and similar institutional structures, but by and large the world's poorest countries (especially in Africa) have fallen behind the richer countries over the post-war period.[9]

Ireland since the mid-1980s provides a clear-cut example of an economy that has made substantial progress towards closing the gap with the world's richest countries. Figure 2.6 plots the annual average growth rates of a selection of OECD countries over the period 1947-91 against the initial 1947 level of output per person.

The convergence hypothesis suggests that countries with lower initial levels of output should have recorded faster growth over the subsequent period. In other words, the points in the graph should trace out a downward-sloping line. This is indeed the case. Countries like Japan and Italy that were relatively poor in 1947

9. See Xavier X. Sala-i-Martin, "The Classical Approach to Convergence Analysis", *Economic Journal*, July 1996, and Lant Pritchett, "Forget Convergence: Divergence Past, Present, and Future", *Finance and Development*, June 1996.

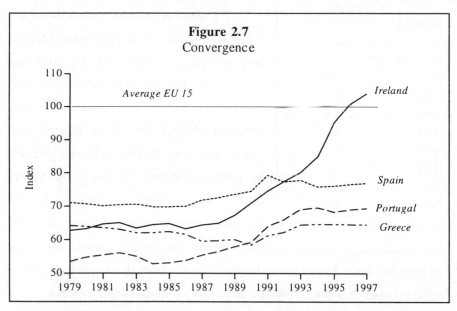

Figure 2.7
Convergence

achieved an above-average growth rate over the following four decades. Ireland, too, started from a relatively low income level and achieved above-average growth subsequently.[10] However, this relatively good performance was not sufficient to prevent Ireland sliding from 14th to 18th place among the nineteen countries shown in Figure 2.6 between 1947 and 1991.

This comparison is strongly affected by Ireland's dismal performance in the 1950s and does not take account of the exceptional performance in the 1990s. A more up to date comparison can be made using EU data. At the start of the 1980s Ireland's standard of living was about 60 per cent of the EU average. This is much the same as when the country joined the EEC in 1973. The failure to catch up over the initial years of membership was disappointing. However, Figure 2.7 shows that as a result of accelerated growth since the mid-1980s Irish living standards by 1997 were three percentage points above the EU average. Whereas in 1980 Ireland lagged behind Spain and Greece, by 1997 it had overtaken these countries.[11]

---

10. The data on which this Figure is based are from the widely used "Penn World Tables": see Robert Summers and Alan Heston, "The Penn World Tables (Mark 5): An Expanded Set of International Comparisons, 1950-88", *Quarterly Journal of Economics,* May 1991.

11. A note of caution must be sounded about comparisons based on Gross *Domestic* Product. As discussed in Chapter 4, GDP includes the value of production by foreign-owned firms, including profits that are eventually remitted abroad. It may overstate the living standards in countries, such as Ireland, where foreign firms account for a significant proportion of the growth of domestic production. While

Table 2.1	
Irish GDP per person as	
a % of UK level	
1913	51.6
1938	48.5
1947	46.6
1961	47.9
1971	62.9
1981	60.9
1991	73.8
1996	103.0
Source: Angus Madison, OECD.	

The long-run position relative to the UK is also informative. Table 2.1 shows Irish GDP per person as a percentage of the UK level from 1913 to 1996. It can be seen that between 1913 and 1961 Irish living standards declined somewhat relative to the UK, but that this trend was reversed over the three following decades. By 1996 the standard of living in Ireland was within 5 percentage points of that in the UK. The poor performance before 1961 creates the suspicion that the policies pursued during the first four decades of Independence hindered any tendency that might have existed for Ireland to catch up with its nearest neighbour and closest trading partner.

2.4 Interpreting the Record

Why did Ireland, a relatively backward economy with a surplus of labour and generally low costs of production, not catch up with the wealthier countries of Europe during the first half of the twentieth century? What changed the country's relative performance so dramatically in the 1990s? While it is not possible to provide definitive answers to these questions, some plausible explanations can be suggested.

Economic policies

An important lesson to learn from economic history is that policies matter. With the benefit of hindsight it is easy to blame Ireland's dismal economic performance in the 1940s and 1950s on bad economic policies.

Initial caution During the first decade of Independence, Ireland pursued basically conservative economic policies. Agriculture, in which half the labour force was

---

Gross *National* Product provides a better measure of the trend in the country's living standards, the GDP figures do not seriously overstate the rate of growth of national income (see William Keating, "Measuring Growth" in *Proceedings* of Conference on Measuring Economic Growth, Dublin, Central Statistics Office and Irish Economic Association 1995).

still engaged, was viewed as the engine of economic growth. It was believed that the country would thrive in a free trade environment that allowed cheap imports of raw materials and open access to export markets. In the monetary and financial areas, continuity with the past was also maintained and no radical initiatives were launched. The government's finances were carefully managed. Although a major state monopoly, the Electricity Supply Board, and a state bank, the Agriculture Credit Corporation, were created in 1927, and some tariffs were erected to help industries that were facing "unfair" competition from abroad, the role of the state in the economy remained limited. It was not until the Great Depression and the collapse of the global free trade system in the early 1930s that more radical and, in the long run, damaging policies were adopted.

Prolonged inward orientation In the 1930s disillusionment with the traditional liberal political economy was widespread, not just in Ireland but throughout the world. The stage was set for a more radical approach. The Fianna Fáil government that took office in 1932 responded by introducing a wide-ranging set of inward-looking policies. Foreign investment was virtually excluded through the Control of Manufactures Acts (1932-4). High tariffs were imposed on imports to protect anyone willing to manufacture products in Ireland. In addition, measures were introduced to encourage the growth of native Irish industry, as well as a more labour-intensive pattern of farming. The level of protection of Irish industry remained extremely high for the next forty years. Even as late as 1966 the average rate of effective protection of Irish manufacturing industry was almost 80 per cent, one of the highest in the western world.[12]

The firms that set up behind these high tariffs were Irish owned, although in many cases all that happened was that British firms went into joint ventures with Irish residents and formed subsidiaries to cater for their existing Irish markets. Due to the small scale of this market, separate production facilities proved very inefficient. An extreme example was the car industry, where British manufacturers had to dismantle new cars, put them in special kits and ship them to Ireland for re-

---

12. Dermot McAleese, *Effective Tariffs and the Structure of Industrial Protection in Ireland*, Dublin: The Economic and Social Research Institute, Paper No. 62, 1971. "Effective protection" measures the extent to which a tariff allows an industry to be inefficient relative to international competitive standards and still survive.

assembly here. A limited number of semi-skilled jobs was created in this manner but at the cost of much higher car prices in Ireland. Within ten years of the ending of protectionism hardly any of these jobs survived.

The fact that between 1932 and 1966 the Irish economy was one of the most heavily protected in the world is probably the single most important reason for the country's relatively poor economic performance over these years. Prolonged reliance on generalised protectionism has not proved to be an effective way of promoting economic development anywhere in the world. Whatever the merits of imposing tariffs on selected "infant industries" at the early stages of industrialisation, there is no example of a country that has successfully used indiscriminate protection extending for over a generation to create a viable industrial sector.[13]

A start was not made on dismantling tariffs until the 1960s. The Anglo-Irish Free Trade Area Agreement (1966) led to the elimination of tariffs between Ireland and Britain. The phased elimination of tariffs with European countries was negotiated as part of the terms of our accession to the EEC in 1973. It is hardly a coincidence that the country's relative economic performance improved dramatically as more outward-looking policies were adopted.

Excessive state involvement in the economy After 1932 numerous state-sponsored bodies (or "semi-state companies") were created to fill what were regarded as gaps left by enterprise. The areas in which they operated included radio and TV broadcasting, turf development, air, sea, road and rail transport, hotels, and food processing, manufacturing steel and chemical fertilisers – the list is long! Most of the state-owned companies enjoyed significant monopoly power and eventually became overmanned and inefficient. They were also asked to achieve a variety of political and social objectives, which burdened them with high-cost operations.

By the 1970s the role of the state in the Irish economy was probably more extensive than in any other country that had not formally adopted socialism. The result was a high tax burden on the economy and a deterrent to private enterprise. By the 1980s it was clear that the expansion of the role of the state in the economy

---

13 For a review of the issues, see World Bank, *World Development Report 1991: The Challenge of Development*, Oxford University Press, 1991.

since the 1930s had not succeeded in its aim of promoting the long-run development of the economy. This recognition – prompted by changes in attitude towards the economic role of the state in Britain and America – led to the gradual introduction of deregulation and privatisation. Some state companies (Nítrigin Éireann, the Irish Life Assurance Company, Irish Steel, the Industrial Credit Corporation, the Agricultural Credit Corporation, the Irish Sugar Company and parts of the Irish Airlines group) have been, or are due to be, privatised. The monopoly privileges of those in areas such as access transport, inter-city bus transport, health insurance, and TV and radio broadcasting have been reduced.

However, despite these changes the state still plays a major role in the productive sectors of the Irish economy. The level of state ownership and regulation of the economy is higher than in many of the former socialist economies of Central and Eastern Europe. We have consistently delayed implementation of EU regulations for liberalisation of civil aviation, insurance and banking.

The level and structure of investment Modern growth theory attributes great importance to the level and structure of investment as a determinant of growth. In the 1950s Ireland had a relatively low savings rate. A high proportion of the funds available for investment was used by government for social overhead projects such as housing and hospital building. The result was a low rate of investment in productive assets. In the 1970s the rate of investment rose but the government directly or indirectly controlled an inordinate proportion of it and its productivity was low. In the 1990s, the investment ratio was lower but the contribution of FDI to raising productivity was very significant.

The legacy of history

Many historical factors also contributed to Ireland's poor economic performance after Independence. We shall briefly consider the principal ones.

The British connection Political independence did little to reduce Ireland's heavy economic dependence on Britain. As late as the 1950s, almost 90 per cent of Irish exports went to the United Kingdom and almost three-quarters of them consisted of live animals and foodstuffs. Our banking system and financial markets remained integrated with their British counterparts. With such close links to Britain it is hardly surprising that the growth rate of the Irish economy was closer to that of Britain than of the continental European countries. The relatively slow growth of the UK economy acted as a constraint on Irish economic development.

The safety valve of emigration Another historical legacy that may have impeded Ireland's quest for higher living standards was the long tradition of emigration. From the beginning of the nineteenth century, emigration from Ireland was encouraged by easy access to Britain and America. The outflow became a torrent after the famines of the 1840s. The growing numbers of Irish people living overseas facilitated further emigration. The persistence of high emigration led to a unique, century-long decline of population which is often cited not just as a symptom of under-achievement but also as a cause of poor economic performance.

- Emigration and a declining population can have a number of adverse effects on economic development.
- A contracting domestic market acts as a deterrent to new investment.
- The psychological and social effects of emigration are negative. It is dispiriting if almost half of the school-leaving cohort leaves the country, as was the case during the 1950s, especially if those who go are the more energetic and enterprising. The remaining population will tend to be conservative and reluctant to take risks.
- Until the 1980s the highest rates of emigration from Ireland were recorded among farm labourers, the sons and daughters of small farmers, and unskilled manual workers. However, in the 1980s higher rates of emigration occurred among those with third level and professional qualifications. This outflow of highly educated young people represented a major loss of human capital and the state enjoyed no return on the public money spent on their education.
- Emigration distorts the age structure of the population, leading to a relatively high proportion of both young and old dependants, and a relatively small proportion of young adults.

The adverse effects of emigration can, however, be exaggerated. Account should also be taken of the compensating benefits. In the absence of emigration the living standards of those who left and of those who stayed would have been even lower. Emigration afforded many young Irish people the opportunity of raising their living standards and relieved pressure on the welfare services in Ireland.[14] When the rate of growth of the Irish economy picked up in the 1990s, return migration proved to be a valuable source of skilled personnel.

2.5 Accounting for the "Celtic Tiger"

Having listed so many possible explanations for Ireland's poor performance during the first four decades of Independence, it behoves us to try to explain why the country performed so much better after 1960, and particularly the factors that account for the unprecedented expansion of the 1990s.[15] To some extent these positive factors are the reverse of the negative factors that we listed as explanations for Ireland's under-performance in earlier years.

Favourable longer-term factors

We discuss first the positive factors that were in place before the boom of the 1990s and which help to explain the improvement in Ireland's economic performance after 1960.

Outward orientation Economists would tend to agree that the most important contribution to turning the Irish economy round was made by the return to free trade in the 1960s. By the end of the 1950s it had come to be recognised that inward-looking economic policies offered little hope of raising Irish living standards. The growing momentum towards free trade in Europe and the prospect

---

14. It is surprisingly difficult to find evidence that high rates of emigration have an adverse effect on the rate of economic growth: see B. M. Walsh, "Testing for Macroeconomic Feedback from Large-Scale Migration based on the Irish Experience, 1948-87: A Note", *The Economic and Social Review*, Vol. 20, No. 3, April 1989, pp 257-66 and J. J. Sexton, B. M. Walsh, D. F. Hannan and D. McMahon, *The Economic and Social Implications of Emigration*, Dublin: The National Economic and Social Council, March 1991.

15. This section draws on Anthony Leddin and Brendan Walsh, "Economic Stabilisation, Recovery, and Growth: Ireland 1979-96", *Irish Banking Review*, Spring 1997, pp 2-17, and Brendan Walsh, "Stabilisation and Adjustment in a Small Open Economy: Ireland 1979-95", *Oxford Review of Economic Policy*, 12 (3), 74-86. For the views of a distinguished group of economists on the Irish economic "miracle", see *International Perspectives on the Irish Economy*, edited by Alan Gray, Dublin: Indecon, 1997.

of eventual entry to the European Economic Community (as it then was) forced Irish policy makers to think about opening up the economy. The belated dismantling of protectionism in the 1960s allowed Ireland to benefit from the growth of the world economy. After 1960, successive governments were consistent in their commitment to export-led growth.

Industrial policy As tariffs were dismantled in the 1960s an elaborate system of industrial grants and tax incentives was introduced. Instead of giving priority to Irish-owned firms willing to substitute for imported goods, the emphasis of policy was switched to attracting export-oriented FDI. The Industrial Development Authority (IDA) and An Foras Tionscal (which had been established in 1949 and 1952, respectively) were given this remit.

The incentives used for this purpose included fixed asset grants and generous capital allowances which lowered the effective tax on companies. Export sales tax relief was introduced in 1958, to be replaced by a 10 per cent rate of tax on profits in manufacturing and traded services in 1981.

This package was regularly criticised by Irish economists, who viewed it as over-generous. The grants to plant and equipment were said to be encouraging capital intensity in a labour surplus economy. Reviews recommended greater emphasis on creating a favourable cost and production environment for firms, while reducing the reliance on tax breaks and grants (*Industrial Policy Review Group*, 1992 – known as the *Culliton Report*). It was argued that the main elements of an environment that would promote economic development are:

- A tax system that provides incentives for enterprise and risk-taking, with few distortions.
- An efficient infrastructure that does not penalise industry relative to its international competitors.
- An educational system that equips job seekers with the technical, vocational and managerial skills required by modern industry.
- The availability of government funds for joint projects with the private sector.[16]

---

16. The Irish incentives are deemed compatible with EU competition policy at least until the year 2010. Under the "regional aid" rubric – the whole country is still classified as a peripheral region. While the

In response to criticism, fixed asset grants were back and tax concessions reduced. The principal remaining incentive is now the 10 per cent rate of corporate profit tax applied to manufacturing industry and some traded financial services. The level of support per job created has fallen steadily. In fact Ireland now spends less than the EU average on state aid to industry.

In addition to grants and the low tax rate, the other factors that are cited as attractions for FDI to locate in Ireland are, first, a highly educated, English-speaking workforce. Second, flexible working practices and fewer institutional rigidities. Most of the new foreign-owned firms that have located in Ireland are not unionised.

External economies Success breeds success. Ireland has established a reputation as a suitable location for new foreign investment. In the microelectronic area, for example, numerous computer companies (Intel, IMB, Digital, Hewlett Packard, Gateway 2000, Dell) have set up and expanded here is a clear signal to other computer companies looking for a suitable location within the EU. There is now a critical mass of workers with experience in computer-related occupations, sub-suppliers are in place and the environment for further investment in this sector is attractive. The same applies to some extent to sectors such as pharmaceuticals, high tech food industries, medical equipment, financial services and telemarketing.

The IDA's record in 1996

- The IDA supported 1,040 companies. These companies employed 97,472 people which accounts for 44 per cent of total manufacturing employment.
- IDA expenditure in 1996 (funded by the Irish government and by transfers from the EU budget) amounted to £136 million. This resulted in a cost per job sustained of £11,920, down from £24,952 in 1983.
- Sales by multinational companies amounted to £13,058 million (30 per cent of GDP). Of this, £12,570 million (96 per cent) was exported.

Irish level of subsidy to industry is high by European standards, it is lower (relative to value added) than that offered by Greece and Spain (Commission of the EU, 1992).

- Irish economy expenditure by multinational firms amounted to 33.7 per cent of total sales, indicating considerable spin-off effects for the domestic economy.
- Productivity (output per worker) in the FDI sectors is much higher than in the rest of Irish industry, but earnings per employee were actually slightly lower in the former. This indicates the vastly greater profitability of the FDI sector. As a consequence, the profits repatriated from the foreign-owned sector amount to about 5 per cent of the value of Ireland's domestic output.

An important feature of Irish industrial policy is that it does not involve the state either in direct participation in industry or in explicitly picking winning sectors or firms. Although sectors such as electronics, pharmaceuticals and medical instrumentation are undoubtedly targeted, the IDA is willing to provide similar assistance to all firms that regard Ireland as a suitable location. This contrasts with, for example, the approach taken in South Korea or Singapore, where the state has been directly involved in directing the pattern of investment.

It is somewhat puzzling, none the less, that Ireland has been far more successful in attracting FDI in the 1990s than in earlier years. As the IDA's expenditure per job created has declined and competition from other countries and regions has intensified, the number of jobs created has risen dramatically. Ireland's share of the FDI coming to Europe from the United States has increased. A possible explanation is that only in the 1990s did Ireland become an attractive location for firms employing skilled labour. This can be attributed to the increased outflow from the Irish educational system of well-educated young workers, English speaking and prepared to work for relatively modest salaries.

While it is true that FDI accounts for most of the growth of industrial employment, output and exports during the current boom, the recovery of "indigenous" Irish industry should not be overlooked. Between 1988 and 1996 employment in Irish-owned manufacturing industry grew by 6.9 per cent, compared with a decline of 14 per cent in industrial employment in the EU.[17] While most of the traditional firms that emerged under the umbrella of

17. Eoin O'Malley, "The Revival of Irish Indigenous Industry, 1987-97", The Economic and Social Research Institute, February 1998.

protectionism have contracted or gone out of business, a core of strong Irish firms has survived and expanded. These firms are increasingly multinationals in their own right. Companies such as Smurfit, CRH, Ryanair, the Bank of Ireland, Allied Irish Banks, Kerry, Elan, Fyffes, Glen Dimplex, Independent Newspapers, Waterford-Wedgwood, Greencore and Waterford-Avonmore, among others, derive large and increasing proportions of their profits from their international activities. Non-Irish investors own significant proportions of their equity. Some are head-quartered in Ireland for historical reasons only. In fact it is becoming increasingly difficult, and less relevant, to distinguish between "Irish" and "foreign" industries.[18] Thus the Irish economy is now thoroughly internationalised. The contrast with the largely self-sufficient, inward-looking economy of the 1950s could not be greater.

Investment in education and the supply of skilled labour We have stressed the importance of investment in human capital in the growth process. It holds the key to raising the productivity of the labour force and attracting high quality FDI. Ireland had achieved a high level of investment in first and second level education by the 1970s, and in the 1980s and 1990s additional resources were devoted to raise the proportion of school leavers participating in third level education. As a result, young people with relatively high qualifications increasingly dominated the outflow from the educational system. The supply of unskilled labour began to dry up. Ireland came to be characterised by its abundant supply of skilled, English-speaking workers available at relatively low cost by EU standards.[19] While in the late 1980s the emigration rate among these young people was very high, the supply of skilled labour played an important role in the unprecedented growth of output and employment recorded in the 1990s.

---

18. Some of the most famous "Irish" branded products, such as Guinness stout, the main Irish whiskies, and Bailey's Irish Cream, are owned by multinational companies.

19. For a detailed discussion of this view, see John Curtis and John D. FitzGerald, "Real Wage Convergence in an Open Labour Market", *Economic and Social Review*, 27 (4), 1991, 321-40.

2.6 Getting Things Right After the mid-1980s

The factors listed in the previous sub-section were put in place gradually over the 1960s and 1970s. They may have allowed Ireland to shake off the stagnation of the 1950s but they did not insulate it from the global recessions of 1973-74 and 1980-85. They certainly do not explain the country's exceptional economic record in the 1990s. For this we must look to another set of influences.

Creating the financial preconditions The macroeconomic situation in Ireland at the start of the 1980s was unsustainable. The country was facing insolvency due to the rising debt/GDP ratio and the exceptional current account balance of payments deficit. The result was a flight of capital from the country and a reluctance of foreign firms to locate here. The rising tax burden encouraged widespread evasion and avoidance (discussed at greater length in Chapter 8). Restoring order to the public finances was a precondition for a resumption of economic growth. The sharp adjustment of 1987 restored private investors' confidence in the economy and laid the foundations for the subsequent expansion of the economy.

External assistance In 1922 the new Irish Free State was cut off from the financial support that it would eventually have enjoyed as a poorer region of the United Kingdom. This loss of support became quite significant as the welfare state was established and various regional policies implemented in the UK after World War II. Ireland did, however, benefit from the European Recovery Programme (Marshall Aid) which was launched by the United States in 1949. Under this programme Ireland received low interest loans amounting to over 3 per cent of GNP for three years. These funds were used to finance the development of agriculture and forestry and local authority housing and hospitals.[20] With the ending of Marshall Aid, however, Ireland had to rely exclusively on its own resources until it entered the European Economic Community (EEC) in 1973. Since then the country has benefited from high prices for farm products paid for through the Common Agricultural Policy and grants from the Regional and Social

---

20. See Barry Eichengreen and Marc Uzan, "The Marshall Plan: economic effects and implications for Eastern Europe and the former USSR", *Economic Policy*, April 1992, pp 13-76, and Bernadette Whelan, "Ireland and the Marshall Plan", *Irish Economic and Social History*, Vol. XIX (1992), 49-70.

Table 2.2

Receipts from and payments to EU

	Receipts from EU	Payments to EU	Net receipts	Net receipts % of GDP
	£m	£m	£m	%
1973	37.1	4.5	32.6	1.3
1974	67.4	5.5	61.9	2.2
1975	109.1	9.8	99.3	2.6
1976	119.5	13.4	106.1	2.3
1977	272.9	22.1	250.8	4.5
1978	410.2	46.1	364.1	5.6
1979	529.1	60.6	468.5	6.1
1980	560.6	88.9	471.7	5.2
1981	506.9	105.4	401.5	3.7
1982	602.1	136.7	465.4	3.7
1983	727.7	184.7	543.0	4.0
1984	866.7	202.5	664.2	4.5
1985	1128.7	213.3	915.4	5.8
1986	1146.6	240.3	906.3	5.2
1987	1100.3	255.2	845.1	4.5
1988	1161.6	247.8	913.8	4.6
1989	1295.3	285.6	1009.7	4.6
1990	1741.0	282.9	1458.1	6.1
1991	2201.2	348.2	1853.0	7.3
1992	1994.0	353.4	1640.6	6.2
1993	2245.3	453.5	1791.8	6.4
1994	1841.4	505.5	1335.9	4.4
1995	2023.4	542.8	1480.6	4.4
1996	2217.9	541.1	1676.8	4.3
1997	2331.6	582.0	1749.6	4.3

Source: The Department of Finance.

Funds. When Ireland joined the European Monetary System in 1979, additional aid was provided to assist in the adjustment. During the 1980s the level of aid under the Social and Regional Funds increased significantly and in the 1990s a new Cohesion Fund was established to narrow the gap between rich and poor countries. Table 2.2 shows Irish payments to and receipts from the EU. Net receipts reached a peak of 7.3 per cent of GNP in 1991. Total net receipts over the period 1973-97 amounted to £21,505 million, an annual average of 4.7 per cent of GNP.

Table 2.3 shows the breakdown of total receipts since 1973. By far the most important source of funding is from the FEOGA guarantee section which is the main channel of funding to the agricultural sector.

Note

FEOGA stands for Fund European Orientation Guidance Agriculture. It is also known as EAGGF which is an abbreviation for European Agriculture Guidance and Guarantee Fund.

EU assistance is often cited as a reason for Ireland's improved economic performance in the 1990s. The timing of the increased inflows was very favourable because they helped counter the impact on the Irish economy of the world

Table 2.3

Receipts from the European Union 1973-97

	FEOGA Guarantee Section	FEOGA Guidance Section	European Social Fund	Regional Development Fund	Cohesion Fund	Misc.	Total
	£m	£m	£m	£m	£m	£m	£m
1973	37.1					0	37.1
1974	63.8		3.6			0	67.4
1975	102.2	0.6	4.0	1.8		0.5	109.1
1976	102.0	2.6	4.6	8.5		1.8	119.5
1977	245.1	7.4	8.2	8.5		3.7	272.9
1978	365.6	9.7	19.3	11.1		4.5	410.2
1979	396.5	18.5	28.8	25.5		59.8	529.1
1980	381.1	31.8	46.7	46.4		54.6	560.6
1981	304.6	41.9	45.3	54.6		60.5	506.9
1982	344.3	59.6	73.2	66.1		58.9	602.1
1983	441.7	63.7	92.7	58.2		71.4	727.7
1984	644.6	49.3	84.3	65.2		23.3	866.7
1985	836.6	55.8	141.3	76.0		19.0	1128.7
1986	884.0	46.6	127.4	77.1		11.5	1146.6
1987	739.6	67.9	193.5	87.4		11.9	1100.3
1988	838.5	64.4	126.8	129.6		2.3	1161.6
1989	963.4	76.7	138.6	112.9		3.7	1295.3
1990	1286.7	93.9	128.5	225.1		6.8	1741.0
1991	1334.4	143.3	370.7	341.9		10.9	2201.2
1992	1113.6	147.4	277.3	444.6		11.1	1994.0
1993	1281.8	125.9	311.6	464.4	41.6	20.0	2245.3
1994	1173.7	130.9	277.1	175.6	68.3	15.8	1841.4
1995	1150.2	142.9	256.2	358.1	102.0	14.0	2023.4
1996	1364.5	150.6	251.4	297.1	137.1	17.2	2217.9
1997	1300.0	201.7	313.7	352.0	137.0	27.2	2331.6

Source: Department of Finance.

recession of the early 1990s. The money was spent on roads and railways, telecommunications, and aid to industry, agriculture and tourism. The strategy was to strengthen the country's productive capacity by upgrading infrastructure, developing the skills of the population and encouraging local initiatives. It was hoped that these measures would raise Ireland's growth rate and lead to convergence in living standards with the richer EU countries. The fact that in the

1990s Ireland did indeed close this gap is often taken as evidence of the success of this approach.

Economists tend to be sceptical about the contribution made by foreign aid to economic development. The international evidence suggests that aid tends to boost consumption rather than investment, and that its long-term contribution to growth is negligible. However, it is interesting to note that a high correlation between aid and investment has been found among a few small countries that have received an exceptionally large volume of aid (generally more than 15 per cent of GDP).[21] Such a high level of aid is no longer fungible (that is, it cannot be diverted to uses other than those for which it is provided) and is therefore likely to produce the desired effect. It is possible that EU assistance to Ireland falls into this latter category of effective, growth-promoting assistance.

Investment in education We have emphasised the potential importance of human capital formation in the growth process. Irish investment in human capital has been high over the years. In fact Ireland had one of the highest levels of participation in second level education of the OECD countries. Ireland had a high rate of investment in secondary education over the period 1960-85 and more recently has invested heavily in third level education.[22] The acceleration in Irish economic growth in the 1990s may reflect the pay-off to high levels of investment in human capital in earlier years. The availability of a well educated, English-speaking labour force at competitive wage rates has acted as a magnet attracting foreign firms in high technology fields to Ireland.

The return to centralised wage bargaining Another factor that has been invoked to explain Ireland's good economic record is the return to centralised wage bargaining or National Wage Agreements (NWAs) in the second half of the 1980s.

---

21. On the basis of data for almost 100 countries over the period 1979-90 a recent study concluded: "Aid does not increase investment and growth, nor benefit the poor as measured by improvements in development indicators, but it does increase the size of the government." Boone Peter, "The Impact of Foreign Aid on Savings and Growth", London School of Economics, Working Paper, June 1994.
22. Mankiw N. Gregory, David Romer and David Weil, "A Contribution to the Empirics of Economic Growth", *Quarterly Journal of Economics*, 107 (2), 407-37.

There were several NWAs in the 1970s, but this approach broke down under the strain of rising inflation and unemployment in the 1980s.[23] The high and rising level of unemployment exercised a harsh discipline on wage claims – real take-home pay fell by about 20 per cent between 1981 and 1986. In order to preserve moderation in wage inflation as the recovery gathered momentum, a new series of NWAs was launched from 1988. The programmes were:

- *The Programme for National Recovery* (1988-90)
- *The Programme for Economic and Social Progress* (1991-93)
- *The Programme for Competitiveness and Work* (1994-95)
- *Programme 2000: Employment, Competitiveness and Inclusion* (1997-2000).

A feature of these agreements has been that in return for low nominal wage demands the government has held out the prospect of a reduction in income taxation, improvements in social benefits and a wide variety of other measures.

Between 1987 and 1997 gross industrial earnings increased by about 15 per cent in real terms, but after-tax earnings rose by a further 9 per cent. Thus reductions in tax rates accounted for about one-third of the rise in real take-home pay.

It is possible that centralised wage bargaining contributed to pay moderation and enhanced Ireland's competitive advantage after 1987. This was certainly a period of moderate pay increases, a commitment to three year wage contracts, and a virtual absence of industrial strife. But the high rates of unemployment and emigration of the mid-1980s were sufficient to ensure wage moderation before the return to centralised pay bargaining in 1988. Other countries, including Britain and the United States, have achieved pay moderation and low unemployment under decentralised pay bargaining. Only in the late 1990s is the Irish system of social partnership being tested by the need to reconcile falling unemployment with moderate wage inflation. It remains to be seen whether it will help sustain the growth of the economy under the changing circumstances.

The falling burden of taxation We noted that part of the approach to centralised pay bargaining adopted in 1988 was a commitment to reducing the burden of

---

23. Centralised wage bargaining is referred to in Ireland and Europe as "Social Partnership". The phrase "corporatism" is also used.

taxation on employees. In 1988 the standard rate of income tax was 35 per cent and the higher rate 58 per cent; by 1998 these rates had been lowered to 24 per cent and 46 per cent, respectively, and the thresholds at which they are applied have been raised in real terms. The rates of social insurance tax on lower paid workers have also been reduced slightly. More broadly, Ireland is one of the few EU countries where the share of taxes in GDP is significantly lower now than ten years ago. Government current receipts as a percentage of GDP peaked in Ireland at 40.9 per cent in 1984; by 1997 they had fallen to 34.7 per cent, whilst in the EU as a whole this ratio rose from 45 to 46 per cent over the same period. Because high rates of taxation act as a disincentive to economic development, especially in a small open economy, the reversal of the upward trend in taxation since the mid-1980s is another factor that contributed to Ireland's improved performance.[24]

Favourable exchange rate developments The launch of the European Monetary System in 1979 provided Ireland with the opportunity of breaking the link with sterling just as that currency began to be seriously overvalued. This fortuitous development was a prelude to a period, extending all the way to 1998, when, through a mixture of good fortune and some good policy management, Ireland maintained a competitive exchange rate. Apart from the quixotic attempt to remain in the narrow band of the exchange rate mechanism after sterling's devaluation in 1992, the currency was kept at a level that enhanced the country's international competitiveness. We discuss this topic in greater detail in Chapter 22. In Chapter 15 we show that over the period 1979-85 Ireland's real exchange rate was rising (causing a loss of competitiveness), whilst after 1985 it fell (leading to a competitive gain).

The list of factors that can be invoked to account for the dramatic improvement in Ireland's economic fortunes since the mid-1980s is long. The financial stabilisation of the 1980s, the reversal of the rising tax burden, the refinement of our industrial policy, the coming on to the labour market of a large

---

24. We must of course acknowledge that the rapid growth of the economy has facilitated tax reductions and it is difficult to disentangle cause and effect. What matters is that since the mid-1980s Ireland has enjoyed a virtuous circle with faster growth leading to lower tax and public debt burdens, which in turn has reinforced the economy's performance.

cohort of well-educated young people, the increased inflow of EU aid, the reintroduction of centralised pay bargaining, favourable exchange rate developments – all played their role. It is not possible to measure the relative importance of the factors. But it is clear that the period since 1986 has been unique in Irish history because never before did so many favourable factors combine and this combination made it possible to attract a steady inflow of high-quality FDI. The inflow of new firms transformed the country's economic base and propelled exports, employment and productivity to heights that were undreamed of in earlier decades.

2.7 Summary

Over the first sixty-four years of Independence (1922-86), little progress was made towards closing the gap in living standards between Ireland and the richer countries of Europe. In fact, several European countries that were poorer at the beginning of the century. Italy, Austria and Spain, for example, overtook Ireland during this period. However, following a dramatic increase in real growth towards the end of the 1980s and in the 1990s Ireland narrowed the gap with the rich industrial countries.

In this chapter we reviewed some factors that help explain Ireland's poor record in the first four decades after Independence. Chief among these was the protracted period of protectionism and other inward-looking policies from the 1930s to the 1960s. In the 1930s global recession and economic nationalism led us to turn our back on the world economy. We persisted with these policies in the changed circumstances of the post-war period, when they cut us off from the rapid expansion of the world economy. We paid a high price through large-scale emigration and stagnant living standards. The ease with which young people could emigrate from Ireland and our continued dependence on the slow-growing British economy aggravated this drag on our economic performance.

The transformation of the economy after 1960 may be attributed in the first place to a switch from inward to outward-looking policies. As Ireland became reintegrated in the world economy, its growth rate surpassed the OECD average. In place of protectionism and barriers to inward investment, subsidies to exports and grants to FDI helped raise the productivity of the industrial sector. While many of the jobs in the traditional, indigenous firms disappeared, they were replaced by jobs with much higher value added in new high tech sectors. A smaller, leaner Irish industrial base survived and expanded both inside Ireland and abroad

The growth rate slumped during the early 1980s as the economy suffered from the global recession and the need to correct the imbalances caused by an unsustainable growth spurt in the late 1970s. Since the mid-1980s, however, the Irish economy has significantly out-performed the rest of Europe and the gap in living standards with the world's richest countries narrowed markedly.

In addition to the consistent outward orientation of the economy and the stabilisation of key macroeconomic indicators, such as the rate of inflation, the current account deficit and the public finances, several factors may be credited with a role in the economy's recent success. These include a substantial inflow of grants and subsidies from the EU. A high rate of investment in education also played a key role by creating a pool of trained and employable workers that attracted FDI in areas such as electronic engineering, pharmaceuticals, and financial services. The reintroduction of centralised wage bargaining in 1988 may also have played a role in enhancing the economy's competitiveness. Favourable exchange rate developments and a falling burden of taxation also played their part.

Ireland's experience shows that "nothing succeeds like success". The inflow of foreign firms is a cumulative process. New firms are attracted by the fact that well-known firms have already decided to locate in Ireland. The size of the trained labour force and the number of suitable suppliers has expanded. The emigration of the best educated is turned into a return flow of experienced workers.

2.8 The Prospects

Writing at the beginning of 1998, Ireland's medium-term economic prospects look favourable. The forecasters are unanimously predicting a high growth rate for 1998. But the economy is now entering a fifth year of exceptionally rapid growth. The growth rate over the last ten years has been considerably above the longer-run average. The spare capacity that existed after the prolonged recession of the 1980s has been used up and constraints on maintaining the rate of expansion are becoming more binding. The most important of these is in the labour market, where shortages of skilled labour are increasingly likely to hinder expansion. Falling unemployment rates – particularly among better-qualified workers – are likely to test the commitment of the social partners to wage restraint. The country's infrastructure, especially the urban road system, is increasingly inadequate for the level of activity it now has to bear. The level of house price inflation in the main urban centres is of concern not only from a social perspective but also because it affects the cost of recruiting employees and the willingness of people to work and live in Ireland. These developments will reduce the attractiveness of the country as a location for FDI and act as a brake on the growth rate in the years ahead. Finally, Ireland's heavy dependence on foreign-owned firms in a few key sectors has increased our exposure to the world business cycle and to conditions in these sectors. A serious downturn in the world microelectronics market, for example, would have grave repercussions for employment in the Dublin region.

But it is hard not to believe that earlier generations of Irish men and women would have preferred to have had the opportunity to face these challenges and risks than to be confronted with the stagnation and lack of opportunities that characterised the Irish economy for so long.

2.9 Conclusion

The main topics covered in this chapter included:

- The long-run economic performance of the economy as indicated by the trends in emigration and the real growth rate
- Convergence
- Factors which constrained the development of the economy prior to 1960, such as protectionism, state involvement in industry, reliance on the UK economy and emigration
- Factors which contributed to the improved economic performance after 1960, such as external assistance, industrial policy and investment in education.

Chapter 3

Introduction to the Theory of Income Determination

3.1   Introduction

We saw in Chapter 1 that the primary objectives of macroeconomic policy are to achieve a high and stable growth rate in national output and to maintain a low level of unemployment. A low rate of inflation is also desirable, both in its own right and because it helps to achieve high and stable growth. In pursuing these objectives policy-makers are constrained by the need to avoid excessive fiscal and current account balance of payments deficits.

In Chapter 2 we discussed Ireland's economic performance over the long term. We explored the factors that influenced the growth and development of the economy. In this chapter we turn to the short term and the issue of fluctuations round the long-run growth path. From the business cycle and unemployment data given in Chapter 1 (Figures 1.2 and 1.3) it is clear that these fluctuations have been very marked. These are the subject of a great deal of commentary and preoccupy economic policy-makers.

To increase our understanding of the short-term economic fluctuations we introduce a simple model of how the economy behaves. We outline two broad schools of thought, classical and Keynesian, and explain how they differ in regard to their conclusions about the workings of the economy and the scope for an active macroeconomic policy.

3.2   The Circular Flow of Income

Macroeconomic theory uses models to explain how the economy works. Model building consists in setting out the way in which variables such as GNP, national income, unemployment and the price level are interrelated. A model can be used to explore how policy variables, such as government expenditure and the exchange

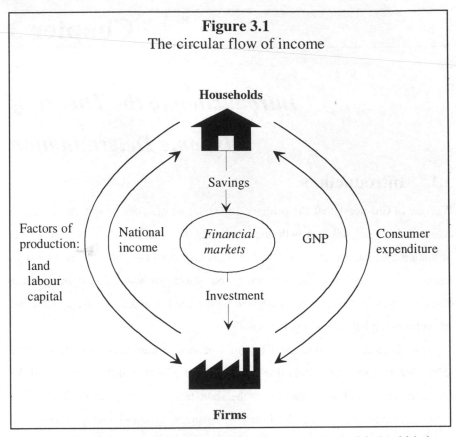

Figure 3.1
The circular flow of income

Households

Savings

Factors of
production:

land
labour
capital

National
income

*Financial
markets*

GNP

Consumer
expenditure

Investment

Firms

rate, affect the economy's performance. A macroeconomic model should help us to:

- explain economic events
- prescribe solutions to economic problems.

It is important to bear in mind that models are based on theories. It is necessary to keep testing economic theories against the facts to make sure that they are consistent with reality. A theory of the Irish economy would not be much use if, for example, it predicted that unemployment would always be low.

Note:
Economists use econometric theory to estimate economic models. This involves using statistical techniques to estimate the parameters or coefficients of a model and to carry out various diagnostic tests. Lawrence Klein developed one of the first large-scale macroeconometric models at the University of Pennsylvania in the 1950s. In Ireland, the two most widely used models have been developed by the Central Bank of Ireland and the Economic and Social Research Institute (ESRI).

In this chapter we develop the theory of income determination which is based on the *circular flow of income*. First attempts to develop such a theory were made by a court physician to Louis XV, François Quesnay (1694-1774), but the modern version owes much to the work of the Cambridge economist John Maynard Keynes (1883-1946), whose influence has dominated macroeconomic theory since the 1930s.

Figure 3.1 presents a simple model of an economy. We assume that there is no government and no foreign trade. We also assume that the *price level is fixed or constant*. These simplifying assumptions will be dropped later, and the model will be elaborated to correspond more closely to the real world.

There are only two kinds of economic agent in our simple economy, namely, households and firms. Consider the two loops on the left-hand side of the diagram. Households own the *factors of production*: land, labour, capital and natural resources. These factors of production are made available to firms in return for payments of rent, wages, interest and profit. Wages are paid for the use of labour, rent for the use of land, interest for the use of capital, and the owners of firms receive profits. The sum of rent, wages, interest and profit equals *national income*.

Note:

If we ignore rent, interest and profits, the two loops on the left-hand side simply represent people going to work and receiving a salary or wage for their labour.

Consider now the two loops on the right-hand side. (Ignore for the moment the flows to and from financial markets.) Firms combine the factors of production to produce goods and services. We do not go into detail about the techniques of production. We shall just assume that inputs of land, labour and capital simply enter a "black box" called the *production function*, and outputs of goods and services emerge on the other side. We shall use the term *GNP* (Gross National Product) to describe the aggregate output of goods and services. To close the loop, households, using the income they have earned (national income), purchase the goods and services produced by firms. We refer to this household expenditure as *private consumer expenditure* (C). Given that the two right-hand loops are equal, that is, expenditure equals output, it follows:

$$GNP \equiv C \qquad\qquad (1)$$

where the symbol ≡ denotes *an identity* or something that is true by definition.

Going a stage further, since all of the money received by firms is passed on to households in the form of wages, rent, interest and profit, it is also true that total expenditure equals national income. Hence:

$$\text{National income} \equiv \text{GNP} \equiv \text{C} \tag{2}$$

The essential message of the simplified circular flow diagram given in Figure 3.1 is that, in the aggregate, we consume what we produce, and we spend what we earn. People go to work and get paid, and spend their income purchasing the goods and services produced by the firms.

Saving and investment

Notice that in Figure 3.1 there are two additional flows relating to *saving* (S) and *investment* (I), which we have not yet mentioned. The flow of savings reflects the fact that households do not spend all of their income. Some proportion of income is saved. This represents a *leakage* from the circular flow. Now given that people must either spend or save their income, it follows that the sum of consumer expenditure and saving equals national income. That is:

$$\text{National income} \equiv \text{C} + \text{S} \tag{3}$$

In the modern economy, household saving are channelled into the financial system (banks and building societies). Firms borrow from these institutions in order to finance *investment* (I). Investment refers to firms' expenditure on new machinery and buildings. Thus, households do not buy all of the goods and services produced by firms. Some firms purchase machines and materials from other firms. Total expenditure now equals consumer expenditure plus investment. Substituting into (2), above, we obtain:

$$\text{National income} \equiv \text{GNP} \equiv \text{Total expenditure} \equiv \text{C} + \text{I} \tag{4}$$

This relationship states that national income equals GNP, which in turn equals total expenditure. Total expenditure, in turn, is divided into households' consumer expenditure and firms' investment expenditure. Note that the the letters or symbols we are using to describe macroeconomic variables have become standard.[1]

---

1. It was not always so. In a paper entitled, "Mr Keynes and the Classics" (*Econometrica*, April 1937) which reviewed *The General Theory*, the Nobel prize-winning economist John Hicks (1904-1989) used

54

The government and foreign sectors

Earlier we made the simplifying assumption that there was no government or foreign sector. The discussion of the national income accounts in Chapter 4 explains in some detail the exact relationship between households, firms, government and the foreign sector. At this stage we make the point that if government and a foreign sector are included, total expenditure expands to include government consumption expenditure (G), exports (X) and imports (M). Total expenditure now consists of five categories:

Private consumer expenditure	C
Investment	I
Government current expenditure	G
Exports	X
minus Imports	– M

In short:

$$\text{Total expenditure} \equiv C + I + G + X - M \qquad (5)$$

Exports are expenditure by foreigners on Irish-produced goods and services; imports are expenditure by Irish people on goods produced in other countries. Imports are deducted from total expenditure to arrive at expenditure on *domestically* produced goods and services. C, G, X and I include expenditure on both domestic and imported goods and services. Subtracting M leaves us with expenditure on the domestically produced goods. The difference between exports and imports $(X - M)$ is referred to as *net exports*, NX, so we can rewrite (5) as

$$\text{Total expenditure (TE)} \equiv C + I + G + NX \qquad (6)$$

Inserting (6) into (4) gives:

$$NI \equiv GNP \equiv C + I + G + NX \qquad (7)$$

This relationship states that national income (NI) equals output which, in turn, equals total expenditure. We use (7), above, to explain how the government can influence output and employment. Before doing so, however, we introduce two further concepts and we explain the role of stocks in macroeconomic analysis.

---

the symbol I for national income. In a letter to Hicks, Keynes wrote: "I regret that you use the symbol I for income. One has to choose, of course, between using it for income and investment. But, after trying both, I believe it is easier to use Y for income and I for investment. Anyhow we ought to try and keep uniform in usage." This letter is reproduced in J. R. Hicks, *Economic Perspectives: Further Essays on Money and Growth*, Oxford University Press, 1977, p. 145.

The basic assumption is that firms have a planned or desired stock level and they set aside a proportion of their output for stock building. If, however, sales fall short of what was anticipated, the firm will have produced too much output and there will be an unplanned accumulation of stocks. Conversely, if sales exceed expectations, the firm will have produced too little output and there will be an unplanned reduction in stocks.

In any given period, therefore, total stock changes (ΔSK) will consist of a planned component (ΔSK$_p$) and an unplanned component (ΔSK$_u$):

$$\Delta SK = \Delta SK_p + \Delta SK_u$$

Now ΔSK$_p$ is classified as a part of investment. However, ΔSK$_u$ is classified as part of GNP and is not included in investment or total expenditure. This means that if GNP exceeds aggregate demand, ΔSK$_u$ is positive and firms will cut production until GNP equals aggregate demand. Conversely, if GNP is less than aggregate demand, ΔSK$_u$ is negative and firms will expand production until GNP equals aggregate demand. Thus changes in unplanned stocks play a crucial role in modern macroeconomics, sending signals to managers on which they base their production plans. The macroeconomy is said to be in equilibrium when GNP equals aggregate demand and ΔSK$_u$ = 0.

Aggregate demand and aggregate supply

We can think of expenditure as *demand*.[2] If someone spends money on a cup of coffee, they contribute to the demand for coffee. Total expenditure is referred to as *aggregate demand* (AD). This is a particularly important concept in macroeconomic analysis.

The total amount of goods and services produced by firms, which we have labelled GNP, may also be referred to as *aggregate supply* (AS). The concepts of AD and AS are at the heart of all macroeconomic models. If AS equals AD, the economy is said to be in *equilibrium*. If AS exceeds AD, there is an *excess supply* of goods and services. If AS is less than AD, there is an *excess demand* for goods and services.

An important role is played by changes in *stocks* or inventories. (See Box 3.1.) *Unplanned* changes in stocks arise if the economy is not in equilibrium. In particular if

$$AS = AD \qquad \text{unplanned changes in stocks are zero}$$

---

2. Prices are, however, fixed, so this demand is not like the demand schedules of microeconomics.

$$\text{AS} > \text{AD} \qquad \text{unplanned stocks increase}$$
$$\text{AS} < \text{AD} \qquad \text{unplanned stocks decrease.}$$

Unplanned changes in stocks send signals to firms whether to increase or decrease production. If unplanned changes in stocks form part of GNP, equation (7) can be rewritten as:

$$\text{NI} \equiv \text{GNP} = \text{C} + \text{I} + \text{G} + \text{NX} \qquad (8)$$

Note that the identity sign ($\equiv$) between GNP and the components of AD has been replaced by an equals sign ($=$) in order to allow for an *equilibrium/disequilibrium* relationship to exist between the two variables. If GNP exceeds total expenditure (AS > AD), firms are producing too much output. This is a signal to cut back on production. Similarly, if GNP is less than total expenditure (AS < AD), firms are producing too little output. This is a signal to increase production. We now turn to the question of how the government can achieve growth and employment objectives.

Fiscal policy

How does unemployment fit into this picture? In the circular flow diagram, land and capital are constant in the short run. Hence, if a firm wishes to expand its output, it will tend to hire more workers. Recall from Chapter 1 that:

$$\text{Labour force} = \text{employed} + \text{unemployed}$$

Assuming the labour force is relatively constant, an increase in employment will be associated with a fall in unemployment. Overall, an increase in GNP or national income should lead to an increase in employment and a fall in unemployment.

What can the government do if output and income are stagnant and there is a high rate of unemployment? One possibility is for the government to boost total expenditure and thereby create an additional demand for goods and services. An increase in government expenditure (G) leads to an increase in total expenditure (TE). Given that the level of output is initially unchanged, the government has created an *excess demand* for goods and services. Firms will recognise the excess demand through falling levels of stocks, and respond by increasing production. To do so, firms must hire more labour, so unemployment will fall. To compensate households for the extra labour they have supplied, more wages will be paid and national income will increase.

In short:

$$\uparrow G \rightarrow \uparrow AD \rightarrow \downarrow U \text{ and } \uparrow NI$$

In terms of equation (8):

$$C + I + \uparrow G + NX = \uparrow GNP \equiv \uparrow NI \rightarrow \uparrow E \rightarrow \downarrow U$$

where E and U denote employment and unemployment respectively. Conversely, a decrease in government expenditure would lead to an excess supply of output. As stocks build up, firms respond by reducing output and workers are laid off. Employment decreases and national income declines.

Note:

The government could also vary total expenditure by changing taxation. An increase in taxation would, for example, reduce consumer expenditure.

This type of policy, where the government uses its own expenditure and/or taxation to influence total expenditure, is referred to as *fiscal policy*. An increase in expenditure is referred to as an *expansionary* fiscal policy and a decrease in expenditure as a *contractionary* fiscal policy. The active use of public spending and taxation in this manner raises a number of important questions about the level of taxation, borrowing, and the manner in which the government spends its money.

3.3   The Theory of Income Determination

We now move beyond the simple circular flow diagram and develop an aggregate demand (AD) and aggregate supply (AS) framework. *The price level is now allowed to vary*. This adds a new dimension to the simplified analysis in the previous section. A demand curve shows the relationship between the price a firm charges and consumers' demand for that product. The higher the price, the lower the demand for the product. Similarly, a supply curve shows the relationship between price and the firm's willingness to supply a product. More will be offered for sale, the higher the price.

The rationale behind supply and demand schedules for individual products is explained in courses in microeconomics. Similar but somewhat different

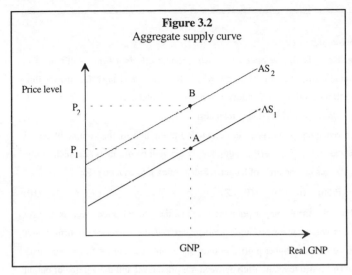

Figure 3.2
Aggregate supply curve

Price level

P_2 .... B

P_1 .... A

GNP$_1$ Real GNP

AS$_2$

AS$_1$

considerations apply to the AD and AS schedules in macroeconomics. At this stage we give a brief, intuitive explanation of why the AD and AS schedules slope downwards and upwards, respectively. A full treatment cannot be presented until we have developed our knowledge of the money and labour markets more fully in later chapters.

Aggregate supply schedule

Figure 3.2 shows an upward-sloping aggregate supply (AS) curve. The price level (P) and real GNP are measured on the vertical and horizontal axes, respectively. (Recall that a change in real GNP amounts to a change in the volume or quantity of goods and services produced or consumed.) An upward-sloping AS curve indicates that an increase in P will lead to an increase in the supply of goods and services. Conversely, a decrease in the price level will lead to a fall in the supply of goods and services. Box 3.2 provides a theoretical explanation as to why this should be the case.

Location of the AS curve

As mentioned, the AS curve is drawn for a given level of input prices or total costs. *If input prices (costs) change, the AS curve will shift.* To see this, consider the point A in Figure 3.2, where the price level, P_1, corresponds to the real output level, GNP$_1$. Suppose that costs increase and firms, in order to maintain profits, pass these higher costs on to customers in the form of higher prices for their products. In terms of equation (10) in Box 3.2, the increase in input prices is reflected in an increase in output prices in order to maintain profit levels. The increase in output prices is shown in Figure 3.2 as a movement from A to B. At B, real GNP is unchanged, but the price level has increased from P_1 to P_2. The supply schedule has shifted upwards to the left, from AS_1 to AS_2. By moving the AS curve upwards in this way, we can examine the relationship between the new, higher price level and the original level of real GNP. Conversely, lower input prices will be reflected in a shift downwards to the right of the AS curve.

An important influence on the location of the AS curve, which we have not yet mentioned, is *productivity*, defined as the ratio of output to inputs. (Total output divided by the quantity of labour employed is referred to as labour productivity.) If more output is obtained from the same, or fewer, inputs, productivity has increased. This occurs as technology improves or there is an improvement in working practices. An increase in productivity reduces costs as more output can be produced with a given amount of inputs. Hence, an increase in productivity shifts the AS curve down to the right, whereas a decrease in productivity shifts the AS curve upwards to the left.

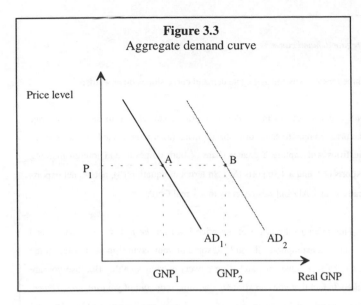

Figure 3.3
Aggregate demand curve

In summary, the key point to note is that an increase in input prices (costs) or a fall in productivity will shift the AS curve to the left. Conversely, a fall in input prices or a rise in productivity will shift the AS curve to the right.

Aggregate demand schedule

As mentioned earlier, total expenditure is referred to as aggregate demand (AD). On the demand side of the economy there is an inverse relationship between the price level and real GNP. This is shown by a downward-sloping aggregate demand (AD) curve (Figure 3.3). It is easy to understand why a change in price would affect the demand for a firm's output. If a firm lowers its price, consumers will switch their spending from alternative products with a higher price. The demand for the firm's product will increase and the demand for the substitute product will fall. But why should a change in the general price level P affect the aggregate level of spending? The theoretical explanation for this is given in Box 3.3.

Location of the AD curve

Let us consider now the factors that determine the location of the AD curve. For a given price level, an increase in any component of AD, such as C, I, G or NX, will shift the AD curve upwards to the right. A fall in any of the components of AD will shift the curve downwards to the left. The government can therefore use fiscal policy to shift the AD curve. To see how, consider the point A in Figure 3.3, which corresponds to a price level P_1 and a real GNP level of GNP_1. An increase

Box 3.3

The slope of the aggregate demand curve

There are basically three reasons why the aggregate demand curve slopes downwards:

International substitution effect A fall in the domestic price level relative to the *foreign* price level will increase the price competitiveness of domestic firms (assuming a fixed exchange rate). As a result, domestic firms will capture a greater share of both domestic and foreign markets. Hence, a $\downarrow$ P $\rightarrow$ $\uparrow$ exports (X) and a $\downarrow$ imports (M). In terms of equation (8), above, net exports (NX) rise, and this leads to an $\uparrow$ AD and subsequently to a $\uparrow$ real GNP.

Real balance effect This refers to the effect of the price level on *the real value of assets* and subsequently on the level of consumption. If you hold some of your savings in cash, a fall in the price level will increase the real value (or purchasing power) of your wealth. Because you are now richer, you are likely to feel that you can afford to consume more out of your income. Hence, a $\downarrow$ P $\rightarrow$ $\uparrow$ households' wealth $\rightarrow$ $\uparrow$ consumption (C) $\rightarrow$ $\uparrow$ aggregate demand (AD). The real balance effect is known as the *Pigou effect* because it was first suggested by Keynes's contemporary at Cambridge University, Arthur C. Pigou (1877-1959).

Inter-temporal substitution Briefly, the argument here is that high interest rates (r) encourage consumers to postpone or abandon expenditure plans because of the high cost of borrowing money. For example, suppose you intend to finance the purchase of a CD player by borrowing from a bank. If interest rates increase, you may decide to make do with your old music system as the cost of finance is too high. On the other hand, low interest rates encourage people to spend as the cost of borrowing is cheap.

As explained in detail in later chapters, there is a relationship between the price level (P) and the interest rate (r). A fall in the price level leads to a fall in the rate of interest. The fall in the interest rate, in turn, leads to increased spending on interest-sensitive components of AD, such as consumer expenditure (C) and investment (I). Conversely, a higher price level increases the interest rate. The higher interest rate should lower C and I and, therefore, aggregate demand.

in G moves the AD curve out to the right. B is a point on the new aggregate demand curve, AD_2. At this point the level of output has risen to GNP_2. By moving the AD curve outwards to the right in this fashion, we can examine the relationship between the old price level and the new higher level of real GNP.

In summary, an increase in C, I, G, X or a decrease in M will shift the AD curve up to the right and vice versa.

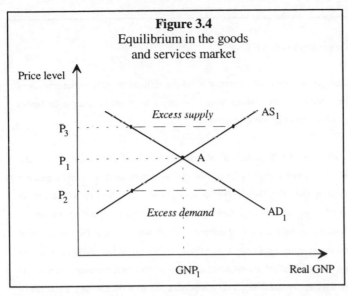

Figure 3.4
Equilibrium in the goods
and services market

Equilibrium

In Figure 3.4, the AS and AD curves are brought together, and we see that the equilibrium price (P_1) and real output (GNP_1) combination is at the point A. Recall that changes in stocks act as a signal to firms as to whether production should be increased, reduced or left unchanged. At the point A, there are no unplanned (unanticipated) changes in stocks. This is the key to the concept of equilibrium in the market for goods and services.

If the price level is lower than P_1, as at P_2, AS is less than AD and there is excess aggregate demand. This excess demand will lead to an unplanned reduction in stocks. In order to ration the available supply among those trying to buy it, firms will raise prices. As the price level rises, this encourages firms to increase production (along the AS curve) and reduces the demand for goods (along the AD curve). Eventually equilibrium will be restored at the point A.

Similarly, if the price level is greater than P_1, as at P_3, AS exceeds AD and there is an excess supply of goods and services. There will be an unplanned increase in stocks. Firms will lower prices in order to clear unwanted stocks. As the price level falls, firms will cut production (along the AS curve) and the demand for goods and services will increase (along the AD curve). Again equilibrium will be reached at the point A.

Note that "equilibrium" simply means that the market clears. It implies nothing about the associated level of unemployment. Point A in Figure 3.4 does not necessarily correspond to the full employment level of output. However, the classical economists believed that there are forces that tend to ensure that equilibrium will correspond to full employment. We turn to this issue now.

Box 3.4

Factors influencing the growth of potential GNP

The growth of the labour force The most important of all the influences on long-run growth of output are the skills and motivation of the labour force. The larger and more productive the labour force, the more goods and services that can be produced.

The growth of the capital stock Increases in a country's stock of productive assets and technological progress allow more output to be produced. Inasmuch as new technologies are usually embodied in new equipment, a high level of investment is vital to sustain a high growth rate of potential output. We showed above (section 3.2) how investment in capital equipment has to be financed from domestic savings in a closed economy. Even when there is the possibility of borrowing from abroad (by running a balance of payments deficit), domestic savings are still by far the most important way of funding investment. Because of this link between savings and investment, economists have always attributed a very important role to thrift among the sources of economic progress.

The supply of raw materials If a country has an abundance of natural resources, such as oil and gas fields, then this will increase the country's potential output. Likewise, scarcities of key raw materials could hinder the growth of the economy. Such scarcities have not, however, been much of a constraint on growth over the years. New sources of supply are always opening up and new technologies are constantly finding ways of economising on raw materials.

3.4 Classical Economics

Classical economics emerged gradually from the writings of the great eighteenth and nineteenth-century British economists, such as David Hume (1711-1776), Adam Smith (1723-1790), David Ricardo (1772-1823) and John Stuart Mill (1806-1873). It provided a strong intellectual justification for a non-interventionist, *laissez-faire* political economy. The classical economists believed that, in the long run at least, the economy tends automatically towards full employment (natural rate of unemployment) without the benefit of active macroeconomic management. The only sound policy was to avoid fiscal deficits: governments, like households, should always balance their books. At the heart of the classical model is the concept of *full employment* or *potential GNP*.

Potential GNP Potential GNP is defined as that level of output that could be

Figure 3.5
Classical model

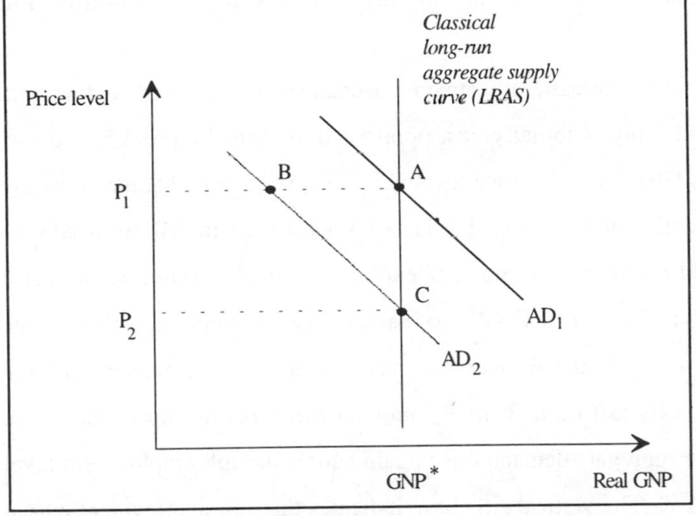

produced in the economy, given the state of technology, the size of the labour force, and without accelerating inflation. If the economy is operating at this level, firms are operating at capacity and there is full employment in the labour market. This level of output is therefore referred to as *potential GNP* or *full employment GNP* and the underlying level of unemployment is referred to as the *natural rate of unemployment.* Box 3.4 outlines the main factors that influence the growth of potential GNP over time.

Note:
Capacity output means that firms have no spare capacity. They cannot produce any more goods or services with their available reserves. Recall that "full employment" does not imply zero unemployment.

The long-run aggregate supply schedule

We saw in the previous section how the economy moves towards equilibrium through firms reacting to unplanned changes in stocks. *The really interesting question is whether this equilibrium will correspond to the full employment or potential level of GNP.* The distinguishing prediction of the classical model is that this will, in fact, be the case.

In Figure 3.5 the price level (P) is represented on the vertical axis, and real GNP on the horizontal axis. The level of GNP corresponding to potential GNP is indicated as GNP^*. If actual GNP is less than the potential level, firms are operating at less than full capacity and unemployment will increase. The classical model holds that the aggregate supply schedule (AS) is vertical at the point corresponding to potential GNP. According to this model there exists an automatic adjustment mechanism which tends to drive the economy towards full employment.

To see how the automatic adjustment mechanism is supposed to function, assume that the economy is initially at a point such as A in Figure 3.5. At this point, GNP equals GNP^* and the price level is P_1. Suppose now that the economy is subjected to a deflationary shock, that is, a leftward shift in AD from AD_1 to AD_2. (This would occur, for example, if exports declined.) Initially, the price level remains at P_1 and output at GNP^*, so that an excess supply equivalent to the distance between points A and B emerges. The classical model predicts that *the price level will quickly fall from P_1 to P_2*, moving the economy down along the AD_2 schedule until aggregate demand once again equals the full employment level of output, GNP^* at C. The vertical AS curve indicates that full employment output is maintained by the rapid adjustment downwards of the price level in the face of excess supply. Thus, excess unemployment proves to be a short-run phenomenon that disappears quickly as the economy reverts, of its own accord, back to GNP^*.

The classical model and economic policy

The policy conclusion that emerges from the classical analysis is that there is no need for intervention on the part of the authorities. The economy automatically reverts back to potential GNP.

Similarly, classical theory predicts that the government cannot increase real GNP beyond the potential level for any length of time. Suppose the economy is at the point A in Figure 3.6, and the government implements an expansionary fiscal policy either by increasing government expenditure and/or lowering taxes. The AD curve shifts outwards to the right, from AD_1 to AD_2, and the economy moves from A to B. At the point B there is an excess demand for goods and services and this puts upward pressure on the price level. As the price level rises from P_1 to P_2, the economy will move back along AD_2 until the point C is reached. At C the economy is once again in equilibrium on the AS schedule. The government's attempt to stimulate the economy has only resulted in an increase in the price level: there has been no long-run gain in output.

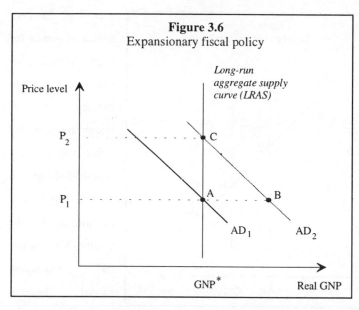

Figure 3.6
Expansionary fiscal policy

In the classical model, therefore, there is no scope for the government to influence the level of output or employment. The only way to increase the level of output is by increasing potential GNP, which requires a rightward shift of the AS curve. This comes about through growth in the skills and expertise of the labour force and investment in new and better capital equipment. Thus, classical economists place the emphasis on supply-side measures rather than on the manipulation of aggregate demand, as the way to achieve lasting increases in the level of output.

Supply-side policies

With demand-side policies ruled out as ineffective and potentially inflationary, the classical model relies on policies designed to shift the AS schedule to the right in order to increase the level of real GNP. Examples are an increase in the productivity of the labour force. The shift in the AS curve results in higher output and a decline in the price level, which is a highly desirable outcome (Figure 3.7). When supply-side policies are successfully pursued, the improvement in real output is accompanied by a fall in the price level.

Events that shift the AS curve to the left have a harmful effect on the economy, resulting in rising prices and falling output, a combination that has been labelled *stagflation*. A leftward shift of the AS curve occurred when the price of energy inputs rose sharply in the 1970s, and again, although only briefly, during the Persian Gulf crisis of 1990-91. The collapse of oil prices in 1986 was a very favourable supply-side shock.

67

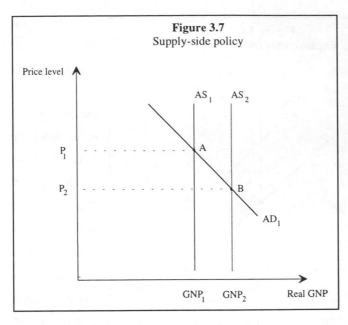

Figure 3.7
Supply-side policy

Concern over a tendency for prices to rise, even when the official indices of unemployment are quite high, led to a renewed interest in supply-side economics in the 1980s. Versions of the underlying model became popular in the US during the Reagan administration and in Britain during the Thatcher era. It was widely believed that the key to greater prosperity lay in shifting the AS curve to the right by increasing the incentives for the unemployed to accept whatever jobs were available and encouraging people to work harder and take greater risks by lowering the top rates of income tax. Demand-side policies were considered to be less effective.

3.5   Keynesian Economics

Keynes, whose most important book was *The General Theory of Employment, Interest and Money* (1936), felt that the classical model was unable to explain the reality of the Great Depression. He believed that it was obvious that very high rates of unemployment tended to persist beyond what could reasonably be called the "short run".[3] He questioned the efficacy of the mechanisms that were supposed to keep the economy at or near full employment. He proposed active management of the economy by government to supplement the self-correcting tendencies of the market.

---

3. Of course it all depends on how long the short run is. Keynes quipped: "In the long run we are all dead." The neoclassical economists, however, countered that Keynes was dead and that they were stuck with the long run!

Keynes remarked in the preface to *The General Theory:*

The composition of this book has been for the author a long struggle to escape . . . The difficulty lies, not in the new ideas, but in escaping from the old ones, which ramify . . . into every corner of our minds.[4]

At the time he was writing, the industrial countries of the world were in the severest depression in modern history. In the US the unemployment rate increased from 3.2 per cent in 1929 to a peak of 25 per cent in 1933, before falling back to 17.2 per cent in 1939. By the time Franklin Delano Roosevelt (FDR) took office in 1933, the depression was much more severe than anything experienced in the past. Unemployment in Britain increased from 10.4 per cent in 1927 to a peak of 22.1 per cent in 1932, before decreasing to 2.4 per cent in 1942. In Ireland, unemployment increased from 22,858 in 1929 to a peak of 133,319 in 1933, and decreased to 83,963 in 1942.[5]

However, not all of the European countries remained mired in depression throughout the 1930s. In Italy, the Fascist regime had embarked on a public works programme in the 1920s and averted the worst effects of the Great Depression. After Hitler's accession to power in Germany in 1933, government expenditure was increased and there was a rapid expansion in output and employment. In Sweden a Social Democratic government had maintained a high level of employment by expending public works programmes. Keynes, in a lecture delivered in University College, Dublin, in 1933, mentioned with approval the fact that European countries "have cast their eyes or are casting them towards new modes of political economy". He praised the protectionist policies of the recently installed Fianna Fáil government as an alternative to the *laissez-faire* recommendations of classical economics.[6]

---

4. J. M. Keynes, *The General Theory of Employment, Interest and Money*, London: Macmillan, 1936, p. viii.

5. We use the numbers unemployed rather than an estimate of the unemployment rate because estimates of the labour force at this time are unreliable.

6. J. M. Keynes, "National Self-Sufficiency" (the first Finlay Lecture at University College, Dublin), reprinted in *Studies*, June 1933, p. 184. Keynes went on to decry "decadent international capitalism" which, he said, "doesn't deliver the goods".

Policy-makers in the English-speaking democracies at this time did not have a macroeconomic model that would have justified action by governments to move the economy out of the depression. Keynes's *General Theory* was devoted to developing such a model. At its crudest, what he proposed was relatively simple. If the economy is in a depression, with high unemployment and plenty of unused capacity, government should increase spending or reduce taxation. This would lead to a higher level of economic activity and lower unemployment.

In fact Keynes's ideas had little immediate impact on policy. The Establishment in America, as well as in Britain, remained intellectually committed to the tenets of orthodox (classical) economics, which predicted that in due course the economy would right itself. Their main concern was with balancing the budget. Taxes were raised and expenditure cut, which had the effect of exacerbating the unemployment problem. Only when government spending on armaments soared and vast numbers were mobilised into active military service, as World War II loomed, did unemployment begin to fall rapidly.

Note:
In times of recession the government's budget automatically worsens. The government pays out more in social welfare to the newly unemployed and collects less in tax revenue. If the government attempts to balance the budget in these circumstances, it must raise taxes or cut expenditure. This will decrease aggregate demand and make the recession worse.

The Keynesian model

To understand how the Keynesian model justifies intervention by government to move the economy towards full employment, consider Figure 3.8. The diagram shows the familiar downward-sloping AD curve. The AS curve, however, is vertical at the potential GNP level (this corresponds with the classical model), but at other levels of real GNP is either horizontal or positively sloped. Keynes argued that the slope of the AS curve is not uniform at all levels of real GNP. When there is a great deal of excess capacity in the economy and the unemployment rate is high, the AS curve is likely to be horizontal. As GNP* is approached, the AS curve becomes steeper and eventually vertical. Keynes, therefore, proposed a kinked AS curve compared to the vertical one proposed by the classics.

Suppose the economy is at A and there is a shift of the AD curve from AD_1 to AD_2. The economy moves along the AS curve to the point B. Note that, in

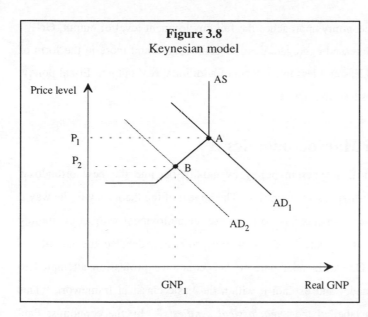

Figure 3.8
Keynesian model

contrast to the classical model, *both the price level and real GNP adjust following the shift of the AD curve.* The relative size of the changes in P and real GNP depend on the slope of the AS curve. If the AS curve were relatively flat, a shift to the left of the AD curve would result in a large decrease in real GNP and a small decrease in the price level. In the classical analysis only the price level changes. The level of output remains at GNP*.

At B the economy can be said to be in equilibrium because the level of output, measured along the horizontal axis, has been reduced to correspond to the level that is demanded. There is no unwanted or unintended accumulation of stocks. However, actual GNP is less than potential GNP, and unemployment over and above the full employment level emerges.

Keynes argued that the economy could remain at the point B in the long run and not merely for some brief period of time. He argued that output gaps could persist and that the economy could get stuck at levels of output below GNP*.

From a policy perspective, note that if the economy is on the horizontal portion of the AS curve, a shift to the right in the AD curve leads to an increase in real GNP without a marked increase in the price level. As the economy approaches full employment, however, the AS curve becomes increasingly steep. Any further shift of the AD curve to the right will lead to an increase in the price level and real output.

Thus Keynes argued that output gaps could persist and that the government should intervene and use fiscal policy to eliminate the resultant unemployment. Fiscal policy would be highly effective along the flat segment of the AS curve.

However, as the economy approaches the full employment level of output, GNP*, the response to increased aggregate demand comes more and more in the form of higher prices, and less and less in the form of additional real output. Fiscal policy, therefore, becomes less appropriate.

3.6 Modern Macroeconomics

After World War II Keynesian policy eventually became the new orthodoxy, especially in English-speaking countries. The appeal of the theory lay in the way it seemed to show governments how to minimise unemployment without enkindling inflation. At the theoretical level the whole profession debated the validity of Keynes's ideas. One influential part of the economics profession attempted to refine Keynes's model and explain it within the basic classical framework. This development was labelled the *"neoclassical synthesis"* by the economist Paul Samuelson.[7]

Between 1940 and the mid-1970s, the neoclassical synthesis was accepted by the majority of economists and much work was carried on refining some of the main theories or concepts identified by Keynes. Among the main advances were:

- The IS/LM model developed by John Hicks (Chapter 11). This model offered a graphical explanation of the Keynesian theory and allowed economists to assess the effectiveness of macroeconomic policy.

- New theories of growth were advanced by economists such as Roy Harrod and Robert Solow.

- New elaborate theories of consumer behaviour were developed independently by Franco Modigliani and Milton Friedman (Chapter 5). These theories offered a long-run perspective on how people make consumption decisions.

- James Tobin expounded new theories of investment and the demand for money (Chapter 10).

During the 1960s the most important debate was between the Keynesians and the monetarists whose intellectual leader was the aforementioned Milton Friedman. The Keynesian/monetarist debate centred on issues such as the relative effectiveness of fiscal and monetary policy and whether or not there is a trade-off

---

7. Paul Samuelson is an American Nobel prize-winner in economics who wrote the first modern textbook of economics aimed at university students.

between inflation and unemployment (Chapters 12 and 13). All of the above-mentioned economists (with the exception of Harrod, who died before the prize was established) have been awarded Nobel prizes in economics. An appendix to this chapter gives a list of winners of the Nobel prize in economic sciences from 1969 to 1997 and a brief description of their contribution and achievement.

However, in the 1970s, following the lead set by the monetarists, a classical counter-revolution gained ground. First, as economies began to experience stagflation (rising inflation *and* rising unemployment), there was increasing scepticism about the Keynesian model and in particular the effectiveness of macroeconomic policy in achieving lasting increases in employment and output.

Second and most important, new sophisticated versions of the classical model emerged that emphasised the role of *rational expectations*. The chief exponents of this new theory were the American economists Robert Lucas (who was awarded the Nobel prize in 1995), Thomas Sargent and Robert Barro. We discuss their ideas in a later chapter. This school of thought, which is known as *New Classical* or *Rational Expectations* macroeconomics, argues that there is no trade-off between inflation and unemployment and that policy-makers cannot use large-scale macroeconomic models to evaluate policy decisions (the Lucas critique).

It is probably fair to say that a new synthesis has now emerged which involves the acceptance of the rational expectations theory set in a Keynesian framework. This new rational expectations synthesis is now accepted by most mainstream economists.

In the context of this new synthesis, macroeconomics has evolved in many directions. Rudiger Dornbush, for example, has been influential in emphasising the importance of the exchange rate in open economy macroeconomics (Chapters 16 to 24). A *New Keynesian* school, associated with economists such as Gregory Mankiw, have focused on imperfections in labour and credit markets and examined the implications of this in the context of the Rational Expectations model.

It will be clear to the reader that there is still a good deal of disagreement between economists, especially in regard to the effectiveness of policies to alleviate the problem of unemployment. It is our task in the chapters that follow to outline the various issues and to outline the different strands to the arguments in this ongoing debate.

3.7 Conclusion

In this chapter we have introduced the broad themes of macroeconomics. These included:

- The idea of a macroeconomic model
- The circular flow of income and the relationship between expenditure, output, income and employment
- The role of unplanned changes in stocks or inventories in maintaining the equilibrium level of production
- The theory of income determination and the concepts of aggregate supply and aggregate demand
- The classical macroeconomic model and the concept of an automatic mechanism tending to maintain the economy at the full employment or potential level of output.
- Keynes's dissatisfaction with the contradiction between the classical model's prediction that the economy always tended to full employment and the reality of widespread, persistent unemployment during the Great Depression
- The Keynesian model of income determination
- The role of policies that affect the supply side of the economy
- Developments in modern macroeconomics.

Appendix

Nobel prize in economic sciences winners: 1969-97

1969   Ragnar Frisch and Jan Tinbergen (joint award)

For the development and the application of dynamic models for the analysis of economic processes.

1970   Paul Samuelson

The development of static and dynamic economic theory and his contribution to raising the level of analysis in economic science.

1971   Simon Kuznets

For his empirically founded interpretation of economic growth which led to a new insight into the economic and social structure and process of development.

1972   John Hicks and Kenneth Arrow (joint award)

For their pioneering contributions to general economic equilibrium theory and welfare theory.

1973   Wassily Leontief

For the development of the input-output method and for its application to important economic problems.

1974   Gunnar Myrdal and Friedrich August Von Hayek (divided equally)

For their pioneering work in the theory of money and economic fluctuations and for their analysis of the interdependence of economic, social and institutional phenomena.

1975   Leonid Kantorovich and Tjalling Koopmans (joint award)

For their contributions to the theory of optimum allocation of resources.

1976   Milton Friedman

For his achievements in the fields of consumption analysis, monetary history and theory and for his demonstration of the complexity of stabilisation policy.

1977   Bertil Ohlin and James Meade (divided equally)

For their contribution to the theory of international trade and international capital movements.

1978   Herbert Simon

For his pioneering research into the decision-making process within economic organisations.

1979   Theodore Schultz and Arthur Lewis (divided equally)

For their contribution to economic development research with particular consideration of the problems of developing countries.

1980   Lawrence Klein

For the creation of econometric models and the application to the analysis of economic fluctuations and economic policies.

1981   James Tobin

For his analysis of financial markets and their relations to expenditure decisions, employment, production and prices.

1982   George Stigler

For his seminal studies of industrial structures, functioning of markets and cause and effect of public regulation.

1983   Gerard Debreu

The incorporation of new analytical methods into economic theory and a reformulation of the theory of general equilibrium.

1984   Richard Stone

His contribution to national income accounting and improving the basis for empirical economic analysis.

1985   Franco Modigliani

His analysis of saving and financial markets.

1986   James Buchanan

His development of the contractual and constitutional basis for the theory of economic and political decision-making.

1987   Robert Solow

For his contribution to the theory of economic growth.

1988   Maurice Allais

For his contribution to the theory of markets and efficient utilisation of resources.

1989   Trygve Haavelmo

His clarification of probability theory foundations of econometrics and his analysis of simultaneous economic structures.

1990   Harry Markowitz, Merton Miller and William Sharpe (one third each)

For their work in the theory of financial economics.

1991   Ronald Coarse

For his discovery and clarification of the significance of transaction costs and property rights and for the institutional structure and functioning of the economy.

1992   Gary Becker

For extending the domain of microeconomic analysis to a wide range of human behaviour and interaction, including non-market behaviour.

1993   Robert Fogel and Douglass North (joint award)

Renewed research in economic history by applying economic theory and quantitative methods in order to explain economic and institutional change.

1994   John Harsanyi, John Nash and Reinhard Selten (joint award)

For their analysis of equilibria in the theory of non-cooperative games.

1995   Robert Lucas

The development and application of the hypothesis of rational expectations, and thereby having transformed macroeconomic analysis and deepened the understanding of economic policy.

1996   James Mirrlees and William Vickrey

Their contribution to the economic theory of incentives under asymmetric information.

1997   Robert Merton and Myron Scholes

For a new method to determine the value of derivatives.

Source: The Nobel Prize Internet Archive.

Chapter 4

Measuring the Economy's Performance: Introduction to National Income Accounting

4.1   Introduction

In this chapter we explore in some detail the relationship between national expenditure, output and income. The treatment is more specialised than that contained in most macroeconomics textbooks because of the complications that arise due to the structure of the Irish economy.

We begin by extending the circular flow of income diagram that we introduced in Chapter 3. We then explain how economic activity can be measured by three different methods: the *output*, *expenditure* and *income* approaches. This is followed by a discussion of the relationship between these measures. We then define Gross National Disposable Income (GNDI) and adjust this measure for both inflation and population growth to obtain what is probably the best indicator of living standards in an economy. The chapter concludes by explaining the relationship between saving, investment and the balance of payments.

4.2   Expanding the Circular Flow of Income Model

Chapter 3 contained a simple circular flow of income and expenditure model that included only firms and households. Figure 4.1 shows an expanded model that also includes the government and the rest of the world. Briefly, the left-hand side of the diagram shows that households supply firms with the factors of production (land, labour and capital). On the right-hand side of the diagram, firms are shown using these factors of production to produce goods and services, the total output of which is known as *(gross) national product* (GNP). Firms have to pay wages, rent, interest and profit to households and these add up to *national income*. Households spend most of their income purchasing goods and services: this is *household consumption*. However,

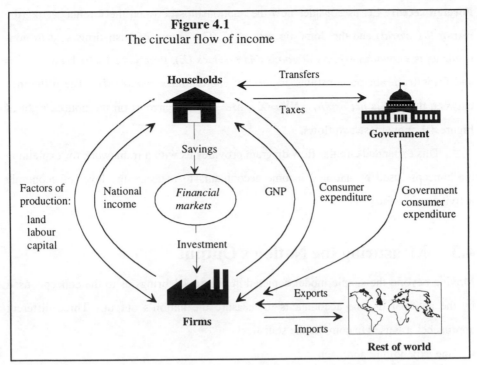

Figure 4.1
The circular flow of income

households also save some of their income, usually by putting money on deposit with banks and building societies. This is *household saving*. Firms borrow from these financial institutions in order to finance *investment* in new plant and machinery. These flows are shown in the centre of the diagram. (Note that not all of the firms' output is sold to households: some is sold to other firms.)

Government The government affects the circular flow of income and expenditure because it levies *taxes* on households and makes *transfer payments* to households under various social welfare schemes. (Transfer payments are payments not in return for any goods or services supplied. They are sometimes called *benefits* or *entitlements*.) We shall denote the difference between taxes and transfer payments as *NT,* the net flow from households to government. The government uses its net tax revenue to pay the people who work in the public sector and to purchase goods and services from private sector firms. These purchases are known as *government consumption expenditure, G,* and are shown on the right of Figure 4.1. (To keep the diagram simple, we have omitted transactions between firms and government.)

Foreign sector Let us consider now the relationships between the foreign sector (the *rest of the world*) and the domestic economy. The output of Irish firms sold to non-residents is known as *exports of goods and services* (*X*). Purchases by Irish households and firms from abroad constitute *imports of goods and services* (*M*). The difference between the two is *net exports*, $NX = X - M$. The two arrows on the bottom right of Figure 4.1 show these two flows.

This expanded circular flow diagram provides us with a framework for explaining the concepts used by national income accountants to measure the level of economic activity in a country.

4.3   Measuring the Nation's Output

Moving beyond the simple model depicted in Figure 4.1 brings us to the concepts used by the national income accountants to measure the nation's output. Three different approaches are used to compile the statistics:

- the expenditure approach,
- the value added or output approach, and
- the income approach.

The expenditure and the value added approach give similar measures of total output, but a number of important adjustments are necessary to go from the expenditure to the income approach.

The expenditure approach

In Figure 4.1, four expenditure arrows point towards the firms. These refer to household consumption expenditure (C), government consumption expenditure (G),[1] investment (I),[2] and exports (X). There is one arrow pointing away from firms to the

---

1. In the *National Income and Expenditure Accounts (NIE)*, government expenditure, *G*, is called "net expenditure by public authorities on current goods and services". It does not include current and capital transfer payments (e.g. social welfare payments, national debt interest paid to Irish residents, IDA grants, etc.) or government investment spending, which is included in *I*. *G* amounted to only 40 per cent of total government spending in 1996.

2. In *NIE* investment is referred to as "gross domestic physical capital formation". It includes both private and government investment. The word "physical" tells us that the value of changes in stocks is included. A fall in the level of stocks is a negative contribution to investment; a rise is a positive contribution.

Table 4.1

Expenditure on Gross Domestic Product at current market prices, 1997

Symbol	Full description	£ billion
C	Personal consumption of goods and services	28.0
+ I	Gross domestic capital formation[1]	10.6
+ G	Net expenditure by public authorities on current goods and services	7.2
+ X	Exports of goods and services	49.9
– M	Imports of goods and services	- 40.2
= GDP		53.5

1. Includes the value of changes in stocks.

Source: *National Income and Expenditure*, 1997, Central Statistics Office, Dublin, 1998.

rest of the world, which represents imports (M). (To keep the diagram as simple as possible, imports by households are omitted.) By adding up C, I, G and X and subtracting M we obtain one measure of the nation's output, which we call gross *domestic* product (GDP) which measures the value of all the *final* goods and services produced in the country over a year:

$$GDP \equiv C + I + G + NX \qquad (1)$$

where the ≡ symbol indicates an identity. Table 4.1 shows the breakdown of expenditure on Irish GDP in 1997. The shares of private consumption (C), government consumption (G) and investment (I) in GDP are respectively 52 per cent, 20 per cent and 13 per cent of the total, which are all close to the corresponding EU averages. However, exports (X) and imports (M) amount to 89 per cent and 75 per cent of GDP, respectively, which are among the highest in the world. Even net exports, (X – M), which amounts to 14 per cent of GDP, is exceptionally large relative to GDP. guarantee

The output approach

The output approach to measuring the value of national production concentrates on the *value added* at each stage of production. Value added is the difference between the value of a firm's output and the cost of the inputs it uses. Assume, for example, that only one good – a book – is produced in the economy. A sawmill produces the timber that it

---

Investment excluding changes in stocks is called *fixed* capital formation. The significance of "gross" is that no allowance has been made for depreciation or "capital consumption". "Domestic" investment takes place in the country. It excludes investment undertaken by Irish firms abroad.

Table 4.2

Illustration of value added approach to measuring domestic production

	Cost of inputs	– Value of output	= Value added
Sawmill	0	2	2
Paper mill	2	5	3
Authors	0	4	4
Publisher	2+3+4 = 9	18	9
GDP			18

sells to a paper mill for £2. The value added at this stage is £2. The paper mill uses the timber to produce £5 worth of paper, which is sold to the publisher. The value added at this stage is £3. The authors produce a manuscript (using no inputs except their own labour) and sell it to the publisher for £4. The value added by the authors is £4. Finally, the publisher combines the paper and the manuscript and produces a book that is sold in the bookshops for £18. The value added by the publisher and distributors is £9.

As shown in Table 4.2, by summing the value added at each stage in the production process we obtain domestic output, which in this case equals £18 (= £2 + £3 + £4 + £9). Only one *final* product – a book – is produced and its value is £18. The same estimate of GDP is obtained using the value added and final output approaches.

The expenditure and value added approaches to estimating GDP in principle yield the same figure and could be used to cross-check the statistical accuracy of the estimates. In reality the information available does not allow both approaches to be completed independently.

Table 4.3

National Income by Category, 1996

	£ billion	%
Income from agriculture, forestry and fisheries	2.4	8.5
Non-agricultural wages and salaries	19.5	68.9
Non-agricultural profits	6.4	22.6
National Income	28.3	100.0

Note: Net factor from the rest of the world and the adjustment for financial services have been taken out of non-agricultural profits.

The income approach

National income is the sum of payments to the factors of production. Traditionally these are described as wages and salaries (payments to labour), rent (payments for the use of land and property), interest (payment for the use of capital), and profits, which can be thought of as a residual payment to entrepreneurs who take risks.

However, the data are not classified in exactly this manner in any table in the Irish *National Income and Expenditure* (*NIE*). Instead the income arising in agriculture is singled out, and non-agricultural income is broken down into two broad categories – wages and salaries ("remuneration of employees") and profits, etc. – and then into several sub-categories. Table 4.3 shows the distribution of national income between the three broad categories in 1996. Since most agricultural income is labour income, it follows that 77 per cent of national income accrues to labour. This is in line with international experience. In the United States, for example, labour's share in national income has been approximately constant at 70 per cent over the post-war period.

4.4 Reconciling the Income and Expenditure Approaches

Three important adjustments have to be made to reconcile the *expenditure* and *income* approaches to measuring the level of national economic activity. These adjustments relate to:

- Net factor income from abroad
- Market prices and factor cost
- Depreciation.

In this section we explain these adjustments.

Net factor payments from the rest of the world Gross *Domestic* Product (GDP) is a measure of the total output of final goods and services *produced in the country*. Gross *national* product (GNP), on the other hand, is a measure of the value of the final output *accruing to the country's residents*. Thus the difference between GDP and GNP is *net factor payments to the rest of world* (F). ("Net" here refers to the difference between the gross inflows and outflows.)

$$GNP \equiv GDP + F \qquad (2)$$

Although GDP is generally used in international comparisons of economic activity, GNP is a better guide to the trend in a country's living standards.

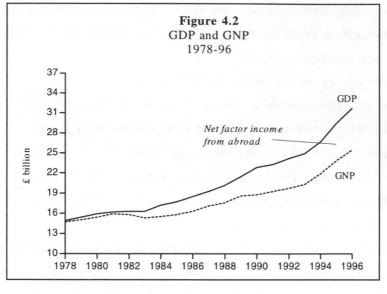

Figure 4.2
GDP and GNP
1978-96

The distinction between GDP and GNP is of unusual importance in Ireland, where F is a large negative number (−£4,826 million in 1996) due to:

- the repatriation of profits by foreign-owned firms operating in Ireland

- interest on our national debt paid to non-residents.

These payments do not constitute part of the nation's income, but they have to be paid from the value of what is produced domestically. Figure 4.2 shows that the gap between the two measures widened rapidly during the 1980s. By 1996 F equalled 12.2 per cent of GDP. For every £8 of income generated in Ireland £1 accrued to non-residents. This is a higher proportion than in any other OECD country.

Note:

The magnitude of F has provoked some misgivings as to the meaningfulness and reliability of the Irish GDP figures. The scale of the profit outflows to foreign-owned firms suggests that they may have been overstated in the first instance due to *transfer pricing*. This is the practice of pricing transactions between subsidiaries of a firm so as to maximise the profits allocated to a country such as Ireland where the tax rate on profits earned in the manufacturing industry is relatively low. It is important to bear in mind that GNP is corrected for any distortion arising from this source.

Market prices and factor cost Taxes levied on expenditure are called *indirect taxes* (T_i). In contrast, *subsidies* (S_u) are like negative taxes. Indirect taxes and subsidies drive another wedge between spending on output and the income of the factors of production. For example, a pint of beer may cost £2.00 in a pub, but indirect taxes (VAT and excises) account for about £1.00 of this. Only £1.00 goes to pay for the

Table 4.4

From GDP to National Income, 1996

		£ billion
GDP$_{mp}$	Gross domestic product at market prices	42.1
− T$_i$	− Indirect taxes	− 6.5
+ S$_u$	+ Subsidies	+ 2.1
= GDP$_{fc}$	= Gross domestic product at factor cost	37.7
− D	− Provision for depreciation	− 4.3
= NDP$_{fc}$	= Net domestic product at factor cost	33.4
+ F	+ Net factor income from rest of world	− 5.1
= NNP$_{fc}$ = NI	= Net national product at factor cost = National income	28.3

Source: *National Income and Expenditure*, 1996, Central Statistics Office, Dublin, 1997

production and distribution of the beer and enters into national income. This requires us to distinguish between magnitudes measured at *market prices* and *factor cost*. The factor cost measure includes only payments made to the factors of production used to produce goods and services.

$$GDP_{fc} \equiv GDP_{mp} - T_i + S_u \qquad (3)$$

where the *fc*, *mp* subscripts refer respectively to factor cost and market prices.

Depreciation Another wedge between the value of production and of income arises due to *depreciation*. The measure of investment (*I*) included in GDP is *gross domestic capital formation,* which is where the *gross* in GDP comes from. No allowance has been made for the using-up or depreciation of capital equipment in the production process. In reality, firms set aside allowances out of their revenue to provide for this depreciation and the eventual replacement of plant and equipment. This is another part of their receipts that is not passed on to households.

Net domestic product (NDP) is equal to gross domestic product *minus* depreciation:

$$NDP_{fc} \equiv GDP_{fc} - D \qquad (4)$$

In practice it is difficult to estimate depreciation and this is why GDP and GNP, rather than their net counterparts, are so often used to describe the economy's performance.

Summary

We are now in a position to reconcile the income and expenditure approaches to measuring economic activity. Table 4.4 summarises the various stages involved using 1996 data. First, an adjustment is made for indirect taxes and subsidies. The second adjustment is to allow for depreciation. Finally, when net factor income from the rest of the world (F) is added to NDP_{fc} we obtain *national income* (NI):

$$NI \equiv NDP_{fc} + F \tag{5}$$

The gap between GDP and NI is almost one third of GDP. This gap is increased by the flow of income abroad due to debt service and profit repatriation.

When estimating national income, the CSO starts by estimating agricultural income from data on crop production, etc. Non-agricultural income (wages and salaries, the income of the self-employed, profits, interest payments and rents) is estimated from data supplied by the Revenue Commissioners and other sources. These estimates of income form the basis of the GDP estimate. The expenditure figure is then reconciled with the income figure by treating personal consumer expenditure (C) as a residual.

4.5   Problems in Measuring GNP

In this section we discuss some of the problems encountered in measuring economic activity.

Double counting When we measure the value of output in the economy, we must avoid *double counting*. In the time-honoured example of a simple economy, in which the only product being produced is bread, we should count only the value of the *final* good (bread), and not the *intermediate* goods (wheat, flour) as well. Bread is a final good because it is consumed and not used to produce any other good. Wheat and flour, on the other hand, are intermediate goods as they are inputs in the production of bread.

The distinction between intermediate and final output is not always as clear cut as in this example. National income accounting, as conventionally measured, treats the value of crime prevention, health care and commuting as if they were final goods and services. However, longer traffic jams and higher bills for policing are really *inputs* to the process of producing and enjoying all the other things we really want: they should not be counted as part of national output. There is therefore a serious element of double

86

counting in the conventional national income accounts. Moreover, since the importance of expenditure on these items tends to increase as a country becomes more urbanised and developed, this problem distorts the comparison of national income between rich and poor countries.

Household production and non-market activities   National income accounting is primarily concerned with activities that are bought or sold. Non-market activities, such as "do-it-yourself" repairs or cooking and cleaning in the home, are not included in GNP as it is measured in most countries. This can give rise to some unsatisfactory results. An old-fashioned example is that if a man marries his housekeeper, the value of national income falls because her work moves out of the market economy and becomes an intra-familial activity. It is possible, in principle, to *impute* the value of non-market work in the national income accounts, but in practice this is done only for a limited range of items. (In Ireland an imputed value of the food produced and consumed on farms is included in national income.) Note also that national income takes no account of the economic value of factors such as a good climate. Leisure, which tends to be scarce in rich countries, is also ignored.

Spillover effects   Spillover effects can be either positive or negative. An example of a negative spillover or *external diseconomy* is the pollution caused by a factory for which the affected parties receive no compensation. (The environmental effects on the Irish sea of the nuclear reprocessing plant in Cumbria is a pertinent example for Irish readers!) An example of a positive spillover or *external economy* is the grounds of a university campus that yield positive benefits to local residents. These spillover effects are not bought and sold and are therefore not included in the national income accounts. Put another way, the *social* costs and benefits are not reflected in the *private* costs or benefits of firms producing national output. In the case of diseconomies, the cost of the firm's output is understated. The national accounts should include a negative item reflecting the damage inflicted on the environment by the production of GNP.

The underground or "black" economy   The underground economy consists of unreported or undetected economic activity. There are, in general, two types of unrecorded transactions: illegal transactions, such as drug trafficking and prostitution,

Table 4.5

GDP and GNDI, 1972 and 1996

		1972 £ million	% of GDP	1996 £ million	% of GDP
GDP	Gross domestic product	2,237.8		42,104	
+F	net factor income from rest of world	29.6	1.3	-5,121	-12.2
= GNP	Gross national product	2,267.4		36,983	
+ R	net transfers from rest of world	41.9	1.8	+1,353	3.2
= GNDI	Gross national disposable income	2,309.3		38,337	

Source: *National Income and Expenditure, 1996*, Central Statistics Office, Dublin, 1997

which are not reported for obvious reasons; and legal transactions (such as small building jobs) that are kept hidden to avoid paying taxes on them. A recent study has estimated that the black economy in Ireland is quite large, amounting to at least 3 per cent of GNP (about £1 billion) and could be as high as 10 per cent (£3.6 billion).[3] While the omission of the black economy from the national income accounts means that the output figures are understated in any given year, this study showed that the growth rate of GNP would not be much affected by including estimates of unrecorded activity in the total.

Multinational companies The activities of multinational companies (MNCs) in Ireland seem to distort our national product figures. Some of these companies are believed to engage in *transfer pricing* (selling components and raw materials at artificially low prices to subsidiary companies in order to maximise profits in low tax countries). This has the effect of artificially boosting the recorded value of their Irish output. The reason they do this is to pay low Irish corporate taxes, rather than the higher rates payable in America, for instance. Because of this, the presence of a large number of multinational companies in Ireland may lead to an overstatement of the value of our output. But much of the distinction caused by this is netted out of GNP, which excludes the profits remitted abroad by the MNCs.

---

3. Gabriel Fagan, "The Black Economy in Ireland", *Irish Banking Review*, Summer 1997.

Table 4.6

Real and nominal GDP

		1992	1993	1994	1995	1996	1997^e	1998^f
Nominal GDP (£ billion)	1	30.0	32.2	34.8	38.6	42.1	47.8	53.5
GDP deflator	2	104.2	108.4	109.4	110.0	111.3	114.1	117.5
(Index: 1990 =100)								
Real GDP 1990 prices	3	28.8	29.7	31.8	35.1	37.8	41.9	45.5
Growth rates: (%)								
Nominal GDP	4	6.4	7.3	8.1	10.9	9.1	13.5	11.9
Real GDP	5	4.0	3.1	7.1	10.4	7.8	10.8	8.6
GDP deflator	6	2.4	4.0	0.9	0.5	1.2	2.5	3.0

Sources: NIE, 1996, Central Statistics Office, Dublin, 1997, Tables 3 and 4. Central Bank of Ireland, *Quarterly Bulletin*, Winter 1997. e = estimate, f = forecast.

4.6 The Disposable Income of the Nation

National income measures the income accruing to the residents of a country, but it takes no account of *net current transfers from the rest of the world* (R). (These differ from F, factor payments from abroad, in that they are not paid in return for goods received or services rendered.) *Gross national disposable income* (*GNDI*) is defined as:

$$GNDI \equiv GNP + R \qquad (6)$$

GNDI is the total amount available to Irish residents to consume and invest. Current transfers received by Ireland from abroad are relatively large, because of the importance of the support to farm prices and other current subsidies received from the European Union (see Chapter 2). They have however declined sharply in recent years. (In the past emigrants' remittances, which also fall into this category, were also important.) Some money is also transferred from Ireland to the rest of the world in the form of overseas development assistance, but this is relatively small.

From Table 4.5 it may be seen that the gaps between GDP, GNP and GNDI have grown markedly since the early 1970s due to the increases in both F and R.

Adjusting for inflation

In Chapter 1 we discussed briefly the distinction between *real* and *nominal* variables. Real GDP, or GDP at *constant prices*, is nominal, or current price, GDP adjusted for inflation. The trend in real GDP measures the trend in living standards. Table 4.6 illustrates how the real growth rate is calculated.

Column 1 shows the level of *nominal* (current prices) GDP from 1992 to 1998. Column 2 shows the GDP *price deflator*. This price deflator is expressed in an index with the base year set equal to 100. To calculate *real* GDP (or GDP in constant 1990 prices) we divide nominal GDP by the price deflator, that is, row 1 by row 2, and multiply by 100.

$$GDP_{constant\ prices} = (GDP_{current\ prices}/GDP\ deflator) \times 100$$

The real GDP figures are given in row 3. The growth rates for nominal GDP, real GDP and the inflation rates are given in rows 4, 5 and 6. Note that the real growth rates are calculated as follows:

$$Real\ growth_{1998} = [(Real\ GDP_{1998} - Real\ GDP_{1997})/Real\ GDP_{1997}] \times 100$$

It can be seen, for example, that the economy grew (in real terms) by 9.0 per cent and 7.88 per cent in 1997 and 1998, respectively. Note that the rate of growth in nominal GDP is approximately equal to the sum of the real growth rate and the rate of inflation. In the *NIE*, data are given for nominal GDP and real GDP. Given these two data series it is possible to calculate the implied GDP deflator.

The GDP deflator is not actually given in *NIE*. However, the data for nominal and real GDP are presented and from these two series it is possible to derive the (implied) GDP deflator. In adjusting GDP for inflation, two approaches, the expenditure and output approaches, are taken. In the expenditure approach each component of expenditure on GDP is deflated using a different price index. *C* is deflated by the consumer price index, *I* by the price index for investment goods, *G* by an index based on rates of pay in the public sector and *X* and *M* are deflated by export and import price indices respectively. The export price index is used to deflate *F* in years when the net flow is negative. (This is on the grounds that a net outflow can be used to purchase imports and ultimately has to be paid for with increased exports.) The import price index is used to deflate *F* in years when the net flow is positive. In the output approach an attempt is made to measure value added in each sector at constant prices. Not surprisingly, the two approaches yield somewhat different figures. There is a persistent tendency for the expenditure approach to yield higher estimates of real growth than the output approach. In 1995 real GDP increased by 10.4 per cent on the expenditure basis but by "only" 9.0 per cent on the output basis. It is usual to take the average of the two when quoting growth rates, as is done in this section.

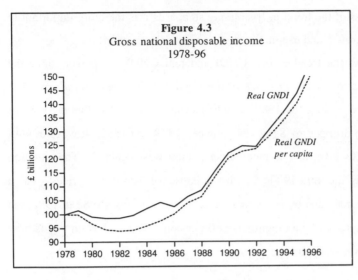

Figure 4.3
Gross national disposable income
1978-96

£ billions

Real GNDI

Real GNDI
per capita

Terms of trade One further aspect of taking account of inflation needs to be discussed. Export and import prices change at different rates. This has important implications for living standards. A country exports in order to earn foreign exchange to buy imports. If the price of its exports rises more slowly that that of its imports, it costs more in terms of exports to acquire a given quantity of imports. This is the *terms of trade effect*. In an economy as dependent on international trade as Ireland this effect can be very significant. It is not reflected in the real GDP figures, but the figures for GNDI at constant prices incorporate a *terms of trade adjustment*. The Appendix explains how this is calculated. The inclusion of this adjustment is another reason for regarding constant price GNDI as the best index of the trend in the country's overall living standards.

Adjusting for population growth

In most developed countries the rate of population growth is low and there is little need to worry about adjusting for it when analysing short-run economic performance. Ireland is unusual in this regard, however. During the 1950s the population declined by over one per cent a year. In the 1970s it grew by about 1.5 per cent a year, the highest growth rate in Europe. In the 1980s the population started to decline due to the resumption of large-scale emigration and the decline in the birth rate. During the 1990s the population started to increase and is now running in excess of one per cent a year.

Our view of the country's recent economic performance would be distorted if we did not take these fluctuations in the rate of population growth into account. In making longer-run comparisons of the trend in Irish living standards it is therefore important to adjust for population growth and use income *per person* (or *per capita*).

Figure 4.3 shows the trend in real GNDI and real GNDI per person since the 1970s. *This is the best available measure of the trend in Irish living standards.* The severity of the recession of the early 1980s may be gauged from the fact that the level of real income per person dropped by 8 per cent between 1979 and 1982. It was not until 1986 that the late 1970s level of real income per person was regained. The situation was transformed from the mid-1980s by the collapse of world oil prices, which improved our terms of trade and by an increase in real income. From 1988 to 1998, the real living standard improved by an impressive 50 per cent. The Irish economy is now half as big again as it was ten years ago.

4.7   Saving, Investment and the Balance of Payments

We now turn to the relationship between saving, investment and economic growth. National saving is one of the main determinants of the growth of living standards in the long run. This is because there is a close correlation between the amount a country saves and invests, and investment is a major source of economic growth. It can be shown (see Box 4.1) that the following identity holds:

$$S - I \equiv CA \tag{7}$$

Where S is saving, I is investment and CA is the current account of the balance of payments. This important identity shows that, whereas in a closed economy S must equal I, this is not true in an open economy. A country that trades with the rest of the world can finance some of its investment by running a current account balance of payments deficit and borrowing from abroad to finance this. Alternatively, it can use up some of its national saving by running a current account surplus, which is invested abroad.[4]

---

4. Despite the possibility of borrowing and lending abroad there is a high correlation across countries between national saving and investment: M. Feldstein and C. Horioka, "Domestic Saving and International Capital Flows", *Economic Journal*, 1980.

Box 4.1

Saving, investment and the balance of payments

Recall from earlier sections in this chapter that:

$$GDP \equiv C + I + G + NX \qquad (8)$$

$$GNP \equiv GDP + F \qquad (9)$$

$$GNDI \equiv GNP + R \qquad (10)$$

Substituting 8 into 9 and 9 into 10 we obtain:

$$GNDI \equiv C + I + G + NX + F + R \qquad (11)$$

In this identity there are three variables that involve transactions with the rest of the world – NX, F and R. The NX variable represents the trade balance in goods and services, F is net income from the rest of the world and R represents international transfers. These three variables together comprise the *current account of the balance of payments*, which we shall label CA:

$$CA \equiv NX + F + R \qquad (12)$$

We can rewrite the definition of GNDI as:

$$GNDI \equiv C + I + G + CA \qquad (13)$$

Now just as a household either spends or saves its disposable income, the nation's disposable income must be either consumed or saved. Consumption consists of private consumption (C) and public sector consumption (G). Hence we can also define GNDI as:

$$GNDI \equiv (C + G) + S \qquad (14)$$

where S equals *gross national saving*. (Gross national saving includes the allowance for depreciation; net national saving does not.)

Combining (13) and (14) yields

$$C + G + S \equiv C + I + G + CA \qquad (15)$$

Cancelling C and G on each side and rearranging yields:

$$I \equiv S - CA \qquad (16)$$

$$S - I \equiv CA \qquad (17)$$

This is identity (7) in the main text. It states that the excess of saving over investment equals the current account surplus.

Note:

We are dealing here with *measured* or *ex post* saving and investment and the relationships above are *identities*, that is, they hold by definition.

The typical experience of New World countries in the nineteenth century was for large investments in infrastructure to be funded by European investors. This was

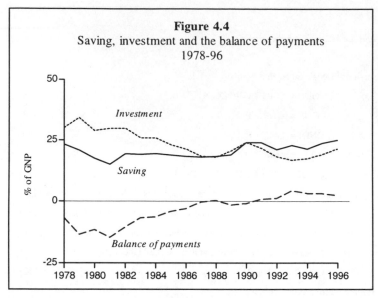

Figure 4.4
Saving, investment and the balance of payments
1978-96

achieved by countries such as the United States running sizeable current account deficits.

On the other hand, Japan in recent years has had a very high national saving rate (36 per cent of GDP in 1996) that has not been matched by an equally high rate of domestic investment. The result has been a large current account surplus, leading to a high level of overseas investment by the Japanese. Much of the outflow of money from Japan during the 1980s was used to buy assets in the US, which financed the US balance of payments current account deficit. The American current account deficit, in turn, reflected a low saving rate relative to a heavy appetite for investment funds. These examples bring out the links between national saving, investment and the balance of payments.

The Irish experience The trend from 1978 to 1996 is illustrated in Figure 4.4.[5] In the late 1970s and early 1980s investment exceeded saving and this was reflected in an exceptionally large current account balance of payments deficit. Investment reached 34 per cent of GNP (one of the highest levels in the OECD) compared to a saving rate of 20 per cent. The current account deficit was 14 per cent. The counterpart of this was heavy borrowing from abroad in order to augment Irish national saving and finance domestic investment.

However, by 1989 the national saving rate exceeded the investment rate and a surplus was recorded on the balance of payments. In 1996, saving amounted to 25 per

---

5. Saving include a small additional item, "capital transfers", which are a further source of funding for investment. These are principally the non-current component of grants from the European Union.

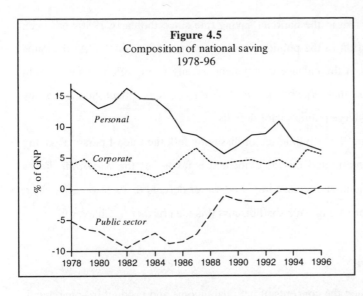

Figure 4.5
Composition of national saving
1978-96

cent of GNP compared to an investment rate of 22 per cent and a balance of payments surplus of 3 per cent. It is interesting to note that the Irish investment rate decreased at a time when exceptional real growth rates in GNP were achieved. Usually, an increase in investment is a pre-requisite for faster growth rates. In Ireland, the lower level of investment was offset by the much higher productivity of that investment.

Public and private saving National saving can be disaggregated into *public* and *private* sector saving. Public sector saving is the excess of current revenue (mainly from taxes) over current expenditure (on transfer payments and debt service as well as on current goods and services, G). Generally this balance has been negative, with the government spending more on day-to-day expenses than it takes in taxes. The current budget deficit is also called *public sector dissaving*.

Private sector saving can be broken down into household or *personal* saving and company or *corporate* saving. (The main component of the latter is the *retained earnings* of the larger corporations.) Figure 4.5 shows that corporate saving rose from a low level in the mid-1980s to 6.2 per cent of GNP in 1995. This reflects the increased profitability of Irish companies.

Personal saving reached over 15 per cent of GNP in 1982 and declined steadily to a low of 6.1 per cent in 1996. In the early 1980s over 20 per cent of personal disposable income was being saved, which was an exceptionally high ratio by international standards and one that could only fall in the longer run.

However, the most dramatic change since the early 1980s has been the reduction in the level of public sector *dissaving*, from −9.5 per cent of GNP in 1983 to 0.3 per cent in 1996. Thus the rise in the national saving rate since the early 1980s has been largely due to the reduction in the public sector's current budget deficit. At the same time the current account of the balance of payments swung from deficit to surplus. In fact it is generally the case that large balance of payments deficits reflect the inadequacy of national saving due to large public sector deficits.

It is also significant that as public sector dissaving fell, the rate of personal saving declined. Some have interpreted this as evidence in favour of the *Ricardian-Barro theorem*, according to which an increase in public sector deficits tends to be offset by a reduction in private sector saving. We shall discuss this idea further in Chapter 6.

4.8 Conclusion

In this chapter we examined the concepts of national income and product in some detail. We discussed the measures that are used in analysing the country's economic performance. Among the key concepts discussed were:

- The effect of government and the foreign sector on the circular flow of income
- Three methods of measuring economic activity: the expenditure, output and income approaches
- The relationship between these three approaches
- Gross national disposable income
- Nominal and real GDP and the GDP deflator
- The relationship between national saving, national investment and the current account of the balance of payments
- The composition of national saving.

Appendix

Adjusting for changes in the terms of trade

We export in order to import. Hence, what matters from the point of view of Irish living standards is how much our exports will allow us to buy in terms of imports. Think of Ireland as a country exporting dairy products and importing petroleum products. If the price of oil rises when that of milk is static, we have to export a larger quantity of milk to pay for a given quantity of imported oil. Conversely, if the price of milk rises relative to the price of oil, we have to give up less milk in order to import a given quantity of oil. In calculating real GNDI account has to be taken of these effects. This is done by adjusting for changes in the terms of trade index, that is, the price of exports, P_x, relative to the price of imports, P_m. (both P_x and P_m are index numbers equal to 100 in the base year).

$$\text{Terms of trade index} = (P_x / P_m) \times 100 \qquad (18)$$

If P_x / P_m increases, the terms of trade are said to have improved because we have to export less in order to obtain a given amount of imports. If the ratio falls the terms of trade are said to have deteriorated.

The *terms of trade adjustment* is the difference between the value of exports deflated by the price of imports and exports deflated by the price of exports, that is:

$$\text{Terms of trade adjustment} = (X/ P_m - X/ P_x) \text{ or } X(1/ P_m - 1/ P_x) \qquad (19)$$

In the base year both P_x and P_m are equal to 100 and hence the adjustment is zero. If in a later year $P_x > P_m$ then the adjustment is *positive* because the terms of trade have improved, allowing the country to buy more imports with the proceeds of a given volume of exports. If $P_x < P_m$ then the adjustment is *negative* because the terms of trade have deteriorated and the country has to export more in order to purchase a given volume of imports. The terms of trade adjustment given in (19) has to be added to GNDI in order to obtain GNDI adjusted for the terms of trade. The procedure has to start arbitrarily from a base year in which the adjustment is zero. The adjustment for any future year is relative to the base year.

The Irish statistician R. C. Geary (1896-1983) did some of the pioneering work on this topic. Dr Geary made important contributions to the theory of national income accounting and index numbers while Director of the Central Statistics Office in Dublin and of the United Nations Statistical Office in New York. He is also remembered for his contributions to economic theory, notably the "Stone-Geary expenditure system".

Table 4.7 shows how movements in the terms of trade have affected real GNDI since 1985, the base year. Because $P_x = P_m = 100$ in the base year, the effect is zero in that year. The adjustment has been significant and variable since then. We gained from the collapse in oil prices in 1986, but weaker agricultural export prices led to a significant loss in the early 1990s. (In fact, some of this loss was offset by larger inflows through R, transfers from abroad, as farmers were compensated for the low prices obtained for their beef exports outside the EU.)

Table 4.9

The terms of trade effect between 1986 and 1993, £ millions

	1990	1991	1992	1993	1994	1995	1996
GNP at constant (1990) prices	24,269	24,743	25,269	26,004	27,967	30,216	32,313
+ Terms of trade adjustment	0.0	– 432	– 639	– 315	– 848	–1,591	–1,633
+ Net current transfers from abroad at constant (1990) prices	1,412	1,570	1,231	1,239	1,064	982	1,205
= GNDI at constant (1990) prices	25,681	25,882	25,861	26,928	28,183	29,607	31,885

Source: *National Income and Expenditure* 1996, Table 8.

Chapter 5

The Consumption Function and Income Determination

5.1   Introduction

Chapter 3 discussed the role of aggregate demand or domestic expenditure in determining output and employment in the economy. In this chapter we discuss the main influences on *short-run* fluctuations in the economy. We do this focusing in some detail on one important component of aggregate demand, namely, consumer expenditure. The first part of the chapter examines issues in consumer theory and in particular the *consumption function,* which plays a key role in macroeconomic theory and policy. The second half of the chapter is concerned with the multiplier model, which is based on the consumption function, and discusses the role of government spending as a regulator of aggregate demand.

5.2   Disposable Income, Consumption and Saving

Personal consumption expenditure (C) in Ireland accounts for about 57 per cent of domestic expenditure or aggregate demand (AD). The study of consumption is therefore important not just in its own right but for our understanding of the determination of output, income and employment.

We start with two important definitions. First disposable income (Y^d) is equal to gross income (Y) *minus* taxation (T).

$$Y^d = Y - T \qquad\qquad (1)$$

Secondly, disposable income is used for consumer expenditure (C) or is saved (S).

$$Y^d = C + S \qquad\qquad (2)$$

The stylised facts

On average, consumption, saving and taxation accounted for 75, 11 and 14 per cent of personal income, respectively, over the period 1958-95. In the 1950s and 1960s, consumption accounted for a much higher proportion of income with correspondingly

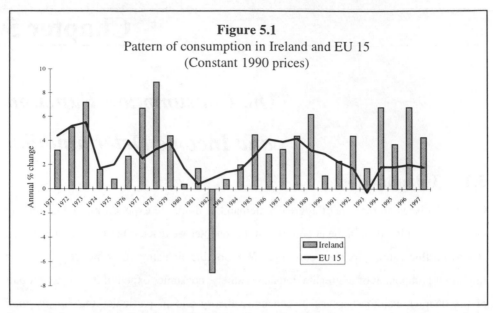

Figure 5.1

Pattern of consumption in Ireland and EU 15
(Constant 1990 prices)

lower saving and taxation rates. Figure 5.1 shows the annual percentage change in private consumption (constant prices) for Ireland and EU 15 from 1979-97. The pattern of consumption would seem to be somewhat out of sync with the rest of Europe and seems to mirror the cyclical swings in the Irish business cycle.

Table 5.1

Composition of personal consumption expenditure, 1996

Category	£ millions	%
Food and non-alcoholic beverages	3,681	15.7
Transport and communication	3,230	13.8
Recreation, entertainment and education	3,034	13.0
Alcoholic beverages	2,690	11.5
Rent	2,675	11.4
Clothing and footwear	1,517	6.5
Household equipment	1,439	6.1
Tobacco	937	4.0
Fuel and power	935	4.0
Miscellaneous	3,180	13.6
Total consumer expenditure	23,318	100.0

Source: *National Income and Expenditure, 1996,* Table 13, Central Statistics Office, Dublin, 1997.

Although we are primarily concerned with consumption expenditure aggregated over all types of consumer goods and services, it is of interest to look at the composition of this expenditure. Table 5.1 shows the breakdown of personal consumption between the different categories of expenditure. The

Table 5.2

Household disposable income, consumption and saving (hypothetical data)

Households	Disposable Income (Y^d)	Consumption (C)	Saving (S)	APC	APS
	£	£	£		
A	10,000	9,000	1,000	0.90	0.10
B	15,000	12,000	3,000	0.80	0.20
C	20,000	15,000	5,000	0.75	0.25
D	25,000	18,000	7,000	0.72	0.28
E	30,000	21,000	9,000	0.70	0.30
F	35,000	24,000	11,000	0.68	0.32
G	40,000	27,000	13,000	0.67	0.33

largest components are food, transport and communications, recreation and entertainment and alcoholic beverages. (By international standards, Irish households spend an unusually large proportion of their income on alcoholic beverages and tobacco.)

The data given in Table 5.1 are an average for all the households in the country. When households are classified by income group, important differences in consumption patterns are apparent. In particular, people on low incomes spend a higher proportion of their income on necessities such as food. As income increases, the proportion of income spent on clothing, transport and leisure activities rises. High income households buy better quality food, but they spend a smaller proportion of their income on it.

The consumption function

The British economist John Maynard Keynes argued that the main determinant of consumer expenditure was current disposable income, Y^d.[1] This function plays a central role in modern macroeconomic theory. The consumption function may be written as:

$$C = \alpha + mpc \times Y^d \tag{3}$$

where α is the intercept term and mpc is the *marginal propensity to consume*. Equation (3) reads "consumption expenditure is a function of disposable income". The direction of causation is running from Y^d to C. Because Y^d *causes* changes in C, Y^d is referred to as the *explanatory* (or independent) variable, and C as the *dependent* variable.

---

1. J. M. Keynes, *The General Theory of Employment, Interest and Money*, Macmillan, 1936.

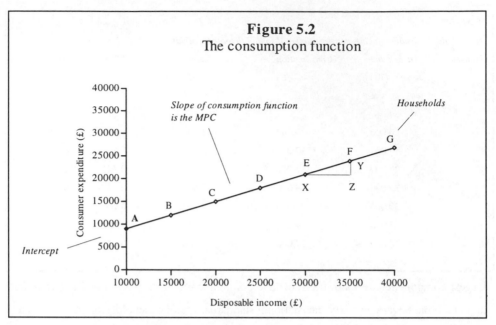

Figure 5.2

The consumption function

In order to explain how the consumption function is derived, consider the data on Y^d, C and S given in Table 5.2 for a hypothetical *cross-section* of households. Household A has an income of £10,000 and consumption of £9,000 per annum. Household B has an income of £15,000 and spends £12,000, and so on for the richer households, C to G.

The main point illustrated in Table 5.2 is that as disposable income increases, households spend less and save more as a proportion of income.

Figure 5.2 plots the relationship between disposable income and consumption given in Table 5.2. Consumption expenditure is shown on the vertical axis and disposable income on the horizontal axis. Point B in Figure 5.2 corresponds to consumption expenditure of £12,000 and income of £15,000. The remaining points in Figure 5.2 correspond to the other households in Table 5.2.

The line joining the points A, B, C etc. is the *consumption function* for this cross-section of households. The *intercept* is the point where the consumption function cuts or intercepts the vertical axis. It corresponds to the α term in equation 3 above. The intercept can be thought of as the level of consumption spending that is independent of the level of Y^d, and is referred to as autonomous consumption.

An important question in macroeconomics is how consumer expenditure *reacts* to a change in disposable income. The *slope* of the consumption function, which is given by the *marginal propensity to consume* (mpc), answers this question. It tells us by how much a household's consumption will increase as a result of a given increase in income. (In

102

economics, the word "marginal" means "extra" or "additional".)

Consider again equation 3. Taking first differences we can write:

$$\Delta C / \Delta Y^d = mpc \tag{4}$$

where Δ denotes change. The mpc shows how C reacts to a given change in Y^d. The mpc is a positive number which is generally greater than zero but less than 1: $0 > mpc > 1$. An mpc of 0.9 means that for every £1 increase in income, spending increases by £0.90.

The hypothetical data on income and consumption in Table 5.2 may be used to calculate the mpc. As household income increases from £10,000 to £15,000, consumption expenditure increases from £9,000 to £12,000. The mpc is therefore 0.6.

$$mpc = \Delta C / \Delta Y^d = (12{,}000 - 9{,}000)/(15{,}000 - 10{,}000) = 0.6 \tag{5}$$

The mpc may also be represented graphically as the slope of the consumption function. Consider the triangle labelled XYZ in Figure 5.2. The distance XZ represents the change in disposable income, and the distance ZY represents the change in consumption expenditure. The slope of the consumption function XY is the ratio ZY/XZ and equals $\Delta C / \Delta Y^d$, which we defined as the mpc.

Note:

Because the consumption function in Figure 5.2 is linear, the mpc is the same at all points on the line. (The reader can confirm this by calculating the mpc for the range of income and expenditure given in Table 5.2.) We have presented a linear consumption function simply for illustrative purposes. In reality, it is possible that the mpc would decrease at higher levels of income because the richer a household becomes, the larger the proportion of any further increase in income it is likely to save. If a line is non-linear, then each point on the line has a different slope. The slope at a particular point on the curve can be calculated by drawing a line tangent to the curve at that point. The slope of the tangent line gives the slope of the curve at that point.

The saving function

Consumption expenditure and saving sum to disposable income. Because C depends on Y^d, it follows that S also depends on Y^d. The relationship between S and Y^d is referred to as the *saving function*. Mathematically, the relationship may be written as:

$$S = \beta + mps \times Y^d \tag{6}$$

where β represents the intercept term and mps the *marginal propensity to save*. The mps shows what proportion of an increase in Y^d is saved. To see this, differentiate equation 6 to obtain:

$$\Delta S / \Delta Y^d = mps \tag{7}$$

An mps of 0.2, for example, indicates that households save £0.20 for every £1

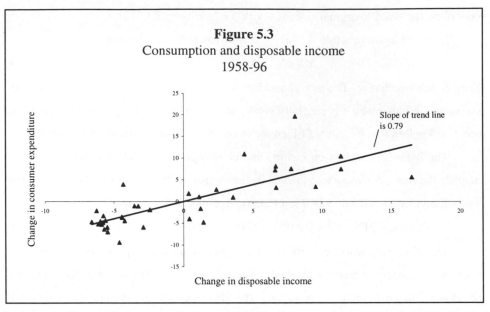

Figure 5.3
Consumption and disposable income
1958-96

increase in disposable income. In terms of Table 5.2, note that as household B's income increases from £15,000 to £20,000, its saving increases from £3,000 to £5,000. Hence, the mps for this household is 0.4:

$$mps = (5,000 - 3,000)/(£20,000 - £15,000) = 0.4$$

Because income is either spent or saved, the mpc and the mps must also sum to one.

$$mpc + mps = 1 \qquad\qquad (8)$$

If the mpc equals 0.6, then the mps must equal 0.4. That is, if a household receives one extra pound in income, 80 per cent is spent and 20 per cent is saved.

The consumption and saving functions are very important building blocks in macroeconomic theory. As we shall see later in this chapter, the consumption function partly determines the effectiveness of fiscal policy.

Evidence from the Irish economy

Using data from 1958 to 1996 it is possible to calculate the mpc for the Irish economy. Defining ΔC and ΔY as:

$$\Delta C^* = \Delta C_t - \Delta C_{mean} \qquad\qquad (9)$$

$$\Delta Y^* = \Delta Y_t - \Delta Y_{mean} \qquad\qquad (10)$$

ΔC^* is the change in consumption adjusted for the average or mean change over the period. It calculates the change in consumption over and above the average change over the period. Similarly, ΔY^* is the change in disposable income again adjusted for the mean change over the period.

The two variables, ΔC^* and ΔY^* are then plotted as a *scatter diagram* as, for example, in Figure 5.3. Each point in the diagram corresponds to the ΔC^*, ΔY^* combination for a particular year. A trend or *regression* line can now be fitted to this scatter diagram and the slope of this line is the marginal propensity to consume.

Applying this procedure to Irish data from 1958-96, the mpc is estimated to be 0.79. This suggests that a change in disposable income (over and above the mean change) leads to a corresponding 79 per cent change in consumer expenditure.[2] Put another way, the equation states that a £1 change in disposable income leads to a £0.79 change in current consumption. The implied marginal propensity to save (mps) is 0.21.

This consumption function is a relatively simple one. It does not take into account any of the influences on consumption other than current year's income. Yet it gives a reasonably good account of the year-to-year variations in consumption and it offers support to Keynesian consumer theory.

Average propensity to consume and save

As mentioned, as disposable income increases, households spend less and save more as a proportion of income. This point can be made more formally by calculating the *average propensity to consume* (APC) and the *average propensity to save* (APS). The APC is defined as being equal to consumption expenditure divided by disposable income, C/Y^d. For example, in Table 5.2, the APC for household B is calculated as follows:

$$APC = C/Y^d = £12,000/£15,000 = 0.8 \qquad (11)$$

An APC of 0.8 indicates that the household spends 80 per cent of its disposable income on consumption goods and services. Similarly, the *average propensity to save* (APS) is defined as being equal to saving divided by disposable income, S/Y^d. Again for household B in Table 5.2:

$$APS = S/Y^d = £3,000/£15,000 = 0.2 \qquad (12)$$

---

2. A number of estimates of the mpc have been published. These include Michael Moore, "The Irish Consumption Function and Ricardian Equivalence", *The Economic and Social Review*, Vol. 19, No. 1, October 1987, who estimates an MPC of 0.67; and Brendan M. Walsh, "Ricardian Equivalence and the Irish Consumption Function: A Comment", *The Economic and Social Review*, Vol. 20, No. 1, October 1988, who estimates an upper value for the MPC of 0.855.

An APS of 0.2 indicates that 20 per cent of disposable income is saved. Because disposable income is either spent or saved, the APC and the APS must sum to 1:

$$APC + APS = 1 \tag{13}$$

Note from Table 5.2 above that as disposable income increases, the APC declines and the APS rises. The low income households save very little of their income, whereas the high income groups save a large proportion of income. Keynes put it as follows in the *General Theory*:

"The fundamental psychological law, upon which we are entitled to depend with great confidence both a priori from our knowledge of human nature and from the detailed facts of experience, is that men are disposed to increase their consumption as their income increases, but not by as much as the increase in income."[3]

Keynes argued, on the basis of his own intuition rather than a detailed study of the data, that as income rose the average propensity to consume (APC) declined. He was influenced by the fact that the rich appear to save a much larger proportion of their income than the poor. This led him to worry about the problem of the economy absorbing an increasing stream of saving. Recall from the circular flow of income diagram that household saving is used to finance new investment. Keynes worried that it would be difficult to find new profitable investment outlets in line with the rise in saving and that, in certain circumstances, this could push the economy into recession.

In a famous passage he praised the ancient Egyptians for building pyramids and the people in the Middle Ages for building cathedrals, because these activities used up their saving and provided employment. Furthermore, because there was no tendency for the *rate of return* from building pyramids to fall:

"Two pyramids, two masses for the dead, are twice as good as one; but not so two railways from London to York."[4]

---

3. *General Theory*, p. 96.
4. *General Theory*, p. 131.

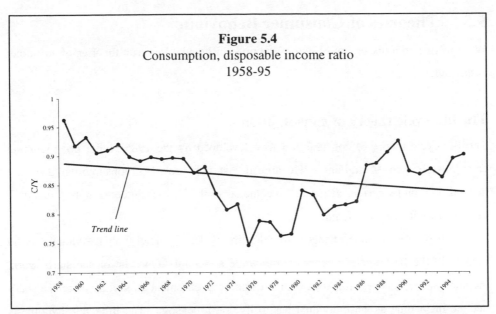

Figure 5.4
Consumption, disposable income ratio
1958-95

The evidence for a declining APC was, however, shaky. In the mid-1940s Nobel prize-winner Simon Kuznets (1901-85) presented evidence that the APC was equal to 0.87 throughout the periods 1869-1898, 1884-1913 and 1904-1933. This meant that the ratio of consumption to income was relatively stable and that the APC did *not* decline as disposable income increased.

In the 1950s, the apparent conflict between Keynes's intuition and Kuznets' findings led to the refinement of theories of consumer behaviour. Two of the most influential contributions have been, first, the *life-cycle hypothesis* and, second, the *permanent-income hypothesis*. Before turning to a discussion of these two theories it is interesting to review the evidence from the Irish economy. Figure 5.4 shows the ratio of consumer expenditure to disposable income for the Irish economy over the period 1958-95. Inserting a trend line confirms that the APC has in fact declined over the years. However, the ratio has fluctuated significantly from year to year. In 1958 the ratio was 0.93 compared to 0.75 in 1973.

Hence, two of the principal tenets underlying Keynesian consumer theory, namely, that the mpc lies between 0 and 1 and, secondly, the APC declines as disposable income increases, are borne out by the Irish evidence.

5.3   Theories of Consumer Behaviour

We now turn to a discussion of two of the most influential long-run theories of consumer behaviour.

The life-cycle theory of consumption

The life-cycle theory of consumption was developed by the 1985 Nobel prize-winning economist Franco Modigliani.[5]   He argued that a household's consumption does not depend only on its *current* disposable income, as in the Keynesian consumption function, but rather on its *lifetime* income.

Disposable income changes over the life cycle. Typically, an individual has no income in the first eighteen years of life, while at school. Once he or she starts work, income rises rapidly reaching a peak in mid-life. On retirement at, say, 60 there is a sharp decline in income as the individual has to live on a pension. The life-cycle hypothesis assumes that people prefer to maintain a constant or slightly increasing flow of consumption over their lifetime to one where consumption depends completely on current income. They can achieve this if they are willing to save at those periods in their lives when their earnings are high and to dissave when their income falls. This would involve dissaving early and late in life, and saving during the peak earning years. This is referred to as *consumption smoothening*.

This pattern of consumption is depicted in Figure 5.5. The upward-sloping consumption line depicts a steadily rising

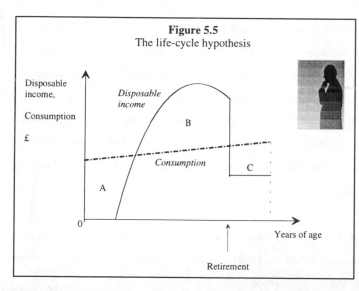

Figure 5.5
The life-cycle hypothesis

Disposable income, Consumption £

Disposable income

B

Consumption

C

A

0

Years of age

Retirement

---

5. The life-cycle hypothesis was developed by Modigliani in conjunction with Richard Brumberg and Albert Ando. See F. Modigliani and R. Brumberg, "Utility Analysis and the Consumption Function", in K. Kurihara (ed.) *Post-Keynesian Economics*, New Brunswick, N.J., Rutgers University Press, 1954.

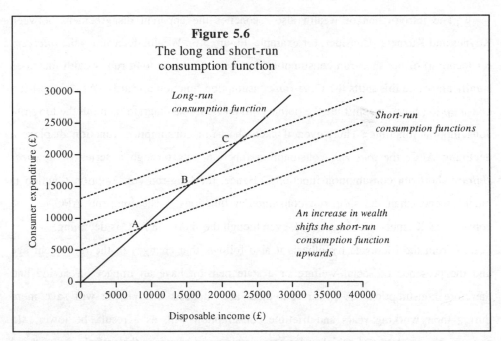

Figure 5.6
The long and short-run
consumption function

Long-run
consumption function

Short-run
consumption functions

An increase in wealth
shifts the short-run
consumption function
upwards

Consumer expenditure (£) (vertical axis): 0, 5000, 10000, 15000, 20000, 25000, 30000

Disposable income (£) (horizontal axis): 0, 5000, 10000, 15000, 20000, 25000, 30000, 35000, 40000

expenditure stream; the inverted U-shaped disposable income line depicts how the typical individual's income might vary over his or her lifetime. Areas A and C in Figure 5.5 are associated with *dissaving*. In area B the individual saves a proportion of income. The saving of one period is used to finance consumption in other periods so that over the life cycle consumption equals income. The dissaving in areas A and C equals the saving in area B. This theory predicts that changes in current disposable income have much less influence on consumption than would be expected from the cruder consumption function we introduced above. Individuals are supposed to take the long view and set their consumption targets in line with their expected lifetime income, rather than simply adjusting consumption to day-to-day fluctuations in income.

The life-cycle hypothesis can be extended in a number of ways. Consumption can be expressed as a function of income and wealth. The greater a person's wealth the higher will be consumption, and vice versa. This means that changes in wealth brought about by a stock market crash can lead to a fall in consumption and thereby help push the economy into recession. This was a feared effect of the stock market crash in October 1987.

Note:
Income, consumption, saving and investment are *flow* variables. They measure how much is earned, consumed, saved and invested over a period of time. Wealth and the capital stock are, on the other hand, *stock* variables. They measure the value of assets at a point of time.

The introduction of wealth also reconciles the apparent disagreement between Keynes and Kuznets. Consider, for example, Figure 5.6. Wealth determines the *intercept* (or location) of the short-run consumption function. Over the long run, wealth increases significantly and this shifts the *short-run* consumption function upwards. As the short-run consumption functions shift up, the points A, B and C in the diagram map out the long-run consumption function. Thus, even if each short-run consumption function displays a declining APC, the *long-run* consumption function cuts through a series of *upward-shifting* short-run consumption functions. Hence, the long-run consumption function is much steeper than the short-run consumption functions. The long-run APC can be constant (as Kuznets' data suggested), even though the short-run APC is declining.

From the life-cycle hypothesis it also follows that changes in the retirement age and the presence of social welfare or a state pension have an impact on saving and therefore consumption. A lower retirement age suggests that people will save more during their working years and lifetime consumption will, as a result, be lower. In contrast, the existence of social welfare or a state pension means that people do not need much saving to maintain consumption in their retirement period. Hence, the saving rate will be lower.

Finally, the age distribution of the population can have an important bearing on aggregate saving and consumption. A stationary or declining population, such as that of many European countries today, implies a high proportion of elderly in the total. This, in turn, implies that many people are living off past saving, which will depress the aggregate saving ratio.

The permanent-income hypothesis

The permanent-income hypothesis was developed by Milton Friedman, 1976 Nobel prize-winner in economics.[6] The permanent-income hypothesis is similar in many respects to the life-cycle hypothesis. The permanent-income hypothesis argues that current consumption depends on *permanent* income (YP):

$$C = f(YP) \tag{14}$$

In Friedman's original exposition of the theory, no precise definition of permanent income was given. However, we can think of permanent income as being equal to a weighted average of *current* and *past* incomes. An example is:

---

6. M. Friedman, *A Theory of the Consumption Function*, Princeton, Princeton University Press, 1957.

$$YP_t = 0.6Y^d_t + 0.3Y^d_{t-1} + 0.1Y^d_{t-2} \qquad\qquad (15)$$

where Y^d_t is disposable income in time t, Y^d_{t-1} is disposable income in time t−1 and Y^d_{t-2} is disposable income in time t−2. Equation (15) says that today's permanent income is equal to 60 per cent of this year's disposable income plus 30 per cent of last year's income plus 10 per cent of income two years ago. Note that the weights used in the calculation tend to get smaller the further we go back in time.

The basic idea underlying equation (15) is that people base their consumption patterns on income averaged over good and bad times. Because permanent income is based on long-run average income, it is similar to lifetime income. The permanent-income hypothesis does, however, have the advantage in that it can easily be applied to aggregate time series data for income, whereas the concept of lifetime income is difficult to measure using aggregate data. The life-cycle hypothesis, on the other hand, allows for a greater role for saving and initial wealth.

Friedman's basic hypothesis is that there is a constant proportional relationship between consumption and permanent income. This means that the APC out of permanent income is constant and the long-run consumption to income ratio is constant. This squares well with Kuznets' findings. Hence, the permanent income can explain why the APC is supposedly constant over time.

However, actual income is highly variable and the proportion of it that is consumed also varies. Income that is not expected to be repeated in the future is referred to as *transitory* (or temporary) income (YT). A good example of such income would be winning the Lottery. According to Friedman's theory this type of unexpected windfall gain should have a weak effect on consumption – most of it will be saved. (In this context it is important to recall that buying consumer durables, such as a car or a stereo set, should be classified as investment rather than consumption.) How do you think most Irish Lottery winners behave in this regard?

The permanent, transitory distinction is important in the context of tax cuts. If a government tries to stimulate spending by cutting taxes, consumers may not respond if they believe the tax cuts will be only temporary. If eventually the government has to revise its tax cuts, households will have enjoyed only a transitory rise in disposable income which will not have much effect on consumption.

5.4   The Keynesian Cross Diagram

In section 5.2 we introduced the consumption function as a relationship between consumption expenditure and disposable income, Y^d. We now make an adjustment to this equation by depicting consumption as a function of GNP rather than Y^d.

$$C = \alpha + mpc \times GNP \tag{16}$$

Figure 5.7 shows the consumption function with GNP, rather than Y^d on the horizontal axis. As we explained in Chapter 4, the gap between GNP and Y^d is due to direct and indirect taxes, subsidies, depreciation and net factor income from the rest of the world. Allowing for changes in these variables, it is reasonable to proxy Y^d by GNP.

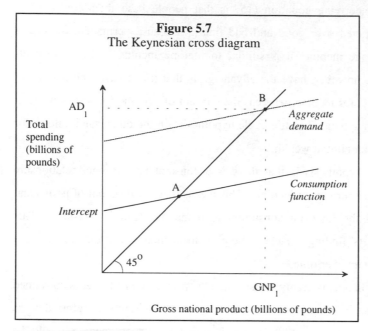

Figure 5.7
The Keynesian cross diagram

Aggregate demand

Recall that total expenditure or aggregate demand (AD) is equal to consumer expenditure (C), government expenditure (G), investment (I) and net exports (NX = X – M):

$$AD \equiv C + I + G + NX \tag{17}$$

We can now derive an aggregate demand function showing the relationship between AD and GNP. Substituting equation (16) into (17), we have:

$$AD = (\alpha + [mpc \times GNP]) + I + G + NX \tag{18}$$

Rearranging:

$$AD = (\alpha + I + G + NX) + (mpc \times GNP) \tag{19}$$

The *intercept* of this line is the sum of α, I, G and NX, while the mpc is the *slope*. Hence the consumption function (Figure 5.2) and the aggregate demand line have the same slope and are parallel lines. This is because I, G and NX are all assumed to be independent of the level of GNP, that is, they are autonomous or exogenous. In Figure

112

5.7, the AD line lies above the consumption function reflecting the contribution of I, G and NX to aggregate demand.

What we have in effect done in Figure 5.7 is to take the consumption function diagram of Figure 5.2 and, by adding the remaining components of total expenditure to the consumption function, we have obtained a diagram depicting the relationship between AD and GNP. Because GNP represents the supply of goods and services, this diagram brings together aggregate demand and aggregate supply. At the point were the AD line cuts the 45° line, aggregate demand equals aggregate supply.

Note:

The point where the AD curve intersects the 45° line is the equilibrium level of GNP. At this point AD equals GNP: the level of spending on the economy's output is equal to the level of output that firms plan to produce. This implies that firms' *actual* stock levels are equal to their *desired* stock levels. At points to the left of the equilibrium the level of AD is higher than GNP. Spending on the economy's output exceeds the level of output being produced. As a result, firms' stocks fall *below* desired levels. Faced with this situation, firms will expand production and move GNP towards the equilibrium level. At points to the right of the equilibrium point, such as C, the level of AD is less than GNP: less is being spent than is being produced. There is unintended accumulation of stocks. In this case, firms cut production and GNP moves back towards its equilibrium level. Hence, changes in stocks send signals to firms to increase or decrease output and this moves the economy towards equilibrium.

This diagram is known as the *Keynesian cross diagram* and has proved very popular in textbooks since it was first introduced by the American Keynesian economist Alvin Hansen (1887-1975) in his exposition of Keynes's theory in 1946.[7] It is important to note that in this model *the aggregate price level (P) is fixed.* All variables are measured in real terms. In other words, it is assumed that the entire effect of a change in AD is on the volume of GNP: there is no impact on the price level. In terms of the AD/AS model of Chapter 3, this is equivalent to assuming that we are on the horizontal segment of the AS line. This may be realistic in a situation where there are considerable unemployed resources in the economy, and demand-pull inflation is not a factor to be reckoned with, which of course was the case when Keynes was writing in the 1930s, but is less obviously true for later periods.

---

7. Alvin Hansen, *A Guide to Keynes*, New York: McGraw-Hill, 1953.

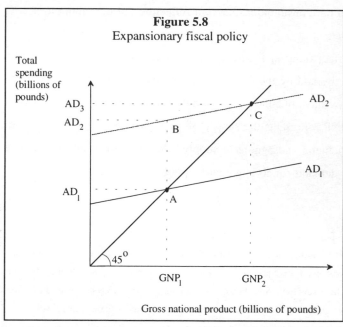

Figure 5.8
Expansionary fiscal policy

Let us now apply this model to the analysis of fiscal policy. Figure 5.8 gives an example of an expansionary fiscal policy. Initially, the economy is at point A and output corresponds to GNP_1. An increase in government expenditure shifts the aggregate demand curve from AD_1 to AD_2 and aggregate demand increases along the vertical axis. The economy moves from A to B. Point B is a disequilibrium point as AD is above GNP and there is an unplanned reduction in stocks. This encourages firms to increase output, so GNP increases along the horizontal axis and, after a time, equilibrium is eventually regained at the point C.

Figure 5.9 highlights an important point. The initial increase in government expenditure is from AD_1 to AD_2, but by the time equilibrium is re-established at the point C, aggregate demand has increased to AD_3. In moving from B to C, aggregate demand increases from AD_2 to AD_3. Thus the final change in GNP is greater than the initial increase in government expenditure. This phenomenon is referred to as the *multiplier*. Let us now examine this concept in some detail.

5.5   The Multiplier

The concept of the multiplier is an integral part of Keynesian economics. The basic idea is that an increase in any of the components of total expenditure, C, I, G or NX, will raise equilibrium GNP by a *multiple* of the initial increase in expenditure. The multiplier is simply a number that relates the initial change in expenditure to the ultimate change in equilibrium GNP. In general:

Change in equilibrium GNP = Initial change in expenditure × multiplier

The idea of the multiplier increased the appeal of Keynesian theory in the 1950s

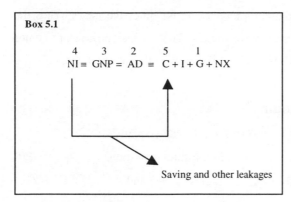

Box 5.1

$$\overset{4}{NI} \equiv \overset{3}{GNP} = \overset{2}{AD} \equiv \overset{5}{C} + I + \overset{1}{G} + NX$$

Saving and other leakages

and 1960s. After all, if every additional £1 million spent by the government boosts GNP by some multiple of £1 million, additional spending would appear to be justified as long as there are any unemployed resources in the economy. Clearly, it is important to be able to say how large the multiplier is under the conditions prevailing in a particular economy.

An intuitive explanation In Figure 5.8 we noted that the equilibrium level of GNP increased by more than the initial increase in government expenditure. The following account of the effects of an increase in expenditure may help the student to understand why this happens. The basic set of relationships underlying the Keynesian model of income determination is shown in Box 5.1. The numbers in the top row indicate the sequence of events. The objective is to show the ultimate effect on output of an initial increase in government expenditure (G). An increase in G (step 1) raises aggregate demand (step 2) by definition. This results in an excess demand for goods and services. Assuming the aggregate supply curve is horizontal, firms respond to the higher level of demand by producing more goods and services at unchanged prices, and GNP (step 3) and NI (step 4) both increase. At the end of this first round, GNP has increased by exactly the amount of the initial increase in G.

That, however, is not the end of the process. In the second round we take account of the fact that the increase in NI raises C (step 5) and this further increases AD and GNP. The link between income (NI) and consumption expenditure (C) is, of course, the consumption function. This function is of crucial importance in the multiplier process. This process will continue into third, fourth and successive rounds because the economy has entered into a rising income-consumption spiral. Every increase in income induces a subsequent increase in consumption which in turn increases income, and so on. The process does, however, eventually come to an end because the mpc is less than 1. In each successive round the increase in consumption is the mpc times the increase in income. If the mpc is equal to 0.8, an increase of £1 million in income will lead to a £0.8 million increase in consumption. In the next round, NI rises by £0.8 million and C rises by a

115

further £0.64 million (that is, the £0.8 million increase in NI times the mpc). Thus the increases in consumption taper off in successive rounds. The expansion therefore comes to a halt sooner, the smaller the mpc. Conversely, it lasts longer the higher the mpc.

Calculating the multiplier formula

In order to derive the multiplier formula, consider the following equations:

$$GNP = AD \qquad \text{Equilibrium condition} \qquad (20)$$

$$AD \equiv C + I + G + NX \qquad \text{Aggregate demand} \qquad (21)$$

$$C = \alpha + (mpc \times GNP) \qquad \text{Consumption function} \qquad (22)$$

To derive the multiplier formula, substitute (21) into (20) to obtain:

$$GNP = C + I + G + NX \qquad (23)$$

Now substitute (22) into (23):

$$GNP = \alpha + (mpc \times GNP) + I + G + NX \qquad (24)$$

Bring the (mpc × GNP) term over to the left-hand side:

$$GNP(1 - mpc) = \alpha + I + G + NX \qquad (25)$$

Divide both sides by (1 − mpc) to obtain:

$$GNP = [1/(1 - mpc)](\alpha + I + G + NX) \qquad (26)$$

We see that if any of the terms (α, I, G or NX) change, the level of equilibrium GNP changes by $1/(1 - mpc)$ times this change. The multiplier therefore equals $1/(1 - mpc)$. For example, if the mpc equals 0.8, the multiplier is:

$$\text{Multiplier} = 1/(1 - mpc) = 1/(1 - 0.8) = 5$$

An increase in G of £1 million would raise GNP or national income by £5 million. If the mpc were 0.9, the multiplier would be 10. We see immediately that the higher the marginal propensity to consume, the larger the multiplier.

We know from our earlier discussion that the mpc and the mps must sum to 1 (see equation 8 above). It follows that (1 − mpc) is equal to mps and the multiplier formula can be rewritten as:

$$\text{Multiplier} = 1/mps$$

An mpc of 0.8 implies an mps of 0.2. Inserting this value for the mps into the above formula, the multiplier again equals 5. The higher the mps, the lower the multiplier; the lower the mps, the higher the multiplier.

We know from Chapter 4 that saving is only one of the three possible leakages from the circular flow of income and expenditure. The other two leakages, which we have ignored in this section, are taxes and imports. It is the sum of these leakages that determines the size of the multiplier. We now turn to a more generalised version of the multiplier formula that takes all three leakages into account.

Generalising the multiplier

The size of the multiplier depends on how much of an initial increase in AD is passed on through an increase in C. In the very simplified model we have just presented, there was only one possible leakage out of domestic expenditure, namely, saving. However, in a more complete model, with a foreign sector and taxes, there are other important leakages.

In an open economy, much of any increase in income will leak abroad in the form of additional imports (M), that is, spending on the output of some other economy. Clearly, this does nothing to stimulate further increases in the level of output in the domestic economy. Similarly, we should take account of the fact that taxes on income and expenditure divert a sizeable proportion of additional consumer income to the government and are another leakage from the circular flow of income. These additional leakages tend to bring the multiplier process to a halt sooner than would be the case in the simple model we discussed above. We now consider how these leakages affect the value of the multiplier. The formula is derived in the Appendix.

Taxation If there is a single flat rate of tax on income, the relationship between tax revenue (T) and GNP is given by the following equation:

$$T = mpt \times GNP \tag{27}$$

where mpt is the marginal tax rate or "marginal propensity to tax", and $0 < mpt < 1$. If the flat rate of tax was 30 per cent, the mpt would equal 0.3. Allowing for a tax of this type, the multiplier formula becomes:

$$\text{Multiplier} = 1/(mps + mpt) \tag{28}$$

Note that the formula has the sum of the "marginal propensities to leak" (that is, to tax and save) in the denominator. Hence, the larger these leakages from extra income, the smaller the multiplier. This general principle holds true even for the most complicated models.

Imports The third possible leakage is due to the relationship between national income and imports. The relationship may be expressed as:

117

$$M = \delta + (\text{mpm} \times \text{GNP}) \qquad\qquad (29)$$

where δ is an intercept term, and MPM is the marginal propensity to import, and $0 <$ MPM < 1. If, for example, mpm equals 0.4, then equation (29) states that 40 per cent of any increase in GNP will be spent on imports. As shown in the Appendix, the multiplier with saving, taxation and import leakages is:

$$\text{Multiplier} = 1/(\text{mps} + \text{mpt} + \text{mpm}) \qquad\qquad (30)$$

Once again, the denominator is the sum of all the leakages from the circular flow of income.

Summary   Any change in the level of investment (I), government expenditure (G), net exports (NX) or the intercept terms of the consumption and import functions affects the equilibrium level of GNP and national income. The change in equilibrium income is greater than the initial change in AD. The ratio between the two is defined as the multiplier. The larger the leakages from the circular flow of income and spending, the smaller the multiplier and, conversely, the smaller the leakages, the larger the multiplier.

Many more complex multiplier formulas can be derived. The models outlined here do not include a financial or money market, which we have not yet discussed. When the model is expanded to include a money market, the multiplier formula becomes even more complex. As a consequence, in recent years simple multiplier analysis of the type presented here has lost much of its prominence in economics.

Another formula that is of some interest is the *balanced budget multiplier* which shows that an equal increase in tax revenue and government expenditure has a multiplier of 1, and not zero as might be expected. Some textbooks elaborate multiplier formulas, presumably in the belief that a bit of algebra is good for the student's soul! However, it is far more important that the student understands the basic concepts, and the issues at stake, in the application of the Keynesian model, than that he or she spends a lot of time deriving complicated multiplier formulas.

The multiplier in the Irish economy

Ireland is a small economy that is extremely open to international trade. Furthermore, the marginal rate of income tax and the indirect tax rates applied to discretionary spending are very high. These considerations would lead us to expect that the multiplier would be very low. A survey of the available research confirms this. There is widespread agreement that mps = 0.26, mpt = 0.24 and mpm = 0.4 are realistic values for the parameters that enter into the calculation of the multiplier. Inserting these values into the formula given above yields the following result:

$$\text{Multiplier} = 1/(0.26 + 0.24 + 0.4) = 1.11 \tag{31}$$

This implies that an increase in G, C, I, or X, or a reduction in M of £1 million would raise GNP by £1.11 million. Under these conditions "multiplier" is somewhat of a misnomer. The leakages are so large that GNP only increases by marginally more than the initial increase in aggregate demand itself. In addition to the fact that large tax and import leakages give rise to small multipliers, there are other considerations, which we shall explore in subsequent chapters, that suggest that fiscal policy will not have any long lasting effect on GNP. Thus one of the alluring features of the simple Keynesian model, the idea that an increase in government spending results in an increase in the equilibrium level of GNP equal to a multiple of the original stimulus, has to be modified to take account of Irish conditions. None the less, increased aggregate demand does tend to increase the equilibrium level of national income.

5.6   Conclusion

The main points discussed in this chapter were:

- The relationship between household disposable income, consumption and saving
- The average and marginal propensities to consume and save
- The consumption and saving functions
- Life-cycle and permanent-income theories of consumption
- The Keynesian cross diagram
- The role of unplanned changes in stocks or inventories in arriving at the equilibrium level of production
- The multiplier effect and how its size depends on the saving, tax and import leakages
- The multiplier under Irish conditions.

Appendix

Deriving the multiplier formula with saving, taxation and import leakages

The notation c, s, t and m is used to denote the marginal propensity to consume (mpc), the marginal propensity to save (mps), the marginal propensity to tax (MPT) and the marginal propensity to import (mpm), respectively. The equilibrium condition is:

$$GNP = C + I + G + X - M \tag{1}$$

The behavioural relationships underlying the equilibrium condition are:

$$C = \alpha + (c\ NI) - T \qquad \text{Consumption function} \tag{2}$$

$$T = t\ NI \qquad \text{Taxation function} \tag{3}$$

$$M = \beta + m\ NI \qquad \text{Import function} \tag{4}$$

The letters α and β denote the intercept term in the consumption and import equations respectively. The coefficients c, t and m show how C, T and M react to changes in NI. The consumption function here differs from the over-simplified multiplier formula given above in that consumer expenditure is determined by gross income and by taxation. Previously, consumer expenditure depended only on gross income. Here the consumption function states that a change in gross income affects consumer expenditure via c, whereas a change in taxation has a *direct* effect on consumer expenditure. In the next section we shall examine the case where consumer expenditure depends on disposable income, that is, gross income *minus* taxation.

Substitute equation (3) into equation (2).

$$C = (\alpha + c\ NI) - (t\ NI) \tag{5}$$

or

$$C = \alpha + (c - t)NI \tag{6}$$

Substitute equations (6) and (4) into the equilibrium condition (1).

$$GNP = \alpha + (c - t)NI + I + G + X - \beta - (m\ NI) \tag{7}$$

Bring the terms involving NI over to the left-hand side and assume GNP = NI.

$$GNP - (c - t - m)GNP = \alpha - \beta + I + G + X \tag{8}$$

or

$$GNP(1 - c + t + m) = \alpha - \beta + I + G + X \tag{9}$$

Recall that s = 1 − c.

$$GNP(s + t + m) = \alpha - \beta + I + G + X \tag{10}$$

Divide both sides by the term in brackets:

$$GNP = [1/(s + t + m)] \times (\alpha - \beta + I + G + X) \qquad (11)$$

The term $[1/(s + t + m)]$ is the multiplier formula when saving, taxation and import leakages are allowed for. Note that the minus sign on the import intercept term, β, indicates that an increase in imports, not brought about by a change in national income, will decrease GNP via the multiplier formula. As before, an increase in α, I, G or X will increase GNP via the multiplier formula, and vice versa.

It is clear that taking taxation and imports into account lowers the value of the multiplier. For example, if s, t and c equalled 0.1, 0.3 and 0.4, respectively, the crude multiplier that ignored taxes and imports would be equal to 10. However, the more realistic multipliers that include taxes and imports would be equal to only 1.25. The latter value would be more relevant in Ireland's very open and taxed economy.

Chapter 6

Fiscal Policy and the National Debt

6.1   Introduction

The Keynesian theory of income determination discussed in Chapters 3 and 5 suggests that governments can use fiscal policy to smooth the economy's growth path. The present chapter explores some implications of this idea.

6.2   Stabilisation Policy

We saw in Chapter 1 that the growth rate of Irish GDP has been very erratic over the years. One of the principal tenets of Keynesian economics is that governments can adjust their spending and taxation to stabilise the rate of growth of GDP. According to this view fiscal policy can be used to keep the *actual* level of GDP close to the *potential* or *full employment* level of output.

Note:

Potential GDP or GDP is the level of output the economy could produce given the state of technology and the size and education of the labour force without generating inflationary pressures. Potential output is sometimes referred to as "full employment output". The unemployment rate associated with potential output is known as the "natural rate of unemployment".

In Figure 6.1, the growth rate of potential GDP is indicated by a horizontal line. This assumes that the economy is capable of averaging a steady 4 per cent annual growth rate over the long run. A higher growth rate would not be sustainable if shortages of skilled labour, capacity constraints and other bottlenecks appeared.

Note:

The long-run determinants of the economy's potential growth rate are the subject of that branch of economics labelled *growth theory*. They include factors such as the rate of investment in physical and human capital, the rate of growth of the labour force, and the general economic environment and institutional framework. We discussed some of these issues in Chapter 2.

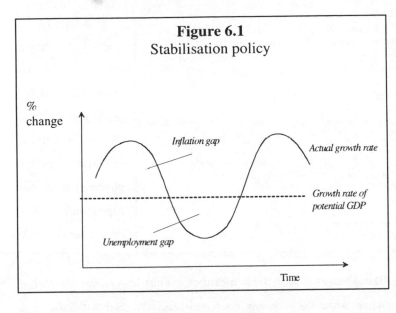

Figure 6.1
Stabilisation policy

% change

Inflation gap

Actual growth rate

Growth rate of potential GDP

Unemployment gap

Time

The actual growth rate of GDP is shown crossing and re-crossing the potential growth rate line. When the actual growth rate is above the rate of growth of potential GDP, firms are operating at above full capacity, labour shortages emerge and there is upward pressure on costs and prices. The result is *demand-pull inflation.* Conversely, when the actual growth rate is below the potential rate, firms find they have excess capacity and workers will be laid off. Employment decreases and cyclical unemployment increases.

The objective of stabilisation policy is to keep actual GDP as close as possible to its potential or full employment level and thereby minimise inflation and cyclical unemployment. A very important motivation for attempting this is the fact that recessions leave additional structural unemployment in their wake. As we discussed in Chapter 14, the "natural" rate of unemployment does not appear to be a constant but drifts upwards after a recession.

Figure 6.2 shows the aggregate demand (AD) and aggregate supply (AS) model developed in Chapter 3. (We assume an upward-sloping AS curve as suggested by Keynesian economics.) The position or *location* of the AD is determined by its component parts: consumption (C), investment (I), government expenditure (G), exports (X) and imports (M). An increase in C, I, G, X or a fall in M will shift the AD curve out to the right and vice versa. Stabilisation policy is an attempt by government to offset the instability caused by fluctuations in the private sector components of aggregate demand. For example, if the economy begins to move into a recession because of a fall in X, the government could counter this fall in demand by increasing G. Alternatively, it could stimulate C by reducing taxes or increasing transfer payments or providing incentives to stimulate I.

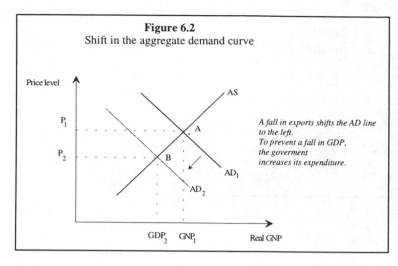

Figure 6.2
Shift in the aggregate demand curve

A fall in exports shifts the AD line to the left.
To prevent a fall in GDP, the goverment increases its expenditure.

Similarly, if prices are rising because of an excess demand for goods and services, the Keynesian prescription is for government to cut expenditure and/or raise taxes, thereby dampening the inflationary pressure. These *discretionary* fiscal measures should be *counter-cyclical* – injecting additional spending when the economy goes into recession, and withdrawing it when the economy is booming. If properly implemented, an active fiscal policy will keep GDP closer to its full employment level than would be the case if the government ignored the business cycle.

Keynes appeared to favour using wasteful public expenditure as a component of stabilisation policy because, unlike productive investment, it is not subject to diminishing returns. He stated that

"If the Treasury were to fill old bottles full with bank notes, bury them at suitable depths in disused coal mines . . . and leave it to private enterprise to dig the notes up again . . . then there need be no more unemployment."[1]

However, those who advocate an active fiscal policy today are aware that government expenditure financed by borrowing should be productive and yield a return to the community adequate to warrant the burden that servicing the debt will impose on future taxpayers.

6.3   Implementing a Stabilisation Policy

The idea of using fiscal policy to stabilise the economy is appealing, but experience has shown that it is in practice very difficult, if not impossible, successfully to fine-tune the economy in this manner. We now consider the reasons why this is the case.

---

1. Keynes pointed out that the "form of digging holes in the ground known as gold-mining" was quite acceptable to those who deplored "wasteful" public spending. See *General Theory*, Book III, Chapter 10.

Lags

If the economy experiences an adverse shock and is going into recession, the government should adopt an expansionary fiscal stance. But the timing of this response is likely to be delayed. It takes time to recognise what is happening to the economy (the *recognition lag*). Only a limited amount of timely economic data is available. Information on key variables becomes available gradually – in Ireland no quarterly GDP estimates are published. The first official national income tables for 1996 were not published until June 1997. While numerous unofficial estimates are prepared, economists often disagree about the direction in which the economy is moving.

In the middle of 1990 the consensus was that the Irish economy would grow by at least 3 per cent in 1991. No forecaster recognised that the economy was at a turning point in mid-1990, but in fact a slow-down occurred after the invasion of Kuwait in August 1990. Since early 1997 many commentators warned that the Irish economy was "overheating" but the rate of inflation has remained low into 1998. No wonder policy makers were in a quandary about the appropriate stance to adopt!

Secondly, policy makers have to implement appropriate policy. This too takes time. More money cannot be spent on road building until project documents have been drawn up, planning permission obtained and tenders approved. Tax changes are usually introduced only once a year, at budget time, and do not take effect until after they have been passed into law. The tax reductions announced in the budget of December 1997 were not reflected in higher take-home pay until April 1998.

These lags are referred to as *inside lags*. There is also the *outside lag* between implementing a policy and when it affects aggregate demand. The impact of the income tax cuts in the 1997 budget that went into effect in April 1998 built up over the second half of the year. By the time a change announced in the budget affected the level of spending, economic conditions had altered. The implication is that the policy could be inappropriate by the time it becomes effective and end up *destabilising* instead of stabilising the economy.

How big a response?

Another difficulty arises from the problem of deciding how much additional demand the government should inject into or withdraw from the economy. The appropriate amount to spend to counter a fall in investment can only be calculated on the basis of an exact knowledge of the investment and fiscal multipliers. But calculating multipliers entails estimating a model of the economy, which is a far from exact science. Different models suggest different policy prescriptions.

Endogenous economic policy

Policy makers are not disembodied technicians, unaware of political realities. In all countries economic policy is influenced by the desire of politicians to get re-elected, which depends on delivering results such as low inflation and unemployment. The relative importance of these objectives differs between countries. German politicians, for example, have believed that low inflation is crucial, while until recently Italian politicians were willing to condone high inflation. Thus economic policies are *endogenous,* a reflection of policy makers' and the public's preferences.

The timing of elections influences policy. During the General Election of 1978, for example, Irish political parties vied with one another in their extravagant promises to the electorate. After the election increases in expenditure and cuts in taxation were implemented when the economy was already booming.

One way around the problem created by the political cycle is to create independent economic policy-making institutions. Following the American and German examples, many European governments, including Britain, have given their central banks increased autonomy and the independence to withstand demands for inflationary financing of government deficits. Countries like Ireland that participate in the European EMU have relinquished control over their monetary policy to the European Central Bank and agreed to observe the Stability Pact (agreed in Dublin in December 1996) in the conduct of their fiscal policy.

6.4 The Government's Budget Constraint

This brings us to the issue of how the government pays for its spending, which has a crucial bearing on the effects of fiscal policy. The government spends money on current consumption, G, and to pay interest on its past borrowing. If we denote the stock of government debt as D and the interest rate payable on this debt as i, total government spending equals $G + iD$. The main source of government revenue is tax receipts, T. (Recall T denotes tax receipts net of transfer payments such as unemployment and other social welfare benefits.)

The *general government deficit* is defined as the shortfall of government spending over tax revenue:

$$G + iD - T \qquad (1)$$

A narrower definition of the deficit excludes interest on past debt. (The government has little control over these interest rate payments.) This is called the *primary deficit:*

$$G - T \qquad (2)$$

There are a number of ways a deficit can be financed. First, the government can borrow from the Central Bank. This form of financing increases the money supply, ΔM^s, in the economy. However, there are narrow limits to how much of the deficit governments can finance in this way. Under the Maastricht Treaty countries planning to participate in the single European currency are precluded from financing fiscal deficits by borrowing from their central banks.

The alternative is for the government to borrow either from the domestic private sector ΔD_{ps} or abroad ΔD_f to pay for its deficit. We can therefore state the *government's budget constraint*

$$G + iD - T = \Delta M + \Delta D = \Delta M + \Delta D_{ps} + \Delta D_f \qquad (3)$$

Increasing the money supply and borrowing from abroad constitute *government monetary financing:*

$$\Delta M + \Delta D_f \qquad (6)$$

(We explain how foreign borrowing increases the money supply in Chapter 9.) Borrowing from the domestic private sector and from abroad increases the stock of *interest-bearing debt* and hence adds to the future burden of debt service, iD. Borrowing from the Central Bank and printing money does not increase the interest the government has to pay the public.

The impact of an expansionary fiscal policy on aggregate demand depends on whether the deficit is financed through an expansion of the money supply or by selling bonds to the domestic public or borrowing from abroad. We discuss now two issues that arise when bonds are issued to finance a government deficit.

Crowding-out

First, there is the question of *crowding-out*. To make bonds attractive to investors their price has to be lowered when the government wishes to issue more of them to finance a deficit. However, lowering the price of a bond is equivalent to raising its yield (see Chapter 10). As a result, selling government bonds puts upward pressure on interest rates. Higher interest rates, in turn, reduce private sector investment and consumer spending. This is referred to as *crowding-out*. If the fall in C and I equals the increase in G, there is *complete* crowding-out. The result is a change in the composition of AD, with no change in its level.

Figure 6.3 uses the Keynesian cross diagram to illustrate the crowding-out argument. Initially, the economy is at the point A and the output level corresponds to GDP$_1$. The increase in government expenditure from G$_1$ to G$_2$ shifts the aggregate demand curve upwards. The economy moves to the point B and an output level of GDP$_2$. However,

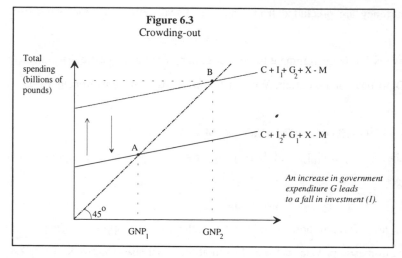

Figure 6.3
Crowding-out

Total spending (billions of pounds)

$C + I_1 + G_2 + X - M$

$C + I_2 + G_1 + X - M$

An increase in government expenditure G leads to a fall in investment (I).

45°

GNP$_1$

GNP$_2$

the increase in government expenditure increases the demand for funds on the money markets and this increases interest rates. The higher interest rates, in turn, reduce private sector investment. As investment falls from I$_1$ to I$_2$ the aggregate demand curve shifts back down and the economy reverts to the point A. The initial increase in G is completely offset by the fall in I and GDP is unchanged. Government expenditure has crowded out investment. In this case, there is 100 per cent crowding-out and fiscal policy has no impact on aggregate demand.

An alternative form of crowding-out is associated with government foreign borrowing. The inflow of foreign exchange associated with foreign borrowing exerts upward pressure on the exchange rate. This tends to crowd out exports and encourage imports. As before, the effect of a fiscal expansion on aggregate demand is less than if the expansion were financed by printing money.

In practice, the degree of crowding-out is likely to be considerably less than 100 per cent. Fiscal policy would therefore affect aggregate demand although by less than the increase in G. The important point is that the ultimate effect on GDP is smaller than that suggested by the multipliers we derived in Chapter 5, which took no account of crowding-out.

Barro-Ricardo equivalence theorem

A second issue relates to the effect of government deficits on the behaviour of households. In an influential article published in 1974, the Harvard economist Robert Barro proposed the idea that increases in government debt could result in a fall in private sector consumption. The classical economist David Ricardo (1772-1823) appeared to have entertained the same idea, hence it is now known as the *Barro-Ricardo equivalence theorem.*

The bones of the proposition are as follows. Suppose the government lowers taxes without cutting its spending and finances the deficit by selling bonds to the public. These bonds must be redeemed (with interest) at some time in the future. Households' *current* disposable income rises due to the tax cut, but *future* disposable income will fall by an equivalent amount because of the necessity of repaying the debt. Thus, households' long-run or permanent income is not increased by the tax cut. If they are rational and care about future generations, their consumption should remain unchanged. However, if the present generation is willing to pass the increased debt on to future generations they would feel better off as a result of the tax cut and their consumption would increase.

As we discuss in greater detail in Chapter 8, the Irish experience offers some support for the Barro-Ricardian equivalence theorem. When the fiscal deficit was very large in the first half of the 1980s, the private sector saving ratio was very high; when the public sector deficit was brought under control in the later 1980s, the private sector saving ratio fell.

Summary   From the above discussion it should be clear that in practice the use of fiscal policy to stabilise the economy is not an easy task. While the basic idea seems simple, its implementation is fraught with difficulties. Moreover, economists have become increasingly sceptical of some of the assumptions underlying the basic Keynesian model. None the less, policy makers continue to try to use budgets to reduce the fluctuations in economic output.

6.5   Some Refinements

In this section we introduce some important refinements to the basic concepts of fiscal policy introduced in Chapter 5.

Endogenous tax receipts and spending

Up to now we have dealt with government spending and taxation as if they were completely *exogenous*, that is, as if they could be set precisely at a level decided by policy makers. In reality, the levels of government spending and taxation are influenced by the behaviour of the economy.

Automatic stabilisers During a recession government net tax receipts fall – as unemployment rises households and companies pay less income tax, VAT receipts decline, and unemployment and other transfer payments increase. The process goes into reverse during an expansion. As a result the budget deficit automatically increases during recessions and falls during booms. Cyclically induced changes in the fiscal balance act as *automatic stabilisers* on the economy.

The effect of the income tax system and transfer payments on the government's budget is illustrated in Figure 6.4. The diagram shows government expenditure on current goods and services, G, and net taxes (tax revenue *minus* transfers) along the vertical axis. Nominal GDP is shown on the horizontal axis.

Government expenditure is assumed to be

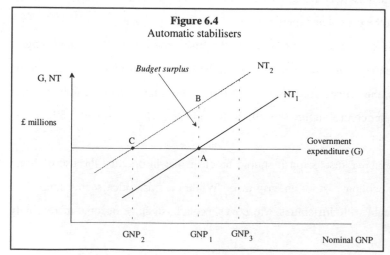

Figure 6.4
Automatic stabilisers

constant at all levels of GDP and is therefore represented as a horizontal line. The net taxes line (NT), on the other hand, is positively sloped. This is because more tax revenue is collected and less is paid out in transfers as GDP increases. Conversely, as GDP falls, less is collected in taxes and more paid out in transfers and NT decreases.

At the point A in Figure 6.4, which corresponds to GDP_1, government expenditure equals net taxes and the budget is balanced. To the left of GDP_1 there is a budget deficit (expenditure exceeds revenue), and to the right a budget surplus (expenditure is less than revenue). It is clear from the diagram that the budget balance automatically changes as GDP changes. If, for example, we start from GDP_2 and move to GDP_3, then net taxes move up along the NT_1 line and the government's budget swings automatically from deficit to surplus. This means that as the economy moves out of a recession, the government's budget surplus will automatically increase. Conversely, as the economy contracts, the budget surplus automatically falls.

The diagram allows us to clarify the distinction between automatic and *discretionary* changes in the budget balance. Discretionary budget changes arise when the government deliberately changes the stance of fiscal policy by changing tax rates, the level of social welfare benefits, or the level of its expenditure on goods and services. A tax increase shifts the NX line upwards to the left, and vice versa. A cut in rates of social security payments or a cut in government consumption shifts the government expenditure line downwards and vice versa. Each of these changes represents a policy decision by the government. They are discretionary as distinct from an automatic reflection of the sensitivity of the tax receipts and payments to changes in the level of economic activity.

It has been estimated that the elasticity of Irish budget receipts with respect to changes in the output gap (actual *minus* potential GDP) is about -0.4, while the elasticity of budget expenditure is about 0.2.[2] This means that every one percentage point increase in the output gap lowers the government's receipts by 0.4 percentage points of GDP, while it raises expenditure by 0.2 percentage points. Given the high variability of Irish GDP over the years, we can see that automatic stabilisers are important.

2. Commission of the European Communities, *1997 Annual Economic Report,* p. 85.

The full-employment budget When there is a discretionary change in any of the budgetary variables, the level of GDP at which the budget will be balanced changes. A tax increase or spending cut lowers the level of GDP at which the budget is balanced, and a tax cut or expenditure increase raises it. For example, following the increase in taxes shown in Figure 6.4, the level of GDP consistent with a balanced budget falls from GDP_1 to GDP_2. The budget surplus is eliminated as we move from B to C because the government collects less in tax revenue and pays out more in transfer payments.

It can be argued that the relevant budget balance from a policy perspective is the *full-employment budget* surplus or deficit (also referred to as the *structural, high-employment,* or *cyclically adjusted* budget surplus or deficit). The government should choose a combination of tax rates and levels of expenditure that would result in a balanced budget *if the economy were at potential GDP*, rather than targeting the actual or *ex post* budget balance. If the economy is in recession the government should tolerate the resultant budget deficit, and run a surplus when the economy recovers.

If the government pursues a policy of always trying to balance the budget, when the economy goes into recession and a budget deficit emerges it would respond by cutting expenditure or raising taxes. This reaction would push the economy further into recession. This is what happened in many countries in the 1930s: governments that wanted to balance the budget pushed their economies deeper into recession by raising taxes and cutting expenditure to correct recession-induced deficits. This intensified the recession: budgetary policy was *pro-cyclical.*

The full-employment budget balance is more relevant than the actual budget balance in gauging the stance of fiscal policy. An examination of the budget balance without adjustment for built-in stabilisers would give a misleading picture of the direction of fiscal policy. For example, if the government's budget is in deficit only because the economy is in recession, it is incorrect to conclude that fiscal policy is expansionary. On the other hand, in the mid-1990s the Irish budget moved towards a surplus as the economy grew exceptionally rapidly. It would be wrong to conclude from this that the stance of fiscal policy was contractionary. Given the exceptionally rapid rate of economic growth, many commentators criticised the government for not running very sizeable budget surpluses.

6.6 Taxation and the Supply Side of the Economy

Up to this point, our emphasis has been on how taxation affects the demand side of the economy. But ever since Adam Smith, economists have recognised that taxation also affects the supply side of the economy by affecting the *incentives to work and save*. This affects the level and composition of output and income. If these effects are large they can have surprising results. It could be that tax cuts increase, rather than decrease, tax revenue. This argument has been put forward by the University of Southern California economist Arthur Laffer, who reputedly first drew the *Laffer Curve* on a napkin in a Washington restaurant to explain the point to a reporter.[3]

The Laffer curve depicts the relationship between the average tax rate (vertical axis) and the yield of a tax (horizontal axis). This is illustrated in Figure 6.5, which shows how much revenue is obtained from different average rates of income tax. There are two rates where no tax revenue is collected – zero and 100 per cent. In the first case, there is no tax and therefore no revenue. If no one works there is no income to tax and revenue is zero. In the second case, all income would be taken in tax and there would be no incentive to work. Between these two extremes, it is argued, revenue first increases and then decreases as the tax rate rises.

Figure 6.5 shows that there is *a revenue maximising tax rate*, T^*. Moreover, the same amount of tax revenue can be obtained at high or low tax rates: T_1 and T_2 generate the same revenue, R_1. It follows, therefore, that government could cut the tax rate from T_1 to T_2 without suffering any loss of revenue. More generally, if the tax rate is below T^* an increase in the tax rate leads to an increase in revenue. This is what is normally expected. However, if the tax rate is above T^*, we have the surprising result that an increase in the tax rate leads to a *reduction* in revenue. In the latter situation, the government raises the tax rate in order to generate extra revenue and finds that its tax receipts fall. If it lowered the tax rate it would generate extra revenue.

The explanation for this paradoxical result centres on work incentives. High tax rates discourage people from working. If people work less, their taxable income falls and so do tax receipts. In 1986 the marginal income tax rate in Ireland was 65 per cent. The rate for evening teaching at a university was £30 per hour. For every £30 earned, the government

---

3. It has been said of the Laffer curve that you can explain it to a politician in half an hour and he can talk about it for six months.

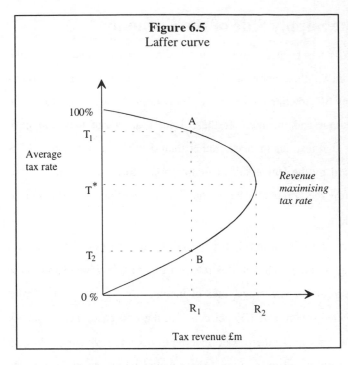

Figure 6.5
Laffer curve

took £19.50 in income taxes and the lecturer received £10.50. When this after-tax income is spent a further 20 per cent or so was taken in indirect taxes. If the lecturer decided that the after-tax purchasing power of the lecture fee was not worth the time and effort involved, (s)he would stay at home in the evenings instead of going out to teach an extra course. If enough people reacted in this way, the course would not go ahead and the government would lose tax revenue. A reduction in the marginal tax rate would make it more worthwhile to put on the course and tax receipts would rise.

In addition to discouraging work effort, high tax rates create many other undesirable incentives. People are encouraged to switch from the formal economy into the informal or "black" economy, to shop in countries where indirect taxes are low, to take money out of the country and place it in foreign tax havens ("capital flight"), and even to emigrate. These responses are all channels that could lead to Laffer's hypothesis being borne out.

When marginal tax rates are high it may therefore be argued that a reduction in tax rates would have a stimulating effect on the economy by encouraging people to work harder and to save and invest more, leading to a rise in national income and ultimately to higher tax revenue.

However, there are a number of reasons why tax cuts may not have the dramatic effects predicted by this theory. It is possible, for example, that lower taxes might encourage people to work less because after the tax cut they can obtain the same level of take-home pay with less effort; they may decide to enjoy more leisure at the same income, which they can now earn by working less. This would offset the effects predicted by Laffer.

Moreover, for the Laffer curve to be bell shaped, the reduction in taxes has to boost output by an amount sufficient to more than compensate for the initial loss of tax revenue. This requires that the elasticity of output with respect to the tax rate be greater than unity. While there may be particular sectors of the economy where this condition is met, it is by no means certain, even at very high levels of taxation, that this holds for the economy as a whole. However, the openness of the Irish economy does imply that we cannot afford to move too far out of line from the tax rates that obtain in the UK. This was illustrated by the manner in which high excises and VAT rates on spirits, petrol and electrical goods led shoppers from the Republic to purchase these items in Northern Ireland in the mid-1980s. When the tax rates were cut towards the end of the decade, more was spent in the Republic and revenue rose. (A reverse flow is occurring in 1998.) Similarly, emigration of qualified people to the UK and the US is encouraged by the relatively low rates of income taxation in those countries. These effects of high tax rates are consistent with the existence of a Laffer curve.

The Laffer curve adds to the uncertainty about the effects of fiscal policy on the economy. Normally, we would expect an increase in the tax rate to increase tax revenue. However, if the tax rate is at or above the optimal tax rate, the opposite might happen.

6.7   Deficits and the Dynamics of the Debt

We noted in section 6.4 that when printing money (borrowing from the central bank) is ruled out as a means of financing a deficit, the government must borrow from the public or from abroad. Budget deficits accumulate in the *national debt,* which we denoted as D. That proportion of the debt that is borrowed at home is referred to as the *domestic* or (*internal*) *debt* and that proportion owed to non-residents is referred to as the *external debt.*

Both forms of debt are a burden on the economy. Taxes have to be raised from the working population to service the entire debt. The fact that the interest paid on the internally held debt is received by other members of the Irish economy does not alter this. These taxes involve *dead-weight losses* because people alter their decisions about working and saving as a result of them. (We discussed some responses to high taxation in the previous section.) There are limits to the capacity and willingness of the public to accept a tax burden arising from past borrowing. Future generations of taxpayers may feel that they benefited little from the spending which gave rise to the debt. *Debt fatigue* can set in, leading to pressure on the government to default on its obligations to its creditors. Thus, a steadily rising national debt/GDP ratio will sooner or later result in a *debt crisis*. Ireland approached a crisis of this type in the 1980s.

The burden of external debt is more worrying than that of domestic debt. In the case of domestic debt we owe the money to ourselves. Although they do involve higher taxes, the debt repayments stay within the country and do not involve an outflow across the balance of payments. External debt, however, involves payments to non-residents (mostly foreign banks). To service the externally held debt a surplus of exports over imports has to be generated in order to transfer purchasing power abroad.

6.8 The Dynamics of Debt Accumulation

The dynamics of debt accumulation was studied by the Polish-American economist Evsey Domar who analysed the implications of US wartime borrowing in an article written in 1944.[4] This paper provides the foundation of the recent literature on *sustainable fiscal policy*.

Let us return to the definition of the government's budget constraint in (3) above,

$$G + iD - T = \Delta M + \Delta D \qquad (3)$$

---

4. E. Domar, "The Burden of the Debt and National Income", *American Economic Review*, Vol. 33, 1944.

If we rule out increasing the money supply as a means of financing the deficit, then $\Delta M = 0$ and the budget constraint becomes

$$G + iD - T = \Delta D \tag{4}$$

If the aim is to stabilise the national debt, $\Delta D = 0$, then the budget constraint becomes:

$$T - G = iD \tag{5}$$

In other words, to stabilise the level of the national debt the government must run a *primary budget surplus* equal to iD. It must pay the interest on past debt out of current tax receipts. Under current Irish circumstances this would involve running a primary budget surplus equal to about 3.5 per cent of GDP.

Stabilising the absolute level of the debt would imply that it was falling as a proportion of GDP. The Maastricht Treaty sets out the condition that countries that wish to participate in the single European currency must bring the debt/GDP ratio down to 60 per cent. We now turn to the question of how to stabilise the national debt relative to GDP.

Stabilising the national debt To see how the debt ratio can be stabilised let us divide the magnitudes in (4) by the level of GDP.

This gives us

$$G/GDP + iD/GDP - T/GDP = \Delta D/GDP \tag{6}$$

Writing ratios to GDP in lower case letters ($G/GDP = g$, etc.) this becomes:

$$g + id - t = \Delta D/GDP \tag{7}$$

(Note that $\Delta D/GDP$ equals the fiscal deficit as a proportion of GDP. This should not be confused with the *change in the debt/GDP ratio,* $\Delta(D/Y)$ or Δd.)

Let us now examine the relationship between the fiscal deficit and the change in the debt/GDP ratio. By definition, $d = D/GDP$. Rearranging:

$$D = d \times GDP$$

Using the mathematical technique known as total differentiation gives:

$$\Delta D = d\, \Delta GDP + GDP\, \Delta d$$

Dividing both sides by GDP yields:

$$\Delta D/GDP = d\, \Delta GDP/GDP + \Delta d$$

Letting y equal the rate of growth of GDP:

$$\Delta D/GDP = dy + \Delta d$$

Substituting from (7) above we obtain

$$g + i\mathrm{d} - \mathrm{t} = \mathrm{d}y + \Delta\mathrm{d}$$

Rearranging:

$$\Delta\mathrm{d} = g + i\mathrm{d} - \mathrm{t} - \mathrm{d}y$$

or

$$\Delta\mathrm{d} = g - \mathrm{t} + (i - y)\mathrm{d}$$

The goal of stabilising the debt/GDP ratio implies setting $\Delta\mathrm{d} = 0$, which implies:

$$g - \mathrm{t} + (i - y)\mathrm{d} = 0$$

or

$$\mathrm{t} - g = (i - y)\mathrm{d}$$

In words this condition says that a stable debt/GDP ratio will be achieved if the primary budget surplus as a percentage of GDP equals (or exceeds) the excess of the rate of interest over the rate of growth of GDP *times* the initial ratio of debt to GDP. (Note that both interest rates and GDP are in nominal terms.)

To stabilise the debt/GDP ratio, therefore, it is necessary to run a primary budget surplus whose size depends on:

- the level of interest rates relative to the rate of growth of GDP, and
- the initial size of the national debt.

In the present Irish situation, with GDP growing at or above the rate of interest on government debt, $y > i$, combined with a primary budget surplus, $\mathrm{t} > g$, the debt/GDP ratio is falling, $\Delta\mathrm{d} < 0$. It is this combination of events – high growth, low interest rates and a primary budget surplus – that has led to a faster fall in the Irish debt/GDP during the 1990s than has been achieved in any other European country.

6.9   Conclusion

The main points discussed in this chapter were:

- Stabilisation policy
- The difficulties in the way of implementing such a policy
- The government's budget constraint
- The crowding-out effect
- Interest rate and exchange rate crowding-out
- Barro-Ricardo equivalence theorem
- Automatic fiscal stabilisers

- The full employment budget deficit
- Taxation and the supply-side of the economy
- The Laffer curve
- The dynamics of the national debt
- The dynamics of debt accumulation.

Chapter 7

The Public Finances

7.1   Introduction

In the preceding chapters we presented the Keynesian argument that the government should intervene to stabilise the economy. Following such an active fiscal policy involves raising and lowering taxes and public expenditure to "fine-tune" the economy. During recessions budget deficits would be incurred to try to keep GNP close to its potential level. If not offset by surpluses during the boom phase of the business cycle, these deficits will accumulate over time in a growing national debt, which would have serious implications for the economy.

In this chapter we examine trends in public spending, taxation and borrowing in Ireland. This analysis provides the background to a discussion of fiscal policy in Ireland in the next chapter.

7.2   The Budget

In Ireland, the government's budget is divided into a *current* and a *capital* account. Current expenditure is of a day-to-day nature. It does not result in the creation of fixed assets. Current revenue is income from taxes and state-owned enterprises. A *current budget deficit* (CBD) arises if current expenditure exceeds current revenue.

Capital expenditure involves the creation of assets such as schools, hospitals and roads. Capital

Table 7.1

The government's budget: 1998

	£ millions	% of GNP
A1. Current expenditure	14,388	32.5
A2. Current revenue	15,497	35.0
A = A2 – A1. *Current budget surplus*	1,109	2.5
B1. Exchequer capital expenditure	2,002	4.5
B2. Exchequer capital revenue	804	1.8
B = B2 – B1. *Capital budget deficit*	1,198	2.7
(C) *Exchequer borrowing requirement* (EBR), (A + B)	– 89	0.2
(D) *General government surplus*	133	0.3

Source: *Budget 1998 (3 December 1997).*

revenue consists of interest on stocks owned by the government, loan repayments and capital grants received from the European Union (EU). The excess of the central government's capital expenditure over capital revenue is called the *capital budget deficit*.

Table 7.1 presents a summary of the government's current and capital budgets for 1998. The sum of the current and capital budget deficits (subtotals A and B) is the *exchequer borrowing requirement* (EBR). This is the total amount of money the central government must borrow to cover the excess of its spending over revenue. The *general government surplus (deficit)* is the budget measure used by the EU in judging fiscal policy. This is a broader measure than the EBR as it takes into account cash flows of local authorities and other grant-aided bodies and also some definitional changes. In 1998 this was projected to be a small surplus. If this is realised, it will be the first time in over fifty years that the Irish budget turned in an overall surplus.

We turn now to an examination of the trends in government expenditure, revenue and borrowing.

7.3   Government Expenditure

Current expenditure

Table 7.2 shows the main headings underlying total government *current* expenditure over the period 1986 to 1998. The largest headings are national debt service, social welfare, health and education. Over the period, spending on social welfare and health increased, whereas spending on education declined. The cost of servicing the national debt has fallen from 25 per cent of GNP in 1986 to 15 per cent in 1998. This is a very favourable trend, but the fact that more is still being spent on debt service than on education illustrates the problems attributable to heavy borrowing in the

Table 7.2

Principal heads of government current expenditure

	1986		1998	
	£ m	%	£ m	%
Service of the public debt	1,988	24.5	2,596	14.8
Social welfare	1,535	18.9	4,866	27.8
Health	1,094	13.5	2,941	16.8
Education	1,479	18.2	2,351	13.4
Gárda Síochána	262	3.2	467	3.2
Defence	253	3.1	462	3.2
Total current expenditure	8,087	100.0	14,388	100.0

Source: *Estimates of Receipts and Expenditure, 1986* and *1998*.

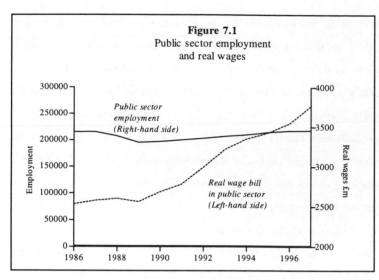

Figure 7.1
Public sector employment
and real wages

Public sector
employment
(Right-hand side)

Real wage bill
in public sector
(Left-hand side)

past.

Government current expenditure has been growing at a very rapid pace in the 1990s. Some categories of spending have risen very rapidly – current spending on health, for example, has risen from £2.1 billion in 1993 to a projected £3.1 billion in 1998. Many commentators have drawn attention to the fact that the extremely buoyant tax revenue in the past three years has allowed current spending to race away, almost out of control. The main contributory factor to this has been the very rapid growth of spending on public sector pay and pensions.

The government formed in 1997 has made a commitment to containing the growth of net current expenditure to 4 per cent a year over its life. There was much criticism of its strategy of bringing a large amount of expenditure that would normally have occurred in 1998 back to 1997 in order to increase the expenditure base. However, despite this subterfuge, the Minister admitted in his 1998 budget speech that the projected increase in current spending in 1999 over the 1998 level is 4.8 per cent on a "no-policy-change" basis. Good resolutions like this have been heard before. It remains to be seen if they will be lived up to this time!

Public sector pay and employment Public sector employment relates to persons working in the civil service, Gárda Síochána, defence forces, education, non-commercial state-sponsored bodies, health boards and local authorities. Commercial state bodies are omitted.

Public services are labour intensive and as a consequence the public sector wage bill accounts for 40 per cent of all government current spending. This bill depends on the numbers employed and the level of wages and salaries in the public sector. In the mid-1980s a policy of reducing public sector employment so as to curtail current expenditure was introduced. However, Figure 7.1 (and Table A in the statistical appendix) shows that public sector employment was relatively constant from 1986 to 1997. However, the public sector wage bill increased by 96 per cent in *nominal* terms and by 49 per cent in *real* terms over the same period. Clearly, the curb on public sector wages introduced in the late 1980s has not been maintained. Further large increases in the public sector wage bill are reflected in the 1998 budget. As the Minister for Finance, Charles McCreevy, stated in his 1998 budget speech:

"The public sector pay and pension bill, £5.6 billion, is expected to increase by 6 per cent over 1997 on top of an increase of 10.2 per cent in 1997 itself. This is totally unacceptable."

Public capital expenditure

Government capital expenditure accounted for 4.5 per cent of GNP in 1998. Although somewhat higher than in recent years, this is much lower than the 17.4 per cent of GNP which went on public capital spending in 1981. This figure was exceptionally high by international standards at the time. The sharp reduction in capital spending in the 1980s was due to the completion of many of the large projects, such as the Moneypoint power station, the Dublin-Cork gas pipeline, the Dublin Area Rapid Transit (DART), and the reduction in capital injections into ailing state-sponsored bodies. Allowing the *public capital programme* (PCP) to shrink proved to be a more palatable way of reducing the overall borrowing requirement in the 1980s than curbing current expenditure or raising taxes. With the rapid growth of the economy in recent years, however, it is recognised that spending on infrastructure (roads, railways, ports etc.) has to be raised to try to keep pace with growing demand.

Changes in capital expenditure have a disproportionate effect on the level of activity in the building and construction sector. This sector is inherently prone to wide cyclical fluctuations and changes in the government's capital budget amplify these fluctuations.

7.4 Government Revenue

Figure 7.2 (and Table B in the appendix) shows that total taxation is broken down into taxes on *income and wealth*, *expenditure*, *capital*, and "other" taxes. The first two are by far the most important sources of revenue for the government. With regard to taxes on

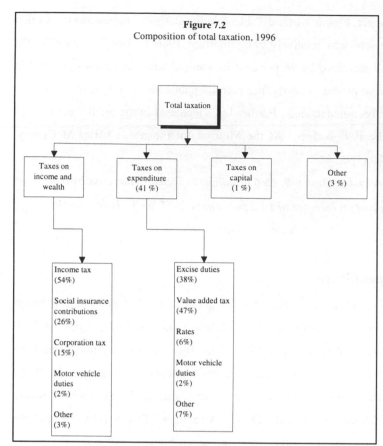

Figure 7.2
Composition of total taxation, 1996

Total taxation

Taxes on income and wealth

Taxes on expenditure (41 %)

Taxes on capital (1 %)

Other (3 %)

Income tax (54%)

Social insurance contributions (26%)

Corporation tax (15%)

Motor vehicle duties (2%)

Other (3%)

Excise duties (38%)

Value added tax (47%)

Rates (6%)

Motor vehicle duties (2%)

Other (7%)

income and wealth, *income tax* and *social insurance* contributions are the largest components. The heavy burden of taxation on employees is reflected in the fact that 55 per cent of all income and wealth tax paid in 1996 came from PAYE.

In the case of taxes on expenditure, *value added tax* (VAT) and *excise duties* are by far the biggest contributors. There are heavy excise taxes on cars, alcoholic drinks, tobacco and petrol, while the standard rate of VAT (21 per cent) also applies to these items and to a wide range of consumer goods.

Note that VAT is an *ad valorem* tax, levied as a percentage of the price of the good or service. The VAT yield rises automatically with inflation. Excise duties, on the other hand, are mostly specific taxes (that is, levied in terms of so much per *unit*) and have to be adjusted to prevent inflation eroding their real value. This is why successive ministers for finance have imposed higher excises on the "old reliables" (tobacco, drink and petrol) in their budgets in order to maintain this source of revenue.

Recent trends in taxation Figure 7.3 (and Table C in the appendix) show that the burden of taxation increased from 22 per cent of GNP in 1962 to a peak of 45 per cent in 1988. Since then it has dropped and by 1998 will amount to "only" 34 per cent of GNP. The increase in the tax burden in the 1980s had serious adverse effects on the economy. In addition to the Laffer curve effects discussed in the previous chapter, it fuelled

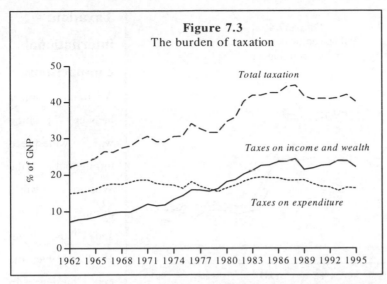

Figure 7.3
The burden of taxation

Total taxation

Taxes on income and wealth

Taxes on expenditure

% of GNP

50 — 40 — 30 — 20 — 10 — 0

1962 1965 1968 1971 1974 1977 1980 1983 1986 1989 1992 1995

inflationary wage claims that impaired the country's international competitiveness. The falling burden of taxation in the 1990s has been a positive factor, contributing to Ireland's rapid economic growth. It is in marked contrast to the trend of the continental EU countries, where the burden of taxation remains at historically high levels.

Taxes on income and wealth more than trebled as a percentage of GDP from 1962 to 1995. Within this category, the yield of *income tax* has increased significantly. Income tax receipts rise automatically as incomes increase if the tax allowances and bands are not adjusted to compensate for inflation. During the 1970s and 1980s failure to adjust fully for inflation increased the real burden of income tax dramatically. But the fastest growth of all has been recorded in *social insurance contributions* as more and more income has been made subject to this levy and higher rates of contribution have been introduced. Also the yield of *corporate profits* tax has also increased very rapidly as many of the tax concessions given to firms in the 1970s were phased out.

Taxes on expenditure rose over the period, but their share in total taxation fell. Within this category, revenue from *VAT* and excise duties have been very buoyant.

The narrow tax base in Ireland remains a problem. It is argued that the PAYE sector contributes a disproportionate amount of total tax revenue, and a fairly narrow range of goods bear high rates of VAT and excise taxes. The result is that the burden of taxation is particularly heavy on groups such as PAYE workers who spend a high proportion of their income on petrol, tobacco and alcoholic drinks. It has been widely suggested that it would be fairer, and more economically efficient, if a larger proportion of the tax burden were borne by taxes on wealth, especially land and property, which cannot be moved out of the country. The abolition of rates on domestic dwellings in 1978, and of the Residential Property Tax in 1997, shows that these proposals are difficult to implement.

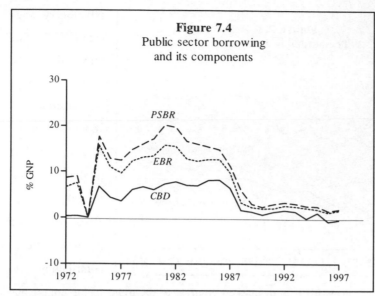

Figure 7.4
Public sector borrowing
and its components

A trend towards heavier taxation was widespread throughout the Western world during the 1970s and 1980s. From 1988 to 1996, the tax burden in Ireland fell below the average of the OECD countries. This change was due to a curb on current expenditure in Ireland and the deterioration in the budgetary situation in countries such as Germany, Greece and Italy. However, the burden of taxation in Ireland is still much higher than in the United States or Japan.

From the perspective of incentives to work and save, *marginal* tax rates are more relevant than average taxation. In Ireland a single worker becomes liable to a high rate of income tax at very low levels of income. Such a high marginal income tax rate does not apply at a comparable income level in any other OECD country.

Moreover, in addition to this high rate of income tax, the level of indirect taxes in Ireland is now significantly above the OECD average. In the European Union (EU), Denmark is the only country where rates of VAT and excise duties are generally higher than in Ireland. A consequence of the widening gap between Irish and UK rates of indirect taxation during the 1980s was the growth of large-scale cross-border trade and smuggling from Northern Ireland.

7.5   Borrowing and the Growth of the National Debt

Government borrowing

Before 1973 Irish budgets were framed so as to "balance the books" in the sense that current revenue should match current expenditure: borrowing for capital purposes was condoned on the grounds that it resulted in the creation of tangible assets. After 1972, however, very large current and capital budget deficits were incurred. Figure 7.4 (and

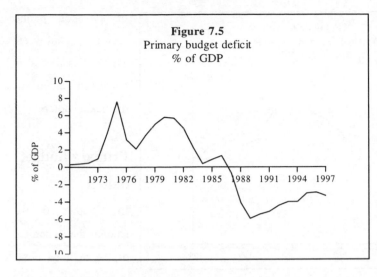

Figure 7.5
Primary budget deficit
% of GDP

(The difference between the CBD and the EBR is government borrowing for capital purposes.) The PSBR also includes borrowing by state-sponsored bodies. In recent years *the general government surplus/deficit* has replaced the PSBR as the broadest measure of fiscal policy.

Table D in the appendix) show the trend in the *current budget deficit* (CBD), the *exchequer borrowing requirement* (EBR) and the *public sector borrowing requirement* (PSBR) as a percentage of GNP since 1972.

The CBD rose from less than 1 per cent of GNP in 1972 to 8.3 per cent in 1986. In addition, borrowing for capital purposes and borrowing by state-sponsored companies pushed the PSBR to a record 20 per cent in 1981, more than double its level ten years earlier.

Overall borrowing started to decline gradually after 1982. Following the introduction of policies to curb government expenditure and increase taxes, a significant decline in the CBD was achieved after 1987. A surplus of £15 million on the CBD (the first in 27 years) was recorded in 1994. By 1998 this has grown to £1,109 million or 2.5 per cent of GNP. Moreover, this surplus was larger than the government's borrowing for capital purposes, so in 1998 an overall budget surplus was projected for the first time in modern Irish history.

While this evolution of the public finances appears satisfactory at first sight, in fact there are some deep underlying problems. The exceptional rate of economic growth recorded in recent years has provided the tax revenue to pay for a very rapid growth of government spending while still allowing room for an improvement in the budgetary balance. Many commentators believe that the current boom should have been used to achieve much faster progress towards reducing the national debt by running significant surpluses, instead of using the opportunity to allow an expansion of the number and rates

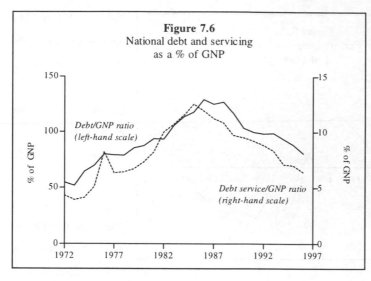

Figure 7.6
National debt and servicing
as a % of GNP

Debt/GNP ratio
(left-hand scale)

Debt service/GNP ratio
(right-hand scale)

of pay of public sector employees. This issue is discussed again in the next chapter.

Primary budget deficit

In Chapter 6 we studied the dynamics of the national debt. A key concept in this regard is the *primary budget deficit* which is equal to the EBR *minus* interest paid on the national debt. A minus sign indicates a primary *surplus*. The basic point is that if there is a primary budget deficit, the debt/GNP ratio will increase over time. In this case, the public finances are on an *unsustainable* trajectory. On the other hand, if there is a large enough primary budget surplus, then the debt/GNP ratio will decline and the public deficits are said to be sustainable.

Figure 7.5 (and Table D in the appendix) shows the primary budget balance as a percentage of GNP since 1972. The deficit reached a peak in 1975 at 7.6 per cent of GNP and remained high until 1981, after which it fell rapidly. By 1987 a small *surplus* was recorded which grew to 6 per cent of GNP in 1989. This surplus declined slightly after 1990, but for 1998 it was projected at 5.2 per cent of GNP.

The national debt

By the early 1970s, the Irish government had accumulated a significant national debt. However, due to a combination of modest levels of borrowing, fairly rapid growth in GDP and low rates of interest, the debt/GDP ratio declined from over 70 per cent in the early 1960s to 54 per cent in 1972. (Note that for EU purposes this ratio is always expressed relative to GDP and not GNP.)

However, following the increase in borrowing in the 1970s and 1980s, the debt/GDP ratio again increased and reached a peak of 129 per cent in 1986. In line with the fall in the primary deficit, the debt/GDP ratio then declined and by 1998 it had fallen

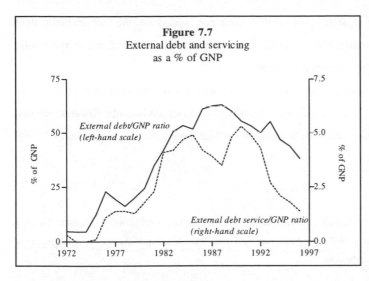

Figure 7.7
External debt and servicing
as a % of GNP

to 61 per cent of GDP (Figure 7.6 and Table E in the appendix). [1]

Interest payments on the national debt increased steadily from 1972 onwards, reaching a peak in 1985. In line with the fall in the debt ratio, they then declined and now cost £2,596 million per annum. As a percentage of the yield of income tax, debt service is now lower than at any time since the early 1970s. However, heavy interest payments will continue to be required to service the national debt well into the next century.

External debt

It is important to distinguish between domestic and external debt. "Domestic" debt is issued in and will be redeemed in Irish pounds; "external" debt is denominated in, and has to be redeemed in, foreign currencies. As discussed in the previous chapter, in the case of the domestic debt we "owe the money to ourselves". Hence the payment of interest and principal remains within the country. Servicing the externally held debt, however, involves a transfer of income abroad. Furthermore, the Irish pound value of the debt denominated in foreign currencies is affected by exchange rate changes. This was a factor behind the reluctance to devalue the Irish pound at the beginning of 1993.

To obtain a complete picture of the government's external liabilities, however, account should also be taken of the "domestic" debt that is owned by non-residents. In the second half of the 1980s foreign investors, Germans in particular, purchased sizeable amounts of Irish government securities because the yield on them was attractive relative to that obtainable in other countries. When the £2,320 million held in this manner and the

---

1. For a discussion of the management of the national debt and related issues, see Michael Somers, "The Management of Ireland's National Debt", paper read to the Statistical and Social Inquiry Society of Ireland, 13 February 1992.

external liabilities of the state-sponsored bodies are added to the government debt denominated in foreign currencies, a figure for the total external liabilities of the public sector of £14,083 million is obtained for 1996.

From Figure 7.7 (and Table F in the appendix) it may be seen that government external debt relative to GNP peaked at 63.1 per cent in 1988. While the absolute amount owed to non-residents has continued to increase, it had declined to 38.1 per cent of GNP by 1996.

Note:

In order to minimise the cost of servicing the national debt, the government established the National Treasury Management Agency (NTMA) in 1990. A separate unit within the NTMA is responsible for the management of the exchange rate risk related to the debt.

Interest payments on the externally held debt peaked at 5.3 per cent of GNP in 1990. Substantial interest payments on the external debt will have to be made well into the next century. However, by comparison with many developing countries, external interest payments have remained low in Ireland. As a result there is no uncertainty about our ability to honour our international debt service obligations. However, the question of how wisely we have used the large amounts borrowed abroad in the past remains a matter for debate.

7.6   Conclusion

In this chapter, we have reviewed the following topics:

- The current budget deficit, the EBR and the PSBR
- The growth of government spending
- Public sector pay and employment
- The trend in government revenue
- The different forms of taxation and the burden of taxation
- The rise of the national debt and debt servicing
- The composition of the national debt
- The distinction between domestic and external debt.

Data appendix

Table A

Public sector employment and the wage bill

	Public service numbers	Public service pay bill £ m	Public service pay bill % of GNP	Public sector pay adjusted for inflation
1986	215,641	2,625	15.7	2,528.9
1987	215,963	2,759	14.5	2,576.0
1988	208,354	2,845	14.2	2,600.5
1989	196,424	2,914	13.1	2,560.6
1990	198,190	3,160	13.0	2,687.0
1991	201,499	3,382	13.3	2,785.8
1992	204,394	3,750	14.0	2,997.6
1993	207,894	4,087	14.2	3,220.6
1994	210,794	4,356	13.9	3,353.3
1995	215,376	4,567	13.3	3,428.6
1996	218,362	4,804	12.9	3,548.0
1997	218,967	5,183	12.8	3,763.9

Sources: *Estimates for the Public Services*, 1994, *Budget Booklet* 1994 and the Department of Finance.

Table B

Taxation: 1995

Composition of total taxation

	£ millions	% of total
Taxes on income and wealth	7548.0	55.0
Taxes on expenditure	5580.0	40.7
Taxes on capital	104.0	0.8
Other taxes	483.0	3.5
Total taxation	13715.0	100.0

Composition of taxes on income and wealth	£ millions	% of total
Income tax	4123.0	54.6
Corporation tax	1148.0	15.2
Motor vehicle duties	139.0	1.8
Training and employment levy	158.0	2.1
Social insurance contribution	1958.0	25.9
Other	22.0	0.3
Total	7548.0	100.0

Taxes on expenditure	£ millions	% of total
Customs duties	8.6	0.2
Excise duties	2115.0	37.9
Value added tax	2615.0	46.9
Residential property tax	12.0	0.2
Rates	321.0	5.8
Motor vehicle duties	113.0	2.0
Agricultural levies	0.2	0.0
Other	395.2	7.1

Table C

Composition of taxation

% of GNP

	Total taxation	Income taxes	Expenditure taxes
1962	22.1	7.2	14.9
1963	22.9	7.8	15.1
1964	23.5	8	15.5
1965	24.6	8.5	16.1
1966	26.4	9.2	.2
1967	26.2	9.7	17.5
1968	27.3	.9	17.4
1969	27.9	9.9	18.0
1970	.5	10.9	18.6
1971	30.6	12.0	18.6
1972	29.1	11.5	17.6
1973	29.1	11.8	17.3
1974	30.5	13.3	17.2
1975	30.6	14.3	16.3
1976	34.0	15.9	18.1
1977	32.6	15.8	16.8
1978	31.6	15.5	16.1
1979	31.6	16.2	15.4
1980	34.5	18.1	16.4
1981	35.8	18.7	17.1
1982	40.2	21.1	19.1
1983	41.9	22.0	19.9
1984	41.9	22.5	19.4
1985	42.6	23.0	19.6
1986	42.6	23.5	19.1
1987	44.3	24.7	19.6
1988	44.7	25.3	19.4
1989	41.7	22.4	19.3
1990	40.8	22.8	18.0
1991	41.0	23.5	17.5
1992	40.9	23.7	17.2
1993	41.2	24.9	16.3
1994	42.0	24.8	17.2
1995	40.2	23.1	17.0

Table D

The public sector borrowing requirement and its components, 1972-97

	Current budget deficit		Exchequer borrowing requirement (EBR)		Public sector borrowing requirement (PSBR)		Primary budget	
	£ m	% of GNP	£ m	% of GNP	£ m	% of GNP	£m	% GNP
1972	6	0.3	151	6.6	197	8.6	66	2.9
1973	10	0.4	206	7.5	248	9	105	3.9
1974	93	-	334	-	385	-	217	7.2
1975	259	6.8	601	15.8	672	17.7	430	11.6
1976	201	4.4	506	11	595	12.9	265	5.9
1977	201	3.6	545	9.7	697	12.5	237	4.4
1978	397	6.1	810	12.4	973	14.9	428	6.6
1979	522	6.8	1,009	13.2	1,230	16.1	535	7
1980	547	6.1	1,218	13.5	1,559	17.3	426	4.7
1981	802	7.4	1,721	15.9	2,204	20.3	668	6.1
1982	988	7.9	1,945	15.6	2,466	19.8	485	3.9
1983	960	7.1	1,756	12.9	2,277	16.7	43	0.3
1984	1,039	7	1,825	12.4	2,375	16.1	− 75	− 0.5
1985	1,284	8.2	2,015	12.8	2,444	15.5	188	− 1.2
1986	1,395	8.3	2,145	12.8	2,506	14.9	− 75	− 0.4
1987	1,180	6.5	1,786	9.9	2,056	11.4	− 575	− 3.0
1988	317	1.7	619	3.3	1201	6	− 1,533	− 7.7
1989	263	1.3	479	2.3	667	3	− 1,671	− 7.7
1990	152	0.7	462	2	588	2.4	− 1,840	- 7.7
1991	300	1.3	510	2.1	762	3	− 1,826	− 7.3
1992	446	1.7	713	2.7	910	3.4	− 1,586	− 6.0
1993	379	1.4	690	2.5	862	3.1	− 1,586	− 5.7
1994	− 15	− 0.1	672	2.2	782	2.6	− 1,633	− 5.5
1995	362	1.1	627	1.9	826	2.5	− 1714	− 5.0
1996	− 292	− 0.8	436	1.2	531	1.5	− 1904	− 5.1
1997	− 193	− 0.5	636	1.6	764	1.9	− 1714	− 4.2

Sources: Central Bank of Ireland, *Annual Report,* 1997, *National Income and Expenditure,* various issues and Economic and Social Research Institute, Medium-Term Review: 1994-2000.

Table E

Government debt and debt service, 1972-1996

	Government debt £ m	Government debt to GNP ratio	Annual debt service £ m	Debt service as a % of GNP	Debt service as a % of income tax
1972	1,251	54.7	100	4.3	n.a.
1973	1,421	51.8	109	3.9	n.a.
1974	1,622	64.4	126	4.1	n.a.
1975	2,651	69.8	195	5.1	n.a.
1976	3,612	80.1	278	8.2	60.2
1977	4,229	79.2	334	6.3	64.0
1978	5,167	79.1	418	6.4	69.1
1979	6,540	85.7	514	6.7	70.2
1980	7,896	87.7	661	7.3	65.2
1981	10,195	93.9	885	8.2	71.2
1982	11,669	93.7	1,249	10	85.6
1983	14,392	105.9	1,456	10.7	87.5
1984	16,821	113.7	1,705	11.5	86.7
1985	18,502	117.9	1,967	12.5	93.5
1986	21,611	129.2	1,989	11.9	83.3
1987	23,691	124.9	2,118	11.2	78.1
1988	25,360	126.8	2,152	10.8	76.8
1989	25,858	116.7	2,150	9.7	76.2
1990	25,083	103.4	2,302	9.5	76.1
1991	25,378	99.8	2,351	9.2	72.8
1992	26,344	98.4	2,355	8.8	69.0
1993	28,358	98.8	2,390	8.3	64.4
1994	29,227	93.5	2,227	7.1	58.0
1995	30209	88.5	2405	7.0	58.2
1996	29912	80.9	2360	6.4	51.7

Source: Various *Budget Books* and Central Bank of Ireland, *Quarterly Bulletin*.

Notes: 1. Debt service includes interest and payments to sinking fund.

2. The data does not include debt incurred by local authorities and state-sponsored bodies.

3. "1974" was a nine-month period as the accounts were changed from a calendar to a financial year.

Table F

Government external debt, 1972-93

	External debt £ m	External debt as a % of total debt	External debt as a % of GNP	Interest on the external debt £ m	Interest on the external debt as a % of GNP
1972	107	8.6	4.7	7	0.3
1973	126	8.9	4.6	9	0.0
1974	311	8.9	4.6	9	0.0
1975	471	17.7	12.4	33	0.1
1976	1,040	28.8	23.0	53	1.1
1977	1,039	24.6	19.4	95	1.4
1978	1,064	20.6	16.3	131	1.4
1979	1,542	23.6	20.2	154	1.3
1980	2,207	28.0	24.5	193	1.8
1981	3,794	37.2	34.9	266	2.3
1982	5,248	45.0	42.1	526	4.1
1983	6,899	47.9	50.7	597	4.2
1984	8,740	59	53.4	720	4.7
1985	9,022	48.7	51.7	795	4.9
1986	10,337	47.8	61.1	761	4.2
1987	11,151	48.3	62.5	804	3.9
1988	12,163	49.4	63.1	703	3.5
1989	12,790	51.5	60.1	1,041	4.8
1990	12,720	48.0	55.5	1,254	5.3
1991	13,288	49.5	53.3	1,220	4.9
1992	13,176	48.5	50.1	730	4.3
1993	15,447	54.2	55.2	769	2.7
1994	14657	50.1	46.9	660	2.1
1995	14914	49.4	43.7	600	1.8
1996	14083	47.1	38.1	535	1.4

Source: *Budget Book*, 1996; the Central Bank of Ireland, *Quarterly Bulletin,* Spring 1997, Table D1 and D2. Interest on the external debt from 1977 onwards taken from *NIE* Balance of Payments tables.
Note: "External" debt includes all debt held by non-residents, regardless of currency denomination. Net external liabilities of the state-sponsored bodies is not included.

Chapter 8

Fiscal Policy in Ireland

8.1   Introduction

In this chapter we examine the role of stabilisation policy in Ireland since the 1950s.[1] We also look at the various approaches to economic planning that have been adopted. As we saw in Chapter 6, stabilisation policy relates to discretionary changes in fiscal policy in an attempt to stabilise the business cycle. An economic plan, on the other hand, is a medium-term plan or programme designed to achieve specific targets relating to growth, employment and other key macroeconomic variables. The distinction between economic plans and stabilisation policy is not entirely clear cut. For example, fiscal policy in 1978 was based on a specific economic plan.   However, there are enough examples of discretionary changes in fiscal policy to justify making the distinction.

The first part of the chapter discusses the various economic plans introduced since the 1950s. The second half of the chapter is concerned with stabilisation policy and its effectiveness.   We conclude by identifying the main difficulties or limitations of implementing fiscal policy in a small open economy such as Ireland.

8.2 Economic Programming and Planning

There is a long tradition of economic planning or programming in Ireland. Numerous government documents have set targets for the future growth of output. These met with varying degrees of success, as may be seen from Figure 8.1, which displays the *projected* or target growth rates in GNP cited in each of the economic programmes or plans since the 1950s with the *actual* growth rate recorded in the relevant period. It can be seen that the projections bear little resemblance to the outcome. This highlights one essential point. In

---

1. For an insider's account readers should consult T. K. Whitaker, "Fiscal Turning Points", in *Interests*, Dublin: The Institute of Public Administration, 1983.

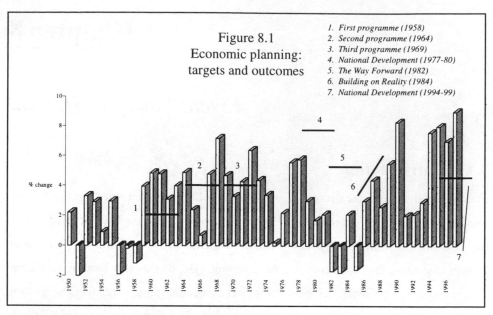

Figure 8.1
Economic planning:
targets and outcomes

1. First programme (1958)
2. Second programme (1964)
3. Third programme (1969)
4. National Development (1977-80)
5. The Way Forward (1982)
6. Building on Reality (1984)
7. National Development (1994-99)

a small open economy it is extremely difficult to regulate the business cycle. We now turn to a detailed description of each of the economic plans introduced over the years.

The origins of economic planning in the 1940s and 1950s

The *Public Capital Programme* was introduced after World War II in an attempt to systematise the public sector's annual spending on capital and development projects. This was linked to our participation in the Marshall Plan because, as a condition of receiving aid, the US authorities wanted to see integrated proposals for spending it. The Department of Finance was opposed to borrowing, even on very favourable terms, for ambitious new projects, but the Department of Foreign Affairs, where Seán MacBride was Minister, prepared a long-term development programme.

These tentative steps towards "planning" were overtaken by the stagnation of the early 1950s and the crisis of 1955-56, when living standards and employment fell and emigration soared. T. K. Whitaker, who was secretary of the Department of Finance at the time, commented:

> *"The mood of despondency was palpable. Something had to be done or the achievement of national independence would prove to have been a futility. Various attempts were made to shine a beam forward in this dark night of the soul."*

158

In early 1958, a survey of the economy was prepared in the Department of Finance and was published in November under the title *Economic Development*. This survey provided the basis for the *First Programme for Economic Expansion*, which was published soon afterwards. To escape from the recession, the *First Programme* proposed three main policies.

- Public expenditure should be switched from non-productive to productive projects. In particular, capital spending on local authority housing and hospitals was to be reduced and spending on agriculture and industry increased.

- Priority was to be given to a significant reduction in taxation, particularly income taxation, because "high taxation is one of the greatest impediments to economic progress because of its adverse effects on saving and on enterprise".

- It was also suggested that the increase in wages and salaries in Ireland should lag behind that in Britain.

The hope was that agriculture would still serve as the engine of growth for the economy.[2] The conflict between trying to increase agricultural output while at the same time maintaining exceptionally high protective tariffs on industrial products was not discussed. In fact, the failure of protectionism (see Chapter 2) and the need to move to an export-oriented strategy were not explicitly addressed. Although it was acknowledged that tariffs "might impair the incentive to reduce costs and increase efficiency", the enthusiasm for free trade was muted:

> *"It is obviously essential that existing industries should become progressively more efficient, but also that new industries should be competitive in export markets and capable of withstanding the challenge presented by the Free Trade Area."*

The *Programme* set an 11 per cent growth in the volume of GNP over the period 1959-63, but growth of 23 per cent was actually achieved. However, the improved

---

2. Out of a total of 212 pages of text in the *First Programme*, 100 were devoted to a detailed discussion of agriculture, forestry and fisheries. (The headline in the *Irish Independent* proclaimed "Easier credit schemes for farmers proposed"!) The same emphasis on rural development was apparent in the reports of the Commission on Emigration published in 1954, which looked mainly to agriculture to halt the outflow of population.

performance was *not* attributable to any of the policies introduced in the *Programme* for the reason that few of its recommendations were implemented.

- The burden of taxation was not eased. Instead, income tax in particular rose inexorably.

- There is no evidence of a rise in the level of manufacturing investment, or its share in GNP, prior to the increase in the growth rate of GNP.

- Agriculture did not prove to be an engine of growth. Even after entry into the EEC and a massive injection of subsidies from the Community, the share of GNP originating in this sector declined steadily and the number employed on family farms continued to fall. The role of economic locomotive was assumed by industry, as the scale of the inflow of foreign capital far exceeded that in the *First Programme's* projections.

- Growth resumed in 1958/59, before any of the new policies could have taken effect.

In reality, the Irish economy recovered more or less spontaneously from the protracted recession of 1954-58 and participated in the rapid expansion of the world economy during the 1960s. This was helped by the opening up of the economy and the dismantling of protectionism, which were not emphasised in the *Programme*.

There is, however, no doubt that the *First Programme* captured the imagination of a much wider population than would normally be aware of a detailed discussion of economic policy.[3] It served to gain acceptance of the importance of economic development as a policy objective, and the need to look outward rather than inward in order to generate this development.

Economic planning: 1960s and 1970s

It was inevitable that the dramatic improvement in the performance of the Irish economy in the years following the publication of the *First Programme* would be attributed to the *Programme* itself. It is not surprising that the planning exercise was repeated in a much more ambitious form in subsequent years. A *Second Programme 1964-70* was published in 1964 and a *Third Programme, Economic and Social Development, 1969-72* in 1969.

---

3. The perception persists that the *First Programme* "installed Keynesian economic principles as the main item on the national agenda", Richard Breen, Damian F. Hannan, David F. Rottman and Christopher T. Whelan, *Understanding Contemporary Ireland: State, Class and Development in the Republic of Ireland*, Dublin: Gill and Macmillan, 1990, p. 5. In fact there was no emphasis on demand management in the document.

These contained much more detailed statistical analyses of the Irish economy than had been attempted in 1958.

Both of these programmes projected a growth rate of 4 per cent a year in real GNP, which was the actual growth rate during the recovery from the deep recession of the 1950s. However, as may be seen from Figure 8.1, the projections of the growth of the economy proved as wide of the mark during the *Second* and *Third Programmes* as they had been in the *First*. The greater sectoral detail contained in the later documents drew attention to their increasing lack of relevance as the planning periods progressed. The *Second Programme* was based on the assumption that Ireland would be a member of the EEC by 1970. France's veto of British entry shortly after its publication provided a rationale for abandoning the *Programme*. It also became clear, after the publication of the *Third Programme* in 1969, that the targets contained in this, especially those relating to employment, would not be achieved. Thus the exercise in planning that was a central feature of Irish economic policy in the 1960s seemed to end in failure.

The degree of disillusionment with the process of planning in the turbulent economic circumstances of the 1970s is reflected in the words of the Minister for Finance, Richie Ryan, in his 1975 budget speech:

". . . of all the tasks that could engage my attention, the least realistic would be the publication of a medium or long-term economic plan based on irrelevancies in the past, hunches as to the present and clairvoyance as to the future . . ."[4]

Economic planning: 1970s and 1980s

Irish economic planning enjoyed renewed popularity after the formation of a new government in 1977. A Department of Economic Planning and Development was created.[5] A plan called *National Development 1977-80* was published, containing specific targets for the growth of output and employment and the reduction in unemployment. It was envisaged that the public sector would provide an initial boost to the economy, after which the private sector would take up the running. This required increased government

---

4. Cited in John Bradley, "Economic Planning: The Lessons of the Past and Future Prospects", *Administration*, Vol, 36, No. 1, 1988.

5. It is of interest to note that T. K. Whitaker, then a Senator, spoke against this step.

spending and recruitment in the public sector. The optimistic projections on which the plan was based were rendered irrelevant by the second oil-price crisis in 1979. With hindsight it is evident that the plan hindered, rather than helped, the adjustment of the economy to this shock.

Subsequent government statements on national development focused on the constraints facing the economy, rather than on specific targets for sectoral output. Following entry into the European Monetary System in 1979, it was recognised that pay moderation was essential if competitiveness was to be improved. In 1981 the Coalition government established a *Committee on Costs and Competitiveness*. Its report set out calculations of a *wage norm* based on forecast increases in our competitors' wage costs and likely changes in exchange rates. The idea was that if this norm were adhered to, there would be no deterioration in the country's competitiveness. Unfortunately, the norm proposed in October 1981 was rendered inappropriate by a weakening of sterling almost as soon as it was published. (The fall in sterling meant that greater wage moderation was required if Ireland was to maintain its competitiveness with the UK.)

A planning document, *The Way Forward*, was prepared by the Fianna Fáil government during 1982 and became the manifesto on which the party fought (and lost) the second general election of 1982. This document contained optimistic forecasts of economic growth based on a dramatic improvement in our international competitiveness, to be achieved by "moderate pay increases combined with increases in productivity".

In March 1983 the new Coalition government established an independent National Planning Board to prepare a study that would form the basis for a new plan.[6] *Proposals for Plan 1984-87* was published in April 1984. This document differed fundamentally from its immediate predecessors, and in some ways returned to the spirit of the *First Programme*, by presenting very detailed sectoral policy recommendations. It contained no fewer than 241 recommendations, ranging over many aspects of economic and social policy. The recommendations included:

- The need to reduce the level of public sector borrowing by expenditure cuts rather than increased taxation.

---

6. One of the authors of the present book, Brendan Walsh, was a member of the Committee on Costs and Competitiveness and of the National Planning Board.

- To increase the efficiency of the public sector through privatisation and deregulation. The high costs of monopolistic state companies were acting as a drag on the ability of the private sector to compete internationally.

- Special targeted measures to alleviate the problem of long-term unemployment.

- The plan emphasised the goal of stabilising the debt/GNP ratio and reducing the level of taxation.

In many respects the package proposed resembled a *structural adjustment programme* of the type supported by soft loans from the International Monetary Fund and World Bank in numerous developing countries in the 1980s.

The Coalition government's plan, *Building on Reality,* was published in autumn 1984. This generally endorsed the policy recommendations contained in *Proposals for Plan.* It forecast that total employment would increase over the next three years as employment in private sector services grew rapidly and industrial employment began to recover from the recession. These projections proved too optimistic. The public finances continued to deteriorate until 1987 and employment did not begin to recover until 1988.

Economic planning: 1980s and 1990s

The minority Fianna Fáil government that was formed in 1987 published a *Programme for National Recovery 1987-90* in October 1987. This did not aspire to be a plan in the way earlier documents had. At its core was an agreement between employers, trade unions and the government to adhere to specified increases in wages and salaries over a three year period. A reduction in the rate of income taxation was promised, and the prospect of increases in employment in selected state-sponsored enterprises was held out.

A similar wage formula was accepted in the *Programme for Economic and Social Progress* (PESP), 1991-94, the *Programme for Competitiveness and Work*, 1994-96, and *Partnership 2000*, 1997-99. Table 8.1 summarises the agreed increase in nominal wages under each of these programmes.

These national agreements have been hailed as examples of co-operation between the social partners (trade unions, employers, farmers and government). Such co-operation is referred to as *corporatism* and credited with maintaining industrial peace, providing a stable framework for business and moderating wage costs. As such they have been

Table 8.1

National wage agreements	Period of agreement	Agreed % change in nominal wages
Programme for National Recovery	1988-90	7.69
Programme for Economic and Social Progress	1991-93	11.14
Programme for Competitiveness and Work	1994-96	8.24
Partnership 2000	Jan 1997- March 1999 (39 months)	7.44

identified by a number of commentators as one of the reasons underlying the economic boom in the 1990s.

However, wage agreements can also be criticised for imposing a uniform wage increase on all sectors of the economy and being tailored to the needs of stronger, unionised sectors (including the public sector), rather than those of small and medium-sized firms facing severe international competition.

In October 1993 the Coalition government published the *National Development Plan: 1994-1999*. This plan envisages spending £22,228 million between 1993 and 1999 on a whole range of areas including industry, natural resources, tourism and transport. Expenditure is to be funded by the EU (39.4 per cent), the public sector (42.2 per cent) and the private sector (18.4 per cent). The basic objective is to create jobs by developing the agricultural, industrial and services sectors, by improving infrastructure and by developing the skills of the workforce through education and training. The plan anticipated an annual real growth rate of 3.5 per cent from 1994 to 1999 and the creation of 200,000 gross jobs. These targets proved too pessimistic. As Figure 8.1 shows, the period since 1994 has been characterised by an unprecedented growth of output and employment that was not anticipated at the time this *Plan* was drafted. This provides yet another illustration of the inability of policy makers to foresee the behaviour of a small open economy.

The spending in the *Plan* is akin to that of a fiscal expansion, with the important difference that it is being financed by large-scale capital grants from abroad. These grants are made available from Brussels under the so called *Community Support Programme,* that is, the "structural funds" made available to the weaker countries and regions of the

EU. (See the discussion of this issue in Chapter 2.) These funds have helped Ireland to raise its potential GDP growth rate by strengthening its infrastructure and raising its stock of human capital. Evaluations undertaken by the Economic and Social Research Institute concluded that these EU structural funds will add between one and three percentage points to the level of potential GDP over the long run.[7]

Summary

Economic planning of the type undertaken by successive Irish governments since the 1950s is now totally out of fashion. With the collapse of the planned socialist economies of the Soviet Union and Eastern Europe in the 1980s, and the success of the American economy in the 1990s, little credibility now attaches to the notion that governments can direct their economies towards desired goals. The last vestiges of this approach are seen in some of the continental EU economies, which have been notably under-performing the "Anglo-Saxon" models of the US and the UK economies in recent years. The Irish experience with economic programming and planning illustrates several problems with this approach:

- Failures to actually implement the policy measures specified in the plans.
- The difficulty in framing policy in a small open economy where even short-run forecasts of key variables can be very wide of the mark.
- Basing plans on unrealistic assumptions about the behaviour of key variables.
- Failure to forecast important events such as the oil crises of the 1970s.
- The difficulty in coming to grips with the serious imbalances that emerged in the economy in the late 1970s and early 1980s, some of which were due to misguided attempts to boost the economy's growth rate.

A key lesson to learn from this history is not that the failures were due to mistakes or lack of dedication on the part of Irish policy makers, but rather that the whole approach was misguided. The evidence from round the world shows that planning or programming offers little prospect of increasing a country's economic performance in the long run. Unpalatable though the message may be to politicians, they should leave the guidance of the economy to market forces!

---

7. See Chapter 3 of *Medium-Term Review: 1997-2003,* Dublin: Economic and Social Research Institute, 1997.

8.3 The Irish Experience with Stabilisation Policy

Stabilisation policy is concerned with the short-run fluctuations in the economy. Even if we accept the conclusion of the foregoing review of economic planning and programming, it is still possible to believe that government fiscal and monetary policy has a role to play in smoothing the economy's growth path by manipulating aggregate demand along the lines described in Chapter 6. In this section we review the Irish experience with stabilisation policy.

Before the 1970s, Irish Ministers for Finance did not consciously attempt to implement an active fiscal policy. (Box 8.1 below identifies the various Ministers for Finance since the foundation of the state.) Annual budgets were framed primarily to raise the money needed to finance the government's day-to-day spending. Although borrowing was incurred to finance the Public Capital Programme, fiscal policy was not consciously used as an instrument of demand management or to try to reduce the level of unemployment. This situation changed radically after the first oil shock in 1973. During the 1970s Irish public finances were transformed by the attempt to use government spending to achieve macroeconomic objectives.

1972-77: Departure from fiscal rectitude

The year 1973 was a watershed in Western economic history. The Organisation of Petroleum Exporting Countries (OPEC) raised crude oil prices from $3 to $12 a barrel. This was a severe shock to both the demand and the supply sides of economies dependent on imported energy. On the demand side, the enormous price rise greatly increased expenditure on imports because there was little scope in the short run for reducing dependence on imported energy.

As Figure 8.2 illustrates, an increase in imports shifts the aggregate demand (AD) schedule down to the left: spending on domestic output is lower at every price level. On the supply side, the increase in the cost of a basic input has the effect of shifting the aggregate supply (AS) schedule up to the left: the price level associated with each level of output rises. Putting the two effects together we see that output falls but whether the price level rises or falls depends on the slopes and the relative size of the shifts in the AD and AS schedules. In Figure 8.2 the shift in AS is larger than that in AD. The economy moves from A to B, a major *output gap* opens up between actual and full-employment or

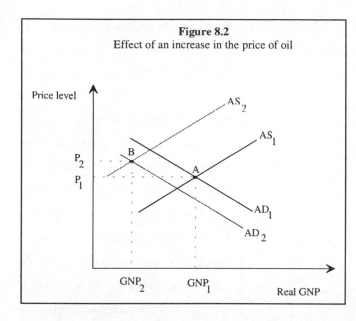

Figure 8.2
Effect of an increase in the price of oil

potential output, unemployment rises sharply and the price level increases. This combination of rising unemployment and higher inflation is known as *stagflation*. This is what happened throughout the developed economies in 1973/4 and again in 1979.

The immediate policy response was to try to maintain the level of aggregate demand by increasing government spending without any corresponding increase in the level of taxation. The *Public Sector Borrowing Requirement* (PSBR) increased from 8.6 per cent of GNP in 1972 to 17.7 per cent in 1975. Both the current budget deficit and borrowing for capital purposes increased. This was justified as a Keynesian response to a demand-side shock.

Note, however, than an expansionary fiscal policy is an inadequate response to the oil price shock. An expansionary fiscal policy will shift the AD curve in Figure 8.2 upwards to the right (not shown). The result will be an increase in real output but also an increase in the price level. Hence the fiscal policy exasperates the inflation problem.

Figure 8.3 shows the relationship between the real growth rate in GNP and the current budget deficit for each of the sub-periods. In 1975 the government recognised the need to dampen the inflationary pressures that were building up. Food subsidies and tax cuts were introduced in a mini-budget in mid-1975 in the hope that this would moderate wage inflation. In fact it increased the current budget deficit and added to inflationary pressures.

In a reversal of policy in 1976 the Minister for Finance (Richie Ryan) raised taxes and curbed expenditure as the economy began to recover. (This earned him the title "Minister for Hardship" and "Red Richie" in the media.) As a result of these corrective measures, combined with a recovery in economic growth, the PSBR fell to 12.5 per cent of

GNP, and the current budget deficit to 3.6 per cent, in 1977. It appeared that the economy had weathered the oil crisis and the public finances were moving in the right direction.

In fact the structural problems created by the oil price shock remained unresolved and Ireland, like most other OECD countries, was still vulnerable to further shocks due to its continued dependence on imported oil and the failure to eliminate the fiscal deficit. It was not until after the second oil price shock, at the end of the 1970s, that investment in energy conservation began in earnest.

1977-81: Going for broke

The General Election of 1977 destroyed the chances of maintaining progress towards restoring order in the public finances. The political parties vied with one another in promising to cut taxes and raise expenditure. (Both major parties claimed credit for having thought of the idea of abolishing rates on private houses at this time.) The incoming Fianna Fáil government exceeded their manifesto commitments to tax cuts and increased expenditure.

The measures introduced by the Minister for Finance, George Colley, in the 1978 budget added about 1.5 per cent of GNP to the current budget deficit and increased the projected EBR to 13 per cent of GNP. A total of 11,250 new posts were authorised in the public sector between mid-1977 and the end of 1978. This occurred at a time when the

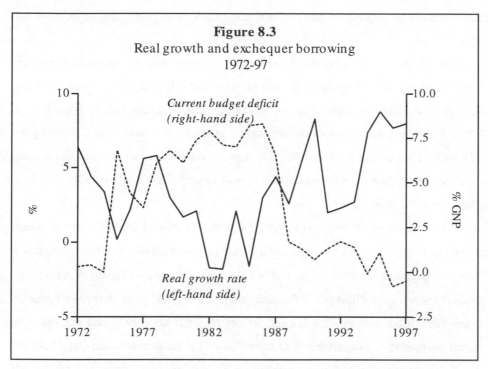

Figure 8.3
Real growth and exchequer borrowing
1972-97

*Current budget deficit
(right-hand side)*

*Real growth rate
(left-hand side)*

economy was already growing at an unsustainable rate: real GNP expanded by 7.0 per cent in 1977 and was forecast to continue to grow rapidly in 1978 even if there had been no fiscal stimulus (see Figure 8.3). Employment and real earnings were increasing rapidly and for the first time ever there was substantial net immigration to Ireland.

The expansionary fiscal policy implemented in the 1978 budget was justified by reference to the need to reduce unemployment which, although falling, was still above its 1973 level. It was argued that the increase in the fiscal deficit would be only a temporary expedient, leading to increased private sector investment which would sustain the economic expansion and tax buoyancy would quickly eliminate the budget deficit. It was claimed that the fiscal stimulus would turn out to be self-financing over the medium term.[8]

---

8. This period in economic policy has been the subject of much criticism, some of it quite colourful. For example, Kevin Myers, in a profile of the civil servant Tom Barrington, wrote, "Fortunately for his mental health, his retirement came in 1977, the year in which Irish politics lurched from mere slovenly venality and genial incompetence to outright criminality. The economy of the country was debauched and local government effectively destroyed: the most brilliant civil service cannot stop credulous electorates choosing recidivist delinquents to represent them, nor prevent the consequences of malfeasant policy." *The Irish Times*, 20 April 1991.

Terms such as "pump-priming" and "self-financing fiscal boost" were used to describe this policy.

Events between 1978 and 1980 confounded the hope that the budget deficit would be quickly eliminated. The rate of growth of real GNP fell to 2.7 per cent in 1979 and remained at that level in 1980. The current budget deficit remained above 6 per cent of GNP and a high level of borrowing for capital purposes was maintained, bringing the PSBR to 17.3 per cent of GNP in 1980. Of even greater significance was the fact that the current account balance of payments deficit rose to 11 per cent of GNP in 1980. The Irish economy was in crisis.

We were therefore ill-prepared to cope with the second oil price shock, which occurred in 1979, as the price of crude oil rose to over $40 a barrel. The fiscal deficit was already so large and the level of the national debt was growing so rapidly that no scope remained for trying to offset the deflationary impact of the oil price increase through an expansionary fiscal policy. The budget deficits incurred after 1973 and our resort to external borrowing to finance them had turned us into a net debtor country by 1980: the level of our external public debt had reached £2,207 million, whereas our official external reserves were only £1,346 million.

This episode illustrates many of the points made in Chapter 6 concerning the problems of successfully implementing fiscal policy.

- There was confusion about how rapidly the economy was growing.
- The policies that were implemented began to take effect long after the conditions they were designed to address had changed.
- The desire of politicians to be elected prevailed over economic realities.

There was little general awareness of the speed with which the country was being plunged into debt and the implications for the future tax burden. Some economists argued that there was no need to worry about further external borrowing because our international credit rating was still sound and additional borrowed money could be used to generate employment and create valuable assets. But in reality much of the borrowed money was wasted – it went to finance day-to-day expenditure or projects with a rate of return that was much lower than the rate of interest. Further borrowing for such purposes was not warranted, regardless of the willingness of international bankers to lend to the country. Moreover, the growth of public sector debt throughout Eastern Europe, Africa and Latin

America was to trigger off an international crisis in 1982 which completely changed the attitude of international creditors to countries in Ireland's situation.

1981-86: Picking up the pieces

In July 1981 the new Coalition government introduced a mini-budget to try to correct the deteriorating fiscal situation. The emphasis was placed on tax increases, rather than cuts in expenditure, to reduce the deficit. This set the pattern for several subsequent attempts to restore order to the public finances. However, due to the absence of revenue buoyancy the current budget deficit actually increased to 7.4 per cent of GNP, bringing the PSBR to 20.3 per cent of GNP, the highest level it had ever reached. This outcome (higher taxation leading to larger rather than smaller current budget deficits) was to be repeated in subsequent years.

The financial and economic crisis intensified in the course of 1981 and 1982. (See Figure 8.3.) The current account balance of payments deficit reached almost 15 per cent of GNP in 1981, while government external debt doubled in sixteen months. Unemployment increased by 38 per cent in one year. By the time of the General Election of November 1982 (the third within 18 months) the gravity of the fiscal crisis facing the country was widely appreciated. The main political parties agreed that restoring order to the public finances had to take precedence over trying to reduce the level of unemployment. The objective of eliminating the current budget deficit was endorsed by all parties and disagreement was confined to the question of how fast this could be achieved and whether it was better to rely on tax increases or expenditure cuts.

The Coalition government tried to tackle the problem over the period 1982-86 both by raising the level of taxation and reducing current expenditure, but without much success for the following reasons.

- A ban on public sector recruitment did not bring the wage bill under control.
- Rising unemployment caused transfer payments to increase.
- The accumulating national debt and rising interest rates caused debt interest payments to increase.
- Higher tax rates did not yield more revenue due to the stagnation of the economy and the Laffer-type effects we discussed in Chapter 6. The most striking illustration of the failure of the tax strategy was provided by Minister for Finance Alan Dukes' 1983

171

budget. This set a record for tax increases but produced hardly any reduction in the current budget deficit.

The result was that between 1983 and 1986 the current budget deficit rose from 7.1 per cent to 8.3 per cent and the debt/GNP ratio rose from 105 per cent to 128 per cent. During the third quarter of 1986 disappointing exchequer returns led to further loss of confidence in the economy, which was manifested in nervousness on the foreign exchange markets and a 3 per cent increase in Irish relative to UK interest rates. This episode marked the beginning of the end of the attempt to reduce the level of borrowing through higher taxation.

It had become clear to all but a small minority that this strategy was self-defeating. The economy was shrinking under the increasing burden of taxation and capital was fleeing the country for more benign environments. (It is estimated that the private capital outflow reached over £1 billion in 1986.) The public finances were on a downward spiral due to falling revenue and rising transfer payments. It was coming to be accepted that the problem had to be tackled through drastic cuts in expenditure rather than further tax increases, but the Coalition government split and fell on this issue. The cuts in current expenditure proposed by the Minister for Finance, John Bruton, in the *draft Book of Estimates* in October 1986 were not acceptable to his Labour Party partners in government, who still favoured maintaining a high level of expenditure and trying to reduce the deficit by increasing taxation.

1987-91 Order restored

The formation of a minority Fianna Fáil government in January 1987 initially increased the economic uncertainty. While in opposition the party had vehemently attacked what they had labelled the "monetarist" or "Thatcherite" policies of the Coalition government. They fought the election with promises of *increased* government spending. However, once in office the new government, with the support of the main opposition parties, tackled the problem of curbing government expenditure head-on. In the 1987 budget, the Minister for Finance, Ray MacSharry, reduced current government spending by more than had been proposed by Fine Gael in the *draft Book of Estimates* that had led to the downfall of the Coalition government (earning him the nickname Mac the Knife).

The restoration of order in the public finances gained momentum in the January 1988 budget when an unprecedented 3 per cent reduction in government spending was passed. This cut in expenditure was with the support or abstention of the main opposition parties and came to be known as the Tallaght Strategy.[9] As a result, in the course of 1988 the level of public expenditure declined in current prices for the first time since the 1930s. This budget also proposed a tax amnesty (known as the Tax Incentive Scheme), with the objective of collecting £30 million in unpaid taxes. In fact, during 1988 over £500 million was raised from this source and from the application of a new system of self-assessment of income tax to the self-employed. These amounts far exceeded the most optimistic forecasts. In addition, other sources of revenue (VAT and excises) were buoyant and expenditure was held below the level projected in the budget.

The performance of the Irish economy during the period 1987 to 1991 was extraordinary. The PSBR and current budget deficit fell to 3.0 per cent and 0.7 per cent of GNP respectively in 1990. Simultaneously, the rate of growth of GNP increased markedly. The fact that a reduction in the fiscal deficit was associated with an increase in economic growth seemed to refute the conventional Keynesian view of fiscal policy. A number of alternative explanations of these developments have been put forward.

It has been claimed that the Irish experience during these years is an example of an expansionary fiscal contraction (EFC).[10] According to this explanation, the contraction in government expenditure (G) actually led to an expansion in economic activity. For this to happen it is necessary that the private sector components of aggregate demand, such as consumer expenditure (C) and investment (I), increased by more than the initial fall in government expenditure. In other words, the fall in G must have been more than offset by increases in C or I, with the result that there was a net increase in aggregate demand. Essentially, an EFC entails a multiplier effect operating in reverse. This could come about through the operation of "crowding-in", the opposite of "crowding-out", which we

9. So called after a speech supporting the cuts was made by the opposition leader Alan Dukes in Tallaght, Co. Dublin.

10. The phrase "Expansionary Fiscal Contraction" was first coined by F. Giavazzi and M. Pagano, "Can Severe Fiscal Contraction be Expansionary? Tales of Two Small European Countries", National Bureau Economic Research, *Macroeconomics Annual*, 1990, O. Blanchard and S. Fischer, editors. See also Dermot McAleese, "Ireland's Economic Recovery", *Irish Banking Review*, Summer 1990; F. Barry, "Irish Recovery 1987-90: Economic Miracle?" *Irish Banking Review*, Winter 1991; and F. Barry and M. Devereux, "The Expansionary Fiscal Contraction Hypothesis: A Neo-Keynesian Analysis", *Oxford Economic Papers,* Vol. 47 (1995).

Table 8.2

General government deficit (−) (% of GDP)

	1995	1996	1997	1998
Unadjusted	− 2.0	− 1.6	− 0.9	− 0.5
Cyclically adjusted	− 3.2	− 3.9	− 3.1	− 2.4

Source: Commission of the EU, 1997 *Annual Economic Report*, Tables 22 and 23.

discussed briefly in Chapter 6. "Crowding-in" could occur if lower government spending and reduced deficits led to lower interest rates which, in turn, stimulated private sector spending.

Note:

Briefly, the EFC argument is that the economy was facing a crisis of confidence arising from the lack of credibility of the government's commitment to restoring order to the public finances. This had led to capital flight and a widening interest rate differential between Ireland and Britain. Once the financial markets became convinced that the government was intent on reducing the borrowing requirement, the capital outflow subsided, and this facilitated a reduction in domestic interest rates. Increased confidence and lower interest rates led to a recovery in private sector investment and consumption, which helped offset the contractionary effects of fiscal retrenchment.

However, other factors also played a role in the recovery. These included the collapse of world oil prices, higher farm prices, and the accelerating growth in the UK economy. These were reinforced by an improvement in our international competitiveness following the successful devaluation of the Irish pound in August 1986. This devaluation contributed to an upsurge in net exports in 1987. Moreover, interest rates began to fall in the wake of the devaluation, *before* the 1987 budget.

The 1990s

During the 1990s, especially after 1993, Ireland experienced an unprecedented combination of rapid growth and low inflation. The stance of fiscal policy moved away from the failed stabilisation policies of earlier years. Policy became dominated by the objective of qualifying for membership of European Monetary Union (EMU) in 1999. This entailed achieving a government deficit of less than 3 per cent of GDP and a debt/GDP of 60 per cent. In May 1998, Ireland was deemed to have met the entry criteria and was invited to join the single currency club. We discussed in Chapter 2 at great length the factors behind the transformation of the Irish economy.

Given this generally satisfactory picture, it none the less remains the case that the stance of fiscal policy was relatively *expansionary* as the Irish economy recorded an

174

unprecedented growth spurt in the mid-1990s. In fact, the stance of fiscal policy in the 1990s has been generally *pro-cyclical*, that is, tending to fuel the flames of the strong expansion that is already under way.[11]

Recall from Chapter 6 the concept of "built-in stabilisers". The point is that rapid growth in the economy *automatically* reduces the budget deficit through tax buoyancy and reduced social welfare spending. Hence, an examination of the unadjusted deficit gives a misleading picture of the stance of fiscal policy. In order to assess the stance of fiscal policy, it is desirable to net out the *automatic* effects (due to tax buoyancy and social welfare spending) and to isolate the *discretionary* changes in fiscal policy.

Table 8.2 shows that the actual budget deficit fell from 2.0 to 0.5 per cent of GDP over the period 1995-98. It could be concluded from this that fiscal policy tightened over these years. The second line of Table 8.2 shows the *cyclically adjusted* deficit (the deficit adjusted for the budgetary effects of the very high growth rates). According to this measure Irish fiscal policy was actually expansionary in 1996. Policy changes such as tax cuts and increased spending increased the deficit from 3.2 to 3.9 per cent of GDP. Many commentators have argued that it would have been appropriate at this time of rapid growth to plan for a large surplus and make significant progress in reducing the national debt.

Table 8.2 suggests that the fiscal situation in Ireland in the mid-1990s is not as healthy as the raw data suggest. The actual deficit has almost disappeared, but the underlying (structural or cyclical) deficit is still in the region of 3 per cent of GDP. Ireland as a member of EMU is bound by the Stability Pact, which obliges us to maintain the budget in balance over the business cycle. Deficits in excess of 3 per cent of GDP will attract fines. There will be little scope for adopting an expansionary fiscal policy should economic conditions deteriorate and the growth rate fall. It would have been better to have used the current exceptional period to prepare for less favourable times in the future.

8.4 Evaluation

As we have seen, the 1970s ushered in a period when fiscal policy was actively used in the hope of getting the economy to grow faster and to reduce the level of unemployment.

---

11. For a discussion of this issue, see Phillip Lane, "On the Cyclicality of Irish Fiscal Policy", *Economic and Social Review,* forthcoming (1998).

There is now widespread agreement that fiscal policy was implemented in a very ill-judged manner, for the following reasons:

- An expansionary fiscal policy was not an appropriate response to the oil crisis of 1973/74. An expansionary policy may boost output but it exacerbates the problem of rising inflation.

- There is general agreement that Irish fiscal policy has been perversely pro-cyclical. Instead of dampening the fluctuations in GDP, successive governments have generally made them larger. This was particularly the case towards the end of the 1970s when the mistake was made of stimulating the economy during a period when the economy was growing at a rapid pace. The gains proved to be short lived.

- In the early 1980s, external developments pushed the Irish economy into recession. The authorities were forced to restore order to the public finances and this aggravated the recession. The government was forced to correct the fiscal imbalance – especially the ever increasing burden of taxation – during a period of rising unemployment.

- Increased government spending led to higher levels of taxation which, in turn, led to higher wage demands and a rise in prices. As taxation increased, wage and salary earners sought compensation by demanding higher wages and this subsequently led to higher prices. (Because much of the additional spending went on increased debt service and transfer payments during the 1980s, the public did not see improvements in the level of public services commensurate with the higher level of taxation they had to shoulder.) The result was a reduction in the competitiveness of the traded sectors of the economy, which reduced the level of employment it could support. In effect, the expansionary fiscal policy generated no lasting increase in the level of employment.

By the end of the 1980s, however, the major imbalances in the public finances had been corrected and a high growth rate maintained without a fiscal stimulus. Lower interest rates and sustained growth in the 1990s have led to a further sharp fall in the debt/GNP ratio. While the cyclically adjusted or structural deficit is higher than revealed by the unadjusted data, fiscal policy in the middle of the 1990s is a sustainable path and the Maastricht fiscal criteria have been met.

8.5　Conclusion

In this chapter, we have reviewed the stance of fiscal policy from the 1970s to date. We showed that:

- The timing of fiscal policy has been pro-cyclical, that is, it has tended to amplify rather than dampen the business cycle

- The most conspicuous effect of deficit spending has been to increase the burden of the national debt

- Since the late 1980s Irish fiscal policy has succeeded in reducing the debt/GDP ratio and meeting the EMU fiscal criteria.

- None the less, recent fiscal policy has continued to be pro-cyclical, fuelling the fires of an already fast-growing economy and paying too little attention to the need to keep something in reserve for less favourable times in the future.

Chapter 9

Money and Banking and the History of the Irish Monetary System

9.1   Introduction

The initial sections in this chapter discuss the functions of money and the types of money used in a modern economy. We then outline the role of the banking system and explain how money is created in a modern economy. This is followed by an account of the role and functions of a central bank. The following sections discuss the development of money and banking in Ireland, the evolution of the Irish currency and the history of the Central Bank of Ireland.   Finally, we outline the situation after Ireland's entry into the European EMU in 1999 and the demise of an independent Irish monetary policy.

9.2   What is Money?

Money performs four basic functions in an economy. The most important of these is its role as a *medium of exchange*. It also serves as a *unit of account, a standard of deferred payment* and a *store of value*. We discuss each of these functions in turn.

Medium of exchange Without money an economy would have to operate on a *barter system*: all transactions would involve the exchange of goods and services directly for other goods and services. A farmer, for example, would have to exchange the output of his farm for clothes and other necessities. A doctor, in return for medical services, would receive goods or services from his patients. Such a system would involve enormous *transaction costs*. To complete a transaction there would have to be a *double coincidence of wants* – each party to a deal would have to want what the other was offering. A hungry doctor and a sick farmer would be able to do business, but in practice most people would find it difficult to complete a transaction. As a result, intermediaries would tend to become involved and the cost of transactions would increase.

Adam Smith in *The Wealth of Nations* (1776) opened with a famous illustration of the benefits of the division of labour based on the working of a pin factory. By specialising in the production of a single item, the workforce became very efficient and output increased significantly. However, under a barter system the cost of transactions would deter people from specialising. They would be forced to be self-sufficient and prevented from concentrating on a particular skill or trade. Occupations requiring a high degree of specialisation such as engineering, accountancy and teaching would not come into existence. As a consequence, productivity would remain low. Barter is costly and inefficient and almost all societies have abandoned it in favour of money.

In a money economy, goods and services can be sold for money that can be used to purchase other goods and services. The use of money as a medium of exchange is a very significant progression away from barter. It greatly reduces the cost of doing business and encourages people to specialise and trade. It allows people to specialise in what they do most efficiently, selling the output that is surplus to their needs, and buying what they want with the proceeds. This is an infinitely more efficient arrangement than a barter system. Far from being "the root of all evil", the use of money is of major benefit to all societies!

Unit of account   Once people become involved in trading, they need a *unit of account* in which to quote prices and compare whether something is dear or cheap relative to other items. Money serves this important function. Usually the same currency is used as a medium of exchange and a unit of account. It is possible, however, to use a unit of account that is not actually in circulation as money. The EU, for example, uses the ECU (European Currency Unit), soon to be replaced by the *euro*, in its contracts. A number of multinational firms operating in Ireland use dollars as their unit of account. In horse racing, the 1,000 and 2,000 guineas are classic races but no bets are accepted or paid out in guineas any more.

Standard of deferred payment and store of value   These functions allow us to link the present with the future when doing business. Loans, leases and other contracts can specify amounts of money to be paid in the future (*standard of deferred payment*). People can save some of their income as cash (*store of value*) and use it to purchase things in the future. This is useful, but there are risks involved. In inflationary periods money loses its value over time. If inflation gets out of control, people will learn to specify contracts in a manner that takes account of inflation (this is called indexation). Similarly, people will look to other assets (foreign currencies, land, works of art, old stamps) to use as a store of value. However, all these ways of coping with inflation involve costs. Thus inflation is a threat to the efficiency of a modern economy.

9.3   Types of Money

Over the centuries, money has taken many forms – whales' teeth were used in Fiji, dogs' teeth in the Admiralty Islands, silk and salt in China, and cowrie shells in Africa. The origins of the "pound sterling" go back over 900 years as the following letter published in *The Irish Times* points out:

"Sir, I am afraid your correspondent (name withheld) has got the wrong end of the stick. He disdains the use of the term 'sterling' to mean the British pound on the grounds that this is just a propaganda term meaning 'the real thing'. On the contrary, English silver penny coins were called 'sterlings' as much as 900 years ago. Thus the pound sterling was, originally, a pound weight of sterlings. It was because of the high quality of these sterlings that – from the late 17th century on – the term came to mean something like 'the real thing'. Soon thereafter the gold guinea, and then the sovereign, wholly replaced silver coins in England, but the term 'sterling' survived. The connotation of excellence has, of course, been rather tarnished in more recent times. What's in a name? Mention of the guinea brings to mind the currency of Guinea, called the *Syli*, and which had the misfortune to live up to its name, before it was eventually replaced. When it comes to our own currency, I confess to a preference (unless *as Gaeilge*) for 'pound' rather than 'punt', if only to avoid the connotation of something small and flat-bottomed, prone to sinking if not looked after properly."[1]

There are two basic types of money, namely, *commodity* money and *token* money.

Commodity money   It was natural that intrinsically valuable commodities would be the first money. Cattle were used in many early societies, including Ireland. (The Latin word for cattle is *pecus* and for money *pecunia*, whence the English word "pecuniary".) Over the centuries silver and gold emerged as the preferred form of commodity money. Their durability, divisibility and scarcity ensured that their value would remain stable. The main disadvantage of commodity money is that it ties up the commodity used as money and diverts it from other uses. When silver is used to make coins, the supply of silver to jewellers and other users is reduced.

---

1. Patrick Honohan, *The Irish Times*, 7 December 1997.

Token money   This is money which does not have any intrinsic value. The notes and coins in circulation in Ireland today fall into this category. Their intrinsic value is very small compared to their value as a medium of exchange. For example, the paper in an Irish £50 note is almost valueless as paper. Our so called silver coins are in fact made from a cheap cupro-nickel alloy. No silver is wasted in making them.[2]

In the past, bank notes were *convertible* into something of intrinsic value, such as gold or silver, but this is generally no longer the case today. Inconvertible notes and coins made from paper and cheap metals are issued by governments which decree that they are the only *legal tender* that may circulate in their country. (Legal tender refers to the currency that must be accepted in payment of debts and taxes.) Because it derives its value ultimately from a government decree, it is known as *fiat money*.

Gresham's law

Whatever commodity, paper or coin is used as money, it must first achieve *circularity in its acceptance*. The only reason people accept paper money is because they are certain that they can use it to purchase goods and services at a later stage. If people had the slightest suspicion that paper money could not be spent, they would not accept it as payment. If token money is to be accepted it must not be easily reproduced or counterfeited. Counterfeiting can be a serious problem for a government because if it were practised on a large scale it would undermine the economy. Vladimir Lenin asserted that the best way to undermine a society was to debauch the currency. During World War II, the Germans attempted to flood Britain with forged currency in order to disrupt the war economy.

Note:

Forged currency can be very sophisticated and bears a close resemblance to the real thing. Soon after the new Irish £20 notes were issued in 1993, forged look-alikes were found in circulation. Shopkeepers in the United States are often suspicious of being paid even moderate amounts in cash as opposed to credit cards. But not all forgery is sophisticated. One of the authors discovered in his change a 10 pence coin battered down to look like a 50 pence coin. The forged coin has, however, six sides instead of the normal seven. It took a lot of hard work to make 40 pence profit!

When gold and silver coins were in circulation, debasing them in one way or

---

2. However, even though the "copper" coins are made of very cheap metal, the process of minting them is quite expensive.

another was brought to a fine art. *Clipping* referred to clipping small pieces off the edges of coins. The authorities responded by milling the circumference of coins. A second practice was *sweating*. People put gold coins into a bag and shook the bag vigorously. The dust at the bottom of the bag that flaked off the coins was the profit. Governments and monarchs were not above cheating by adding a cheap metal alloy to the precious metals in the manufacture of legal tender.

The English financial expert Thomas Gresham (1519-1579) asserted that bad money tends to drive out good. This is known as *Gresham's law*. To understand the idea, consider what would happen if a country originally had coins minted with a high silver content (as was the case with the Irish florins and half-crowns until the 1940s). If the government puts into circulation coins of substantially lower silver content *but with the same face value* (as happened in the 1940s) the latter will quickly replace the former: anyone coming across an older coin, with a high silver content, will hoard it. As a result you will never receive an old 2/- in change today: it is worth far more than 10p for its silver content.

In the US in the nineteenth century both gold and silver coins circulated as legal tender (this system is known as *bimetallism*). The ratio of the value of gold to silver was set at various ratios to try to ensure that both types of coins remained in circulation, but in 1873 silver was demonetised, leaving America on the gold standard. However, a shortage of gold (reduction in the money supply) led to falling prices. The fall in the value of silver caused an outcry from silver-producing states such as Nevada. William Jennings Bryan ran for election in 1896 on the slogan "We shall not crucify mankind on a cross of gold." He lost! The new goldmines in the Klondike and South Africa provided enough gold to meet the demand for monetary purposes by the end of the nineteenth century.

9.4　The Banking System in a Modern Economy

Banks are deposit-taking institutions. They accept funds from the public and place them in accounts. There are two principal types of accounts – current (checking) and deposit (savings) accounts.

Note:

No interest is paid on a current account, but cheques can be drawn on it. Interest is paid on money in a deposit account, but cheques cannot be drawn on it, and notice may be required before money can be withdrawn.

Table 9.1

Money supply, June 1997

	£ m
Currency	2,008
+ Current accounts	+ 4,042
= M1	= 6,050
+ Deposit accounts	+ 31,881
= M3E	= 37,931

Source: Central Bank of Ireland, *Quarterly Bulletin*, Winter 1997, Table A3.

1. M3 does not include non-residents' deposits or cash held by the licensed banks, but it does include foreign currency deposits held by residents at within-the-state offices of licensed banks.

In Ireland two measures of the money supply are used: the *narrow* and the *wide* money supply, referred to as M1 and M3E, respectively. (There used to be an intermediate concept, called M2, but this is no longer used.) As illustrated in Table 9.1, M1 is equal to notes and coins in circulation plus current accounts in banks. Current accounts are included because a cheque may be used to transfer money from the person writing the cheque to the payee. This is a very efficient way of transacting business. Any amount of business can be transacted with a cheque. The banks charge about 30 pence for *clearing* a check through the system – that is, debiting your account and crediting the account of the person you are paying. Notes and coins make up only a small component of the total money supply (7.2 per cent of M3).

The broad money supply, M3E (henceforth referred to as M3) is obtained by adding deposit accounts at the banks and the Post Office Savings Bank to M1. Money in deposit accounts can be easily accessed and as such forms an important part of the money supply. Note, however, that any definition of the money supply is somewhat arbitrary because it is very hard to draw a borderline between "cash" and "non-cash". Deposits with building societies and

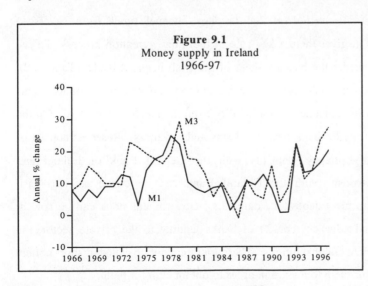

Figure 9.1
Money supply in Ireland
1966-97

Table 9.2

Licensed banks' balance sheet (vis-à-vis residents), June 1997 £ millions

Assets		Liabilities	
Reserves	878	Current accounts	4,042
Lending	27,719	Deposit accounts	20,826
Other	17,572	Other	19,419
	46,169		44,287

Source: Central Bank of Ireland, *Quarterly Bulletin*, Autumn 1997, Table C4.
Note: Assets do not equal liabilities as we are only considering the balance sheet *vis-à-vis* residents of the Republic of Ireland. When non-residents are included the two sides of the balance sheet are equal. Because the Irish banks operate in Northern Ireland, dealings with non-residents are very important.

credit cards can readily be used to purchase things, but neither is included in M3.

Figure 9.1 shows the annual percentage change in M1 and M3 between 1966 and 1997. The variability of both series is striking. It is also noticeable that the two series have not always moved in tandem. In 1974 and 1990, for example, M3 increased as M1 declined. This poses the question: which measure of the money supply should the Central Bank try to control? As we shall see in Chapter 10, changes in the money supply can have an important influence on the inflation rate. Hence, it is desirable to control the money supply in the economy.

The fractional reserve banking system

Banks act as *financial intermediaries*, that is, they channel funds from savers to borrowers. This function gives them a key role in the money-creation process. To see that this is the case, consider the balance sheet of the Irish licensed banks (Table 9.2). The important entries on the liability side are the current and deposit accounts. This money is owed to depositors and hence is a liability from the banks' perspective. On the asset side, there are entries for bank reserves, loans and advances. Reserves consist of the banks' holdings of currency, deposits with the Central Bank of Ireland and government stock. Deposits with the Central Bank can be converted into cash immediately and used to meet depositors' demands. Government stock can be sold at short notice. Loans and advances consist of banks lending to the private sector, the government and other financial institutions. These loans cannot be called at short notice: the banks have to wait for them to mature in order to obtain cash for them.

Modern banking is based on a system of *fractional reserves*. The banks operate on the basis that it is not necessary to keep 100 per cent of deposits in cash. When £1 is deposited, the bank need keep only a fraction in reserve. The rest can be either lent out or used to purchase interest-bearing securities such as government stock or corporate bonds. Over time, new deposits are likely to match withdrawals so that all that is really necessary is to keep a small amount of "till money" to meet occasional net outflows. If a bank has sufficient reserves to meet normal requirements, the public's confidence in it will remain high and the fractional reserve system will work well. The bank will earn interest from its loans and advances, and the public will enjoy the convenience of having money on deposit.

Note:

The fractional reserve system was developed by the goldsmiths of the Middle Ages. People used to place gold and other valuables with them for safe-keeping. At first they simply stored the gold in a vault for a small fee and issued receipts that could be used at a later stage to reclaim the gold. However, it soon became apparent that it was most unlikely that all of the depositors would withdraw all of their gold at the same time. It was therefore possible to make profits by lending out money (gold) and charging interest on the loans. Of course, a certain proportion of the gold had to be kept on hand to meet any withdrawals that would arise. This would reassure depositors, and as long as they had confidence in the system, only a small proportion of the gold would actually be withdrawn. The rest could be put to work to earn interest for the goldsmiths turned bankers.

Reserve requirements

To minimise the risk of default and failure, in most countries banks are required by law to keep minimum reserves in relation to deposits. They can keep excess reserves if they wish, but since they earn less on their reserves than on other assets, they tend not to do so.

In Ireland the Central Bank of Ireland sets a required liquidity ratio known as the *primary ratio*. This ratio applies to all banks and building societies. In 1997 the primary ratio stipulates that 3 per cent of "relevant resources" must be kept in reserve.

Primary liquidity ratio = 3 per cent of relevant resources

Primary liquid assets consist of banks' holdings of notes and coins and deposits at the Central Bank. "Relevant resources" comprise mainly current and deposit accounts. Thus, for every £100 the banks have in current and deposit accounts, a minimum of £3 must be kept in notes and coins plus deposits at the Central Bank. The purpose of the primary reserve ratio is to ensure that the banks have adequate liquid assets to meet

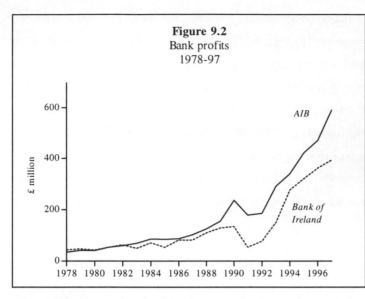

Figure 9.2
Bank profits
1978-97

demands for cash by their depositors.

Note:

Until recent years the Central Bank also required a secondary reserve ratio. This ratio dictated what proportion of relevant resources must be kept in government stock. The secondary reserve ratio was abolished in December 1993.

Bank profits and bad debts

The rate of interest paid by banks on deposits is lower than the rate they charge on loans.

Table 9.3 *Interest margins in Europe*	%
Ireland	183.2
Britain	158.3
Norway	158.1
Finland	156.6
Portugal	148.3
Netherlands	143.7
Spain	141.8
Austria	136.4
Italy	136.4
Belgium	135.5
Sweden	133.2
France	129.4
Denmark	129.3
Switzerland	125.5
Germany	123.4
Greece	122.1

Source: Datamonitor European Banking database.

For example, in 1997 the associated banks paid 0.25 to 0.75 per cent on deposits less than £5,000 and charged 10.25-10.95 per cent to category A borrowers (i.e. personal and retail borrowings) on term loans. This *interest differential* is the main source of bank profits. (Banks charge for all transactions to cover their day-to-day operating costs. There are nearly thirty different types of charges relating to a current account.) As Table 9.3 shows, an independent survey in 16 European countries found that Irish financial institutions (banks and building societies) had the highest interest margins over the five years 1992-96. That is, the Irish institutions made more profit on their lending and deposit business than their counterparts in other countries. Within Ireland, the TSB had the highest interest margin (defined as bank earnings from loan interest as a percentage of interest paid on deposit).

186

Figure 9.2 shows the profits before tax at AIB and Bank of Ireland for the period 1978 to 1996. Profits increased significantly after 1992 reaching £463 million and £363 million for AIB and Bank of Ireland respectively in 1996.

Bank profits are reduced by *bad debts*, that is, loans that are not repaid. Obviously, the lower the provision that has to be made for bad debts, the higher bank profits will be. In the case of AIB, for example, bad debts declined from £178 million in 1992 to £52 million in 1996. As the economy booms, the banks suffer less from bad debts, but during a slump bad debts mount.

To minimise bad debts, banks screen and monitor borrowers very carefully. Yet bankers are influenced by the psychology of the moment, and when a boom in property or land starts they lend to speculators to buy at prices that are unjustified by the underlying value of the assets being bought. When boom turns to bust, the value of the assets used as collateral falls, and even if a bank forecloses it cannot realise its loans. There has been much criticism of bankers in several countries for the role they played in the property boom of the 1980s. In several countries – the US and France, for example – these booms ended in the banks being bailed out at taxpayers' expense. In Japan the big banks loaned money for office properties that fell sharply in value in the 1990s, resulting in large-scale panics and bank failures in 1997.

When very large banks become insolvent governments feel they must be rescued because otherwise they might bring the whole financial system crashing down. This is known as the "Too Big To Fail" syndrome. But if governments bail out banks that have lent money recklessly there is a *moral hazard*: why should the banks worry about taking risks? If things go right they will make big profits; if things go wrong someone else will pick up the cost!

9.5 Money Creation in a Modern Economy

In a modern economy, where bank money is the most important type of money and the banks operate on fractional reserves, an inflow of cash will cause a *multiple expansion* of the money supply. This process is illustrated by the simplified example in Table 9.4. It is assumed that (a) there is only one bank in the country, (b) that the primary reserve requirement is 10 per cent, and (c) that the bank does not keep any excess reserves. On the liability side of the balance sheet are deposits. On the asset side, there are entries for bank reserves and bank lending.

Table 9.4

Money creation with fractional reserve banking

Licensed banks' balance sheet

Assets				Liabilities			
Increases in round:	1	2	3		1	2	3
Reserves	100	90	81	Deposits	1,000	900	810
Loans	900	810	729				

Let us explore what happens when there is a net inflow of reserves (cash) to the bank. Suppose someone takes £1,000 in cash from under the mattress and deposits it in the bank. The bank immediately gains excess reserves, because the new deposit is 100 per cent backed by cash. It lends out as much as it can, which in view of the assumed 10 per cent reserve requirement is £900. Suppose the loan of £900 is used to purchase a car. A local garage receives £900 in exchange for the car and lodges it with its bank. Hence the car loan has, in the second round, resulted in the creation of a deposit of £900, fully backed by cash reserves. The bank again keeps 10 per cent (£90) of the new deposit in reserve and loans out the remainder (£810). The process need not end there. The borrower of £810 from the bank purchases a CD player from a local store. The store, in turn, deposits the £810 with its bank. A deposit of £810 is created, fully backed by reserves, and once again the bank will keep 10 per cent in reserves and lend out the rest. This process will go on, but the amount loaned out at each successive stage dwindles.

Table 9.5 shows what happens to M3 as this process unfolds. As bank deposits increase in each round, so too

Table 9.5

The process of money creation with fractional reserve banking

Round	Δ M3 =	Δ (Currency + Current and deposit accounts)
	£	£
1	1,000	1,000
2	900	900
3	810	810
4	729	729
.	.	.
n	.	.
Total	10,000	10,000

Note: The symbol Δ denotes the change in the magnitude.

188

does the money supply. Given a primary reserve ratio of 10 per cent, the initial £1,000 deposit will eventually lead to a £10,000 increase in the money supply. However, if somewhere along the line someone hoarded the money and kept it out of the banking system, then the expansion of the money supply would halt. The money-creation process only works when the money lent out finds its way back into a bank as a deposit. (Of course, the process also works in reverse. If a bank loses reserves, there will be a multiple contraction of credit.)

Money multiplier The final increase in the money supply can be calculated using a formula for the money multiplier.

$$\text{Money multiplier } (m) = 1/\text{reserve requirement}$$

In the above example, $m = 1/0.1 = 10$, so that

$$\text{Change in M3} \quad = \quad (m) \times (\text{initial increase in reserves})$$
$$£10,000 \quad = \quad 10 \times £1,000$$

Note that the higher the reserve requirement, the lower the money multiplier. A reserve requirement of 20 per cent (0.2), for example, gives a money multiplier of 5, but a reserve requirement of 3 per cent (0.03) gives a money multiplier of 33.3. The less money that has to be held in the form of reserves, the greater the final increase in the money supply following an initial increase in reserves. However, we must bear in mind that this example is based on a very unrealistic example in which no reserves are lost through spending on imports. In Appendix 1 to this chapter a more realistic example, which allows for currency leakage, is worked out.

Note:

The money multiplier should not be confused with the fiscal multiplier discussed in Chapter 5. The fiscal multiplier relates increases in aggregate demand to increases in the equilibrium level of GNP, whereas the money multiplier relates a change in a bank's reserves to the final change in the money supply.

9.6 The Role of a Central Bank

The main functions of a central bank are:

- Issue the currency in the economy.
- Act as banker to both the commercial banks and the government.
- Supervise the orderly operation of the financial system.
- Conduct monetary and exchange rate policies so as to safeguard the *integrity of the country's money*.

189

Table 9.6

Central Bank of Ireland balance sheet: £ m, June 1997

Assets		Liabilities	
External reserves	5,092	Currency	2,213
Loans:		Licensed bank reserves	688
Banks	1,786		
Government	132	Government deposits	2,518
Other	332	Other	1,923
Total	7,342	Total	7,342

Source: Central Bank of Ireland, *Quarterly Bulletin*, Autumn 1997.

Note: Currency includes cash reserves held by the licensed banks. The figure is therefore larger than the figure given earlier in Table 9.2.

We discuss how the central bank can protect the integrity of the currency in the following section. Consider first its roles in issuing the currency and banker to the commercial banks and the government. Table 9.6 shows the structure of the Central Bank of Ireland's balance sheet. The liability side of the balance sheet contains Irish currency in circulation. The central bank has the sole authority to issue currency. The central bank also accepts deposits from both the licensed banks and the government. In effect, the central bank serves as a "bankers' bank" and the government's banker.

On the *asset* side, the most important entry is the official external reserves. These are the country's official holdings of foreign currency, gold and other reserves This is in effect what backs the Irish currency. The central bank is willing to exchange foreign currency, such as sterling, dollars and yen, for Irish pounds and, conversely, to buy back Irish pounds with these currencies. It is the fact that Irish pounds can be converted into other currencies that maintains confidence in the currency.

Complementing its deposit-taking role, the central bank also provides loans to both the commercial banks and the government. There are two important issues relating to the above functions that we now discuss – seigniorage and *lender of last resort*.

Consider first seigniorage. A central bank is a profitable institution. The surplus of the income earned on the country's official external reserves over the Central Bank of Ireland's operating expenses (profit) is turned over to the Department of Finance. In 1996 the Department of Finance received £103 million from this source. However, the

Box 9.1

Seigniorage and the inflation tax

Seigniorage refers to the revenue raised by a government or central bank through issuing money. The *inflation tax* refers to the revenue accruing to government as a result of inflation. The two concepts are closely linked.

Let us define *seigniorage* first. The term comes from tne French word *seigneur*, meaning lord. In the Middle Ages, feudal lords had the right to mint coins on their estates. Today, central banks have a monopoly on this right. A central bank can issue money by purchasing bonds, for example, on the open market and paying for them with a cheque drawn on itself. Anyone selling a bond to the central bank is happy to accept the bank's cheque because they can lodge it with their bank without any difficulty. (The bank gains reserves by accepting the lodgement of a cheque drawn on the central bank, and the money supply increases.) The central bank has now gained an interest-earning asset (the bond) in exchange for an increase in its non-interest-earning deposits. The profit the central bank makes by expanding the money supply in this way is eventually transferred to the government.

The inflation tax refers to the consequence of the increase in the money supply that results from the central bank printing money to finance government expenditure. As we shall see in our discussion of the Quantity Theory of Money in Chapter 10, an increase in the money supply will increase the inflation rate. This reduces the *real* value or the purchasing power of money. For example, if the annual inflation rate is 10 per cent, then £100 today will buy 10 per cent less goods and services in a year's time. Hence, inflation acts as a form of tax on holders of money. The fall in the value of the outstanding money supply benefits the central bank and government by reducing the real value of their liabilities. The losers are, of course, the public who hold money and see its purchasing power decline.

Under certain conditions, the inflation tax and the rate of seigniorage will be the same.

central bank is also able to raise revenue (or reduce its liabilities) by printing money. This particular concept is explained in Box 9.1.

An important function related to its role as banker to the commercial banks is the role of *lender of last resort*. To understand what this entails, recall that commercial banks do not have all of their depositors' money available on demand. Most of it is given out in short and medium-term loans that cannot be called in immediately. However, the central bank is ready to lend to banks that need cash to redeem their obligations to depositors. This ultimately ensures that the banks can operate on fractional reserves and still retain the confidence of their depositors. But while the central bank can act as a lender of last resort in times of crisis and provide the liquidity that stops a run on the banks, it is important that it should not encourage the banks to lend money recklessly. Monitoring the solvency of the banks is therefore an important responsibility of the central bank. (See the discussion of solvency in Box 9.2.)

9.7   Instruments of Monetary Policy

We now turn to the question of maintaining the integrity of the nation's currency. The key to success in this objective lies in curtailing inflation. Central banks are judged successful if they achieve a low rate of inflation and, linked to this, prevent the currency from falling in value (depreciating) relative to other currencies. Most central banks are of the opinion that there is a close link between changes in the money supply and inflation. This relationship is based on the *Quantity Theory of Money*. If central banks can control the money supply, they can control the inflation rate.

In exercising its control over the money supply, a central bank can use the following instruments of monetary policy.

Setting reserve requirements   The central bank sets the reserve requirements that apply to all the banks in the country, who have to comply with these requirements or be penalised. The primary reserve ratio is set well above the level deemed prudent from the banks' point of view and it ensures that they have sufficient liquid assets on hand to meet day-to-day withdrawals. If the central bank increases the reserve ratio the banks have to contract their lending in order to meet the new requirement. In fact, because it is a relatively blunt instrument that could lead to severe changes in liquidity, the reserve ratio is changed only infrequently.

Open market operations   Open market operations consist of buying and selling government stock on the "open market" in order to influence the money supply. If the central bank buys government stock, it pays money for it. When the seller lodges the money in a bank, the bank's reserves increase. By buying government stock, the central bank injects liquidity into the system. On the other hand, by selling stock, the central bank causes a reduction in the reserves of the banking system and hence in the money supply. Thus, decisions about buying and selling government stock form an important part of monetary policy.

Credit guidelines   A central bank can try to dictate to the banks by how much they can increase their lending over a specified period of time. If the banks exceed the guideline, then they can be subject to penalties. Credit guidelines are asymmetrical in the sense that banks can be restrained from exceeding the ceiling but cannot be forced to go up to it. If the demand for credit is weak, banks will not be able to reach the ceiling. Credit guidelines were first used in Ireland in the mid-1960s and were abandoned in the 1980s.

The discount rate   The interest rate a central bank charges on its lending to the commercial banks and the government has different names in different countries. In Britain it used to be known as the Bank Rate, then the Minimum Lending Rate, but now the only rate set by the Bank of England is the *Bill Discounting Rate*. In the US the rate charged by the Federal Reserve Board to the commercial banks is known as the *Discount Rate*. In Germany the Bundesbank sets the *Lombard Rate*. In Ireland the key rate is that charged on the *short-term credit facility* (STCF), which is an overdraft facility for the banks at the Central Bank of Ireland. The banks can only use this facility to top up their reserves to meet the reserve requirement. They cannot borrow from the central bank and on-lend the money to the public. As the STCF rate charged to the banks is higher than the rate they earn on their reserves, they are in effect being penalised for having to borrow to meet the reserve requirement. An increase in the STCF rate discourages the banks from borrowing from the central bank and thus restricts lending throughout the economy. Moreover, the banks will tend to pass an increase in the STCF rate through to their customers. This allows the central bank to influence the whole structure of interest rates in the economy. More often than not, a central bank uses the discount rate to indicate its intentions (or "send a signal") to the commercial banks. When it raises the bank rate, this is taken as a signal to the commercial banks to curtail credit.

Many textbook accounts of how a central bank conducts open market operations and interest rate policy are based on the American banking system. The principal assets held by the Federal Reserve Board are US government bonds. Purchases and sales of these through the Fed's Open Market Committee is the most important monetary policy-making instrument in the world. American interest rates have a major influence on interest rates all over the world, but foreign interest rates do not have much effect on them, so the Fed is relatively free to conduct an independent policy in this area.

In Ireland the context of monetary policy is very different. The ability of the Central Bank of Ireland to operate an independent monetary policy is severely limited by the openness and smallness of the economy. The Irish money market is dominated by external influences and flows across the foreign exchanges. With the launch of EMU in 1999 the monetary policy of the participating countries will be taken over by the European Central Bank, located in Frankfurt. Countries like Ireland will cease to control any of the traditional instruments of monetary policy. Chapter 23 provides a discussion of the manner in which European monetary policy will operate in EMU.

9.8 The Development of the Irish Currency

This section provides a brief history of the development of Irish money.

Early history

Gold and silver were used in Ireland as a medium of exchange in ancient times, although the units took the form of rings and bracelets rather than coins.[3] Money, however, took many other forms as the following quote suggests:

> "*The Annals of the Four Masters, originating from* A.D. *106, state that the tribute (Boroimhe meaning literally 'cow-tax') paid by the King of Leinster consisted of 150*

---

3. P. Nolan, *A Monetary History of Ireland*, London, 1926.

Table 9.7

A brief history of the Irish pound

Date	Exchange rate	Movement of Irish currency in terms of sterling relative to previous date
1200	Par	
1487	IR 1.5 silver coins/ UK 1 silver coin	Depreciation
1561	IR 1.3 silver coins/UK 1 silver coin	Appreciation
1601-1602	IR 4 silver coins/UK 1 silver coin	Depreciation
1603	IR 1.3 silver coins/UK 1 silver coin	Appreciation
1650	Par	Appreciation
1689	IR 13 pence/UK 12 pence	Depreciation
1797-1826	Irish currency floated against UK currency	Depreciation
1826	Abolition of independent Irish currency	Par
1927	Creation of Saorstát pound	Parity with sterling
1979	The Irish currency depreciated following Ireland's entry into the Exchange Rate Mechanism (ERM) of the European Monetary System. Followed by appreciation	Depreciation
1990-1992	Entry of Britain into the ERM	Stability at about IR£ = STG£0.92
1992 (September)	Sterling is devalued on foreign exchanges and drops out of the ERM	
1993 (August)	Margins of fluctuation in ERM widened to 15 per cent.	
1993-99	Irish pound the strongest currency in the ERM.	
1998 (March)	Irish pound revalued by 3 per cent in ERM realignment.	
1999 (January)	Irish pound permanently fixed to the euro. Irish pound ceases to be a currency and becomes a unit of account	
2002	Irish currency withdrawn from circulation and replaced by euro notes and coins.	

cows, 150 pigs, 150 couples of men and women in servitude, 150 girls and 150 cauldrons.''[4]

The first coinage in Ireland can be traced to the Norse settlement in Dublin in the 990s.[5] The amount of coinage in circulation was relatively small and largely confined to

---

4. P. Einzig, *Primitive Money*, New York: Pergamon, 2nd edition, 1966, p. 239.

5. See P. McGowan, *Money and Banking in Ireland: Origins, Development and Future*, Institute of Public Administration, 1990, for an extended analysis of money and banking in Ireland. Also Cormac Ó Gráda,

the main trading towns. The use of coinage increased after the arrival of the Normans in 1169. In 1460 the Irish parliament that met in Drogheda established the first separate Irish currency and devalued it relative to the English currency: 15 Irish pence were worth 12 English pence (or one English shilling), so the exchange rate was 15:12.[6] Over the centuries the exchange rate between the Irish and English currencies has varied considerably. A summary of the fortunes of the Irish pound is given in Table 9.7.

In the sixteenth century the English monarchy allowed the so called Harp coinage (sometimes referred to as "white money") to be issued. In doing so, the monarchy acknowledged the existence of a separate Irish currency unit. This was followed in 1601 by an issue of copper coinage by Queen Elizabeth I.

By the 1680s, when banking-type activities first began to emerge, the currency situation in Ireland was unsatisfactory for a number of reasons. First, there was a general shortage of coins and the economy still operated partly on a barter system. James II had melted down cannons to manufacture coins. This was the so called "gun money" which gave rise to the expression "not worth a brass farthing". The coinage in circulation consisted of a mix of Spanish, French, Portuguese and English coins, which were of different quality and design, and this lack of uniformity impaired its ability to function as a medium of exchange (recall our discussion of Gresham's law, above).

In the early 1720s a Mr Wood received a patent to issue coinage (Wood's half-pence) which would have increased the copper coinage in circulation by about a quarter. However, this patent was withdrawn two years later, partly because of the argument used by Jonathan Swift in *The Drapier's Letters* that the increase in currency would raise prices. A general shortage of coinage continued in Ireland, but as the poorer people in the country areas still lived in a subsistence and semi-barter economy, this had little effect on them. Merchants issued their own coins in order to facilitate trade.

From the eighteenth century to Independence

Throughout the eighteenth century, the Irish currency was at a discount of about 8 per cent relative to the English currency: 13 Irish pence equalled 12 English pence. In 1797, during the turmoil of the Napoleonic Wars, the convertibility of Irish and British specie

---

Ireland 1780-1939: A New Economic History, Oxford University Press, 1994, p. 42.

6. See J. Moore McDowell, "The Devaluation of 1460 and the Origins of the Irish Pound", *Irish Historical Studies*, xxv, No. 97 (May 1986) pp 19-28.

(that is, coins) to gold was suspended, and in 1803 the Irish currency depreciated sharply. A parliamentary inquiry was established which issued a report known as the *Irish Currency Report* (1804). This *Report* argued that excessive credit expansion caused the depreciation and that the exchange rate could be stabilised if the growth of credit were controlled.

After 1804 the Irish currency gradually stabilised at a 13:12 exchange rate against sterling. By the time gold convertibility was resumed in 1821, this rate was sufficiently re-established for the Bank of Ireland to accept responsibility for maintaining the Irish currency at this rate. Following the implementation of the monetary provisions of the 1800 Act of Union in 1826, full political and monetary union was established between Ireland and Great Britain, and the Irish currency was abolished. Thereafter both British coins and notes circulated freely in Ireland.

Note:

The *Irish Currency Report* influenced thinking in the "bullionist controversy" in England (1796-1821) and is an important document in the history of monetary economics. The key issue it addressed was whether there could be an "excessive" growth in the money supply. The *Report* set out what came to be the orthodox view that an "excess" increase in the money supply would lead to an increase in the price level and this, in turn, would make exports less competitive and cause the exchange rate to depreciate. This reasoning was influential in the development of the modern *Quantity Theory of Money*.

Developments since Independence

Following the foundation of the Irish Free State in 1922, the *Coinage Act* of *1926* was passed in order to enable the Minister for Finance to issue new Irish coins. These coins were used in Ireland until 1971, when a new design was introduced and the coinage decimalised.[7]

A banking commission was set up in 1926 to advise the government on the establishment of an Irish pound. This was known as the Parker-Willis Commission, after its chairman, Professor Henry Parker-Willis (1874-1937) of Columbia University, a former secretary of the Federal Reserve Board (the US Central Bank). The commission's final report was signed in January 1927. It recommended that a new currency unit, the

7. Until the 1950s the "silver" coins minted for Ireland in fact contained significant amounts of silver. Some of them became very valuable as the price of silver rose. The two shilling and half-crown coins from the early 1940s are now worth hundreds of pounds. Hence, following Gresham's law, they have entirely disappeared from circulation.

Saorstát pound, be created. In order to ensure public confidence in the new currency, it should be backed 100 per cent by sterling reserves, British government stock and gold reserves, freely convertible into sterling, and its value in terms of sterling could not be changed without the introduction of additional legislation. Thus the new currency would, in effect, be sterling with an Irish design. This would ensure that it would be acceptable alongside sterling as a medium of exchange. The commission also recommended the establishment of a new body, confusingly to be called the Currency Commission, to oversee the issue of the new legal tender notes.

The recommendations of the Parker-Willis Commission were incorporated into law in the *Currency Act 1927*. The Currency Commission was established and remained in existence until 1942, when its powers were transferred to the new Central Bank. Its only chairman was Joseph Brennan (1887-1976), who became the first governor of the Central Bank of Ireland. The first Irish notes were issued in September 1928.

Note:

Under the new arrangements the commercial banks were allowed to issue a certain quantity of private bank notes which bore the banks' names. These were called the Consolidated Bank Note issue and the notes were known as ploughman notes because of their design. These notes were finally withdrawn from circulation in 1953.

The share of Irish legal tender notes in the total supply of money in circulation is believed to have reached about two-thirds by the beginning of World War II. This represents another example of the benefits of seigniorage. To understand how seigniorage profits arise, consider the following example. In 1928 the Irish public exchanged their holdings of sterling for the new Irish currency. The Currency Commission (which issued the new Irish notes) received sterling in return and this sterling was placed on the London money markets and earned interest. The interest received by the Currency Commission (allowing for expenses) represented seigniorage profits. It has been estimated that the value of the seigniorage amounted to about 0.2 per cent of national income at the time.[8]

9.9   The Evolution of Central Banking in Ireland

In this section, we present an overview of the development of central banking in Ireland.

8. Cormac Ó Gráda, *Ireland 1780-1939: A New Economic History*, Oxford University Press, 1994, p. 42.

In nineteenth-century Ireland there was no central bank. In particular, there was no lender of last resort to bail out the commercial banks when they got into trouble. A key date in Irish banking history is 1783 when the Bank of Ireland was founded by royal charter. It performed some of the functions of a central bank. It issued notes and managed the government's account. Because of its size it was able to lend money to banks that were in distress, but it was not always willing or able to provide enough support to avert bank failures. Following the Act of Union in 1801 and the abolition of the Irish currency in 1826, the Bank of England was given some responsibility for supervising banking in Ireland. Greater competition in the banking sector following the *Bankers' (Ireland) Act of 1845* forced the Bank of Ireland to evolve along commercial lines. This reduced its willingness to help out other banks in times of crisis.

Note:

Because there was no lender of last resort, the Irish private banks were very vulnerable in times of crisis. In 1820, for example, at the end of the Napoleonic Wars there was a slump in agricultural prices and widespread bankruptcy among the merchants to whom the banks had loaned money. When depositors got wind of this there was a "run on the banks", which did not have enough cash on hand and could not call in their loans from bankrupt clients. In one month thirty banks failed in Munster alone and the crisis spread throughout the country, leaving only ten banks solvent outside Dublin.[9] As the banks were private companies, when they failed the partners who owned them lost their capital and frequently had to sell off their town houses and country estates as well. Depositors were lucky if they got back half the money they had lodged with the banks.

The question of the appropriate way to regulate the banking system emerged as an issue after independence. It was recognised that a serious conflict of interest would have emerged if the Bank of Ireland were asked to act as the Central Bank in the Free State. None the less, the Minister for Finance in the new provisional government asked the

---

9. McGowan notes that the banks ". . . were primarily concerned with facilitating the transfer of agricultural output from the countryside to Dublin and abroad and placing the proceeds of the sale of that output at the disposal of the landlords" (op. cit., p. 10). Merchants borrowed from the banks to pay farmers for crops which were sold on the domestic market and exported. The farmers used the bank notes to pay the landowners' rent and the landowners returned the notes to the private banks in exchange for gold, silver or foreign currency. Hence the private banks facilitated a transfer of resources from tenant farmers to landowners. The private banks were superseded by joint stock banks following the banking crises of the 1820s. These had at least six major shareholders (who accepted unlimited liability) and they were therefore better able to withstand crises. See Eoin O'Kelly, *The Old Private Banks and Bankers of Munster*, Cork University Press, 1959; and Kevin Hannon, "The Limerick Savings Bank", *Old Limerick Journal*, No. 3, 1980.

Bank of Ireland to continue to manage the government's account. The Banking Commission which reported in 1927 did not intend that the Currency Commission would become a fully fledged central bank. It was not given the power to act as a lender of last resort, nor could it set reserve requirements for commercial banks. It did not gain control over the commercial banks' sterling assets, which continued to be kept in London. Furthermore, the commission did not manage the government's account, nor did it advise the government on monetary matters.

Perhaps the main reason a central bank was not established in the 1920s was that there was little such an institution could usefully do as long as the country remained in a monetary union with Great Britain. There was a fixed exchange rate between the Irish currency and sterling and there was no money market in Ireland. Under these circumstances, a central bank could not control the money supply or have any influence on the price level, output or employment. All that was needed was some type of *currency board*, to issue local currency in exchange for approved assets such as sterling. This function was discharged by the Currency Commission.

Another possible reason why a central bank was not established after independence was:

"... a conviction that central banks were being promoted as antidotes to backward or unduly risk-adverse commercial banking systems. Accordingly, creating an Irish central bank might be seen as both a slight and a threat to the long-established commercial banks."[10]

When in September 1931 the UK terminated the gold standard and sterling was devalued by 25 per cent against gold, there were misgivings in some quarters in Ireland that the Irish currency was automatically devalued due to the link with sterling. The Fianna Fáil government established a second Banking Commission in 1934 to report on money and banking in Ireland. The new commission included Joseph Brennan (chairman of the Currency Commission), George O'Brien (professor of national economics at University College, Dublin) and the Swedish economist Per Jacobsson who later became president of the International Monetary Fund. (John Maynard Keynes was

---

10. Ó Gráda, op. cit., p. 27. In the same vein, when government asked the commercial banks to underwrite a flotation of government stock in the 1930s, the banks were reluctant and wished to know how the government intended to spend the proceeds.

considered but was not invited, possibly because of his support for the Irish government's protectionist policies in a lecture in Dublin in the previous year.)[11] A bishop was included, but Dr McNeely was

". . . unaware of any reasons why he should have been appointed, except to add an atmosphere of respectability to the Conference".[12]

This second Banking Commission deliberated for nearly four years and reported in 1938. As one commentator put it:

"The opinion of the majority report on the system of banking and currency may be summarised as a recommendation to leave things as they were."[13]

The creation of an Irish central bank, as such, was not recommended, but it was suggested that the Currency Commission be allowed to engage in open market operations and that its name be suitably altered to "indicate that the monetary authority envisaged in these recommendations is a central banking organisation". Thus, the commission tried to steer a course between outright advocacy of a central bank and the status quo. In the days before the start of World War II, the Bank of Ireland approached the Bank of England to see if it would act as a lender of last resort to the Irish banks in an emergency. The Bank of England replied that it was not in a position to provide assistance and suggested that "as Eire was a separate political entity it should have a central bank of its own".[14] Perhaps in the light of this rebuff the Irish commercial banks, who had been heavily represented on both banking commissions and had staunchly opposed the creation of a central bank, had second thoughts on the issue.

In any event,

"The government chose to ignore the Report, and used the threat of war to produce central banking legislation. In the end, the Central Bank Act of 1942 was a

---

11. See John Maynard Keynes, "National Self-Sufficiency", the first Finlay Lecture delivered at University College, Dublin, April 1933, reprinted in *Studies*, June 1933.

12. Ó Gráda, op. cit., p. 42.

13. James Meenan, *The Irish Economy since 1922*, Manchester University Press, 1970, p. 222.

14. Ó Gráda, op. cit., p. 39.

compromise between, on the one hand, Brennan and the Department of Finance [who
did not wish to establish a Bank], and the majority of ministers [who did] on the
other."[15]

The *Central Bank Act* was passed in 1942 and soon afterwards the Central Bank of Ireland was established, with Joseph Brennan, the former chairman of the Currency Commission, as the first governor. To date there have been eight governors of the Central Bank (see Box 9.3). The primary function of the new Central Bank was to "safeguard the integrity of the currency". Its powers were, however, limited. It could act as lender of last resort and use open market operations to influence liquidity in the money market, but it could not set reserve requirements or act as a banker to either the government or the commercial banks. The government continued to hold its account with the Bank of Ireland and the commercial banks held most of their reserves in the London money markets. Thus, little changed in Irish banking immediately following the establishment of the Central Bank of Ireland.

Box 9.3	
Governors of the Central Bank of Ireland	
Joseph Brennan	1943-53
James J. McElligott	1953-60
Maurice Moynihan	1961-69
T. Kennedy Whitaker	1969-76
Charles H. Murray	1976-81
Tomás Ó Cofaigh	1981-87
Maurice F. Doyle	1987-94
Maurice O'Connell	1994 -

The 1960s, however, were a period of rapid development in Irish banking. A number of new banks began operations in Ireland and there was a wave of mergers among the established ones. The Bank of Ireland acquired the Hibernian Bank in 1958 and the National Bank in 1965. The Allied Irish Bank group was formed with the merger of the Munster and Leinster Bank, the Provincial Bank and the Royal Bank of Ireland in 1966. Appendix 2 to this chapter discusses the structure of the banking sector in Ireland today.

In 1965, the Central Bank of Ireland first issued "letters of advice" (or credit guidelines) to the banks, telling them to restrain credit expansion in order to curtail the growing balance of payments deficit. The Central Bank began to promote new markets in foreign exchange, government stocks and money. Because of these developments, it was becoming increasingly clear that the 1942 Central Bank legislation was inadequate.

---

15. Ó Gráda, op. cit.

In response the *Central Bank Act, 1971*, was passed. This Act significantly increased the powers of the Central Bank. Its main features were:

- The Central Bank became the licensing authority for banks.
- The government's account was transferred from the Bank of Ireland to the Central Bank.
- The commercial banks were required to keep their reserves with the Central Bank.
- The Central Bank was given the power to issue primary and secondary reserve ratios (these were first issued in August 1972).
- The new legislation made it possible to break the sterling link by government order. This power was exercised in March 1979, following Ireland's entry to the European Monetary System.

The *Central Bank Act, 1989,* brought money brokers, financial futures traders and companies associated with the new International Financial Services Centre (IFSC) under the supervision of the Central Bank. In addition, commercial bank charges were brought under its control and, as mentioned earlier, a deposit protection scheme was established to protect the savings of small depositors. Under the *Building Society Act, 1989*, and the *Trustee Savings Bank (TSB) Act, 1989*, the Central Bank gained responsibility for supervising the building societies and the TSBs.

If the Central Bank is to discharge its commitment to safeguarding the value of the currency, it must maintain strict control over the growth of credit to government and the commercial banks. High rates of inflation have invariably been accompanied by a loss of control by the Central Bank over lending to government and the commercial banks. To maintain this control the Central Bank must be politically and economically independent of government. (Full central bank independence is laid down in the Maastricht Treaty as a prerequisite for participation in the proposed single European currency.) The Fed in the United States and the Bundesbank in Germany are viewed as being very independent of government and free to pursue the monetary policies they believe will result in low inflation. In Italy, on the other hand, the central bank has traditionally been subservient to government and not strong enough to keep inflation low. The Central Bank of Ireland is viewed as lying somewhere in the middle, having a moderate degree of political and economic independence.

Irish policy makers are now committed to the radical step of abandoning the independent Irish currency and replacing it with the euro. This entails surrendering monetary independence to the European Central Bank. The Governing Council of the

ECB, which will include the governors of the central banks of the participating countries, will formulate European monetary policy after 1999.

In effect Ireland will have had an independent currency for less than 20 years – between breaking the link with sterling in March 1979 and the fixing of the value of the Irish pound in terms of the euro in January 1999.

9.10 Conclusion

In this chapter we introduced the subject of money and banking and reviewed their history in Ireland from the earliest times to the present. The main points discussed included:

- Money performs a number of functions. The most important is its role as a medium of exchange
- The evolution of currency and banking in Ireland
- Fractional reserve banking
- How bank lending results in an increase in bank deposits
- How inflows (outflows) of cash cause a multiple expansion (contraction) of the money supply
- The money multiplier
- The role of a central bank
- The origins of the Central Bank of Ireland
- The instruments of monetary policy used by central banks include open market operations, changes in the reserve requirements, discount rates and credit guidelines.
- The prospect of joining the European EMU and adopting the euro as our currency.

Appendix 1

High-powered money and the money multiplier

The Central Bank's liabilities are referred to as *high-powered money* or the *monetary base*. The reserves of the commercial banks are included in this total. It is called high-powered because, as we have seen, changes in reserves have a multiple or expanded impact on the money supply. Ignoring, for simplicity, government deposits and "other liabilities" on the liability side of the Central Bank balance sheet (see Table 9.5), high-powered money (H) is equal to currency (CU) plus licensed bank reserves at the Central Bank (RE).

$$H = CU + RE \tag{1}$$

Using this definition we can now present a more complete version of the money multiplier than the simple one introduced earlier in section 9.5. We assume that people hold currency in proportion to their current and deposit accounts (D):

$$CU = c_pD \tag{2}$$

where $0 < c_p < 1$. If c_p was equal to, say, 0.1, this means that for every £1 held in current and deposit accounts, the public holds 10 pence in currency. Because of the primary liquidity ratio, licensed bank reserves at the Central Bank are also related to current and deposit accounts.

$$RE = r_bD \tag{3}$$

Again, $0 < r_b < 1$. If the primary reserve ratio were 10 per cent, r_b would be at least 0.1. The banks can, however, keep excess reserves if they wish. If equations (2) and (3) are inserted into equation (1), we obtain:

$$H = (c_p + r_b)D \tag{4}$$

Recall now that M3 is equal to currency plus current and deposit accounts.

$$M3 = CU + D \tag{5}$$

Substitute equation (2) into equation (5):

$$M3 = (c_p + 1)D \tag{6}$$

The final step in deriving the relationship between M3 and H is to take the ratio of equation (6) to equation (4):

$$M3/H = (c_p + 1)/(c_p + r_b) \tag{7}$$

or

$$M3 = (c_p + 1)/(c_p + r_b)H \tag{8}$$

This version of the money multiplier relates high-powered money to the overall money supply and allows for currency leakages. If $c_p = 0$ (the public does not increase currency holdings as deposits increase) we obtain the earlier version of the multiplier.

We can calculate the money multiplier in the Irish economy for December 1993 using the data in Tables 9.2 and 9.5.

$$c_p = CU/D = 2,213/24,868 = 0.089$$
$$r_b = RE/D = 878/24,868 = 0.035$$

The money multiplier is equal to

$$(c_p + 1)/(c_p + r_b) = (0.089 + 1)/(0.089 + 0.035) = 8.78$$

This means that an increase of £1 in high-powered money would lead to an increase of £8.78 in the money supply. An increase in currency holdings in relation to deposits (c_p) will reduce the money multiplier. For example, if c_p increased from 0.089 to 0.2, the money multiplier would fall to 1.47. Similarly, as we noted earlier, an increase in r_b will decrease the money multiplier.

High-powered money is increased whenever the Central Bank increases its assets or its liabilities. It follows, therefore, that if the Central Bank can control currency in circulation and bank deposits with the Central Bank, it should be able to control the money supply. In practice, however, controlling the money supply has proved to be a very difficult task. During the early 1980s UK economic policy relied heavily on trying to control sterling M3 by controlling the stock of high-powered money. However, control of high-powered money did not translate simply into control of the money supply. It was found that the money multiplier was very unstable, perhaps because the UK banking system was undergoing a profound transformation under deregulation. There is also the possibility that if the Central Bank tries to control one definition of the money supply, the public will switch into near substitutes to side-step this control. This tendency has been called "Goodhart's law", after Professor Charles Goodhart of the London School of Economics who drew attention to this problem.

Despite the problems of fine-tuning the money supply, international experience shows that it is not possible to have a sustained expansion of the money supply without an increase in the monetary base. Hence the Central Bank's balance sheet is at the centre of the stage of monetary policy.

Appendix 2

The structure of the Irish financial sector

Although small, the Irish financial sector is quite complex. For historical reasons, a variety of different categories of banks exist and different regulations, including reserve requirements, are applied to them. The various types of financial institutions specialise in different segments of the market, attracting their deposits from different types of depositors and lending to different types of borrowers. The main categories of financial institutions are as follows:

Associated banks (Allied Irish Bank, Bank of Ireland, National Irish Bank and the Ulster Bank). These are public quoted companies which provide a full range of lending and deposit facilities and together they constitute the backbone of the Irish retail banking system which meets the banking needs of the general public. The term "associated banks" comes from the *Central Bank Act, 1942,* and indicates that a special relationship exists between these banks and the Central Bank. It should be noted that the associated banks have important subsidiaries operating in other segments of the banking market and in hire-purchase finance. The Irish retail banking system is characterised by a few large banks with hundreds of branches. In this it resembles the British and Canadian systems. Banking in the US, on the other hand, is still characterised by thousands of small, independent and localised banks, although regional and national banking networks are being established.

Non-associated banks This category is subdivided into:

1. Merchant and commercial banks (Allied Irish Investment Bank, Algemene Bank Nederland, Guinness and Mahon, the Bank of Nova Scotia, Citibank, etc.). These banks cater to the wholesale end of the market, which includes large personal and corporate accounts. They also provide investment management and consultancy services.

2. Industrial banks (Allied Irish Finance, Bank of Ireland Finance, Bowmaker Bank, Lombard and Ulster, UDT Bank, etc.). These specialise in providing fixed interest loans to the personal sector for consumer durables and to industry for machinery and other equipment. Note that the associated and non-associated banks comprise the licensed banks.

State-sponsored financial institutions (The Industrial Credit Corporation and the Agricultural Credit Bank). These are state-owned banks which were established to act as development banks in industry and agriculture, respectively. They are likely to be privatised in the near future.

The post office savings bank This is a government-owned savings bank. All deposits are used to purchase government securities. The post office also administers an instalment savings scheme and issues savings certificates on favourable tax terms.

Trustee savings banks Approximately 80 per cent of the deposits of these banks are lent to the government and the remainder is lent to the public. These banks are owned by trustees on behalf of their depositors.

Building societies (First National Building Society, Educational Building Society, Irish Permanent Building Society, etc.). Building societies now act very much like banks, but they were founded as mutual societies (owned by members or policy shareholders) to help small savers acquire money for house purchase against the security of the property. The 1989 legislation has brought them more into line with ordinary banks. There has been a wave of demutualisation in many countries in recent years. In Ireland, there are now just two mutual building societies down from fourteen some twenty years ago.

Hire-purchase finance companies (Allied Finance, Advance Finance, etc.). These companies are similar to the industrial banks in that they provide fixed interest loans for the purchase of consumer durables and machinery for industry. Many of them are subsidiaries of the associated banks.

Credit unions Credit unions are localised, co-operative banks whose main business is lending to their members on a non-profit basis. The following data indicates the growth of the credit unions over the last forty years.

	1959	1997
Number of credit unions	3	532
Members	200	2,100,000
Savings	£415	£2,820,000,000

In recent years the main insurance companies have launched a number of schemes to attract savings. These offer attractive returns by taking advantage of the favourable tax treatment of life insurance premiums. They compete with the banks and other financial institutions for the public's savings.

Bank profits were the subject of much criticism in the 1920s. The Irish Banks' Standing Committee (IBSC) was set up in 1920, comprised of representatives of both southern and northern banks, to agree common interest rates and bank charges. This suggested that a cartel had been formed with the objective of making supranormal profits from bank customers. Criticism focused, in particular, on the spread between deposit and lending rates. It was pointed out that deposit rates were lower and lending rates higher than similar rates in the UK. The concern at the outflow of large deposits from Ireland to the UK added weight to this argument. The IBSC continues to exist, but it no longer sets interest rates for the banks, and its influence has been eroded by the entry of new financial institutions into the banking market. Despite this growth, the Irish financial sector remains small by international standards. The London clearing banks (the counterpart of our associated banks) have combined deposits totalling almost £300 billion, compared with £7 billion in Irish banks.

The interest rate charged by the industrial banks is roughly double that charged by the associated banks. In October 1991 the associated banks' overdraft and term loan rate to A borrowers was 12.5 per cent. In contrast, the *annual percentage rate* (APR) charged by the industrial banks varied from 18 per cent to 25 per cent, and the rates charged by hire-purchase finance companies were at least as high. (The APR must now be displayed on all advertisements for loans, hire-purchase arrangements, etc. This requirement was resisted by the financial institutions.) The reason for the higher interest rate charged by finance houses is that their loans are riskier and involve higher administration costs than those entered into by the banks. The hire-purchase finance companies do not take deposits from the public but borrow from banks and other sources and on-lend this money at much higher interest rates to the public.

Over the years, a significant shift in market share has occurred. In 1966 the associated banks and the building societies had approximately 80 per cent and 6 per cent of the deposit market, respectively. The building societies and other financial institutions have gained at the expense of the banks. The building societies' gain was partly due to increased demand for housing and, up to 1986, the confidentiality and favourable tax treatment of their interest payments. The Finance Act 1986, however, moved some way towards creating a "level playing field" for all financial institutions. Since 1986 all have to deduct the deposit interest retention tax (DIRT) at the standard rate from deposit interest paid, which is not disclosed to the Revenue Commissioners.

Despite the smallness of the Irish financial market, in the past the number of regulatory bodies responsible for it was quite large. The situation was rationalised in the *Central Bank Act, 1989*, when the building societies, the trustee savings banks and hire-purchase finance companies were all brought under the control of the Central Bank, which was already responsible for the licensed banks. The Department of Finance regulates the Post Office Savings Bank. The Department of the Environment, in conjunction with the Registrar of Friendly Societies, controls credit unions. The Department of Enterprise, Trade and Employment is responsible for insurance companies and firms operating under the Money Lenders' Acts.

The years ahead will see further important changes in Ireland's financial services. The opening of the IFSC has created a new layer of activity which, however, is largely offshore, that is, dealing with non-Irish deposits and transactions, and subject to special regulations and enjoying special tax concessions. Tax harmonisation and the abolition of exchange controls within the European Union will allow Irish residents a wider choice in regard to where they place their money or from whom they borrow. At the same time, Irish banks will continue to seek to diversify internationally, so that the Irish banking sector will become increasingly closely integrated with other centres abroad.

Banks continue to come under criticism from time to time for their "failure" to lend money on favourable terms to new start-up and small businesses. The need to funnel capital to new ventures is a recurrent theme in the commentaries on banking systems. It is difficult to strike a balance between the desire to foster enterprise, on the one hand, and the need to manage depositors' funds prudently on the other.

Chapter 10

Interest Rates and Money in a Closed Economy

10.1   Introduction

We begin this chapter by outlining the quantity theory of money, which is the classical theory of how the price level and the rate of inflation are determined in a closed economy. This is followed by a discussion of the Keynesian theory of the demand for money. We then show how the supply and demand for money determine the rate of interest. This analysis of the money market is incorporated into the simple Keynesian model developed in earlier chapters. The key relationship between the rate of interest and the level of investment is highlighted. Using the expanded Keynesian model, issues such as the relative effectiveness of fiscal and monetary policy are discussed.

We emphasise at the outset that much of what we say in the course of this chapter has to be modified to take account of the environment of a small open economy such as Ireland. We shall undertake these refinements in later chapters.

10.2   The Quantity Theory of Money

The quantity theory of money explains the price level and hence the rate of inflation. In its simplest form, it states that the larger the quantity of money in the economy, the higher the price level. Alternatively, the more rapid the rate of increase in the money supply, the higher the rate of inflation.

Note:

The discovery of large silvermines in Mexico, Bolivia and Argentina led to a vast increase in the stock of silver coins in circulation in Europe from the sixteenth century onwards. The rise in the price level experienced at the same time was attributed by many observers to the increase in the quantity of money. This is the origin of the modern quantity theory.

To set out the quantity theory in algebraic terms, we define the *velocity of circulation of money* (V) as nominal GNP divided by the stock of money:

$$V \equiv GNP/M^S \tag{1}$$

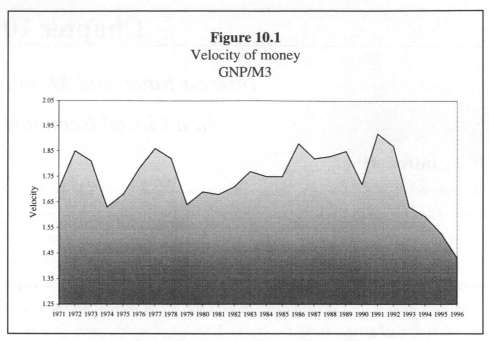

Figure 10.1
Velocity of money
GNP/M3

Using the M3 definition of money, the 1996 figures for Ireland are:

$$V \equiv \pounds36{,}983 \text{ million}/\pounds27{,}038 \text{ million} = 1.36$$

This means that each £1 of notes and coins, current and deposit accounts in banks financed £1.36 worth of expenditure on final goods and services. In other words, the average monetary unit was used one and a third times during the year. This is what is meant by "velocity". Figure 10.1 shows the velocity of circulation of money in Ireland over the period 1971 to 1996. Velocity has varied within a fairly narrow range up to 1992 but since then it has declined significantly. The average velocity figure over the period was 1.73.

If nominal GNP is divided into the price level (P) and real GNP, identity (1) can be written:

$$V \equiv (P \times \text{real GNP})/M^S \qquad (2)$$

Multiply both sides of (2) by M^S:

$$M^S \times V \equiv P \times \text{real GNP} \qquad (3)$$

The quantity theory is a cornerstone of that school of economics that has come to be known as *monetarism*. The monetarists argue that identity (3) can be used to explain the price level if we assume:

- V is relatively stable, and
- real GNP is at or close to the full employment level.

Given these assumptions, it is clear that if the money supply, M^S, is increased the brunt of the adjustment must come through an increase in P, the price level. This, in a nutshell, is the explanation of inflation that follows from the quantity theory of money: *increases in the money supply lead to higher prices.*

Since real GNP tends to the full employment level, any increase in the money supply will cause the price level, rather than real GNP, to rise. It follows, therefore, that attempts to use monetary policy to stabilise the economy are doomed to failure. On the basis of these arguments, monetarists believe there should be no *discretionary* monetary policy. Instead, the authorities should simply maintain the growth in the money supply in line with the predicted growth in real GNP. If this *monetary rule* is followed, the growth in the money supply will support the growth in the real economy without inflation.

Note:
The exact mechanism by which increases in the money supply are transmitted into a higher price level is not specified. The quantity theory is a kind of "black box" theory.

As support for the quantity theory, monetarists point to the close correlation between inflation and the growth in the money supply over the long run in different countries and at different periods of time. Milton Friedman's *A Monetary History of the United States: 1867-1960* (written with his wife Anna Schwartz)[1] found support for the monetarist point of view in the experience of the United States since the nineteenth century. Friedman also found support for the quantity theory in inflation-prone countries such as Brazil, Bolivia and Israel. These countries have had high growth rates in their money supplies and rapid inflation. This led Friedman to conclude: "Inflation is always and everywhere a monetary phenomenon."

Keynesian perspective Keynesian economists, in contrast, argue that velocity is not constant and that an increase in the money supply will lead to a fall in velocity. If this is the case, an increase in the money supply may have little or no effect on nominal output. In terms of equation 3, if the increase in M^S is matched by a fall in V, then the right-hand side of the equation is unchanged. The implication is that monetary policy will be ineffective. In addition, Keynesians contend that the economy will take a long time to

1. M. Friedman and A. Schwartz, *A Monetary History of the United States: 1867-1960*, Princeton University Press, 1963.

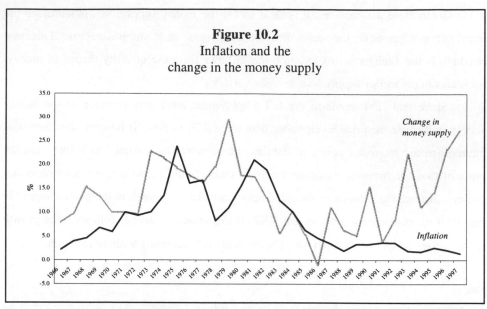

Figure 10.2
Inflation and the
change in the money supply

revert to potential GNP following some disturbance. For all intents and purposes, the "automatic adjustment" mechanism advocated by the monetarists does not occur except in the long run. In so far as a change in the money supply does affect nominal GNP, it could be real GNP, rather than the price level, which adjusts.

Another serious criticism of the quantity theory is that *causation* may run from nominal GNP to the money supply and not the other way round.[2] In other words, the money supply is "demand led". As we shall explain later in this chapter, an increase in nominal GNP will increase the demand for money. If the money supply is held constant the result will be an increase in interest rates. Politicians may now put pressure on the Central Bank to increase the money supply in order to prevent an increase in interest rates. (In effect a shift of the demand curve to the right is matched by a similar shift of a supply curve to the right and the result is that the interest rate remains constant. See Figure 23.3 on page 530, for example.) If this happens then the causation in equation 3 is running from right to left. Changes in nominal GNP have resulted in an expansion of the money supply.

Evidence from the Irish economy The quantity theory of money is essentially a theory of inflation in a closed economy. Note, however, once *purchasing power parity* (PPP) theory is incorporated, the quantity theory becomes an *open economy monetary model*.

2. For a quirky view, see N. Kaldor, *The Scourge of Monetarism*, Oxford University Press, 1982.

This model is discussed in detail in Chapter 20.

It is of interest to review the relationship between the change in the money supply and inflation in Ireland. In Figure 10.1 we saw that the velocity of circulation of money declined significantly in recent years. Figure 10.2 shows the relationship between the growth in the Irish money supply (M3) and Irish inflation over the period 1966 to 1997. The money supply series has been lagged one period in order to allow for the time it takes for changes in the money supply to translate into inflation. (For example, the rate of growth of the money supply in 1996 would be expected to affect inflation in 1997.) It can be seen that there is a very weak relationship between the two series. This is particularly evident after 1991 when the money supply increased significantly while the inflation rate remained low. The lack of a relationship between the money supply and the rate of inflation is important even in a small open economy such as Ireland.

10.3 Monetary Policy

In the remaining sections of this chapter, we explain how changes in the money supply impact on aggregate demand, output and employment. Figure 10.3 presents an overview of the key diagrams underlying the analysis. The lower diagram shows equilibrium in the *money market*. In this market, the supply (M^s) and a demand (M^d) for money determines the *nominal* interest rate (i). An increase in the money supply, for example, will shift the M^s line out to the right and this reduces the interest rate.

The centre diagram shows the *marginal efficiency of investment* (MEI) line. This line illustrates an inverse relationship between the interest rate and investment (I). An increase in interest rates leads to a reduction in investment and vice versa.

Finally, the upper diagram represents *equilibrium in the goods and services market*. This is the familiar aggregate supply (AS) and demand (AD) developed in Chapter 3. The main point is that changes in investment (brought about by changes in the interest rate) shift the AD line. An increase in investment will shift the AD line up to the right and vice versa.

Taking the three diagrams together, the central bank can influence real output and the price level as follows. An increase in the money supply leads to a fall in interest rates. Via the MEI line, this leads to an increase in investment. The rise in investment shifts the AD curve out to the right and both real GNP and the price level increase. A reduction in the money supply would have the opposite effect.

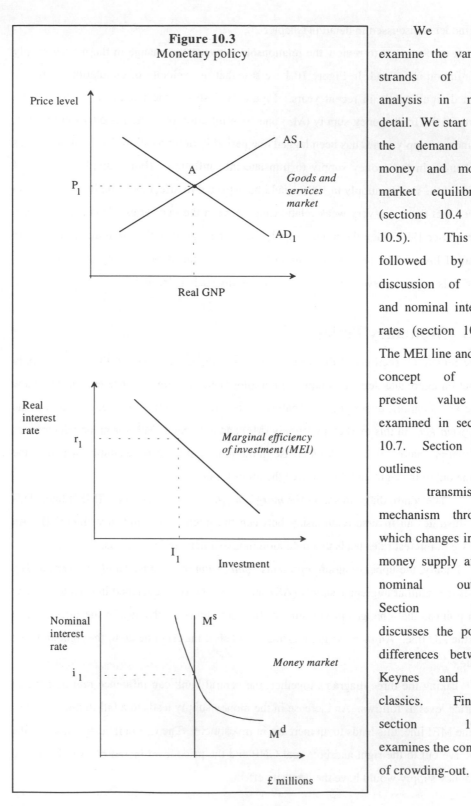

Figure 10.3
Monetary policy

Price level

AS$_1$

A

P$_1$

*Goods and
services
market*

AD$_1$

Real GNP

Real
interest
rate

r$_1$

*Marginal efficiency
of investment (MEI)*

I$_1$

Investment

Nominal
interest
rate

M^s

i$_1$

Money market

M^d

£ millions

We now examine the various strands of this analysis in more detail. We start with the demand for money and money market equilibrium (sections 10.4 and 10.5). This is followed by a discussion of real and nominal interest rates (section 10.6). The MEI line and the concept of net present value is examined in section 10.7. Section 10.8 outlines the transmission mechanism through which changes in the money supply affect nominal output. Section 10.9 discusses the policy differences between Keynes and the classics. Finally, section 10.10 examines the concept of crowding-out.

10.4 The Demand for Money

In this section we discuss the Keynesian *theory of liquidity preference* or the demand for money. At first sight, the concept of the demand for money (M^d) may appear rather odd. If you ask someone what is her "demand for money", the answer is likely to be "infinite" or something to that effect. However, the term "demand for money" is used by economists in a rather special way and does not refer simply to the desire to be rich.

To understand what economists mean by the demand for money, we start from the consideration that *wealth* can be stored in many forms: money, government stocks, company shares, works of art, houses and so on. Why do people keep some of their wealth in money as opposed to the alternatives?

There are two important differences between money and the alternatives.

- Money is *liquid*, that is, its value is known and it can be easily and quickly converted into purchasing power. On the other hand, government stocks, company shares and other stores of value give a return, but they are in varying degrees *illiquid*, that is, they cannot be used as a medium of exchange and it can take time to convert them into cash. Moreover, the value of these assets can change, giving rise to some uncertainty as to how much they are really worth.

- Money does not give a *return* over time whereas the other assets give a return. Note, however, that the borderlines between the different categories of assets are not rigid. Some liquid assets such as deposit accounts and some current accounts earn interest.

These considerations shed light on the reasons why people forgo the return available on other assets and keep some of their wealth in money or cash.

Transaction and precautionary motives

Keynes developed his theory of liquidity preference to account for people's desire to hold cash.[3] He analysed the reasons for holding cash under the headings of the *transaction*, *precautionary* and *speculative* motives. Let us now examine each of these in turn.

People need cash for *transaction* purposes, that is, to do their shopping, buy lunch, pay bus fares, etc. No matter how rich one is, it is hard to purchase a meal or a suit of clothes without paying with cash or something very close to cash (such as a credit card). Keynes described the transaction motive for holding money as the need "to bridge the

---

3. J. M. Keynes, *The General Theory of Employment, Interest and Money*, London: Macmillan, 1936.

interval between the receipt of income and its disbursement".[4] The more frequently people are paid, the smaller this interval and hence the smaller the demand for cash balances for this purpose. Also, improvements in the banking system have made it easier to transfer money between accounts and hence to minimise the amount of actual cash that has to be held for transaction purposes.

The *precautionary* motive is the desire to hold money to cater for unexpected contingencies (accidents, illness, etc.) or opportunities that may arise. According to Keynes, people hold cash to "provide for contingencies requiring sudden expenditure and for unforeseen opportunities of advantageous purchases".[5]

It is reasonable to assume that the amount of money demanded for transactions and precautionary reasons depends on the level of income. The richer a person is, the more expensive her lifestyle and the more money she needs for transaction and precautionary reasons. The same is true at the macro level. As national income or GNP increases, there is an increase in the demand for money for transaction purposes. An increase in GNP leads to an increase in the demand for money and a fall in GNP reduces the demand for money. The transaction and precautionary motives for holding money may therefore be written as:

$$M^d = f(GNP) \qquad\qquad f_1 > 0 \qquad\qquad (4)$$

Equation (4) states that the demand for money is *a function of* nominal GNP. The $f_1 > 0$ indicates that an increase in GNP results in a higher demand for money.

Note:

Causation runs from the variable inside the brackets to the variable on the left-hand side. As a result, the variables inside the bracket are referred to as *explanatory* or *independent* variables and the variable on the left-hand side is the *dependent* variable.

The speculative demand for money

In addition to the desire to hold money to finance day-to-day transactions and eventualities, Keynes believed that people hold money with the "object of securing profit from knowing better than the market what the future will bring forth".[6] He called this the *speculative motive*. To understand the speculative motive we need to look at the workings

---

4. J. M. Keynes, op. cit., p. 195.

5. J. M. Keynes, op. cit., p. 196.

6. J. M. Keynes, op. cit., p. 170.

Table 10.1			
The relationship between interest rates and bond prices			
1. Interest rate on bank deposit	20%	10%	5%
2. Fixed bond coupon	£10	£10	£10
3. Price of bonds	£50	£100	£200
4. Yield on bonds (– coupon/price)	20%	10%	5%

The bond market Bonds issued by a company differ from shares in the company in a number of important ways.

- Shareholders own a proportion of the company and have voting rights which give them some control over the operations of the company. This ownership entitles them to an uncertain dividend which depends on the profits of the company.

- In contrast, bondholders lend money to a company for a specific period of time and do not have any control over the company's affairs; bonds pay a fixed monetary return (*coupon*) until the maturity date, so the bondholder knows with certainty how much income she will receive from the bond. For example, a bond with a face value of £2,000 and a coupon of £100 that matures in the year 2010 entitles the bondholder to a sum of £100 every year until 2010 and repayment of the £2,000 principal in 2010. A bond which is never redeemed but which pays an income indefinitely is known as a *perpetuity*.

The government is the largest issuer of bonds in most modern economies, and government bonds provide a convenient medium for speculators trying to make *capital gains*. To see how this may be done, we need to consider what determines bond prices and bond yields. Consider the data in Table 10.1.

- Line 1 displays three rates of interest on bank deposits.

- Line 2 shows the *fixed coupon* payable on a government bond. This is assumed to be £10.

- *Arbitrage* should now ensure that the yield (per cent) on the bond is equalised with that on bank deposits. The yield on a bond is defined as the coupon divided by the price of the bond. If the coupon is £10 and the price of the bond is £100 then the yield is 10 per cent. (See Box 10.1 for a discussion of the concept of arbitrage.) The price of the bond required to ensure that the bond yield is the same as the interest rate is given in line 3.

- The only way for the yield on bonds to change, given that the coupon is fixed, is for the *price* of the bond to vary. (We assume that it is a perpetuity, so that what matters to an investor is its current and future yields, rather than its value at maturity.) Line 4 shows the yield on bonds that is equalised with that on bank accounts.

- Notice what happens when the interest rate falls from 20 to 10 to 5 per cent. Arbitrage will ensure that the yield on government bonds also falls from 20 to 10 to 5 per cent. For this to happen, the price of the bond must rise from £50 to £100 to £200. Therefore, as interest rates fall, bond prices rise and, conversely, as interest rates increase, bond prices fall.

Note:

There are many different interest rates, for example, the rates on short and long-term government stocks, on low and high-risk company bonds (the latter became known as "junk bonds" during the 1980s), as well as the rates charged by the banks on loans and paid on deposits. All these rates tend to move together, allowing us to refer to an average or representative interest rate as "the" interest rate.

Speculation   The inverse relationship between interest rates and bond prices means that bondholders stand to make a capital *gain* when interest rates *fall* and a capital loss when interest rates rise. Investors should therefore buy bonds if they expect interest rates to fall and sell them if they expect interest rates to rise. This strategy provides the basis of the Keynesian speculative motive for holding cash.

Keynes's "normal rate of interest"   Keynes believed that a "normal" rate of interest existed. He argued that departures from this rate are viewed as temporary. If interest rates rise above the normal rate, the expectation will be that they will eventually fall. Similarly, if interest rates fall below the normal rate, the expectation will be that they will rise.

Suppose, for example, that the normal rate of interest is considered to be 10 per cent and interest rates increase from 10 per cent to 11 per cent. Investors holding bonds suffer a capital loss. However, the expectation is now that interest rates will fall back to the normal level of 10 per cent. Investors should therefore reduce their money holdings and purchase bonds in anticipation of making a capital gain sometime in the future. Hence the rise in the interest rate is associated with a fall in the demand for cash balances. Conversely, a fall in the interest rate (associated with the expectation that interest rates will rise) leads to an increase in the demand for money.

The relationship between the interest rate (i) and the demand for money can be written:

$$M^d = f(i) \qquad\qquad f_1 < 0 \qquad\qquad (5)$$

where $f_1 < 0$ indicates that an increase in the interest rate causes a *fall* in M^d, and vice versa.

Note:

The inverse relationship between the interest rate and the demand for money could also be explained in terms of the *opportunity cost* of holding cash. As we saw above, wealth held as cash does not earn a return, whereas wealth held as bonds or in other assets does. By holding cash, a person is therefore forgoing the interest that could have been earned on bonds, for example. Thus, when the interest rate is high, the opportunity cost of holding cash balances is also high, and it is to be expected that the public will economise on their holdings of cash. It is therefore only realistic to include the rate of interest among the determinants of the demand for money.

Combining the transaction, precautionary and speculative motives

Combining equations (4) and (5) we can account for all the motives for holding money and write the demand for money function as:

$$M^d = f(GNP, i) \qquad\qquad f_1 > 0, f_2 < 0 \qquad\qquad (6)$$

Equation (6) states that the demand for money is a function of nominal GNP and the interest rate. As before, f_1 and f_2 indicate how the explanatory variables influence the dependent variable. Separating nominal GNP into its real and price components, equation (6) can be rewritten as:

$$M^d = f(\text{real GNP}, P, i) \qquad\qquad f_1 > 0, f_2 > 0, f_3 < 0 \qquad\qquad (7)$$

Equation (7) states that the demand for money is positively related to both real GNP and the price level (P), but negatively to the rate of interest. Rearranging:

$$M^d/P = f(\text{real GNP}, i) \qquad f_1 > 0, f_2 < 0 \tag{8}$$

Equation (8) expresses the demand for money in real terms or the demand for *real money* or *real cash balances* (M^s/P). This is a function of real GNP and the rate of interest. An increase in real GNP increases the demand for real cash balances and a rise in the rate of interest reduces it.

A demand for money schedule is drawn in Figure 10.4. The downward-sloping line shows the inverse relationship between the rate of interest on the vertical axis, and the demand for money on the horizontal axis. An increase in the interest rate reduces the demand for money and, conversely, a fall in the interest rate increases the demand for money.

Note:

that the slope of the demand for money curve is not linear. At low interest rates the curve is flat or horizontal. The reason for this is that at low interest rates there may be unanimity among investors that interest rates will rise in the future, and if this happens bond prices will fall. In order to avoid speculative losses in the bond market investors therefore keep their wealth in cash balances. Therefore, as the rate of interest falls to a low level, the demand for money increases very rapidly. This is reflected in the diagram in the flat portion of the demand for money curve.

Nominal GNP determines the *position* (or location) of the demand for money schedule. Whereas the relationship between the interest rate and the demand for money is shown by movements *along* the line, the relationship between GNP and the demand for money is shown by *shifts* of the line. An increase in GNP shifts the M^d schedule to the right; a fall in GNP shifts it to the left. (To understand why certain variables cause curves to shift, refer to the discussion of the factors that shift the

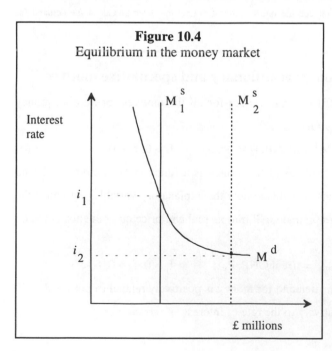

Figure 10.4
Equilibrium in the money market

222

aggregate supply and demand curves in Chapter 3.)

10.5 Money Market Equilibrium

In Figure 10.4 the *money supply* (M^s) schedule is combined with a demand for money (M^d) schedule. The money supply is shown as a *vertical* line which indicates that changes in the interest rate do not affect the supply of money. This assumes that the money supply is completely controlled by the monetary authorities or central bank. Put another way, we are assuming that the money supply is exogenous. (If changes in interest rates had a positive effect on the money supply, the M^s curve would slope upwards to the right.)

The important point here is that the interaction of the supply and demand for money determines the nominal interest rate (i). In other words, the rate of interest is the price of money and, like other prices, it is determined by the forces of supply and demand. At an interest rate of i_1, the supply and demand for money are equal. The money market is in equilibrium.

Note:

If the interest rate is above i_1, there is an excess supply of money and the interest rate will fall towards the equilibrium rate. If the interest rate is below i_1, there is an excess demand for money and the interest rate will rise to the equilibrium rate.

Figure 10.4 also illustrates what happens to the interest rate when the central bank increases the money supply through, for example, open market operations. The money supply (M^s) line moves out to the right and the interest rate falls from i_1 to the new equilibrium level, i_2. An increase in the money supply therefore reduces the interest rate. Conversely, a reduction in the money supply leads to an increase in the interest rate.

As mentioned in the previous section, the demand for money schedule is horizontal at low interest rates. An increase in the money supply along the flat portion of the demand for money curve would not lower interest rates and, as we shall see, monetary policy would be ineffective. This situation is known as the *liquidity trap*.

Note that an increase in nominal GNP will shift the demand for money (M^d) curve upwards to the right. The resulting excess demand for money increases the interest rate from i_1 to i_2. Similarly, a fall in nominal GNP will shift the M^d curve downwards and interest rates will fall.

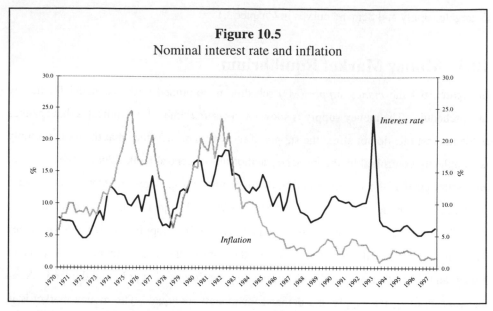

Figure 10.5
Nominal interest rate and inflation

10.6 Nominal and Real Interest Rates

In referring to "interest rates" we have made no distinction between *real* and *nominal* rates. In fact we have been referring to the nominal interest rate, *i*, which is the rate quoted in the newspapers or by banks and issuers of bonds. The *real* rate, r, is defined as the nominal interest rate *minus* the inflation rate, π

$$\text{Real interest rate} = \text{nominal interest rate} - \text{inflation rate}$$

or

$$r = i - \pi \tag{9}$$

Equation (9) is referred to as the *Fisher equation* after one of America's greatest economists, Irving Fisher (1867-1947), who taught at Yale University. Since interest rates are forward looking (interest is paid or charged over the next six months or a year), and as we do not know what the rate of inflation will be in the future, the Fisher equation should be stated in terms of *expected* inflation, that is, π^e

$$r = i - \pi^e \tag{10}$$

Rearranging equation (10), we can also state that the nominal interest rate is equal to the real interest rate plus the inflation rate.

$$i = r + \pi^e \tag{11}$$

According to this equation, if the real interest rate is stable, a rise in the expected rate of inflation will lead to a one-to-one increase in the nominal interest rate. This is known as the *Fisher effect.*

224

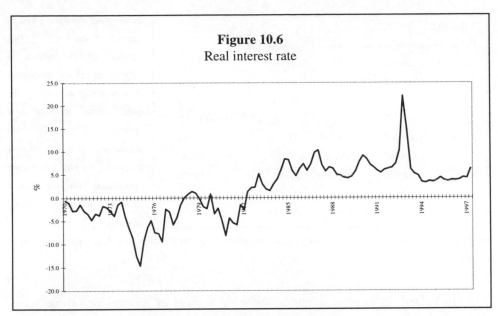

Figure 10.6
Real interest rate

Figure 10.5 shows the nominal interest rate and the inflation rate in Ireland between 1970 and 1997. The difference between the two series is the real interest rate. Figure 10.6 shows the real interest rate. It can be seen that in the 1970s and early 1980s, the real interest rate was negative, while a high positive real rate was recorded in the late 1980s and 1990s. From 1970-81 and 1982-97 the average real interest rate was –3.8 and 5.8 per cent respectively. The average over the entire period was 1.5 per cent.[7]

10.7 Investment and Interest Rates

Investment consists of acquiring or creating assets that generate future streams of income. Examples are building roads, factories and houses, and purchasing plant and equipment. Consider a firm that is contemplating investing in, say, new plant or machinery. It has three possible ways of financing this:

- Using retained earnings or profits
- Borrowing from a bank
- Selling new shares in the company on the stock exchange.

Note:
In the national income accounts, the magnitude corresponding to what we have labelled investment, I, is referred

---

7. The large "spike" in interest rates at the end of 1992 and early in 1993 was due to the currency crisis, which we discuss in a later chapter.

Table 10.2

Calculating net present value using a 5% discount rate

Year	Net income at end of year £ (1)	Discount factor £ (2)	Present value £ (3) = (1) × (2)
1	100,000	$1/(1.05) = 0.9524$	95,238
2	110,000	$1/(1.05)^2 = 0.9070$	99,773
3	105,000	$1/(1.05)^3 = 0.8638$	90,703

Total = £315,000   Project's NPV = £285,714

to as *gross domestic physical capital formation*. This totalled £7,524 million in 1996. Some of this investment is undertaken directly by the public sector; some of it is financed in part by state grants; and the rest is privately financed. In what follows we concentrate on the factors affecting privately financed investment, but similar considerations should apply to public sector investment, although political factors tend to complicate matters in this area

In Ireland, as in most countries, the main sources of finance for private sector investment are retained earnings and bank borrowing. (The stock market is mainly a market in existing, rather than new, shares, and most smaller and medium-sized companies are not listed on the stock exchange.) Because banks charge interest on their loans, it is easy to see why a higher rate of interest will tend to discourage borrowing, while a lower rate will tend to encourage it. But the rate of interest should also be taken into account when internally generated funds are being considered for use to finance a project. Firms should not regard these funds as free: they should take account of the opportunity cost of ploughing retained profits back into the firm. These funds should not be used for any purpose that does not promise at least as high a rate of return as could be earned from placing them in a bank deposit or buying bonds with them. Similarly, a firm's ability to raise money through the stock market depends on whether it can convince investors that it will use the funds profitably, guaranteeing them a return that is comparable to what they could earn from alternative uses of their money. Thus, the rate of interest will affect a firm's investment plans, *regardless of which of the three sources of funds it uses.*

Net present value   The effect of changes in the rate of interest on the profitability of an investment plan can be shown by employing the concept of the *net present value* (NPV), which is now routinely used in the evaluation of projects by firms, banks and governments.

To illustrate its use, let us suppose that you have the opportunity of investing in a

226

Table 10.3	
NPV and the interest rate	
Interest	NPV
rate	
%	£
0	315,000
2.5	299,763
5	285,714
7.5	272,731
10	260,706

project that is forecast to generate income over a three year period. For simplicity, we assume that no assets remain at the end of the three year project. We also ignore inflation, so that the above income flows are given in constant (year 1) prices.

How much would you be prepared to pay to buy into such a project? To answer this, we must *discount* the projected income stream to calculate its NPV.[8] Discounting is the inverse of the more familiar concept of compounding, according to which a sum of money, £x, invested today at r per cent is worth £x(1 + r) at the end of the year. Discounting inverts this process and asks: how much is £x to be paid at the end of a year worth today? What is its present value? The answer is £x/(1+ r). Extending this logic, the same sum paid at the end of two years has a present value of $£x/(1+r)^2$. Assuming a real interest rate of 5 per cent (r = 0.05), Table 10.2 shows how the net present value of the income stream given above is calculated. We use the *real* interest rate, r, to discount because this is the key rate in making investment decisions.

These calculations tell us that while this project yields an undiscounted income stream of £315,000, the discounted value or NPV of this income stream is £285,714, given an interest rate of 5 per cent.

The NPV can be thought of as the *demand price* of an investment project: it is the maximum that a person would be willing to pay to buy into it. If more than £285,714 has to be paid to invest in the above project, the investor would be better off putting his money in the bank and earning 5 per cent interest on it. If he can get in on the project for less than £285,714, then he should accept the opportunity as he will make more from the project than from the alternative use of the money.

Table 10.3 shows how the NPV of the hypothetical investment project falls as the interest rate increases. (The student should replicate the calculations in Table 10.3 using different discount rates to confirm these numbers.) It may be seen that the higher the rate of interest, the lower the value of the project to a prospective investor. As a consequence,

---

8. The significance of the "net" in NPV is that the income stream is net of costs: we are calculating the net income or profit from the investment.

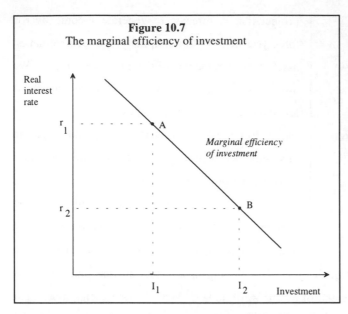

Figure 10.7
The marginal efficiency of investment

a rise in the interest rate can make a previously profitable project unprofitable. A fall in the interest rate can make an unprofitable project profitable. The interest rate has a greater effect on the NPV of projects that are long lived: some very capital intensive investments that have a very long life, such as electricity-generating projects, can only be profitable at low rates of interest.

Marginal efficiency of investment   It follows from this that an increase in the rate of interest will reduce the number of investment projects that people will want to undertake, and choke off the demand for funds for investment, while a fall in the rate of interest will increase the number of projects it is worth undertaking and increase the demand for investment funds.   There is, therefore, an inverse relationship between the interest rate and the demand for funds for investment.   This relationship is known as the *marginal efficiency of investment* (MEI) schedule and it is illustrated in Figure 10.7.   The interest rate is measured along the vertical axis and the level of investment along the horizontal axis.   If changes in the rate of interest have a weak effect on investment, then the MEI curve will be steep (inelastic).   If, on the other hand, changes in the rate of interest have a strong effect on investment, the curve will be flat.   The magnitude of the effect depends on the type of projects being considered: if they are mainly capital-intensive, long-lived projects, then the MEI will be very flat (elastic).

10.8 Monetary Policy in a Closed Economy

Let us now incorporate our model of the money market into the model of the economy we developed in earlier chapters. We shall not assume, as is done in the quantity theory of money, that the economy is at full employment: instead, we assume that there are

228

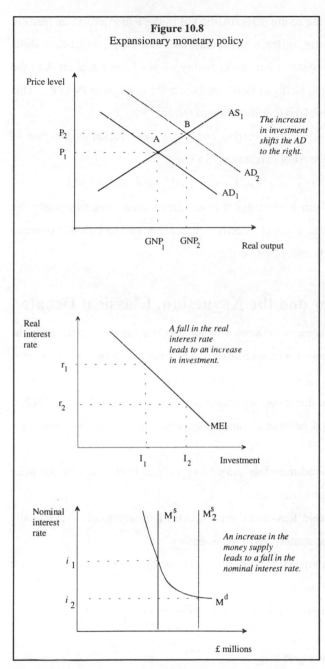

Figure 10.8
Expansionary monetary policy

The increase in investment shifts the AD to the right.

A fall in the real interest rate leads to an increase in investment.

An increase in the money supply leads to a fall in the nominal interest rate.

unemployed resources and that the level of real output and prices can change in response to changes in aggregate demand.

The expanded model of the economy contains two markets: the goods or product market and the money market. In the goods market, equilibrium occurs when aggregate supply (GNP) is equal to aggregate demand (or total expenditure). The demand side of a closed economy can be broken down in its components, private and public consumption expenditure and investment (C, G and I). In the money market, the supply and demand for money determine the interest rate. The link between the goods and money market is the MEI curve.

The authorities have two *policy instruments,* government expenditure and taxation (*fiscal policy*) and the money supply and interest rates (*monetary policy*), with which to influence output, income and prices.

Figure 10.8 illustrates the effect of an increase in the money supply. In the lower diagram, the central bank increases the money supply from M^s_1 to M^s_2. The interest rate falls from i_1 to i_2. The fall in the nominal interest rate leads to a fall in the real interest rate via the Fisher equation. In the centre diagram, the fall in the real interest rate leads to an increase in investment. Finally, in the top diagram, the increase in investment shifts the aggregate demand schedule upwards and the economy moves from the point A to the point B. Real GNP increases from GNP_1 to GNP_2 and the price level from P_1 to P_2. This increase in real output should also lead to lower unemployment.

Thus, the link between the money market and the goods market is the rate of interest through its effect on the level of investment. In short:

$$\uparrow M^S \rightarrow \downarrow i \rightarrow \downarrow r \rightarrow \uparrow I \rightarrow \uparrow AD \rightarrow \uparrow GNP \rightarrow \uparrow NI \rightarrow \downarrow U$$

Note that fiscal policy is much more direct in its effects than monetary policy: an increase in G increases aggregate demand directly, whereas an increase in M^S operates indirectly through its effect on the rate of interest.

10.9   Monetary Policy and the Keynesian, Classical Debate

We shall now discuss the differences between Keynes and the classics concerning the effects of fiscal and monetary policy on the economy. The extreme *Keynesian* position is that:

- fiscal policy is effective and that monetary policy is ineffective in influencing GNP.

In contrast, neoclassical economists and monetarists such as Milton Friedman argue that:

- fiscal policy is ineffective and monetary policy has a significant effect on the price level and little or no impact on real output.

The disagreement between Keynesian and neoclassical economists essentially revolves about two relationships, namely, those between:

- the interest rate and the demand for money. This is referred to as the *interest elasticity of the demand for money.*

- the interest rate and investment, that is, the *marginal efficiency of investment* curve.

Keynesian position   Keynesians argue that:

- the demand for money curve is relatively *flat*. This means that an increase in the money supply leads to a *small* decrease in the interest rate.

- the MEI curve is relatively steep (inelastic). Changes in the interest rate have a *weak* effect on investment. He emphasised factors such as changes in the level of business confidence and in expectations about the growth in national income which could easily swamp the influence of the rate of interest.

The effect of these two assumptions is that monetary policy has a weak effect on output and employment. A given increase in the money supply leads to a small change in the nominal interest rate. This, in turn, will have a weak effect on investment. Overall, the AD curve will not move very much to the right and there will be little or no change in real output and the price level. (We suggest that the reader experiments with Figure 10.8 in order to verify that this is the case.)

Note:

If the demand for money curve is horizontal at low interest rates, an increase in the money supply along this portion of the M^d curve will have no effect on the interest rate. In this case, monetary policy cannot be used to increase output and employment. This is known as the *liquidity trap*.

Classical position Neoclassical economists, [9] on the other hand, argue that:

- the demand for money curve is *steep* (inelastic). An increase in the money supply will lead to a large fall in the nominal interest rate.
- the MEI curve is relatively *flat* (or elastic). Changes in the interest rate have a strong effect on investment.

Taking these two assumptions together, an expansionary monetary policy leads to a significant fall in interest rates, which in turn provokes a large rise in investment. However, the classical school also argues that the AS curve is *vertical* at full-employment (potential) GNP. The shift of the AD curve to the right leads to a large hike in the price level and has no effect on real output and employment.

The classical position is illustrated in Figure 10.9. The implication is that monetary policy (changes in the money supply) will have an important effect on aggregate demand and the price level. This outcome is in accordance with the conclusions of the quantity theory of money discussed in section 10.2.

Neoclassical economists also believe that fiscal policy has little or no effect on GNP. At first sight this appears rather odd. After all, an increase in government expenditure (G) boosts aggregate demand and GNP. Hence changes in government expenditure must influence GNP. Neoclassical economists, however, point to *crowding-*

---

9. An early exposition of the classical position is given in Irving Fisher, *The Purchasing Power of Money*, New York: Macmillan, 1911. An early and very influential paper is Milton Friedman, "The Quantity Theory of Money: A Restatement", in Milton Friedman (ed.) *Studies in the Quantity Theory of Money*, University of Chicago Press, 1956.

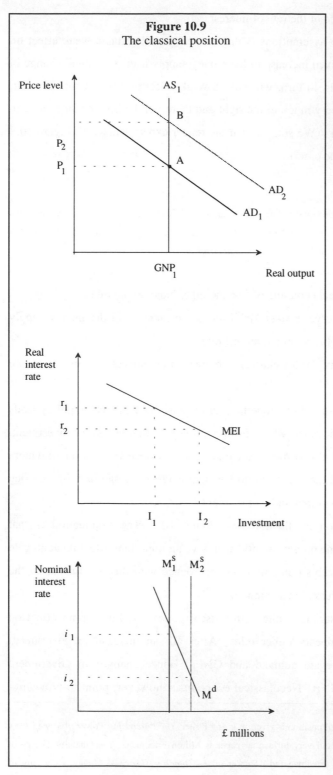

Figure 10.9
The classical position

out as a reason why fiscal policy is ineffective. We shall examine this issue in the next section. A brief review of the Irish literature relating to the demand for money and the MEI curve is given in the Appendix.

10.10 Crowding-Out

If there are unemployed resources and the economy is operating at less than full capacity, then the *short-run* AS curve may be upward sloping. If this is the case, then fiscal policy (changes in government expenditure and taxation) must lead to changes in aggregate demand and therefore GNP. However, neoclassical economists would still not accept that fiscal policy is an effective policy instrument. The reason is the crowding-out effect.

Briefly, the argument is as follows: an expansionary fiscal policy may increase aggregate demand and real output. In

232

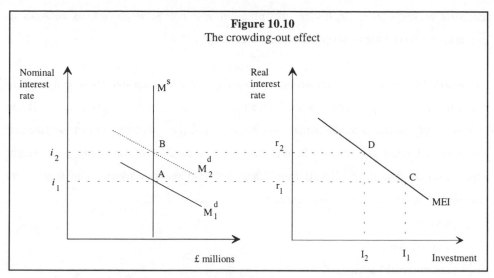

Figure 10.10
The crowding-out effect

short:

$$\uparrow G \rightarrow \uparrow AD \rightarrow \uparrow \text{nominal GNP}$$

However, the increase in GNP increases the demand for money (M^d) via the transactions motive. If there is no increase in the money supply this will push up interest rates. The rise in interest rates will, in turn, lower the level of investment. The initial increase in government expenditure thus leads to a reduction in private sector spending. Investment has been crowded out by government expenditure

$$\uparrow GNP \rightarrow \uparrow M^d \rightarrow \uparrow i \rightarrow \uparrow r \rightarrow \downarrow I$$

If $\uparrow G = \downarrow I$, there is 100 per cent crowding out. In this case, AD and GNP revert back to their original level and fiscal policy is completely ineffective. This is the extreme neoclassical position.

Figure 10.10 illustrates the crowding-out effect. The expansionary fiscal policy increases GNP. The increase in GNP, in turn, shifts the demand for money curve upwards from M^d_1 to M^d_2 (left-hand diagram). The interest rate rises from i_1 to i_2 along the vertical axis. In the right-hand diagram, the increase in the real interest rate reduces investment. In terms of the components of aggregate demand, the fall in investment offsets the initial increase in government expenditure and aggregate demand may revert back to its initial level.

The elasticity of the MEI schedule is what determines the degree of crowding-out. The neoclassical contention that the MEI is flat (elastic) at the current interest rate means that a small increase in the interest rate will have a relatively large effect on investment. If this is the case, crowding-out will be important. If, however, as the Keynesians argue, the MEI curve is steep (inelastic), crowding-out will not be important, as changes in interest rates have little or no effect on investment.

Monetary financing   It is important to note that the crowding-out effect only occurs when the money supply remains unchanged in the face of a fiscal expansion.   If the money supply increases as the demand for money rises, the interest rate need not rise and crowding-out need not occur.   In this context, the method of financing government expenditure is important.   Recall from Chapter 6 that the government can finance its borrowing requirement from four sources:

i.   abroad

ii.   Central Bank

iii.   commercial banks

iv.   domestic non-bank public.

Sources i, ii and iii are referred to as *government monetary financing (GMF)*. Borrowing from these sources increases the money supply.   Borrowing from source iv does not affect the money supply.

In Ireland, government borrowing has relied heavily on monetary financing. Consequently, increases in government expenditure have tended to be accompanied by increases in the money supply and interest rates have not been unduly affected. Moreover, in a small open economy such as Ireland, higher interest rates tend to attract capital inflows from the rest of the world.   Both these considerations reduce the risks of crowding-out.   These are points that we shall develop more systematically in a later chapter.

In the course of our discussion of Ireland's economic performance during the second half of the 1980s, it was pointed out that a contractionary fiscal policy was followed by a period of increased growth (Chapter 8).   One possible explanation of this episode is that a form of "reverse crowding-out" or "crowding-in" occurred.   According to this view, the reduced pressure on the domestic money market due to the lower deficit led to a reduction in interest rates, which stimulated private sector investment.   For this interpretation of events to be valid, private sector spending would have had to increase by *more* than the reduction in public sector spending.   This is more extreme than the case of complete crowding-out on which the classical case for the ineffectiveness of fiscal policy is based.

10.11 Conclusion

In this chapter we have extended our basic macroeconomic model by incorporating a money market. The extended model consists of a goods market and a money market and the authorities can influence the economy through fiscal policy or monetary policy. The key points covered in this chapter included:

- The quantity theory of money as a theory of inflation
- The demand for money. Changes in nominal GNP and interest rates affect the demand for money
- The interaction of the supply and demand for money determine the nominal rate of interest
- The Fisher equation which distinguishes between nominal and real interest rates
- The link between interest rates and investment is known as the marginal efficiency of investment schedule (MEI)
- Monetary policy. Changes in the money supply affect aggregate demand and GNP via the real rate of interest and its influence on the level of investment
- The differences between Keynes and the classics with regard to fiscal and monetary policy and the concept of crowding-out.

Appendix

Review of the Irish evidence relating to the demand for money and the MEI curve

A number of authors, including Pratschke and O'Connell (1973), Browne and O'Connell (1978), Browne (1984) and Hurley and Guiomard (1989), have studied the demand for money function for Ireland.[10] Browne and O'Connell estimate that the interest elasticity of the demand for money is − 0.18. This means that a one per cent increase in the interest rate leads to a 0.18 per cent decrease in the demand for money. Hurley and Guiomard find a weak relationship between the interest rate and the demand for money (in fact the interest rate sometimes appears with a positive rather than a negative sign). These two studies therefore tend to offer support for the monetarist case. The demand for money curve for Ireland appears to be steep (inelastic).

What evidence there is for Ireland indicates that interest rates have a weak effect on investment, that is, the MEI is steep. A recent survey of the evidence concluded that "a one per cent increase in interest rates has a negligible effect in the first year and, after three years, the effect is to leave GNP one-third of a percentage point lower that would otherwise have been the case".[11]

The evidence on the effects of interest rates on the Irish economy, therefore, tends towards a Keynesian view of the demand for investment funds, but towards a classical view of the demand for money.

---

10. J. L. Pratschke and T. O'Connell, "The Demand for Money in Ireland, 1948-60, A preliminary Report", mimeo, Central Bank of Ireland, 1973. F. X. Browne and T. O'Connell, "The Demand for Money Function in Ireland: Estimation and Stability", *The Economic and Social Review*, April, Vol. 9, 1978. F. X. Browne, "The Short Run Demand for Money with Exogenous Money Creation in an SOE", *Technical Paper*, 10/RT/84, Central Bank of Ireland, 1984. M. Hurley and C. Guiomard, "Determinants of Money Demand in Ireland 1971 to 1988: Rounding up the Usual Suspects", *The Economic and Social Review*, Vol. 21, No. 1, October 1989.

11. Jim Nugent and Tom O'Connell, "The Effect of Interest Rates on the Economy". Paper to ESRI Banking Research Centre Conference, *Interest Rate Movements: Causes and Effects*, 9 December 1993. See also F. X. Browne, "Loan Market Price and Quantity Effects in a Production Smoothing Model of Inventory Investment", Central Bank of Ireland, *Technical Paper*, 11/RT/84, November 1984. A. Leddin, "The Impact of Credit Control on Consumer Durable Expenditures and Fixed Investment in the Irish Economy", *Irish Business and Administrative Research*, Vol. 8, No. 20, 1986.

Chapter 11

Aggregate Demand and the Money Market: A More Complete Model of the Economy

11.1 Introduction

In this chapter we bring the elements of the analysis outlined in the previous chapters together into a more complete model of the economy. We do this by using IS and LM curves, which depict equilibrium in the goods and money markets respectively. The focus is on a closed economy and we assume that the *price level is fixed*. In later chapters we shall extend the model to analysing the open economy and the problem of inflation.

The "I" in IS stands for investment and "S" for savings. The "L" in LM denotes liquidity preference (demand for money) and "M" the money supply. The Nobel prize-winning English economist John Hicks (1904-1989) developed the IS-LM framework very shortly after the publication of Keynes's *General Theory*.[1]

11.2 Equilibrium in the Goods Market: IS

The IS line describes the market for goods and services or, simply, the goods market. Equilibrium in this market requires that the value of what is being produced (GNP) equals total spending or aggregate demand (AD). Aggregate demand, in turn, is identically equal to the sum of consumer expenditure (C), investment (I) and government current consumption (G). In this closed economy, we ignore exports and imports.

$$GNP = AD \equiv C + I + G \qquad (1)$$

We now return to the consumption function, which was outlined in Chapter 5. In its simplest form, the consumption function states that consumer expenditure is a function of income or GNP.

---

1. J. R. Hicks, "Mr Keynes and the Classics, A Suggested Interpretation", *Econometrica*, Vol. 6 April 1937.

$$C = a + c \, \text{GNP} \qquad (2)$$

The intercept term a represents autonomous consumer expenditure, that is, expenditure not influenced by changes in income or GNP. The coefficient c indicates what proportion of extra income is consumed and is referred to as the marginal propensity to consume (MPC).

We now introduce the relationship between investment and the (real) interest rate (r). Note that as the inflation rate is assumed constant we can use either nominal or real interest rates. As we saw in the previous chapter, when discussing the marginal efficiency of investment (MEI) line, an increase in interest rates leads to a fall in investment and, conversely, a fall in the interest rate increases investment.

$$I = d - b \, \text{r} \qquad (3)$$

The intercept term d indicates autonomous investment, that is, investment in plant and machinery not influenced by changes in the interest rate. The coefficient b indicates how investment reacts to changes in the interest rate (r). Substituting (2) and (3) into (1) we have:

$$\text{GNP} = a + c \, \text{GNP} + d - b \, \text{r} + G \qquad (4)$$

Rearranging:

$$\text{GNP}(1 - c) = (a + d + G) - b \, \text{r} \qquad (5)$$

Let total autonomous expenditure $(a + d + G) = Z$ then:

$$\text{GNP} = (Z - b \, \text{r})/(1 - c) \qquad (6)$$

It can be seen from (6) that there is a negative relationship between GNP and r. Basically, what happens is that an increase in the interest rate lowers the level of investment which in turn reduces aggregate demand and ultimately GNP, and vice versa. In short:

$$\uparrow \text{r} \rightarrow \downarrow \text{I} \rightarrow \downarrow \text{AD} \rightarrow \downarrow \text{GNP}$$

Figure 11.1 outlines the effect of a decrease in the interest rate using the Keynesian cross diagram. In the upper diagram a reduction in the interest rate from r_1 to r_2 increases investment. The aggregate demand line shifts upwards and the economy moves from the point A to the point B. GNP increases along the horizontal axis from GNP_1 to GNP_2. In the lower diagram the point C represents the initial combination of interest rates and output, which is one point on the IS line. Similarly, the point B represents the r_2, GNP_2 combination, which is a second point on the IS line. By shifting

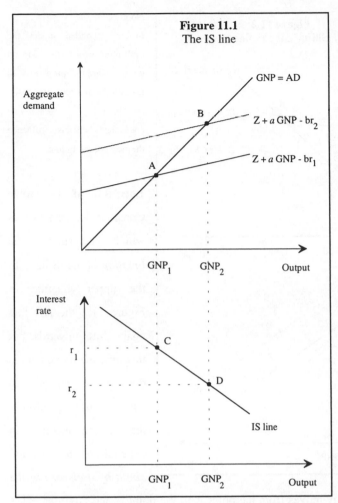

Figure 11.1
The IS line

the AD line in this way we can trace out each equilibrium interest rate, GNP combination, and construct the complete IS line. Each point on the IS curve represents equilibrium in the goods market.

Slope of IS curve The slope of the IS line indicates how a change in the interest rate affects GNP. It can be seen from equation (6) that the interest rate affects GNP via the b coefficient and the $1/(1-c)$ term. Hence the slope of the IS line depends on:

- the b coefficient, which represents the link between the interest rate and investment (the MEI line).

- the $1/(1-c)$ term which reflects the link between investment and GNP (the multiplier).

    It follows therefore that:

- The IS curve will be flat (elastic), [a given change in the interest rate will have a large effect on investment] if b is large (elastic MEI line) and/or $1/(1-c)$, (the multiplier) is large.

    Conversely,

- The IS curve will be steep (inelastic) if b is small and/or the multiplier $1/(1-c)$ is small.

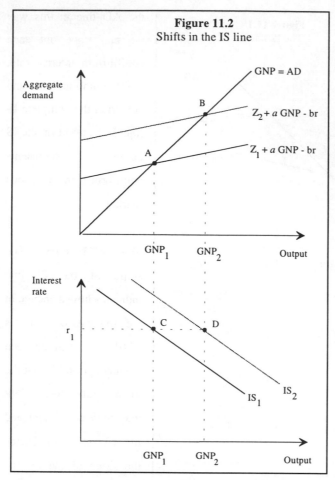

Figure 11.2
Shifts in the IS line

Note:

In an expanded model the multiplier would also depend on the marginal propensity to tax and the marginal propensity to import. These two coefficients will also influence the slope of the IS line.

Location of IS curve

Consider now the factors which determine the *location* of the IS line. In the upper diagram in Figure 11.2 the AD line again shifts upwards, but this time the movement is due to a change in autonomous expenditure, that is, an increase in expenditure *not brought about by a change in the interest rate*. The economy moves from the point A to the point B and GNP increases along the horizontal axis.

In the lower diagram, the point C represents the initial r_1, GNP_1 combination. The increase in autonomous expenditure has increased output from GNP_1 to GNP_2. This means that the point D is a point on the new IS line. The point D represents the original interest rate, r_1, and the new higher level of output, GNP_2. A change in any of the components of autonomous expenditure, consumption (C), investment (I) or government expenditure (G), will shift the IS line. An increase in C, I, or G causes the IS line to shift outwards. Thus an expansionary fiscal policy will shift the IS line to the right and a deflationary fiscal policy will shift it to the left. (In an open economy, changes in the level of net exports, X – M, will also shift the IS line upwards.)

240

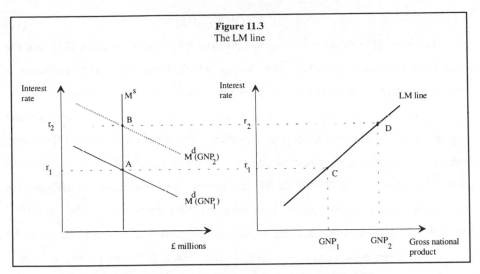

Figure 11.3
The LM line

11.3   Equilibrium in the Money Market: LM

Consider now the relationship between the interest rate and GNP as reflected in the money market. The level of nominal GNP and the interest rate determine the demand for money.

$$M^d = e\, GNP - f\, r \qquad (7)$$

There is a positive relationship between GNP and M^d. The coefficient e indicates how a change in GNP influences the demand for money and is referred to as the *income elasticity of the demand for money*. The larger the coefficient e, the greater the effect GNP has on M^d. The interest rate reflects the speculative demand for money. There is an inverse relationship between r and M^d. The coefficient f shows how changes in the interest rate affect the demand for money and is referred to as the *interest elasticity of the demand for money*.[2]

It is assumed that the central bank controls the money supply (M^s). Hence the equilibrium condition in the money market is:

$$M^s = M^d \qquad (8)$$

Substitute equation (7) into (8) to obtain:

$$M^s = e\, GNP - f\, r \qquad (9)$$

Solving equation (9) for the interest rate, we have:

---

2. The demand for money is a function of the *real* interest rate, r, whereas in Chapter 10 we related it to the *nominal* interest rate, i. (We can reconcile these two treatments by assuming that inflationary expectations, π^e, are zero.)

241

$$r = (e \text{ GNP} - M^s)/f \qquad (10)$$

Equation (10) shows that there is a positive relationship between GNP and the interest rate in the money market. The LM line, which shows the r, GNP combinations consistent with equilibrium in the money market, is therefore upward sloping.

Figure 11.3 illustrates why this positive relationship exists. The left-hand diagram shows equilibrium in the money market. The supply and demand for money interact to determine the interest rate on the vertical axis. Recall from the previous chapter that changes in GNP shift the M^d line upwards, and vice versa. Initially, we are at the point A in the money market. Suppose now GNP increases from GNP_1 to GNP_2. The M^d line shifts upwards and the money market moves to the point B, with the interest rate increasing to r_2 along the vertical axis. Hence, in the money market there is a positive relationship between the level of GNP and the interest rate that is consistent with equilibrium in the money market. This is represented in the right-hand diagram as an upward-sloping line labelled LM. In short:

$$\uparrow \text{GNP} \rightarrow \uparrow M^d \rightarrow \uparrow r$$

In the right-hand diagram the point C represents the r_1, GNP_1 combination. This is one point on the LM line. The point D, in turn, indicates the new r_2, GNP_2 combination and is another point on the LM line. By shifting the M^d line in the money market we can trace out the various interest rate, GNP combinations consistent with equilibrium in the money market. These points lie on the LM line.

Slope of the LM curve Consider now the factors which determine the slope of the LM line. A steep LM line means that a given change in GNP has a large effect on the interest rate and vice versa. An examination of equation (10) indicates that the effect of changes in GNP on the interest rate depends on the coefficients e and f. Hence:

- The LM curve will be steep (inelastic) if e (income elasticity of the demand for money) is large and/or f (interest elasticity of the demand for money) is small.
- The LM curve will be flat (elastic) if e is small and/or the coefficient f is large.

Location of LM curve The location of the LM line depends on the level of the money supply. An increase in the money supply shifts the LM line to the right and a decrease to the left. For example, in the left-hand diagram in Figure 11.4 the money market is initially in equilibrium at the point A. This equilibrium point corresponds to r_1 and

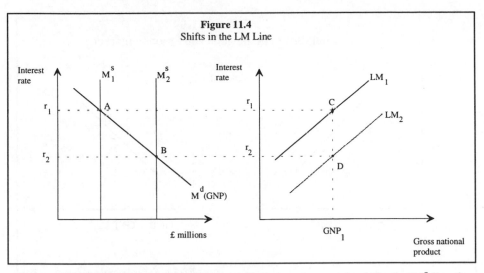

Figure 11.4
Shifts in the LM Line

GNP_1. Holding GNP constant, an increase in the money supply shifts the M^S line from M^S_1 to M^S_2 and the interest rate falls from r_1 to r_2. In the right-hand diagram the point C corresponds to the initial r_1, GNP_1 combination. The point D corresponds to the new r_2, GNP_1 combination. Both of these are points on the new LM line.

11.4   Equilibrium in the Goods and Money Markets

Figure 11.5 includes an IS and an LM line. Recall that points on the IS line are consistent with equilibrium in the goods market, and points on the LM line are consistent with equilibrium in the money market. Hence, at the point F, where the two lines intersect, there is equilibrium in *both* the goods market and the money market. At this point, and only here, aggregate demand equals planned production and the stock of money equals the desired holdings of cash balances by the public.

If a disequilibrium situation should arise, either because the interest rate or GNP is too high or too low, then it can be shown that the economy will adjust back to equilibrium. To establish this, consider the two diagrams at the top of Figure 11.5. The diagram on the top left shows the IS line. The point A corresponds to r_1 and GNP^* and the goods market is in equilibrium. Suppose, however, that output is at GNP_1 so that the economy is at the point B, to the left of the IS line. Since GNP is lower than what is necessary for equilibrium, there must be an excess demand for goods and services. Hence:

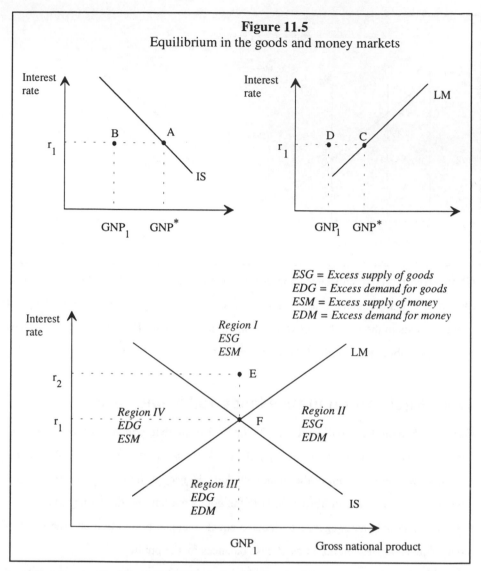

Figure 11.5
Equilibrium in the goods and money markets

ESG = Excess supply of goods
EDG = Excess demand for goods
ESM = Excess supply of money
EDM = Excess demand for money

- all points to the *left* of the IS line are associated with an excess *demand* for goods and services.

- all points to the *right* of the IS line are associated with an excess *supply* of goods and services.

Consider now the LM line in the top right-hand diagram. At the point C, r_1 and GNP^* represent the interest rate and the level of output consistent with money market equilibrium. If, however, output is less than GNP^*, say GNP_1, and the market is at a point such as D, then there is an excess supply of money. The reason is that GNP and therefore the demand for money is lower than that necessary for equilibrium. It follows, therefore, that:

- points to the left of the LM line represent an excess supply of money.

- points to the right of the LM line are associated with an excess demand for money.

We can divide the area in the diagram in the bottom panel of Figure 11.5 into four regions, corresponding to combinations of excess supply and demand in the goods and money markets. The economy will adjust towards equilibrium (represented by the point F) because:

- output rises whenever there is an excess demand for goods and vice versa.

- the interest rate rises when there is an excess demand for money and vice versa.

Region I Points in region I correspond to an excess supply of goods and an excess supply of money. If the economy were at a point such as E in this region, the effect of the excess supplies in both the goods and money markets would be to drive both the interest rate and GNP down until equilibrium is reached at F.

Region II Points in region II correspond to an excess supply of goods but an excess demand for money. In this situation, the interest rate will rise and GNP will fall until equilibrium is reached at the point F.

Region III Points in region III correspond to an excess demand for goods and an excess demand for money. Both GNP and the interest rate will rise until equilibrium is reached at F.

Region IV Finally, if the economy is in region IV, there is an excess demand for goods and an excess supply of money. GNP will rise and the interest rate would fall until equilibrium is re-established.

Thus the combination r_1 and GNP_1 represents a stable equilibrium to which the economy will return if the economy is subjected to a shock.

11.5 Government Spending and Private Investment: Crowding-out

In this section the IS-LM model is used to explore how an increase in government spending may affect private sector investment spending. Suppose that there are unemployed resources and the government embarks on an expansionary fiscal policy. This is shown in Figure 11.6 as the IS line shifting outwards from IS_1 to IS_2. If, as was assumed in the early chapters, we ignore the effects of this on the monetary sector, the

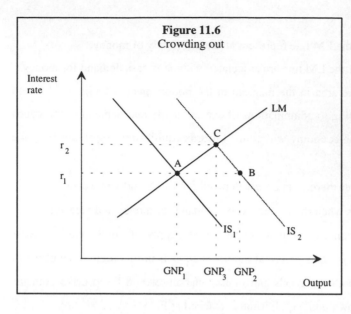

Figure 11.6
Crowding out

economy would move from the point A to the point B and GNP would increase to GNP$_2$. However, when we take account of the possible repercussions of the fiscal expansion on the money market, we see that the economy moves up along the LM line and equilibrium is established at the point C. Output increases only to GNP$_3$, which is lower than the level, GNP$_2$, that would have been reached if there had been no monetary repercussions.

The reason for the smaller increase in GNP is the *crowding-out effect*. Basically, what happens is that the rise in GNP leads to an increase in the demand for money. Given a constant supply of money, the increase in money demand pushes up the interest rate (along the vertical axis in Figure 11.6) and this, in turn, reduces investment expenditure. Hence, increased government expenditure is partly offset by a reduction in investment and the impact of fiscal policy on GNP is reduced. The crowding-out effect reduces the effectiveness of fiscal policy.

In practice, however, the crowding-out effect may be reduced if the government implements an *accommodating monetary policy* simultaneously with an expansionary fiscal policy. Instead of

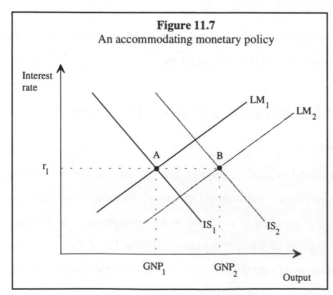

Figure 11.7
An accommodating monetary policy

246

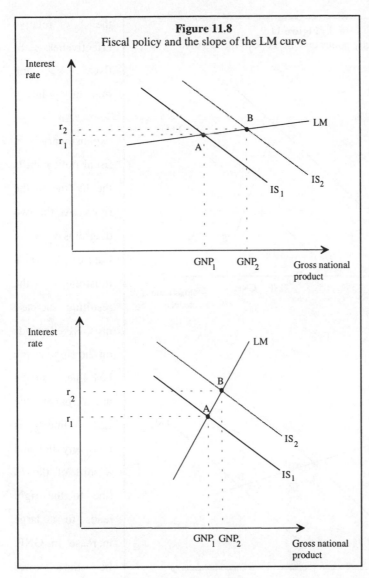

Figure 11.8
Fiscal policy and the slope of the LM curve

assuming that the money supply is held constant, let us suppose that the expansionary fiscal policy is accompanied by an increase in the money supply. In Figure 11.7 an increase in the money supply shifts the LM line upwards from LM_1 to LM_2. The economy moves to the point B, GNP increases to GNP_2, and because there is no increase in the interest rate along the vertical axis investment expenditure is not crowded out. In Ireland successive governments have engaged in an accommodating monetary policy during fiscal expansions by borrowing abroad to finance increased government spending. The increase in foreign indebtedness to £14 billion in 1997 is ample evidence of an accommodating monetary policy.

11.6 The Relative Effectiveness of Fiscal and Monetary Policy in the IS-LM Model

The IS-LM framework can be used to illustrate issues raised in Chapter 10 concerning

247

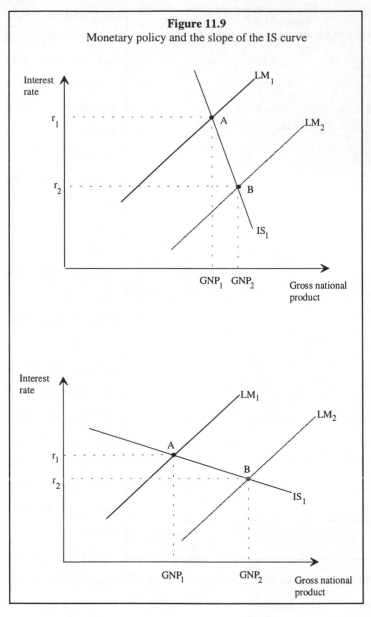

Figure 11.9
Monetary policy and the slope of the IS curve

the relative effectiveness of fiscal and monetary policy.

An expansionary fiscal policy shifts the IS line to the right. As the two diagrams in Figure 11.8 illustrate, the resulting increase in GNP depends on the slope of the LM line. In the upper panel, the LM line is relatively flat and a shift of the IS line to the right leads to a large increase in GNP. In the lower panel, the LM line is steep and a similar shift of the IS line has a small effect on GNP. The reason for the difference in the change in GNP is the crowding-out effect. When the LM line is flat, there is a small increase in the interest rate on the vertical axis and the crowding-out effect is insignificant. On the other hand, if the LM line is steep, there will be a large increase in the interest rate and the crowding-out effect will be significant.

Figure 11.9 examines the case of an expansionary monetary policy (shift of the LM line to the right). In the upper panel, the IS line is steep and an expansionary

248

monetary policy has a small effect on GNP. The reason is that investment is not very sensitive to interest rate changes and, as a result, the decrease in the interest rate on the vertical axis has an unimportant effect on investment. As a result, monetary policy has only a small effect on the level of output and employment.

In the lower panel, the IS line is relatively flat because investment is sensitive to changes in the interest rate, and a shift of the LM line to the right has a large effect on GNP. As a consequence, a change in the money supply has a relatively large effect on GNP.

The Keynesian-classical debate The debate between the Keynesian and classical views of macroeconomics can be summarised in terms of the IS-LM model. The Keynesian view requires

- a *flat* LM line and a *steep* IS line (upper diagram in Figures 11.8 and 11.9).

Fiscal policy has a significant effect on GNP and monetary policy has little or no effect on GNP. An extreme Keynesian position is the concept of a *liquidity trap* when the LM line is horizontal. Under this condition, there is no crowding out of investment and fiscal policy is very effective.

The classical view is just the opposite, namely:

- a *steep* LM line and a *flat* IS line (lower diagrams in Figures 11.8 and 11.9).

Now government spending crowds out private sector investment and fiscal policy is ineffective. In contrast, changes in the money supply have an important effect on the level of nominal GNP. The extreme classical case is that the LM line is vertical and an expansionary fiscal policy has no effect on output. With a vertical LM line there is 100 per cent crowding-out. This conclusion is in accordance with the quantity theory of money discussed in Chapter 10.

As is often the case, it is possible to compromise and to suggest that the truth lies between the extremes represented by the Keynesian and classical views. When interest rates are low, for example, an increase in interest rates may not crowd out investment and the Keynesian view that fiscal policy is effective may be valid. On the other hand, when interest rates are relatively high any further rise in interest rates may lead to significant crowding-out of investment. In this case, the classical view that fiscal policy is ineffective may be valid. However, it is clear that the interest elasticity of the demand for money is of crucial importance in assessing policy prescriptions. Over a half a century since Keynes launched his *General Theory* the economics profession has still not reached a consensus on the controversies it provoked.

11.7   The Fiscal-Monetary Policy Mix

If we assume that there are unemployed resources in the economy, the question naturally arises: which mix of fiscal and monetary policies should the government use to reduce unemployment?   In Figure 11.10, the economy is initially at the point A which corresponds to an interest rate of r_1 and output of GNP_1. Suppose that the vertical line corresponding to GNP* indicates potential or full employment GNP. If the government implements an expansionary fiscal policy the economy will move to the point C. Output increases but the interest rate rises along the vertical axis. This implies some crowding-out of private sector spending.

If, alternatively, the government pursues an expansionary monetary policy, the economy moves to the point B. This time the increase in output is accompanied by a reduction in the interest rate, which would stimulate an increase in private sector investment. It might appear that this outcome is preferable, but we have not considered the longer-run implications of the increase in the money supply and the reduction in interest rates for inflation.

The choice between an expansionary fiscal or monetary policy is clearly in part a political one. Conservative politicians tend to prefer tax cuts over increases in public expenditure.   They would also worry about the longer-run inflationary implications of an expansionary monetary policy. Left-wing politicians, who generally favour increases in public expenditure, tend not to be as worried about

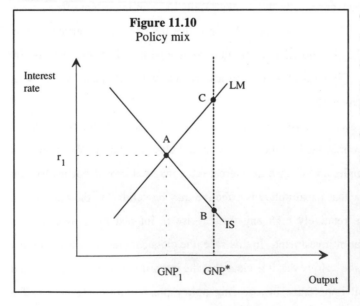

Figure 11.10
Policy mix

250

inflation as are conservatives.

11.8 Conclusion

In this chapter we introduced the IS-LM model and used it to analyse how the economy responds to fiscal and monetary policy. The key points covered included:

- The IS line shows the combinations of the interest rate and GNP that give an equilibrium in the market for goods and services
- The LM line shows the combination of the interest rate and GNP that give an equilibrium in the money market
- The intersection of the IS and LM lines represents a simultaneous equilibrium in both the goods and money markets
- The Keynesian case is represented by a flat (elastic) LM line and a steep (inelastic) IS line
- The classical case is represented by a steep (inelastic) LM line and a flat (elastic) IS line
- The crowding-out effect is important in the monetarist case but unimportant in the Keynesian model
- Expansionary fiscal and monetary policies have different implications for interest rates.

Our treatment at this stage does not include the issues that arise in a small open economy and we cannot shed light on the problem of inflation.

Chapter 12

Unemployment and Inflation

12.1   Introduction

In the last chapter we developed a model of the economy in which prices were fixed. We looked at the effect of the level of real output of changes in monetary and fiscal policy. This framework did not allow us to develop a theory of inflation or the relationship between the level of unemployment and the rate of inflation. The present chapter takes up this task. Our approach is first to expand the AS-AD analysis of Chapter 3 by showing how the AS schedule is derived from a production function and the interaction of the supply and demand of labour. We then use this expanded model to illustrate the differences between the Keynesian, monetarist and neoclassical schools of thought. As we shall see, different assumptions about price expectations lead to different conclusions about policy towards inflation and unemployment. In the following chapter we explore the evidence concerning this trade-off in greater detail.

12.2   The Aggregate Production Function

In any economy, land, labour and capital are the three basic factors of production. These are used as inputs in the production of goods and services and are combined with the technology available to produce the output of the economy. This relationship is described by the *aggregate production function* that can be written as

$$GNP = f(C, L, N) \tag{1}$$

where N = the labour input or hours worked, L = land, and C = the capital input or the quantity of plant and machinery employed. Land is clearly not a variable input, at least in the short run. If we assume that the amount of capital available is fixed or constant in the short run, we can examine the relationship between output and employment for a given level of technology in the simple diagram shown in Figure 12.1.

In the upper half of this diagram, increasing employment along the horizontal axis leads to an increase in output on the vertical axis. For example, employment of N_1 is associated with output GNP_1. The curve relating these two variables becomes flatter as the level of employment increases. This means that as more and more labour is hired, output continues to increase, but at a *diminishing rate*. In Figure 12.1, the

252

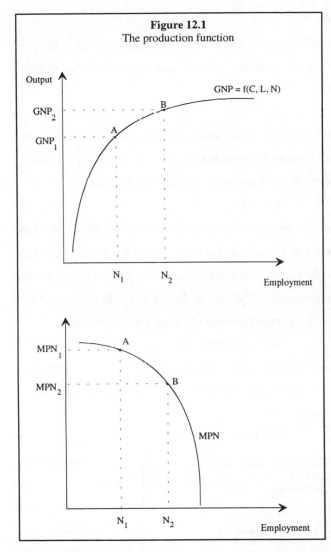

Figure 12.1
The production function

increase in employment from N_1 to N_2 leads to a less than proportional increase in GNP. This reflects the assumption of diminishing returns to labour. As more and more labour is applied to fixed amounts of land and capital, the *marginal product of labour* falls.

The lower diagram in Figure 12.1 shows the marginal product of labour (MPN) relative to the level of employment. The MPN measures the extra output produced by hiring one extra worker. The diagram has been drawn to reflect the assumption that, as employment is increased along the horizontal axis, the MPN decreases along the vertical axis. The slope of the production function determines the MPN curve. Most important, the MPN underlies the demand curve for labour.

12.3 The Labour Market

In this section we explain how the supply and demand for labour determine the wage rate (W) and the level of employment (N). We begin by deriving the demand for labour schedule.

The demand for labour

The basic rule for profit maximisation is that a firm will increase output up to the point where the marginal cost (MC) of producing an extra unit is equal to the marginal revenue (MR) from selling it:

$$MC = MR \tag{2}$$

In a competitive market, each firm is so small in relation to the overall market that increases in its output will have no effect on the market price and marginal revenue is therefore equal to output price (P). The profit-maximising rule becomes:

$$MC = P \tag{3}$$

Consider now the cost of producing an extra unit of output, MC. We have assumed that the only variable input is labour: land and capital are fixed in the short run. MC is therefore equal to the cost of hiring one extra worker divided by the number of units of extra output (s)he produces. The cost of the worker is the wage rate (W) and the output of the worker is the marginal product of labour (MPN). Hence:

$$MC = W/MPN \tag{4}$$

If, for example, the wage rate is £100 a week and an additional worker produces 20 units of output in a week, the MC of a unit of output is £5. Substituting equation (4) into (3), a firm maximises its profits when:

$$W/MPN = P \tag{5}$$

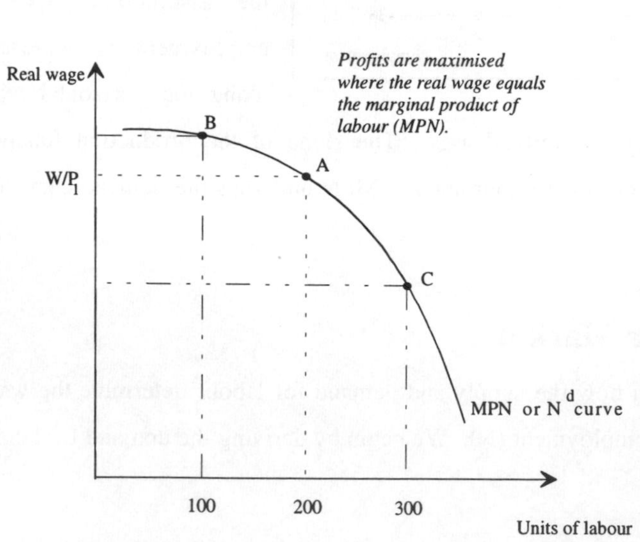

Rearranging, the profit maximisation rule can be written as:

$$W/P = MPN \tag{6}$$

Equation (6) states that a firm's profits are maximised when the real wage rate (W/P) is equal to the marginal product of labour, MPN. Figure 12.2 shows the MPN schedule and

Figure 12.2
The demand for labour

Profits are maximised where the real wage equals the marginal product of labour (MPN).

254

the real wage on the vertical axis and the level of employment on the horizontal axis. If the real wage is $(W/P)_1$ the profit-maximising level of employment is 200 workers. If the firm hired only 100 workers the MPN would exceed the real wage and profits could be increased by hiring additional labour. Similarly, if the firm hired 300 workers, then the MPN is less than the real wage and the firm is incurring a loss on the last 100 workers hired. The firm could increase profits by reducing its workforce to 200.

It follows that the point A in Figure 12.2 is one point on the demand for labour schedule. In fact, the demand for labour curve coincides with the MPN curve. For any level of W/P we can read off the profit-maximising level of employment by moving horizontally over to the MPN curve and then vertically down to the X-axis. Each point where W/P cuts the MPN curve corresponds to a point on the demand for labour schedule. Because the MPN schedule is downward sloping due to diminishing returns, the demand for labour schedule is also downward sloping.

If the MPN curve in Figure 12.2 is re-labelled the demand for labour (N^d) curve, it can be seen that the number of workers hired depends on (i) the location of the demand for labour schedule, and (ii) the level of the real wage. The location of the demand for labour schedule depends on the influences we have held constant, such as the level of capital and other inputs that are combined with labour, and the level of technology used in the economy. The more capital available and the better the level of technology employed, the higher will be the marginal productivity of labour at each level of employment and the more labour will be employed at a given wage rate. But for a given level of technology and capital, the higher the wage rate the less labour will be employed. Anything that makes workers more productive – technical progress, having more capital to work with, better education and training – shifts the MPN schedule outwards and increases the demand for labour at each wage rate. Reductions in the wage rate increase the demand for labour for a given level of MPN by moving firms down along a given demand for labour schedule.

In the upper panel of Figure 12.3 is a demand for labour schedule, with the real wage along the vertical axis and employment along the horizontal axis. The curve is labelled N^d(MPN) to indicate that the demand for labour is a function of the marginal productivity of labour.

Alternatively, the demand for labour can be plotted as a function of the nominal wage. Rearranging, equation (6) can be written:

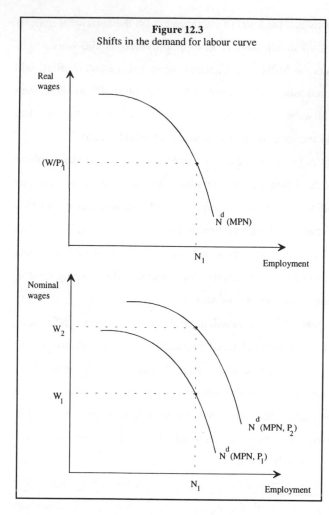

Figure 12.3
Shifts in the demand for labour curve

$W = P \times MPN$ (7)

Using this rule, firms hire workers up to the point where the nominal wage equals the value of the output produced by workers.

Note:

The term $P \times MPN$ is the value of workers' output and is referred to as the *marginal revenue product* (MRP).

The demand for labour now depends on the nominal wage, the price level and MPN:

$N^d = F(W, P, MPN)$ (8)

This is drawn in the lower diagram in Figure 12.3. Movements along the N^d curve show the relationship between the nominal wage, W, and the quantity of labour demanded. A change in P shifts the N^d curve. If the price level rises, each nominal wage rate is associated with a higher level of employment. This is illustrated in the lower panel of Figure 12.3, where the demand for labour shifts out as the price level rises from P_1 to P_2. As a result of the rise in the price level, the level of employment associated with the initial nominal wage, W_1, increases from N_1 to N_2. Conversely, they would wish to hire fewer if the price level fell but the nominal wage remained unaltered.

An important qualification is necessary. An employer hires labour with a view to producing additional output and selling it profitably. This is a forward-looking decision and involves expectations of the wages that will have to be paid to workers and the prices that will be obtained for selling the output. To simplify our analysis we will assume throughout this chapter that firms can predict future wages and prices

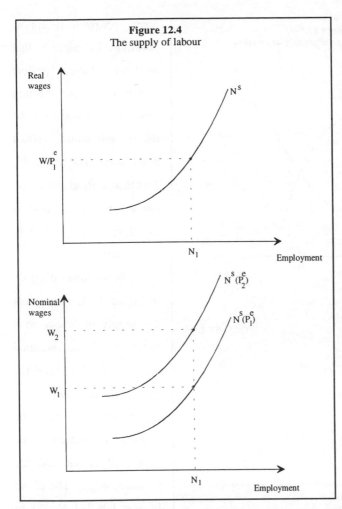

Figure 12.4
The supply of labour

accurately. If we write P^e for the expected price level, then we are assuming that for firms, $P^e = P$. This assumption allows us to use P throughout this chapter as the variable affecting the demand for labour.

The supply of labour

We start from the basic assumption that the supply of labour depends on the real wage, W/P. This reflects the common-sense belief that people must be paid more if they are to work longer hours and that it takes a higher wage rate to induce inactive people into the labour force. What matters is the *real* wage that prevails over the period for which the worker agrees to accept a given nominal wage. This is not known when a worker accepts an offer of employment. In effect, (s)he makes the decision to accept a job offer on the basis of a nominal wage (W) and the price level (s)he expects (P^e) will prevail for the duration of the wage agreement or contract. The relevant real wage is therefore (W/P^e). The question of how workers form their *inflation expectations* is brought to the centre of the stage by this consideration. The supply of labour function is written:

$$N^s = f(W/P^e) \tag{9}$$

This relationship is shown in the upper diagram in Figure 12.4. The labour supply curve (N^s) is upward sloping, indicating that firms must offer higher real wages in order to encourage workers to supply more labour or to induce entrants to the labour

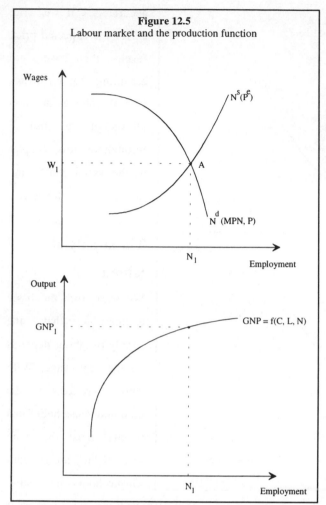

Figure 12.5
Labour market and the production function

force. Now it is not as plausible to assume that workers have perfect foresight about future inflation as it was to make this assumption about employers. The use of P^e, as distinct from P, in the labour supply function is therefore highly significant.

In the lower diagram in Figure 12.4, we express the supply of labour as a function of the nominal wage and the expected price level separately. The N^s curve describes the relationship between the supply of labour and the nominal wage. The curve is now labelled $N^s(P^e)$ to indicate that changes in P^e shift the N^s curve. If P^e rises, the N^s curve shifts to the left: for a given nominal wage, workers will supply less work effort, the higher the price level expected to prevail over the period of the wage contract. Conversely, if P^e falls, the N^s curve shifts to the right: workers will supply more work effort for a given nominal wage, the lower they expect the price level to be.

Equilibrium in the labour market

The labour market and the production function describe the supply side of the macroeconomy. Figure 12.5 shows how they interact. In the upper diagram, the demand and supply of labour determine the nominal wage rate and the level of employment, at W_1 and N_1. A level of employment equal to N_1 allows the economy to produce output equal to GNP_1 as shown in the lower panel of the diagram. What

258

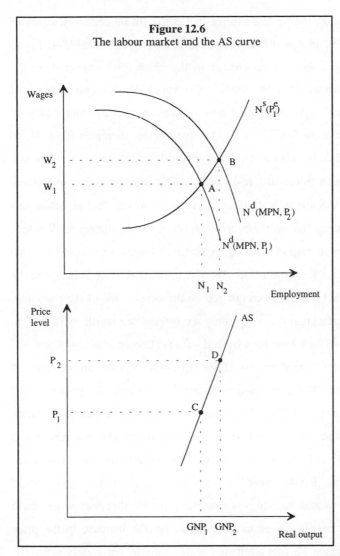

Figure 12.6
The labour market and the AS curve

happens now if there is an increase in the price level? Assuming both workers and firms correctly anticipate this increase, the labour supply schedule will shift inwards and the labour demand schedule outwards. The result will be a higher nominal wage, W_2, but no change in the real wage: nominal wages and the price level increase in equal proportions, so:

$$(W_1/P_1) = (W_2/P_2)$$

and there is no change in the level of employment or output, which remain at N_1 and GNP_1.

12.4 Aggregate Supply

Let us now expand the model of aggregate supply we introduced in Chapter 3 to incorporate these ideas about how the labour market operates. It will be recalled that the aggregate supply (AS) schedule showed a positive relationship between prices and real GNP. The process was as follows:

$$\uparrow \text{Output Prices (P)} \rightarrow \uparrow \text{Profits} \rightarrow \uparrow \text{Real GNP}$$

The important underlying assumption is that costs, and wages in particular, remain constant as P increases. As a result, an increase in output prices leads to an increase in profits and this, in turn, encourages firms to expand output. Figure 12.6 shows the labour market and the associated aggregate supply (AS) curve. Suppose output prices increase from P_1 to P_2. We assume that firms are immediately aware of this and as a result there is an upward shift of the N^d curve (from N^d(MPN, P_1) to N^d(MPN, P_2). If, however, there is no change in the price level expected by the workers, the supply of labour does not shift. The result of this combination of assumptions is that nominal wages and employment increase as the economy moves up along the supply of labour curve from A to B. As employment increases (from N_1 to N_2), the level of real GNP rises. Hence, on the supply side of the economy there is a positive relationship between prices and real output. This is shown as a movement along the upward-sloping AS curve, from C to D. Note, however, that to obtain this result it is necessary to assume that workers' price expectations are incorrect. Workers have supplied more labour in response to higher nominal wages without taking into account the fact that the price level has risen. The rise in the real wage is less than the rise in the nominal wage, but this has been ignored on the supply side of the economy. Workers are under the illusion that the wages they are offered are worth more than in reality is the case. In a sense they have been tricked. This is known as *money illusion*.

If money illusion exists, the steepness of the AS curve depends on the slope of the labour supply (N^S) curve. The flatter (more elastic) the N^S curve, the flatter the AS curve. To see this point, note that if the N^S curve is flat a given increase in the price level will lead to a large increase in employment and, via the production function, a large increase in real GNP. A large increase in real GNP, in response to a given price increase, indicates a relatively flat AS curve.

Consider now what would happen when workers realise that real wages have fallen and demand higher money wages to compensate for the increase in the price level. This is shown in Figure 12.7 as a leftward shift of the labour supply schedule. Equilibrium in the labour market is now at point B. We have drawn the diagram so that the increase in W equals the increase in P and the real wage returns to its initial level. (This corresponds to the situation depicted in Figure 12.5.) At point B employment remains at its original level. The increase in money wages also shifts the AS curve upwards. In the lower panel of Figure 12.7 this is shown as a shift from AS_1 to AS_2. Prices have increased but real GNP is unchanged. The economy moves from C to D. This implies that the upward-sloping AS schedule is only a short-run phenomenon. The AS schedule slopes upward only for as long as workers suffer from money illusion. As soon as workers demand higher wages to compensate for higher output prices, the short-run AS schedule shifts to the left. The movement of short-run AS schedules

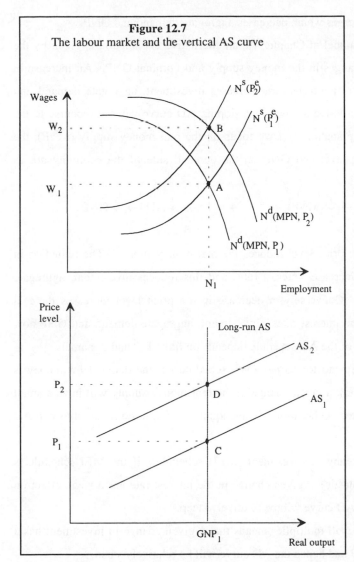

Figure 12.7
The labour market and the vertical AS curve

enables us to map out the long-run AS schedule. C and D are two points on the long-run AS curve, which is vertical. Increases in output prices do not lead to any increase in real output in the long term. This is because only N_1 workers are willing to accept employment at the original real wage level. Furthermore, at this real wage N_1 is the full employment level of employment. Any remaining unemployment is voluntary, reflecting an unwillingness to accept jobs at the prevailing real wage. These ideas are crucial to the neoclassical model and its vision of an economy that always tends to full employment.

12.5 Aggregate Demand

In Chapter 3 we stated that on the demand side of the economy there is an inverse relationship between prices and real GNP. We explained this in terms of the link between the price level, international competitiveness and the current account of the balance of payments. An increase in the domestic price level leads to a loss of competitiveness and this results in a decrease in exports and an increase in imports. A trade account deficit emerges which decreases aggregate demand and GNP.

In the expanded model of Chapter 10, an alternative explanation is given by the relationship between changes in the money supply and nominal GNP. An increase in the money supply lowers interest rates, increases investment, aggregate demand and GNP. This allows us to derive a downward-sloping AD curve without recourse to the balance of payments explanation. If we focus on the real money supply (M^S/P), the links between the price level and GNP on the demand side of the economy are as follows:

$$\uparrow P \rightarrow \downarrow (M^S/P) \rightarrow \uparrow r \rightarrow \downarrow I \rightarrow \downarrow AD \rightarrow \downarrow GNP$$
$$\qquad\qquad\quad 1 \qquad\quad 2 \qquad 3$$

An increase in the price level reduces the real money supply. The reduction in the real money supply increases interest rates and this reduces investment, aggregate demand and real GNP. Conversely, a decrease in the price level increases the real money supply and lowers interest rates. Investment, aggregate demand and GNP now increase. The steepness of the AD schedule depends on links 1, 2 and 3, namely:

1. The slope of the demand for money (M^d) schedule. If the demand for money is relatively flat (elastic), a given change in the real money supply will have a small effect on interest rates. Other things being equal, this implies a relatively steep AD curve.

2. The marginal efficiency of investment (MEI) schedule. If the MEI schedule is relatively steep (inelastic), a given change in the interest rate has a weak effect on investment and the AD curve will be relatively steep.

3. The multiplier. A small multiplier means that a given change in investment has a small effect on GNP and hence the AD curve will be relatively steep.

If the AD curve is steep, this implies that a given change in the price level has a small effect on real output. This occurs if the demand for money curve is flat and the MEI curve steep. We saw that Keynesians believe these assumptions to be valid. A flat AD curve implies that a given change in the price level has a large effect on real output. This would be the case if the demand for money is relatively inelastic with respect to the rate of interest and the level of investment is relatively elastic, as is assumed by the classical economists.

The location of the AD line depends on the level of private and public consumption expenditure (C and G), investment (I), net exports ($NX = X - M$), and the

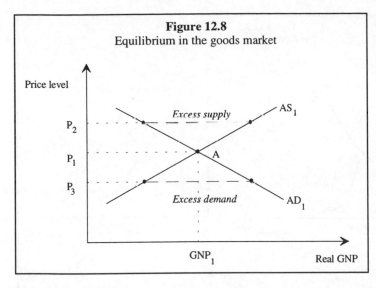

Figure 12.8
Equilibrium in the goods market

Price level

P_2

P_1 A

P_3

Excess supply AS_1

Excess demand AD_1

GNP_1 Real GNP

money supply (M^S). An increase in C, I, G, NX, or M^S shifts the AD curve to the right (assuming no change in the price level). Expansionary fiscal or monetary policy shifts the AD schedule outward.

Equilibrium In Figure 12.8, the upward-sloping short-run AS schedule derived in the previous section is combined with the AD schedule. The interaction of these two schedules determines the equilibrium price level (P) and the level of GNP. If the economy is not at point A it is assumed that firms will quickly adjust both prices and output so that equilibrium is re-established. This diagram is very similar to that discussed in Chapter 3. The main difference is that we have expanded the analysis underlying the two schedules. A labour market and a production function now underlie the AS schedule and the goods and money markets underlie the AD schedule. We shall use this framework to clarify some key issues in modern macroeconomics, particularly the relationship between the level of unemployment and the rate of inflation, as viewed by Keynesians, monetarists and neoclassicals.[1]

---

1. These terms mean different things to different economists. In fact, the term "classical economist" was first coined by Karl Marx to describe orthodox nineteenth-century British economics. A representation of the classical model was given by Keynes in Chapter 2 of the *General Theory* so that he could replace it with his own "Keynesian" model. Mark Blaug has commented that "perhaps the recent proliferation of definitely new but conflicting interpretations of the essential meaning of classical economics is simply an expression of the fact that modern economists are divided in their views and hence quite naturally seek comfort by finding (or pretending that they can find) these same views incorporated in the writings of the past". See "Classical economics" in *The New Palgrave: A Dictionary of Economics*, edited by John Eatwell, Murray Milgate and Peter Newman (London, Macmillan, 1987).

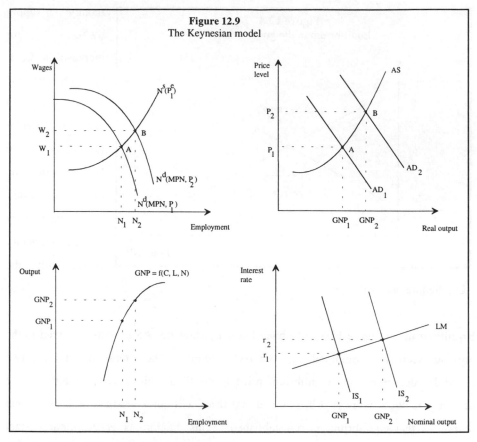

Figure 12.9
The Keynesian model

12.6   The Keynesian Model

Return, for the moment, to the fixed-price model of the previous chapter. Figure 12.9 gives an outline of the Keynesian model. The Keynesian theory of aggregate demand is shown in the IS-LM diagram in the lower right-hand corner. The IS line is steep and the LM line is flat, representing the Keynesian belief that fiscal policy is effective and monetary policy ineffective as a means of influencing output and employment.

Incorporating this in an AS-AD framework requires us to assume that wage contracts are fixed into the future. In order to maintain real wages, workers have to anticipate or forecast changes in the price level for the duration of the contract. Hence, given that the nominal wage is known, the supply of labour depends on the expected price level (P^e) rather than the actual price level.

Consider now the effects of an expansionary fiscal policy on output and employment. An increase in government expenditure shifts the IS line from IS_1 to IS_2 (diagram, bottom right). Nominal output rises along the horizontal axis and, because of the flat LM line, there is only a small increase in the interest rate on the vertical axis.

264

This means that the crowding-out effect will be very small. The increase in government expenditure also shifts the AD curve from AD_1 to AD_2, and because the AS line is positively sloped, both real output and the price level increase (diagram, top right).

The increase in the price level shifts the N^d curve from $N^d(MPN, P_1)$ to $N^d(MPN, P_2)$ (diagram, top left). However, because the supply of labour depends on the expected price level, the N^s curve does not immediately shift. In the Keynesian model, workers formulate price expectations by looking at the historical trend in prices. Price expectations are, in effect, backward looking. This is not an unreasonable assumption. If someone asks what the inflation rate in Europe will be in 1999, a reasonable answer might be: "Much the same as in 1998." Of course if a shock were to occur, such as an increase in energy prices or a breakdown of EMU, then you would want to change your forecast.

In the Keynesian model, an expansionary fiscal policy leads to an unexpected increase in the price level. Initially, people are not aware that the price level has increased. They work longer hours, or enter the labour force, in response to the higher nominal wage – which is perceived as a higher real wage. In reality, the real wage has risen less than was initially believed to be the case. The public is suffering from money illusion. Because the N^s curve does not immediately shift, employment increases and this enables firms to produce more goods and services. The failure of the N^s curve to shift to the left following an increase in the price level also explains why the AS curve is positively sloped.

In the longer term people will recognise the effect of higher prices on real wages. They will demand an increase in nominal wages to compensate. The supply of labour shifts to the left and employment and output revert back to their initial levels. In the Keynesian model, an expansionary fiscal or monetary policy can influence the level of output and employment in the short run but there is no effect in the long run.

12.7 Monetarism

Monetarism is a variant of the classical economics that incorporated some of Keynes's ideas but modified them significantly. The monetarist model is outlined in Figure 12.10. The theoretical structure of the monetarist model is not very different from the Keynesian model. On the supply side of the economy, the monetarists accept the Keynesian view that workers do not have perfect information on future price

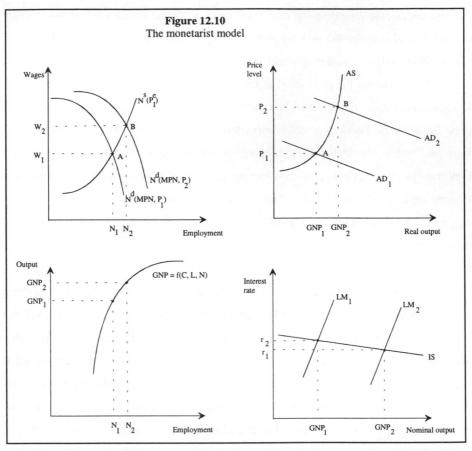

Figure 12.10
The monetarist model

movements and that errors are made in forecasting. As a result, the N^S curve is positively sloped and this, in turn, implies that the AS curve is also upward sloping.

The difference between the monetarists and Keynesians lies in the slope of the IS and LM lines. Figure 12.10 shows the monetarist view that the LM line is steep and the IS line is flat. This means that fiscal policy has a relatively small effect on output and employment. For example, an increase in government expenditure would shift the IS line upwards to the right (not shown). The large increase in the interest rate along the vertical axis would crowd out investment with the result that there is a small increase in real output on the horizontal axis.

Monetary policy, on the other hand, has a very significant effect on nominal output. In Figure 12.10 (diagram, bottom right) an increase in the money supply shifts the LM line from LM_1 to LM_2 and nominal output increases along the horizontal axis. The increase in the money supply also shifts the AD line from AD_1 to AD_2 (top right) and both real output and the price level increase. Real output increases because in the

266

labour market the N^S line does not shift to the left following the unanticipated increase in the price level. Workers are supplying more labour in response to a higher nominal wage even though in terms of real wages they are no better off. The essential theoretical difference between the monetarists and the Keynesians is the proposition that changes in the money supply have a significant effect on nominal output, whereas fiscal policy has an insignificant effect.

Monetarists argue that monetary policy should not be used to influence output or stabilise the business cycle. They reason that in the longer run increases in the money supply will, via the quantity theory of money, lead to an equal increase in the price level. The process is as follows. In the labour market, workers eventually realise that real wages have not risen and demand an increase in nominal wages to compensate for the higher price level. The N^S line shifts to the left and real output and employment revert to their original levels. This means that in the long run the AS and the N^S lines are vertical. An expansionary monetary policy has no long-run effect on real variables such as output and employment, but it results in a higher price level.

Second, monetarists argue that there is a long and variable lag between changes in the money supply and changes in nominal output. They argue that changes in the money supply have been one of the major sources of instability in the economy. Active monetary policy is likely to destabilise the economy. The monetarists therefore conclude that, given the role of money as a medium of exchange, the government should allow the money supply to increase in line with the predicted growth in real GNP.[2] The targets should be announced beforehand and the government should adhere to this *monetary rule*.

Thus the monetarists' position is that the government should not adopt an active policy stance. They argue that the economy is inherently stable and gaps that emerge between the actual and full-employment level of output will be eliminated quickly by the automatic tendency of the labour market to clear. In the Keynesian model the AD line is very steep and the price level has to fall significantly in order to return the economy to full employment GNP, but in the monetarist model the AD line is flat. This means that only a small fall in the price level is necessary to restore the economy to full employment GNP. Output gaps tend to be closed quickly.

---

2. This is a rough rule of thumb. Account should be taken of the income elasticity of demand for real cash balances.

Note:

For the monetarist model to work, the labour market has to be flexible. Minimum wage legislation, trade union closed shops, employment protection legislation and similar rigidities slow down wage adjustments and impede the movement back to full employment GNP. If wages can be made more responsive to shifts in the supply and demand for labour, the adjustment process will be speeded up.

12.8 The Neoclassical Model

The controversy surrounding the effectiveness of fiscal policy has developed largely around the way economic agents (firms and households) form expectations about key variables such as the rate of inflation. In this section we examine alternative approaches to forming expectations in some detail.

Expectations formed on the basis of the current levels of economic variables are known as *static expectations*. The shortcoming with this approach is that it allows for no feedback from errors in previous forecasts. *Adaptive expectations* are adjusted on the basis of previous forecast errors. But even this approach can lead to systematic forecasts. In a period of accelerating inflation, for example, the expected rate of inflation will always be less than the actual rate. Surely the public will learn from its mistakes and adopt a more sophisticated approach to formulating expectations?

Rational expectations avoid systematic forecast errors. They are formed on the basis of all available information and knowledge of how the economy works. This approach does not result in systematic errors. This does not imply that the forecasts will be always accurate – just that there will be no tendency to consistently over or under-predict a variable such as the rate of inflation. In recent years, rational expectations have become a very influential way of thinking about the economy. This approach is associated with the name of Robert Lucas of the University of Chicago, who was awarded the Nobel prize in economics in 1996.[3]

A rational forecast of inflation is based on all available information and a correct knowledge of what causes inflation. A belief in monetarism will lead the public to anticipate an increase in the rate of inflation when the rate of growth of the money

---

3. Robert Lucas, "Rules, Discretion and the Role of the Economic Advisor", in Stanley Fischer (ed.) *Rational Expectations and Economic Policy*, University of Chicago Press, 1980. Rational expectations originated in a paper that attracted little attention when it was first published: John Muth, "Rational Expectations and the Theory of Price Movements", *Econometrica*, 29 July 1961. Other influential economists who developed the rational expectations approach include Thomas Sargent of the University of Chicago and Robert Barro of Harvard University.

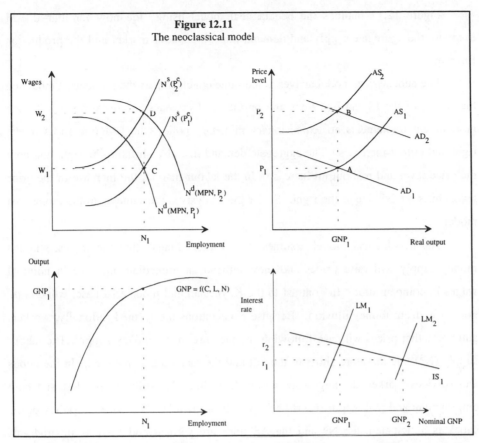

Figure 12.11
The neoclassical model

supply increases. If the economy is close to full employment and the government pursues an expansionary monetary policy, firms and households will anticipate that the rate of inflation will increase. A key feature of neoclassical economics is that *anticipated* inflation will not fool firms or households into believing that an increase in nominal variables represents an increase in real variables. The *money illusion* that we discussed earlier in this chapter can only come about through *surprise* or *unanticipated* inflation. Policy makers can only achieve this result by an *unannounced* change of policy that takes firms and households by surprise.

Note:

Inflation expectations can influence actual inflation. If workers expect the rate of inflation to increase they will demand increases in nominal wages in compensation. If households anticipate a rise in inflation, they will rush to buy at today's prices. These reactions will of themselves tend to push up the rate of inflation. Feedback from expectations to outcomes is very important in economics. Things are very different in meteorology: unfortunately, a forecast of fine weather is not enough to ensure that the weather will be fine!

Figure 12.11 outlines the neoclassical model using the now familiar IS-LM diagram, the aggregate supply and demand lines, the labour market and the production function.

The neoclassical model arrives at the same conclusion as the monetarist model on the slopes of the IS and LM lines and on the ineffectiveness of fiscal policy. If the government implements an expansionary monetary policy, the LM line shifts to the right and output increases. The aggregate demand line also shifts to the right and both the price level and real output increase. In the labour market, the increase in the price level shifts the N^d line to the right. So far the analysis is the same as in the monetarist model.

The neoclassical model assumes that workers realise that the increase in the money supply will raise prices and they demand an immediate increase in nominal wages in compensation. In contrast to the Keynesian and monetarist case, workers do not suffer from money illusion. Because expectations are formed rationally, workers anticipate that prices will rise following the increase in the money supply. The labour supply (N^s) line therefore shifts to the left and the real wage is restored. In the goods and services market, the aggregate supply (AS) line also shifts to the left and both employment and real output revert back to their original levels. Once the policy or the shock is anticipated, the N^s and the AS lines are vertical and there is no trade-off between inflation and unemployment other than in the very short run.

Note:
Both employers and employees forecast an increase in prices equal to the increase in the money supply. This forecast takes account of any secondary increases in the price level due to a shift of the AS line.

The analysis of fiscal policy is similar except that fiscal policy is even less effective due to crowding out of investment. (The Barro-Ricardian Equivalence Proposition, according to which increases in government deficit spending lead to a reduction in private consumption as the public anticipates higher taxes in the future, is another reason why the neoclassical analysis believes that fiscal policy is ineffective. We discussed this idea in Chapter 6.)

Even in a neoclassical world it is possible, in the short run, to raise output above the level corresponding to full employment or the natural rate of unemployment. This can occur through an *unanticipated* increase in the price level or the rate of inflation.

This could be engineered through a surprise fiscal or monetary expansion. As before, the aggregate demand schedule will shift to the right and real output and the price level will increase. If, however, workers do not anticipate the increase in prices, neither the N^S line nor the AS line will shift to the left. Under these circumstances, real output and employment will rise. Thus only unanticipated changes in monetary and fiscal policy can result in changes in real output. Moreover, such surprises do not last: the public quickly learns from the evidence and adjusts its expectations, so that only in the very short run do these shocks have any effect on real output.

Note:

The neoclassical aggregate supply function can be written:

$$GNP = GNP^* + \alpha \, (\pi - \pi^e) \qquad (10)$$

where GNP^* and GNP represent full employment GNP and actual GNP, respectively. Output can exceed full employment output only if the price level (or rate of inflation) exceeds the expected price level (or expected inflation). If expectations are formed rationally, such unanticipated inflation will not persist for long.

Neoclassical economists argue that there is no role for a Keynesian stabilisation policy to offset the instability in the private components of aggregate demand. Because shocks are unanticipated, the government cannot offset them. Both the private and the public sector are caught unawares. Once a shock occurs economic agents will forecast its implications. Expectations, formed rationally, will *on average* correctly anticipate the consequences of the shock for the rate of inflation. In the labour market, firms and workers will quickly adjust the supply and demand for labour schedules to ensure that the economy reverts to the natural rate of unemployment. For these reasons, neoclassical economists are sceptical about governments' ability to "fine-tune" the economy in response to shocks. As Lucas comments about economists: "As an advice-giving profession we are in way over our heads."[4]

---

4. Robert Lucas, "Rules, Discretion and the Role of the Economic Advisor", in Stanley Fischer (ed.) *Rational Expectations and Economic Policy,* University of Chicago Press, 1980. Lucas also argued that changes in policy change the slope of the Phillips line. These ideas are key parts of what is called "New Classical Economics" and were developed by University of Chicago economists Robert Lucas and Thomas Sargent, Neil Wallace of the University of Minnesota and Robert Barro of the University of Rochester and Harvard University. See R. E. Lucas, "Some International Evidence on Output-Inflation Tradeoffs", *American Economic Review,* 63(3), September 1973, pp 326-34, and T. J. Sargent and N. Wallace, "Rational Expectations, the Optimal Monetary Instrument, and the Optimal Money Supply Rule", *Journal of Political Economy,* 83(2), April 1975, pp 241-54.

12.9 The Speed of Adjustment and the Persistence of Output Gaps

Beliefs about the nature of the aggregate supply schedule have a crucial bearing on the appropriate response to deflationary shocks and lie at the heart of modern macroeconomic controversies. Figure 12.12 illustrates the implications of an adverse demand shock for the economy, using the IS-LM framework. In the upper panel, a decrease in investment shifts the AD line from AD_1 to AD_2 and the economy moves from point A to B. Both real output and the price level fall. In the labour market the decrease in the price level shifts the N^d line to the left and the equilibrium moves from point X to Y. The decrease in nominal wages is smaller than the fall in the price level and as a result the real wage rises. Employment decreases along the horizontal axis. This implies an increase in unemployment. The N^s line does not immediately shift because the change in the price level was unexpected.

After a time, workers realise that the price level has fallen and they accept a cut in the nominal wage so as to restore the real wage. In the labour market, the N^s line shifts to the right so as to intersect the N^d line at the point Z. At this point, the fall in the nominal wage is equal to the fall in the price level and the original real wage is restored. In the goods market, the fall in nominal wages causes the AS line to move to the right and the economy moves to the point C, where employment and output are back to their original levels, but the level of wages and prices has fallen. Thus, a *disinflation* has restored the economy's real variables to their original levels.

Note:

The movement of the AS line brings forth yet another fall in the price level from P_2 to P_3. This means that in the labour market, the N^d line again shifts to the left (not shown) and employment falls. In order to restore the real wage, workers will again have to revise their price expectations downwards and this process will continue for as long as workers fail to anticipate the changes in the price level. Eventually, workers will come to anticipate the effect of a shift of the AS line on the price level and equilibrium will be achieved, but in the transition there may be a protracted period of high unemployment.

The key question is: how long will the unemployment that emerges as a result of the adverse shock to AD persist? Those who believe in a smooth-functioning, self-regulating economy claim that prices and wages will fall quickly in response to the emergence of unemployment and spare capacity. A reason for believing this is that expectations are formed rationally, and workers anticipating a decline in the rate of

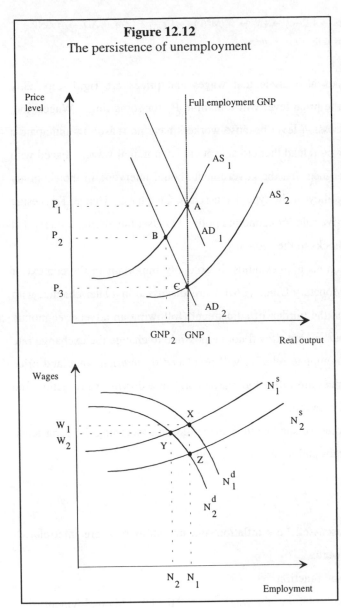

Figure 12.12
The persistence of unemployment

the AD line is steep (inelastic). Large changes in the price level are necessary before equilibrium at full employment GNP is re-established.

Note:

In the General Theory, Keynes identified the process by which an economy would adjust back to full employment GNP following an adverse shock. The process is as follows: the increase in unemployment (following the shock) reduces wages and therefore firms' costs. This, in turn, leads to a reduction in the price level, an increase in the real money supply, lower interest rates and an increase in investment and in real GNP. In short:

inflation will be willing to moderate their nominal wage claims in the knowledge that their real wages will not be affected. Flexibility of wages and prices speeds up the adjustment process. It allows an economy to achieve a relatively painless disinflation following a supply-side shock such as a rise in oil prices.

Recall a point raised earlier. Monetarists believe that the AD line is relatively flat (elastic) and as a result only small changes in the price level are necessary for the economy to revert back to full employment GNP. The Keynesians, on the other hand, believe that

Unemployment $\rightarrow \downarrow$ Wages $\rightarrow \downarrow$ Costs $\rightarrow \downarrow$ P $\rightarrow \uparrow (M^S/P) \rightarrow \downarrow r \rightarrow \uparrow I \rightarrow \uparrow$ AD $\rightarrow \uparrow$ GNP

This adjustment process is known as the *Keynes effect*.

Keynesian economists also argue that wages and prices are rigid, especially downwards. As a result, the price level will remain at P_1 for some time. Wages, too, will remain at their pre-recession level because workers have no reason to anticipate a fall in the price level that would lead them to accept cuts in nominal wages. Faced with these rigidities, it can be argued that the government should intervene in the economy and pursue a stabilisation policy of the type discussed in Chapter 6. Hence, Keynesian economists advocate an active role for economic policy to offset the unemployment that results from deflationary shocks to the economy.

The speed with which economies adjust is crucially important in the context of membership of European Monetary Union (EMU). As discussed in a later chapter, with a single currency in Europe the burden of adjustment (following an adverse economic shock) will fall on the labour market. It will not be possible to change the exchange rate to help in the adjustment: complete reliance will be placed on internal wage and price flexibility. If wages and prices are inflexible, particularly in a downward direction, the result could be a protracted recession.

In the following chapter we shall explore the evidence concerning the persistence of unemployment, output gaps and inflation in Ireland.

12.10 Conclusion

In this chapter we have discussed how inflation and unemployment are interrelated. The main topics discussed were:

- The aggregate production function
- The supply and demand for labour, the wage rate and the level of employment
- The role of price expectations, the concept of money illusion and the aggregate supply schedule
- The Keynesian, monetarist and neoclassical models.

Chapter 13

The Inflation-Unemployment Trade-off

13.1 Introduction

In this chapter we examine the relationship between inflation and unemployment. The New Zealand economist A. W. Phillips (1914-75), working at the London School of Economics in the 1950s, presented evidence which showed an inverse relationship between movement in wages and prices (inflation) and unemployment.   A curve depicting this inverse relationship has come to be known as the *Phillips curve*. We begin this chapter by discussing the original version of the Phillips curve and its implications for economic policy.   This is followed by a discussion of subsequent modifications and critiques of the Phillips curve. We review where the debate stands today.   We conclude by looking at the relevance of the Phillips curve to the Irish economy.

13.2 The Original Phillips Curve

Phillips noted that between 1861 and 1957 in Britain there was a tendency for periods of low unemployment to coincide with periods of rising wage rates.[1]   Conversely, during periods of high unemployment, the rate of increase in wages moderated. The Phillips curve simply shows the inverse relationship between the rate of unemployment and the rate of increase in nominal wages. Phillips drew a diagram depicting this inverse relationship. Variants of it have appeared in macroeconomic textbooks ever since. One modification is to replace the rate of increase in nominal wages by the increase in prices or the inflation rate. This adjustment, in effect, assumes that prices are set as a *mark-up* over wages. If wages rise, so too will the price of output, and vice versa. Expressed in terms of price inflation, the Phillips curve can be written as:

$$\pi = f(U) \qquad f_1 < 0 \qquad\qquad (1)$$

---

1. See A. W. Phillips, "The Relation Between Unemployment and the Rate of Change of Money Wages in the United Kingdom, 1861-1957", *Economica*, Vol. 25, November 1958. In fact Irving Fisher published a similar study for the United States in 1926: see Robert Barro, "I Discovered the Phillips Curve", *Journal of Political Economy*, April 1973.

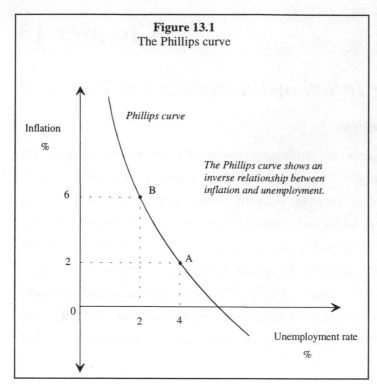

Figure 13.1
The Phillips curve

Phillips curve

Inflation %

The Phillips curve shows an inverse relationship between inflation and unemployment.

6 ┈┈ B

2 ┈┈ A

0

2   4

Unemployment rate %

where π is the rate of inflation and U the unemployment rate. Equation (1) states that the inflation rate is a function of the rate of unemployment. The $f_1 < 0$ indicates that we expect an increase in unemployment to lead to a fall in the rate of inflation and vice versa.

Phillips suggested that the best fit to the historical data was a non-linear one, as shown in Figure 13.1. As unemployment fell to very low levels, the rate of inflation accelerated more rapidly, while at very high levels of unemployment inflation levelled off or even became negative.

The economic rationale underlying this relationship is the Keynesian belief that shifts of the AD curve to the right lead to increases in both inflation and real GNP. As the economy approaches full employment, the AS curve becomes increasingly steep and the price level increases more rapidly.

The thinking behind the Phillips curve was enormously influential in the 1960s. It led macroeconomic policy-makers to believe, in a phrase used by Paul Samuelson and Robert Solow (both Nobel prize laureates teaching at the Massachusetts Institute of Technology) in 1960, that there exists a "menu for policy choice".[2] This led to the belief that there was a *trade-off* between the two evils of inflation and unemployment. It

2. Samuelson and Solow coined the phrase "the Phillips curve". They warned explicitly that their analysis was a short-run one and that the relationship between unemployment and inflation might shift under conditions of full employment. See P. A. Samuelson and R. M. Solow, "Analytical aspects of anti-inflation policy", *American Economic Review, Papers and Proceedings,* May 1960.

is not possible to enjoy a low rate of inflation *and* a low rate of unemployment at the same time, but it is possible to have less of one if more of the other is tolerated. Countries have to decide how much extra inflation they are prepared to tolerate in order to achieve a reduction in unemployment. For example, suppose the economy is initially at point A in Figure 13.1, where an inflation rate of 2 per cent is combined with an unemployment rate of 4 per cent. If the government now uses a fiscal or monetary policy to move the economy to point B, unemployment is reduced to 2 per cent but inflation rises to 6 per cent. The gain in terms of lower unemployment has been paid for in terms of a higher rate of inflation. The choice between these two evils is essentially a political one. Conservatives might prefer low inflation and ignore the high unemployment that this entails, whereas Labour or left-wing parties might tend to opt for low unemployment and accept the consequences in terms of inflation.

Various attempts were suggested in the 1960s to improve the trade-off. For example, a *prices and incomes policy* could be used to constrain the rise in inflation. With inflation held constant along the vertical axis, fiscal or monetary policy could then be used to lower unemployment. The result would be to shift the Phillips curve down to the left and improve the trade-off.

However, attempts to exploit the trade-off between unemployment and inflation led to increasing disillusionment. The emphasis during the 1960s was on keeping the rate of unemployment low, and a fair degree of success was achieved in this regard; but in many countries it became evident that the rate of inflation associated with what was considered full employment was rising. Even worse was the experience of the mid-1970s when the rate of inflation began to increase at a time of rising unemployment. This became known as *stagflation*. It appeared that the policies designed to move the economy up the Phillips curve were in fact causing the curve to shift outwards. The inflation/unemployment relationship, which apparently had been stable for over a hundred years, appeared to be breaking down.

There was much discussion of possible explanations for this: increased trade union militancy, the aggregate supply curve shifting to the left due to an increase in oil prices, a growing mismatch between the skills of the job seekers and the requirements of employers, a more generous social welfare system, and so on. However, none of these explanations seemed to go to the heart of the matter. For this, a fundamental reformulation of the Phillips curve idea was required.

13.3 The Revised Phillips Curve

A fundamental critique of the Phillips curve analysis was advanced independently by the monetarist economists Milton Friedman and Edmund Phelps of Columbia University in the late 1960s.[3] Basically, they argued that the original Phillips curve ignored the role of price expectations in wage negotiations. They incorporated *price expectations* into the Phillips curve and showed that in the long run there is no trade-off between inflation and unemployment: the long-run Phillips curve is vertical. Furthermore, they argued that this vertical Phillips curve would intersect the horizontal axis at the *natural rate of unemployment*. This "natural" rate is also known as the non-accelerating inflation rate of unemployment or NAIRU.[4] Attempts to hold unemployment below this rate result in accelerating inflation.

Note:

Friedman and Phelps deserve credit for foreseeing in the 1960s the acceleration of inflation that occurred in the 1970s and for providing a theoretical framework that divorced an understanding of the rate of inflation from the rate of unemployment.

The starting point is to reformulate the Phillips curve in terms of how workers bargain for wage increases. Here it is essential to distinguish between nominal wages (W) and real wages. Because wage contracts last into the future, workers will try to anticipate the rate of inflation in order to protect their real wages for the duration of the contract. For example, if inflation is expected to be 20 per cent over the coming year, workers will demand a 20 per cent increase in wages to compensate for anticipated inflation and maintain real wages at the present level. Hence the variable that matters in wage bargaining may be defined as $(\Delta W - \pi^e)$, where ΔW is the rate of change in wages and π^e is expected price inflation.

Note:

The real wages are nominal wages adjusted for the rate of inflation. This is usually done *ex post*, using realised or actual inflation. But wage bargaining is forward looking and has to be based on an anticipated or *ex ante* rate of inflation.

---

3. See M. Friedman, "The Role of Monetary Policy", *American Economic Review*, March 1969; and E. Phelps, *Inflation Policy and Unemployment Theory*, Norton, 1973.

4. The phrase NAIRU was introduced by James Tobin, of Yale University. It has the merit of avoiding the moralistic overtones of the "natural" rate.

Given that prices are set as a mark-up over wages, it follows that an increase in inflationary expectations will increase wage demands which, in turn, will increase the inflation rate. In short:

$$\uparrow \pi^e \rightarrow \uparrow \Delta W \rightarrow \uparrow \pi$$

The second main strand in the Phelps-Friedman theory is to incorporate the natural rate of unemployment into the analysis. They argue that inflation depends on the *gap* between the actual unemployment rate (U) and the NAIRU (U_n), that is, inflation is influenced by ($U - U_n$), rather than U. If U is greater than U_n, there is downward pressure on inflation and, conversely, if U is less than U_n, there is upward pressure on inflation. Unemployment does not affect inflation when U is equal to U_n.

Taking the above two adjustments together, the revised or *expectations-augmented* Phillips curve may be written:

$$\pi_t = \pi^e_t - \alpha(U - U_n) \tag{2}$$

where α is a coefficient which indicates how the rate of inflation reacts to the difference between the unemployment rate and the NAIRU ($U - U_n$). As in the original Phillips curve an increase in unemployment leads to a fall in inflation, and vice versa. Equation (2) states that the inflation rate in time t depends on the expected rate of inflation (π^e_t) plus an adjustment based on the difference between the actual rate of unemployment and the NAIRU.

How are expectations formed?

In the Keynesian model, workers formulated expectations about inflation by assuming that this year's inflation rate will recur next year, that is, $\pi^e_t = \pi_{t-1}$, where the subscript t indicates the year. This assumes that if inflation is 3 per cent in 1997, the same inflation rate is expected for 1998. This is a backward-looking approach to formulating expectations, and in periods of volatile inflation it is likely to lead to serious errors in the anticipated rate of inflation. Inserting this formulation of expectations into equation (2), we have:

$$\pi_t = \pi_{t-1} - \alpha(U - U_n) \tag{3}$$

Equation (3) states that the inflation rate in time t depends on inflation in the previous year plus an adjustment based on the unemployment gap.

The accelerationist theory of inflation

The expectations-augmented Phillips curve is illustrated in Figure 13.2. The Phillips curve is again downward sloping, indicating an inverse relationship between inflation and unemployment. We have also inserted a vertical line labelled the *long-run Phillips curve*.

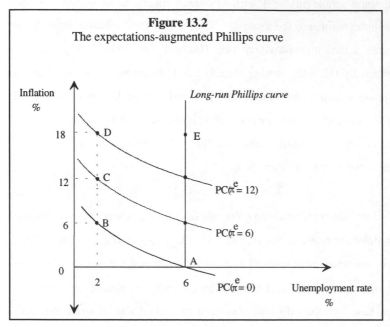

Figure 13.2
The expectations-augmented Phillips curve

For reasons which we shall explain, the long-run Phillips curve is located at the natural rate of unemployment which for illustrative purposes may be taken to equal 6 per cent unemployment.

Suppose now that the expected inflation (π^e) equals zero and that the actual unemployment rate equals the natural rate. Phelps and Friedman argue that under these circumstances the inflation rate will also be zero. This means that in Figure 13.2 the Phillips curve cuts the horizontal axis at the point A. At this point, zero inflation is combined with a 6 per cent unemployment rate. Note that the Phillips curve is labelled $PC(\pi^e = 0)$ to indicate that expected inflation is zero.

Let us suppose that the government decides that 6 per cent is an unacceptably high rate of unemployment and uses monetary or fiscal policy to increase nominal GNP. Initially, inflation increases to 6 per cent and unemployment falls to 2 per cent, and the economy moves to point B on $PC(\pi^e = 0)$.

The movement from A to B in Figure 13.2 is a satisfactory outcome from the government's point of view. An expansionary macroeconomic policy has increased real output and lowered unemployment to 2 per cent at the cost of a 6 per cent increase in inflation.

However, at point B the economy is not in long-run equilibrium. Inflation has increased from 0 per cent to 6 per cent, but people are still expecting it to be zero. Consequently, workers are confusing increases in nominal wages with increases in real wages, and hence are willing to increase their supply of labour. This money illusion will not continue for ever. Workers will revise their inflation expectations upwards and as a result the Phillips curve will shift upwards and to the right, from PC($\pi^e = 0$) to PC($\pi^e = 6$), corresponding to an increase in price expectations from 0 per cent to 6 per cent. The upward-sloping Phillips curves are in effect only *short-run* Phillips curves. Changes in inflation expectations cause these short-run curves to shift upwards or downwards.

Note:
When actual unemployment equals the NAIRU, actual inflation is determined by expected inflation. In other words, the short-run Phillips curve intersects the long-run Phillips curve at the point corresponding to the expected rate of inflation.

If, in the new situation, policy-makers persist in trying to maintain the rate of unemployment at 2 per cent, the economy will move to the point C on PC($\pi^e = 6$). At this point, 2 per cent unemployment is combined with an inflation rate of 12 per cent. Why has the inflation rate increased from 6 per cent to 12 per cent? Because the revision in price expectations from 0 per cent to 6 per cent resulted in an increase in wage demands. This (via the mark-up model) added a further 6 per cent to the inflation rate.

However, as before, point C is not a long-run equilibrium point, because the expected inflation rate of 6 per cent falls behind the actual inflation rate of 12 per cent. Workers will eventually revise their inflation expectations upwards once again, from 6 per cent to 12 per cent, and the Phillips curve will shift upwards from PC($\pi^e = 6$) to PC($\pi^e = 12$). The economy now moves to the point D, where 2 per cent unemployment is combined with an 18 per cent inflation rate.

The crucial point is that as long as policy is dedicated to maintaining the rate of unemployment below its natural level, the economy cannot reach equilibrium. Inflation will have to go on accelerating in order to maintain the money illusion which is necessary to increase the level of output above the level corresponding to the NAIRU.

Note:

The above analysis could also be conducted in terms of the Phillips curve. Recall from equation (3) that:

$$\pi_t = \pi_{t-1} - \alpha(U - U_n)$$

The expansionary monetary policy reduced U below the natural rate of unemployment and this added 6 per cent to π_t in the first year. In the second year this increase in inflation feeds back into the π_{t-1} term and this pushes the actual inflation rate to 12 per cent. In the third year the increase in inflation again feeds back into the π_{t-1} term and inflation again rises, and so on.

The consequences of trying to maintain the rate of unemployment below its natural rate are very unsatisfactory. The price of the reduction in unemployment is an ever rising rate of inflation. The expansionary macroeconomic policy has not just caused a once-off increase in inflation but has led to an accelerating rate of inflation. Eventually, workers will adjust their price expectations to take account of previous forecast errors. The increase in wages will catch up with inflation and the economy will revert back to the NAIRU. Equally, the policy-maker will come to view the inflation problem as more serious than the unemployment problem, and policies will be introduced to stop inflation accelerating.

By joining points such as A and the point at which we return to the natural rate, we obtain the long-run Phillips curve. We can see that it is *vertical* because we started at the natural rate and ultimately we end up back at the NAIRU. The inflation rate may differ, but the unemployment rate will in the long run be the same. Given that we started from the NAIRU and that we have now ended back at this rate, what has been gained by the expansionary macroeconomic policy? The answer is: *a temporary reduction in the rate of unemployment and a permanent increase in the rate of inflation.*

This is obviously less attractive than the permanent reduction in unemployment that was promised by the original version of the Phillips curve. If the cost of maintaining unemployment below the NAIRU is accelerating inflation, the attempt to do so would eventually have to be abandoned in order to prevent the breakdown of economic life. Accelerating inflation would lead to *hyperinflation* of the sort experienced in central Europe after World War II and in many east European countries in recent years. Such inflation is so disruptive that it undermines normal economic processes and leads to a sharp decline in living standards. (See Box 13.1.)

On the basis of their critique of the earlier Phillips curve analysis, therefore,

Phelps and Friedman rejected the notion that in the long run unemployment could be reduced by accepting a higher rate of inflation. The *accelerationist theory* of inflation, as this theory has been called, left little or no room for expansionary macroeconomic policy as an instrument for lowering the rate of unemployment.

13.4 Deflation, Expectations and Credibility

So far we have concentrated on accepting a higher inflation rate in order to lower unemployment. But what of the opposite case where a government is willing to accept higher unemployment in order to bring down inflation? This is essentially the type of "monetarist" policy introduced by Mrs Thatcher in Britain in 1979 and by Paul Volcker, chairman of the Federal Reserve Board in America in the same year. This deflation policy is the reverse of the expansionary policy discussed in the previous section.

Consider Figure 13.3, where the economy is initially at the natural rate of unemployment at A. Suppose also that inflation is 19 per cent and that this rate is unacceptable to the government. To reduce inflation the government introduces a deflationary fiscal or monetary policy. (This is akin to a shift to the left in the aggregate demand curve.) As a result, the economy moves from the point A to the point B along the Phillips curve labelled PC ($\pi^e = 19$). This Phillips curve is associated with inflation

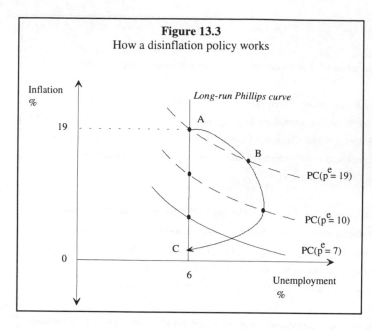

Figure 13.3
How a disinflation policy works

Long-run Phillips curve

Inflation %

19

A

B

$PC(p^e = 19)$

$PC(p^e = 10)$

$PC(p^e = 7)$

C

0

6

Unemployment %

expectations of 19 per cent. At the point B unemployment has risen but actual inflation has fallen below 19 per cent. At the point B the economy is said to be experiencing an *inflationary recession*.

In the next period, workers realise that inflation is lower than expected and they revise downwards their inflation forecast, and this is reflected in a shift downwards in the Phillips curve. As price expectations are revised downwards, over time the Phillips curve will gradually shift downwards. Eventually the government will become satisfied with the new low level of inflation and it will relax its deflationary fiscal or monetary policy. The economy will revert back to the natural rate. The final outcome may be at a point such as C, where the natural rate of unemployment is combined with a new lower level of inflation.

The cost of reducing inflation is the lost output and the rise in unemployment associated with the policy-induced recession. How much unemployment has to be increased in order to reduce inflation by one percentage point is referred to as the *sacrifice ratio*. This ratio depends on the size of the initial deflationary policy and how rapidly inflationary expectations are revised. If inflation expectations are quickly revised downwards, the adjustment costs will be relatively small. Conversely, if inflation expectations are slow to change, the adjustment costs will be relatively high.

Note:

The sacrifice ratio is defined as the number of *point years of excess unemployment* needed to reduce inflation by 1 per cent. For example, suppose unemployment exceeds the natural rate by 4 per cent for two years. This is equivalent to 8 points of excess unemployment (4 per cent excess unemployment × 2 years = 8 points).

Economists such as Robert Lucas of Chicago University, who believe in rational expectations, argue that the sacrifice ratio may be small under certain circumstances. Individuals take policy changes into account in formulating their expectations. If the central bank announces a reduction in the money supply, individuals would anticipate the reduction in inflation and adjust their expectations accordingly. In this case, the adjustment to low inflation could happen quite quickly and the unemployment costs involved would be small. An extreme form of rational expectation is the "full information" assumption. According to this, price expectations prove correct not just on average but in all cases. If wages and prices are completely flexible and the public is well informed, then the adjustment to low inflation will be instantaneous and the costs of deflation will be negligible.

However, the evidence does not support this point of view. In the UK Mrs Thatcher's monetarist experiment resulted in a painful transition. Inflation fell from 18 per cent in 1980 to 4 per cent in 1983, but GDP fell by 3 per cent between 1981 and 1983 and unemployment increased from 1.1 million in 1979 to 3 million in 1984. Similarly, in the US, the Fed under Paul Volcker pursued a deflationary monetary policy that reduced US inflation from 13.5 per cent in 1979 to 4 per cent in 1983. However, the real growth rate averaged only – 0.3 per cent from 1980 to 1982 and unemployment increased from 5.5 per cent in 1979 to 10 per cent in 1983. It took several years to return to the 5.5 per cent level.

Classical economists, however, emphasise the *credibility* of the policy-maker in bringing about costless adjustment. If the policy is credible, then firms and workers will quickly adjust prices and wages to take account of the new policy. However, if the policy-maker lacks credibility then adjustment will be prolonged and the costs will be high. Factors influencing the "credibility" of the policy-maker include:

- An ability to significantly reduce, if not eliminate, excessive budget deficits.
- Central bank independence. In particular, the central bank should not monetise public deficits by printing money or making loans to the government.
- An ability to communicate the new policy effectively to the public.
- In a small, open economy pegging the currency to a "hard" currency such as the deutschmark and then implementing appropriate fiscal, monetary and incomes policies to back up the peg. The ultimate logic of this approach is to abandon an independent monetary policy and a separate currency, as Ireland has now done by entering the EMU. This effectively removes responsibility for Irish inflation from

285

Dame Street in Dublin to the European Central Bank in Frankfurt.

Another issue relates to whether the policy-maker should introduce a "gradualist" or "cold turkey" approach in deflating the economy. That is should the policy-maker slowly deflate the economy and move gently towards a low inflation rate? The alternative is to introduce a once-off deflationary policy which hits the economy so hard that market participants cannot but recognise the government's intention and therefore revise their expectations. The movement to a low inflation rate should happen very quickly and the cost in terms of lost output is small.

The problem with the "cold turkey" approach is that it can lead to a severe recession which leads to civil unrest and political instability. In this context, one of the authors noticed the following headline in a Polish newspaper: "Sachs obcial psu ogon przy szyi." Literally translated this means "Sacks cuts dog's tail off at neck."! This is a reference to the American economist Jeffery Sacks who was responsible for introducing economic reforms in Poland during the late 1980s. Obviously, the media felt he had overdone the "cold turkey" approach![5]

13.5   Is there an Irish Phillips Curve?

The Phillips curve was developed to explain inflation in large economies that are relatively closed to international trade. It is still widely applied to economies such as the United States and probably to the post-EMU European economy. The relevance of this theory to a small open economy such as Ireland is less obvious.[6] This is because inflation in small open economies is strongly influenced by external factors. For a given exchange rate, the domestic price of traded goods is determined on world markets. On theoretical grounds, therefore, we would not expect a close relationship between inflation and unemployment in a small open economy, although clearly there should be some relationship between the rate of unemployment and the rate of wage inflation.

Figure 13.4 shows price inflation and the unemployment rate in Ireland from 1960 to 1997. The raw data do not indicate a close relationship between the two

---

5. However, the international evidence shows that the sacrifice ratio tends to be lower, the quicker the disinflation. See Laurence Ball, "What Determines the Sacrifice Ratio?" in N. G. Mankiw (ed.) *Monetary Policy*, University of Chicago Press, 1994.

6. The causes of Irish inflation are discussed in some detail in Chapters 18 and 22.

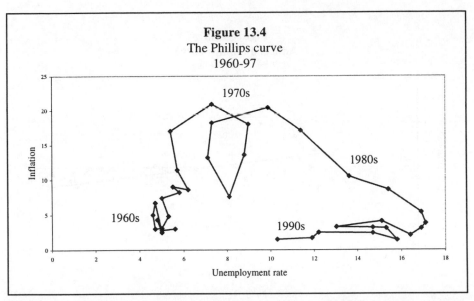

Figure 13.4
The Phillips curve
1960-97

variables. In fact, only during the 1980s is the inverse relationship predicted by the Phillips curve evident. The curves for the 1960s, the 1970s and the 1990s bear little resemblance to either the downward-sloping short-run Phillips curve or the vertical long-run Phillips curve discussed above. It is possible, however, that we are looking at a collection of short-run Phillips curves that shift over time.

■ In the 1960s low unemployment was combined with low inflation so the Phillips curve was down towards the left-hand corner.

■ In the 1970s low unemployment was associated with high inflation. This suggests that the Phillips curve representing this decade moved up towards the right.

■ In the 1980s high unemployment was associated with a high, but falling, inflation rate. The Phillips curve may have moved downwards from right to left.

■ In the 1990s, low inflation was combined with a falling unemployment rate. The Phillips curve appears to be shifting back towards the right-hand corner.

If the short-run Phillips curves have in fact shifted in this manner, then it would follow that the natural rate of unemployment in Ireland is not constant. It may have increased during the 1980s and declined again in recent years.

The sacrifice ratio Was the rise in unemployment in the 1980s the price of squeezing inflation out of the economy? If so, the "sacrifice ratio" was high. The number of "point-years" of excess unemployment 1981-97 has totalled 73, while inflation has fallen by 15 percentage points. This suggests a sacrifice ratio of 4.9, almost twice the

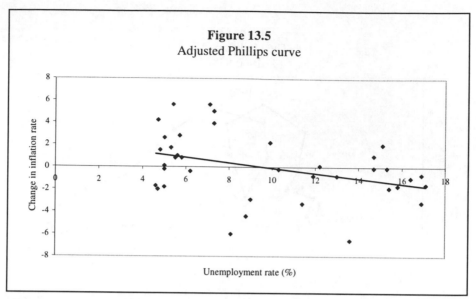

Figure 13.5
Adjusted Phillips curve

ratio attributed to the Volcker disinflation in the United States. High unemployment seems to be a very costly mechanism for reducing inflation in an Irish context.

This evidence of a Phillips curve type relationship in the 1980s is, however, somewhat tentative. Other factors played an important role in the inflationary process.

- The collapse of world energy prices in 1986 and the subsequent decline in global inflation.

- The fixed exchange rate between the Irish pound and the deutschmark led to low German inflation being transmitted to Ireland.

- High Irish unemployment led to a "disciplining" in the labour market in that it persuaded the trade unions to accept moderate increases in nominal wages.

Some empirical evidence

It would be informative if we could estimate the trend (regression) line running through the scatter diagram of the inflation-unemployment rate combinations for the entire period 1960 to 1997. However, estimating equation 3, above, is problematic because the natural rate of unemployment is unobservable. An alternative to equation 3 is to estimate the following equation:

$$\Delta \pi_t = \beta - \alpha U \qquad (4)$$

This equation examines the relationship between the *change* in the inflation rate and the unemployment rate. The β term is the intercept which may reflect how firms mark up prices over wages and other rigidities in the system such as national

Box 13.2

Deriving the Phillips curve

Equation 4 in the main text states that:

$$\Delta \pi_t = \beta - \alpha\, U \qquad\qquad (4)$$

We start with a definition. The natural rate of unemployment is the level of unemployment that prevails when actual inflation equals expected inflation. That is when $\Delta \pi_t = 0$. Setting equation 4 equal to zero and substituting the natural rate of unemployment for the actual rate we have:

$$0 = \beta - \alpha\, U_n \qquad\qquad (5)$$

Rearranging:

$$\alpha\, U_n = \beta \qquad\qquad (6)$$

Return now to equation 4 above. This equation can be rewritten as:

$$\pi_t = \pi_{t-1} + \beta - \alpha\, U \qquad\qquad (7)$$

Substitute equation 6 into 7 to obtain:

$$\pi_t = \pi_{t-1} + \alpha\, U_n - \alpha\, U \qquad\qquad (8)$$

Rearranging:

$$\pi_t = \pi_{t-1} - \alpha(U - U_n) \qquad\qquad (9)$$

which is equation 3 in the main text. Hence equations 3 and 4 are equivalent.

---

wage agreements and so on. The α term shows how the change in inflation reacts to the unemployment rate. Box 13.2 demonstrates that equation 4 is consistent with equation 3 (the accelerationist theory of inflation). Equation 4 can easily be estimated without having to make any assumptions about the natural rate of unemployment.

Figure 13.5 shows the scatter diagram for the *change in* inflation and unemployment over the period 1960-97. The trend (regression) line is estimated to be:

$$\Delta \pi_t = 2.0 - 0.2\, U \qquad\qquad (5)$$

The estimate for α is relatively low and indicates a very favourable trade-off. A one per cent reduction in the unemployment rate, for example, should lead only to a 0.2 per cent increase in inflation. Estimates for the United States would put this coefficient closer to one. However, the overall fit to the Irish data is not particularly good. Underlying statistics (not reported) indicate that the unemployment rate explains only 13 per cent of the variation in the change in inflation over the period. Clearly, there are other variables influencing Irish inflation which are omitted from equation 5.

As shown in Box 13.2, we can use the findings to get an indication of the natural rate of unemployment over the period. From equation 9 in Box 13.2, we can write:

$$U_n = \beta/\alpha \qquad (6)$$

Using the estimates in equation 5, the natural rate of unemployment is approximately 10 per cent ($U_n = 2/0.2 = 10$ per cent).

13.6 Conclusion

In this chapter we have discussed how inflation and unemployment are interrelated. The main topics discussed were:

- The Phillips curve
- The Phelps-Friedman critique of the Phillips curve analysis
- The long-run Phillips curve is vertical at the natural rate of unemployment or NAIRU (the non-accelerating inflation rate of unemployment). Holding the rate of unemployment below this rate will lead not just to a higher, but to accelerating inflation
- An inflationary recession – stagflation
- Evidence of the link between price and wage inflation and the rate of unemployment in Ireland. We leave to later chapters an explicit discussion of the inflationary process in a small open economy.

Chapter 14

The Labour Market and the Persistence of Unemployment

14.1 Introduction

The gap between European and American unemployment rates widened markedly during the 1990s. Unemployment in 1998 was close to 11 per cent in the EU, compared with only 4.5 per cent in the United States.[1] The persistence of a high unemployment rate is the most intractable problem facing Europe today.

In 1997, after four years of unprecedented economic growth, the Irish unemployment rate fell below the European average for the first time ever. None the less, the Irish unemployment rate remains very high and a serious problem of long-term unemployment persists among many sectors of the population. In this chapter we focus on the macroeconomic and labour market aspects of unemployment, with special reference to the Irish situation.

The structure of the chapter is as follows. We start with a brief description of the demographic influences on the Irish labour force. We then discuss the behaviour of employment and unemployment in Ireland since 1960. This is followed by an account of the dynamics of unemployment – that is, the flows of population into and out of the labour force, the links between economic growth and changes in unemployment, and the relationship between unemployment in Britain and in Ireland. We then look in more detail at the characteristics of unemployment. Finally, we explore the reasons why high unemployment persists and the policies that might reduce it.

14.2 The Demographic Background

We saw in Chapter 2 that between Independence in 1922 and 1961 the population of Ireland stagnated. After 1961 it started to grow, slowly at first but rapidly in the 1970s and 1990s. Changes in population have been mainly a reflection of the growth of

---

1. We use the OECD "standarised unemployment rates" in our international comparisons.

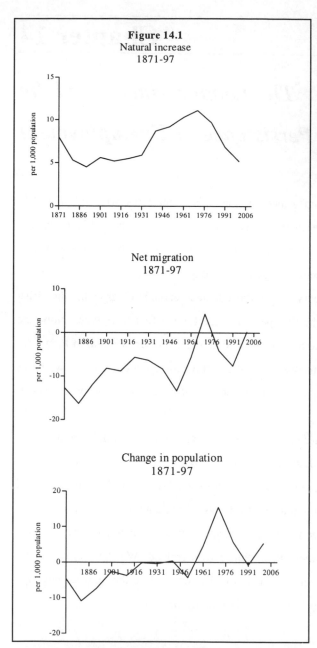

Figure 14.1
Natural increase
1871-97

Net migration
1871-97

Change in population
1871-97

employment in Ireland. In periods of stagnant or falling employment, high emigration has led to falling population; during booms emigration has given way to immigration and the population has grown rapidly.

The rate of population change is the sum of the rate of natural increase (that is, the excess of the birth rate over the death rate) and the net migration rate. The upper diagram in Figure 14.1 shows the rate of natural increase from 1871 to 1997. The centre diagram shows the net migration rate and the lower diagram the rate of population change.

The rate of natural increase rose steadily up to 1971 and then declined sharply as the birth rate fell. Over most of the period between 1871 and 1961, and again in the 1980s, there was a high emigration rate. This offset the natural increase and as a consequence the population fell. During the 1990s there has been a net inflow of population and for the first time in our modern history this has been accompanied by sustained growth of employment and falling unemployment.

While the population stagnated during the first four decades of Independence, over the past 35 years it increased by almost a third – from 2.8 million in 1961 to over

3.6 million today. It is now growing more rapidly than that of any other country in Europe.

14.3 The Labour Force

The labour force (or the economically active population) is the sum of the employed and the unemployed:

$$\text{Labour force} = \text{employed} + \text{unemployed} \tag{1}$$

A person is classified as employed if he or she is working for pay or profit or in a family business for one hour or more during the week.[2] The employed include employees, farmers, those working in family businesses, and the self-employed.

A person is classified as unemployed if he or she is (i) not working, and (ii) actively seeking, and available for, work. People who are neither working nor looking for work are classified as economically inactive. They do not form part of the labour force. Calling unpaid workers in the home, such as housewives and farmers' wives, "inactive" is clearly a misnomer. However, it is consistent with the convention of excluding unpaid home production from GNP.

The unemployment rate (UR) is the proportion of the labour force that is unemployed:

$$UR = (\text{unemployed/labour force}) \times 100 \tag{2}$$

The unemployment rate can be calculated separately for specific population groups (men, women, by age group, etc.).

Note:

In most countries the principal source of information on employment and unemployment is a household survey, such as the Current Population Survey in the United States or the Labour Force Survey (LFS) in Europe. The first Irish LFS was undertaken by the Central Statistics Office (CSO) in 1975. Annual surveys were conducted between 1983 and 1996 and a quarterly survey introduced in 1997. A sample of about 45,000 households is interviewed. The questionnaire has been refined over the years by the Irish CSO, the Statistical Office of the EU and International Labour Office (ILO).

---

2. These are the International Labour Office (ILO) definitions. Data on the labour force on this basis are obtained from the Labour Force Survey. Appendix 1 contains a detailed discussion of how unemployment is measured.

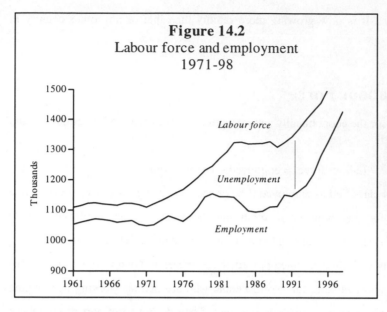

Figure 14.2
Labour force and employment
1971-98

Figure 14.2 shows the trend in employment, unemployment and the labour force over the period 1961-97.[3] Over the period 1961-71 the labour force stagnated, but between 1971 and 1998 it grew by 40 per cent. Initially much of this growth was reflected in rising unemployment. However, between 1986 and 1998 employment grew by 30 per cent – an unprecedented growth in the numbers at work. No other country in the OECD recorded a comparable rate of increase in employment over this period.

Labour force participation rate

The labour force participation rate (LFPR) is the proportion of the population that is in the labour force:

$$LFPR = (labour\ force/population) \times 100 \qquad (3)$$

In 1998 there were 1.6 million people in the labour force out of a population of 3.7 million, giving an LFPR rate of 43 per cent. There has been a steady rise in the LFPR since the late 1980s (Figure 14.3). The two influences on the aggregate LFPR are:

The ratio of the working-age population to the total population. In the past this ratio was low in Ireland, due to the relatively high birth rate and to emigration. This has changed dramatically since the 1980s, however. The falling birth rate has reduced the proportion of children in the population and net immigration is also raising the ratio of working-age people in the population.

---

3. Data on employment and unemployment are contained in the Appendix to this chapter.

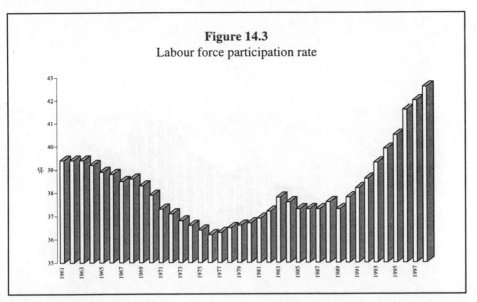

Figure 14.3
Labour force participation rate

The labour force participation rate of the working-age population. This depends on factors such as:

- Educational participation rates. The higher the participation rate in second and third level education, the lower the labour force participation rate among young adults. Educational participation rates rose sharply in Ireland during the 1980s and 1990s, and this tended to depress the LFPR.

- Age at retirement. In most western countries there has been a marked trend towards earlier retirement, especially among men. This has also tended to depress the LFPR.

- Women's labour force participation rates. In the past in Ireland the LFPR among adult women was very low due to the tendency for women with young children not to remain in paid employment. (Until the 1970s, women had to retire from employment in the civil service and the banks if they got married!) However, in recent years women are having fewer children and those with children are less likely to retire from the labour force.

There has also been a contrasting trend in LFPRs among older men and younger women. There has been a dramatic increase in the LFPR among women aged 25-44, while it has fallen significantly among men aged 45-64. Rising educational standards, and the fall in the marriage rate and in family size have contributed to more women remaining in the labour force, while the fall in the demand for older, unqualified

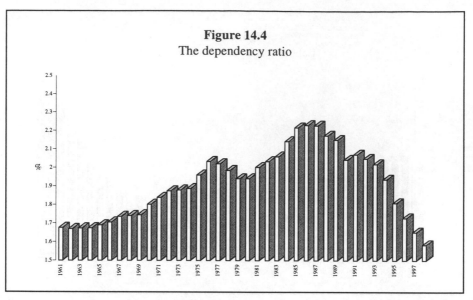

Figure 14.4
The dependency ratio

workers has led to many men dropping out of the labour force at a relatively early age. The net result of the changing age structure of the population and changes in LFPRs within population groups has been a marked rise in the overall LFPR.

The dependency ratio

A measure that takes account of the unemployment rate as well as the LFPR is the employment dependency ratio, that is, the ratio of the non-employed to the employed. This gives an indication of the burden that has to be borne by the employed (through taxation or transfers within households) to support those who are not employed.

From Figure 14.4 it may seen that there was a steady rise in this ratio over the years 1961 to 1985: the employed as a proportion of the population fell due to the high birth rate, the stagnant level of employment and the rising unemployment rate. This rising dependency ratio acted as a drag on the improvement in living standards. However, since the mid-1980s the dependency ratio has been falling and this has allowed living standards to rise rapidly. The sharp drop in dependency since the mid-1980s reflects:

- the rising proportion of the population in the working-age groups, and
- the falling unemployment rate.

Assuming no rise in the unemployment rate, the employment dependency ratio will continue to fall over the coming decades. This will considerably ease the burden on

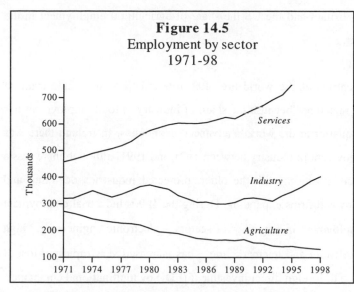

Figure 14.5
Employment by sector
1971-98

the working population of providing for the young and the elderly. Ireland is much better situated in this regard than are the continental European countries and Japan, where the burden of dependency is rising rapidly due to the ageing of the population.

The growth of employment

After a long period of stagnation, an exceptional rate of employment growth has been recorded since the late 1980s. Over the past ten years the Irish economy has created proportionately more employment than any other OECD country. Whereas in the 1980s there was widespread pessimism regarding our ability to absorb our rapidly growing population into employment, in the last few years labour shortages have become widespread. This is all the more remarkable because in the 1980s we still had a large agricultural sector, in which employment was declining, and we went through a fiscal correction that involved some reduction in the numbers employed in the public sector. The rate of growth of private sector, non-agricultural employment has been little short of astounding. Figure 14.5 shows the change in sectoral employment (services, industry and agriculture) over the period 1971-96.

Agriculture Employment in agriculture fell by almost 3 per cent a year over the past two decades. Productivity grew very rapidly. Much more is being produced by a greatly reduced workforce. The share of agriculture in total employment is now down to 10 per cent, compared with 26 per cent in 1971. The decline in agricultural employment is likely to continue – in Britain and the US the share of agricultural employment in the total is below 2 per cent.

Industry The rich countries of the world are often referred to as the "industrialised countries" but this is a misnomer because the share of industry in total employment has fallen well below one quarter in the world's advanced economies. In Ireland there was no net increase in employment in industry between 1971 and 1991, although there was a radical change in its composition, with the older, protected industries declining and newer, mostly foreign-owned firms expanding. During the 1990s industrial employment has grown rapidly. Employment in a number of sectors – electronic engineering, "high tech" food, computer software and telemarketing – has increased very rapidly. Most of this growth has been due to foreign direct investment (FDI) by multinational companies. Ireland now has significant clusters of firms in these sectors, attracted here by factors such as the availability of a relatively skilled, English-speaking labour force, competitive labour costs, and the 10 per cent corporate profit tax rate. The country is no longer attractive to low-wage, labour-intensive industries because of rising labour costs for unskilled workers. In 1998, most successful Irish manufacturing firms have reached maximum employment levels in Ireland and are now expanding abroad.

Services In the advanced countries of the world employment is expanding rapidly in the services sectors. These include marketed and non-market services. Non-marketed services refers to those sectors that are provided directly by central and local government, by state-owned companies, and by tax-financed hospitals, schools, colleges and universities. Employment in these sectors grew rapidly in the 1970s but the retrenchment in public spending reversed this trend in the late 1980s. Market services include a variety of sub-sectors such as banking, financial, professional and business services, hotels and restaurants, and retail and wholesale distribution. Employment in these sectors has increased steadily over the long term and accelerated in the 1980s and 1990s.

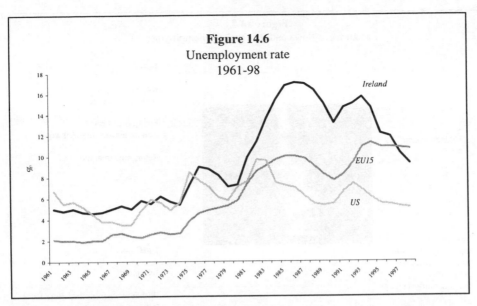

Figure 14.6
Unemployment rate
1961-98

Note:

Believers in the importance of industry argue that service sector employment is "unproductive". This is as fallacious as was the eighteenth-century physiocratic view that only agricultural employment was genuinely "productive". Productive jobs are simply those that respond to consumers' needs. As people become wealthier they spend a rising proportion of income on services rather than on physical products. As a consequence, in rich countries the standard of living depends increasingly on the efficiency of the service sector rather than on industry and agriculture. Furthermore, employment in areas such as tourism and international financial services is a basis for economic development. Ireland can be regarded as a region whose economic base comprises manufacturing industry and traded services. The rapid growth of other service sector employment since the 1980s has been induced by the expansion of this base.

The services sector can act as an "employer of last resort", providing jobs when no other employment opportunities are available. This is often the case in low-income countries where many young people are only able to find jobs like selling cigarettes or polishing shoes on the street corners. In the United States much of the recent employment growth has been in relatively low-wage service jobs, giving rise to the label the "working poor". In the past young Irish people preferred emigration to the prospect of low-wage service employment at home. However, during the current boom the services sector has provided some of the best-paid and most sought-after employment opportunities.

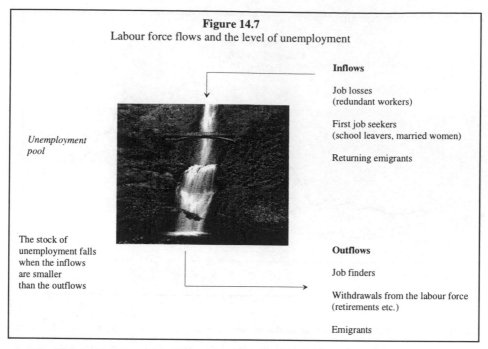

Figure 14.7
Labour force flows and the level of unemployment

Inflows

Job losses
(redundant workers)

First job seekers
(school leavers, married women)

Returning emigrants

Unemployment pool

The stock of
unemployment falls
when the inflows
are smaller
than the outflows

Outflows

Job finders

Withdrawals from the labour force
(retirements etc.)

Emigrants

14.4 The Dynamics of Unemployment

The behaviour of the unemployment rate is an important economic indicator. As we saw in Chapter 1, a low unemployment rate is one of the principal goals of macroeconomic policy. Figure 14.6 shows the unemployment rate in Ireland, EU15 and the US from 1961-98. The Irish unemployment rate has been highly unstable over the past four decades. The pattern of Irish unemployment is similar to that found in other European countries. Unemployment in Europe has been very slow to return to the levels recorded in the 1960s. In the US, on the other hand, the unemployment rate has not drifted upwards from decade to decade.

The unemployment rate refers to a stock of people measured at a point of time. Changes in stocks reflect the difference between inflows and outflows. The main flows into and out of the unemployment pool are illustrated in Figure 14.7. This simple framework allows us to highlight some important points.

▪ Unemployment falls when the numbers leaving the pool of unemployment exceeds the inflow. The best way to increase the outflow from unemployment is to increase the rate at which job seekers find jobs. This depends above all else on the rate at which the economy generates job opportunities.

- For a given rate of growth of employment opportunities, the rate at which unemployment falls depends on the matching of vacancies with job seekers. This in turn depends on factors such as the skills of the unemployed and their willingness to accept the available jobs.

- A less favourable way to increase the outflow is by encouraging people to withdraw from the labour force or to leave the country. In Ireland in the past we tended to blame our high unemployment on the rapid growth of the labour force, but more recently the rapid growth of the economy has been attributed to the abundant supply of labour. Internationally, the rate of unemployment is not related to the rate of growth of the labour force.

A key question, of great social and economic importance, is: how long does the typical entrant to the pool of unemployment remain unemployed? The *duration* of unemployment spells matters because the social costs of unemployment increase with the duration of a spell of unemployment. Long-term unemployment is more costly than short-term unemployment because:

- Savings may tide households over a short spell of unemployment.

- The long-term unemployed tend to lose motivation and self-esteem and come to be regarded as "unemployable".

- The long-term unemployed lose contact with the labour market. They exercise little influence on the wage-bargaining process. Short-term unemployment, on the other hand, moderates inflationary wage pressures.

The rate of long-term unemployment varies more between countries than does short-term unemployment. In 1996, the long-term unemployment rate ranged from 0.7 per cent in the US to 10.6 per cent in Spain, and was 9.5 per cent in Ireland. This highlights the seriousness of the unemployment problem in countries like Spain and Ireland. It is surprising that in 1996 the rate of short-term unemployment in Ireland was lower than in the US.

Figure 14.7 suggests that if people are finding jobs faster than they are losing them, unemployment will fall. This highlights the link between the rate of growth of the economy and changes in the unemployment rate. This relationship is summarised by Okun's law, which we introduced in Chapter 1. This law states that changes in the unemployment rate can be related to the rate of growth of output:

$$u_t - u_{t-1} = \alpha + \beta \, \Delta GNP$$

where u = the rate of unemployment, ΔGNP = the rate of growth of output, and α and β are parameters to be estimated statistically. Using Irish data for GNP and unemployment over the period 1978-97 the following relationship has been estimated:

$$u_t - u_{t-1} = 1.41 - 0.38 \, \Delta GNP$$

This estimated relationship is quite satisfactory from a statistical point of view. Two-thirds of the variation in the change in the unemployment rate over the last twenty years can be "explained" by the GNP growth rate. It suggests that

$$\Delta GNP = 3.7 + u_t - u_{t-1} = 0$$

that is, unemployment is stable if GNP grows at 3.7 per cent. Faster growth leads to a fall in unemployment, slower growth to a rise. For each percentage point that GNP grows above (below) 3.7 per cent, the rate of unemployment falls (rises) by almost 0.4 percentage points.[4]

This equation is a systematic way of accounting for the behaviour of the unemployment rate shown in Figure 14.6. We can summarise it as follows:

1961-73 Over this period the economy grew at a rate sufficient to maintain the unemployment rate in the region of 5 per cent. Fluctuations in output and unemployment were relatively minor.

1974-79 The stability of the 1960s came to an end with the oil price shocks of the 1970s. Unemployment soared during the recession of 1974-75 and, although it fell during the 1977-78 growth spurt, it rose again at the end of the 1970s, long before it fell to its previous "equilibrium" level.

1979-86 There was an unprecedented rise in the unemployment rate over these years. This was due to the prolonged recession. Although other countries also experienced rising unemployment as governments squeezed inflation out of their economies, the crisis in Ireland was aggravated by the youthful age structure of the population. With the safety valve of emigration closed off by the high levels of unemployment in Britain and the US, the rapidly growing labour force was reflected mainly in the rising numbers out of work.

1986-1989 The unemployment rate finally peaked in 1986. By then the combination of very high unemployment in Ireland and falling unemployment rates in Britain and the

---

4. For further discussion of this relationship see Brendan Walsh, "The Persistence of Unemployment in a Small Open Economy: The Case of Ireland" in Frank Barry (ed.) *The Celtic Tiger: Recent Economic Growth and Structural Change in Ireland,* (ed.) London Macmillan, 1998.

US led to a resumption of net emigration at a rate not seen since the 1950s. The recovery in the Irish economy was slow to translate into increases in employment: the initial increase in the demand for labour was readily met from the inflow of young people, women and returning emigrants to the labour force. Unemployment fell towards the end of the decade as the rate of growth of output rose.

1989-92 Despite the increased inflow of EU structural funds, the global recession slowed the growth of the economy over this period and the unemployment rate rose. This illustrates the operation of Okun's law: as the output growth rate fell below 4 per cent, unemployment increased.

1992-to date Since 1992 the exceptionally rapid growth of the economy has progressively lowered the unemployment rate. Despite an inflow of population – returning emigrants and genuine immigrants – the growth of employment has been so rapid that the rate of unemployment has fallen sharply. Once again, this outcome is in line with Okun's Law.

After the rate of growth of output in Ireland, the most important influence on Irish unemployment is probably the economic situation in Britain. We noted above the important influence of migration on the Irish labour market. Some economists have argued that this influence is so strong that the Irish unemployment rate is determined primarily by UK labour market conditions. On the basis of the behaviour of the numbers of registered unemployed over the period 1971-91 the evidence suggests that

> *". . .trends and fluctuations in UK unemployment . . . have a decisive long-term influence on Irish unemployment."*[5]

In Figure 14.8 we show the Irish and British unemployment rates since 1961. The general tendency for unemployment in the two countries to move in tandem is clear, but so is the fact that the gap between the two rates has varied. It almost disappeared during the sudden growth spurt in the late 1970s, and it widened considerably during the 1980s. It is not clear why people preferred to remain unemployed in Ireland than to migrate to Britain at this time. Two possible explanations are:

- The Irish social welfare system became relatively generous and encouraged the unemployed to stay in Ireland rather than emigrate to Britain.

---

5. Patrick Honohan, 1992, "The Link between Irish and UK Unemployment," *Quarterly Economic Commentary* (Spring) 33-44.

Figure 14.8
Unemployment in Ireland and the UK

- Migration to Britain depends not just on the gap between Irish and British unemployment but also on the absolute level of unemployment in Britain. The unprecedented high level of British unemployment in the first half of the 1980s may account for the low level emigration from Ireland and the widening gap between Irish and British unemployment at the time.

14.5 What is the Natural Rate of Unemployment?

We argued in the previous section that the main influences on fluctuations in Irish unemployment are the rate of growth of output and the level of unemployment in Britain. But these factors do not explain the equilibrium or natural rate of unemployment. They do not account for the puzzling fact that after six years of exceptionally rapid growth, the unemployment rate in 1998 remains much higher than would have been regarded as normal in the 1960s.

The persistence of a high unemployment rate in the wake of the recessions of the 1970s and 1980s is a distinguishing feature of European labour markets. In contrast, by the mid-1980s unemployment in the United States had fallen back to its "natural rate" and the sustained growth of the 1990s has pushed it close to a historical low. This raises the question of how to define the "equilibrium" unemployment rate or "full employment".

These concepts should be related to the trade-off between unemployment and inflation discussed in Chapters 12 and 13. There we saw that economists accept that some unemployment is a normal feature of a dynamic economy. Full employment can be thought of as a situation where only minimal frictional unemployment remains. This level of unemployment is referred to as the natural rate of unemployment (or non-accelerating inflation rate of unemployment, NAIRU).

Note:
We used to think we could set precise "full employment" targets. The National Industrial Economic Council in 1967 specified 2 per cent as the target unemployment rate. The National Economic and Social Council (NESC) published a study in 1975 that defined it as 4 per cent. In 1977 the NESC used a rate of 5 per cent as equivalent to full employment. The use of numerical targets was then abandoned. Studies of unemployment by the Economic and Social Research Institute (ESRI) and official documents, including the Programme for National Recovery (1987), the Programme for Economic and Social Progress (1990), Programme for Competitiveness and Work (1994), and Programme 2000 (1997) have avoided specifying targets for employment or unemployment.

Looking at the Irish unemployment record in Figure 14.9, the manner in which the unemployment rate ratcheted up after every recession is striking. Although unemployment fell during the growth spurt of the late 1970s, it did not fall back to the 5 per cent that was normal in the 1960s. Similarly, even after the exceptional growth of the 1990s the unemployment rate was still almost 10 per cent in 1998 and inflationary pressures were building up in the labour market. Is the unemployment rate that was normal in the 1960s no longer relevant? Has the natural rate of unemployment increased?

Economists use the concept of hysteresis when exploring this issue.[6] Hysteresis refers to a situation where the equilibrium value of a variable depends on the actual value assumed by it. If there is hysteresis in the labour market, the natural unemployment rate changes over time in response to changes in actual unemployment. The equilibrium rate might have been 5 per cent in the 1960s but increased to 10 per cent in the late 1990s. The view that the natural rate of unemployment jumps around

6. See Richard G. Layard, Stephen J. Nickell and Richard A. Jackman, *Unemployment: Macroeconomic Performance and the Labour Market*, Oxford: Oxford University Press, 1991; and George Lee, "Hysteresis and the Natural Rate of Unemployment in Ireland", *Journal of the Statistical and Social Inquiry Society of Ireland*, 1989/90.

from decade to decade has led Robert Solow to question the usefulness of the concept: "A natural rate that hops around from one triennium to another under the influences of unspecified forces, including past unemployment rates, is not natural at all."[7]

Note:

Think of what would happen if every time you got the flu your body's normal temperature rose. Even after you had recovered, your temperature would remain above 37° Celsius. It would be exhibiting hysteresis. It sounds unpleasant!

To understand why the natural rate has risen over time we have to appeal to changes in the labour market. A higher proportion of long-term unemployed in the total, for example, would lead to high equilibrium unemployment, with the absence of inflationary pressures. We discuss these aspects of the labour market below.

14.6 Who are the Unemployed?

We can gain a better understanding of the causes of unemployment, and its persistence, by studying the characteristics of the unemployed. The risk of being unemployed differs greatly between population groups. The following is a summary of the factors that have been found to affect the risk of unemployment in Ireland.[8]

Educational attainment There is a very striking association between educational attainment and the risk of unemployment. Those with low educational qualifications are much more likely to be unemployed than better-educated individuals. Furthermore, once they become unemployed, poorly educated individuals are more likely to remain unemployed − their risk of long-term unemployment is high. Finally, they are more likely to drop out of the labour force by ceasing to look for employment. This holds for women as well as men.

---

7. Robert Solow, "Unemployment: Getting the Questions Right", *Economica*, 1986 (Supplement) p. S54.

8. These are *ceteris paribus* findings based on research into the returns of the Labour Force Survey: see Anthony Murphy and Brendan Walsh, "Male Unemployment and Non-employment in Ireland", *Economic and Social Review,* Vol. 27, No. 5 (October 1996) pp 467-90, and *Aspects of Employment and Unemployment in* Ireland, National Economic and Social Forum Report No. 13 (Dublin, May 1997).

Age The youth unemployment rate is higher than that among people of prime working age. Teenagers and those with little or no employment experience have the highest unemployment rate. The lowest rate is among those aged 45-64.

Marital status Other things being equal, unmarried men are most likely to be unemployed and their situation has deteriorated in recent years. This could be because single people have become less committed to holding down a job or, alternatively, because those who cannot get a job are less eligible for marriage. It is difficult to decide the direction of causation between these two variables.

Area of residence Men living in large urban areas are more likely to be unemployed than their rural counterparts. Employment opportunities for men appear to be more plentiful in rural areas. There is some evidence of the reverse pattern for women.

The presence of young children in the household Both men and women are less likely to be employed when there are young children present in the household. Men, as well as women, may choose to devote time to child rearing rather than taking paid employment, and the social welfare and tax systems make it less attractive for those with families to accept offers of employment.

Housing tenure When all other factors are allowed for, those who live in local authority rented accommodation are significantly less likely to be employed than those in other types of housing. The negative effect of this factor is very strong, but it is not clear what mechanism is at work. Employers may discriminate against people with addresses in local authority estates, or residents in these estates may lack the networks that would help them find out about jobs, or they may be influenced by a culture in which unemployment has come to be regarded as normal.

Household composition Living in a household with other unemployed and/or inactive adults. It seems that like cluster with like.

While these findings do not help explain the reasons for fluctuations in the rate of unemployment, they should be taken into account in formulating policy towards the unemployed. They also highlight an issue that has emerged in most western economies

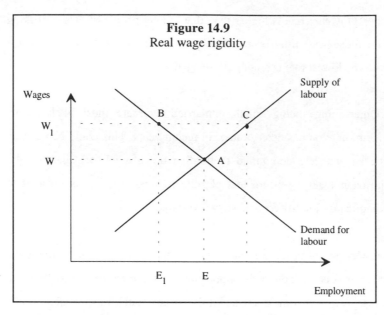

Figure 14.9
Real wage rigidity

Wages

Supply of labour

W_1

B C

W .... A

Demand for labour

E_1 E

Employment

in the 1980s and 1990s, namely, the growing economic disadvantage of poorly educated men and women. Not only are they increasingly at risk of becoming unemployed, they are also most likely to be employed at low wages, and the gap between the earnings of educated and uneducated workers has widened. These trends have been blamed on many factors, such as:

- The way in which new technologies have reduced the demand for unskilled, manual workers.

- The growth of competition from developing countries where unskilled labour is extremely cheap.

14.7 Why Doesn't the Labour Market Clear?

Why should there be any significant unemployment over and above some minimal level of frictional unemployment? Why does the labour market not clear? The persistence of high unemployment in Europe has provoked an enormous amount of research on this topic in recent years.[9] We now review the main explanations that have been suggested.

---

9. For a review of this literature see Charles R. Bean, "European Unemployment: A Survey", *Journal of Economic Literature*, Vol. XXXII, No. 2 (June 1994) pp 573-619, and Stephen Nickell, "Unemployment and Labour Market Rigidities: Europe versus North America", *Journal of Economic Perspectives,* Vol. 11, No. 3 (Summer 1997) pp 55-74.

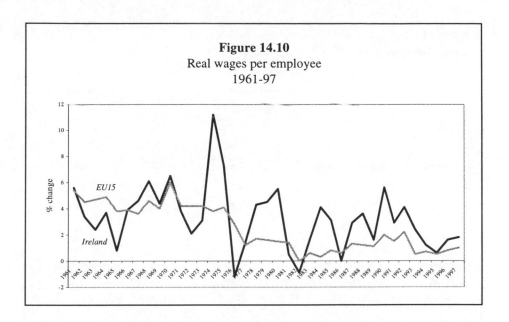

Figure 14.10
Real wages per employee
1961-97

Real wage rigidity

In microeconomics students learn that excess supply in any market leads to a fall in the price until the market clears. Figure 14.9 shows the labour market analysis developed in Chapter 12. The supply and demand for labour determines the real wage (vertical axis) and employment (horizontal axis). The equilibrium real wage is W and the associated employment level is E. (If the price level is assumed to be constant, then W represents the real wage.) If, however, the actual real wage is W_1 firms will only hire E_1 workers, and unemployment emerges. By definition, a non-market clearing real wage results in unemployment. But why does unemployment not lead to a fall in the real wage rate, encouraging employers to move down their demand for labour schedules and hire more workers until unemployment is eliminated?[10] If real wage cuts are resisted, unemployment will persist. This explanation of unemployment is called the real wage resistance hypothesis.

Figure 14.10 shows the annual percentage change in real wages per employee in Ireland and the EU15 from 1961-97. Among the points to emerge from this chart are:

- Annual average change in real earnings was 3.2 per cent in Ireland compared to 2.4 per cent in the EU15.

---

10. We can think of the equilibrium situation as one in which unemployment is at the natural rate. When the real wage is above the market-clearing level, unemployment rises above the natural rate.

Table 14.1

National wage agreements

		Agreed increase nominal wages % change	Inflation	Real Wages
		A	B	C = A - B
Programme	1988 (Jan. - Dec.)	2.5	2.6	– 0.1
for National	1989 (Jan. - Dec.)	2.5	4.71	– 2.21
Recovery	1990 (Jan. - Dec.)	2.5	2.68	– 0.18
Programme	1991 (Jan. - Dec.)	4	3.62	0.38
for Economic	1992 (Jan. - Dec.)	3	2.36	0.64
and Social	1993 (Jan. - Dec.)	3.75	1.43	2.32
Progress				
Programme for	1994 (Jan. - Dec.)	2	2.43	– 0.43
Competitiveness	1995 (Jan. - Dec.)	2.5	2.37	0.13
and Work	1996 (Jan. - Jun.)	2.5	0.82	1.68
	1996 (July - Dec.)	1	0.87	0.13
Partnership 2000	1997 (Jan. - Dec.)	2.5	1.5	1.0
	1998 (Jan. - Dec.)	2.5	na	na
	1999 (Jan. - Sept.)	1.5	na	na
	1999 Oct. - 2000 Mar.	1	na	na

na = not available

- There were only two years (1976 and 1982) when real wages declined in Ireland. There is also little correlation between real earnings and unemployment in Ireland. During the recession of 1974 and in the mid-1980s, there was a significant increase in real wages despite high and rising unemployment.

310

The wage-bargaining process

To say that unemployment is high because the labour market does not clear due to "real wage rigidity" only pushes the explanation back one stage. What accounts for this resistance to wage cuts in the face of high unemployment?

Many explanations have been offered. Most of them have to do with the wage-setting process and the role of trade unions. Trade unions exist in part to ensure that real wages do not fall. In inflationary periods unions look for indexation of wages, that is, automatic increases in nominal wages to compensate for rises in the cost of living. In Ireland during the 1970s and 1980s wage bargaining quickly focused on real, post tax pay. Trade unions sought to protect their members not only from inflation but also from the effects of higher taxation.

Different approaches have been tried to make the behaviour of real wages more responsive to the level of unemployment. Co-operation between the "social partners" (unions, employers and government) or corporatism is advocated. It has been argued that where a high degree of corporatism exists, as in Scandinavia and Austria, the growth of real wages has been moderated to prevent unemployment from rising. At the other extreme, a very decentralised wage-bargaining process, as exists in the United States, may also impose a discipline on the labour market. The worst outcome is associated with situations where individual trade unions struggle to increase their members' pay but accept no responsibility for the effect of their actions on the national economy. This was the situation in Britain before the Thatcher government broke the power of the unions in the 1980s.

In Ireland, four national wage programmes have been agreed since 1988. The increase in nominal wages under each programme is summarised in Table 14.1, column A. Columns B and C show the inflation rate and associated real wages increase for each sub-period. It can be seen that real earnings declined during the Programme for National Recovery (1988–91) and again in 1994. However, in addition to the agreed increase in nominal wages, employees could also negotiate further increases at a local level and the government held out the prospect of tax reductions at budget time. These additional concessions would have boosted workers' real take-home pay. Overall, the national wage agreements have been credited with helping to combine industrial peace with rapid growth in employment since the 1980s.[11]

Efficiency wages

Karl Marx (1818-83) believed that the capitalists of his day used the "Reserve Army of the Unemployed" to force wages down to the bare subsistence minimum. Industrial relations are not so simple today. The unemployed do not knock at employers' doors offering to work for less than the going rate. If they did employers would probably be reluctant to hire them, suspecting that only a problem worker would offer to work for less than the going rate. Nor is it usual for employers to ask their employees to accept wage cuts or to threaten to replace them with new recruits at lower wages. In most firms there is an explicit or implicit contract between employers and workers which guarantees a certain stability of wages and employment.

The efficiency wage hypothesis says that employers use wages to recruit, retain and motivate their workers. By paying above the odds, firms retain a more productive labour force than they would get if they set wages in accordance with fluctuations in the supply and demand for labour. The employers have valid reasons for not allowing the existence of unemployment to drive wages down to the market clearing level.

Labour market rigidity

A number of special features of European labour markets have been blamed for the reluctance of employers to take on workers at the same rate that occurs in the United States. Among these are:

Firing costs In many European countries employers have to offer more or less permanent employment to their workers. It is difficult and costly to get rid of workers once they are hired. Understandably, this makes employers reluctant to take on workers in the first place. Paradoxically, the attempt to protect employment may result in less employment!

---

11. See A. Leddin and B. M. Walsh, "Economic Stabilisation, Recovery and Growth: Ireland 1979-1996", *The Irish Bank Review*, Summer 1997.

Restrictive work practices It is more costly for employers to do business if workers oppose flexible working arrangements, such as part-time and shift working. Demarcation rules could stipulate that employers hire two craftsmen where one would be sufficient. The result may be that no one is hired.

Skills mismatch A mismatch between the skills of the unemployed (particularly the long-term unemployed) and job vacancies can lead to shortages in key occupations even when the overall rate of unemployment is high. The evidence suggests increased mismatch in many economies since the 1980s.

High reservation wages A relatively generous social welfare system leads to high reservation wages, that is, the minimum wage that must be offered before a vacancy can be filled. The unemployed search longer for a "suitable" job rather than taking the first job they are offered.

Labour mobility Immobility of the unemployed to search for jobs reduces the efficiency of the labour market and increases the natural rate of unemployment. Factors such as the difficulty of obtaining housing in expanding regions or the desire to retain a subsidised council house affects labour mobility.

Maximum working week The Maastricht Treaty includes a "Social Charter" that lays down numerous regulations concerning conditions of employment. One of them stipulates that employees may not work more than 48 hours a week – even if they want to! The United Kingdom has consistently opposed this approach to the labour market, citing its own better record at reducing unemployment than that of the continental economies. It obtained an "opt out" from the Social Charter and advocates greater flexibility in the labour market as the way to reduce unemployment. New Labour has adopted the old Conservative view on this issue.

The replacement ratio

High unemployment benefits combined with high rates of income tax can create an "unemployment trap" which removes the incentive to accept a job. An unemployed person may find that going back to work may entail a fall in net income. One measure of this disincentive effect is the replacement ratio. This is defined as:

Replacement ratio = net income while unemployed as % of net income while employed

For example, in 1998 a single person earning a gross wage of £175 a week (about £4.50 an hour) would have to pay £23 a week in PAYE and a further £3.30 a week in PRSI, leaving £148.70 a week in after-tax income. When unemployed he or she could be entitled to £70.50 a week in unemployment benefit. Hence:

Replacement ratio = £70.50/£148.70 = 47%

This may seem relatively low, and hardly enough to dissuade a person from accepting a job offer, but several other factors need to be taken into account. The numerator should include other benefits such as:

- rent allowance
- medical card
- subsidised local authority housing
- family income supplement (FIS).
- non-cash benefits (fuel allowances, etc.)

The denominator should reflect work-related expenses such as commuting and child care costs. Some unemployed persons are able to work occasionally in the gray economy while still registered as unemployed. The upshot is that the interaction of the tax and social welfare systems can create situations in which an unemployed person does not find it very attractive to "sign off" the Live Register and accept an offer of employment.

The poverty trap

A related problem is the "poverty trap". This arises because employees face high marginal tax rates over certain income ranges. Table 14.2 shows that a married man with two dependent children could be little better off earning £14,000 a year than he would be earning £7,000. He would actually be worse off earning £11,000 than £7,000! The reason is that as his income rises, the worker has to pay PAYE and PRSI at higher rates, becomes liable for income levies, and loses FIS (Family Income Supplement), the medical card and pays higher local authority rent. The worker may also lose "secondary

Table 14.2 Illustration of the "Poverty Trap", 1995-96	
Gross Annual Income	Net Weekly Income[1]
£	£
7,000	153
8,000	152
9,000	151
10,000	147
11,000	149
12,000	158
13,000	166
14,000	176

1. Including estimated value of non-cash benefits
Source: Department of Social Welfare, *Report of the Expert Working Group on the Integration of the Tax and Social Welfare Systems*, June 1996, Table 2.1.

benefits " (fuel allowance, Christmas bonus, school clothing and footwear allowance and food vouchers).

How important are these disincentive effects due to the replacement ratio (previous section) and the poverty trap? There is no agreement on this issue, but it is hard to believe that situations like those shown in Table 14.2 do not reduce the willingness of people to work in the official, taxed labour economy.

There is evidence that countries where the unemployed are entitled to extended benefits have higher levels of long-term unemployment than countries where entitled is limited. In the US there is no Federal unemployment insurance system, and most state and occupational systems do not provide benefits after six months' unemployment. In Ireland, on the other hand, entitlement to unemployment benefits (UB) can last up to 15 months. If still unemployed after 15 months, a person has to move to the means-tested unemployment assistance (UA), but entitlement to this can last indefinitely and the rate of benefit is much the same as for UB. It is not surprising, therefore, that the rate of long-term unemployment is so much higher in Ireland than it is in the US.

The tax wedge

Taxes drive a wedge between what it costs the employer to hire a worker and what the employee actually takes home in pay. The difference between the two is known as the tax wedge. This arises due to the taxes levied on income and expenditure. The demand for labour depends on gross wages plus any levies the employer has to pay (such as employer's PRSI at 12 per cent in Ireland today). The supply of labour depends on the after-tax purchasing power of the worker's income. This is reduced not only by income

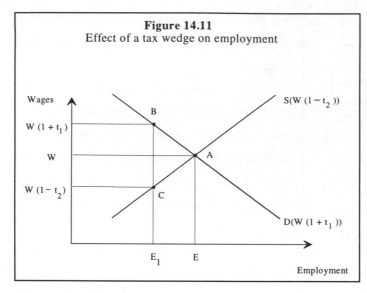

Figure 14.11
Effect of a tax wedge on employment

taxes (PAYE) and social security levies (PRSI) but also by indirect taxes (VAT and excise taxes) that are levied on expenditure. Taxes drive a large wedge between the cost of hiring a worker and the purchasing power of his or her wages.

For example, if the total cost of hiring a worker is £190 (£175 gross wages + 12% employer's PRSI),[12] take-home pay will be £149. VAT and excise taxes reduce the purchasing power of this by about 25 per cent or £34. Thus it costs the employer £196 to give the employee a net-of-tax purchasing power of £115. The wedge between the cost of hiring to the employer and the take-home pay of the employee is much higher now than it was in the 1970s. The rise in this wedge contributed to our poor employment record in the 1980s.

The effect of the tax wedge is to move the employer back up along the demand for labour schedule and the worker back up along the supply of labour schedule, leading to a reduction in employment. In Figure 14.11 (where, with a constant price level, we depict the real wage as W), equilibrium in the absence of taxes would be at W and E. If the tax rate on employers is t_1 and that on employees is t_2, the cost of hiring a worker is $W(1+t_1)$ and the after-tax income of the employee is $W(1 - t_2)$. The gap between these two magnitudes is the tax wedge. The new equilibrium is at E_1. Employment falls by $(E - E_1)$. The size of this fall in employment depends on the slopes of the demand and supply schedules. The more elastic (flat) the schedules, the greater the impact.

---

12. Employers' PRSI rises to 12% on wages above £270 a week.

Note:

In Ireland both labour supply and labour demand are likely to be relatively elastic: the supply of labour because of the possibility of emigrating or working in the "black" economy rather than accepting low after-tax wages; the demand for labour because much of our employment is in internationally-traded sectors, where Irish employers are not able to raise their prices in response to higher domestic costs.

14.8 Reducing Unemployment

There is a reasonable consensus among economists as to what has to be done to tackle Europe's problem of high unemployment. However, among politicians there is still a contrast between the flexible labour market approach favoured by the British and the more solidary approach favoured by the EU and the French in particular. The following is an outline of current economic thinking on how to reduce Europe's unemployment rate.

Maintain a high and stable growth rate A high and stable growth rate is the single most important factor in reducing unemployment and keeping it low. Unemployment has risen mainly because of adverse shocks, such as the recessions caused by the oil price increases in the 1970s. Once it has risen it tends to remain high. We have seen from the Irish experience in the 1990s that even several years of very rapid economic growth are not sufficient to ensure that unemployment falls to its former equilibrium level. The challenge facing European economies today is to get labour markets to adjust and to eliminate persistent high unemployment. This will require appropriate labour market policies as well as successful macroeconomic management.

Real wage moderation A favourable cost and wage structure has helped Ireland to generate rapid employment growth in the 1990s. While the costs of employing unskilled workers in Ireland is relatively high by comparison with Britain in particular, the cost of skilled workers is low by international standards. This has come about:

- Because of an increase in the supply of educated young people eager to work in Ireland at rates of pay that are relatively low by European standards.
- Despite the tax wedge discussed above, non-wage costs (such as social security charges) are low in Ireland by comparison with continental Europe.

- Because of moderate increases in wage costs due to the national wage agreements and reductions in income tax which have boosted after-tax income.

Reform of the tax and social welfare systems The social welfare system should place a floor under those who are unable to support themselves by their own efforts, but it should not create a "culture of dependency" by blunting the incentive to obtain employment. Many people blame the welfare state and the relatively generous support offered to the unemployed for the persistence of high unemployment in Europe. In the US, and more recently in Britain, the welfare system has been restructured to incorporate some form of "workfare". After a relatively short spell of unemployment, able-bodied people are required either to accept an offer of retraining or to enroll on a public works scheme. In the United Kingdom the Restart Programme, and the "welfare-to-work" programme, introduced in 1997, has reduced unemployment by inviting the unemployed for an interview after six months.

There has been a reluctance to adopt this approach in Ireland, despite the evidence that the Live Register figures are inflated by social welfare abuse and the growing number of unfilled job vacancies in recent years. However, several reforms have been introduced to reduce the disincentive effects of the tax and social welfare systems. These include:

- It is now permissible to work "short-time" – up to three days a week – and retain some entitlement to unemployment benefits.
- A "back to work allowance" has been introduced to allow a long-term unemployed person who returns to work to retain part of his/her unemployment assistance (on a sliding scale). Provision was made in the 1998 budget for 27,000 places on this scheme.
- The 1998 budget included further measures designed to remove some anomalies from the tax and social welfare system:
- Family Income Supplement will now be calculated on net rather than gross pay.
- Employers can claim a double tax allowance for hiring a long-term unemployed person.

318

In April 1998 the government announced an Action Plan to reduce unemployment to 7 per cent by the year 2000 and to 5 per cent five years later.[13] A key feature of this plan is "to intervene with unemployed persons systematically to prevent their drift into long-term unemployment". Specifically, persons under 25 years of age who are on the Live Register will be offered a job or other employment support. A similar programme (the Restart Program) has had a considerable impact on unemployment in the UK. A similar approach is long overdue in Ireland.

14.9 Conclusion

The main topics discussed in this chapter were:

- The influences on the growth of the labour force
- The structure of employment and unemployment in Ireland today
- Short-term influences on unemployment – the rate of growth of output and the rate of unemployment in Britain
- The factors that affect an economy's equilibrium rate of unemployment. These include the wage-bargaining process, the social welfare system and the structure of the labour force
- The characteristics associated with the risk of becoming and remaining unemployed. The importance of education was emphasised
- The reasons why the equilibrium rate of unemployment has risen over time. The concept of hysteresis
- Policies that will reduce the level of unemployment.

---

13. If the economy keeps growing at the rate achieved in 1997-98, Okun's law suggests that the unemployment rate would fall to 5 per cent long before the year 2005!

Data Appendix

Basic Labour Force Data

	Total Population (thousands)	Employed (thousands)	Unemployed (thousands)
	1	*2*	*3*
1961	2,818.0	1,053.0	56.0
1962	2,830.0	1,060.0	54.0
1963	2,850.0	1,066.0	56.0
1964	2,864.0	1,071.0	53.0
1965	2,876.0	1,069.0	51.0
1966	2,884.0	1,066.0	52.0
1967	2,900.0	1,060.0	56.0
1968	2,913.0	1,063.0	60.0
1969	2,926.0	1,066.0	56.0
1970	2,950.0	1,053.0	65.0
1971	2,978.0	1,049.0	61.0
1972	3,024.0	1,052.0	69.0
1973	3,073.0	1,067.0	65.0
1974	3,124.0	1,082.0	62.0
1975	3,177.0	1,073.0	85.0
1976	3,228.0	1,064.0	105.0
1977	3,272.0	1,083.0	105.0
1978	3,314.0	1,110.0	99.0
1979	3,368.0	1,145.0	88.0
1980	3,401.0	1,156.0	91.0
1981	3,443.0	1,146.0	126.0
1982	3,480.0	1,146.0	147.0
1983	3,504.0	1,144.1	180.7
1984	3,529.0	1,122.0	204.2
1985	3,540.0	1,099.3	221.4
1986	3,541.0	1,095.1	226.5
1987	3,546.0	1,097.5	225.0
1988	3,530.7	1,111.7	217.3
1989	3,509.5	1,113.2	197.3
1990	3,505.8	1,151.6	174.5
1991	3,525.7	1,147.3	197.8
1992	3,554.5	1,165.2	206.6
1993	3,574.1	1,183.1	220.1
1994	3,585.9	1,220.6	211.0
1995	3,601.3	1,281.7	177.4
1996	3,626.1	1,328.5	179.0
1997	3,660.6	1,379.9	159.0
1998f	3,695.5	1,430.0	146.0

	Labour force	Unemployment rate	Labour force participation rate	Employment rate
	(thousands)	(%)	(%)	(%)
	(4) = (2)+ (3)	(5) = (3)/(4)	(6) = (4)/(1)	(7) = (2)/(1)
1961	1,109.0	5.0	39.4	37.4
1962	1,114.0	4.8	39.4	37.5
1963	1,122.0	5.0	39.4	37.4
1964	1,124.0	4.7	39.2	37.4
1965	1,120.0	4.6	38.9	37.2
1966	1,118.0	4.7	38.8	37.0
1967	1,116.0	5.0	38.5	36.6
1968	1,123.0	5.3	38.6	36.5
1969	1,122.0	5.0	38.3	36.4
1970	1,118.0	5.8	37.9	35.7
1971	1,110.0	5.5	37.3	35.2
1972	1,121.0	6.2	37.1	34.8
1973	1,132.0	5.7	36.8	34.7
1974	1,144.0	5.4	36.6	34.6
1975	1,158.0	7.3	36.4	33.8
1976	1,169.0	9.0	36.2	33.0
1977	1,188.0	8.8	36.3	33.1
1978	1,209.0	8.2	36.5	33.5
1979	1,233.0	7.1	36.6	34.0
1980	1,247.0	7.3	36.7	34.0
1981	1,272.0	9.9	36.9	33.3
1982	1,293.0	11.4	37.2	32.9
1983	1,324.8	13.6	37.8	32.7
1984	1,326.2	15.4	37.6	31.8
1985	1,320.7	16.8	37.3	31.1
1986	1,321.6	17.1	37.3	30.9
1987	1,322.5	17.0	37.3	30.9
1988	1,329.0	16.4	37.6	31.5
1989	1,310.5	15.1	37.3	31.7
1990	1,326.1	13.2	37.8	32.8
1991	1,345.1	14.7	38.2	32.5
1992	1,371.8	15.1	38.6	32.8
1993	1,403.2	15.7	39.3	33.1
1994	1,431.6	14.7	39.9	34.0
1995	1,459.1	12.2	40.5	35.6
1996	1,507.5	11.9	41.6	36.6
1997	1,538.9	10.3	42.0	37.7
1998[f]	1,576.0	9.3	42.6	38.7

Appendix 1

Measuring unemployment

The measurement of unemployment can be a controversial matter. Economists think of an unemployed person as someone who is *involuntarily out of work*. This implies that the person is actively seeking a job but unable to find a suitable one. But what is meant by "actively" seeking work? What is a "suitable" job? A job seeker usually will not take the first job he or she is offered: generally a job will have to meet certain requirements relating to wages and working conditions. If job seekers have unrealistic expectations about the sort of work they want, should they continue to be classified as "involuntarily" unemployed?

There are no hard and fast answers to these questions. In practice unemployment statistics come from two principal sources:

- Household labour force surveys.
- Unemployment registers.

The primary source of survey information through Europe is now the *Labour Force Survey (LFS)*. In Ireland two measures of the labour force are derived from the LFS:

- *The International Labour Office* (ILO) measure. This is based on questions about employment and job search in the week prior to the survey.
- *The Principal Economic Status* (PES) measure. This is based on the answers to questions about the respondent's "usual status with regard to employment".

In addition, data on registered unemployment are available from

- *The Live Register* (LR). This is the monthly record of the numbers registered as unemployed for social welfare purposes.

These three measures of unemployment are shown for the total, males and females, in Figure 14.12. The LR figure is consistently the highest of the three measures. In April 1997, for example, unemployment was measured as follows:

ILO   159,000

PES   179,000

LR   255,500

The discrepancy between the LFS and LR measures of unemployment has attracted considerable public comment and the factors behind the discrepancies have been researched in detail.[1]

---

1. See Anthony Murphy and Brendan Walsh, *Aspects of Employment and Unemployment in Ireland*, National Economic and Social Forum Report No. 13 (Dublin, May 1997).

Figure 14.12
Total unemployment in Ireland

Female unemployment in Ireland

Male unemployment in Ireland

Several factors help account for the discrepancy between the LFS and LR measures of unemployment.

- *Definitions.* The LR is compiled from administrative records of those entitled to unemployment benefit (UB) or unemployment assistance (UA): it does not purport to measure unemployment in the sense of "being available for, and actively seeking, employment". On its monthly LR releases, the Central Statistics Office (CSO) explicitly warns that:

"The Live Register is not designed to measure unemployment. It includes part-time workers (who work up to three days a week), seasonal and casual workers entitled to Unemployment Benefit and Unemployment Assistance."

- *Entitlement to UB or UA.* People tend to claim unemployment benefit or assistance if they are legally entitled to do so, regardless of whether they are actively seeking employment. People taking early retirement, or women retiring from the labour force to rear children, may be entitled to claim UB for up to 15 months. On the other hand housewives who are seeking employment would be included in the ILO measure but may not be on the LR because they are not entitled to UB or UA.

- *Changes in coverage.* The regulations concerning entitlement to UB and UA have changed frequently and it is impossible to obtain a consistent series covering any length of time. Recently, for example, the regulations were changed so that some people working part time can continue to claim welfare.

- *Social welfare fraud.* While there is much anecdotal evidence of widespread fraud in relation to social welfare, a CSO survey conducted in 1996 provided more systematic evidence. A sample of those claiming UB or UA were selected for detailed interview. About 25 per cent could not be located at their stated address. Only 50 per cent of those that were located would have been classified as "unemployed" on the LFS definition. These findings showed that the LR figures are seriously misleading as to the numbers genuinely seeking, and available for, work.

The LFS measures of unemployment, on the other hand, are based on a consistent set of questions specifically designed to measure labour force status. The ILO definition provides a measure of unemployment that is internationally comparable.

The ILO measure may, however, be criticised for excluding those who have stopped looking for work because they believe that no jobs are available. They are classified as inactive rather than unemployed. It may be argued that people in this situation constitute a type of hidden or disguised unemployment. An increase in this phenomenon is part of the reason for the recent fall in the labour force participation rate among older men.

Figure 14.12 shows that for males the PES measure of unemployment is higher than the ILO measure, but the reverse is the case for women. A significant number of males cease to look for employment but continue to regard themselves as "unemployed". If they were included in the ILO definition, the unemployment rate would rise by about 10 per cent. On the other hand, many women state they are looking for work (and hence classified as ILO-unemployed) but do not regard themselves as "unemployed". The difficulty of measuring female unemployment is illustrated by the fact that in 1997 there were 62,000 unemployed women according to the ILO definition, only 48,000 according to the PES measure, but 97,000 according to the LR.

The reader may be forgiven for feeling confused between the three measures of unemployment discussed here – the ILO and PES measures from the Labour Force Survey and the LR number. For most purposes, however, the ILO measure is clearly superior as an indicator of unemployment in the economic sense. We have used this measure in Chapter 14.

Chapter 15

The Foreign Exchange Market and Exchange Rates

15.1 Introduction

In this chapter we introduce the student to some concepts essential to the study of open economy macroeconomics. We begin by explaining the balance of payments and its relationship with the foreign exchange market. This leads to a discussion of the factors that influence exchange rates in the short run. The final sections discuss various definitions of exchange rates.

15.2 The Balance of Payments

The balance of payments is a record of a country's economic transactions with the rest of the world. The basic rules in drawing up the balance of payments accounts are:

- Items, such as exports, that lead to a receipt of foreign exchange are positive entries or inflows.

- Items, such as imports, that lead to payments of foreign exchange are negative entries or outflows.

Table 15.1 presents a simplified version of the Irish balance of payments for 1996. There are four sub-headings:

- the current account,

- the capital account,

- changes in the official external reserves, and

- the net residual.

The current account Within the current account there are four further sub-accounts, showing the balance on:

- merchandise trade,

- trade in services,

- net factor income from abroad, and

Table 15.1

The balance of payments, 1996

		£ millions
1.1 Merchandise trade		8,416
1.2 Services		− 3,598
of which		
1.2.1	International freight	475
1.2.2	Tourism and travel	188
1.2.3	Royalties, licences	− 2,087
1.2.3	Other services	− 2,364
1.2.4	Remuneration of employees	190
1.3 Investment income		− 5,310
of which		
1.3.1	Direct investment income	− 5,319
1.3.2	Other income	7
of which:		
	National debt interest	− 908
1.4 Current transfers		1,353
1.5 Balance on current account		862
2.1 Private capital		− 105
2.2 Official capital		38
of which		
2.2.1 Government foreign borrowing		− 986
2.2.2 Government securities sold abroad		1,024
2.3 Banking transactions		− 1,229
3 Change in official external reserves		55
4. Balance on capital account		− 1,241
5 Net residual = (1) + (2) + (3)		379

Source: Central Bank of Ireland, *Quarterly Bulletin*, Spring, 1998, Table B7.

Note: Rounding error of +£1 million on current account.

- current transfers.

Each of these sub-accounts is now considered briefly.

Merchandise trade refers to exports and imports of goods. In 1996, Irish merchandise exports exceeded imports by £8,416 million. This substantial surplus reflects the very strong export performance of Irish industry.

Figure 15.1 shows exports and imports as a percentage of GDP over the period 1960-97. The difference between the two series is the *balance of trade*. Note that both exports and imports have increased substantially as a percentage of GDP over the years. Exports now amount to 75 per cent of GDP compared to only 30 per cent in 1960. This documents the extreme openness of the economy. Ireland's trade account was in deficit up to 1985, but since then we have recorded a growing trade surplus.

The *services* sub-account records transactions such as international freight, tourism and travel. There was a sizeable deficit of £3,598 million under

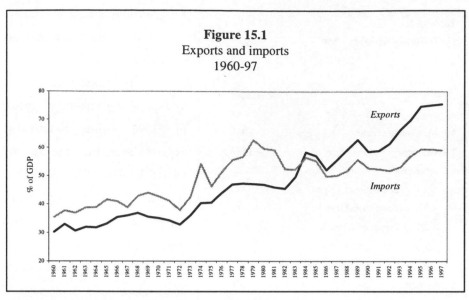

Figure 15.1
Exports and imports
1960-97

Exports

Imports

this heading in 1996. Thus our trade surplus is partly used to pay for the services we import from the rest of the world. Some of these are related to the dealings of multinational companies. The value of these companies' exports is enormous but they have to pay significant amounts for services they buy from abroad. This is one reason why the entry for royalties and licences shows such a substantial deficit.

The *investment income* sub-account records dividends and interest on foreign and domestic investments. The interest paid by the government on foreign debt is also shown under this heading. In 1996 a deficit of £5,310 million was recorded in this sub-account. This reflects the importance of *profit remittances* by the multinational companies and the external payments on our national debt.

Finally, the *current transfers* sub-account includes inflows such as current transfers to Ireland from the European Union (see Chapter 2), remittances from emigrants and, as an outflow, Irish aid to less developed countries.

Putting these sub-accounts together, the result was an overall surplus on the current account equal to £862 million in 1996. This is due primarily to the large surplus on merchandise trade.

It is important to stress how the operation of *multinational companies* in Ireland affects the current account. These companies account for much of the enormous surplus in merchandise exports, but their payments of royalties, interest, and dividends to parent companies and shareholders are recorded as outflows in the other sub-accounts of the current account. Most of the effects of *transfer pricing* cancelled out in

328

the overall current account. This point has been much misunderstood in recent discussion of the issue.

Note:

Transfer pricing occurs when multinational firms try to maximise the profits attributable to their operation in a low tax country, such as Ireland, with its 10 per cent corporate profits tax on manufacturing industry and internationally traded services. A subsidiary company in a high tax country can sell inputs at a low book cost to a subsidiary company in a low tax country thereby boosting profits in the low tax country. In due course most of these profits will be remitted abroad from the low tax country. While this is undoubtedly an important feature of the operation of foreign companies in Ireland, we should note that foreign tax authorities do their best to police it and to minimise their loss of tax revenue due to transfer pricing.

The capital account The capital account of the balance of payments records purchases and sales of *assets* such as bonds, stocks and shares, and land. Foreign borrowing by the government, banks, and the private sector are also included here. Capital transfers from the EU are included as an inflow.

The sub-accounts of the capital account record:

- private sector transactions,
- government transactions, and
- banking sector transactions.

In recent years there has been a net inflow on the government account due to the sale of government bonds to non-residents, but there has been a larger deficit on the banking sector sub-account, leading to an overall capital account deficit.

Central Bank reserves These are the *official foreign exchange reserves* held, until the end of 1998, by the Central Bank of Ireland. They consist primarily of bank deposits in foreign currencies (including those with the IMF), and a small amount of gold. At the end of 1997 these were valued at just under IR£6 billion, compared with a mere IR£2 billion in 1983. From 1999 onwards the reserves of all the countries participating in the EMU will be centralised in the European Central Bank.

In order to understand the role played by the Central Bank of Ireland (until the end of 1998) in foreign exchange transactions we should note that

- A *receipt* by an Irish resident from abroad leads to a *demand for Irish pounds* on the foreign exchange market. (This market is discussed below.) Suppose, for example, an Irish exporter sells goods in the UK and receives sterling in return. The sterling receipts are exchanged for Irish pounds in a bank and this leads to a

329

demand for Irish pounds.

- Similarly, a foreign *payment* by an Irish resident leads to a *supply of Irish pounds* on the foreign exchange market. If an Irish importer needs to obtain sterling to pay his UK supplier, Irish pounds are exchanged for sterling in a bank. The importer is in effect supplying Irish pounds and demanding sterling.

Now the overall balance of payments should sum to zero. This is because it takes two parties to complete a transaction. If someone is supplying (selling) Irish pounds on the foreign exchange market, then someone else must be demanding (buying) them. Hence, in the simple case, the current account (CA) surplus and the capital account (CP) deficit should sum to zero:

$$CA + CP = 0 \qquad\qquad (1)$$

However, in the past the Central Bank frequently intervened in the foreign exchange market either buying or selling Irish pounds to stabilise the value of the Irish pound on the foreign exchange markets. The Central Bank's external reserves played a key role in this operation. The Central Bank used these reserves to intervene in the foreign exchange market. If, for example, there were an overall balance of payments deficit (an excess supply of Irish pounds), the Central Bank could have bought Irish pounds using the foreign currency in its external reserves. Conversely, if there were an overall balance of payments surplus (an excess demand for Irish pounds), the Central Bank could have supplied Irish pounds to the market, which would have increased its external reserves. Hence:

- Balance of payments *surplus* ⇒ external reserves *increase*
- Balance of payments *deficit* ⇒ external reserves *decrease*

Note:

If the Central Bank does not intervene in the foreign exchange market, any net surplus or deficit on the combined accounts would cause the exchange rate to move so as to clear the market. This important issue is explained in section 15.5 below.

The net residual on the balance of payments Rewriting equation 1 to allow for changes in the external reserves (ΔR):

$$CA + CP = \Delta R \qquad\qquad (2)$$

Independent estimates provide data of these three magnitudes. Using the data in Table 15.1 we find that:

$$£862 - £1,241 \neq - £55$$

A current account surplus of £862 million and a capital account deficit of −£1,241 million gives an overall balance of payments deficit of − £479 million. The official external reserves should have decreased by this amount. However, the external reserves actually fell by £55 million leaving a discrepancy of £324 million. To reconcile the accounts, it is necessary to include a *net residual*.

This reflects unrecorded transactions, and errors and omissions in the current and capital accounts. (The residual includes money that is being moved illegally into and out of the country and similar "hidden economy" transactions.)

Inserting a residual item (NR) into equation 2:

$$CA + CP + NR = \Delta R \tag{3}$$

Using again the data from Table 15.1 we have:

$$£862 - £1,241 + 324 = -£55$$

Note that when the ΔR (− £55 million) is taken over to the left-hand side in equation 3, it appears with a positive sign. This is why it is given as a positive £55 million in Table 15.1.

The net residual has been small in recent years compared to the situation in the 1980s. In 1989, for example, the residual was − £908 million. There has been an improvement in the accuracy with which the individual components of the balance of payments are tracked.

The significance of the balance of payments It is easy to think of a current account surplus as good and a deficit as bad. This reflects the *mercantilist fallacy*[1] according to which a country should maximise its exports. In fact exports are only valuable in that they allow us to purchase imports. There is nothing inherently bad in a current account deficit provided there is a capital account surplus to offset it. If there was no capital account surplus, however, then the alternative is to decrease the external reserves or engage in foreign borrowing. The latter, however, increases future debt service obligations. Foreign exchange markets take a dim view of a country that runs persistent large balance of payments deficits. There were crises in Mexico in 1995 and in Malaysia, Thailand and several other South Asian countries in 1997 due to panics over

1. Named after the seventeenth-century economists who believed that a country grew powerful by amassing gold obtained from running balance of trade surpluses.

their ability to continue to borrow abroad to finance balance of payments deficits.

A current account surplus can easily be financed by accumulating foreign assets and reserves. However, beyond a certain level it does not make sense to continue exporting just to accumulate foreign assets. Perhaps the best advice is that given by Polonius in *Hamlet:* "Neither a lender nor borrower be . . ."

Note:

A distinction is made between *autonomous* and *accommodating* transactions. An autonomous transaction is an "ordinary" transaction, such as an export or an import or purchases of land or government stock by private individuals. If autonomous transactions on current and capital account result in an overall deficit, the Central Bank has either to finance that deficit or allow the exchange rate to depreciate. If the Central Bank is pursuing a fixed exchange rate policy, the deficit can be financed by running down the official external reserves or by borrowing foreign currency abroad. The change in the external reserves plus government foreign borrowing are referred to as accommodating or financing transactions. The accommodating transactions ensure that the overall balance of payments adds to zero. The balance of accommodating transactions is sometimes referred to as the *official settlements balance*.

Terms of trade

When discussing trade flows it is important to distinguish between price changes and quantity changes. We can write:

$$X = P_x \times Q_x$$

$$M = P_m \times Q_m$$

where X and M denote the value of exports and imports, respectively, P_x and P_m denote the price of exports and imports, and Q_x and Q_m indicate the quantity of exports and imports, respectively.

What matters for living standards and employment are quantity changes. Firms hire more workers to produce a greater quantity of goods and services. However, price changes have a direct effect on the balance of payments. Starting from an equilibrium position, an increase in P_x relative to P_m will result in a trade account surplus because the value of exports increases relative to the value of imports. (This is a short-run effect; over time, the quantities traded will respond to the change in relative prices.) The *terms of trade* are defined as P_x/P_m. An increase in this ratio is referred to as an *improvement* in the terms of trade. When such an improvement occurs, we need to export fewer goods and services to import a given quantity of imports. Conversely, a decrease in the ratio is referred to as a *deterioration* in the terms of trade. We now need

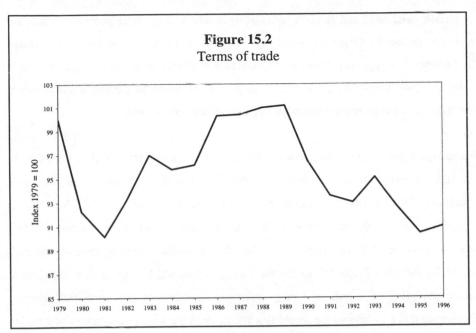

Figure 15.2
Terms of trade

to export more Irish goods in order to import a given quantity of imports.

Figure 15.2 shows the terms of trade index (1979 = 100) for Ireland over the period 1975-96. This index is strongly influenced by changes in the price of petroleum products on the import side, and of agricultural products on the export side. There was an adverse movement in the terms of trade between 1978 and 1982, but this was reversed between 1982 and 1986. In 1990 there was a deterioration in the terms of trade, due mainly to the fall in agricultural export prices. We explored the impact of these movements in the terms of trade on the population's standard of living in Chapter 4 and saw how important it has been in the case of Ireland.

15.3 The Foreign Exchange Market

Most countries have their own individual currencies. The *foreign exchange market* is the market where these currencies are bought and sold. This market is essential for trade between countries that use different currencies. If, for example, an Irish co-operative sends a shipment of beef to France and the French importer pays the Irish exporter in francs, the Irish exporter will exchange these francs for Irish pounds on the foreign exchange market. This completes the transfer of purchasing power from the French importer to the Irish co-operative.

The foreign exchange market spans the globe by means of telephones, computers and telex machines, and is open twenty-four hours a day. It is possible to sell, for example, dollars for German marks (DM) in Tokyo and buy sterling for German marks in Dublin. The opening hours of the markets in different centres round the world overlap. Quotations for the current exchange rates between all the major currencies of the world can therefore be obtained at any time of the day or night.

Exchange rates   The exchange rate is the price of one currency in terms of another. In Ireland, the exchange rate is defined as the foreign price of a unit of the domestic currency. In May 1998, for example, an Irish pound was worth $1.40, Stg£0.82 or DM2.51. This was the value of an Irish pound in terms of the foreign currencies. This way of quoting exchange rates is the British convention, used in Ireland, the UK, Australia and New Zealand. The alternative (American and European) convention is to quote the price of a unit of foreign currency in terms of the domestic currency. Following this convention, we would say that in 1998 the Irish pound prices of a dollar, a pound sterling and a German mark were IR£0.71, IR£1.22 and IR£0.40, respectively.[2]

If a currency falls in value relative to the foreign currency, it *depreciates*; if it rises, it *appreciates*. For example, if the dollar rate moved from $1.40 to $1.55 this would be an appreciation of the Irish pound. Irish residents would obtain more dollars than before. If, on the other hand, the sterling exchange rate moved from £0.82 to Stg£0.80, this would be a depreciation. Less sterling would be obtained for every Irish pound.

An advantage of the British convention is that when a currency appreciates, its exchange rate rises, when it depreciates its exchange rate falls. This is more natural than what happens under the American convention, with a rise in the exchange rate implying a depreciation, and a fall an appreciation. We follow the British convention in this book.

Bid and offer exchange rates   Bureaux de change and banks charge hefty commissions for small transactions in foreign currencies. As a result, converting small amounts of currency is expensive. In addition to commission charges, banks earn a profit by quoting different exchange rates for buying and selling foreign currency.

---

2. The reason for the different conventions is that it is awkward to express the price of foreign currencies in the old pounds, shillings and pence *(£ s. d.)* used up to the early 1970s in Ireland and the UK.

Table 15.2

Bid and offer rates for the dollar, Irish pound, exchange rate: December 1997

Bid	Offer
1.472	1.542

Source: Allied Irish Banks, International Department.

Note: Exchange rates quoted relate to transactions less than £1,000. The spread decreases on transactions greater than £1,000.

These rates are known as the *bid rate* (the rate at which banks will buy Irish pounds or sell foreign currency) and the *offer rate* (the rate at which banks sell Irish pounds or buy foreign currency). The difference between the bid and offer rates is known as the *spread*. Table 15.2 shows bid and offer $/IR£ rates quoted by the banks for December 1997.

The introduction of the euro in 1999

The US economy operates with a single currency; but the European Union, whose economy is larger than the US, in 1998 still used fifteen different currencies. A lot of resources are devoted to dealing in pounds, francs, escudos and so on. The necessity of changing money from one currency into another adds to the cost of doing business. This cost has been estimated to be in the range £100-£150 million in Ireland. The gain from eliminating these costs is one of the motivations for adopting a single European currency, the euro, which will come into force as a currency in its own right at the start of 1999.

From January 1998, the exchange rates between the national currencies of the eleven countries that will participate in EMU will be *irrevocably fixed*.[3] In effect, the national currencies will cease to exist as independent currencies. They will be units of account based on the euro. In Chapter 17 we explain how the conversion will occur.

The rise and fall of the Irish foreign exchange market

Up to the early 1970s there was virtually no foreign exchange market in Ireland. The sterling/Irish pound exchange rate was fixed at a one-to-one parity, a very large proportion of Irish trade was with the UK, and the commercial banks held their reserves in sterling in London. The Irish demand for currencies such as dollars and francs was easily dealt with on the London foreign exchange market. In 1969, the Money Market Committee set up by the Central Bank of Ireland under the chairmanship of Professor

---

3. The eleven countries that agreed to form an EMU in May 1998 are: Austria, Belgium, France, Finland, Germany, Ireland, Italy, Luxembourg, the Netherlands, Spain and Portugal.

Table 15.3

Daily volume of turnover on the Irish foreign exchange market: April 1995

1.	*Total daily turnover*	£1 billion - £1.5 billion
2.	*Irish pound turnover*	
	of which:	
	$/IR£	11.4 %
	Sterling/IR£	5.3 %
	DM/IR£	3.7 %
3.	*Non-Irish pound turnover*	
	of which	
	$/DM	19.4 %
	Sterling/$	11.4 %
	Sterling/DM	21.1 %
	ECU/DM	7.9 %
	DM/Franc	3.4 %

Note: ECU denotes European currency unit. Source: Robert Hutchinson, The Financial Services Sector, in T. Baker, J. Fitzgerald and P. Honohan, *Economic Implications for Ireland of EMU*, The Economic and Social Research Institute, Dublin, 1996, p. 239.

W. J. L. Ryan, recommended that the Central Bank of Ireland (CBI) should help develop a foreign exchange market. In line with this recommendation, in the early 1970s the Licensed Banks' reserves were transferred from London to the CBI and the banks were requested to conduct their foreign exchange business directly with the CBI. In 1976 the CBI quoted for small amounts of foreign exchange. This encouraged the banks to hire and train dealers and to conduct more of their business directly between themselves and on world foreign exchange markets.

Table 15.3 shows that daily turnover on the Irish foreign exchange market varied between £1 and £1.5 billion in April 1995. The vast majority of deals involve currencies such as sterling, the DM or the dollar. Deals involving the Irish pound account for only about 20 per cent of total turnover. One reason for this is that the Irish pound market has little "depth". Dealers are unwilling to act as price-makers for the Irish pound when they cannot spread the risk with other dealers or banks. Also foreigners have little interest in buying and selling Irish pounds, other than the small amounts needed to finance foreign trade. As a result, dealers find it easier and safer to deal in foreign currencies.

Until 1979 the Irish pound was pegged to sterling. In March of that year, Ireland entered the exchange rate mechanism (ERM) of the European Monetary System (EMS) but the pound sterling did not. Following the termination of the sterling link, the banks began to quote a sterling/Irish pound exchange rate, something that had not been required before. (The first deal in sterling was done for STG£500,000 at an exchange rate of IR£1 = STG£0.9975 on 30 March 1979. Many firms with large sterling debt lost heavily as the Irish pound unexpectedly depreciated against sterling.) The banks coped

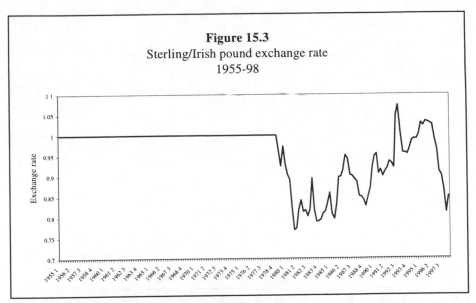

Figure 15.3
Sterling/Irish pound exchange rate
1955-98

very well with the new arrangements. However, they are now faced with the prospect of seeing that part of their foreign exchange business that relates to the European currencies disappear. With the adoption of the euro in 1999 there will no longer be any possibility of a change in the value of one EMU currency in terms of the other. If the EMU develops according to plan, in the year 2002 national currencies will cease to circulate and be replaced by the euro in trade between the eleven participating countries. This will entail a considerable loss of business for the banks. The numbers employed in foreign currency dealing will fall considerably.

15.4 The Exchange Rate of the Irish Pound

Figures 15.3, 15.4 and 15.5 show the value of the Irish pound in terms of sterling, the deutschmark and the US dollar, over the period 1955-98. These were the most important *bilateral* rates of the Irish pound.[4] Up to 1979, the sterling/IR£ rate was fixed on a one-to-one basis. Since then this exchange rate has moved fairly widely in both directions but it has not drifted far from the original parity. The following are some of the main trends in the value of the Irish pound since 1979:

- Following the break in the link with sterling, the Irish pound depreciated sharply, falling as low as Stg£0.72 in 1981. In the later half of the 1980s it gained relative to sterling, culminating in the crisis of 1992, when sterling depreciated sharply

---

4. We use the past tense to refer to the Irish pound here because the Irish currency is now permanently fixed to the euro.

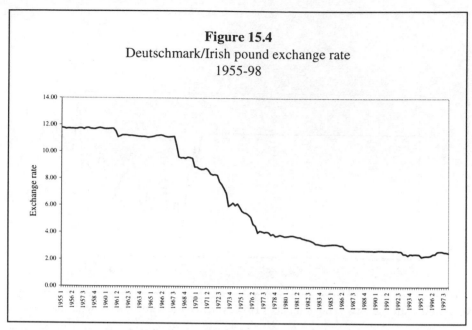

Figure 15.4
Deutschmark/Irish pound exchange rate
1955-98

against the EMS currencies and the Irish pound rose to Stg£1.10. Following the devaluation of January 1993 the Irish pound traded at lower levels, depreciating sharply as sterling strengthened in 1997-98.

■ Relative to the German mark there was a sustained depreciation until 1987. Between 1987 and 1993 the value of the Irish pound was virtually unchanged in the region of IR£1 = DM2.67. The devaluation of the Irish pound in January 1993 moved it down but in March 1998 it was revalued and its final central rate in the ERM was set at IR£1 = DM2.48.

■ The US$/IR£ exchange rate has fluctuated widely, reflecting the movement of the dollar against the European currencies, as well as the fluctuations of the Irish pound relative to the latter. The dollar was weak in 1980 but climbed to a peak in 1985 (when for a brief period the IR£1 was worth less than $1), but in the latter half of the 1980s it weakened considerably. The dollar strengthened in the mid-1990s. The absence of a clear trend in the value of the dollar is sometimes referred to as the "dance of the dollar".

Importance of exchange rate movements

Buying and selling goods and services across international borders involves *exchange rate risk.* Consider, for example, the case of an Irish exporter selling goods into the UK

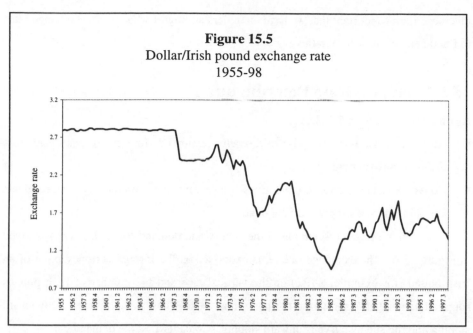

Figure 15.5
Dollar/Irish pound exchange rate
1955-98

market. Suppose the exporter expects to receive STG£1 million in one month's time and anticipates that the exchange rate will be STG£0.96/IR£1. At this exchange rate, Irish pound receipts will be:

$$IR£1,041,667 = (Stg£1 \text{ million}/0.96)$$

Suppose, however, that the Irish pound unexpectedly appreciates to STG£0.98. The exporter's receipts will only be:

$$IR£1,020,408 = (Stg£1 \text{ million}/0.98)$$

This is IR£21,259 less than was anticipated and could render the deal unprofitable. Hence, even small changes in the exchange rate can result in large profits or losses. Traders naturally wish to minimise this type of risk. In Chapter 19 we outline a number of different *hedging techniques* which have been developed for this purpose. However, these hedging techniques only offer short-term protection against exchange rate risk. In the longer term the firm will have to accept the consequences of exchange rate movements.

From a macroeconomic perspective, a change in the exchange rate will affect a country's competitive position. This, in turn, affects the aggregate demand curve and, therefore, inflation, the real growth rate and unemployment. An overvalued exchange rate will adversely effect a number of key macroeconomic variables. Conversely, an undervalued exchange rate will have a beneficial effect. The value of the currency, or the competitive position of the economy, is vitally important in macroeconomics. For

339

this reason, it is important that we have an understanding of what causes exchange rates to fluctuate. We now turn to this issue.

15.5 Exchange Rate Determination

As discussed in section 5.2 above:

- Any transaction that gives rise to a *receipt* (export) of foreign currency leads to a *demand* for Irish pounds.

- Conversely, any transaction that gives rise to a *payment* (import) by Irish residents abroad leads to a *supply* of Irish pounds.

A graphical representation of the supply and demand for Irish pounds is given in Figure 15.6. The exchange rate, e, is expressed as the foreign currency price of an Irish pound (for example, $/IR£) on the vertical axis and the number of Irish pounds supplied/demanded is shown on the horizontal axis. The demand curve is downward sloping and the supply curve is upward sloping. Consider first the demand curve.

The demand for Irish pounds A downward-sloping demand schedule implies that a depreciation increases the demand for Irish pounds. When the Irish pound depreciates Irish exporters can reduce their prices abroad. Irish exports become more competitive and, as a result, more are demanded. The demand for Irish pounds increases. As an example, suppose the exchange rate were IR£1 = $2. Ignoring transport costs, taxes and other factors, if the price of an Aran sweater is IR£40 in Dublin, at this exchange rate the price in New York would be $80. Suppose now the Irish pound depreciates to IR£1 = $1.50. If Irish prices and costs do not change in the short run the sweater will still cost IR£40 in Dublin and the exporter could afford to lower the New York price to $60. At the lower price in New York more sweaters are sold and as a result the demand for Irish pounds increases.

Alternatively, the exporter could decide to leave the New York price at $80 and allow her profits to benefit in full from the depreciation. Assuming no change in the number of sweaters sold, the demand for Irish pounds would still increase because the Irish pound equivalent of $80 would rise from IR£40 to IR£53.33. Thus a devaluation must increase the value of exports denominated in the home currency. This is why the demand curve for the home currency slopes downwards.

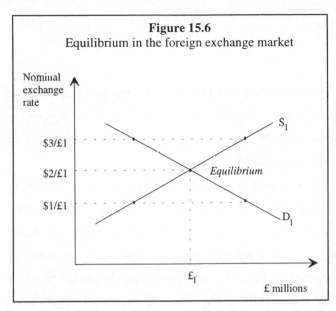

Figure 15.6
Equilibrium in the foreign exchange market

Nominal exchange rate

$3/£1

$2/£1 — — — — — — — — Equilibrium

$1/£1

S_1

D_1

$£_1$

£ millions

The supply of Irish pounds An upward-sloping supply curve for Irish pounds indicates that a depreciation reduces the supply of Irish pounds on the foreign exchange market and an appreciation increases it. The logic behind this is that a depreciation makes imports more expensive and consequently less are sold. For example, at an exchange rate of IR£1 = $2, a pair of jeans selling for $30 in New York would sell in Dublin for IR£15. If the Irish pound depreciates to IR£1 = $1.50, the Dublin price would rise to IR£20 unless some of the depreciation were absorbed as lower profits by the US exporter. As the price increases the quantity of imports falls. Provided the demand for imports is price elastic the Irish pound value of imports will fall, leading to a reduction in the supply of Irish pounds to the foreign exchange market.

Equilibrium in the foreign exchange market The equilibrium exchange rate is determined by the intersection of the supply and demand schedules. In Figure 15.6 at a rate of IR£1 = $2 the supply and demand for Irish pounds are equal. At an exchange rate higher than this, say, IR£1 = $3, there is an excess supply of Irish pounds. This is equivalent to a balance of payments deficit on the combined current and capital accounts. The value of the country's payments is greater than that of its receipts. At a lower exchange rate, say IR£1 = $1, there is an excess demand for Irish pounds which, under a floating exchange rate regime, leads to an appreciation.

The crucial point is that the foreign exchange market must clear. When there is an excess demand for a currency, its value rises (the exchange rate appreciates) and when there is an excess supply, its value falls (the exchange rate depreciates). Appreciation or depreciation continues until supply equals demand. Hence under a floating exchange rate system the current and private capital accounts of the balance of payments must sum to zero.

Exchange rate regimes

There are different ways of organising the foreign exchange market for a currency. The dominant arrangement, which currently applies to the world's main currencies, is *floating exchange rates.* This means that currencies are free to move up or down in response to shifts in the supply and demand for currencies.

When the exchange rate is floating, in principle governments and central banks do not intervene to *peg* or *fix* the value of currencies. As a consequence, exchange rates may be very unstable or *volatile.* But in fact it is difficult to find a situation where exchange rates are allowed to float completely free of central bank intervention. Central banks buy and sell foreign exchange in order to stabilise the market and keep currencies in informal *target ranges.* Even when there is no formal target range, bankers and ministers for finance are prone to pronouncing that their currencies are "too high" or "too low" and trying to nudge the market in a certain direction. This is known as "dirty floating".

The alternative to floating is a *fixed exchange rate regime.* Under this arrangement the values of currencies are fixed or pegged relative to each other. Governments and central banks are committed to maintaining the declared parities. The Gold Standard and the post-war Bretton Woods system were examples of such a regime. Between 1979 and 1993 the EMS was a *quasi-fixed exchange rate regime.* Exchange rates were not rigidly fixed, but formal target (or central) rates were set and currencies were expected to be kept within a ± 2.25 per cent band round these rates. In mid-1993 this system was greatly weakened. The margin of fluctuation was widened to ± 15 per cent in recognition of the strains caused by trying to maintain narrower bands.

15.6 The J Curve

The foreign exchange market does not always adjust in the well-behaved manner described above. It is possible that a depreciation increases the Irish pound value of imports and the supply curve slopes down. To see how this could happen recall that:

$$\text{Value of imports} = P_m \text{ x } Q_m$$

where P_m and Q_m are the price and quantity of imports. A depreciation leads to a rise in P_m and a fall in Q_m, but whether the value of imports (in Irish pounds) rises or falls

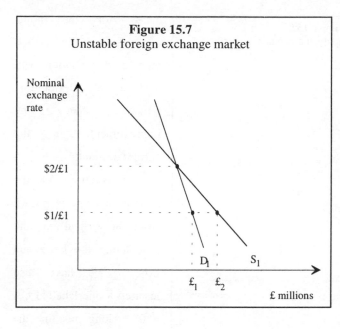

Figure 15.7
Unstable foreign exchange market

Nominal exchange rate

$2/£1

$1/£1

D_1 S_1

$£_1$ $£_2$

£ millions

depends on the price elasticity of demand for imports.

If the price elasticity is less than one (inelastic), then as P_m increases following a depreciation, Q_m will fall less than proportionately and (P_m x Q_m), will increase. This could happen if a large proportion of imported goods have no domestically produced substitutes. An example of such imports would be petroleum products in Ireland. Under these circumstances the supply curve of Irish pounds is downward sloping and the foreign exchange market *unstable*. This is illustrated in Figure 15.7. The market is initially in equilibrium at an exchange rate of $2/IR£1. If the exchange rate fell to $1/IR£1 there would be an excess supply of Irish pounds, leading to further depreciation. The exchange rate would move away from equilibrium.

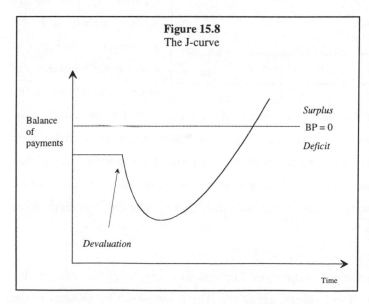

Figure 15.8
The J-curve

Balance of payments

Surplus
BP = 0
Deficit

Devaluation

Time

The slope of the supply curve for the domestic currency has implications for the effect of a depreciation or devaluation on the current account of the balance of payments. If there is a downward-sloping supply

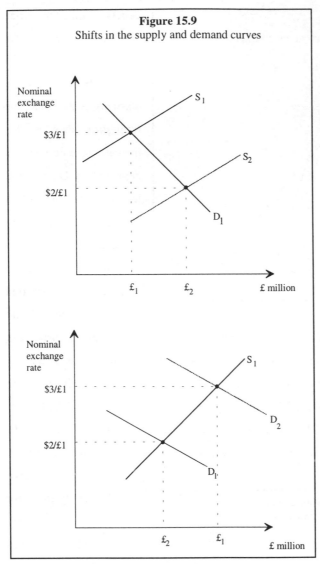

Figure 15.9
Shifts in the supply and demand curves

curve for the home currency, as in Figure 15.7, then a depreciation will lead to a deterioration, rather than an improvement, in the current account.

In Figure 15.8 the current account is shown along the vertical axis and time along the horizontal axis. We have also inserted a line labelled CA = 0. Along this line the current account is zero. Points above the line are associated with a current account surplus and points below with a deficit. Suppose that the country is experiencing a current account deficit and the government decides to devalue the currency in order to correct this. If the supply curve of domestic currency is downward sloping, the devaluation initially leads to a deterioration in the current account. In due course, however, the price effects work in the correct direction (the long-run elasticity of demand for imports is greater than one), so there is eventually an "improvement" in the current account. The curve which maps out how the current account reacts to a devaluation under these assumptions is known as the *J-curve*.

Shifts in the supply and demand curves The equilibrium exchange rate changes due to shifts in the demand and supply schedules. These are caused by changes in the

344

factors such as income, world prices and preferences. The following are some examples of developments that would shift these schedules:

- A fall in the demand for exports due to a global recession would shift the demand for Irish pounds to the left.

- A rise in world interest rates that increased Irish debt service payments abroad would shift the supply of Irish pounds to the right.

- A rise in the demand by non-residents for Irish land would shift the demand for Irish pounds to the right.

- An increase in foreign borrowing by Irish banks or the government would shift the demand for Irish pounds to the right.

If the exchange rate is floating, the first two events would cause a depreciation, the second two an appreciation. Figure 15.9 illustrates an increase in the demand for imports due, for example, to higher oil prices. This shifts the supply schedule of Irish pounds to the right. If the exchange rate is floating it will depreciate from IR£1 = $3 to IR£1 = $2. The lower panel shows an increase in the demand for Irish exports brought about, for example, by a successful marketing campaign for Irish exports, and the exchange rate appreciates from IR£1 = $2 to IR£1 = $3.

Note:

The terms *depreciation* and *appreciation* are used for changes in a floating exchange rate. *Devaluation* and *revaluation* are applied when a fixed or pegged exchange rate is moved down or up.

15.7 Purchasing Power Parity and Real Exchange Rates

In principle, the price of goods that are traded internationally should be the same throughout the world. Allowing for differences in transportation costs and local taxes, there is no reason to expect the price of a litre of petrol to differ significantly from one country to another. This is known as *the law of one price*. But it has frequently been found that this law does not hold. An oft-quoted example is based on a comparison of the price of Big Macs around the world. A Big Mac cost IR£1.85 in Dublin in April 1998. The same product cost DM4.95 in Frankfurt. Are Big Macs more expensive in Ireland or Germany? To answer this question we can convert the Irish price into the German price using the current exchange rate of $e = DM2.50/IR£1$:

$$P_{irl} \times e = P^*_{DM} \qquad (4)$$

$$£1.85 \times 2.50 = DM4.62$$

345

Table 15.4

The hamburger standard

Country	Big Mac Price In Dollars	Implied e_{PPP} rate	Actual exchange valuation %	Local currency under(−)/over(+)
United States	2.56	-	-	-
Australia	1.75	1.04	1.51	− 32
Britain	3.05	1.39	1.66	+19
Canada	1.97	1.09	1.42	− 23
Czech Republic	1.58	21.1	34.4	− 39
France	2.84	6.84	6.17	+11
Germany	2.69	1.93	1.84	+5
Ireland	2.55	1.38	1.38	0
Italy	2.47	1,758	1,758	− 3
Russia	2.00	4,688	4,688	− 22
Spain	2.40	146	146	− 6

Source: *The Economist*, 11 April 1998.
Note: Exchange rates are units of local currency per dollar, except for Ireland and Britain, which are dollars per pound.

where P_{irl} is the Irish price in Irish pounds, P^*_{DM} is the Irish price in DM. The calculation shows that a Big Mac in Dublin costs DM4.62 compared to DM4.95 in Frankfurt. Thus Big Macs are DM0.33 or 6.6 per cent cheaper in Ireland than in Germany. Alternatively, the same result could be obtained by converting German prices into Irish pounds:

$$P_{DM} (1/e) = P^*_{irl}$$
$$DM4.95 \times 0.4 = £1.98$$

The Irish pound price of a Big Mac in Frankfurt is £1.98, which is 13 pence dearer than the Dublin price. This difference is very small and it may therefore be concluded that the market exchange rate is close to that which is predicted on the basis of the Big Mac Standard.

Note:

Since it was first published by *The Economist* in the 1980s the Big Mac Standard has come in for a lot of criticism. After all, Big Macs are not traded internationally and as a result the price could vary considerably from country to country. None the less, it has stood up well to criticism and earned grudging respect from academics. It is possible, and perhaps more logical, to turn the tables on *The Economist* and see whether the prices quoted on its cover confirm the theory of the law of one price. In April 1998 the magazine cost Ir£2.50 in Dublin and $3.95 in New York. This implies an IR£/$ exchange rate of $1.58 compared with an actual rate of about $1.40. The magazine is relatively cheap in Ireland.

The above example illustrates how to compare prices using the nominal exchange rate. A related concept is the exchange rate that would *equalise* prices in the two countries. This is known as the *purchasing power parity* exchange rate. Rearranging equation (4) above:

$$e_{PPP} = P_{dm}/P_{irl} \qquad\qquad (5)$$

Using the prices for a Big Mac in Dublin and Frankfurt:

$$e_{PPP} = DM4.95/IR£1.85 = 2.68$$

If the exchange had been at this level a Big Mac would have been the same price in a common currency in both countries. To the extent to which this is not the case an exchange rate can be said to be *over* or *undervalued*. In April 1998, the market exchange rate was DM2.50/IR£1 compared with a PPP exchange rate of DM2.68/IR£1. On the basis of Big Macs, at least, we could claim that the Irish pound was 7 per cent *undervalued* relative to the DM.

Table 15.4 shows the "hamburger standard" for a number of countries relative to the United States. It can be seen that countries such as Australia, Canada, the Czech Republic and Russia are relatively cheap compared to the United States. American tourists to France and Britain, on the other hand, must feel a little "cheesed off" at local prices!

The real exchange rate

The real exchange rate (ε) is simply the ratio of Irish and German prices expressed in a common currency. Rearranging equation 4 above we can write:

$$\varepsilon = (P_{irl} \times e)/P_{DM} \qquad\qquad (6)$$

The real exchange rate is the nominal exchange rate adjusted for relative prices. The importance of the real rate is that it is a measure of whether a country is becoming more or less *price competitive* relative to its trading partners over time.

- A rise in the real exchange rate implies a loss of competitiveness because either domestic prices have risen relative to foreign prices and/or the nominal exchange rate has appreciated.

- Conversely, a fall in the real exchange rate implies a gain in competitiveness.

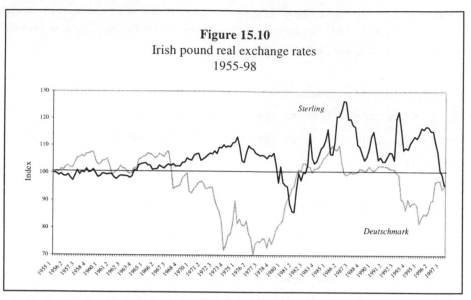

Figure 15.10
Irish pound real exchange rates
1955-98

Either domestic prices have fallen relative to foreign prices and/or the nominal exchange rate has depreciated.

Note that the real exchange rate index only monitors movements in competitiveness relative to the base year: it says nothing about the relative position of the economies in that year.

Figure 15.10 shows Ireland's real exchange rates relative to the DM and sterling over the period 1955 to 1998 based on indices equal to 100 in 1955. Ireland lost competitiveness relative to sterling in the mid-1970s and again in the 1980s. The recent fall in the nominal Stg£/IR£ exchange rate has restored competitiveness *vis-à-vis* the UK back to where it was forty years ago. This may make present exchange rates favourable for entry into the EMU, but of course we cannot predict how sterling will change relative to the euro in the years to come.

Against the DM, the Irish economy enjoyed a competitive gain during the 1970s, but this gain was subsequently eroded. Despite much short-term volatility, the competitive position between the two currencies today has hardly changed. relative to what it was in the 1950s

One point to note from Figure 15.10 is that there has been no consistent long-run trend in any of the real exchange rates. That is, the real exchange rates tend to revert to a stable long-run average. This is called the property of *mean reversion* and it is an implication of purchasing power parity.

After 1999 what will matter to us will be the value of the euro relative to non-

Table 15.5

Trade-weighted exchange rate index

(Hypothetical data)

Country	Trade weight	Bilateral exchange rate index		Trade-weighted exchange rate index	
		1998	1999	1998	1999
	(1)	*(2)*	*(3)*	*(4) =*	*(5) =*
				(1)×(2)	*(1) × (3)*
UK	0.43	100	96.0	43.0	41.3
Germany	0.14	100	97.4	14.0	13.6
US	0.14	100	106.8	14.0	14.9
France	0.10	100	100.7	10.0	10.1
Netherlands	0.06	100	99.5	6.0	5.97
Italy	0.04	100	104.4	4.0	4.17
Belgium	0.04	100	99.5	4.0	3.98
Japan	0.03	100	111.4	3.0	3.34
Denmark	0.02	100	101.9	2.0	2.04
Total	1.0			100	99.4

EMU currencies such as the dollar and sterling. We discuss exchange rate policy in the EMU in Chapter 23.

15.8 The Trade-weighted Exchange Rate Index

It is useful to have a single statistic that summarises a currency's external value. The summary statistic that is most widely used for this purpose is the trade-weighted exchange rate index, also referred to as the *effective exchange rate index*. This is an index of the average value of the Irish pound in terms of foreign exchange. The index is based on the bilateral exchange rates weighted in accordance with the importance of various currencies in Ireland's international trade.

In Table 15.5 we show how the trade-weighted exchange rate index is calculated. Column 1 lists Ireland's trading partners according to their share in Ireland's imports and exports. (Only nine countries are used in compiling the index because they account for virtually all our trade.) Column 2 shows the trade weight for each country. The UK has the largest weight of 0.43 (43 per cent of Ireland's trade is with the UK), Germany

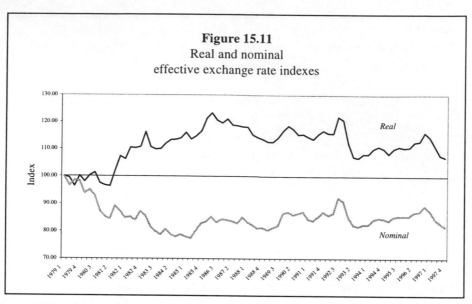

Figure 15.11
Real and nominal
effective exchange rate indexes

has a weight of 0.14 and so on down to Denmark which has a weight of 0.02. These weights sum to 1.0.

The first step in deriving the trade-weighted exchange rate index is to express the bilateral exchange rates as indices. The exchange rates are set equal to 100 in a base year and the index for subsequent years is calculated with reference to this base. For example, if the $/IR£ exchange rate was IR£1 = $1.60 in 1998 and IR£1 = $1.50 in 1999, the dollar exchange rate index would be 100 in 1998 and 93.75 in 1999. Hypothetical exchange rates for 1998 are given for several countries in column 4 of Table 15.5. It is assumed that over the year the Irish pound depreciated against the UK, German, Dutch and Belgian currencies but appreciated against the other currencies on the list.

The trade-weighted exchange rate index is calculated by multiplying each exchange rate index by its trade weight and summing for all countries. This is done in columns 5 and 6 for 1998 and 1999 respectively. Column 6 shows that in 1999 the trade-weighted exchange rate index had fallen to 99.4. This indicates that, on average, the Irish pound depreciated slightly over the two years.

Figure 15.11 shows Ireland's nominal trade-weighted exchange rate index (1979 = 100) over the period 1979-97. It can be seen that the Irish pound depreciated by approximately 21 per cent between 1979 and 1985 and then appreciated by approximately 9 per cent between 1985 and 1990. The effect of the 10 per cent devaluation in January 1993 on the index is noticeable.

350

Note:
The trade-weighted exchange rate index graphed in Figure 15.11 is based on data published in the *Quarterly Bulletin* of the Central Bank of Ireland. The Central Bank does not publish the trade weights used in its calculation, which are likely to differ slightly from those given in Table 15.5. After 1999 this index will no longer be published. The euro will replace the Irish pound and the competitiveness of the Irish economy relative to the rest of the EMU will depend only on price and cost developments in Ireland.

The real trade-weighted exchange rate In Figure 15.11 we also show Ireland's *real* trade-weighted exchange rate index over the period 1979 to 1997. This index is calculated by trade-weighting real exchange rates over time. This is identical to the calculation in Table 15.4 except that nominal exchange rates have been replaced by real exchange rates. The real trade-weighted exchange rate index rose between 1979 and 1992. This means that Ireland suffered a sustained loss in competitiveness against the average of our main trading partners over the period. Since 1997, however, there has been a significant depreciation, indicating a gain in competitiveness for the Irish economy.

15.9 An Alternative Measure of Competitiveness

In deriving the real exchange rate index, the choice of the price index to be used poses some problems. It is possible to use an index of consumer prices, of manufacturing output prices or of wholesale prices. These usually move closely together but sometimes a different picture can emerge depending on which price index is used. The real exchange rates given in this chapter were calculated using the consumer price index.

An alternative measure of the real exchange rate uses an index of *real unit labour costs in a common currency (RULC)*. This measures the cost of labour in the country relative to that in its trading partners. This allows for (i) the trend in relative wages, (ii) the trend in relative labour productivity, and (iii) movements in the exchange rate. Taking all these factors into account provides the best measure of how competitive a country is. Since the mid-1980s there has been a sharp and almost uninterrupted decline in Ireland's RULC index. This reflects the rapid growth of labour productivity in Irish manufacturing industry, which has not been offset by rising labour costs or by an upward movement of the exchange rate. On the basis of this index the country has enjoyed a steady and quite exceptional improvement in competitiveness over the ten

351

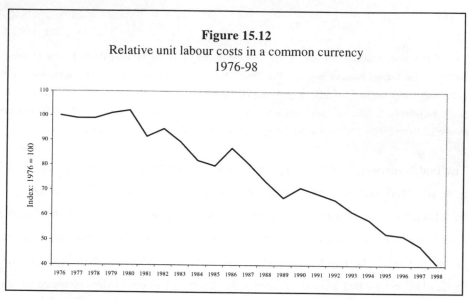

Figure 15.12
Relative unit labour costs in a common currency
1976-98

years, rather as if there had been a continual depreciation of the nominal exchange rate. This has been reflected in an unprecedented export boom.

15.10 Conclusion

In this chapter we have discussed a number of topics relating to the balance of payments and the determination of exchange rates. The main issues and concepts covered included:

• The balance of payments is a record of a country's economic transactions with the rest of the world. Apart from errors in measurement, the current, capital, and official external reserves accounts must sum to zero.

• The foreign exchange market

• How supply and demand for foreign exchange determine the nominal exchange rate

• The trend in the exchange rate of the dollar, DM and sterling relative to the Irish pound

• Deriving real exchange rates

• The nominal and real trade-weighted exchange rate index.

Data appendix

Irish pound real exchange rates

	German mark	Sterling	US dollar	Real Effective exchange rate
1979 1	100.00	100.00	100.00	100.00
1979 2	104.45	96.16	99.51	99.40
1979 3	105.96	89.17	103.33	96.30
1979 4	106.85	95.02	105.24	100.11
1980 1	109.25	89.71	105.56	98.02
1980 2	115.94	89.17	107.99	100.24
1980 3	119.35	88.85	112.17	101.27
1980 4	120.90	82.83	104.25	97.42
1981 1	123.85	79.49	97.04	96.65
1981 2	124.37	79.06	88.86	96.33
1981 3	130.45	87.15	85.79	102.10
1981 4	132.91	93.07	94.26	107.24
1982 1	132.27	90.49	90.61	106.20
1982 2	136.15	94.01	91.79	110.47
1982 3	136.05	92.72	87.46	110.27
1982 4	134.50	95.23	86.33	110.73
1983 1	134.36	106.79	90.14	116.24
1983 2	131.47	97.83	84.82	110.69
1983 3	133.12	96.10	80.65	109.83
1983 4	133.25	97.14	79.66	110.00
1984 1	134.29	99.72	79.76	111.99
1984 2	135.97	101.98	80.21	113.35
1984 3	138.32	102.44	74.89	113.42
1984 4	139.36	104.34	72.05	113.99
1985 1	140.89	108.15	68.71	116.03
1985 2	142.63	99.72	72.77	113.54
1985 3	144.43	99.12	79.24	114.81
1985 4	142.93	103.34	85.89	116.64
1986 1	142.35	112.52	93.98	121.38
1986 2	144.81	112.75	100.40	123.30
1986 3	136.46	114.75	100.37	120.65
1986 4	131.42	117.79	99.78	119.60
1987 1	130.39	117.66	107.41	121.08
1987 2	131.06	111.81	108.87	118.82
1987 3	131.79	111.56	106.29	118.66

1987 4	131.21	109.41	113.18	118.21
1988 1	131.46	109.41	115.33	118.20
1988 2	131.86	103.16	112.84	115.26
1988 3	133.28	102.15	103.09	114.31
1988 4	133.12	99.75	107.70	113.62
1989 1	132.67	97.71	100.91	112.67
1989 2	132.68	98.72	98.23	112.65
1989 3	134.61	101.19	99.28	114.37
1989 4	133.93	106.06	104.46	116.88
1990 1	133.73	108.41	111.42	118.69
1990 2	134.82	104.63	112.81	117.45
1990 3	135.55	98.18	117.79	115.38
1990 4	134.64	98.39	122.72	115.59
1991 1	134.47	97.05	108.38	114.59
1991 2	134.51	96.99	102.54	113.73
1991 3	134.20	98.49	112.25	115.60
1991 4	133.23	100.05	121.90	116.86
1992 1	133.15	99.89	113.07	115.92
1992 2	133.01	97.29	122.36	115.85
1992 3	131.24	111.22	129.83	122.00
1992 4	130.38	113.68	112.74	120.85
1993 1	118.94	107.64	105.02	112.22
1993 2	117.75	100.64	98.15	107.27
1993 3	113.68	101.28	98.72	106.77
1993 4	118.54	100.78	96.46	108.20
1994 1	115.50	103.01	98.81	108.19
1994 2	116.71	104.15	104.82	110.14
1994 3	117.14	105.33	106.84	111.03
1994 4	115.85	104.61	105.60	110.28
1995 1	107.08	106.04	110.68	108.30
1995 2	109.78	108.15	111.86	110.23
1995 3	111.69	107.71	110.53	110.96
1995 4	111.23	108.72	108.90	110.54
1996 1	112.51	108.52	106.70	110.76
1996 2	117.50	107.12	107.54	112.63
1996 3	118.29	107.13	107.86	112.93
1996 4	127.00	103.32	113.66	116.17
1997 1	127.40	100.28	105.05	114.38
1997 2	127.52	93.80	101.12	111.08
1997 3	123.65	92.22	97.09	107.77
1997 4	124.46	88.67	95.36	107.10

Chapter 16

Fixed Exchange Rate Systems: Theory and History

16.1 Introduction

Proponents of fixed exchange rates believe that freely floating rates create uncertainty and discourage international trade and investment. It is claimed that speculative flows may drive exchange rates significantly above or below their equilibrium levels, distorting the pattern of trade and investment between countries. When exchange rates are fixed, so the argument goes, uncertainty is reduced and trade and investment are promoted. This in turn should increase output and employment. These arguments have been very influential as justifications for trying to establish a single currency between the member states of the EU.

In this chapter we first examine some general arguments in favour of fixed as opposed to floating exchange rates; we then examine in some detail how fixed exchange rate systems operate and why they tend to break down. Finally we look at some lessons from earlier attempts to operate fixed exchange rates.

16.2 Fixed or Floating Exchange Rates?

In principle, countries have a choice between fixed exchange rate systems and floating, or various compromises between these two systems. Orthodox economic opinion has varied as to the relative merits of the alternatives. In this section we examine the arguments on both sides of this debate.[1]

---

1. An early discussion on the advantages and disadvantages of fixed and flexible exchange rates is contained in Milton Friedman, "The Case for Flexible Exchange Rates", in Milton Friedman, *Essays in Positive Economics*, Chicago: University of Chicago Press, 1953. For more recent discussions see Jacques Artus and John Young, "Fixed Versus Flexible Exchange Rates: A Renewal of the Debate", *IMF Staff Papers*, 26 December 1979, and Rudiger Dornbusch, "Exchange Rate Economics: Where Do We Stand?", *Brookings Papers on Economic Activity*, No. 1, 1980, and Maurice Obstfed and Kenneth Rogoff, "The Mirage of Fixed Exchange Rates", *Journal of Economic Perspectives,* Vol. 9, No. 4, Fall 1995, pp 73-96.

Advantages of floating exchange rates The basic argument in favour of floating is that the foreign exchange market should be allowed to function free of government intervention and find its own equilibrium through the interaction of the forces of supply and demand. Attempts by governments to set targets and peg exchange rates are, according to this view, as misguided in this market as they would be in the market for apples or shoes. How do governments know what the "correct" exchange rate is? How can they distinguish a temporary fluctuation in the supply and demand for foreign exchange (which should be smoothed out) from a fundamental adjustment (which should not be resisted)? How can they avoid handing speculators sure bets by merely delaying a devaluation or revaluation?

Even if governments are successful in maintaining a fixed exchange rate, the result can be a misalignment. This gives rise to *problems of adjustment*. If, for example, a current account balance of payments deficit indicates that the exchange rate is overvalued, but the government is committed to a fixed exchange rate, measures will have to be taken to reduce domestic costs and prices. The required deflationary policies will have an adverse effect on output, employment and unemployment, in the short run at least, and are politically difficult to implement.

Furthermore, domestic firms may be unable to compete with foreign firms because an overvalued currency has rendered domestic costs too high relative to the international competition. Under these circumstances it is unrealistic to expect employees and trade unions to understand that they should accept cuts in nominal wages so as to restore the country's international competitiveness. (See Chapter 12 for a discussion of how wages and prices adjust to an adverse economic shock.) The best that can be hoped for is to hold domestic costs down while foreign costs rise, but this can take a long time to yield the desired result. A more realistic approach would be for the authorities to devalue the currency while trying to ensure that there is no offsetting rise in domestic money wages and costs.

Floating exchange rates avoid all these problems. Moreover, when currencies are floating there is no need for central banks to intervene to stabilise exchange rates and they can run down the level of their external reserves.

Disadvantages of floating exchange rates The most frequently made argument against allowing currencies to float freely is that left to its own devices the foreign exchange market tends to be dominated by speculative flows. These are based on the

356

hope of making gains by moving into currencies that appreciate and out of currencies that depreciate. In principle, this should not be a problem if speculators base their actions on the "fundamentals" that ultimately determine the relative value of currencies (see Chapter 15). However, at times speculators' expectations appear to lack an anchor. It is possible for floating exchange rates to be volatile. It is also possible for them to move away from what is generally believed to be their equilibrium values over long periods. For example, in the early 1980s most people believed that the US dollar was "too strong" but it continued to rise until 1986. In the short run, currencies can gyrate widely in response to all sorts of news and rumours. An argument in favour of fixed exchange rates is that they avoid the uncertainty and volatility that occur when currencies are allowed to float freely. However, there is surprisingly little evidence that this volatility actually reduces the level of international trade and investment.

Note:

Following the collapse of the Bretton Woods system in the 1970s, the United States was committed to floating exchange rates, especially as far as the dollar was concerned.[2] An important change in US policy took place in 1985, however, when the world's seven main industrialised nations (known as G-7) met in the Louvre to "co-ordinate" a depreciation of the dollar against the other currencies. Since then there have been periodic meetings of this exclusive club to co-ordinate exchange rates. These meetings restore stability to the foreign exchange markets for a while, but do not remove the potential for further tensions. Because of its importance in world trade and because it is the most widely held reserve currency, the dollar always occupies centre stage. This is despite its periodic weaknesses and the long-run decline in its value relative to the German mark and the Japanese yen. It remains to be seen how its role in the world monetary system will be affected by the launch of the euro in 1999. In fact, Argentina recently adopted a currency board which was only allowed to issue local currency against the backing of dollars.

A further potential disadvantage of flexible exchange rates is that depreciation may provoke a depreciation-inflation spiral. This occurs when an initial depreciation increases domestic costs and prices and generates pressure for further depreciation and so on. Why do we have such high inflation? Because the exchange rate is depreciating. And why is the exchange rate depreciating? Because we have high inflation. The experience of a number of South American countries illustrates how difficult it can be to stop this spiral.

---

2. Given the size and relatively closed nature of the US economy, the authorities tend to regard the dollar as the "n^{th} currency", that is, the currency to which all others have to adjust. We discuss this topic in Chapter 17.

Note:

In Chapter 13 we illustrated the problem of *hyperinflation* with reference to Argentina's recent woes. Soaring inflation has undermined the value of the country's currency in terms of foreign currencies. The austral was introduced in 1985 when it was worth $1.25. By mid-1991, there were 10,000 australs to $1 and the government announced plans to replace it with a new currency, which would be called the (new) peso. This was only the most recent in a series of new currencies introduced as inflation undermined the old ones: one new peso would be worth 10,000 *billion* of the old pesos that were in use in the 1960s. To avoid uncertainty about future purchasing power people tend to use a foreign currency, such as the dollar, in preference to the local one. This process is called *dollarisation*. Pegging the exchange rate to a hard currency is a way of breaking the inflation-depreciation spiral.

Policy co-ordination

For a fixed exchange rate system to succeed, the chosen rates must accurately reflect the relative costs of doing business in the participating countries. It is essential that fundamental misalignments be avoided if the system is to endure. It is also essential that the participating countries pursue similar macroeconomic policies so as to avoid the emergence of misalignment over time. If the currencies are misaligned to start with, or divergent policies create misalignments with the passage of time, persistent current account deficits and surpluses will arise, as will a tendency for some countries to experience excess unemployment. These symptoms of disequilibrium will eventually lead to realignments and the possible breakdown of the system of fixed exchange rates.

An example of the tensions caused by unco-ordinated policies is provided by the early years of the ERM. In 1983 France was pursuing an expansionary fiscal policy while Germany was implementing a deflationary monetary policy, while both were committed to maintaining stable exchange rates within the EMS. The result was an increasing balance of payments deficit in France and a surplus in Germany. Speculators, anticipating a devaluation of the French franc, converted large amounts of money from francs into German marks. Eventually the French franc was devalued, rewarding the speculators. It was only after France abandoned its expansionary fiscal policy that the speculation subsided. The Irish currency crisis of 1992/93 reflected similar issues.

The lesson to be learned is that fixed exchange rate systems can only reduce exchange rate uncertainty if macroeconomic policy in the individual states is consistent. This can be achieved by explicit or implicit *policy co-ordination*.

Despite the problems inherent in operating a system of fixed exchange rates, policy-makers and economists are often persuaded of the merits of some arrangement whereby rates are fixed or pegged. We need, therefore, to examine in more detail the technicalities of operating an exchange rate peg and the reasons why such pegs have almost always been abandoned.

16.3 How a Fixed Exchange Rate System Works

As we saw in Chapter 15, when exchange rates are allowed to float the foreign exchange market is just like any other market. The price (exchange rate) adjusts automatically to equate supply and demand. There is no need for central banks or governments to become involved. Fixed exchange rate systems, on the other hand, require countries to observe elaborate "rules of the game" and we shall see, despite repeated attempts to make them work, they tend not to endure.

Exchange rate *target zones* are a modified version of fixed exchange rates. Under this arrangement central banks agree on *central* exchange rates and on *upper* and *lower limits* within which the market rate should be maintained. For example, the European Monetary System (EMS) operated a system of target zones known as the Exchange Rate Mechanism (ERM) since it commenced in March 1979.

Table 16.1

Ireland's official external reserves, June 1997

	£ millions	%
Foreign exchange	4,303	84.5
ECU	404	7.9
SDR	110	2.1
Reserve position at IMF	195	3.8
Gold	80	1.5
Total	5,092	100.0

Source: Central Bank of Ireland, *Quarterly Bulletin*, Autumn 1997, Table A1.

In order to operate a system of fixed exchange rates, central banks must be prepared to intervene on the foreign exchange markets to support a currency at a target level. The official external reserves play a key role in central bank intervention.

The official foreign exchange reserves are a central bank's holdings of foreign currencies and other external monetary assets. Table 16.1 gives a breakdown of Ireland's official external reserves as of June 1997.

In addition to foreign currencies and gold, the reserves consist of assets created by international agencies like the International Monetary Fund (IMF). *Special Drawing Rights* (SDRs), sometimes referred to as "paper gold", are reserve assets created by the IMF in order to supplement the world's monetary reserves. SDRs were first issued in

1970 to member countries in return for subscriptions in their own currencies. The SDR is a basket of the currencies of five of the main industrial nations. An SDR was worth IR£0.93 at the end of 1997. If a central bank needs to borrow foreign currencies in order to stabilise the exchange rate, its SDR allocation at the IMF can be used for this purpose. Because one country is borrowing from another, the IMF debits the SDR account of the borrower and credits the account of the lender.

The *European Currency Unit* or ECU is the numéraire of the EMS. It is based on a basket of European currencies. An ECU was worth IR£0.76 at the end of 1997. The ECU is used by European central banks as a reserve currency. The European Monetary Institute (EMI) which is the European equivalent of the IMF supervises any borrowing or lending involving ECUs. The exchange rate of the new European currency, the euro (which will be launched in 1999), will be set equal to one ECU. Thereafter the ECU will cease to exist as a currency.

Ireland's official external reserves have been held by the Central Bank of Ireland. They may be used to purchase Irish pounds from the foreign exchange market and stabilise the exchange rate. This operation is called *intervention*. After the start of the EMU in 1999 the reserves of all eleven participants will be held by the European Central Bank, which will use them to intervene and stabilise the value of the euro on the world's foreign exchange markets.

Central bank intervention

Figure 16.1 illustrates the principles underlying central bank intervention to stabilise an exchange rate. Participating central banks agree on a *central exchange rate* and on *upper* and *lower limits* within which the exchange rate should be maintained. We can illustrate this using the *narrow band* exchange rate mechanism (ERM) of the European Monetary System that operated between 1979 and 1993. In 1992 the central rate of the Irish pound against the German mark was DM2.67. The permissible fluctuation margin was a range of 2.25 per cent around this rate. The upper limit to this band would be DM2.73 = IR£1 and the lower limit DM2.61 = IR£1. The Irish and German Central Banks were committed to intervene if these limits were about to be breached.

In Figure 16.1 the market is in equilibrium at DM2.67 = IR£1. An increase in imports would shift the supply schedule for Irish pounds to the right (S_1 to S_2). At the new equilibrium B the Irish pound would have depreciated to DM2.50 = IR£1. This exchange rate is below the agreed lower limit of DM2.61. To prevent the pound falling

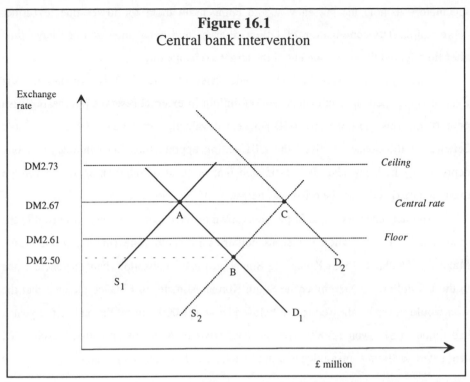

Figure 16.1
Central bank intervention

outside the target zone, the Central Bank of Ireland (CBI) and the Bundesbank must buy Irish pounds and sell German marks on the foreign exchange market. In effect, they create an artificial demand for Irish pounds and an artificial supply of German marks. The CBI must use up some of its external reserves for this purpose, whereas the Bundesbank acquires additional reserves in the form of Irish pounds. The purchase of Irish pounds would have the effect of shifting the demand curve for Irish pounds to the right (D_1 to D_2). The new equilibrium would be at C and the exchange rate would have been kept within the agreed band.

Conversely, central banks can keep the exchange rate from rising above the upper limit of the agreed band by selling pounds and buying marks. The CBI sells Irish pounds and the Bundesbank buys them. This will keep the exchange rate within the band.

When a currency is depreciating a central bank ability to support it is limited by its holdings of reserves of foreign exchange. Were reserves to fall below the minimum level believed to be prudent (often expressed as a multiple of the country's monthly import bill), the bank would be unable to continue to support the exchange rate. More damaging is the fact that central banks will also raise interest rates to encourage speculators to hold the currency and to compensate them for losses due to further depreciation. The combination of falling reserves and penal interest rates have time after time forced the abandonment of the target exchange rate.

This happened during the Irish currency crisis of 1992-93. It is estimated that the Central Bank spent approximately £8,000 million in external reserves purchasing Irish pounds, but this did not avert a 10 per cent devaluation in January 1993. The futile defence of the pound involved the CBI selling appreciating German marks to buy depreciating Irish pounds. It is estimated that the cost of intervening in the foreign exchange market during the crisis was between £350 million and £500 million.[3]

Another recent example of the breakdown of fixed exchange rates occurred in the second half of 1997 when numerous countries in South Asia (including Indonesia, Malaysia, Thailand, South Korea and Singapore) had to abandon their currencies' peg to the US dollar. In November the South Korean Minister of Finance pledged that the won would never be allowed to fall below $1= won 1,000, but by the end of the year it had fallen to $1= won 1,5000. The financial crisis in Asia (the so called "Asian flu") originated partly in a misguided attempt to adhere to fixed exchange rates.

The automatic adjustment mechanism

The theory of fixed exchange rates relies on the concept of an *automatic adjustment mechanism*. To illustrate how this is supposed to operate, consider the case of a country with a relatively high inflation rate. Because its inflation rate is high, its goods become expensive on world markets and a deficit emerges on the current account of its balance of payments. If it adheres to a fixed exchange rate there is, in theory, a mechanism that will reduce its inflation rate and move its current account back into equilibrium.

Note:

The automatic mechanism was outlined by Richard Cantillon, who was from County Kerry, in his *Essai Sur la Nature du Commerce en Général* (published in 1755 but written 20 years earlier) and by David Hume in *Political Discourses* (1752).

This mechanism operates through the intervention of the central bank in the foreign exchange markets to maintain the fixed exchange rate in the face of a current account deficit. Recall from the Appendix to Chapter 9 that high-powered money (H) is

---

3. Patrick Honohan, "Costing the Delay in Devaluing 1992 - 93", *The Irish Bank Review*, Spring 1994.

equal to the external reserves (R), plus central bank credit to the government and the commercial banks, (C_{cb}).

$$H \equiv R + C_{cb} \tag{1}$$

In appendix 1 in Chapter 9, we showed that high-powered money affects the money supply (M^s) via the money multiplier (η).

$$M^s = \eta \, H \tag{2}$$

If follows from these two equations that changes in external reserves affect high-powered money which, in turn, causes a change in the money supply.

$$\Delta R \rightarrow \Delta H \rightarrow \Delta M^s$$

When the central bank intervenes in the foreign exchange market and buys domestic currency to support the exchange rate, the external reserves fall and the money supply contracts. Conversely, if the central bank sells domestic currency to the foreign exchange market to avert an appreciation, the external reserves increase and the money supply expands. The key conclusion is:

- When a country adheres to a fixed exchange rate it loses control over its money supply.

Taking the analysis one stage further, we recall that changes in the money supply affect the inflation rate. The quantity theory is written as:

$$M^s \times V \equiv P \times \text{Real GNP} \tag{3}$$

Where V is the velocity of circulation of money and P is the price level. Assuming V and real GNP are constant, it follows that the price level (P) is the variable that adjusts in response to changes in the money supply.

Now consider the case of a country with relatively high inflation and an associated current account deficit. How does that economy adjust back towards equilibrium? (Under flexible exchange rates, the balance of payments deficit would result in depreciation.) Under a fixed exchange rate, the central bank intervenes by buying its currency on the foreign exchange market and the external reserves fall. This leads to a fall in H and M^s, which in turn leads to a fall in the price level (or the rate of inflation):

$$\text{Current account deficit} \rightarrow \downarrow R \rightarrow \downarrow H \rightarrow \downarrow M^s \rightarrow \downarrow \text{Inflation}$$

The decline in inflation improves the country's competitive position, exports increase and imports fall, leading to the elimination of the current account deficit. Conversely, a country with a current account surplus sees its external reserves and money supply rise. This increases the rate of inflation, making the country less competitive. Exports fall, imports rise and the current account surplus is eliminated.

This automatic adjustment mechanism is a key feature of fixed exchange rate systems. There are, however, limits to the willingness of countries to surrender control over the money supply and to suffer externally caused changes in the rate of inflation.

Sterilisation

Sterilisation is a way of trying to break the link between changes in the external reserves and changes in the domestic money supply. It is often tried when a country is experiencing an inflow of foreign exchange that threatens to increase the domestic money supply and eventually increase the rate of inflation.

Consider the following identity which can be derived from the *consolidated balance sheet* of the banking system:

$$M^S \equiv DC + R \tag{4}$$

Earlier in Chapter 9 we defined the money supply as being equal to cash and bank deposits. Identity (4) is an alternative definition which states that the money supply equals domestic credit (DC) plus the external reserves (R). This identity is simplified for exposition purposes. In the Appendix to this chapter we derive the complete identity from the consolidated balance sheet of the Irish banking system.

Identity (4) can also be presented in terms of changes:

$$\Delta M^S \equiv DCE + \Delta R \tag{5}$$

where DCE = domestic credit expansion, that is, the change in domestic credit.

Note:

Identities 4 and 5 provide the basis of the *monetary approach to the balance of payments* (MAB).[4] This theory provides a rationale for using credit guidelines to achieve an external reserves target. The modern version of MAB dates from the work of the English Nobel prize-winning economist James Meade (b. 1907) in the 1950s and Harry Johnson (1923-1977) in the 1970s. Under the influence of Jacques Polak this approach became the foundation of the International Monetary Fund's (IMF) operational practices. Many countries that borrowed from the IMF are tied to policy programmes based on the MAB.

---

4. For a collection of essays on MAB theory, see J. A. Frenkel and H. G. Johnson (eds) *The Monetary Approach to the Balance of Payments*, London, Allen and Unwin, 1976. A useful survey of the early literature is given in M. E. Kreinin and L. H. Officer, "The Monetary Approach to the Balance of Payments: A Survey", *Princeton Studies in International Finance*, No. 43, Princeton University Press, 1978.

Consider now the case where the central bank is intervening in the foreign exchange market to prevent its exchange rate appreciating. This intervention will lead to a rise in the external reserves (R). In terms of identity (4), the strategy of sterilisation consists of trying to reduce DC as R rises thereby keeping the money supply relatively constant. In other words, as R rises the central bank can try to maintain M^s stable by engineering a fall in DC. This it can do by open market operations, described in Chapter 9. To reduce DC, however, the central bank would sell bonds. To entice the public to hold more bonds their price would have to be lowered, which implies that interest rates would have to rise. At higher interest rates, the demand for money is reduced.

However, the ability of a central bank to reduce DC in this manner is limited. Higher interest rates would tend to attract a larger inflow of funds from abroad. They would also be harmful to the domestic economy. A country experiencing such an inflow would sooner or later find it more attractive to allow its exchange rate to rise rather than to continue to resist the appreciation through attempts at sterilisation.

If the problem is an outflow of reserves due to a balance of payments deficit, the central bank has to try to replace the loss of reserves by increasing the domestic component of the money supply. This will entail open market operations in which bonds are bought. This implies driving their price up and lowering interest rates. But this will encourage a further outflow of funds and reinforce the problem it was designed to tackle.

History shows that sterilisation is of limited effectiveness. It is usually abandoned after a short trial period. A good example is provided by the response of the German Central Bank to the inflow of dollars when the Bretton Woods system was breaking down in the early 1970s.

Why fixed exchange rates do not endure

To understand why it has repeatedly been found impossible to maintain fixed exchange rates between countries, consider the chain of events involved in trying to defend a currency that comes under speculative attack.

Assume that foreign exchange dealers become convinced, for their own good reasons, that a currency is overvalued. Each dealer (or speculator, if you prefer) now has an incentive to speculate against a currency. Suppose, for example, you think the Irish pound will be devalued by 10 per cent, from DM2.67 to DM2.41. You could borrow, say, Ir£1 million pounds from your bank and convert them for deutschmarks at an exchange rate of DM2.67. Total deutschmark receipts are DM2.67 million. If the devaluation now occurs you can convert back from deutschmarks to Irish pounds at an exchange rate of DM2.41. Total Irish pound receipts are Ir£1,107,884. You now re-pay the bank £1 million and the speculative profit is £107,884. Since you borrowed the money with which to speculate, your only cost has been the interest charges incurred over the month. Unless the Central Bank pushes interest rates very high, these interest charges will not eat up much of your profit. If the devaluation fails to materialise you lose on the difference between the interest you earned on your deutschmarks and the interest you paid on your Irish pounds.

To avert this sequence of events, the Central Bank – committed to the fixed exchange rate – will increase interest rates in an attempt to persuade investors to hold the domestic currency and discourage them from selling it on the foreign exchange market. The process of defending the exchange rate can become very painful if the Central Bank is determined to push interest rates high enough to beat off the speculative attack. During the currency crisis of 1992-93, for example, central banks around Europe raised interest rates to astronomical levels to defend their currencies. During the currency crisis of September 1992, the Swedish Central Bank raised its rate to 500 per cent, in January 1993 the Central Bank of Ireland raised its rate to 100 per cent and the Danish Central Bank did likewise in February. But these high interest rates were not sufficient to prevent speculators from continuing to sell the currencies short. All the currencies that were attacked were eventually devalued and the speculators made handsome profits. One of these speculators was the billionaire George Soros, who was credited (or blamed) for having forced Britain out of the European Monetary System in 1992.

Rising interest rates, rather the exhaustion of foreign exchange reserves, tend to break governments' resolve to support fixed exchange rates. In one instance after another, high short-term interest rates have proved extremely damaging to consumer and investor confidence. (In Ireland and Britain, high short-term interest rates are particularly unpopular because so many households hold variable rate mortgages.) Politicians quickly decide that the possible benefits of a fixed exchange rate do not merit the unpopularity caused by the measures needed to defend it. Speculators are aware of this weakness in the commitment to the exchange rate target and are encouraged to continue to sell the currency in order to make a speculative profit.

The level of official external reserves sets a limit to how long a central bank can continue to intervene to support its currency. But many central banks have more than enough reserves to repurchase all of the domestic money supply. In June 1997, for example, Ireland's official external reserves stood at £5 billion compared to a narrow money supply (M1) of £6 billion. If the Central Bank of Ireland (CBI), acting on the instructions of the government, were prepared to subjugate all other economic objectives to the defence of a fixed exchange, it could beat off the most sustained speculative attack by selling its foreign exchange reserves until there was almost no more Irish currency outstanding! Furthermore, if the Irish exchange rate target were supported by other central banks, and they were prepared to buy Irish pounds in unlimited amounts, they could easily absorb all the Irish money available to speculators. In reality, however, no government would be willing to commit itself so fiercely to the defence of a fixed exchange rate because to do so would involve a severe contraction of the money supply and force short-term interest rates up to an unacceptable level. The possible benefits of a fixed exchange rate do not merit such heroism!

Foreign borrowing and the external reserves

After Ireland joined the ERM in 1979 the CBI intervened heavily to maintain the exchange rate of the Irish pound. Some idea of the extent of this intervention can be had by comparing government foreign borrowing and the change in the external reserves.

To understand this point note that foreign currency borrowed abroad is exchanged at the central bank for domestic currency. The central bank adds the foreign

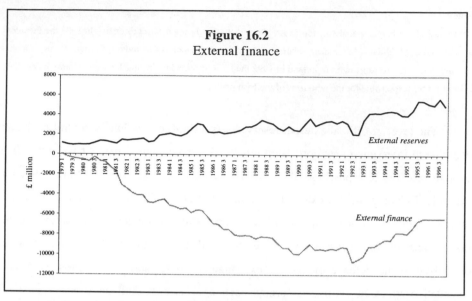

Figure 16.2
External finance

currency to its external reserves and credits the government's account with Irish pounds. The government is then in a position to implement its expenditure plans. If the central bank were not intervening in the foreign exchange market, the external reserves would rise by an amount equal to government foreign borrowing.

We can define *external finance* (EF) as being equal to the external reserves (R) minus official foreign borrowing (FB):

$$EF = R - FB$$

A decrease in EF indicates that the central bank is using the proceeds of foreign borrowing to intervene in the foreign exchange market and stabilise the exchange rate.

Figure 16.2 shows the trend in external finance and the level of the external reserves over the period 1979-96. The decrease in external finance, particularly over the period 1979-1986, indicates that the CBI was intervening to support the Irish pound. This means that it would not have been possible to maintain the exchange rate of the pound at the level that actually prevailed had the bank not used the inflows of foreign exchange that resulted from government external borrowing for this purpose. In recent years there has been a marked increase in external finance indicating that the CBI has not had to use foreign borrowing to support the currency.

The Irish pound could be said to have been overvalued for much of the 1980s. (This is also the conclusion that would be drawn from the appreciation of the real exchange rate discussed in Chapter 15.) An overvalued exchange rate impairs the competitiveness of domestic firms. Exporters and firms competing with importers find it difficult to maintain market share and a fall in output and employment in the traded sectors of the economy can result. However, since the mid-1980s this tendency has been offset by the steady fall in relative unit labour costs due to the steady gain in productivity associated with foreign direct investment (FDI) in Ireland.

Despite intervention the Irish pound depreciated since the 1970s (see Chapter 15). Hence the CBI used appreciating foreign exchange to buy depreciating Irish pounds. Irish taxpayers are now saddled with the burden of servicing this external debt in more expensive foreign exchange.

Having outlined how fixed exchange rate systems operate and the difficulties of sustaining them, we turn now to a brief account of the most important historical examples of fixed exchange rate systems, the Gold Standard, the Bretton Woods System and the precursor to the European Monetary System. (We discuss the EMS in detail in the following chapter.)

16.4   Fixed Exchange Rate Systems in History:
The Gold Standard

The most famous example of a system of fixed exchange rates is the gold standard, which was in full force from 1870 to the outbreak of World War I in 1914.[5] Over this period the values of the world's major currencies were fixed in terms of gold. This determined their value relative to each other. For example, a US dollar was worth 23.22 grains of gold and a pound sterling 113 grains, so the parity between the pound and the dollar was £1= $4.8665 (= 113/23.22).[6]

The gold standard relied on the automatic adjustment mechanism (explained earlier in this chapter) to correct current account balance of payments surpluses and

5. The account of the gold standard in the text draws on the article on "Money" in the *New Encyclopaedia Britannica* (15th edition), which was contributed by Milton Friedman, and on Robert A. Mundell, "Do Exchange Rates Work? Another View", International Monetary Fund, Research Department, WP/91/37, April 1991; Barry Eichengreen, *Gold Fetters: The Gold Standard and the Great Depression 1919-1939*, New York: Oxford University Press, 1992; and the review of this book by Richard N. Cooper, "Fettered to Gold? Economic Policy in the Interwar Period", *Journal of Economic Literature*, Vol. XXX (December 1992), pp 2120-28;

6. As there are 480 grains in a Troy ounce, an ounce was worth $20.66 or £4.25. The ounces used in buying and selling gold are "Troy ounces", which are slightly heavier than the more familiar (avoirdupois) ounces. One Troy ounce = 1.097 avoirdupois ounce.

deficits. If, for example, a country were experiencing a current account deficit, gold would flow out of the country. This reduction in the money supply (gold) would put downward pressure on the price level. Lower prices, in turn, improved competitiveness, increased exports and reduced imports. The incipient current account deficit would be automatically eliminated by this redistribution of the world's gold supply. Similarly, a country with a current account surplus would experience an increase in its money supply and rising prices. The loss in competitiveness would choke off the current account surplus. The monetary authorities in these countries should not intervene to prevent these flows or their effects on the price level: this was an essential part of the "rules of the game".

Under the full-blown gold standard, current account surpluses or deficits would not persist: factors of production (labour and capital), as well as money, would flow from the deficit to the surplus country, and there would be rapid adjustment as the level of economic activity declined in the former and rose in the latter. This is what happens today between the regions of a country. In the US, for example, cut-backs in the defence industry hit California hard, its current account went into deficit, the state went into a severe recession and resources flowed out. A rise in oil prices, on the other hand, would lead to a current account surplus in Texas, money and resources would flow into the state and the economy would boom. A similar adjustment mechanism will operate throughout the EU after the euro has been adopted.

During World War I, France and Britain suspended convertibility of their currencies into gold and, although the US maintained limited convertibility of the dollar, this marked the end of the full-blown gold standard. At the time the suspension of convertibility was regarded as temporary, like the suspension of gold payments during the Napoleonic wars, and a major aim of British post-war policy was to return to the gold standard at the pre-war value of sterling. In 1925 Winston Churchill, then Chancellor of the Exchequer, put the pound back on the gold standard at the pre-war parity. Orthodox financial opinion in Britain was gratified at the thought that the pound was once again worth $4.8665, but as Britain had experienced considerably more inflation since 1914 than the US, sterling was now overvalued. France went back on the gold standard in 1928 but at a realistic, lower exchange rate that more than compensated for the inflation that had occurred since 1914.

When recession hit Germany in 1928 and then America in 1929 it was quickly transmitted throughout the world by the gold standard. It is now widely agreed that the restoration of the gold standard in the 1920s and the attempt to adhere to its rules were reasons why this recession intensified into the Great Depression. The financial panics and bank failures that followed in the wake of the stock market crash of 1929 led to the collapse of the gold standard. Britain suspended sterling convertibility to gold in 1931 and in 1933 dollar convertibility was suspended,[7] to be restored in 1934 at the higher gold price of $35 an ounce. Most other countries abandoned the gold standard completely.

John Maynard Keynes regarded the financial world's obsession with gold as a "barbarous relic". He thought Mr Churchill's decision to re-establish the pre-war gold value of sterling in 1925 was a quixotic blunder that imposed a severe deflation on the British economy. When Britain abandoned the gold standard Keynes wrote:

"There are few Englishmen who do not rejoice at the breaking of our gold fetters. We feel that we have at last a free hand to do what is sensible. The romantic phase is over, and we can begin to discuss what policy is for the best."[8]

The factors that brought the gold standard to an end were:

- As international trade increased there was an associated increase in the demand for gold to act as reserve backing for currencies. Increases in the gold supply, however, depended on new discoveries and these occurred erratically in the course of the nineteenth century, in California, South Africa and Australia. Consequently

---

7. J. M. Keynes, "The End of the Gold Standard" in *Essays in Persuasion*, London, Rupert Hart-Davis, 1952. Keynes was visiting Ireland, to give the Finlay Lecture in University College, Dublin, in March 1933 when the news arrived that the dollar's convertibility had been suspended. The lecture was followed by a dinner and some of the best-known wits of Dublin were invited. The dinner was a total failure. Keynes was called to the telephone in the middle of the meal. When he came back, he said: "You may be interested to know that the United States has just left gold." The short silence that was felt appropriate was broken by [Oliver St John] Gogarty: "Does that matter?" James Meenan, *George O'Brien: A Biographical Memoir*, Dublin: Gill and Macmillan, 1980, p. 171.

8. It is interesting to ask why Keynes should have placed such emphasis on a relatively minor misalignment. Mundell (op. cit.) points out that the magnitude of the British overvaluation was estimated by Keynes to be 10 per cent and "it seems silly to observers in an age accustomed to wild gyrations of major currencies to blame so many of the ills of the world on this little event". Mundell believes that the fundamental problem was not the overvaluation of sterling but that the entire post-war monetary system was unstable due to the undervaluation of gold. The pound may have been overvalued relative to the dollar, but the dollar itself was about 35 per cent overvalued relative to gold. This meant that there was a deflationary bias in the world monetary system that asserted itself with a vengeance in the 1930s.

there was a tendency for periodic shortages of international liquidity to develop.

- One of the major partners in world trade, Britain, adopted an overvalued exchange rate in terms of gold after World War I. The adjustment to this mistake was slow and painful. It has always been difficult for countries to adjust to an over-valuation, because it requires price and wage cuts. Unemployment and cuts in wages in England in the late 1920s led to riots and widespread social unrest.

- Governments were not willing to abide by the "rules of the game". In the United States the Federal Reserve System, created in 1913, was unwilling to accept the consequences of the gold standard in the inter-war period. As a surplus country it experienced an inflow of gold from the rest of the world but in order to avert inflation the Fed prevented these inflows from increasing the US money supply. It operated a form of sterilisation, which thwarted the automatic adjustment mechanism on which the gold standard rested.

As the recession of 1929 intensified into the Great Depression, governments abandoned the commitment to fixed exchange rates, adopting instead a policy of "beggar thy neighbour" devaluations. They devalued in order to secure a competitive gain over their rivals in trade, but the countries that were adversely affected retaliated by devaluing in turn. The result was that no country gained a lasting advantage. The instability of the floating exchange rate system during the 1930s caused policy makers to attach a high priority to re-establishing a fixed exchange rate system after World War II.

The Bretton Woods system, 1945-71

In Bretton Woods, a mountain resort town in New Hampshire, representatives of 44 nations met in July 1944 (three weeks after D-Day) to discuss the arrangements for the post-war world monetary system. They hoped that when the war ended there would be no going back to the chaotic international financial system that had prevailed after the gold standard broke down in the 1930s. They believed that only a system of fixed exchange rates could provide the stable framework required for economic reconstruction.

As a result of its role in financing the war, the US held most of the western world's gold reserves by 1945. Consequently it was natural that the dollar should assume the role of the new reserve currency for the western world. The agreement was that the dollar would remain fixed at its 1934 value of $35 per ounce of gold and that all other countries would keep their exchange rates within a one per cent band of an agreed parity with the dollar. Central banks would buy or sell currencies as appropriate to keep exchange rates within the agreed band. This *dollar exchange standard* was, therefore, an attenuated form of the old gold standard.

The principal architects of the new system were J. M. Keynes and an American economist, Harry Dexter White. This was Keynes's last major contribution to public affairs before his death in 1946.

The *International Monetary Fund* (IMF) was set up to assist countries experiencing balance of payments difficulties and to help maintain fixed exchange rates. The *International Bank for Reconstruction and Development* (IBRD or the *World Bank*) was set up to help finance post-war reconstruction. (The IMF and World Bank are still known as the "Bretton Woods Institutions".) Central banks could borrow foreign exchange from the IMF and use it to support their currency on the markets. If, however, a country was experiencing a "fundamental disequilibrium" in its balance of payments it could devalue. The IMF could not veto a devaluation if it was less than ten per cent, but its permission was required for devaluation in excess of ten per cent.

The provision for devaluation marked a crucial difference between the Bretton Woods system and the old gold standard. No longer did countries have to suffer the protracted deflation of the automatic adjustment mechanism in order to correct a balance of payments problem. Instead they could obtain international agreement on devaluation.

The Bretton Woods system worked well during the 1950s and into the 1960s. The major currencies held to fixed exchange rates for long periods of time. For example, between 1949 and 1967, sterling was worth $2.80 (and because the Irish pound was fixed at one-to-one parity with sterling it too was worth $2.80). For 18 years this was a fact of economic life and no one bothered to look up the newspapers to see if there had been any change. Trade and investment between the nations of the western world expanded rapidly under the fixed exchange rate regime.

However, strains began to be felt in the late 1960s. The rising rate of inflation in the US, which was running budget deficits to fight a War on Poverty at home and a War on Communism in south-east Asia, led to massive US current account deficits and undermined confidence in the dollar. The other main industrial countries were unwilling to revalue their currencies to help eliminate the US deficit. For a while, central banks were glad of additional dollars to augment their reserves, but the continued loose US monetary policy soon created an excess supply of the currency. In 1968 a two-tier gold price was established, with the market price rising far above the official price. The major nations decided to discontinue supplying their gold reserves to the world gold markets at the official price. Thus most of the world's gold was immobilised. By 1970 the German and Japanese Central Banks held so many dollars that if they had been allowed to obtain gold in exchange for them, American gold reserves would have been completely depleted. (In 1969 the German money supply grew by 25 per cent in a week due to the inflow of dollars and the Bundesbank proved powerless to offset this through sterilisation. This is an important illustration of the limits to sterilisation, discussed above.) There was growing reluctance to continue to absorb the dollars flooding on to world foreign exchange markets. The dollar exchange standard was breaking down.

Finally, in August 1971 President Richard Nixon officially terminated the convertibility of the dollar into gold, which had already ceased to operate. In December 1971, at the Smithsonian Agreement (which was concluded at the Smithsonian Institution, a museum in Washington, D.C.), raised the price of gold to $38 an ounce, which in effect devalued the dollar by almost 8 per cent. Most of the other major currencies also devalued in terms of gold. This final attempt to patch up the Bretton Woods system did not succeed. There was a further devaluation of the dollar in February 1973 (which raised the price of gold to $42.22 an ounce), but instead of restoring confidence in the system, this encouraged the countries of Europe to terminate their links with the dollar and to float their currencies.

The instability of the international payments system and the decline of the dollar relative to gold opened the way for one of the greatest periods of inflation in the history of the world. There was a direct link between the fall of the dollar and the decision of the Organisation of Petroleum Exporting Countries (OPEC) to quadruple the dollar price of oil when the opportunity presented itself during the Arab-Israeli War late in 1973.

The rise in oil prices in turn fuelled the massive global inflation that occurred between 1973 and 1985. Over this period the Irish price level rose fivefold. It is understandable, in the light of this chain of events, that governments yearn for a return to some form of backing for their currencies that will prevent a recurrence of this experience, but a new standard for the world's money has so far proved elusive.

The European snake, 1972-74

Instability in the foreign exchange markets was unsettling for the European Economic Community (as it then was). It made it very difficult to operate the Common Agricultural Policy, whose goal was to establish a common price for agricultural products throughout the Community. How could this be done if the currencies of Europe were fluctuating wildly on the foreign exchange markets? But it also undermined the long-standing aim of the Community to establish a common European currency and a single European market for goods and services.

In 1972 the EEC central banks agreed to intervene in the foreign exchange markets to minimise fluctuations. Countries were expected to hold their currencies in a band ± 1.125 per cent around a central rate (the "snake"). They also had to maintain their exchange rates in a ± 2.25 per cent band against the dollar (the "tunnel"). This system became known as the "snake in the tunnel" because the European currencies slid up and down within the "tunnel" as they followed the movements of the dollar. In March 1973, the European currencies decided to float against the dollar and the "tunnel" part of the system came to an end. The remaining snake had a short life. The UK joined at the start, but left after two months because it proved impossible to maintain the value of sterling at the target level. (The Irish pound entered and left the snake along with sterling.) France left and rejoined as the franc rose and fell against the DM. By the mid-1970s the snake was dead. However, renewed currency instability increased the awareness of the need for a system that would stabilise exchange rates in Europe and led to the initiatives that culminated in the launch of the European Monetary System (EMS) in 1979.

The main reason for the failure of the snake was the same as that which led to the downfall of the gold standard and the Bretton Woods system, namely, the lack of economic policy co-ordination between the participating countries. If countries do not have similar monetary policies, leading to similar rates of inflation, they cannot hope to maintain their balance of payments in equilibrium under a system of fixed exchange rates. During the 1970s France and the UK pursued much more expansionary fiscal and monetary policies than Germany. As result they tended to run chronic current account deficits, while Germany ran surpluses. These imbalances eventually forced exchange rate changes and killed off the snake.

This episode illustrates the basic point that countries can only maintain fixed exchange rates if they pursue similar monetary and fiscal policies. Consistent policies are difficult to achieve as long as national governments believe they can improve their countries' economic performance by pursuing independent policies. If a system of fixed exchange rates is to be successful, it requires that the participants surrender or at least curtail their independence in economic policy making.

How significant a sacrifice this is depends on how effective these policies are in the first place. We reviewed the Irish experience with expansionary fiscal policies in Chapter 8 and saw that very few lasting results were obtained. The expansionary policies pursued by Britain and France in the 1970s, which led to the break-up of the snake, resulted in higher inflation but no extra growth. The apparent ineffectiveness of monetary and fiscal policies is an argument in favour of fixing exchange rates.

16.5   Concluding Reflections on Fixed Exchange Rates

The main lesson to be learned from this chapter is that all previous experiments with fixed exchange rate systems have been relatively short lived. Ultimately they have all broken down. Apart from very small countries that choose to peg their currency to that of a larger neighbour (Luxembourg and Belgium, for example) there are few examples anywhere in the world of independent countries that have maintained their currencies in a fixed exchange rate for any long period of time. The ultimate reason for this is that countries operate different monetary and fiscal policies, and this is incompatible with maintaining a fixed exchange rate.

Central banks can try to preserve fixed exchange rates by intervening on the foreign exchange markets. But there are limits to this approach. Intervention to prop up a weak currency puts upward pressure on domestic interest rates and this proves too painful for governments to endure for very long. Whilst intervention may be a reasonable way of smoothing out short-term fluctuations, it can become an expensive and futile exercise if governments try to adhere to an unrealistic target exchange rate. A fixed exchange rate that is initially realistic and defensible will become inappropriate over time as underlying fundamentals shift. This is why systems of fixed exchange rates, from the Gold Standard to the European snake, have broken down. During 1997 another illustration of the fragility of fixed exchange rates was provided by the turmoil in Asia, where several currencies that had for long been pegged to the US dollar, were forced to break this link.

Yet despite the difficulties of operating fixed exchange rate systems, in Europe the desire to establish stability on foreign exchange markets remains very strong in official circles. This has led to the attempt to create a "zone of monetary stability" in the European Monetary System in the late 1970s, and when it collapsed in 1993 attention switched to building a European monetary union (EMU), the final stage of which is due to commence at the beginning of 1999. We explore these experiments in detail in the following chapters.

16.6 Conclusion

In this chapter we have discussed the following topics:

- The operation of a fixed exchange rate system
- The official external reserves and their composition
- The limitations to central bank intervention on foreign exchange markets
- The advantages and disadvantages of floating and fixed exchange rates
- The Gold Standard
- The Bretton Woods system
- The European snake.

We have left a discussion of the European Monetary System and the move towards a single currency to the following chapters.

Appendix

The monetary approach to the balance of payments (MAB)

We illustrate the MAB using the consolidated balance sheet of the Irish banking system in 1997.

Consolidated balance sheet of banking system.

December 1997, £ millions

Liabilities

1. Capital employed	6,395
2. Government deposits at the Central Bank	1,191
3. Currency	2,260
4. Current accounts	5,199
5. Deposit accounts	33,904
6. Accrued interest	364
$M^3 = 3 + 4 + 5 + 6$ (money supply)	49,313
7. Net external liabilities of all credit institutions	3,197
8. Acceptances	0
9. Other liabilities	4,011
Total liabilities	56,521

Assets

10. Non-government credit	44,154
11. Accrued interest	228
12. Government credit	4,256
13. Official external reserves	4,636
14. Fixed assets	1,030
15. Other assets	2,218
Total assets	56,521

Source: Central Bank of Ireland, *Quarterly Bulletin*, Spring 1998, Table C1.

Using the row numbers from this table and bearing in mind that Assets = Liabilities, we can define the money supply, M^3, as follows:

$$M^3 \equiv 10 + 11 + 12 + 13 + 14 + 15 - (1 + 2 + 7 + 8 + 9)$$

$$\equiv (10 + 11) + (12 - 2) + 13 - 7 - (1 + 8 + 9 - 14 - 15)$$

$$\equiv NGL + BLG + R - NEL - NNDL$$

where

NGL = Bank lending to the non-government sector

BLG = Bank lending to the government

R = External reserves

NEL = Net external liability of domestic banks

NNDL= Net non-deposit liabilities of domestic banks

Consider changes over a period of, say, one year.

$$\Delta M^3 \equiv \Delta NGL + \Delta BLG + \Delta R - \Delta NEL - \Delta NNDL \qquad (1)$$

Now from the balance of payments (see Chapter 15, Table 15.1):

$$\Delta R = BOP + GEB + PCI + \Delta NEL \qquad (2)$$

where:

BOP = Balance of payments on current account (deficit –, surplus +)

GEB = Government external borrowing

PCI = Private capital inflow

ΔNEL = Change in net external liabilities of banks

Substitute (2) into (1):

$$\Delta M^3 \equiv \Delta NGL + \Delta BLG + BOP + GEB + PCI + \Delta NEL - \Delta NEL - \Delta NNDL$$

$$\equiv \Delta NGL + \Delta BLG + GEB - \Delta NNDL + BOP + PCI$$

$$\equiv DCE - \Delta NNDL + BOP + PCI$$

where DCE is *domestic credit expansion* in the economy, i.e. the increase in bank lending to the private sector (ΔNGL), plus monetary financing of the government ($\Delta BLG + GEB$). If $\Delta NNDL$ and PCI are both assumed to be zero, this accounting identity states that:

$$\Delta M^3 \equiv DCE + BOP$$

or

$$\Delta M^3 - DCE \equiv BOP$$

If we regard the change in M^3 to be equivalent to the growth in resources in the banking system, this states that if resource growth is less than the growth of claims on resources (DCE) there will be a balance of payments deficit and vice versa.

To see how MAP theory can be used for policy purposes consider again identity (1):

$$\Delta M^3 \equiv \Delta NGL + \Delta BLG + \Delta R$$

where NEL and NNDL are assumed to be constant. A further key assumption is that the supply of money is determined by the demand for money (M^d). That is, the money supply is assumed to respond to demand. This assumption is consistent with the fact that the central bank cannot control the money supply in a small open economy when the exchange rate is fixed. However, the MAB suggests that it can influence the *composition* of the money supply by restricting domestic credit expansion. For any given growth in the demand for money, the slower the rate of domestic credit expansion, the faster the rate of accumulation of external reserves. This suggests that *credit guidelines* can be used to achieve an external reserves target.

Note:

Credit guidelines may be issued by central banks as a means of curtailing the growth in bank credit. Typically, these guidelines stipulate by how much the banks can collectively increase their lending over a period such as a year. If the banks exceed the guideline they have "excess" lending, while if the growth of bank lending falls short of that specified by the guideline they have a "deficiency" in lending relative to the guideline. Since loans are the principal component of the banks' assets, credit guidelines are equivalent to placing a ceiling on the assets of the banking system. If a borrower is refused a loan because of a credit guideline, he is said to have experienced *credit rationing*. Banks have a profit incentive to meet a demand for credit provided they have the necessary reserves, even if this involves breaching a credit guideline. As a result, central banks are normally obliged to accompany credit guidelines with some form of enforcement measure. The Central Bank of Ireland has imposed *special deposits* on the banks for this purpose. These try to ensure that a bank makes a loss on excess lending.

The following steps illustrate how a credit guideline can be used to achieve an external reserves target:

(1) Estimate the growth in the demand for money for the forthcoming year, which gives the target for the growth in the money supply. Typically this estimate is based on a forecast of the change in nominal GNP and the interest rate.

(2) Decide on the external reserves target. Usually some rule of thumb such as building up a certain number of months' import cover is used.

(3) Estimate the growth in Central Bank and licensed bank lending to the government (ΔBLG).

(4) Issue a credit guideline to ensure that the change in bank lending to the private sector (ΔBLP) is consistent with the external reserves objective.

Suppose, for example, that the Central Bank predicts that the demand for money will increase by £100 million and that bank lending to the government will increase by £25 million. If the objective is to increase the external reserves by £25 million, from the MAB identity the growth in licensed bank lending to the private sector should be restricted to £50 million. Given the various estimates and the external reserves objective, the credit guideline is in effect calculated as a residual.

MAB is a theory of the balance of payments because changes in the external reserves equal the overall balance of payments. A balance of payments deficit leads to a fall in the external reserves. Hence, an external reserves target is tantamount to a balance of payments target.

A credit guideline restricts the growth of bank credit and therefore curtails the growth in one of the counterparts of the money supply. If the demand for money exceeds this, an excess demand for money emerges which raises interest rates and reduces aggregate expenditure. This is expected to reduce expenditure on imports and lead to a capital inflow. As a result, the balance of payments deficit falls and the external reserves increase. The Central Bank can thus achieve an external reserves target by pursuing a tight monetary policy. However, the capital inflow represents foreign borrowing, which will have to be repaid at a later stage.

It is important to note that a key assumption implicit in the MAB theory is that the demand for money is a *stable* function of a few variables such as nominal GNP and the interest rate. If, however, the demand for money fluctuates unpredictably over time, so too will the amount of additional money that can be absorbed by the economy, and an identity like (1) will be of little value for policy purposes.

Chapter 17

EMS and the Push for a
Single European Currency

17.1 Introduction

In the last chapter we explained how fixed exchange rate systems operate. We sketched the evolution of the world monetary system up to the collapse of the European snake in the 1970s. We saw that at the end of World War II there was strong support for a return to fixed exchange rates, which led to the establishment of the Bretton Woods system. After its collapse in the 1970s there was a desire to re-establish fixed exchange rates between the major European currencies. This led to a number of attempts to form a regional, European system of fixed exchange rates in the 1970s. After the failure of the snake, the next initiative was the launch of the European Monetary System (EMS) in 1979.

The EMS has survived several setbacks since its launch, and it is now about to be superseded by the European Economic and Monetary Union (EMU). In this chapter we explain how the EMS operated, what it achieved, why it broke down in 1993, and the subsequent decision to forge ahead with an EMU among eleven of the European Union countries. [1]

17.2 The European Monetary System, 1979 -1998

We have noted that exchange rate stability is regarded as essential for the proper functioning of the Common Market. Despite the failure of the snake, during the second half of the 1970s the EC Commission pressed ahead with plans for a European monetary union. The interim goal was to create a "zone of monetary stability" in Europe. By 1978 there was agreement between the French President, Valéry Giscard

---

1. For further reading, see Peter B. Kenen, *Economic and Monetary Union in Europe,* Cambridge University Press, 1995, and Paul De Grauwe, *The Economics of Monetary Integration*, Third Edition, Oxford University Press, 1997.

Table 17.1

The European currency unit (ECU): November 1993

		Units of currency	Weight (%)
1.	German mark (DM)	0.6242	30.1
2.	French franc (FF)	1.332	19.0
3.	Dutch guilder (HFL)	0.2197	9.4
4.	Belgian franc (BFR) ⎤	3.30	
5.	Luxemburg franc (LFR) ⎦	0.13	7.9
6.	Italian lira (LIT)	151.8	10.15
7.	Danish krone (DKR)	0.1976	2.45
8.	Irish pound (IR£)	0.0085	1.1
9.	Pound sterling (STG£) 0.0878	13.0	
10.	Spanish peseta (PTA)	6.885	5.3
11.	Greek drachma (DR)	1.15	0.8
12.	Portuguese escudo (ESU)1.393	0.8	
		1 ECU	100.0

D'Estaing, and the German Chancellor, Helmut Schmidt, that fixed exchange rates and eventually a common currency were desirable for Europe. After long and difficult negotiations the European Monetary System (EMS) commenced on 13 March 1979. More details of the chronology of events surrounding the EMS are provided in Appendix 1 to this chapter.

How the EMS operated

At the heart of the EMS was a system of quasi-fixed exchange rates, known as the *Exchange Rate Mechanism* (ERM).[2] The ERM was based on the *European Currency Unit* (ECU), a basket of currencies.[3] Table 17.1 shows the contribution of the individual currencies to the basket in November 1993, when the composition of the ECU was frozen. The amount of each currency in the ECU was based on the country's GDP and intra-EC trade. The German mark (DM) had by far the largest weight, reflecting the size of the German economy and its dominant role in European trade. The Irish pound accounts for only 1.1 per cent of the value of an ECU – the basket

2. We have tended to use the past tense in referring to the EMS and ERM because by the end of 1998 they will have ceased to exist in the form described here.

3. The écu was a medieval French coin. There is ambiguity as to whether "ECU" refers to this or is simply an acronym of European Currency Unit.

Table 17.2			
Calculating the ECU exchange rate for the Irish pound			
	Basket	Exchange rate November 1997	Converted to IR£
	(1)	*(2)*	*(3) = (1)/(2)*
DM	0.6242	2.4046	0.2595
FF	1.332	8.2158	0.1621
HFL	0.2198	2.6982	0.0814
BFR	3.301		
LFR	0.13	49.49	0.0669
LIT	151.8	2,408.59	0.0630
DKR	0.1976	9.4537	0.0209
IR£	0.008552	1	0.008552
STG£	0.0878	0.9835	0.0893
PTA	6.885	197.73	0.0348
DR	1.44	362.79	0.0039
ESU	1.393	244.43	0.0056
Total =	1 ECU		0.7964

(which was worth almost IR£0.80) contains less than one Irish penny! It may be seen that the German mark, French franc and pound sterling accounted respectively for 30, 19 and 13 per cent of the ECU, together accounting for over 60 per cent of its value.

Note:

The basket of currencies comprising the ECU was first defined when the EMS commenced in 1979. It was redefined in 1984, 1989, and a final set of weights was agreed in November 1993.

In Madrid in 1995 it was decided that the currency to be adopted by the countries joining the EMU in 1999 would be called the euro. At the start of EMU in January 1999, one ECU will be equal to one euro but thereafter the ECU will cease to exist. This is because the basket of currencies comprising the euro will not be the same as the ECU. The euro will only contain the currencies participating in the single currency system. Sterling, the Danish krone, the Greek drachma and the Swedish krona will not be included in the calculation of the euro.

The Irish pound/ECU exchange rate was calculated by converting the amount of each currency in the basket to Irish pounds and summing. This procedure is shown in Table 17.2 using the exchange rates prevailing in November 1997.

A number of points should be noted about the way the ECU was constructed.

■ It included currencies, notably the pound sterling, that were not in the ERM and will not join EMU in 1999.

384

Table 17.3

Central rates and intervention margins for IR£: May 1998

	HFL	B/LFR	DM	PTA	FF	LIT
Central Rate + 15 %	3.2177	58.903	2.8554	242.995	9.57835	2827.85
Central Rate	2.798	51.22	2.483	211.3	8.329	2459
Central Rate – 15 %	2.3783	43.537	2.1105	179.605	7.0796	2090.15

Note: If all the currencies in the system were at their central rates, the Irish pound could move by a maximum of 30 per cent. This would occur if the Irish pound was at the top of the band (+ 15 per cent) and fell to the bottom of the band (– 15 per cent). However, at any one time, no two currencies can be more than 15 per cent apart. Hence if any other currency were at the bottom of the band, the Irish pound could not move above its central rates.

- When a currency weakened (depreciated) on foreign exchange markets its contribution to the value of the ECU fell.

The key feature of the ERM was the commitment by the central banks of the participating countries to keep exchange rates within a specified band. Each participating currency declared a *central rate* against all others. These rates were then used to calculate the *parity grid*. That is the ceiling and the floor relative to the central rate. The idea is that a central bank would not intervene to influence a particular exchange rate while it remains inside the band. The central bank will only intervene if an exchange rate threatens to go through the ceiling or fall through the floor of the system. (See section 16.3 for a discussion of central bank intervention.)

Table 17.3 shows the central rates at which each currency will be locked to the euro in January 1999. Technically, each exchange rate can fluctuate by ± 15 per cent relative to the central rate up to that date. For example, this gives an upper and lower boundary for the deutschmark/Irish pound exchange rate of 2.8554 and 2.1105 respectively relative to a central rate of 2.483. In practice, exchange rates are not likely to deviate very much from their central rates prior to the locking of currencies in January 1999.

The *European Monetary Co-operation Fund* (EMCF) was an important part of the EMS. It was designed to help countries maintain their central rates in the ERM. In 1979 it received 20 per cent of all members' foreign reserves. In return, each member was credited with an equivalent amount in ECUs. The EMCF provided ECU credits to countries experiencing current account balance of payments deficits. It operated a

"Very Short-Term Financing Facility" (VSTFF) which allowed central banks to borrow ECUs for the purpose of defending a currency in the ERM. These credits had to be repaid in due course.

There were two important features of the EMS that conveyed a degree of flexibility to the system. The first was that *realignments* were permitted. A realignment was an adjustment of a currency's central rates against the other ERM currencies. Thus if circumstances warranted it, the parity grid was altered. Between 1979 and 1998 there were 21 changes in the ERM central rates. The dominant trend was for the German mark and the Dutch guilder to be revalued, and the French franc, Italian lira and the other smaller currencies to be devalued. The exception was a 3 per cent revaluation of the Irish pound against all the other currencies, including the deutschmark, in March 1998.

The second source of flexibility in the EMS was the *margin of fluctuation* around the central rates. Until August 1993 the maximum permissible deviation of the strongest and weakest currencies in the ERM from their central rates was ± 2.25 per cent. (The Spanish peseta, the Portuguese escudo and the pound sterling were allowed a ± 6 per cent fluctuation margin.) The combination of periodic realignments and the margin of fluctuation round the central rate meant that the EMS was a compromise between a rigidly fixed exchange rate system like the gold standard or the Bretton Woods system and free floating.

17.3 What Did the EMS Achieve?

The EMS was a system of quasi-fixed exchange rates that relied on *indirect policy co-ordination* for its success. There was no mechanism to force the participating countries to harmonise their monetary policies, yet it was recognised that stable exchange rates could not be maintained between the German mark and, for example, the French franc and Italian lira if Germany pursued a tight monetary policy, but France and Italy continued to tolerate high inflation. This was exactly what happened in the early years of the EMS with the result that realignments were frequent – two in every year from 1979 to 1983. (Table 17.4 shows how realignments affected the central rates of the currencies in terms of the ECU after 1979.) Italy, for example, devalued the lira eight times between 1979 and 1987. The French franc was also weak during the early 1980s when the Mitterrand administration implemented several new socialist measures. If

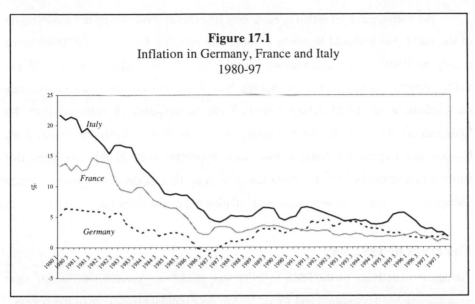

Figure 17.1
Inflation in Germany, France and Italy
1980-97

realignments had continued at this frequency the EMS would have been undermined. (We discuss the performance of the Irish pound in the ERM in Chapter 22.)

A major change occurred in 1983 when the Mitterrand administration abandoned its attempt at domestic expansion in favour of a programme of austerity and stabilisation. Between 1983 and 1986 the system became more stable and transformed into a more rigidly fixed exchange rate system. The Basle-Nyborg Agreement of September 1987 extended the use of the VSTFF, pledging central banks to unlimited intervention and to the use of interest rates to defend ERM parities.

Between 1987 and 1992 there were no major realignments and the margin of fluctuation between the main currencies narrowed to a *de facto* ± 1 per cent. Spain, Portugal and Britain entered the ERM, and Italy moved from the broad to the narrow band. Stability was helped by the fact that the participating countries were implementing broadly consistent economic policies and their rates of inflation were much lower and more uniform than was the case during the early 1980s. These were the golden years of the EMS. The trajectory of inflation in Italy and France, relative to Germany, is shown in Figure 17.1. This illustrates the dramatic narrowing of inflation differentials between the beginning and the end of the 1980s.

In 1979 countries like Italy, Ireland and France had much higher inflation rates than Germany, but by the end of the 1980s this was no longer the case. Inflation had fallen in all countries and the differentials between formerly high-inflation countries – such as Italy, Ireland and France – and low-inflation Germany had almost disappeared.

The convergence of inflation rates may be cited as evidence of the achievement of the ERM, but it should be borne in mind that inflation fell in all OECD countries during the 1980s. The major reasons were the collapse of energy prices in 1986 and tighter monetary policies. There is not much evidence to show that the countries that participated in the ERM achieved more rapid convergence of inflation than did European countries that remained outside, such as the United Kingdom, Switzerland, Norway and Sweden, for example. Even more important, there is little to suggest that participation in the ERM reduced the *sacrifice ratio,* that is, the cost in terms of extra unemployment associated with squeezing inflation out of the economy.[4]

The crisis of 1992-93

The apparent stability of the EMS in 1992 was deceptive. A number of factors were soon causing serious tensions and would lead to the eventual breakdown of the system.

These problems had their origin in the increasing dominance of German monetary policy over the countries participating in the ERM. While initially the spread of the anti-inflationary reputation of the Bundesbank was welcome, it became less attractive as German monetary policy was tightened in order to reduce the inflationary pressures building up in the wake of reunification in 1990. The nth *currency problem* came to the surface.

When exchange rates are pegged, there is one fewer exchange rate than there are countries to the agreement. If, for example, there are two countries, as under the Irish pound-sterling link, there is only one exchange rate, the Irish pound/sterling rate. Under these circumstances, it is sufficient for one country's central bank to intervene to hold the target exchange rate. (If they both intervene, they have to co-ordinate their intervention so that they are working towards the same target rate.)

In the EMS the nth currency was the DM and the Germans had the freedom to set their monetary policy to achieve a particular inflation target. Essentially, the Bundesbank controls the money supply and this results in relatively low German inflation. Low inflation, in turn, results in a "hard" or appreciating DM and low nominal interest rates.

The other *n–1* countries then attempt to "feed off" Germany's success by fixing their exchange rates to the DM. The theory of purchasing power parity (PPP) predicts

---

4. For a discussion of this issue, see De Grauwe, op. cit.

that if a country fixes its exchange rate to the DM then German inflation will be transmitted to that country. (See Chapter 18.)

The reason why Germany was accepted as the dominant or anchor country in the EMS is to do with the *credibility* of the Bundesbank. Effectively, the other n−1 countries had little faith in their own central banks to control their money supplies and inflation. They preferred the alternative approach of fixing their currencies to the DM thereby inheriting the low German inflation rate.

However, this favourable view of Germany was weakened by the repercussions of the reunification of Germany in July 1990. This led to a slow-down in the German economy, a rise in inflation and a weakening of the DM on the foreign exchange market. Furthermore, as was seen very clearly during the crisis of 1992-93, the Bundesbank's commitment to ERM parities was secondary to its concern for the domestic economy. In other words, the Bundesbank was prepared to implement policies to deal with domestic problems even if these policies were wholly inappropriate for Europe as a whole. Increasing strains were evident in the EMS experienced in the early 1990s due to the following developments:

- European and US monetary policy became markedly out of sync in the early 1990s. To stimulate the US economy, the Federal Reserve Bank lowered short-term interest rates in 1992 to their lowest levels for 29 years. In Germany, on the other hand, the Bundesbank raised rates to moderate the inflationary pressures arising from the fiscal expansion required to finance German reunification in 1990. This led to a widening of the gap between European and US unemployment rates in the 1990s.

- Because of the commitment to fixed exchange rates, higher German interest rates were transmitted to the other EMS countries.

- The combination of lower interest rates in America and higher rates in Germany caused a capital outflow from the dollar into the German mark, leading to its appreciation. This strained the ERM parity grid.

- Rising interest rates and appreciating currencies were painful for countries such as Italy, the UK and Spain, which were in recession.

- Despite the fixed exchange rates, inflation remained higher in several of the peripheral ERM countries than in Germany. The result was a loss of competitiveness.

- With hindsight it is now clear that these currencies were vulnerable to a speculative attack in the early 1990s. The only question was when it would begin.

Note:

A recurrent problem with the EMS was the fact that when money flows into Europe from the rest of the world, European currencies – even those participating in the ERM – were not regarded as perfect substitutes. The German mark was favoured over other currencies, putting upward pressure on it and generating strain in the ERM.

The factor most frequently blamed for precipitating the currency crisis was the Danish "No" vote in a referendum on the Maastricht Treaty (2 June 1992). At the same time opinion polls predicted a 50/50 split in the French referendum, which was to be held in September. Since the Maastricht Treaty contained the timetable for moving forward to "irrevocably" fixed exchange rates and the adoption of a single European currency, its rejection by a major European country would have caused a full-scale political as well as monetary crisis. The French voted "Yes" by a narrow margin but the uncertainty caused by the referendum drew attention to the shaky political foundations on which the project rested.

Meanwhile speculators focused their attention on the real appreciation of the lira, the peseta and the escudo, as well as the unsustainable level at which sterling had joined the ERM.

Late in August speculators launched concerted attacks on the ERM currencies they believed were overvalued. (Note that it is impossible to have a speculative attack on a floating currency because it will simply adjust up or down in response to market forces. The possibility of a speculative killing only arises when central banks attempt to prevent a currency from adjusting, that is, when it is pegged.) Despite massive intervention by central banks, a number of currencies quickly fell below their permitted ERM floors. Early in September, the Finnish markaa abandoned its unofficial peg to the German mark. Both the Bank of England and the Bank of Italy raised short-term interest rates to defend their currencies, but on 12 September the lira was devalued by 7 per cent. Speculation against the pound and the peseta intensified. On 16 September, "Black Wednesday", the Bank of England spent an estimated £10 billion supporting sterling and the Bank of France and the Bundesbank bought sterling heavily. British interest rates were raised from 10 to 15 per cent.

This was not enough to dissuade speculators from continuing to sell sterling, so the British government withdrew sterling from the ERM. On the following day the

Italian government withdrew the lira, and the Spanish peseta was devalued by 5 per cent. Pressure then switched to the French franc, the Danish krone, the Irish pound, the Portuguese escudo and the peseta (again!). The Banque de France raised short-term interest rates to 13 per cent and with the help of the German authorities fought off the attack on the franc. The successful defence of the franc was the only achievement of central bank intervention during the crisis, but it was an important one for it preserved the commitment of France and Germany to continue to peg their currencies.

Pressure in the system gradually lessened late in 1992, especially after the peseta and the escudo were devalued in November and the Swedish krone (which had been informally pegged to the German mark) was floated.

Following sterling's departure from the ERM, UK interest rates fell to 8 per cent. Lower interest rates and the competitive gain from the devaluation were instrumental in making the UK economy's recovery from recession more rapid than that of the continental European countries. In recognition of how well the economy subsequently fared some of the British media renamed the day Britain left the ERM "White Wednesday".

Despite the extreme pressure on the Irish pound following sterling's departure from the ERM and depreciation in autumn 1992, the Irish authorities resisted a devaluation of the Irish pound until January 1993. We examine this episode in Irish exchange rate policy in detail in Chapter 22.

By early 1993 virtually all the currencies of the ERM had been devalued relative to the German mark. After a long and painful period of turbulence, the result was much the same as would have followed from a unilateral revaluation of the German currency in 1992. It is believed that the German authorities offered to revalue the mark in mid-1992 but the French and British authorities resisted this because they did not wish to see their currencies devalued. If this was the case, then this is another example of irrational pride in the nominal value of currencies overriding sound economic policy.

Note:
As mentioned in Chapter 16, the way speculators moved from one currency to another during the crisis of 1992-93 is an interesting example of *contagion*. Having profited from the vulnerability of one currency to an attack, speculators were quick to realise that other currencies were also vulnerable.

There was a period of stability in the first half of 1993 when the ERM appeared to have weathered the storm and settled back into a stable parity grid. But by the summer renewed speculative pressures emerged as markets came to view the Spanish peseta and French franc as overvalued. The EU finance ministers finally threw in the towel in August 1993 and announced that the ERM fluctuation margins were being widened to ± 15. To all intents and purposes the ERM was dismantled. It is important to note, however, that the French franc survived the crisis without devaluation and with its peg to the German mark almost intact.

The responses to the 1992-93 crisis

There were two possible responses to the effective demise of the ERM. The first, perhaps most obvious, reaction would have been to abandon the notion of fixed exchange rates and allow all the currencies of Europe to float freely, following the example of sterling and the lira. The second possible reaction was to push ahead for a full monetary union instead of the halfway house of the ERM. This was the option preferred by "convinced Europeans". It was argued that a European Central Bank, managing a single European currency, would conduct monetary policy in the interests of all member states. Whereas the ERM had relied on indirect policy co-ordination, and failed because this was not achieved, an economic and monetary union would co-ordinate policy directly. The nth problem would be removed and the dominance of Germany over European economic policy reduced. The irrevocable fixing of exchange rates and the eventual replacement of national currencies by a single European currency would eliminate the possibility of future speculative attacks.

While these arguments were attractive to countries other than Germany, the latter would have to be convinced that it stood to gain something by participating in the proposed EMU. Given that the German mark had been the lowest-inflation currency in Europe for decades, what gain was there to Germany in replacing it with an artificial currency based on a basket of national currencies, some of which had been highly inflation prone in recent years? To assuage German fears on this front, strict *convergence criteria* were included in the Maastricht Treaty. These would have to be met by countries hoping to qualify for entry to EMU. Another argument to recommend the EMU to Germany was the prospect that the mark would no longer attract speculative inflows during currency crises. These inflows had repeatedly driven up the value of the German mark in the past, rendering the economy less competitive. This problem would be removed by replacing the German mark with a common European currency.

A further argument for pushing ahead towards a full-blown monetary union was that the completion of the internal market could never be accomplished as long as prices were quoted in national currencies.

These were the immediate arguments that provided the impetus for the Commission of the EU to bring forward plans for an Economic and Monetary Union in the 1990s. While the blueprint that was proposed was a descendant of the prototype outlined in the Werner Report of 1970, it was more radical than anything that was deemed possible when the EMS was launched in 1979.

17.4 The Run-up to Economic and Monetary Union

My annals have it so:[5]
A thing my mother saw,
Nigh eighty years ago
With happiness and awe.

Sight never to forget:
Solemn against the sky
In stately silhouette
Ten emus walking by.

It now appears virtually certain that an Economic and Monetary Union (EMU) will be launched in Europe at the start of 1999. The remainder of this chapter contains a brief discussion of the EMU project (a detailed account of the chronology of events leading to its formation is contained in Appendix 2). The operation of the European Central Bank and the costs and benefits to Ireland of participating in EMU are discussed in Chapters 23 and 24 respectively.

European monetary union is seen by the EU as part of a wider process of Economic and Monetary Union (EMU). The design of the EMU dates back to a meeting of the European Council in June 1988 in Hanover, when a committee was given the task of "studying and proposing concrete stages leading towards [economic

---

5. M. Fullerton, "Emus" in Douglas Stewart (ed.) *Poetry in Australia*, Vol. 1, University of California Press, 1965, p. 193.

and monetary] union".[6] The committee was chaired by the commission President Jacques Delors and consisted of the governors of the central banks of the twelve member states (including Ireland's Maurice Doyle), a commission representative and three invited experts. The committee published its report (the Delors Report) in April 1989.

We summarise the proposals on economic union briefly. An economic union entails:

- A single market within which persons, goods, services, and capital can move freely (the four freedoms). The implementation of the 1987 Single European Act went a considerable way towards achieving this objective.

- A common competition policy. To establish a "level playing field" governments should not subsidise firms. State aids to industry were to be reduced. However, during the recession of the 1990s many European governments in fact stepped up their aid to industry. Following reunification, Germany became one of the main offenders on this front. Ireland's special 10 per cent profit tax rate on industry has come in for increased criticism although it is not officially regarded as a state aid to industry.

- Structural and regional convergence. It was recognised that a monetary union between countries at very different levels of development was unlikely to succeed.[7] In acknowledgment of the difficulties faced by "peripheral regions" a Cohesion Fund was established to help in the transition to a single market. The subsidies received by Ireland from this Fund were discussed in Chapter 2, where we also looked at the progress that has been made in bringing standards of living of the European regions closer together. (This process is sometimes called *real convergence.*)

Our concern in this Chapter is mainly with the proposals for monetary union. A monetary union entails:

- The complete liberalisation of capital transactions and full integration of banking

---

6. Committee for the Study of Economic and Monetary Union, *Report on Economic and Monetary Union in the European Community*, Office for the Official Publications of the European Communities, 1989, foreword. This report is known as the Delors Report, not to be confused with the White Paper, *Growth, Competitiveness and Employment*, published by the EU in 1993, which is also known by this name.

7. In this context it is interesting to note that the North American Free Trade Area agreement (NAFTA) contains no provision for a currency union between Mexico, the US and Canada.

and other financial markets. A directive passed in June 1988 provided for complete liberalisation by 1992. (The implementation of this coincided inconveniently with the currency crisis.)

- The introduction of a single currency. It was decided in Madrid in 1995 to call this the euro.

- Monetary and exchange rate policy in EMU will be conducted by the European Central Bank. Its basic objective will be to ensure price stability in Europe. The participating countries will surrender control over their monetary and exchange rate policy to the ECB. The manner in which the ECB will operate is discussed in detail in Chapter 23.

The framers of the Maastricht Treaty were very conscious of the fact that before full EMU could be launched the participating countries should first have achieved a high degree of *nominal convergence*. Accordingly they laid down several convergence criteria that would have to be met by any country that wanted to join the EMU. These related to inflation and interest rate differentials, the levels of the fiscal deficit and the national debt. The actual criteria proposed were originally framed for the purpose of excluding traditionally inflation-prone countries such as Italy from EMU, but as circumstances changed during the 1990s, it became difficult for even France and Germany, the core of the proposed EMU, to meet them. Consequently, in May 1998, the criteria were loosely applied and eleven countries were deemed eligible to participate in EMU. These countries are: Austria, Belgium, France, Finland, Germany, Ireland, Italy, Luxembourg, the Netherlands, Spain and Portugal. Sweden, Britain and Denmark have opted out for domestic political reasons and because of their misgivings about the soundness of the project. The only country that might have been interested in joining but was not deemed eligible was Greece. A more detailed account of these criteria and how they were applied is contained in Appendix 3 to this chapter.

The fact that eleven EU countries will be in, and three outside, implies that the process of economic and monetary union will now progress at different speeds in Europe. This will become even more apparent when the EU is enlarged to include Poland, the Czech Republic, Hungary and Croatia at the end of the century. These new members are unlikely to adopt the euro for some years to come.

The remaining steps towards EMU

The Delors Report envisaged Europe evolving towards EMU in three stages. These stages were subsequently modified by the Maastricht Treaty which was drafted in 1992 and at a number of inter-governmental conferences, in particular the summit meeting in Madrid in December 1995. Stages I and II were concerned with completing the internal market and launching the European Monetary Institute (EMI) (the precursor of the European Central Bank). These have been completed and need not detain us here.

The final stage, Stage III, of EMU will commence in January 1999. This will involve:

- The exchange rates at which the eleven participating currencies will be converted into euros will come into effect in January 1999. The mechanics of the transition from the ECU to the euro are outlined in Chapter 23.

- 1 July 1998, the EMI will be replaced by the European Central Bank.

- The euro will become "a currency in its own right". The exchange rates between the national currencies (the German mark, French franc, etc.) will technically be "conversion factors" for units of the euro.[8]

- All inter-bank, money and foreign exchange markets will be conducted in euros.

- All new government debt will be issued in euros.

- The euro will be introduced in a *non-cash* form on a "no compulsion, no prohibition" basis. Firms will be encouraged to switch from using the national currency to the euro in transactions. Payments can be made, and bank accounts held, in euros. Notes and coins, however, will continue to be in national currencies.

- As early as possible in 2002 euro notes and coins will be introduced and all notes and coins denominated in national currencies will be withdrawn. The transition to EMU will then be complete.

Between now and the year 2002 shocks may blow this timetable off course. The Maastricht Treaty contains no provisions for reserving the procedures outlined above, but the EU cannot force a country to continue along the road if national politicians decide to back out of EMU. It remains to be seen whether the countries that are about to embark on the most radical experiment ever in European economic history are in fact sufficiently similar in economic and financial terms to form an enduring monetary union.

---

8. Except for the Irish pound, all the national currencies will be non-decimal sub-units of the euro. Only the Irish pound will be worth more than a euro.

17.5 The Prospects for EMU

The evidence of history is that systems of fixed exchange rates do not endure. From the gold standard to the EMS, attempts to stabilise the world's currency markets have collapsed. The most important reason is that, despite being committed to maintaining stable exchange rates, sovereign countries have retained the right to implement independent economic policies. Sooner or later incompatibilities between national economic policies have led to strains, speculative attacks, and ultimately the abandonment of fixed exchange rates.

The breakdown of the EMS was due to fundamental strains created by incompatible monetary and fiscal policies and different inflation rates among the participants. The most important example of this was the expansionary fiscal and tight monetary policy stance adopted in Germany in the early 1990s.

The collapse of the ERM convinced many that the best way forward would be to abolish national currencies and adopt a single European currency. They argue that only when the commitment to fixed exchange rates is made "irrevocable" in this manner will the full benefits of a stable international financial system be enjoyed in Europe. Others interpret the history of the EMS since 1979 as evidence of the dangers inherent in trying to fix exchange rates between sovereign countries. They point to the risks involved in the single currency project. For the moment the argument in favour of a single European currency has won. It remains to be seen whether they will prove correct in the long run.

17.6 Conclusion

In this chapter we have discussed the following topics:

- The design of the European Monetary System (the EMS)
- The way it functioned between 1979 and 1993
- The proposal to create an economic and monetary union (EMU) in Europe

The design of the proposed European EMU and the timetable for its implementation

In appendices to this chapter we present:

- A chronology of events leading to the establishment of EMU
- A discussion of the Maastricht convergence criteria.

Appendix 1

Chronology of main events relating to the EMS

- European Monetary Co-operation Fund (EMCF) established in April 1973. It is designed on the lines of a European IMF, to help countries maintain fixed exchange rates by supplying them with credits during currency crises.

- European unit of account (EUA) – a basket of currencies – introduced in 1975. The ECU was subsequently based on the same basket of currencies.

- At the European Council meeting in Copenhagen in April 1978, the German Chancellor Schmidt and the French President Giscard d'Estaing propose the creation of a European Monetary System (EMS). The EMS is intended to create a zone of monetary stability in Europe. This was the beginning of the Franco-German co-operation that has ever since been behind the push for monetary union in Europe.

- July 1978: EC heads of state and governments meet in Bremen and agree on the structure of the EMS.

- December 1978: The European Council meeting in Brussels agrees on the mode of operation of the EMS. Ireland is committed to joining.

- The EMS commences operation in March 1979. Within the narrow band of the Exchange Rate Mechanism (ERM) currencies are to fluctuate within a maximum of ± 2.25 per cent of the central rates. All the currencies of the member states as of 1979 entered the narrow band ERM, except the Italian lira, which was put in a wider band (± 6 per cent), and sterling, which did not join. The Spanish peseta joined the wide band in June 1989. In January 1990 the lira came into the narrow band and in September sterling joined the wide band. The Portuguese escudo joined the wide band in April 1992.

- September 1992. Following intense speculative pressure, UK and Italy leave the ERM. The Finnish markaa, which had been informally pegged to the ERM, is floated.

- September 1992 - January 1993. After prolonged speculative attacks, the peseta, the escudo, and the Irish pound are all devalued and the Swedish and Norwegian krona abandon their ERM pegs.

- August 1993. Renewed speculative pressure against the French franc, the Belgian franc and Danish krone force a decision to widen the ERM band to ± 15 per cent for all except the German mark and Dutch guilder. The Irish Finance Minister Bertie Ahern states that the plan to create a single currency in Europe is "now on the back-burner".

- 1995-96: Following the enlargement of the EU, the Austrian schilling joined the ERM in January 1995 and the Finish markaa in October 1996.

- 1997: Of the currencies of EU countries, only the Greek drachma and the Swedish krona have never been in the ERM. The Swedish government commissioned a study of the proposed single currency that recommended that Sweden should not enter in the first wave. The new Irish government, with Mr Ahern as Taoiseach, endorses the policy of Ireland adopting the single currency even if Britain does not. The new Labour government in the UK announces that, while not opposed in principle to the EMU, Britain will not participate in the first wave.

Appendix 2

Chronology of the EU and EMU

- April 1951: France, West Germany, Italy, Belgium, the Netherlands and Luxembourg sign the Treaty of Paris, which establishes the European Coal and Steel Community (ECSC).

- March 1957: These six countries sign the Treaty of Rome that establishes the European Economic Community (EEC). One of the objectives of the Treaty is to establish a customs union where there is free movement of goods, services and capital. The Treaty also refers to the desirability of achieving international monetary stability. The EEC and the ECSC constitute the European Communities (EC).

- January 1962: The EC Common Agricultural Policy (CAP) commences with the aim of establishing a common market and prices for agricultural produce.

- October 1962: A Commission report to the Council proposes to form a monetary union by 1971. Germany objects on the grounds that the Bretton Woods system is working well.

- February 1969: Barre Report on the co-ordination of economic and monetary policies is published.

- December 1969: At a conference of European governments in The Hague, the German Chancellor Brandt called for establishing economic and monetary union in stages. This followed the devaluation of sterling in 1967 and the realignment of the French franc and German mark in 1969. His proposal was based on the Barre Report and was adopted by the European Council and a working party chaired by Mr Pierre Werner (Prime Minister of Luxembourg) was set up to examine the issues.

- October 1970: The Werner Report is published. The Report calls for the creation of a monetary union, in stages, by 1980. Monetary union will entail (i) fixing European currencies irrevocably or introducing a single currency, (ii) free movement of capital, (iii) the establishment of a European central bank, and (iv) co-ordination of macroeconomic policy. The Report called for "parallel progress" towards monetary union, involving co-ordination of fiscal and monetary policies at the same time as progress was being made towards fixing exchange rates. The Report suggested that economic policies are co-ordinated and exchange rate fluctuations reduced so that after a period of ten years exchange rates could be irrevocably fixed.

- March 1971: The Council adopts a resolution to achieve economic and monetary union by 1980.
- March 1972: As the Bretton Woods system collapses, European governments agree to maintain exchange rates within a ± 2.25 per cent band relative to each other (the snake). The snake did not succeed in stabilising European exchange rates and the remaining stages proposed in the Werner Report were postponed.
- January 1973: Denmark, Ireland and the UK join the EC.
- March 1979: The European Monetary System (EMS) commences operation.
- June 1985: The EC Commission submits a report on completing the internal market. The report identifies measures to remove barriers to the free movement of goods, services, capital and labour (the four freedoms).
- February 1986: Signing of the *Single European Act* which came into force in July 1987, after its adoption by referendum in Ireland. Its aim is to complete the internal market.
- June 1988: Council of Ministers directive to liberalise capital movements by July 1990. Transition period extended for Ireland, Portugal, Greece and Spain.
- June 1988: A committee of central bank governors and other experts is formed at a meeting of the European Council in Hanover to study how economic and monetary union could be achieved. EC Commission President Jacques Delors chairs the committee.
- January 1989: Commission President Jacques Delors proposes that the EC and the European Free Trade Association (EFTA, which includes the Nordic countries, Austria and Switzerland) create a European Economic Area (EEA).
- April 1989: The Delors Report is published.
- June 1989: European Council at a meeting in Madrid agrees to implement the first stage of the Delors Report starting July 1990.
- 1989: EC and EFTA begin formal negotiations to create a European Economic Area (EEA).
- December 1989: European Council meeting in Strasbourg agrees to establish the institutional changes necessary to implement Stages 2 and 3 of the Delors Report.
- July 1990: Beginning of Stage 1 of the process leading to EMU.
- July 1990: After more than forty years of separation, the economically strong

Federal Republic of Germany united with the economically weak German Democratic Republic in an economic, monetary and social union.

- October 1990: German economic integration made irreversible by political unification.

- October 1990: European Council meeting in Rome agrees to start the second stage of EMU in January 1994.

- October 1991: The twelve countries of the EC and the seven countries of the European Free Trade Association (EFTA) agree to create a European Economic Area (EEA) in which there will be free movement of goods, services, capital and labour, starting January 1993. This will be the world's richest free trade area with a population of 380 million.

- December 1991: At a meeting in Maastricht, in the Netherlands, the heads of state of the EC countries agree to create a single currency by 1997 or 1999 at the latest. Details contained in the Maastricht Treaty. Britain obtains an "opt out" from the proposed single currency.

- May 1992: Ireland votes "yes" in a referendum to adopt the Maastricht Treaty

- June 1992: Denmark rejects the Maastricht Treaty by a narrow margin.

- August 1992: France passes the Maastricht Treaty by a narrow margin.

- January 1994: The second phase of the EMU commences with the establishment of the European Monetary Institute (EMI). June 1994: Norway, Sweden, Finland and Austria sign treaties of accession to the EU on 1 January 1995. Austria (July 1994), Finland (October 1994) and Sweden (November 1994) vote "yes" in referendums on accession. Norway (November 1994) votes "no".

- 1996: Irish government commissions the Economic and Social Research Institute to prepare a report on the merits of participation in EMU. The Report concludes that, on balance, Ireland would gain by joining.

- 1996: Swedish government appoints an independent commission of economists to examine the merits of joining the EMU. The Commission favours a "wait and see" policy. In 1997 the Swedish government endorses this view, partly because of the growing unpopularity of the EU in Sweden.

- 1996 (December): At the Dublin Summit the Growth and Stability Pact was drafted. This constrains fiscal policy in countries that join EMU.

- 1997: The new British Labour Government unveils its policy on EMU. Unlike its Conservative predecessor it is not *in principle* opposed to the project but it does not believe that the British economy is sufficiently convergent with the continental economies to warrant joining in the first wave. In particular, attention was drawn to the fact that the British business cycle is not synchronised with the rest of the EU. It is stated that it is unlikely that the UK will join in the lifetime of the present government.

- 1997: Despite the declaration that sterling will remain outside the EMU, the new Irish government reaffirms the intention of joining EMU in the first wave.

- 1998 (May): At a meeting of Heads of Governments in Brussels eleven EU countries – Austria, Belgium, France, Finland, Germany, Ireland, Italy, Luxembourg, the Netherlands, Spain and Portugal – were deemed eligible to join the EMU. The exchange rates at which their national currencies will be converted to the euro were announced and the deadline for a January 1999 launch of Stage III was reaffirmed.

Appendix 3

The Maastricht convergence criteria and their application

The Maastricht convergence criteria stipulated that to be eligible to participate in EMU:

- A country's rate of inflation should be within 1.5 per cent of the average of the three lowest inflation rates in the Community.

- Its long-term interest rate should be within 2 per cent of the average interest rate of the three lowest inflation countries in the Community.

- Its fiscal budget deficit should not exceed 3 per cent of GDP. However, if its deficit is above this limit, it could still be deemed to meet this criterion provided the deficit is falling rapidly or if there are exceptional or temporary reasons for the excess deficit.

- The country's public debt/GDP ratio should be no more than 60 per cent or falling rapidly to that level.

- The currency should have been within the normal margins of fluctuation of the ERM and not devalued unilaterally for at least two years.

    In addition the following general conditions were to be met:

- The country's central bank should be independent of all political influences and there must be no monetary financing of fiscal deficits such as government borrowing from the central bank.

- A high degree of genuine economic and financial convergence should be attained between the countries before EMU is started.

    The economic situation in Europe changed dramatically after the Maastricht Treaty was adopted. The prolonged recession that emanated from Germany led to high unemployment and little tax buoyancy. Fiscal deficits widened in the main European countries and even Germany and France no longer looked likely to meet the Maastricht criteria. On the other hand, countries like Italy, Spain and Portugal made impressive progress towards lowering inflation and correcting their fiscal imbalances.

    As the deadline for making the examination on which countries were eligible for entry to EMU approached countries indulged in a certain amount of financial window dressing. Privatisation plans were speeded up and the proceeds used to lower the budget deficit. In France, a £5 billion France Telecom pensions rebate to the government was used to improve the budget figures. Many countries postponed

Table 17.4

EMU qualification

EU member	Deficit (Surplus)/GDP	Debt/GDP ratio	Inflation	
Target	3%	60%	2.7%	
Austria	2.5	66.1	1.1	✓
Belgium	2.1	122.2	1.4	✓
Denmark	(0.7)	65.1	1.9	●
Finland	0.9	55.8	1.3	✓
France	3.0	58.0	1.3	✓
Germany	2.7	61.3	1.4	✓
Greece	4.0	108.7	5.4	✗
Ireland	(0.9)	66.3	1.2	✓
Italy	2.7	121.6	1.8	✓
Luxembourg	(1.7)	6.7	1.4	✓
Netherlands	1.4	72.1	1.8	✓
Portugal	2.5	62.0	1.8	✓
Spain	2.6	68.8	1.9	✓
Sweden	0.8	76.6	1.9	●
UK	1.9	53.4	1.9	●

Does not qualify ✗   Opt-out ●   Member ✓

expenditure to 1998 and accelerated receipts in 1997. Italy imposed a once-off EMU tax in 1997, which has been repealed in 1998. Even the German government indulged in creative accounting, postponing tax refunds until 1998, and at one stage proposing the use of the Bundesbank's gold reserves to reduce the fiscal deficit.

The decision on eligibility to participate in the EMU was taken over the 1998 May Day weekend at a summit held in Brussels. It was based on data for the fiscal outcomes for 1997. The outcome for each member state published by the European Commission in March 1998 are shown in Table 17.4. It may be seen that (partly because of the creative accounting procedures just discussed) almost all countries met, or came close to meeting, the deficit/GDP criterion. Only Greece was clearly outside the limit. There was much less success in meeting the debt/GDP criterion, however, with countries like Belgium and Italy far outside the limit. There was no likelihood that EMU would have been launched without Belgium, so little attention was paid to the failure of several countries to meet this criterion. Even more worrying, from the perspective of the prospects for EMU enduring, is the fact that the fiscal deficit will probably rise in many of the countries deemed eligible in May 1998, and the debt/GDP ratio is continuing to increase in most of them. With regard to inflation, all member states were inside the target.

We have seen that when the Maastricht criteria were originally framed they were designed to reassure Germany that the EMU club would be an exclusive one, with inflation-prone countries like Italy excluded. Developments after 1992 altered the situation radically. Considerable progress has been made by many of the high deficit countries – combined with backsliding by German and other low-deficit countries – so that it proved politically impossible to exclude the "Club Med" countries from EMU.

However, in order to reassure the Germans that there would be no further backsliding once EMU has been launched a *Growth and Stability Pact* was agreed at the summit in Dublin in December 1996. This stipulates that the general government deficit (GGD) must be less than 3 per cent of GDP. If it rises above this level a fine of between 0.2 and 0.5 per cent of GDP may be imposed. If, for example, Ireland breached the restriction a fine of between £100 to £125 million would have to be paid. There are, however, exceptional circumstances such as if an economy goes into recession where a country will not be required to pay the fine.[9] We discuss how this will affect fiscal policy in Chapter 23.

---

9. For a detailed discussion of the stability pact and its implications for Ireland, see J. Peter Neary, "The EU Stability Pact and the Case for European Monetary Union", Centre for Economic Research, University College, Dublin, Working Paper, WP 97/28, November 1997.

Chapter 18

Inflation and Interest Rates in Open Economies

18.1 Introduction

In this chapter we discuss the factors that influence inflation and interest rates in open economies.   We develop two concepts that were mentioned in earlier chapters – purchasing power parity (PPP) and uncovered interest rate parity (UPT).   We apply these in a discussion of the factors that determine inflation and interest rates in open economies.

18.2 Purchasing Power Parity

The theory of purchasing power parity (PPP) states that the prices of similar goods, expressed in a common currency, should be the same in all countries.[1] The strong version of PPP, also referred to as *absolute PPP*, can be stated in an Irish context as:

$$P_{irl} \times e = P_f \qquad (1)$$

where P_{irl} and P_f are the Irish and "world" or foreign price levels, respectively, and e is the nominal exchange rate (expressed as the foreign currency price of a unit of Irish pounds).   This states that Irish prices will equal "world" prices when converted using the current exchange rate.

Note:

It may transpire that equation (1) does not hold. In this case, we can define the PPP exchange rate, e^{PPP} , as $e^{PPP} = P_f / P_{irl}$. This is the exchange rate that ensures that PPP holds. The PPP exchange rate is simply the ratio of domestic to world prices.

---

1. See Gustav Cassel, "Abnormal Deviations in International Exchanges", *Economic Journal*, 28 December 1918. J. M. Keynes, *A Tract on Monetary Reform*, Macmillan and St Martin's Press, 1971, Chapter 3, suggests that purchasing power parity theory can be traced to the writings of David Ricardo in the nineteenth century.

If we define the UK as the rest of the world we have:

$$P_{irl} \times e = P_{uk} \qquad (2)$$

PPP holds if prices in the two countries (converted at the exchange rate) are equal. Under the old sterling link, for example, e was equal to 1, and so $P_{irl} = P_{uk}$. In this situation it was easy to compare prices in the two countries. Similarly, with the introduction of the new European currency, the euro, price comparisons in different European countries will become much more transparent.

The reason why Irish and foreign price levels expressed in a common currency should be equal is based on the *law of one price*. This is the tendency for the same price to prevail for a good everywhere in the world. This tendency depends on *arbitrage*, which occurs when people spot an opportunity of making a profit by buying cheap in one market and selling dear in another. If, for example, shirts were $30 each in New York and £30 in Dublin, and the exchange rate were £1 = $1.5, traders could make a profit by buying in New York and selling in Dublin. The increased demand would drive up the price in New York and the increased supply would drive the Dublin price down. Arbitrage would thus ensure that the prices in the two cities would converge.

An illustration of how the prices of internationally traded goods tend to equalise is provided by the Irish experience in the 1980s. Due to movements in the exchange rate and higher rates of indirect taxation in the Republic, a whole range of goods, including petrol, drink and electrical appliances, became cheaper (in Irish pounds) in Northern Ireland than south of the border. Excursions were organised throughout the Republic for shoppers to go to Newry and Belfast in search of bargains. Similarly, people living in border areas bought all their petrol and drink in the North. Garages and supermarkets in the Republic, unable to cut their prices because of high taxes, went out of business and those in the North expanded. The Irish Minister for Finance was forced to reduce indirect taxes on selected items in the Republic.

This was an example of arbitrage forcing prices to converge. It simply was not possible for major price discrepancies to persist north and south of the border. However, many factors can impede the operation of the law of one price.

- Transportation costs. It takes time and money to shop across national borders or to transport goods.
- Trade restrictions. Tariffs and quotas drive a wedge between prices in different countries.

- Firms do not immediately adjust prices as exchange rates fluctuate.

- Product differentiation and brand loyalty. Also customers worry about after-sales service on items bought abroad.

- Firms can exploit monopoly positions by charging different prices in different markets. Why do brand-name jeans cost more in pounds in Dublin than they cost in dollars in New York?

- PPP is only expected to operate for *traded goods*. An increasing proportion of consumer expenditure is on *non-traded services* – everything from housing rents to haircuts to health care. It is quite possible for inflation in non-traded items to differ between countries and even between regions of a country. Inflation in house prices in 1998 was much higher in Dublin than in other parts of Ireland, for example. Rents are correspondingly higher.

Given the obstacles to the operation of the strong version of PPP it is hardly surprising that PPP may not hold in the short term. Note that one way of observing if PPP holds is to examine the real exchange rate. In Chapter 15 we defined the real exchange rate as:

$$\varepsilon = (e \times P_{irl})/P_f \tag{3}$$

Expressing equation (3) as an index with the base year set equal to 100, PPP holds if the right-hand side of this equation is always equal to 100. In other words, PPP holds if the real exchange rate is a constant, which can be arbitrarily set equal to 100.

The way in which PPP is expected to operate is illustrated in Figure 18.1. The Irish price level and exchange rate are measured on the vertical and horizontal axis respectively. A PPP line is drawn for a constant foreign (UK) price level. At all points on the PPP line the real exchange rate is constant. To see this consider the movement from A to B. The increase in the Irish price level from P_1 to P_2 is exactly matched by a depreciation of the exchange rate from E_1 to E_2. As P_{uk} is constant, the real exchange rate is unchanged between A and B.

The real exchange rate is *overvalued* at all points above the PPP line. For example, at the point C the Irish price level is higher than that consistent with PPP and the real exchange rate is overvalued. Conversely, the exchange rate is *undervalued* at all points below the PPP line. At the point D, P_{irl} is lower than the level consistent with PPP.

The foreign price level determines the *location* or position of the PPP line. An

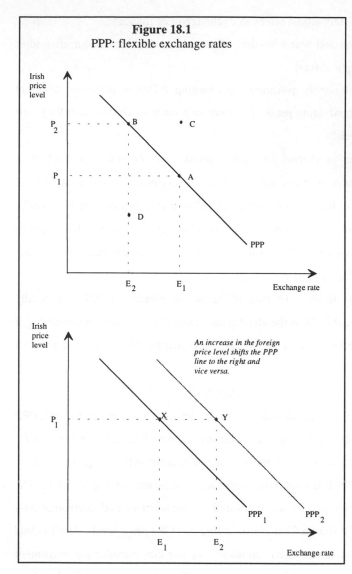

Figure 18.1
PPP: flexible exchange rates

An increase in the foreign price level shifts the PPP line to the right and vice versa.

increase in P_{uk} shifts the PPP line out to the right. Conversely, a decrease in P_{uk} shifts the PPP line to the left. For example, in the lower diagram in Figure 18.1, an increase in P_{uk} shifts the PPP line to the right and the economy moves from X to Y. The nominal exchange rate appreciates from E_1 to E_2 along the horizontal axis and this offsets the rise in P_{uk} so that the real exchange rate is unchanged. We shall use this diagram below to illustrate the policy implications of PPP theory.

Relative PPP

Believers in PPP are not too worried by the existence of price differentials between the prices of similar goods in two countries (expressed in a common currency) provided there is no tendency for the *divergence* to increase over time. For this reason, a weaker version of PPP, which expresses equation (1) in terms of rates of change, is more relevant to testing if PPP holds:

$$\pi_{irl} + \Delta e = \pi_f \qquad (4)$$

where π_{irl} and π_f are the rates of inflation in the domestic economy and the rest of the world respectively. Δe is the percentage change in the nominal exchange rate. Equation (4) allows for the possibility that prices in different countries may not be the same in any particular period. However, given the initial difference, the change in relative prices should be similar and therefore the prices should not diverge any further over time.

18.3 PPP Under Flexible Exchange Rates

Rearranging equation (4) above we can write:

$$\Delta e = \pi_f - \pi_{irl} \tag{5}$$

Equation (5) states that changes in the nominal exchange rate will be offset by differentials in inflation rates between countries. If, for example, the rate of inflation in Ireland exceeds the British rate, the Irish pound should depreciate.

$$\pi_f < \pi_{irl} \quad \Rightarrow \downarrow \Delta e$$

Conversely, if Irish inflation is less than British inflation, the Irish pound should appreciate:

$$\pi_f > \pi_{irl} \Rightarrow \uparrow \Delta e$$

In terms of Figure 18.1 above, the upper diagram illustrates the case where a rise in prices in Ireland leads to exchange rate depreciation. Conversely, the lower diagram illustrates the case where a rise in the UK price level leads to an appreciation of the exchange rate.

Hence, PPP theory implies that price or inflation differentials are the most important determinant of exchange rates. Countries with low inflation, such as Germany, will generally have strong, appreciating currencies. Conversely, countries with high inflation rates will have weak or depreciating currencies.

History shows that the loose version of PPP is a good general guide to the behaviour of exchange rates. When exchange rates are free to adjust, it is invariably true that high inflation currencies tend to depreciate sharply relative to low inflation currencies. For example in 1921 the dollar/German mark exchange rate was $1 = Reichsmark 270, but by October 1922 the mark had depreciated to $1 = Reichsmark 25,000 million reflecting the hyperinflation in Germany. In the early 1990s hyperinflation in Russia and many of the former socialist economies, such as Yugoslavia and the Ukraine, rendered their currencies worthless on foreign exchanges. For example, at the beginning of 1992 there were 300 roubles to the dollar; by the end

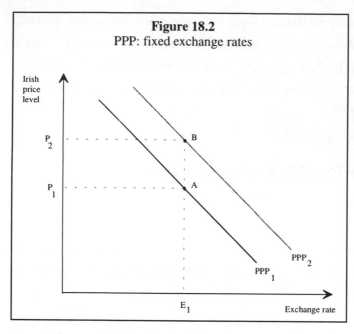

Figure 18.2
PPP: fixed exchange rates

of 1998 there were 6,000. This reflected high inflation in Russia relative to the US. The same is true of the Latin American countries that have experienced hyperinflation: their currencies have become worthless on the foreign exchange markets.

18.4 PPP Under Fixed Exchange Rates

For a small economy with a pegged or fixed exchange rate PPP can become a theory of inflation. Rearrange equation (4) again:

$$\pi_{irl} = \pi_f - \Delta e \tag{6}$$

If the exchange rate is constant ($\Delta e = 0$), then Irish inflation should equal British inflation. Since Irish firms are in general *price-takers* with little or no market power, the *causation* must run from British to Irish inflation. This view of inflation is very important in a small open economy such as Ireland.

If in Figure 18.2 the nominal exchange rate, *e,* is fixed, an increase in P_{uk} shifts the PPP line upwards and the economy moves from A to B. If PPP holds, the Irish price level will rise along the vertical axis until PPP is restored. Conversely, a fall in British inflation would shift the PPP line downwards and this would lead to a fall in Irish prices along the vertical axis.

We discuss, in the final section of this chapter, how this theory can be applied to controlling inflation via an exchange rate peg.

Note, however, that the small open economy version of the PPP equation (6) states that domestic inflation is primarily caused by foreign inflation and changes in the exchange rate. This means that domestic variables (such as changes in firm costs and wages) have no, or very little, effect on domestic inflation. This is an issue which has

412

attracted much attention from Irish economists. A recent review of the evidence concluded that since the mid-1980s "the contribution of domestic inflationary impulses, relative to foreign ones, has been largely subdued".[2]

Following the launch of the final stage of EMU in 1999 there will be no exchange rate between the participating countries. They will share a single currency, the euro. Apart from relatively small local variations, due to different rates of inflation in non-traded goods and services, there should be a single rate of inflation throughout the EMU countries. This is the same as occurs in the US, where a single rate of inflation is quoted for the whole economy, even though there are some regional variations. However, we must bear in mind the factors mentioned earlier that impede the operation of the law of one price. Attention will, in any event, shift from the national economy to Frankfurt, where the European Central Bank will be responsible for monetary policy in EMU and for ensuring that the euro is a low inflation currency.

18.5 PPP and the Real Exchange Rate

We stated above that if absolute PPP holds, the real exchange rate will be *constant*. We now elaborate on this point more fully. To see that PPP is consistent with a constant real exchange rate, consider the following examples:

- Under flexible exchange rates: for PPP to hold an increase in P_{irl} must be fully offset by a fall in *e*. From equation (3) it follows that the real exchange rate will remain unchanged.

- Under fixed exchange rates: for PPP to hold an increase in P_{uk} must lead to a similar increase in P_{irl}. From equation (3) we see again that the real exchange rate will remain constant

Figure 18.3 shows an alternative representation which brings out more clearly the dynamics in the PPP relationship. Equation (1) can be rearranged as follows:

$$e = P_f / P_{irl} \qquad (7)$$

This equation states that PPP holds if the exchange rate is equal to the ratio of foreign to domestic prices. If, for example, all prices in the US were twice those in Ireland, then PPP would predict that a dollar would cost IR£0.50. If this rate does not obtain, then one of the countries will seem relatively expensive, and the other relatively

---

2. G. Kenny and D. McGettigan, "Inflation in Ireland: Theory and Evidence", Central Bank of Ireland, Annual Report, 1996, p. 89.

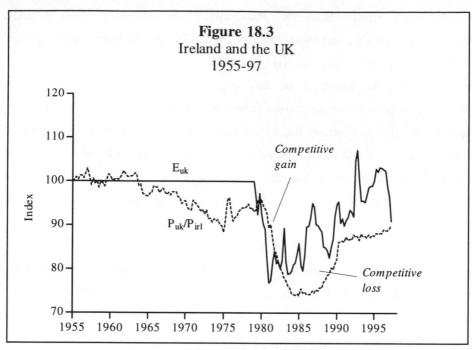

Figure 18.3
Ireland and the UK
1955-97

cheap. Hence deviations from the PPP exchange rate imply gains or losses of competitiveness.

If the nominal exchange rate, e, and changes in the price ratio, P_f/P_{irl}, move together the real exchange rate remains constant. However if,

- P_f/P_{irl} line falls below the e line $\Rightarrow$ *loss* of competitiveness (*e* is higher than what is necessary for equilibrium).

- P_f/P_{irl} line rises above the e line $\Rightarrow$ *gain* in competitiveness (*e* is lower than what is necessary for equilibrium).

We now apply this representation to the Irish experience. (An alternative method of illustrating PPP is given in Chapter 22.)

18.6 PPP: Evidence from the Irish Economy

We turn now to an examination of the evidence based on the Irish experience both before and after we joined the ERM in 1979. Figures 18.3 to 18.5 illustrate the Irish experience relative to the UK, Germany and the US from 1955 to 1997. For each pair of countries we give (i) the ratio of price levels (P_{uk}/P_{irl}) and (ii) the nominal exchange rate, e. If PPP holds, and the real exchange rate is constant, then the two lines should move closely together. If the line describing the price ratio rises above the exchange

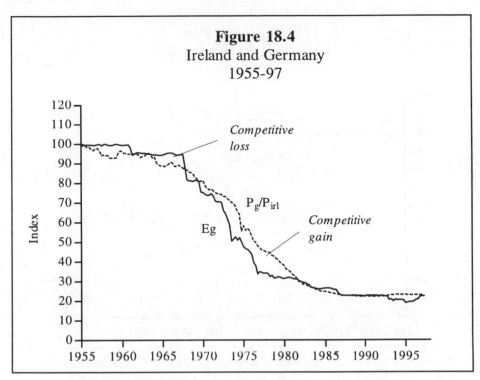

Figure 18.4
Ireland and Germany
1955-97

rate line, there is a real exchange rate depreciation or a competitive gain. Conversely, if the line describing the price ratio falls below the exchange rate line, there is a real exchange rate appreciation or a competitive loss.

We now summarise the experience relative to the three currencies.

Sterling The Stg£/IR£ exchange rate was fixed, on a one-to-one, no margins, basis from 1955 to 1979.[3] This fixed exchange rate was broken in March 1979 when Ireland joined the EMS and the UK declined to participate. Hence in Figure 18.3 the nominal exchange rate is represented as a straight line up to 1979. In relation to the PPP hypothesis, the diagram highlights a number of points.

- Up to 1979, relative prices varied even though the exchange rate was constant. In the 1960s there was a fairly significant loss of competitiveness in Ireland.

- From 1979 to 1984, the Stg£/IR£ exchange rate depreciated sharply and this was quickly followed by a fall in relative prices. In other words, as predicted by the PPP hypothesis, the price ratio fell as P_{irl} rose relative to P_{uk} following a depreciation of the exchange rate.

---

3. The link goes back to 1826 when the Irish currency was abolished. A new Irish currency was introduced in 1927 following the foundation of the Irish Free State in 1922.

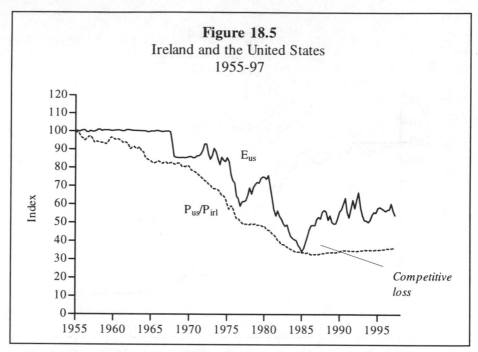

Figure 18.5
Ireland and the United States
1955-97

- Similarly, the exchange rate appreciation from 1984 to 1992 resulted in a rise in the price ratio. Consistent with the PPP hypothesis, *e* appreciation led to a rise in the price ratio as the Irish inflation rate fell below the British.

- By 1997, following the sharp fall in the exchange rate, the two series had converged.

This suggests that PPP is a good guide to the relationship between the Irish pound and sterling over the long run.

The German mark The centre diagram shows the experience relative to Germany. There is a strong correlation between relative prices and the exchange rate which favours the PPP hypothesis.

US Relative to the US (lower diagram), the nominal exchange rate is again very volatile compared to the price series. From 1965 to 1985, the exchange rate and price series tend to move in tandem as PPP would suggest. However, since 1985 this relationship seems to have completely broken down.

Overall, it seems clear that there can be significant deviations from PPP in the short run. However, over a long period of time, the Irish experience relative to the UK and German experience supports the theory.

Evidence from other countries would seem to concur with this view. PPP appears to be a poor guide to the behaviour of exchange rates in the short run. Persistent deviations from PPP have been documented in studies of the major industrial countries. A recent study concluded after a review of the literature that the hypothesis that arbitrage quickly equates goods prices internationally has probably been rejected more decisively by empirical evidence than any other hypothesis in the history of economics.[4]

While these departures from PPP have been important, there has none the less been a tendency over the long run for exchange rates to return to levels that relate to the internal purchasing power of the currencies.

18.7 Speculation

When discussing the balance of payments in Chapter 15, we assumed that the demand and supply of foreign exchange arise because people wish to import and export goods and services or to deal in assets such as stocks and shares across national boundaries. However, the reality of foreign exchange markets today is that they are dominated by speculative flows, that is, individuals and institutions trying to make money by dealing in currencies. This can be done by correctly anticipating movements in exchange rates.

Speculators can shift vast amounts of money from one currency to another in the course of a few minutes. It is estimated that global imports and exports amounted to $5.8 trillion in 1989, but that total foreign exchange transactions amounted to $150 trillion or 26 times the value of trade. Thus foreign exchange transactions amount to about $600 billion per working day, the preponderance of which are not trade related.

A speculator tries to buy a currency cheap and sell it dear. The profit is derived from correctly anticipating an exchange rate movement. A simplified example would be if a speculator believed today's exchange rate of IR£1 = $1.40 is too high. He expects the dollar to appreciate. If he buys IR£1 million worth of dollars at $1.40 he obtains $1.4 million. If the dollar then appreciates to IR£1 = $1.30 he can sell these dollars and obtain IR£1,076,923 – a profit of almost 7.7 per cent. Not all of this will be pure profit, however, because the speculator probably had to borrow the money used in this deal. The net profit depends on the interest rate paid on the loan, the interest rate

---

4. M. Obstfeld and K. Rogoff, "Mirage of Fixed Exchange Rates", *Journal of Economic Perspectives*, Fall 1995, pp 73-96.

earned on the dollars, and the length of time the speculator had to wait for the anticipated devaluation to materialise. Of course, if the devaluation did not materialise he would have made a loss due to the cost of the borrowed funds.

Selling short

Real world speculators frequently *sell a currency short*, that is, they sell the currency on the forward market (for delivery sometime in the future) and hope to be able to complete the contract by buying the currency at a lower price when the time comes. We discuss the forward foreign exchange market in Chapter 19.

Speculative attacks developed on the currencies of the ERM during the crisis of 1992-93. Speculators take the view that the value of a particular currency is too high and begin to sell it short in anticipation of making a profit when it is devalued. This is how the ERM was undermined in 1992-93. Under a floating exchange rate regime there is no scope for this type of attack: as soon as dealers begin to sell the currency, it depreciates. Fixed or pegged exchange rates offer speculators opportunities of gains that are absent under floating.

In September 1992 the Hungarian-born financier George Soros, among others, became convinced that the British Government would not be able to maintain sterling at its level in the EMS. He speculated that the pound would be devalued and is estimated to have made a profit of £1 billion on "Black Monday" when sterling withdrew from the system and fell sharply on the foreign exchanges. There is a sense in which speculators can create a *self-fulfilling prophecy* – by heavy selling of a currency they help force its devaluation. However, it does not always work that way. Mr Soros speculated against the French franc during the currency crisis, but eventually became convinced that concerted action by France and Germany would be sufficient to maintain the parity set in 1987.

Note:
During the East Asian currency crisis of 1997, politicians blamed Mr Soros, amongst others, for undermining confidence in the fixed exchange rates of the currencies.

Speculation may make exchange rates volatile. Following the outbreak of the Gulf War, in January 1991, the US dollar rose on the foreign exchange markets. Dealers, suddenly expert in military matters, read the results of the first day's air strikes as an indication that Saddam Hussein's forces could not put up any real resistance. As the week went on and the battlefield situation became less clear, the dollar lost all its gains. Later in the month, as the military defeat of Iraq became inevitable, the dollar began to appreciate again. Speculators respond almost instantaneously to any news that is likely to affect the long-run value of a currency.

Countries sometimes introduce *exchange controls* to try to prevent speculative inflows or outflows. Since 1992 this is no longer permissible between EU states. Moreover, speculation is very difficult to stop. It can take many forms. *Leading* and *lagging* by companies has been an important type of speculation in Ireland. It works as follows: if an exporter to the UK expects the Irish pound to depreciate relative to sterling in the near future, he will delay (lag) converting his sterling receipts into Irish pounds because they will be worth more after the depreciation has taken place. Similarly, an importer may speed up (lead) payments to his UK supplier in order to avoid paying more after the depreciation. Because of the size of Ireland's trade in relation to GNP, leads and lags in payments and receipts can put tremendous pressure on the exchange rate.

Speculators must base their expectations on the underlying "fundamentals" – they must have reasons for believing a currency is over or undervalued. When they act to correct a misalignment of a currency, that is, to force down a currency that is overvalued or to force up an undervalued currency, speculation is beneficial. If, however, speculation is uninformed it can destabilise a currency, increasing volatility and uncertainty in the market. This is undesirable. Some economists, including the Nobel prize-winning James Tobin, have proposed that taxes be imposed on speculative gains to curb the level of speculation, but most reject the notion of a "Tobin tax" as unworkable, because it would be impossible to distinguish between "speculative" and "non-speculative" deals. It may also be unnecessary because there is no agreement that speculation is harmful to any significant degree. Countries that are really concerned about speculation can always allow their currency to float. This deprives speculators of a target to attack.

18.8 Uncovered Interest Rate Parity (UIP)

The above account of speculation was greatly simplified. For a deeper understanding of the forces at work we need to explore the relationship between the interest rates prevailing in different countries and expectations of how their exchange rates will vary, which requires an understanding of the theory of uncovered interest rate parity (UIP).

Consider the case of an investor who is trying to decide whether to invest in Ireland or the US. A straightforward comparison of interest rates in the two countries would be misleading. The investor has to take into account *expected* changes in the exchange rate. To see why, compare the return from an investment government bond in Ireland to a similar investment in the US. The return from the d*omestic* investment is given by:

$$(1 + i_{irl})$$

For example, if the interest rate, i_{irl}, is 10 per cent then an investment of IR£1,000 will yield a total return of IR£1,100.

$$IR£1,000(1 + 0.1) = IR£1,100$$

There is no need to consider the exchange rate in calculating this return, since the money stays in Ireland. The return from the US investment is more complicated. The steps involved are as follows:

1 January 1999

- Convert Irish pounds into dollars using today's spot exchange rate, e_t.

- Invest the dollars in US and receive a total return of $(1 + i_{us})$.

31 December 1999

- Convert the total dollar return back into Irish pounds using the spot exchange rate $(1/e^e_{t+1})$. The term e^e_{t+1} denotes the *expected* exchange rate twelve months from now. We are dealing with the expected exchange rate as we have no way of knowing the future spot exchange rate. The Irish pound could rise or fall relative to the dollar over the period. The subscript t+1 indicates the spot rate next December. We also use $1/e^e_{t+1}$ because we are converting from dollars into Irish pounds.

The US return, expressed in Irish pounds, is given by:

$$(1 + i_{us})e_t / e^e_{t+1}$$

As an example consider an investment of IR£1,000 in US treasury bills.

- The spot exchange in January is e_t = \$1.599/IR£1. Hence, IR£1,000 will translate into \$1,599.

- If that money is invested in the US at an interest rate of i_{us} = 8.25 per cent, the return will be \$131.90. The total return (principal *plus* interest) will be \$1,730.90.

- Suppose, next December, the actual spot exchange rate turns out to be e_{t+1} = \$1.5734/IR£1. Using this exchange rate, the total return in Irish pounds is IR£1,100.

- Note that the US investment gave a return of £100 or 10 per cent (the same as in Ireland) despite the fact that the interest rate in the US was only 8.25 per cent. The reason for this is that there are two parts to foreign investment:

- The interest rate in the currency.

- Gain or loss on the foreign exchange market. In the example the Irish pound depreciated from \$1.599/IR£1 to \$1.5734/IR£1. Hence the investor made a gain as he was holding dollars.

Arbitrage The basic theorem of UIP is that investors will move money between countries so as to ensure that the total returns from investment in different places are equalised through arbitrage. This involves seeking out the highest returns, which leads to an equalisation of returns the available opportunities. Setting the domestic investment equal to the US investment, we have:

$$(1 + i_{irl}) = (1 + i_{us})e_t / e^e_{t+1}$$

Bring e^e_{t+1} and e_t over to the right-hand side.

$$(e^e_{t+1}/e_t)(1 + i_{irl}) = (1 + i_{us})$$

Now bring $(1 + i_{irl})$ over to the left-hand side.

$$(e^e_{t+1}/e_t) = (1 + i_{us})/(1 + i_{irl})$$

Subtract 1 from both sides and rearrange to obtain:

$$(e^e_{t+1} - e_t)/e_t = (i_{us} - i_{irl})/(1 + i_{irl}) \tag{8}$$

This is the equation underlying *uncovered* interest parity (UIP) theory. This condition is readily interpretable. It says that if the market expected the exchange rate to depreciate in the future, domestic interest rates will exceed foreign rates.

- Expect depreciation $\Rightarrow$ foreign < Irish interest rate.

Conversely, if the exchange rate is expected to appreciate, domestic interest rates will be less than foreign rates.

- Expect appreciation $\Rightarrow$ foreign > domestic interest rate.

Note that it is possible for a US investment to give a higher return even though the US interest rates are lower than Irish rates. This would happen if the dollar appreciated more than the interest rate differential. If investors knew that the exchange rate would move like this, they would rush to invest in New York. But a flow of funds into New York would set the forces of arbitrage in motion. Interest rates would be bid down and/or the dollar bid up. Only the fast movers would benefit because the inflow of money to New York would quickly equalise returns in Europe and New York. Because exchange rates are sensitive to interest rate differentials, a central bank that wishes to strengthen its currency will raise interest rates.

The UIP theorem is very relevant to the phenomenon of speculative attacks. If a speculator expects a currency to depreciate he will only hold it if the interest rate earned is high enough to compensate for the currency's expected loss of value. If a currency comes under speculative attack, the central bank can try to fend off this attack by raising interest rates above those prevailing abroad. While this is unpopular at home, it may persuade speculators to hold the currency and abandon their attack on it. However, we shall see that this strategy failed repeatedly in the history of the EMS.

Covered and uncovered interest parity

We used the word "uncovered" to describe the situation in equation (8) because the investor is exposed to exchange rate risk. He does not know with certainty what the future exchange rate will be. An investor can *hedge* against exchange rate risk by entering into a *forward rate* agreement. The investor is now "covered" in the sense that he is no longer exposed to unexpected movements in the exchange rate. If the forward exchange rate is inserted into equation (8) in place of the expected exchange rate, then we have an alternative version of the theory called *covered interest rate parity* (CIP) theory. Hedging and the forward exchange rate are discussed in Chapter 19.

18.9 The Irish Experience Before 1979

Between 1826 and 1927 Ireland was in a monetary union with the UK, and between 1927 and 1979 the Irish pound was rigidly fixed to sterling on a one-to-one, no margins basis. Exchange rate expectations did not enter into the comparison of Irish and UK

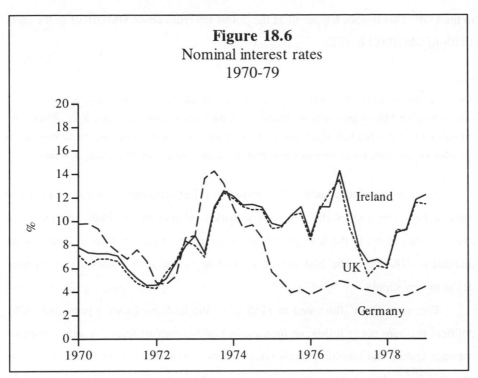

Figure 18.6
Nominal interest rates
1970-79

interest rates during the period 1926 to 1979 because there was no possibility of the exchange rate link being terminated. In fact, as mentioned in Chapter 9, until the *Central Bank Act* of *1971* the government did not possess the legal authority to break the sterling link. The only reasonable assumption was that the sterling exchange rate would remain at parity and there was no possibility of incurring a capital loss or gain by moving money between Ireland and Britain. Some allowance for the greater risk of investing in the small Irish economy might be made, but otherwise there was no reason for Irish and UK interest rates to differ.

Figure 18.6 shows the trend in Irish, UK and German interest rates between 1970 and 1979. (Interest rates are three month inter-bank interest rates.) It is evident that Irish interest rates were more or less the same as UK rates over the period. On the other hand, following the floating of the DM against sterling and the dollar in 1973, a significant gap opened up between Irish and UK interest rates, on the one hand, and German rates, on the other. The average gap between Irish and UK rates over the period was 0.31 per cent compared with 2.14 per cent between Ireland and Germany. In late 1976 the Irish-German gap widened to 9.3 per cent. This differential reflected an expectation that sterling (and the Irish pound) would continue to depreciate relative to the DM. This is what happened as the pound fell from about DM8/IR£1 in the early 1970s to DM4/IR£1 in 1976.

Note:

There is a whole spectrum of interest rates in a country. Different rates are charged to different types of customers and on different types of loans. Short-term, medium-term and long-term rates differ. Irish interest rates always tended to be a little higher than those in London, reflecting the narrowness of the Irish market and allowing some premium for the greater risk, from an outsider's perspective, of investing in Ireland.

From Independence until 1979 Ireland in effect remained in a monetary union with Britain. The size of the UK money market relative to the Irish, and the fixed exchange rate between the Irish pound and sterling meant that Irish interest rates were dictated by UK rates. The Irish authorities had no control over domestic interest rates or the money supply.

This was clearly illustrated in 1955 when the Irish banks were prevailed on by political pressure not to follow an increase in London interest rates. A gap opened up between Dublin and London interest rates. The net external assets of the Irish banking system fell by about 8 per cent of GNP during the year, as capital flowed out of the country in response to the higher returns available abroad. This led to panic among the Irish authorities and forced them to take corrective action, which contributed to the recession that followed.[5]

18.10 Irish Interest Rates Since 1979

Following Ireland's entry into the EMS and the termination of the sterling link in 1979, exchange rate uncertainty became an extremely important consideration for an investor comparing returns in Dublin and London. The difference between Irish and UK interest rates now reflected exchange rate expectations. When the Irish pound was expected to appreciate, Irish interest rates were lower than UK rates. Conversely, when the Irish pound was expected to depreciate, Irish interest rates were higher than UK rates. Figure 18.7 shows Irish, UK and German interest rates for the period 1979 to 1997. On average, Irish interest rates exceeded UK rates by 0.5 per cent and German rates by 4.08 per cent over the period. We can conclude that the market believed that the Irish pound

---

5. For an account of this episode from a monetary perspective, see Patrick Honohan, "How Well Can a Currency Board Work?", Working Paper, The Economic and Social Research Institute, August 1994.

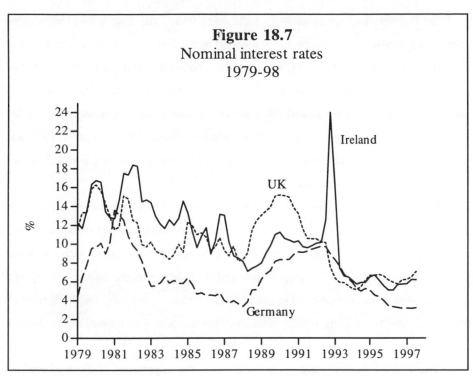

Figure 18.7
Nominal interest rates
1979-98

was likely to depreciate relative to both sterling and the DM for most of this period.

One of the arguments put forward in favour of Ireland's entry into the EMS was that Irish interest rates would quickly converge to the lower German rates. It was argued that given a fixed Irish pound/DM exchange rate, Irish interest rates could not remain above German rates without causing a capital inflow into Ireland. In fact this outcome did not materialise, at least until 1988. Markets were not convinced of the Irish commitment to holding the exchange rate within the EMS: they consistently anticipated devaluation. However, they were too pessimistic on this score. A German investor would have been more than compensated by the high rate of interest in Dublin for the loss on the exchange rate suffered by moving funds from Frankfurt to Dublin over most of the period from 1979 to 1987.

On three occasions – in 1983, 1986 and 1992 – there was a sharp widening of the Irish-German interest rate differential. On each occasion there were speculative outflows of capital which arose from expectations that the Irish pound would be devalued. The market took this view due to a weakening of sterling relative to the DM. Speculators believed that the resultant appreciation of the Irish pound relative to sterling could not be maintained due to the pressure it placed on Irish exports and, ultimately, employment.

On the first two occasions – in 1983 and 1986 – the Irish authorities reacted quickly and obtained a devaluation of the pound in the EMS. Once the appreciation of the Irish pound in terms of sterling was reversed, confidence returned to the market and the Irish-German differential narrowed. In 1992, however, the Irish Government resisted devaluing the Irish pound for a period of four months. Interest rates in the Dublin money market were raised to unprecedented levels – in November 1992 and January 1993 the Central Bank raised the overnight rate to 100 per cent. The one month rate peaked at 44 per cent.

Despite these drastic measures it was clear, when sterling weakened again at the end of January 1993, that the Irish currency was overvalued and that devaluation was inevitable. A 10 per cent devaluation of the Irish pound was agreed with our ERM partners on 30 January. This quickly restored confidence in the Irish currency and money flowed back to Dublin. Domestic interest rates eased and the Irish-German differentials narrowed more rapidly than even the advocates of an earlier devaluation had anticipated.

The 1983, 1986 and 1992 episodes illustrate the importance of the sterling/Irish pound exchange rate as an indicator of the sustainability of the Irish exchange rate within the ERM. When sterling – outside the ERM – weakened against the DM, the Irish pound (pegged to the DM in the ERM) rose against sterling. Markets took the view that the loss of competitiveness would lead sooner or later to a devaluation of the Irish pound in the ERM. Irish interest rates rose to compensate investors for the anticipated capital loss associated with holding Irish pounds.

In May 1998, Ireland joined the single currency zone and from January 1999 the DM/IR£ exchange rate will be irrevocably fixed. When this happens, the Irish interest rates must converge to the German levels. In June 1998, however, the Irish interest rate was 6.82 per cent compared to 3.24 per cent in Germany. Hence, the expectation is that Irish interest rates will fall in late 1998 and this will add further fuel to an already overheating economy.

18.11 Exchange Rate Overshooting

One of the implications of UIP is that interest rates in an open economy can only deviate from world interest rates for as long as the exchange rate is above or below its

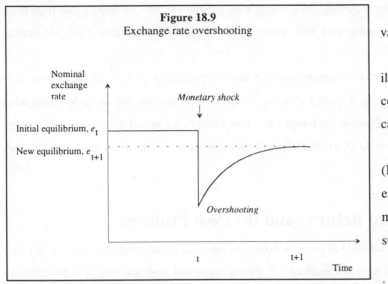

Figure 18.9
Exchange rate overshooting

Nominal exchange rate

Monetary shock

Initial equilibrium, e_t

New equilibrium, e_{t+1}

Overshooting

t   t+1

Time

equilibrium value.[6]

To illustrate this, consider the case of a country (Ireland) that experiences a monetary shock, such as an unexpected increase in the money supply. Before the shock, exchange rates were in equilibrium and interest rates were equal to world (US) interest rates. From equation (8) above we have:

$$(e^e_{t+1} - e_t)/e_t = 0 \implies i_{us} = i_{irl}$$

In the aftermath of the shock the stock of money in circulation is higher than the amount the pubic wishes to hold. For the money market to clear there must be a fall in interest rates, that is, interest rates must fall below the world level. But this can only happen if the spot exchange rate falls below its long-run equilibrium value. Put another way, the exchange rate is expected to appreciate at a later stage:

$$(e^e_{t+1} - e_t)/e_t > 0 \implies i_{us} > i_{irl}$$

The monetary expansion caused Ireland's exchange rate to *overshoot,* that is, to fall below its new long-run equilibrium value. It will eventually return to its long-run equilibrium because the Irish price level will rise (reflecting the effects of the monetary expansion) and real cash balances are reduced to equate supply and demand for money. The domestic interest rates rise to world interest rates.

Figure 18.9 shows how the exchange rate adjusts to a nominal shock, such as a monetary expansion. In the immediate aftermath of the monetary expansion the exchange rate falls below its new long-run equilibrium. This allows interest rates in Ireland to be lower than "world" interest rates because there is the expectation of an

6. The concept of overshooting was developed by Rudiger Dornbusch, "Expectations and Exchange Rate Dynamics", *Journal of Political Economy*, 84, 1976, pp 1161-76.

exchange rate appreciation. In the long run, at time t+1, the exchange rate rises to its new equilibrium value and Irish interest rates are once again equal to world interest rates.

The concept of overshooting is a useful application of UIP to show how open economies adjust to monetary shocks. It relies on the notion that the price level takes longer to adjust than the exchange rate. This reflects the speed with which the foreign exchange markets react to "news", such as evidence of laxity in a country's monetary policy.

18.12 Excess Returns and the Peso Problem

The UIP theory outlined above was based on the notion that arbitrage tends to equalise expected returns between markets. If this is combined with the idea that expectations are on average correct, then there should be no *excess returns* to be earned from investing in one financial centre rather than another. The movement of the exchange rate should, on average, cancel out higher or lower interest rates.

In reality, this has not been found to hold *ex post.* Many countries have had much higher interest rates than were warranted after the fact by the weakness of their currency. For example, after Ireland joined the ERM in 1979, Irish interest rates were not just higher than German rates, but also higher than were needed simply to compensate for the subsequent weakness of the Irish pound relative to the German mark. That is:

$$(e^e_{t+1} - e_t)/e_t \neq (i_{us} - i_{irl})$$

When this inequality, rather than the equality contained in equation (8), holds, *excess returns* are said to obtain. A German investor willing to take the risk would have done better by putting her money on deposit in Dublin rather than hold it on deposit in Frankfurt. (This extra return was quite significant over the period 1979-92.) Similar excess returns have been noted for many other currencies, including several in Latin America in recent years.

What is the explanation for this apparent breakdown of economic theory? One explanation that is given is called the *peso problem.* This refers to the risk – associated with Mexico and other Latin American countries – of a radical change in polices (due to a revolution, perhaps) which results in a major fall in the value of the currency. In the 1980s there was some risk that Ireland's economic crisis would become so bad that

428

it would have defaulted on its foreign debt or dropped out of the ERM. Although such events were not observed, the risk that they could occur was present and taken into account by investors. A *risk premium* was, in effect, attached to the currency. We return to this point, which is relevant to Ireland's expected gains from adopting a common currency in EMU, in Chapter 19.

18.13 Putting It All Together

In this section we summarise the factors that influence inflation in open economies. In the course of our discussion of inflation and exchange rates we developed the following key theories:

$M^s \times V \equiv P \times GNP$	*The Quantity Theory of Money*
$\Delta e_t = \pi_f - \pi_{irl}$	*Purchasing Power Parity*
$i_n = i_r + \pi^e$	*The Fisher Equation*
$(e^e_{t+1} - e_t)/e_t = (i_{us} - i_{irl})/(1 + i_{irl})$	*Uncovered Interest Parity*

PPP and UIP were discussed earlier in this chapter. The quantity theory of money and the Fisher equation were explained in Chapter 10. We can apply these to understanding inflation in different types of economies.

There is a good deal of evidence to show that independent central banks have a better inflation record than those central banks subservient to national governments. If a country's central bank is independent, in the sense of being free from political control and committed to an anti-inflationary policy, it will pursue policies that achieve a low rate of inflation. If it relies on a monetarist approach, its main instrument will be to control the rate of growth in the money supply (M^s). Using the quantity theory of money approach, and assuming that velocity (V) is constant and real income is growing at, for example, 3 per cent, it follows that a steady increase of 3 per cent in the money supply will result in price stability.[7] Alternatively, the central bank may pursue an *inflation target*, and respond to any signs of increasing inflation by raising interest rates. Either way it will achieve a low inflation target.[8]

If a country's rate of inflation is low compared to other countries then this will have two important effects.

---

7. It is also necessary to assume that the income elasticity of demand for money is unity.

8. For a review of the evidence on this issue, see Manfred Gärtner, *A Primer in European Macroeconomics,* Prentice Hall, London, 1997, Chapter 10.

- First, via PPP theory, it will result in a stable or appreciating spot exchange rate.

- Secondly, via the Fisher equation, it will result in low nominal interest rates (i_n). We assume here that the real interest rate (i_r) remains constant. Low nominal interest rates will, via UIP theory, lead to the expectation that the exchange rate will appreciate in the future.

The central banks of countries such as Germany and the United States have achieved good anti-inflation reputations, attributable to their independence from political control. In 1990 the Central Bank of New Zealand was made politically independent and charged with minimising the rate of inflation. In 1997 the new Labour government in the UK gave the Bank of England increased independence in setting inflation targets and controlling interest rates. Similar moves have also been made in France and other European countries. The Central Bank of Ireland is rated as reasonably independent in international comparisons. An independent central bank is a precondition for participation in the EMU.

There is a stark contrast between countries with independent central banks and those countries – in the former Soviet Union, in Latin America and many parts of the developing world – where governments run huge budget deficits and expect the central bank to finance them. In these countries large annual increases in the money supply are associated with high rates of inflation, as predicted by the quantity theory. This, in turn, results in weak, depreciating currencies and high nominal interest rates.

An approach to achieving low inflation that has often been adopted in small open economies is to peg the exchange rate to a hard currency. The most frequent choices are the German mark and the US dollar. This amounts to announcing that the change in the exchange rate in the PPP equation will be zero ($\Delta e = 0$). If the PPP theory holds, then the inflation rate in the small economy will in large part be determined by German or US inflation. This low inflation should then translate (via the Fisher equation) into low nominal interest rates. This approach to economic policy is known as *borrowing anti-inflationary credibility* or *reputation* from an independent central bank.

The launch of the EMU in 1999 goes a stage further than the attempt to borrow the reputation of a "hard-nosed" central bank through an exchange rate peg. It entails eleven countries replacing their national currencies with the single European currency, the euro, and handing over control of monetary and exchange rate policy to the new European Central Bank. In addition, they will lose a great deal of freedom for manoeuvre in the area of fiscal policy. We discuss how this experiment will operate in Chapter 23.

18.14 Conclusion

In this chapter we have discussed a number of topics relating to the determination of inflation and interest rates in open economies. The main issues and concepts covered included:

- The theory of purchasing power parity
- The effect of speculative flows on exchange rates
- The link between expected changes in the exchange rate and the difference between foreign and domestic interest rates. The theory underlying this relationship is known as uncovered interest rate parity theory
- The concept of overshooting
- The concept of excess returns and the peso problem
- The link between key relationships, such as the quantity theory of money, PPP and UIP theories.
- Central bank independence and inflation
- An exchange rate peg as an anti-inflation commitment.

Appendix

The determinants of Irish inflation and PPP

A large body of literature has now emerged on the causes of Irish inflation. This Appendix provides a brief review of the issues in the debate and highlights areas where consensus has not as yet emerged.

Box 18.1 lists four different models plus a miscellaneous category which help explain the causes of Irish inflation.[1] The *PPP model* emphasises the importance of foreign inflation (π_f) and the nominal exchange rate (e) in the inflation process. The *mark-up model* stresses the importance of real wages (W), productivity and other input costs. Firms strive to maintain a "normal" profit and any increase in wages and other input costs, over and above changes in productivity, are passed on in the form of higher output prices. *Monetary models* of the inflation process highlight the importance of variables such as credit, interest rates (i) and the money supply (M^s). *Growth models* stress the importance of the business cycle as a determinant of inflation. If, for example, the real growth rate exceeds the potential growth rate, the economy will overheat and this results in demand-pull inflation. The real growth rate, in turn, can be influenced by a large number of variables including the IDA's industrial policy, EU grants and fiscal policy. Unemployment (U) may also be an important explanatory variable within the context of growth models. Finally, there is a miscellaneous category which includes variables such as competition in the retail sector and migration.[2]

In the Irish literature, the PPP and mark-up models have, by far, received the most attention. In contrast, very little work has been done on the monetary and growth models. In a recent study of Irish price inflation, Kenny and McGettigan (1996) found evidence to support both the pure PPP model and the mark-up model. As such they argue that a *hybrid model* best explains the inflation process in Ireland. The findings in this study suggest:

- The main influences on Irish inflation are foreign inflation, the exchange rate and real wages (over and above that warranted by productivity growth).
- Wages and prices track each other closely over time, with strong evidence of causality running in both directions. The competitive position of the economy, as measured by the real exchange rate, also has a direct effect on wages. This means that a simple exogenous cost-push wage model is invalid.
- The significance of domestic "demand" conditions is found to be mixed. There is some support for the role of output, but no role being found for unemployment.
- The link between wage inflation and unemployment also appears to be weak.

---

1. Kenny and McGettigan (1996) outline some of these models in their survey paper. Leddin (1995) also offers a survey of the Irish inflation literature.

2. Irish inflation started to rise in mid-1998. Among the factors contributing to this rise are: (i) a 12 and 20 per cent depreciation of the effective and sterling exchange rates respectively; (ii) an unsustainable real growth rate which averaged 8 per cent per annum over the previous four years; (iii) a 30 per cent increase in private sector credit. Factors operating to constrain inflation include low wage inflation due to *Partnership 2000*, a benign external inflation environment, depressed commodity, including oil, prices and intensive competition in the retail sector. This list illustrates the point that the various determinants of inflation can come from different models and work in opposite directions. For example, within the PPP model, π_f appears to be curtailing domestic inflation, whereas e is increasing it.

The causes of Irish inflation

Domestic inflation	*Influenced by:*		*Model*
π	π_f		
	e		*PPP*
	W		*Mark-up model*
	Credit, i, M^s		*Monetary model*
	$\Delta GNP - \Delta GNP^*$, U		*Growth model*
	Miscellaneous (Retail competition, migration)		

We now relate these findings to the other work in the inflation literature.

Mark-up model A large number of papers find support for the mark-up model. Geary, Henry and Pratschke (1970) use an input-output model, Geary and McCarthy (1976) and Geary (1976a) estimate a small open economy type model, and Hackett and Honohan (1981) specify a mark-up model. All find a significant relationship between wages and consumer price inflation. Browne (1982) estimates a model of export supply and demand and finds that the "variable cost of production" is the most important variable explaining the price of exports. Browne (1983) uses an open economy monetarist model and somewhat reluctantly admits, "Contrary to our expectation wage cost pressure seems to have an enduring effect on domestic inflation" (p. 33). Fountas and Lally (1993) use Granger causality tests to examine an expectations augmented Phillips curve. They conclude that "wages have a very strong predictive power with respect to prices" (p. 5). They also find that prices are marked up over wages adjusted for productivity.

The only dissenting voices appear to be Callan and FitzGerald (1989) who find that "Domestic wage costs play only a minor role in price determination while foreign price influences are dominant" (p. 184). Similarly, the OECD (1997) conducted a comparative analysis using annual data to estimate the relationship between wages and price inflation for 21 countries over the period 1970-95. The Irish equation proved to be badly specified indicating a weak relationship between the real wage demands and price inflation.

As mentioned in relation to the Kenny and McGettigan (1996) paper, a simple exogenous cost-push model of wages may not be appropriate. This is because of the close link between UK and Irish wages. Changes in UK productivity and inflation influence UK wages which, in turn, affect Irish wages and ultimately Irish inflation. Curtis and FitzGerald (1994) estimate that 60 per cent of an increase in UK wages will be passed on in the form of higher Irish wages. Hence there is a rapid, but not an instantaneous, adjustment of Irish wages to UK wages. These authors also find that unionisation and the tax wedge have an important bearing on Irish wages.

A number of authors report a weak relationship between wages and unemployment. In line with the Kenny and McGettigan (1996) result, Geary and Jones (1975), Geary (1976a), Curtis and FitzGerald (1994) and the OECD (1997) all find small and insignificant links between unemployment and wage inflation. This is surprising because a tightening labour market, and falling unemployment, should be associated with higher wage claims.

PPP   The findings in early papers by Geary and McCarthy (1976), Geary (1976a) and Geary (1976b) are generally not supportive of the *short-run* PPP hypothesis. For example, Geary (1976b) finds that it takes over two years before changes in UK inflation are fully transmitted to Irish inflation. However, Bradley (1978) uses an alternative model to "cast doubt on the reality of the long lags found by Geary". He finds that the lags in the transmission of UK to Irish inflation are "of very short duration, usually less than one quarter" (p. 154). This means that a competitive gain resulting from a devaluation of the sterling/Irish pound exchange rate would be fully offset by higher domestic inflation within three months. In a similar vein, Browne (1983a) finds that both Irish importers and exporters are price takers with regard to UK trade.

However, subsequent studies tend to support Geary's earlier findings and reject the short-run PPP hypothesis. Flynn (1986) found that the competitive gain from devaluation still exists after two years. Honohan and Flynn (1986) examined the relationship between foreign prices, import prices, consumer prices and wages, and conclude that the "response times are much longer than those estimated by Bradley" (p. 179). O'Connell and Frain (1989) report that the cumulative effect of a one per cent change in the exchange rate on inflation is only 0.44 per cent, which is significantly less than unity as predicted by PPP. Leddin (1988), using both consumer and manufacturing output prices, found that absolute PPP did not hold in the short run between Ireland and the UK or between Ireland and Germany. Similarly, Callan and FitzGerald (1989) found that PPP does not hold in the short run. Leddin and Hodnett (1995) found that a short-run PPP relationship held between Ireland and the UK over the period 1947 to 1974, but that the relationship broke down thereafter.

With regard to the *long-run* PPP hypothesis, Callan and FitzGerald (1989) found a long-run PPP relationship between Ireland, on the one hand, and a weighted average of both the UK and Germany, on the other, after entry to EMS (1979-87) but not over the longer period 1976-87. They also report that a change took place in the pricing behaviour of Irish firms after 1979, with Germany having a stronger effect on Irish inflation than formerly. However, FitzGerald and Shortall (1998) contradict this result. They found that the inclusion of the German inflation rate adds very little to explaining Irish inflation. Thom (1989) tested for equilibrium between the nominal exchange rate and the foreign/domestic price ratio. His results suggest that long-run PPP does not hold between Ireland and the UK and the US. His results were inconclusive in the case of Germany. However, Wright (1993a) found that the long-run PPP relationship holds if it is augmented by short-term interest rates. Wright (1993b) found that PPP offered a poor description for the UK/Irish data but, in the case of Germany, the degree of error was small so that PPP may after all provide an empirically acceptable approximation.

One way of examining the long-run PPP model is to calculate the response time it takes the economy to adjust back to equilibrium following a disturbance. Kenny and McGettigan (1996) find that deviations from PPP (brought about by shock changes in π, π_f or e) and trend stationary real wages (brought about by shock changes in wages) lead to a 6.8 and 10.8 per cent change respectively in domestic inflation in the first quarter. Hence, the adjustment to disequilibrium is quite protracted and can take up to 20 quarters before equilibrium is re-established. The ESRI report (1996) on Ireland's entry into EMU found that Irish prices react reasonably quickly to changes in the UK price level, with 50 per cent of the adjustment occurring over the first three quarters. The reaction to exchange rate changes is slower, with 50 per cent adjustment taking one year (p. 94). Similarly, FitzGerald and Shortall (1998) estimate that changes in UK prices are passed through fully within two quarters. Exchange rate changes are much slower, with only 65 per cent of the change passed on after six quarters. One reason for this is that firms are uncertain about the future path of the exchange rate and are reluctant to pass on what they perceive to be temporary changes. Overall, the findings do not support short-run PPP but do offer support for long-run PPP (two years or more).

Monetary and growth models   Geary (1981) applied the quantity theory of money to Irish data. A one per cent rise in the money supply was estimated to lead to a 0.75 per cent rise in the domestic price level after one year. The results also support the monetarist view that changes in velocity are relatively unimportant. Howlett and McGettigan (1994) estimated impulse response functions and found that the broad money supply explains over 50 per cent of the variance of domestic prices. No support could be found to support the Browne (1983a) result that inflation is mostly imported from abroad through the capital (as opposed to the current) account of the balance of payments.

Very few studies include output gaps or measures of excess demand in their analysis. One exception is O'Connell and Frain (1989). In a model which tests the inflation, exchange rate nexus, they find that variables representing excess domestic demand and taxation have an important bearing on domestic inflation.

In general, variables representing credit, interest rates and output gaps are virtually ignored by most studies in the Irish literature. This is a matter of concern because it raises the question of whether the various models are correctly specified. If key variables are omitted from the analysis, this can have an important bearing on the findings.

In conclusion, it would appear that a hybrid model, containing elements of PPP, wage, monetary and growth theories, best explain the Irish inflation process. PPP appears to hold in the long run but not in the short run. The response times to shocks are protracted and this has important implications for Ireland's membership of EMU. (See the discussion of the "adjustment problem" in Chapter 24.) Wages and other costs of production are important and this highlights the contribution of successive national wage agreements to the record real growth rates achieved in recent years. Now that the exchange rate, interest rate and credit controls are no longer available as policy instruments and fiscal policy is constrained by the stability pact, incomes policy will, in future, play a key role in the policy formulation process.

Note:

The references cited in this Appendix are given in A. Leddin, "The Causes of Irish Inflation: a Survey", forthcoming October 1998.

Chapter 19

Some Aspects of International Financial Markets

19.1 Introduction

In this chapter we explore some technical aspects of international financial markets. It takes up a set of topics that are not necessary for an understanding of the main stream of open economy macroeconomics. Students not interested in an introduction to international finance may, without loss of continuity, skip this chapter.

Ireland is a small and open economy that is deeply integrated into the global economy. Buying and selling across international borders between countries that use different currencies involves *exchange rate risk*. This will continue to be a problem for Irish exporters and importers even after 1999, when we have joined the EMU and adopted the common European currency. Trade between Ireland and the UK, the US, Japan and other countries outside the EMU will involve exchange rates. It is also worth noting that even if a firm's sales are entirely in Irish pounds, it may still be exposed to exchange rate risk if it imports some of its inputs from another country.

To see how significant this risk can be, it is relevant to consider the case of a firm exporting to the United Kingdom. As long as the UK remains outside the EMU, the pound sterling will fluctuate in terms of the euro, and hence its Irish pound value will also fluctuate. Consider, for example, an exporter who expects to receive STG£1 million in one month's time and anticipates that the exchange rate will be STG£0.84/IR£1. At this exchange rate, Irish pound receipts will be IR£1,190,476 = (Stg£1,000,000/0.84). Suppose, however, that the Irish pound unexpectedly appreciates to STG£0.86. The exporter's receipts will translate into only IR£1,162,791. This is IR£27,685 less than was anticipated and could render the deal unprofitable. Traders naturally wish to minimise this type of risk.

Because of its importance to a country like Ireland, in this chapter we provide a quick survey of some technical aspects of foreign exchange markets. We describe the various techniques that have been developed to *hedge* against exchange rate risk. Much of the discussion relates to the *forward* exchange rate, which is the most important external hedging technique. We examine the topic of forward market efficiency and the unbiased predictor hypothesis (UPH). The concluding sections discuss how *futures contracts* can be used to hedge against interest rate risk.

19.2 Internal Hedging Techniques

In this section we outline some of the more common internal hedging techniques. These techniques are less costly than external hedging techniques, but can achieve the same objective.

Use domestic suppliers   One way of eliminating exchange rate risk is to switch from a foreign to a domestic supplier. This may not, however, be possible because many of the raw materials imported into Ireland have no domestic substitutes. If local suppliers cannot be found, then a supplier operating out of a weak currency country is preferable to a strong currency country supplier. If the foreign currency depreciates, imports will cost less in Irish pounds.

Invoice in Irish pounds   If a company can invoice in Irish pounds, then exchange rate risk is eliminated. In effect, the exchange rate exposure is transferred to the other party in the transaction. Whether or not this is possible will probably depend on the relative strength of the parties to the deal. For example, a large buyer may be able to pressurise a small supplier into accepting the exchange rate risk. On occasions, both parties may agree to trade on the basis of a mutually acceptable hard currency such as the US dollar or, after 1999, the euro.

Match assets (liabilities) against liabilities (assets) in the same currency   Consider the case of an Irish firm with foreign assets, such as a subsidiary company in Britain. All of the assets and liabilities of the company in Britain will have to be translated from sterling to Irish pounds in order to prepare the balance sheet of the parent company in Ireland. If sterling appreciates on the foreign exchange market, then the Irish pound value of the British subsidiary will fall and this will lower the value of the parent company. This type of exchange risk is referred to as *translation exposure*. One way to avoid or minimise it is to match overseas assets with liabilities in the same currency by,

437

for example, borrowing in sterling. Then if the Irish pound appreciates, the value of both assets and liabilities will fall. However, there is some debate as to the importance of translation costs and gains in determining a firm's stock price. Modern security analysis should disclose translation gains and losses in income statements and, as such, should not unduly influence prospective buyers of the firm's stock.

Foreign currency accounts   Another way of reducing exchange rate exposure is to match foreign currency receipts (from the sale of output) against foreign currency payments to suppliers. That way a loss on receipts will be matched by a reduction in payments. This technique will not, however, be possible unless the firm has a reasonable two-way flow in the same foreign currency.

To use this technique a firm will normally operate a *foreign currency account*. This is an account denominated in a currency other than Irish pounds. These accounts allow the trader to match inflows and outflows in the same currency. Another technique relates to a trader who has payments in one foreign currency (dollars) and receipts in another foreign currency (sterling). It is possible to convert from sterling to dollars using the cross exchange rate and thereby reduce conversion charges. Normally, the trader would convert his sterling receipts to Irish pounds and then use the Irish pounds to obtain dollars. However, the greater the number of conversions, the higher the charges and the lower the revenue to the trader.

Borrowing foreign currency   Consider the case of an exporter who expects to receive a certain amount of sterling in one month's time. He could borrow the sterling now and convert it into Irish pounds at the current spot exchange rate. The foreign borrowing is subsequently repaid by the proceeds from the exports. By using this technique the exporter avoids exposure to exchange rate risk for the period he is waiting to be paid.

Leading and lagging of payments or receipts   In Chapter 15 we discussed how importers and exporters can speculate on future exchange rate movements by leading and lagging. Importers and exporters can also minimise exchange rate losses through leading (importers paying before time) and lagging (exporters delaying receipts for as long as possible). If, for example, the Irish pound were expected to be devalued in an EMS realignment, importers would pay their bills as soon as possible and exporters would delay converting their foreign currency receipts into Irish pounds. Given the very high exports/GNP and imports/GNP ratios, a concerted use of this strategy can have a very significant impact on the level of Irish external reserves.

Transfer pricing Transfer pricing is concerned with setting intra-firm prices so as to minimise tax burdens. It is also possible to use transfer pricing to reduce exchange rate exposure. For example, suppose a company has two subsidiaries, one in a strong currency country and the other in a country whose currency is expected to depreciate. If the subsidiary in the weak currency country sells at cost to the other subsidiary, profits are maximised in the hard currency country and minimised in the weak currency country. The company will then gain if currencies move in the expected direction.

In recent years the main banks in Ireland have introduced a market information service to help customers implement hedging techniques. For example, Bank of Ireland introduced *Netlink* in 1995. This offers the customer a daily, weekly and monthly commentary on key economic and political developments and how they could affect exchange rates and interest rates. The same bank also offers *TreasuryLink* which delivers market news and rates to the screen of customers' mobile phones. AIB bank offers a PC package called *FX Tactician* which enables the customer to formulate better hedging strategies.

19.3 External Hedging Techniques: The Forward Market

In this section we describe one of the most widely used external hedging techniques, the use of the *forward exchange rate*.

Forward exchange contracts

A forward exchange contract consists of an agreement between a bank and a customer to:

- buy or sell a specified amount of foreign currency *for delivery some time in the future* at an exchange rate agreed today.
- Payment and delivery are not required until the maturity date.

Consider the example of an Irish firm importing cars from Germany. The cars will arrive in three months' time and the Irish importer will be required to pay, say, DM2,400,000 at that time. If the current *(spot)* exchange rate is DM2.40/IR£1, the importer's bill will be IR£1 million. The importer, however, may be worried that over the next three months the Irish pound could depreciate against the DM and not be prepared to take the exchange rate risk. (If the Irish pound fell to DM2.35/IR£1, the importer's bill would increase by IR£21,277.)

To remove this uncertainty the importer could enter into a contract which provides *forward cover* and removes the exposure to exchange rate risk. For example, he could arrange today to have DM2,400,000 delivered in three months' time at an exchange rate (the three month forward rate) agreed today. (Forward exchange rates are quoted for one, two, three, six and twelve months, and contracts can be arranged for longer periods. The rates are available from the banks and are published in the financial newspapers.) Table 19.1 shows the spot and six month forward exchange rates for the Irish pound against sterling and the dollar in January 1998.

Recall from Chapter 15 that:

- the *bid* rate is the rate at which banks buy Irish pounds (or sell foreign currency)
- the *offer* rate is the rate at which the banks sell Irish pounds (buy foreign currency).

The spot rates given in Table 19.1 indicate that a bank dealer will buy Irish pounds at STG£0.8570 and sell Irish pounds at STG£0.8600. The difference between the bid and offer rates is referred to as the "spread" and it provides the banks' profit from foreign exchange transactions.

The six month forward rates in Table 19.1 are the rates at which sterling and the dollar can be purchased or sold forward. Suppose, for example, an Irish importer wishes to obtain sterling six months from now. The bank will sell sterling forward to the importer (delivery is in six months' time) at an exchange rate of STG£0.8625/IR£1. Similarly, an exporter who is due to receive a certain amount of sterling in six months' time can eliminate exchange rate risk by selling sterling to the bank. The bank will buy sterling at a forward exchange rate of STG£0.8645.

The forward exchange rate is normally at a *premium* or a *discount* relative to the spot exchange rate. Using indirect quotes (i.e. STG£/IR£), which is the convention in Ireland, if the forward exchange rate is *lower* than the spot rate, the Irish pound is said to be at a *discount* relative to the foreign currency. Conversely, if the forward rate is *higher* than the spot rate, the Irish pound is said to be at a *premium* relative to the foreign currency.

Comparing the spot and forward rates in Table 19.1, we see that more sterling could be obtained for Irish pounds delivered in the future than today and hence the Irish pound was at a premium relative to sterling. Fewer dollars could be obtained in the future for Irish pounds and hence the Irish pound was at a discount relative to the dollar. If the spot and forward rates are exactly the same, the forward price is said to be *flat*.

Note:

There are two types of forward contracts. A *fixed* contract is where a specific date is chosen to fulfil the contract. This is used when the exact payment date is known. An *option* contract is where the customer can chose two specified dates to fulfil the contract. This type of contract will be used when the customer is unsure about the actual payment date. It is not an option to take or leave the contract.

How hedging can result in a loss of revenue

It is important to note that while a hedging strategy minimises exchange rate losses, it also removes any possibility of making windfall profits from exchange rate movements.

As an example, suppose an exporter expects to receive STG£1 million in three months' time. He has a choice as to whether to sell sterling forward and avoid exchange rate risk, or sell sterling spot in three months' time and accept the exchange rate risk. Using data for 1980 quarter 4, the alternative outcomes would have been as follows:

- If he had sold STG£1 million three months earlier at a forward exchange rate of $(1/F_t) = (1/.8710)$, his receipts would have been IR£1,148,106.
- If he accepted the exchange rate risk and sold STG£1 million on the spot market at $(1/e_{t+1}) = (1/.8038)$, his IR£ receipts would have been IR£1,244,091.

It is clear from this example that because F_t was not equal to e_{t+1}, the exporter's receipts differed significantly depending on which option he chose. If he had decided to hedge, his receipts would have been £95,985 or one per cent *lower* than if he had accepted the exchange rate risk and sold sterling on the spot market.

In the above example the exporter would have forgone a profit by contracting forward. However, an importer would have gained by entering into a forward contract. The reason is that the importer is buying foreign currency when the exporter is selling. The two cases are mirror images of the same transaction.

This illustrates how hedging can entail forgoing a significant profit. In practice, treasury managers and others concerned with international cash flows do not always attempt to eliminate exchange rate risk because taking risks (or speculating) on foreign exchange movements can be profitable. For this reason, currency management is an integral part of treasury management in any large firm whose business involves extensive foreign exchange dealings.

Forward currency options contract

A variation on the forward currency contract is the *forward currency options contract*. This gives the holder the right, but not the obligation, to buy or sell currency in the future. For this right, the holder will be charged a fee (or a premium) expressed as a percentage of the total amount of money involved. The right to sell a currency is referred to as a *put option* and the right to buy is known as a *call option*. The distinctive feature of option contracts is that while the holder can avoid exchange rate losses (downside risk), she can benefit from any favourable movements in the exchange rate (upside potential), or vice versa. Take, for example, an Irish exporter who expects to receive $1 million in three months' time. To avoid exchange rate risk she enters into an options contract to convert dollars to Irish pounds at an exchange rate of, say, $1.60/IR£1. If the spot dollar exchange rate depreciates (Irish pound appreciates) to $1.70/£1, the exporter should exercise her option contract in order to avoid incurring an exchange rate loss. If, however, the spot dollar exchange rate appreciates (Irish pound depreciates) to, say, $1.50/IR£1, the exporter should allow the options contract to lapse and instead convert the dollar receipts to Irish pounds on the spot market. In this case she will gain from the exchange rate movement.

If the exporter had used a normal forward currency contract, she would have avoided any exchange rate loss but would also have forgone any gains. (A fee or commission is charged on these contracts, otherwise they would be preferable to using the forward market.)

Note:

There are two types of foreign currency option contracts. An *American* option is where the customer can exercise the option on any business day between the granting of the contract and the expiry date. A *European* option is where there is a single expiry date and a single settlement date. The customer must tell the bank if he or she intends exercising the contract on a particular date.

A variation of the forward option contract is a *participating forward contract*.

442

This is where the trader has an options contract for *part* of her exposure and a fixed rate contract for the remainder. This allows the customer to benefit from exchange rate movements using only a part of their exposure. Another variation is known as a *zero-cost cylinder*. This involves buying a currency call option while simultaneously selling a currency put option. The details are rather technical, but the principle is essentially the same. The idea is to reduce exchange rate exposure while still being able to benefit from any windfall gains that might emerge due to currency movements. While the options contract allows for greater flexibility, in general, the simple forward currency contract is the most extensively used method of hedging against exchange rate risk.

19.4 Interest Rate Parity Theory

As explained earlier in Chapter 18, the uncovered version of interest rate parity theory (UIP) relates the difference between domestic and foreign interest rates to the expected change in the exchange rate. In this section we outline the *covered* version of interest rate parity theory (CIP).

Covered interest parity

In Chapter 18 the UIP formula was given as:

$$(e^e_{t+1} - e_t)/e_t = (i_{us} - i_{irl})/(1 + i_{irl}) \qquad (1)$$

This equation says that the expected change in the exchange rate, $(e^e_{t+1} - e_t)$, should equal the difference between foreign and domestic interest rates, $(i_{us} - i_{irl})$. If the market expects the exchange rate to depreciate in the future, domestic interest rates will exceed foreign rates and vice versa.

The covered version of interest rate parity (CIP) is based on the same equation except that the forward exchange rate (F_t) replaces the expected exchange rate variable (e^e_{t+1}). Hence:

$$(F_t - e_t)/e_t = (i_{us} - i_{irl})/(1 + i_{irl}) \qquad (2)$$

CIP states that the forward premium or discount (left-hand side) equals the interest differential (right-hand side). If the Irish pound is at a premium ($F_t > e_t$), the foreign interest rate will exceed the domestic interest rate. Conversely, if the Irish pound is at a discount ($F_t < e_t$), the Irish interest rate will exceed the foreign interest rate.

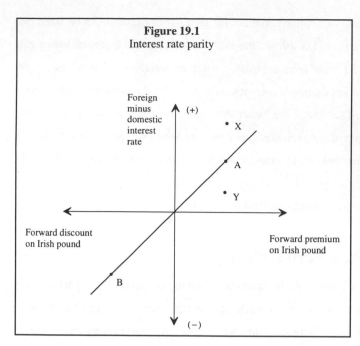

Figure 19.1
Interest rate parity

Foreign minus domestic interest rate

(+)

X

A

Y

Forward discount on Irish pound

Forward premium on Irish pound

B

(−)

Note:

We have used the dollar in the above example to develop the basic IRPT equation, but the theory can be generalised to include any currency and foreign interest rate. Hence in equation (2) the US can be replaced by the more general term "interest rate in the rest of the world".

Figure 19.1 gives a graphical representation of CIP. The interest differential (foreign *minus* domestic) is given on the vertical axis, and the premium (+) or discount (−) on the Irish pound is given on the horizontal axis. The diagonal line represents the parity condition. At points on this line, such as A and B, CIP holds because the forward premium or discount is equal to the interest differential. If the interest differential exceeded the premium, as at point X, it is profitable to borrow in Ireland and invest in the UK. This is true for all points above and to the left of the parity line. It is also true for points in the south-west quadrant of the diagram. At a point such as Y the premium on the Irish pound exceeds the interest differential. If this were the situation, it would be profitable to borrow in the UK and invest in Ireland.

Note:

It is possible that exchange controls might prevent arbitrage restoring the values on the left and right-hand sides of the CIP equation. However, the leading and lagging by exporters and importers, respectively (see Chapter 15), cannot be prevented by exchange controls, and this would have the effect of re-establishing any divergence from interest rate parity.

The available evidence for the Irish economy and elsewhere suggests that CIP holds. In fact, banks tend to set forward exchange rates by looking at interest rate differentials. Hence, it is the interest rate differential which determines the forward exchange rate. The next step is to ask whether the forward exchange rate is a *good predictor* of the future spot rate. This is the unbiased predictor hypothesis to which we now turn.

19.5   The Unbiased Predictor Hypothesis (UPH)

It is natural to ask whether the forward exchange rate is a *good indicator* of the future spot rate, that is, if the forward rate is a good predictor of exchange rate expectations. The forward exchange rate is said to be an unbiased predictor of the future spot rate if, over time, the forward rate is equal to the future spot rate *plus* or *minus* a random error. Mathematically, the *unbiased predictor hypothesis* (UPH) may be written:

$$e_{t+1} = \alpha + \beta\, F_t + u_t \qquad (3)$$

where e_{t+1} is the spot exchange rate in time t+1, F_t is the forward exchange rate in time t and u_t represents the forecast error. This error should be random with a mean of zero and a constant variance. If F_t is an unbiased predictor of e_{t+1}, the coefficients α and β will equal 0 and 1, respectively. F_t will equal e_{t+1} on average. If the UPH holds, today's forward rate is the best indicator of what the spot exchange rate will be in the future.

Why F_t should reflect movements in e_{t+1} Suppose that the six month sterling forward rate (F_t) is currently STG£0.98/IR£1 and that a speculator expects the spot exchange rate in six months' time (e^e_{t+1}) will be STG£0.97/IR£1. If the speculator's expectations prove correct, she could profit from the situation by:

- Contracting to buy, say, STG£1 million forward at STG£0.98/IR£1. The Irish pound cost would be IR£1,020,408.
- Then in six months' time sell the STG£1 million on the spot market at STG£0.97/IR£1 and receive IR£1,030,927.
- Her profit on the transaction would be IR£10,519.

In general, if the speculator expects $e^e_{t+1} < F_t$, she should buy the foreign currency forward today and sell it on the spot market in the future. However, if a sufficient number of speculators believe this to be the case, their actions will have the effect of forcing F_t to converge to e^e_{t+1}. Buying sterling forward (selling Irish pounds forward) drives down F_t and selling sterling on the spot market (buying Irish pounds) drives up e^e_{t+1}.

Conversely, if the speculator expects $e^e_{t+1} > F_t$, she should sell the foreign

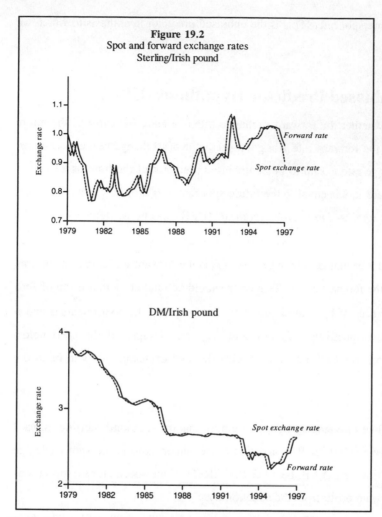

Figure 19.2
Spot and forward exchange rates
Sterling/Irish pound

currency forward and buy it on the spot market in the future. Again the effect will be to force F_t to converge to e^e_{t+1}. Selling sterling forward (buying Irish pounds forward) drives up F_t and buying sterling on the spot market (selling Irish pounds) drives down e_{t+1}. Hence, F_t should reflect what the market believes the future spot exchange rate will be. If this is not the case, the actions of speculators in the pursuit of profits will force a convergence of the forward and the future spot exchange rates as predicted by UPH.

Note:

The profit on such a deal cannot be expressed in percentage terms as no capital is actually invested when the speculator enters into the forward contract. The profit is simply the return from risk-taking. The amount that can be invested in this type of speculation will be limited by the amount of credit the speculator can draw down. There is, therefore, considerable scope for profitable speculation on the foreign exchange markets.

It is important to note that the type of speculation discussed above is not permitted under Irish exchange controls. Up to January 1988 firms could only buy or sell currency forward if the transaction was *trade related*. Those dealing in services had to use some alternative hedging technique or accept the exchange rate risk.

446

However, the exchange controls were relaxed in January 1988 to allow service industries access to forward cover, and in January 1992 to allow capital transactions and debt repayments cover. However, speculative transactions continue to be excluded.

The Irish experience In Figure 19.2 *today's* sterling and DM forward rates (F_t) are compared with the spot rates *three months* from now (e_{t+1}). It is evident that these rates are not identical. In particular it is noticeable that the forward rate consistently *fails to predict turning points* in the future spot exchange rate. As such, the forward rate does not appear to be a particularly good indicator of the future spot rate. However, it may still be the case that UPH holds. UPH does not require F_t to be an "accurate" predictor of e_{t+1}. While the period to period forecast errors could be large, so long as they are random, then UPH may hold and no better guide than F_t can be found for predicting e_{t+1}.

A key question therefore is: can any rule be devised which can out-perform the forward rate as a predictor of the future spot rate? If such a rule could be developed then, in theory, unlimited profits are available from speculating in the forward market. The answer to this question is uncertain. The very limited empirical evidence available for the Irish currency is inconclusive and as such the jury is still out on the validity of UPH.[1]

19.6 Forward Market Efficiency

Related to the UPH are tests for *forward market efficiency*.[2] A market is said to be

---

1. In the Irish context, very little work has been published to date on UPH. Leddin, 1988, "Interest and Price Parity and Foreign Exchange Market Efficiency: The Irish Experience in the European Monetary System", *The Economic and Social Review*, Vol. 19, No. 3, April 1988, found evidence to support UPH. B. Lucy, "Efficiency in the Forward Exchange Market: An Application of Co-Integration", *The Economic and Social Review*, Vol. 20, No. 1, October 1988, using the co-integration technique, presents evidence to the contrary. Lucy's findings are however disputed in A. Leddin, "Efficiency in the Forward Exchange Market: An Application of Co-Integration: A Comment", *The Economic and Social Review*, Vol. 20, No. 3, April 1989.

2. Surveys of forward market efficiency are given in R. A. Hodrick, *The Empirical Evidence on the Efficiency of Forward and Futures Foreign Exchange Markets*, Harwood Academic Publishers, 1987; R. M. Levich, "Empirical Studies of Exchange Rates, Price Behaviour, Rate Determination and Market Efficiency", in R. H. Jones and P. B. Kenen (eds) *Handbook of International Economics*, Vol. II, North Holland, 1985; R. Baille and P. McMahon, *The Foreign Exchange Market: Theory and Evidence*, Cambridge University Press, 1990.

Box 19.1

Expected value

As an example of how expected values are calculated, consider a lottery where half the tickets sold carry no prize money and the other half carry a prize of £10. This means that if someone were to purchase a ticket there is a 50 per cent change of winning £10 and a 50 per cent change of winning nothing. The following table shows the two possible outcomes and their associated probabilities (note that the sum of the probabilities add to one.) The third column shows the product of column 1 and column 2. The sum of the two products is the expected value. In this case the expected value is £5. What this means is that if someone were to buy, say, 100 tickets, they would expect to win on average £5. The first few tickets may or may not carry any winnings, but on average over a hundred or so tickets the purchaser could expect average winnings of £5. The expected value is, in effect, the most likely average outcome from purchasing tickets. Note that no one ticket actually carries a prize of £5. In formulating a forecast of the exchange rate, the task of deciding on the probabilities associated with each possible outcome will, of course, be considerably more complex than in this example.

Outcome	Probability	Outcome × Probability
£0	0.5	0
£10	0.5	£5
Expected value		£5

efficient if prices fully reflect all available information. If this is not the case, unexploited profit opportunities are available and the stock market is said to be inefficient.[3] Efficiency requires that, first, investors are rational in the sense that they process all available information and use it to prepare forecasts of the future exchange rate. If these conditions hold, then the forecast of a currency in time t+1 formulated in time t (which we shall write as $_{t+1}e^e_t$) will equal its mathematically expected value, denoted $EV(e_{t+1})$. The expected value is a weighted average of all possible outcomes, where the weights are determined by the probability of the outcome. (See Box 19.1 for an explanation of the expected value concept.) $EV(e_{t+1})$ is, in effect, the most likely outcome given current available information and will, on average, be correct. This, in turn, means that the forecast errors are randomly distributed about a mean of zero.

$$_{t+1}e^e_t = EV(e_{t+1}) \tag{4}$$

---

3. E. F. Fama, "Efficient Capital markets: A Review of Theory and Empirical Work", *Journal of Finance*, 25, 1970, p. 383-417, distinguishes between three forms of market efficiency. Weak form efficiency is where current prices reflect only the information contained in historical prices. Semi-strong efficiency is where current prices reflect all public information. Strong efficiency is where current prices reflect all information, including insider information.

The second requirement for market efficiency is that exchange rate expectations are reflected in the forward exchange rate. As explained in the previous section, if a speculator believes that the future spot exchange rate of the Irish pound differs from that suggested by the forward rate then speculative profits are available. However, if a sufficient number of speculators share this view, the forward rate will converge to the future spot rate and this will remove the profit opportunity.

In summary, if the forward market is efficient, all available information will be accurately processed by investors in calculating the expected value of the future spot rate. Because of arbitrage, the forward rate will converge towards $_{t+1}e^e_t$, which will embody all the currently available information about the future spot exchange rate. If this happens, the forward market is said to be efficient. Thus *simple market efficiency* may be stated as:

$$F_t = EV(e_{t+1}) \tag{5}$$

Exchange rate expectations prove correct on average and the forward exchange rate equals the expected future spot rate.

UPH and market efficiency If the simple market efficiency hypothesis is correct, then it follows from conditions (4) and (5) that:

$$_{t+1}e^e_t = F_t \tag{6}$$

Subtracting E_{t+1} from both sides:

$$_{t+1}e^e_t - e_{t+1} = F_t - e_{t+1} \tag{7}$$

or

$$v_t = F_t - e_{t+1} \tag{8}$$

where $v_t = {}_{t+1}e^e_t - e_{t+1}$ is the forecast error in time t. Rearranging (8):

$$e_{t+1} = F_t - v_t \tag{9}$$

When coefficients representing the intercept and slope are inserted into (9) we obtain the UPH equation given in (3) above. (v_t is an error term equivalent to μ_t. Because the mean of the error term is zero the sign change is of no consequence.) Hence, the unbiased predictor hypothesis is closely related to the forward market efficiency hypothesis. If UPH holds, then it is likely that the forward market is efficient.[4]

---

4. Associated with the unbiasedness and market efficiency hypothesis is the concept of a *random walk*. A variable is said to follow a random walk if changes from one period to the next are unpredictable or random,

Risk premium

Even if UPH does not hold, the foreign exchange market may none the less be efficient. The explanation could be that the market allows a *risk premium* on forward contracts. In the previous example speculators, in an attempt to make profits, drive F_t towards $_{t+1}e^e_t$. In practice, F_t need not exactly equal $_{t+1}e^e_t$ because at some point speculators may demand a risk premium in order to compensate them for the possibility of being wrong.

Market efficiency now requires that

$$F_t = {}_{t+1}e^e_t + RP_t \qquad (10)$$

where RP_t is the risk premium demanded by investors. (The simple market efficiency hypothesis can be restored by assuming that investors are risk neutral, so that the risk premium does not enter into the analysis.) This is known as the *general efficiency hypothesis* and it requires that the forward rate embody all publicly available information on the future exchange rate (through $_{t+1}e^e_t$) as well as the market's attitude towards risk (given by RP_t). The important point to emerge from this discussion is that the relationship between F_t and e_{t+1} is no longer unambiguously defined. If a researcher estimates equation (1) and finds that F_t is a biased predictor of e_{t+1}, it does not necessarily follow that the forward market is inefficient. It can be argued that the general rather than the simple market efficiency hypothesis holds and that the researcher did not properly account for the risk premium. However, to avoid this rationalisation becoming a tautology, we need to have some measure of risk. If there is such a measure, say Z, the researcher can estimate an equation of the form:

$$e_{t+1} = \alpha + \beta F_t + \chi Z_t + u_t \qquad (11)$$

Unfortunately, current research indicates that the risk premium can change signs over time and this makes it extremely difficult to measure.

Note:

There is a further complication in testing for market efficiency. Investors may not, in fact, be rational in formulating forecasts. In testing for market efficiency the researcher must therefore correctly measure both the manner in which expectations are formed and the risk. If the market efficiency hypothesis is rejected, it

---

which will ensure that it tends to return to its original value. For example, a drunk wandering along the street might follow a random walk. His next step could be to the left, to the right, straight ahead or even backwards. He could end up going round in circles. There is some evidence that the Irish pound exchange rate follows a random walk. The implication is that historical exchange rate data cannot be used to forecast the future exchange rate.

may be because expectations or risk or both were incorrectly modelled. This issue makes it extremely difficult to test the market efficiency hypothesis.

At the present time the evidence in the international literature is very mixed. The consensus would appear to be that UPH does not hold or, at least, there are important deviations from it. The implication is that a rule can be developed to out-perform the forward exchange rate in forecasting the future spot rate and profits could be made from forward market speculation. The results relating to market efficiency are less decisive and, because of the estimation difficulties involved, will probably never be satisfactorily resolved.

19.7 Other External Hedging Techniques: Futures Contracts

Futures markets have been around in one form or another for over 150 years. Initially, participants on the market agreed prices for the future delivery of commodities (oil, metal, wheat and sugar). Over the last 30 years *financial futures* have evolved which are designed to reduce risk relating to movements in exchange rates, interest rates and stock market prices. Hence, the function of a financial futures contract is to enable companies and individuals with positions in money, securities and foreign exchange markets to reduce their exposure to risk.[5] Financial futures trading is conducted on the floor of an organised exchange. The main futures exchanges include (the year indicates the starting date):

- International Money Market (IMM) of Chicago   1972
- Singapore International Monetary Exchange (SIMEX)   1979
- New York Futures Exchange   1979
- London International Financial Futures Exchange (LIFFE) 1982

There are also other exchanges in Sweden, New Zealand, France and Canada and other parts of the world. In terms of trading volume, the IMM is by far the largest and most important exchange. In May 1989 the Irish Futures/Options Exchange (IFOX) commenced trading but was voluntarily closed down in August 1996. IFOX used to trade in three different types of contracts:

---

5. For an introductory textbook on futures markets, see J. Hull, *Introduction to Futures and Options Markets*, Prentice Hall, 1991. For a more advanced treatment, see D. Duffie, *Futures Markets*, Prentice Hall, 1989.

- Future on long-term Irish gilt

- Future on short-term Irish gilt

- Future on three month DIBOR (Dublin inter-bank offer rate).

Each of these contracts has its own specifications. The contracts are for a standardised amount and are delivered on a standardised date in the future. The reason IFOX closed down was due to a lack of demand for the product. Turnover fell from 27,000 contracts in 1990 to an infeasible 7,000 in 1996. The DIBOR contract proved to be the only real success. One of the main reasons for the lack of demand was that the Irish market was too small and this led to a lack of liquidity. If someone wanted to sell a particular contract it was often very hard to find a buyer. As a result investors sought alternative hedging techniques. In particular, investors used the sale and repurchase ("repo") market and the broker Garban Butler to hedge their positions in Irish gilts. In addition only 25 shareholders were allowed to trade on the exchange and this further restricted the size of the market. Other traders and smaller institutions who were not members were directly excluded from participating on the exchange.

In what follows we give an example of how the three month DIBOR contract might be used in practice. This contract can be used to hedge against *interest rate* risk. The operation of this contract is very similar to what happens on the other futures exchanges around the world.

Interest rate risk   As an example of interest rate risk consider the case of a treasury manager who, in July 1998, anticipates a cash surplus of IR£1 million between mid-September and mid-December 1998.   The treasury manager proposes to place this money in a bank deposit. The current interest rate is 10 per cent but the treasury manager expects interest rates to fall to 8 per cent sometime in September. If interest rates do fall, then the interest received on the deposit will be reduced. For example, if the interest rate equals 10 per cent the return on the deposit is:

$$\text{Deposit interest} = \text{IR£1 m} \times 10/100 \times 90/360 = \text{IR£25,000}$$

that is, the deposit interest equals the sum deposited multiplied by the interest rate multiplied by the duration (90 days). If the interest rate falls to 8 per cent:

$$\text{Deposit interest} = \text{IR£1 m.} \times 8/100 \times 90/360 = \text{IR£20,000}$$

Hence a reduction in interest rates from 10 per cent to 8 per cent leads to a loss of IR£5,000 on deposit interest. (If the treasury manager was borrowing money instead of depositing it, the opposite would be the case.) It is possible to hedge against this type

452

of risk by using the three month DIBOR contract.

Interest rate futures contract The specifications of the DIBOR contract are:

Contract size:	IR£100,000
Settlement date:	Third Wednesday of March, June, September, December
Quotation price:	100 *minus* the rate of interest
Tick size	0.01 per cent
Tick value	IR£2.50
Contract	cash settlement.

The DIBOR contract is a standardised size of IR£100,000. The standardised settlement dates are the third Wednesday of March, June, September and December. The quotation price is calculated as 100 *minus* the interest rate (the Dublin inter-bank offer rate). Hence, if the interest rate is 10 per cent, the quotation price is $100 - 10 = 90$. If the interest rate is 8 per cent, the quotation price is $100 - 8 = 92$. This means that if interest rates decrease, the quotation price increases and (as explained below) the buyer of the futures contract gains. If, on the other hand, interest rates increase, the quotation price falls and the buyer incurs a loss.

The *tick size* is the minimum price movement and is set at 0.01 per cent. The tick value is calculated as the value of the contract multiplied by the tick size multiplied by the duration of the contract (3 months or 90 days).

$$\text{Tick value} = IR£100,000 \times 0.0001 \times 90/360 = IR£2.50$$

This means that the price has to move by IR£2.50 before the price movement will be recorded.

Hedging To hedge against falling interest rates the treasury manager enters into a futures contract. The basic idea is to set up in the futures market an equal but opposite position to that in the deposit or cash market. If interest rates fall, the value of the futures contract will increase and the profits on the futures contracts will compensate for the loss of interest on the deposit.

In order to "lock in" to an interest rate of 10 per cent on a deposit of IR£1 million, the treasury manager must purchase ten contracts of IR£100,000. (A borrower in the cash market would sell futures contracts.) Ten contracts at a price of 90.00 would cost IR£225,000.

$$10 \text{ contracts} \times 9,000 \text{ ticks} \times IR£2.50 = IR£225,000$$

453

Suppose that in September the treasury manager's expectations are realised and interest rates fall from 10 per cent to 8 per cent and the contract price rises from 90 to 92. Having bought the 10 contracts for IR£225,000, the treasury manager now sells the 10 futures contracts for IR£230,000.

$$10 \text{ contracts} \times 9200 \text{ ticks} \times IR£2.50 = IR£230,000$$

The profit on the futures contract of IR£5,000 exactly offsets the loss on the deposit interest. In effect, the treasury manager has achieved a "perfect hedge".

The profit (or loss) on the futures contract can also be calculated using the tick values. The difference between the sell price (92) and the purchase price (90) is equivalent to 200 ticks. The profit is equal to the number of ticks multiplied by the tick value multiplied by the number of contracts.

$$\text{Profit on futures contract} = 200 \times IR£2.50 \times 10 = IR£5,000$$

The treasury manager, by "fixing" the interest on a floating rate deposit, also trades away any potential gains. If interest rates increased over the period, the gain made on deposit interest is offset by a loss on the futures contract. It should be borne in mind that it takes two parties to complete a transaction. If someone is purchasing a futures contract, someone else must be selling. This means that the two parties are taking opposing views on how interest rates will move in the future. If the buyer of the futures contract gains, the seller of the contract loses, and vice versa.

Note:

Because of arbitrage between the cash and futures markets, the interest rates on futures contracts are very closely related to the interest rates embodied in the yield curve. (The yield curve shows the term structure of interest rates. See Chapter 22.) Hence, if the yield curve is upward sloping, indicating that interest rates will increase in the future, the interest rate on futures contracts will be greater than current interest rates. This means that futures contracts only offer insurance against unexpected changes in interest rates, that is, changes in interest rates over and above changes reflected in the yield curve.

Variation margin The purchaser of a futures contract is required to deposit, as collateral, with the clearing exchange a sum of money known as the *initial margin*. This money is returned on completion of the contract. Each day the clearing exchange marks all accounts to the current market value and the purchaser is refunded or required to pay a maintenance margin, known as the *variation margin*, in cash each day. The variation margin is equivalent to the difference between yesterday's and today's closing price. This feature of futures contracts is known as *marking-to-market*. As an example

454

Table 19.2

Variation margin

Day	Price	Initial margin IR£	Variation margin IR£
Monday	90	3,000	
Tuesday	89		(2,500)
Wednesday	87		(5,000)
Thursday	92		+ 12,500
Close			+ 5,000

Note: + sign indicates a payment from the futures exchange whereas (–) indicates a payment from the depositor to the futures exchange.

of how the variation margin works, consider the data in Table 19.2.

On Monday the treasury manager buys 10 contracts at a price of 90. Each contract requires an initial margin of IR£300. Hence the manager must deposit IR£3,000 with futures exchange. Suppose the contract price falls on Tuesday to 89, a decrease equivalent to 100 ticks, reflecting an increase in interest rates.

Because the price has fallen the manager must now pay the futures exchange IR£2,500 as a variation margin. This is calculated as:

$$10 \text{ contracts} \times IR£2.50 \times 100 \text{ ticks} = IR£2,500$$

Suppose that on Wednesday the contract price again falls, this time to 87. The treasurer must pay a further variation margin of IR£5,000.

$$10 \text{ contracts} \times IR£2.50 \times 200 \text{ ticks} = IR£5,000$$

Finally, suppose that on Thursday interest rates decrease and the contract price rises to 92. The treasury manager now receives IR£12,500 from the futures exchange.

$$10 \text{ contracts} \times IR£2.50 \times 500 \text{ ticks} = IR£12,500$$

Having incurred a loss of IR£7,500 on the first two days and a profit of IR£12,500 on the third day, the treasury manager has made an overall profit of IR£5,000. She may now close out her position by selling the 10 contracts. As mentioned, the gain on the futures contract offsets losses in the cash market. The main point about the variation margin is that gains and losses are paid for on a daily basis. If the purchaser cannot pay the variation margin, the clearing exchange will close out his position and make good any losses from the initial margin. In this regard, the clearing exchange guarantees the performance of the futures contract.

Forward and futures contracts Foreign currency futures contracts are very similar to forward contracts. The two types of contracts differ, however, in a number of respects.

- Forward contracts are negotiated with a bank at any location. Futures trading is conducted by brokers on the floor of an organised exchange.

- Banks will enter into a forward contract for any amount. Futures contracts are for a standard size contract for delivery at a standard maturity date in the future.

- Forward contract prices are expressed by a bank in the form of bid and offer rates. Some futures prices are determined on the floor of the exchange by an "open outcry" system.

- Futures contracts require the purchaser to put up an initial margin as a good-faith gesture. A variation margin is then required each day as the price of the contract is mark-to-market. Forward contracts require no margin prior to the settlement date. This is one of the most important differences between futures and forward contracts.

- Unlike the futures contract, there is no minimum price movement on forward contracts.

19.8   Conclusion

The main points discussed in this chapter were:

- Exchange rate risk and how it impacts on the operation of exporters and importers

- The various internal hedging techniques that can be used to reduce exposure to exchange rate risk.

- The definition of a forward exchange transaction

- The concept of a premium or discount on forward exchange rates

- The link between the forward discount/premium and the differential between domestic and foreign interest rates. The theory underlying this relationship is known as "covered interest parity theory"

- Covered interest rate arbitrage is the process that ensures that "covered interest parity" holds

- The hypothesis that the forward exchange rate is an unbiased predictor of the future spot exchange rate states that on average the forward exchange rate is a good predictor of the future spot rate and that the prediction error will be random

- The concept of forward market efficiency

- The role of risk premiums

- Financial futures contracts can be used to reduce interest rate and exchange rate risk
- A foreign currency futures contract is similar to a forward contract. One of the main differences is that in a futures contract the purchaser is required to put up an initial margin as collateral.

Chapter 20

The Open Economy Monetary Model

20.1 Introduction

In this chapter we outline a monetary model of the open economy. This is a classical-type model that assumes prices are flexible. We use it to explore the effects of monetary policy, supply-side policies, and changes in foreign prices on output and employment under both fixed and flexible exchange rates. In the concluding sections we illustrate the application of the model by analysing the Irish decision to enter the EMS in 1979.

20.2 The Open Economy Monetary Model

The open economy monetary model is essentially an open economy version of the classical model that was developed in Chapter 12. A key assumption underlying this model is that workers do not suffer from money illusion. They are assumed to use rational expectations to form their inflation expectations. Prices are assumed to be flexible in both directions. As a result of these assumptions the economy quickly reverts to full employment following a disturbance. Output gaps are short lived.

Figure 20.1 provides a graphical representation of this model. The diagram on the far right represents equilibrium in the goods market. The aggregate supply (AS) schedule is vertical at full employment GNP. This reflects the assumption that prices and wages are flexible. If unemployment or over-employment should emerge, the real wage consistent with full employment GNP will be quickly restored. By implication the long-run Phillips schedule is vertical and there is no trade-off between inflation and unemployment.

Superimposed on this vertical AS schedule is a downward-sloping aggregate demand (AD) schedule. Changes in the money supply (monetary policy) and changes in the components of aggregate demand (consumption, investment, public expenditure and net exports) determine the position of the AD schedule. An expansionary monetary policy, for example, would shift the AD schedule out to the right. In the classical

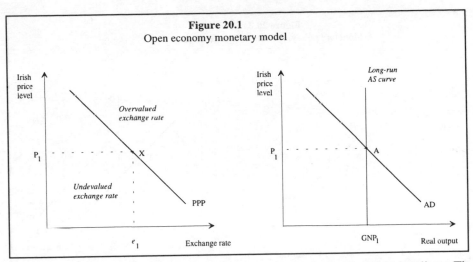

Figure 20.1
Open economy monetary model

model, monetary policy has a much stronger effect on output than fiscal policy. The reason for this is the crowding-out effect, whereby increased public spending results in a rise in interest rates, which depresses private spending and leaves total spending unchanged.

Note:

An expansionary fiscal policy increases nominal GNP in the short run. However, with a constant money supply this raises the demand for money and therefore interest rates. Higher interest rates, in turn, reduce investment. If the fall in investment is equal to the original increase in government expenditure, there is 100 per cent crowding out. This is the extreme classical position. We do not discuss the effects of fiscal policy in detail in this chapter.

The model can be expressed in terms of rates of change, with inflation on the vertical axis, and the change in the exchange rate and the growth rate in real GNP on the horizontal axis. This is perhaps more realistic because, while a reduction in the price level is rarely observed, we have experience of both decreases and increases in the rate of inflation.

The diagram on the left shows a PPP relationship between the Irish pound and sterling. This diagram was developed in Chapter 18. The PPP line shows the combinations of the domestic price level (vertical axis) and the nominal exchange rate (horizontal axis) that maintain international price competitiveness (that is, a constant real exchange rate). PPP holds at all points on the PPP line. The position or location of the PPP line is determined by the foreign price level. An increase in the foreign price level shifts the PPP line upwards. Points above the PPP line indicate an overvalued

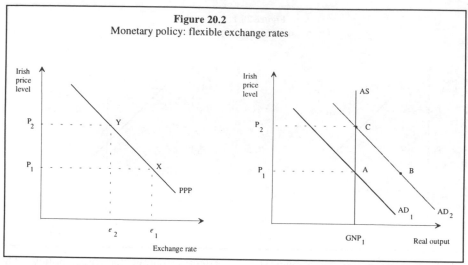

Figure 20.2
Monetary policy: flexible exchange rates

exchange rate and points below it an undervalued exchange rate.

The essence of the monetary model is that inflation is determined in accordance with PPP, while the real economy remains at full employment. We now use this model to explore the effects of an expansionary monetary policy, a supply-side policy and a change in the foreign price level under both floating and fixed exchange rates.

20.3 Applying the Model under Floating Exchange Rates

Monetary policy

An increase in the money supply shifts the AD schedule from AD_1 to AD_2, as shown in the right-hand panel in Figure 20.2. Initially, there is an excess demand for goods measured by the vertical distance AB. This causes the price level to rise until equilibrium is re-established at C. In accordance with the quantity theory of money, the increase in the money supply is matched by a rise in the price level. There is no increase in real output as workers anticipate the change in prices and adjust their demands for higher nominal wages accordingly.

The increase in the price level initially leads to an overvalued exchange rate. This is depicted in the left-hand panel of Figure 20.2. The loss of competitiveness reduces exports and increases imports, creating a current account balance of payments deficit. This causes the exchange rate to depreciate from e_1 to e_2. The economy moves from X to Y along the PPP line. Competitiveness is restored and the real exchange rate reverts to its original level.

460

The expansionary monetary policy results in a higher price level and a lower exchange rate. Conversely, a decrease in the money supply leads to exchange rate appreciation. Real output and unemployment are unaffected.

The impact of an expansionary fiscal policy depends on the strength of the crowding-out effect. An expansionary fiscal policy initially shifts the AD schedule out to the right (not shown). However, as interest rates rise, investment is crowded out and the AD schedule reverts back to its original position. If there is complete crowding out, real output, employment, prices and the exchange rate will all be unaffected. In so far as the price level increases (less than 100 per cent crowding out), it will be matched by an exchange rate depreciation.

In this model therefore neither fiscal nor monetary policy is effective in boosting output and employment. This is why classical economists believe in a non-interventionist policy stance. They do not favour trying to fine-tune the economy through a monetary or fiscal policy. Instead, they recommend that central banks should adopt a monetary rule such as allowing the money supply to increase in line with the long-run growth rate of real output. This would eliminate the possibility of inflation being caused by a monetary expansion. To ensure that prices and wages are more responsive to the forces of supply and demand, and that wage-price flexibility quickly eliminates output gaps, markets (including the labour market) should be deregulated.

Supply-side policies

An increase in full employment GNP could come about through improvements in technology, infrastructure, education, or greater efficiency in the labour market. The effect is to shift the AS schedule to the right. As the AS schedule moves out, an excess supply of goods and services emerges. This is equal to the vertical distance AB in Figure 20.3. This drives the price level down from P_1 to P_2 and equilibrium is re-established at C. The fall in the price level results in an undervalued exchange rate (left-hand panel). As a result of this improvement in competitiveness, a current account surplus emerges, causing the nominal exchange rate to appreciate. The economy moves from X to Y and the original real exchange rate is restored. Eventually equilibrium is reached at C and Y. Hence, a supply-side change that increases real GNP has the effect of reducing prices and causing the exchange rate to appreciate.

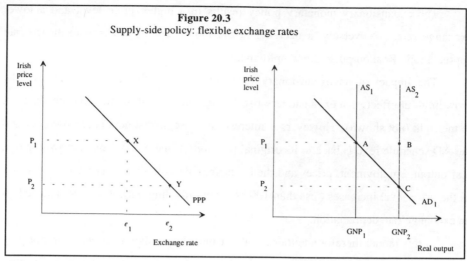

Figure 20.3
Supply-side policy: flexible exchange rates

Note:

This outcome contrasts with that predicted by the Keynesian model where increases in real output are associated (via the marginal propensity to consume) with an increase in imports and a balance of payments deficit. The classical model reaches the opposite conclusion because it emphasises the impact on the demand for money, which is a function of nominal GNP. Nominal GNP is equal to real output multiplied by the price level. The initial rise in nominal output (brought about by the supply-side policy) increases the demand for money and, for a constant money supply, creates an excess demand for money. An excess demand for money, however, implies an excess supply of goods and services, which leads to lower prices until the demand for money reverts to its original level. While nominal GNP is unchanged, its composition has been altered. The real output component has gone up and the price level has gone down.

Conversely, a policy or a shock that moves the AS schedule to the left results in a fall in real output, a rise in the price level and an exchange rate depreciation.

Changes in the foreign price level

An increase in the foreign price level shifts the PPP line out to the right (left panel in Figure 20.4). At the initial price level (P_1) and the nominal exchange rate (e_1) there is a gain in competitiveness for the domestic economy. This results in a balance of payments surplus that in turn causes the exchange rate to appreciate from e_1 to e_2. The economy moves from X to Y and PPP is restored. The domestic price level and real output are unaffected. Conversely, a decrease in the foreign price level will shift the PPP line downwards. If the domestic price level does not change, the exchange rate will depreciate. There is no effect on real output. As long as the exchange rate is flexible, changes in the foreign inflation rate have no effect on real output in the

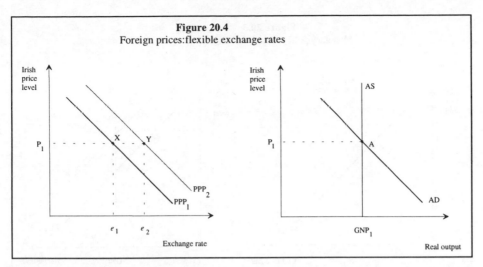

Figure 20.4
Foreign prices:flexible exchange rates

domestic economy.

We may thus conclude that a flexible exchange rate can insulate the domestic economy from changes in world inflation. If a country's exchange rate is completely flexible, the model shows that it can attain any price level (or rate of inflation) depending on the rate of domestic monetary expansion.

20.4 Applying the Model under Fixed Exchange Rates

In this section we discuss the impact of disturbances on the economy when the exchange rate is fixed. The main difference with the previous section is that the central bank now intervenes in the foreign exchange market to stabilise the exchange rate. This takes the form of buying and selling Irish pounds. For example, to prevent an exchange rate depreciation, the Central Bank must buy (create an artificial demand for) Irish pounds. This has the effect of reducing the bank's reserves of foreign exchange. Conversely, to stop exchange rate appreciation the Central Bank must sell Irish pounds. This will increase the reserves of foreign exchange. (See Chapter 16 for a detailed discussion of this mechanism.)

The second point to note is that central bank intervention in the foreign exchange markets affects the domestic money supply. This is because changes in the central bank's external reserves cause changes in high-powered money (H) which in turn affects the overall money supply in the economy (see the Appendix to Chapter 9). In short:

$$\Delta \text{ External reserves } \rightarrow \Delta H \rightarrow \Delta M^s$$

463

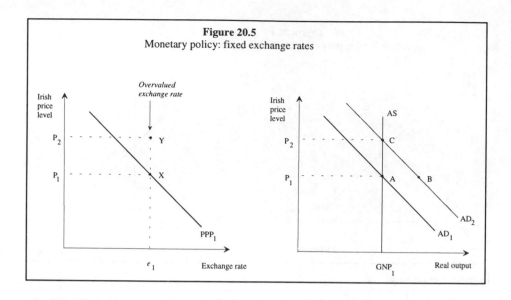

Figure 20.5
Monetary policy: fixed exchange rates

Note:

It is not inevitable that changes in reserves affect the domestic money supply. Central banks can try to break the link between the external reserves and H by reducing the domestic component of the money supply. This is *sterilisation*. There are limits to central banks' ability to sterilise flows across the foreign exchanges.

Monetary policy

We now examine the effectiveness of an expansionary monetary policy when the exchange rate is fixed. An increase in the money supply shifts the AD schedule upwards from AD_1 to AD_2 (right-hand panel of Figure 20.5). Initially there is an excess demand for goods, equal to AB. This leads to an increase in the price level from P_1 to P_2 and a new equilibrium is established at C. As predicted by the Quantity Theory of Money, the increase in the money supply has been matched by an equal increase in the price level.

The exchange rate is fixed at e_1 (left-hand panel). Because of the increase in the price level the economy moves from X on the PPP line to a point such as Y. At Y, the exchange rate is overvalued and the economy experiences a loss of competitiveness.

Consider now how the economy adjusts back towards equilibrium. The overvalued exchange rate makes exports more expensive and imports cheaper. As a result, a current account balance of payments deficit emerges. In the absence of central bank intervention this would lead to a depreciation of the exchange rate. If the Central Bank buys Irish pounds with foreign currency from its reserves, it can stabilise the exchange

464

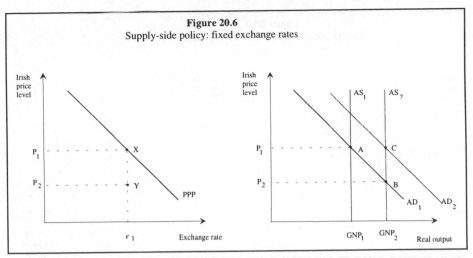

Figure 20.6
Supply-side policy: fixed exchange rates

rate but its reserves of foreign exchange will be depleted. This leads to a contraction in the domestic money supply, shifting the AD schedule downwards. The economy moves back to its original position at A and X. As this happens the price level falls and the overvaluation of the exchange rate is eliminated. The effect of the expansionary monetary policy has been to reduce the Central Bank's holdings of external reserves. All other variables, such as the price level, real output and the real and nominal exchange rates, are unchanged.

The effects of an expansionary fiscal policy depend on the degree of crowding out. A high degree of crowding out will result in only a small and temporary increase in the price level. The ultimate fall in the external reserves will be smaller. On the other hand, a small crowding out effect will be associated with a relatively large fall in the external reserves.

Supply-side policies

Consider now the effect of a supply-side policy which shifts the AS schedule to the right. A shift to the right in the AS schedule moves the economy from A to B (right-hand panel of Figure 20.6). At B real output is higher and the price level has fallen from P_1 to P_2. As the domestic price level falls relative to the foreign price level, the economy moves from X to Y and the real exchange rate becomes undervalued (right-hand panel). The associated gain in competitiveness leads to a current account balance of payments surplus. In the absence of Central Bank intervention the exchange rate would appreciate.

465

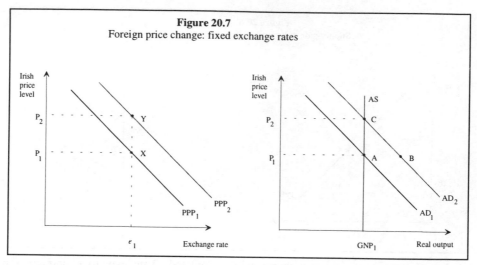

Figure 20.7
Foreign price change: fixed exchange rates

However, in a fixed exchange rate system the Central Bank intervenes – buying foreign currency in exchange for Irish pounds. The external reserves increase, causing a rise in the domestic money supply, which has the effect of shifting the AD schedule out to the right (AD_1 to AD_2) until it intersects the new AS schedule at C. The overall effect of the supply-side policy is to increase real output and employment and increase the Central Bank's external reserves, leaving the price level unchanged.

Note:

Again this conclusion differs radically from that of the standard Keynesian model where increases in output are associated with a current account deficit and a fall in the external reserves.

Changes in the foreign price level

This model may be used to explore the effects of an increase in foreign inflation (or a rise in the foreign price level) that is relevant to understanding the Irish experience in the EMS. An increase in the foreign price level shifts the PPP line upwards from PPP_1 to PPP_2 (Figure 20.7). At X the Irish pound exchange rate is undervalued and Ireland's competitive position has improved. As a result, exports increase, imports fall, and a current account surplus emerges. The Central Bank now intervenes in the foreign exchange market to stop the exchange rate appreciating. It sells Irish pounds in exchange for foreign currencies and this increases the bank's reserves and the money supply. The AD schedule shifts upwards from AD_1 to AD_2 (right-hand panel of Figure 20.7). As the economy moves from A to C the domestic price level increases, which restores PPP at Y. The overall effect of the rise in foreign price level is to increase the

466

Table 20.1

Predictions of the open economy monetary model

Exchange rate regime: floating

Policy	*Effect on:*		
	GNP	*Price level*	*Exchange rate*
Expansionary monetary and fiscal policy	-	↑	↓
Supply-side policy	↑	↓	↑
Increase in foreign price level	-	-	↑

Exchange rate regime: fixed

Policy	*Effect on:*		
	GNP	*Price level*	*External reserves*
Expansionary monetary and fiscal policy	-	-	↓
Supply-side policy	↑	-	↓
Increase in foreign price level	-	↑	↑

external reserves and also the domestic price level. Domestic output and employment remain unchanged.

20.5 Assessment

In Table 20.1 we summarise the conclusions of the two previous sections. According to the monetary model of an open economy, expansionary monetary and fiscal policies do not affect the level of real output. Their only impact is on the rate of inflation and the nominal exchange rate. Supply-side policies, on the other hand, will affect the level of real output and leave all nominal variables unchanged. If the exchange rate is flexible, expansionary monetary and fiscal policies raise the domestic price level and cause the exchange rate to fall. An increase in the foreign price level causes the exchange rate to

467

rise and leaves the domestic price level unaltered. Under fixed exchange rates, on the other hand, expansionary policies result in a fall in the external reserves, which is a limiting factor on the extent to which such policies can be pursued. Under fixed exchange rates, domestic inflation reflects foreign inflation.

It is clear that extending the macroeconomic model developed in Chapter 13 to take account of the factors that are relevant in an open economy complicates life considerably. In addition to specifying whether prices and wages are rigid or flexible, it is necessary to spell out assumptions about the exchange rate (fixed or floating). The number of possible combinations of assumptions grows multiplicatively and radically different conclusions about the effectiveness of monetary and fiscal policy follow from different combinations of assumptions. The student may well wish for a "correct" model and a single answer to burning policy issues, but unlike the physical sciences, economics is not a subject in which hard and fast, well-established results have been derived by testing alternative models against the evidence. This is exasperating, but it reflects the lack of consensus about how economies function.

In the concluding sections to this chapter we explain how interest rates fit into the economic models and we discuss the effectiveness of devaluation as a policy instrument.

20.6   Interest Rates and the Exchange Rate

Interest rate parity theory (IRPT), which we developed in Chapter 18, is a corner-stone of the open economy monetary model. Uncovered interest parity (UIP) theory states that:

$$(e^e_{t+1} - e_t)/e_t = (i_g - i_{irl})/(1 + i_{irl}) \tag{1}$$

where i_{irl} is the domestic interest rate, i_g is the rate of interest in Germany (the "rest of the world"), e_t is today's DM/Irish pound exchange rate and e_{t+1} is next period's exchange rate. Since e_{t+1} is not known, we have to replace it with next period's *expected* exchange rate, e^e_{t+1}. Ignoring the denominator on the right-hand side, we can rearrange equation (1) as:

$$i_{irl} = i_g - \Delta e^e/e_t \tag{2}$$

Equation (2) states that domestic interest rates should equal foreign interest rates *minus* the expected rate of appreciation of the currency. If the Irish pound is expected to appreciate, Irish interest rates will be lower than world interest rates, and vice versa.

Suppose that the exchange rate is fixed and there is no expectation of any change. If equation (2) is to hold, an increase in i_g must be matched by an equal increase in i_{irl}. Hence, under fixed exchange rates, interest rates in the domestic economy are determined by foreign interest rates. This was one of the beliefs that influenced the decision to join the EMS. It was believed that if the Irish pound was tied to the DM, then Irish interest rates would converge to the relatively low German interest rates. However, as we shall see in Chapter 22, this did not happen in the early years of membership. The failure of interest rates to converge indicated that the market did not believe that the fixed exchange rate commitment was credible.

If the exchange rate is fixed, domestic interest rates cannot remain above or below the foreign rate for very long. If i_{irl} increases relative to i_g, this will provoke a capital outflow until the money supply and domestic interest rates revert to their original levels. Thus in this model under fixed exchange rates a small country's interest rates are exogenously determined.

Overshooting exchange rate

Under floating exchange rates, interest rate differentials provide a guide to market expectations about the future course of the exchange rate. In Chapter 18 we outlined the theory of exchange rate *overshooting* (see Chapter 18). If a country experiences a monetary contraction, prices and costs should fall and the exchange rate appreciate. However, if prices are sticky the initial effect of the contraction on M^S is a fall in the real money supply, M^S/P. Given that the demand for money has not changed, the interest rate must rise to maintain equilibrium between supply and demand. Now, according to UIP the only way domestic interest rates can rise, given the level of world interest rates, is if the exchange rate appreciates above its equilibrium level, creating an expectation that it will fall back to its equilibrium level sometime in the future. This can be seen from equation (2), which shows that if the market expects the currency to depreciate, domestic interest rates will be above world interest rates. This raises the possibility that part of the process of adjusting to monetary shocks requires exchange rates to over or undershoot their eventual equilibrium levels.

If the market believes the exchange rate is overvalued, then investors must be compensated for the risk of a capital loss that holding the currency entails. This requires that domestic interest rates pay a premium over foreign rates. Thus an over-valued exchange rate tends to be associated with relatively high domestic interest rates.

The problem of an exchange rate misalignment is compounded by high interest rates. This is very relevant to the sequence of events in Ireland during the currency crisis of 1992-93, when the Central Bank of Ireland intervened massively to support the Irish pound at a level that was viewed as unsustainable by the markets. The result was that the problems of high interest rates, needed to persuade people to hold Irish pounds, were added to the problem of the overvalued exchange rate.

A more favourable combination can be produced if the markets believe that the currency is undervalued. The US dollar in the early 1990s was widely regarded as below its long-run equilibrium level (as indicated, for example, by PPP) and US interest rates were lower than those in Europe. The combination of an undervalued currency and low interest rates was effective in moving the US economy out of recession.

20.7   How Effective are Devaluations?

We can use the monetary model to explore how a change in the exchange rate affects the economy. Starting from a point such as X on the PPP line in the left panel of Figure 20.8, we illustrate the effects of lowering the exchange rate from e_1 to e_2. At Y the currency is undervalued and the associated gain in competitiveness should result in a balance of payments surplus. This shifts the AD schedule upwards from AD_1 to AD_2 (right-hand panel). The price level rises and a new equilibrium is established at C. The rise in the price level erodes the competitive gain brought about by the devaluation and PPP is restored at Z. The overall effect of the devaluation has been to create a temporary balance of payments surplus. The increase in the price level is equal to the original devaluation and all the real variables (output, employment and the real exchange rate) are unchanged.

Note:

Devaluation causes the price of imports to rise, which erodes some of the competitive gain which exporters and import-competing firms initially enjoyed. Workers will soon seek compensation for the fall in their standard of living caused by the rise in the cost of living. If these claims are conceded, the domestic price level would quickly rise by the same proportion as the exchange rate has fallen, completely offsetting the initial gain in competitiveness. There is no lasting gain in output and employment. The end result of the devaluation is a higher price level and a lower nominal exchange rate.

The following points also have a bearing on the appropriateness of devaluation:

■   By decreasing the price of exports and increasing the price of imports a devaluation

470

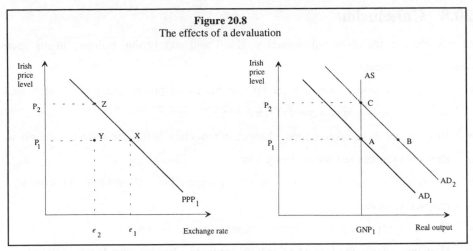

Figure 20.8
The effects of a devaluation

causes a deterioration in the terms of trade. The home country must now export more goods and services to import a given amount of goods and services. Thus a devaluation reduces domestic living standards in the short term so as to raise output and employment in the longer run. It is not a "soft option" that improves the balance of payments without domestic sacrifice.

- A vicious cycle of inflation and depreciation can start. A lax monetary policy will lead to high domestic inflation, initially causing an overvalued exchange rate. If the government devalues in response, this gives another twist to the inflationary spiral. If the stance of monetary policy is not changed, the underlying rate of inflation will continue to be high and further devaluations will be necessary to restore competitiveness. When devaluations are frequent people anticipate them, domestic prices adjust more quickly and the competitive advantage of the devaluation is short lived. An inflation-devaluation spiral of this type is destabilising. It can lead to the substitution of foreign currency for the domestic currency in more and more transactions.

Note:

In many countries where high inflation has led to the rapid depreciation of the domestic currency it has almost lost its store-of-value function. Residents prefer to use foreign currencies for this purpose. The "dollarisation ratio" (the share of foreign currencies in the domestic money supply) has reached about 70 per cent in Bolivia, and about 40 per cent in many of the countries of the former Soviet Union.

20.8 Conclusion

In this chapter we discussed monetary, fiscal and supply-side policies in an open economy. We discussed:

- An open economy monetary model that builds on purchasing power parity and assumes that aggregate supply is fixed
- How, under these assumptions, changes in monetary policy are reflected mainly in changes in prices and the exchange rate
- If exchange rates are fixed, a monetary expansion will deplete the country's external reserves
- How a supply-side policy can raise output and employment
- How increases in the foreign price level are transmitted into the domestic economy
- The relationship between exchange rate expectations and changes in domestic interest rates
- The effects of devaluation.

Chapter 21

The Adjustment of the Open Economy in the Short Run

21.1 Introduction

In the previous chapter we studied how the economy adjusts to shocks when prices are flexible. In the short run prices are not flexible, especially downwards, and output bears the brunt of the adjustment. This was the situation emphasised by Keynes and later developed into a model of the open economy by John Fleming, an Oxford economist, and Richard Mundell, a Canadian economist teaching at Columbia University. In this chapter we use the Mundell-Fleming model to explore the effects of fiscal, monetary and exchange rate policies on output and employment. This supplements our analysis in the previous chapter, where the same issues were addressed using a model that allowed prices as well as quantities to vary.

21.2 Internal and External Balance

In an open economy a key issue is how the policy-maker can achieve simultaneously both full employment (*internal balance*) and balance of payments equilibrium (*external balance*). To start, we need to extend the IS-LM framework we introduced in Chapter 11 to analyse a closed economy with fixed prices. In Figure 21.1 we reproduce this IS-LM diagram. The IS line shows the combinations of GNP and the real interest rate consistent with equilibrium in the goods market. The LM line shows the combinations of GNP and the real interest rate consistent with equilibrium in the money market. At A the two lines intersect and there is, simultaneously, equilibrium in both the goods and money markets.

Note:

In Figure 21.1 we actually use nominal (i), and not real (r), interest rates on the vertical axis. The substitution of the nominal for the real interest rate does not affect the analysis because, with prices fixed, a change in the real interest rate will be completely reflected in a change in the nominal interest rate. The reason for making this substitution is to incorporate into the analysis capital flows through the balance of payments. These capital account flows are responsive to changes in nominal interest rates.

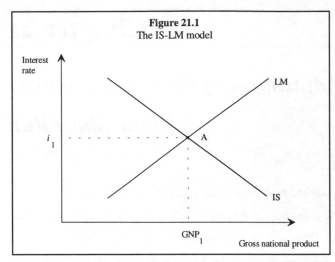

Figure 21.1
The IS-LM model

Any change in the components of aggregate demand (consumption, investment, government expenditure and taxation) shifts the IS schedule. An expansionary fiscal policy, for example, would shift the IS curve to the right. On the other hand, a change in the money supply (monetary policy) will shift the LM schedule.

In an open economy we have to take account of the fact that net exports (NX = X – M), where X and M are exports and imports respectively, are an important component of aggregate demand. An increase in NX will shift the IS curve out to the right, and vice versa. In Chapter 15 we saw that the real exchange rate $[(e \times P)/P_f]$, where P and P_f are domestic and foreign prices respectively and e is the nominal exchange rate, is one of the determinants of NX. It follows, therefore, that changes in the real exchange rate affect the position of the IS curve in an open economy.

In a closed economy, the position of the LM curve depends on the money supply, which in turn was determined by domestic monetary policy. As we shall see, in an open economy the domestic monetary authorities (the country's central bank) have much less control over the money supply. If the exchange rate is fixed or pegged, a surplus (deficit) in the balance of payments will cause the external reserves to rise (fall) and shift the LM curve. Thus in an open economy, with a fixed exchange rate, macroeconomic policy cannot be exclusively concerned with internal targets such as maintaining full employment. The balance of payments acts as a constraint on the freedom to pursue the goals of economic policy.

External balance In Chapter 15 we pointed out that under flexible exchange rates the balance of payments always balances in the sense that the current account surplus (deficit) is always offset by an equal deficit (surplus) on the capital account. If the exchange rate is fixed these surpluses (deficits) will be reflected in an increase (decrease) in the official reserves of foreign exchange held by the central bank.

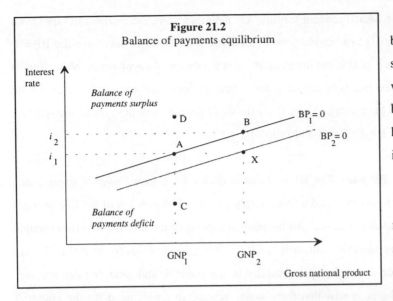

Figure 21.2
Balance of payments equilibrium

Interest rate

Balance of payments surplus

• D

B

i_2

A

i_1

X

Balance of payments deficit

• C

$BP_1 = 0$

$BP_2 = 0$

GNP_1

GNP_2

Gross national product

"External balance" can be said to exist when the central bank docs not have to intervene in the foreign exchange market to stabilise the exchange rate. This implies that the sum of the current account and private capital flows is zero. This balance could happen even though there is a large current account deficit, provided it is financed by a private capital inflow.

In Figure 21.2 we draw a reference line BP = 0 which shows the combinations of GNP and the interest rate which result in the overall balance of payments being zero. (Later in this chapter we shall look at the conditions required to achieve a balance on the current account, that is, NX = 0.) The BP = 0 line slopes upwards because increases in the interest rate and in GNP have opposing effects on the balance of payments. Consider first the effect of an increase in the interest rate. If the exchange rate is fixed, an increase in the domestic interest rate relative to the world rate leads to a capital inflow as investors move funds to the country that offers the highest return. This tends to restore domestic interest rates to the world level.

■ i (relative to the interest rate in the rest of the world) → ↑capital inflows → surplus on the capital account of the balance of payments.

On the other hand, an increase in GNP leads to an increase in imports via the marginal propensity to import (MPM) and a fall in net exports, that is, a rise in the deficit on current account.

■ ↑ GNP → ↑ M → rise in current account deficit

The BP = 0 line is drawn so that the positive effect of higher interest rates offsets the negative GNP effect and the overall balance of payments remains in equilibrium. In Figure 21.2, as the economy moves from A to B the interest rate increases from i_1 to i_2

475

and this leads to a capital account surplus. On the other hand, the increase in GNP from GNP_1 to GNP_2 leads to a current account deficit. If the economy is above the BP = 0 line, at a point such as D in the diagram, there is a balance of payments surplus. This is because the interest rate is higher than that necessary for equilibrium. If it is below the BP = 0 line, at C for example, there is a balance of payments deficit. (The interest rate is lower than that required for equilibrium.)

Location of the BP line   The BP = 0 line is drawn for a given level of exports and imports, world interest rates and a fixed exchange rate. The position of the line changes if any of these variables change. An increase in exports or a fall in imports (not brought about by a change in GNP) will shift the BP = 0 line downwards to the right. To see why, suppose that the economy is initially at the point A and interest rates are kept constant at i_1. Suppose now that there is an increase in the demand for the country's exports. By shifting the BP = 0 line to the right we can again achieve BP equilibrium. The point X, for example, in Figure 21.2 is on the lower BP = 0 line. At X the rise in GNP from GNP_1 to GNP_2 has increased imports sufficiently to offset the increase in exports and the balance of payments returns to equilibrium.

A fall in world interest rates or an exchange rate depreciation would also shift the BP = 0 line downwards. A fall in exports, a rise in imports (not due to changes in GNP), an increase in world interest rates or an exchange rate appreciation would shift the BP = 0 line upwards to the left.

Slope of the BP line   The slope of the BP = 0 line depends on (1) the degree of capital mobility, and (2) the marginal propensity to import (MPM). If capital flows are very sensitive to interest differentials then the BP line will be relatively flat. Only a small change in the interest rate (relative to the world rate) is necessary to attract sufficient capital to compensate for the increased imports due to a given increase in GNP and maintain the balance of payments in equilibrium. If there is *perfect capital mobility*, the BP = 0 line will be horizontal. A small change in the domestic interest rate would lead to unlimited capital inflows or outflows. In this case, only the world interest rate, i^*, is consistent with balance of payments equilibrium whatever the level of GNP. Changes in exports, imports and the exchange rate will *not* shift the BP = 0 line because enough capital will always flow in to finance the current account deficit. On the other hand, if capital flows are restricted by exchange controls, the BP = 0 line will be relatively steep. A large change in interest rates would be needed to attract the capital inflows to finance the current account deficit due to a given increase in GNP.

A large MPM means that a given increase in GNP will lead to a relatively large increase in imports and interest rates will have to increase accordingly to compensate; hence the BP = 0 line will be steep. In general:

- If there is a high degree of capital mobility and the MPM is small, then the BP line will be relatively flat.

- If there is a low degree of capital mobility and the MPM is large, then the BP line will be relatively steep.

At the present time the Irish economy is best described by a horizontal BP = 0 line because the degree of capital mobility between Ireland and the rest of the world is very high. It is true that the Irish MPM is relatively large, but the increase in imports as GNP rises is likely to be dominated by the effect of an incipient rise in interest rates on the capital account. The BP = 0 line was horizontal in Ireland up to 1979 when the Irish pound was pegged to sterling and capital flowed freely between Ireland and the UK. Between December 1978 and December 1988 exchange controls restricted capital movements between Ireland and other countries. It is possible that during this period the BP = 0 line sloped upwards, allowing the Irish interest rate to deviate from that in the rest of the world. However, with the complete abolition of exchange controls in 1992, it is likely that there is now near perfect capital mobility between Ireland and other countries.

21.3 Introduction to the Mundell-Fleming Model

We can now extend our IS-LM analysis to include the effect of changes in the level of economic activity on interest rates and the balance of payments. The Mundell-Fleming model was developed for this purpose.[1] The model is based on several assumptions.

---

1. See J. M. Fleming, "Domestic Financial Policies under Fixed and Floating Exchange Rates", *IMF Staff Papers*, 9, 1962, and R. A. Mundell, "The Appropriate Use of Monetary and Fiscal Policy Under Fixed Exchange Rates", *IMF Staff Papers*, 9, 1962. The reader may also consult R. A. Mundell, *International Economics*, New York: Macmillan, 1968. See also Rudiger Dornbusch, "Expectations and Exchange Rate Dynamics", *Journal of Political Economy*, 84, 1976, and P. J. K. Kouri and M. G. Porter, "International Capital Flows and Portfolio Equilibrium", *Journal of Political Economy*, 82, 1974. Surveys of the literature are given in P. B. Kenen, "Macroeconomic Policy: How the Closed Economy was Opened", in R. W. Jones and P. B. Kenen (eds) *Handbook of International Economics*, Vol. 2, North Holland, 1985.

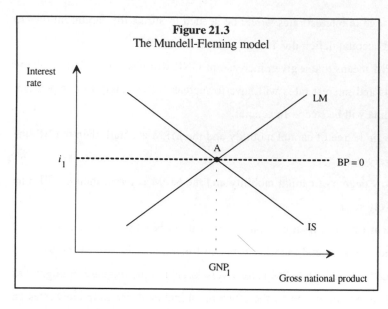

Figure 21.3
The Mundell-Fleming model

- First, and most important, it assumes that *the price levels in the domestic country and the rest of the world are constant.* (Recall that the open economy monetary model discussed in the previous chapter assumed flexible prices.)

- Secondly, the model assumes that the economy is not supply constrained.

- Thirdly, crowding out is less than complete and the Ricardian Equivalence effect does not offset fiscal policy.

    These three assumptions imply that the aggregate supply curve is perfectly horizontal and that changes in real output and employment are determined only by changes in aggregate demand.

- Fourthly, we assume that an expansionary fiscal policy is financed in a non-monetary way and does not result in an increase in the money supply.

- Finally, we assume perfect capital mobility so that the BP = 0 line is horizontal. (Later in the chapter we show how imperfect capital mobility would alter the conclusions of the model.)

    Figure 21.3 incorporates these assumptions. A horizontal BP = 0 reference line is amalgamated with the IS-LM model. At the point A the IS and LM curves intersect with the BP = 0 line. At this point the goods and money markets and the balance of payments are all in equilibrium.

    In the next section we use the Mundell-Fleming model to analyse the effects of fiscal and monetary policy on output and the balance of payments when the exchange rate is both fixed and flexible. In what follows, it is important to bear in mind that under fixed exchange rates the central bank intervenes in the foreign exchange market to stabilise the exchange rate. As a result, balance of payments deficits or surpluses are

478

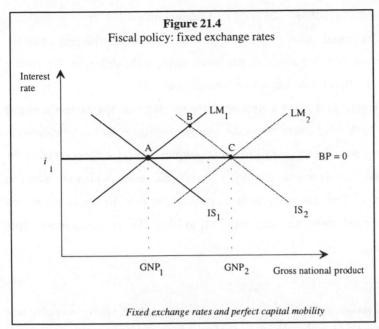

Figure 21.4
Fiscal policy: fixed exchange rates

Fixed exchange rates and perfect capital mobility

reflected in changes in the external reserves, which in turn affect the domestic money supply and shift the LM curve. If the exchange rate were floating, then the central bank would not intervene in the foreign exchange market and balance of payments surpluses or deficits would result in an appreciation or depreciation of the currency. As we shall see, the effect of fiscal and monetary policy on output and employment is very different, depending on whether the exchange rate is fixed or floating.

21.4   Applying the Model Under Fixed Exchange Rates

Fiscal policy

In Figure 21.4 we show the effect of an increase in government expenditure on output when the exchange rate is fixed. An increase in government expenditure shifts the IS curve outwards from IS_1 to IS_2 and the economy moves from A to B. At B, GNP has increased and there is a balance of payments surplus as the economy is above the BP = 0 reference line.

An expansionary fiscal policy results in a balance of payments surplus because:

- The increase in GNP leads to an increase in imports via the marginal propensity to import and this results in a deficit in the current account of the balance of payments.

- The increase in GNP increases the demand for money and therefore the domestic interest rate. This results in a capital inflow and a surplus on the capital account of the balance of payments.

$$\uparrow GNP \rightarrow \uparrow M^d \rightarrow \uparrow i \rightarrow \text{capital inflow}$$

Given perfect capital mobility, the second effect dominates the first, with the result that there is an overall balance of payments surplus: the deficit in the current account is more than offset by the surplus on the capital account.

Point B in Figure 21.4 is not a final equilibrium. Because the exchange rate is fixed, the central bank must intervene in the foreign exchange market to stabilise it following the emergence of a balance of payments surplus. This intervention takes the form of selling Irish pounds and accumulating foreign currencies, which are added to the external reserves. The rise in the external reserves, in turn, increases the money supply and the LM curve shifts outwards from LM_1 to LM_2. The economy moves from B to C.

Note:

Changes in the external reserves lead to changes in the domestic money supply. If, however, the central bank engages in *sterilisation,* it can try to offset this effect. Sterilisation is discussed in Chapter 23. At this stage we assume that the central bank does not engage in sterilisation.

At C the domestic interest rate is again equal to the world rate and the overall balance of payments is zero. The current account is in deficit but this is offset by the capital account surplus. The level of GNP has risen as a result of the fiscal expansion. Fiscal policy is therefore effective when the exchange rate is fixed and capital is perfectly mobile. The magnitude of the impact of fiscal policy depends on the slopes of the IS-LM curves, as we discussed in Chapter 11.

Note:

If there is imperfect capital mobility, the BP = 0 line will slope upwards. If the degree of capital mobility is such that the BP = 0 line is steeper than the LM curve, the reader can verify that an expansionary fiscal policy will result in a balance of payments deficit. The LM curve will then shift upwards to the left, reflecting a fall in the central bank's external reserves, and the increase in GNP will be smaller than when there was perfect capital mobility. The greater the degree of capital mobility, the more effective is fiscal policy.

Monetary policy

Figure 21.5 shows the effect of an expansionary monetary policy when the exchange rate is fixed. The increase in the money supply shifts the LM curve from LM_1 to LM_2 and the economy moves from A to B. At B, GNP has increased, but the economy is

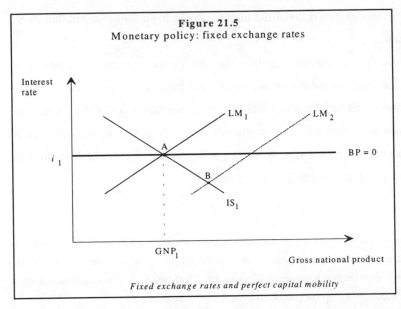

Figure 21.5
Monetary policy: fixed exchange rates

Fixed exchange rates and perfect capital mobility

below the BP = 0 line, indicating that there is a balance of payments deficit.

The balance of payments deficit arises for two reasons:

- The increase in the money supply leads to a fall in the domestic interest rate relative to the world interest rate, and this results in a capital outflow and a deficit on the capital account of the balance of payments.

$$\uparrow M^s \rightarrow \downarrow i \text{ (relative to the world rate)} \rightarrow \text{capital outflow}$$

- The increase in GNP leads to an increase in imports (via the marginal propensity to import) and a current account deficit.

$$\uparrow GNP \rightarrow \uparrow M \rightarrow \text{current account deficit}$$

An expansionary monetary policy therefore results in a deficit in both the current and capital accounts of the balance of payments, giving rise to an overall balance of payments deficit. The economy will not remain at B. Because the exchange rate is fixed, the Central Bank must intervene in the foreign exchange market to offset the balance of payments deficit. It does this by buying Irish pounds with foreign exchange from the official external reserves. The fall in the reserves results in a contraction in the money supply. This is shown by the backward shift in the LM curve, which continues until the economy returns to its original position at A. At this point, the domestic interest rate is again equal to the world rate and GNP has returned to its initial level. From this sequence of events we see that:

- when the exchange rate is fixed the money supply is no longer controlled by the central bank.

Because capital is perfectly mobile, the fall in the interest rate leads to an immediate capital outflow and the money supply and the interest rate quickly return to their original levels. Given the speed with which capital flows out of the country, the interest rate does not remain below the world rate long enough to have any effect on the level of domestic economic activity. Monetary policy is therefore ineffective when the exchange rate is fixed and capital is perfectly mobile.

Note:

The degree of capital mobility does not change the result that monetary policy is ineffective when the exchange rate is fixed. The reader can verify that even if the BP = 0 line is upward sloping, an expansionary monetary policy will again result in a balance of payments deficit and the economy will eventually return to the initial level of output. With imperfect capital mobility this will take longer.

Summary Our analysis shows that fiscal policy is effective, and monetary policy ineffective, when the exchange rate is fixed and capital is perfectly mobile.

21.5   Applying the Model under Floating Exchange Rates

Fiscal policy

In Figure 21.6 an expansionary fiscal policy shifts the IS curve outwards from IS_1 to IS_2 and the economy moves from A to B. At B, GNP has increased and there is an overall balance of payments surplus because the capital account surplus (brought about by higher interest rates) dominates the current account deficit (due to the increase in GNP).

However, if the exchange rate is floating and the central bank does not intervene in the foreign exchange market, the balance of payments surplus will result in exchange rate appreciation. The external reserves and the money supply remain unchanged. The LM curve is therefore not affected. But the rise in the exchange rate reduces exports and increases imports, and the IS curve shifts backwards to the left. This process will continue until the economy reverts to point A. The increase in GNP was therefore only temporary. In effect, under floating exchange rates, an expansionary fiscal policy crowds out net exports (exports *minus* imports) through exchange rate appreciation. Fiscal policy is therefore ineffective when the exchange rate is floating and there is

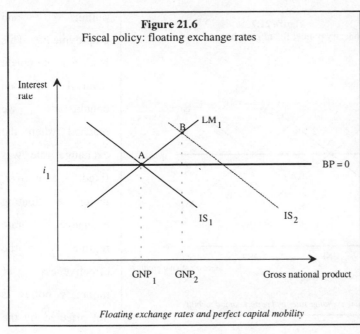

Figure 21.6
Fiscal policy: floating exchange rates

Floating exchange rates and perfect capital mobility

perfect capital mobility.

Note:
If the BP = 0 line is steeper than the LM curve due to imperfect capital mobility, an expansionary fiscal policy will result in an increase in GNP and a balance of payments deficit. In this case, the exchange rate depreciates and this results in a further increase in GNP. The reader can verify that under these circumstances fiscal policy will have a greater effect on output and employment than in the case of fixed exchange rate and perfect capital mobility. But note that we are assuming there are no supply-side constraints and that no domestic inflation follows from the exchange rate depreciation.

Monetary policy

Figure 21.7 illustrates the case of an expansionary monetary policy under floating exchange rates with perfect capital mobility. The increase in the money supply shifts the LM curve from LM_1 to LM_2 and the economy moves from point A to point B. At B, GNP has increased and a deficit has emerged on both the current and capital accounts of the balance of payments.

The exchange rate now depreciates and this increases net exports. The IS curve shifts outwards from IS_1 to IS_2 and the economy moves from B to C. GNP again increases and equilibrium is restored to the balance of payments. This implies that monetary policy is very effective when exchange rates are floating, capital is perfectly mobile, and there are no supply-side constraints. This result is not changed if the BP = 0 line is upward sloping, reflecting imperfect capital mobility.

Summary Under floating exchange rates with perfect capital mobility, monetary policy is very effective and fiscal policy ineffective in terms of achieving increases in

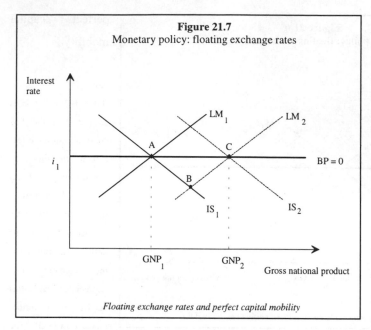

Figure 21.7
Monetary policy: floating exchange rates

Interest rate

LM_1
LM_2

A
C
i_1
B
BP = 0

IS_1
IS_2

GNP_1
GNP_2
Gross national product

Floating exchange rates and perfect capital mobility

output and employment. This is a complete reversal of the conclusions we reached when the exchange rate was fixed. Moreover, under a floating exchange rate regime the effectiveness of monetary policy is not affected by the degree of capital mobility. However, imperfect capital mobility allows fiscal policy to be effective when the exchange rate is floating. Table 21.1 summarises our conclusions for fixed and floating exchange rate cases.

21.6   Exchange Rate Policy

We now extend the model to look at how the economy adjusts to changes in the exchange rate. To do so, we have to abandon the assumption that domestic and world price levels are constant.

Devaluation, output and employment

Recall from the discussion in Chapter 15 that:

$$\text{Value of Exports} = P_x \times Q_x$$
$$\text{Value of Imports} = P_m \times Q_m$$

where P_x and P_m are export and import prices, and Q_x and Q_m are the quantities of exports and imports sold. We saw that a devaluation must increase the value of exports, $P_x \times Q_x$, measured in domestic currency. Similarly, a devaluation will increase P_m measured in domestic currency, leading to a fall in Q_m. Provided the elasticity of demand for imports is large enough, the value of imports, $P_m \times Q_m$, measured in domestic currency, will also fall. Thus a devaluation will lead to an improvement in the

Table 21.1

The effect of fiscal and monetary policy on output

Exchange rate	Fixed	Floating
	(regardless of degree of capital mobility)	
Monetary policy	Ineffective	Effective
Fiscal policy	*Capital mobile*	
	Effective	Ineffective
Fiscal policy	*Capital immobile*	
	Relatively ineffective	Effective

trade balance and an increase in output and employment.

Devaluation, by changing the price of exports relative to the price of imports, is an *expenditure switching* policy that shifts demand from imports to domestically produced goods and leads to an expansion of output, which should lower unemployment:

$$\text{Devaluation} \rightarrow \uparrow X \text{ and } \downarrow M \rightarrow \uparrow AD \rightarrow \uparrow GNP \rightarrow \downarrow U$$

However, it should be noted that the improvement in the home trade balance resulting from exchange rate devaluation has to be matched by an increase in some other country's trade deficit. An increase in Irish exports implies a rise in imports in some other country and a fall in our imports implies a drop in someone else's exports. Hence the gain in output and employment at home must be at the expense of a reduction in output and employment in some other country. This gives rise to the accusation that devaluation is a "beggar thy neighbour" policy in that the devaluing country is attempting to "export its unemployment" to other countries.

As happened in the 1930s, countries adversely affected by a devaluation are likely to retaliate by devaluing their currencies in order to restore competitiveness. This can result in a series of competitive devaluations, with countries retaliating to other countries' devaluation in order to maintain output and employment. If this happens, there will be no net increase in aggregate demand in the countries concerned. It is therefore frequently argued that if a number of countries are suffering from high unemployment, the best policy is for them not to try to solve the problem through competitive devaluations, but instead to co-operate and implement a co-ordinated expansion in aggregate demand in all countries. This would result in an overall increase in output and employment.

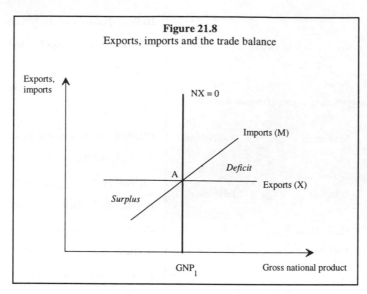

Figure 21.8
Exports, imports and the trade balance

Exports, imports

NX = 0

Imports (M)

Deficit

A

Exports (X)

Surplus

GNP$_1$ Gross national product

Devaluation and the trade balance

An expansionary fiscal or monetary policy increases GNP, but in doing so creates a trade deficit (or reduces a trade surplus). This happens because the increase in GNP leads to an increase in imports via the marginal propensity to import (MPM). Devaluation, on the other hand, increases GNP through an improvement in the trade balance. Devaluation is therefore a particularly useful policy instrument if there is a trade deficit and high unemployment. The policy dilemma that can exist between achieving a trade balance and full employment can be resolved by devaluation.

In Figure 21.8 we elaborate on this point by developing an NX = 0 reference line. The analysis is the same as it would be for the BP = 0 line, with zero capital mobility: we are now concentrating on the balance of trade because capital flows do not enter into aggregate demand. With GNP on the horizontal axis and exports and imports on the vertical axis, the import schedule is shown as sloping upwards. This reflects the fact that imports increase as GNP rises. The slope of this line is determined by the MPM. The larger the MPM, the steeper the import schedule. The export schedule is shown as a horizontal line, indicating that changes in GNP do not affect the level of exports, which are determined by aggregate demand in the rest of the world. At GNP$_1$, exports equal imports and the trade account is balanced. We draw a vertical NX = 0 reference line to indicate this level of GNP. To the right of the NX = 0 line there is a trade deficit (imports exceed exports), and to the left there is a trade surplus. A devaluation will shift the import schedule down to the right and the export schedule upwards. The NX = 0 line will now shift to the right and the equilibrium level of GNP will move to the right along the horizontal axis.

Figure 21.9 shows an NX = 0 line which corresponds to a trade balance at GNP$_1$

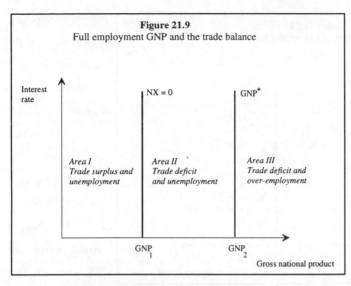

Figure 21.9
Full employment GNP and the trade balance

and a full employment reference line denoted by GNP*. As drawn, the NX = 0 line is situated to the left of the GNP*. The economy can be in area I, II or III. These areas are characterised as follows:

Area I   Trade surplus and unemployment.

Area II   Trade deficit and unemployment.

Area III   Trade deficit and over-employment.

If the economy is in area I or III there is no conflict between achieving a trade balance and full employment. For example, if the economy is in area I, an expansionary fiscal or monetary policy can be used to reduce unemployment *and* reduce the trade surplus. Similarly, if the economy is in area III, a deflationary fiscal or monetary policy can be implemented to reduce over-employment *and* reduce the trade deficit. A dilemma does however arise if the economy is in area II. An expansionary fiscal or monetary policy would aggravate the balance of trade deficit, whilst a contractionary fiscal or monetary policy would aggravate the problem of unemployment. In the early 1980s, when the balance of trade deficit was about 15 per cent of GNP and unemployment was high and rising, the Irish economy was clearly in area II. In the late 1990s, with a large balance of trade surplus and a relatively high unemployment, we are in area I.

The dilemma between the internal and external policy objectives that exists when the economy is in area II can be resolved by introducing an additional policy instrument. Exchange rate policy is such an instrument. A devaluation could be used to resolve the policy dilemma. This is illustrated in Figure 21.10. A devaluation would shift the NX = 0 line towards GNP* and move the IS curve from IS_1 to IS_2 as NX increases. As a result, full employment could be restored while at the same time maintaining a balance in the trade account.

487

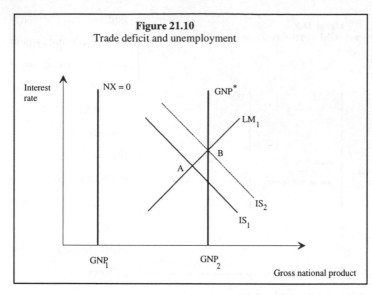

Figure 21.10
Trade deficit and unemployment

but because of the shift to the right of the IS curve, the economy moves to the point B. At the point B, there is over-full employment and the trade account continues to be in deficit. The reason the trade deficit increases is that the increase in GNP leads to an increase in imports. Overall devaluation should improve a trade account position, but the increase in imports associated with the rise in GNP offsets some of the improvement. In this situation a deflationary fiscal or monetary policy is required to move the economy back to GNP*. This example shows that if the economy is close to full employment, devaluation will have to be accompanied by an *expenditure reducing* policy if the objectives of internal and external balance are to be achieved simultaneously. Put another way, if the objective of devaluation is simply to improve the trade account without increasing output and employment, an expenditure reducing policy will have to accompany it.

Suppose, however, the economy is at a point such as A in Figure 21.11, which corresponds to full employment and a trade *deficit*. A devaluation would move the NX = 0 line towards GNP*,

These applications illustrate how economists can analyse the appropriate policy mix for an open economy.

21.7 Conclusion

In this chapter we discussed how the open economy adjusts in the short run when all prices are not flexible. The Mundell-Fleming model was used to show that:

- Fiscal policy is effective and monetary policy ineffective when the exchange rate is fixed and there is perfect capital mobility

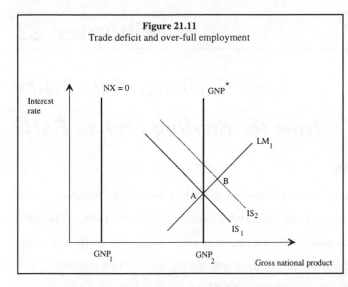

Figure 21.11
Trade deficit and over-full employment

- If the exchange rate is floating and capital perfectly mobile, fiscal policy is ineffective and monetary policy effective
- Devaluation is an expenditure switching policy that increases output and employment by increasing the trade surplus. However, this is a "beggar thy neighbour" policy which could lead to retaliation by other countries
- Devaluation must be accompanied by a deflationary fiscal or monetary policy if the objective is to remove a trade deficit
- When an economy faces high unemployment and a balance of payments surplus, devaluation is an appropriate policy, provided the other assumptions of the model hold.

Chapter 22

Irish Exchange Rate Policy from the Sterling Link to EMU

22.1 Introduction

In this chapter we examine Irish exchange rate policy from Independence to the decision to join the European Economic and Monetary Union in 1998. The most important event during this period was the decision, taken at the end of 1978, to enter the Exchange Rate Mechanism (ERM) of the European Monetary System (EMS). This eventually led to the decision to participate in EMU.

The chapter deals with the sterling link, from 1922 to 1979, the decision to enter the EMS in 1979 and our experience as a member of EMS, with particular reference to the crisis of 1992. The concluding section discusses exchange rate policy in the run-up to joining EMU.

22.2 The Sterling Link, 1922-79

A link with sterling was the logical policy for Ireland in the 1920s. Sterling had been the strongest currency in the world until World War I, and in the 1920s was still regarded as a reliable store of value, despite the wartime inflation and suspension of convertibility into gold. Ireland's trade was predominantly with Britain and the Irish and British banking systems were closely linked. Preserving the sterling link minimised transaction costs for Irish importers and exporters.

The rationale for maintaining the sterling link can also be understood by referring to the purchasing power parity (PPP) theory developed in Chapter 18. According to PPP

$$\pi_{irl} = \pi_{uk} - \Delta e_{uk} \tag{1}$$

where π_{irl} and π_{uk} are the Irish and UK inflation rates respectively and e_{uk} is the sterling/Irish pound exchange rate. If the exchange rate is fixed so that $\Delta e_{uk} = 0$, then PPP theory predicts that UK inflation will be transmitted to Ireland so that $\pi_{irl} = \pi_{uk}$. This is because Ireland is a small economy relative to the large UK economy and the

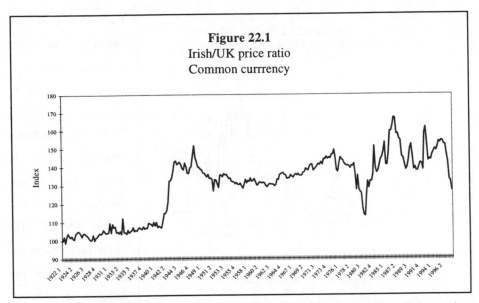

Figure 22.1
Irish/UK price ratio
Common currrency

causation is running from the UK to Ireland. Hence, PPP theory predicted that as long as the Irish pound was pegged to sterling we had to experience the same rate of inflation as Britain. In the early years of the independent Irish state sterling appeared to be a stable, low-inflation currency to which it made sense to peg our currency. Although its pre-eminence was undermined by its departure from the gold standard in 1931 and subsequent devaluations relative to the dollar, no real alternative to the sterling link was open to Ireland over these years. Doubts were expressed about the merits of maintaining the sterling link at the time of the devaluations of 1949 and 1967, but the debate remained academic in the absence of a realistic alternative arrangement.

The Irish experience under the sterling link

Did Ireland experience the same rate of inflation as Britain under the sterling link, as predicated by PPP? Figure 22.1 shows the ratio of the Irish and UK price (P_{irl}/P_{uk}) levels from 1922 to 1998. It is evident that over the period 1922-1940 and again between 1945 and 1979 the two price levels moved closely together. They diverged significantly only during World War II, when rationing and price controls were in operation in Britain. Thus, with the exception of the war period, the prediction that Ireland would experience the same inflation rate as Britain is broadly supported by the evidence. However, following the termination of the sterling link in March 1979, the series becomes much more volatile as the sterling/Irish pound exchange rate enters the calculation. (That is, the price ratio is expressed in a common currency by adjusting the

491

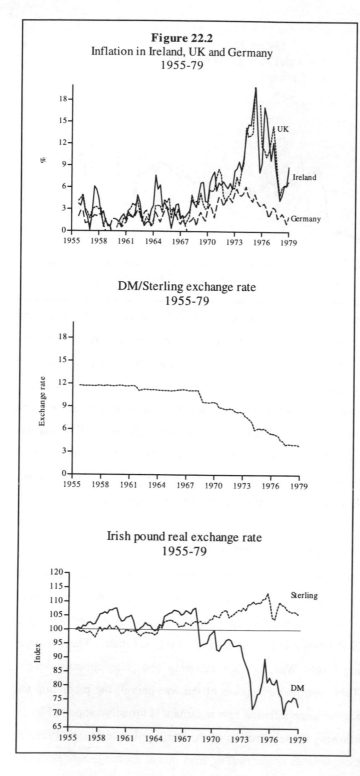

Figure 22.2
Inflation in Ireland, UK and Germany
1955-79

DM/Sterling exchange rate
1955-79

Irish pound real exchange rate
1955-79

Irish price for changes in the exchange rate.)

The upper diagram in Figure 22.2 compares inflation rates in Ireland, the UK and Germany over the period 1955-79. Up to the oil crisis in the mid-1970s, the inflation rates in all countries were very similar. However, between 1974 and 1979, the inflation rate was much lower in Germany. The average inflation in Ireland, the UK and Germany was 5.4, 5.1 and 2.5 per cent respectively over that period.

PPP predicts that the relatively high inflation in the UK would have caused the pound to depreciate relative to the DM. This was indeed the case. As can be seen from the centre diagram in Figure 22.2, the pound fell from DM11 = £1 in

492

1964 to DM4 = £1 in 1978. Since the Irish pound was pegged to sterling throughout this period, its value in terms of the DM fell at the same rate as sterling. However, PPP theory makes the stronger prediction that real exchange rates should have remained constant. It may be seen from the lower diagram in Figure 22.2 that there was no clear trend in the Irish pound/sterling rate over the entire period; there was a 10 per cent rise over the 1969-1975 sub-period but most of this was subsequently reversed. However, the DM/Irish pound real exchange rate fell by almost 30 per cent between 1964 and 1973 and stabilised at the lower level. The reason for this is that high Irish inflation was more than offset by the fall in the nominal exchange rate. Contrary to the prediction of a stable real exchange rate, a significant real depreciation occurred and the Irish economy enjoyed a competitive gain relative to Germany.

22.3 The Rationale for Joining the EMS

During the 1960s and 1970s there was increasing concern in Ireland that the sterling link condemned us to high inflation and a depreciating currency relative to the DM. An argument in favour of breaking with sterling and switching to a low-inflation or "hard" currency, such as the DM, was that Ireland would then enjoy low inflation. Equation (1) above would now be replaced by:

$$\pi_{irl} = \pi_g - \Delta e_{dm} \tag{2}$$

where π_g and e_{dm} are the German inflation rate and the DM/Irish pound exchange rate respectively. If e_{dm} is fixed so that $\Delta e_{dm} = 0$, then the German inflation rate should be transmitted to the Irish economy.

High British inflation was one factor predisposing Ireland to contemplate breaking the link with sterling. The move towards a system of fixed exchange rates in Europe was the other. In Chapter 17 we outlined the history of the move to form a "zone of monetary stability" in Europe in the aftermath of the breakdown of the Bretton Woods system of fixed exchange rates. This provided Irish policy-makers with a concrete alternative to continuing the link with sterling. As proposals to launch the European Monetary System (EMS) were put forward in 1978 the Governor of the Central Bank of Ireland[1] justified Ireland joining, even if this entailed breaking the link with sterling, in the following terms:

---

1. C. H. Murray, "The European Monetary System: Implications for Ireland", The Central Bank of Ireland, *Annual Report*, 1979.

- The inappropriateness of continuing the sterling link. He believed ". . . that a floating, unstable (but generally depreciating) pound [sterling], and a steady fall in (the relative importance of) Ireland's trade with the UK, had diminished the attractiveness and appropriateness of the link".

- The benefits in terms of a reduction in inflation to be obtained from adherence to a hard currency regime. "It would be prudent to assume that, in the longer run at any rate, membership of the EMS involves a harder currency regime than non-membership."

He also believed that Ireland should make a commitment to a major Community initiative, and that support would be forthcoming in the form of a "transfer of resources" from the Community.

However, evidence to support some of these arguments was lacking. Figure 22.2 shows that the PPP relationship had not held between Ireland and Germany in the pre-EMS period. This should have served as a warning against dogmatic predictions, derived from PPP, about the effects of joining the EMS on Irish inflation. It was a major leap of faith to assume that when the currency peg was switched to the DM a new PPP relationship between Germany and Ireland would quickly become established. Britain had been our main trading partner for centuries, the two banking systems were closely interwoven, and there were no barriers to the movement of money between the two countries. In contrast, in 1979 our financial links with the EMS countries were relatively weak, exchange controls hindered the flow of money between Ireland and the continent, and the narrow-band EMS countries accounted for only about one-third of our trade.

Policy credibility and the speed of adjustment

A key issue is how long it would take Ireland's inflation rate to converge to the lower German rate. Figure 22.3 shows two possible *convergence paths*. Inflation is measured along the vertical axis and time along the horizontal axis. We start in 1979 when Irish inflation exceeds German inflation. It is important to note that with the *nominal* exchange rate, e_g, fixed, as long as P_{irl} is rising faster than P_g the *real* exchange rate will increase and the Irish economy will suffer a loss of competitiveness.

Path A If the economy follows path A, then the adjustment period is relatively short. In this case there will be no significant loss of competitiveness and the cost of

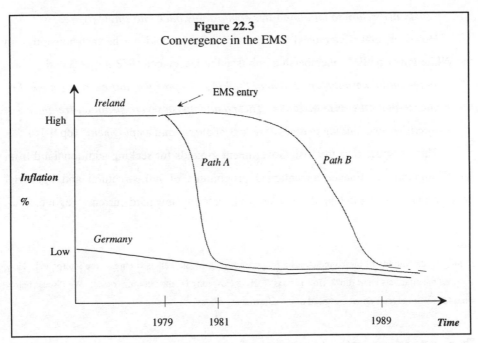

Figure 22.3
Convergence in the EMS

adjustment, as measured by the lost output and employment, will be small.

Path B If, however, the economy follows path B, then as long as the Irish price level is rising relative to the German, the real exchange rate will rise and the Irish economy will suffer a prolonged loss of competitiveness. This will tend to reduce output and raise unemployment. Under this scenario the costs of joining the EMS are high.

It was hoped that participation in the ERM would confer a *credibility bonus*, allowing us to reduce inflation at minimum cost in terms of lost output and increased unemployment. Another way of putting this point is to say that the Irish authorities hoped to borrow an *anti-inflationary reputation* from the Bundesbank by announcing a nominal exchange rate peg between the Irish pound and the DM.

At the time, it was widely expected that disinflation would be relatively painless once we were members of the EMS. To quote the Governor of the Central Bank again:

> *"The Central Bank's calculations suggest that, given sensible domestic policies, the adjustment problems will be manageable and of relatively short duration."*[2]

Similarly, a Central Bank economist wrote:

> *"After a decade of inflation, we can now contemplate the prospect of an early and*

---

2. C. H. Murray, op. cit., p. 106.

sustained return to inflation rates comfortably back into single figures.[3]

However, others cautioned that the adjustment would not be instantaneous. In the White Paper on EMS membership published in December 1978 it was stated:

". . . in the initial period of operation of the EMS, the parity of our currency might be higher than it otherwise would be. This could impose severe strain on Ireland's competitiveness, leading to a possible loss of output and employment" (pp 9-10).

This prospect gave the Irish Government grounds for seeking additional aid from the Community to finance an enlarged programme of infrastructural and industrial development in order to help the economy adjust to the new hard currency regime.

Note:

In judging the validity of these predictions a lot depends on how the italicised phrases are interpreted. How short is "the relatively short run"? How soon is "early"? How long is "the long-run trend"? We discuss below what the record reveals about the speed of the adjustment process.

Wage rate adjustment The behaviour of wages plays a crucial role in determining which path the economy follows. The speed at which the rate of inflation falls depends on how quickly workers reduce their nominal wage demands and firms reduce the rate of increase in output prices. If the government's commitment to the ERM had been credible in 1979, wage and price increases would have immediately moderated and disinflation would have been rapid and relatively painless. (This is very similar to the analysis in Chapter 13 on the Phillips curve, the cost of deflation and the credibility of the policy-maker.) The economy would have followed Path A in Figure 22.3. On the other hand, if the commitment to the EMS lacked credibility, disinflation would only come through the effect of high unemployment on wage and price expectations and the deflationary effect of an overvalued exchange rate working its way through the economy. These forces would take time to operate and an output gap would persist during this interval.

Note:

Different countries adopted different strategies to adjust to inflation and recession at the end of the 1970s. In the UK the Thatcher government opted to curb inflation by controlling the money supply rather than by

---

3. C. McCarthy, "The European Monetary System and Irish Macroeconomic Policy", The Central Bank of Ireland, *Annual Report*, 1979, p. 109.

participating in the ERM.[4] UK inflation fell from 18 per cent in 1980 to 4.5 per cent in 1983, but the cost of this disinflation in terms of lost output and unemployment was considerable. Output fell by nearly 3 per cent in 1981 and 1982, and unemployment increased from 1.1 million in 1979 to three million in 1984.

22.4   The Experience in the EMS

Ireland was offered the possibility of joining the EMS and participating in the exchange rate mechanism (ERM)[5] at its inception in 1979. On 5 December 1978 the British Government announced that the UK would not participate in the ERM. The main reason for this decision was the fear that the commitment to a fixed exchange rate would involve loss of control over the money supply (sterling M3) which at the time was being used as the main instrument in the fight against inflation in the UK. Ten days later the Irish Government announced that we would participate in the narrow band ERM – that is, we would try to hold our exchange rate within ± 2¼ per cent of the central rates we announced against all the other participating currencies. At the same time, exchange controls were imposed on movements of funds from Ireland to Britain.

With the coming into operation of the EMS on 13 March 1979, the Irish authorities were committed to holding the pound to announced central rates in the narrow band of the ERM. Sterling, however, continued to float relative to the currencies in this band. If sterling had stabilised after March 1979, it might have been possible for Ireland to maintain the sterling link and participate in the ERM, but to the surprise of most forecasters, within weeks of the launch of the EMS sterling strengthened sharply relative to the DM. It soon proved impossible for Ireland to maintain the sterling link and remain in the narrow band of the ERM simultaneously. We chose the ERM and the break with sterling came on 30 March 1979. For the first time since Independence the Irish pound and sterling diverged in value. Furthermore, for the first time ever, Northern Ireland and the Republic were separated by an exchange rate.

---

4. The assumption that sterling would remain a weak, inflation-prone currency, although widespread in 1978, proved invalid. The adoption of monetarist policies by the UK Labour government in 1978, the possibility of a Conservative Party victory under Mrs Thatcher in the 1979 election, and the effects of the rise in oil prices on an oil-producing country like the UK were not given due weight. The issue of what would happen to the sterling exchange rate if oil prices increased on world markets was raised by Patrick Honohan, "Some Effects of North Sea Oil on the Irish Economy", *The Economic and Social Review*, Vol. 9, No. 2, 1978.

5. The ERM was the core of the EMS – the grid of quasi-fixed exchange rates. See Chapter 17.

Figure 22.4
Inflation in Ireland, UK and Germany
1979-97

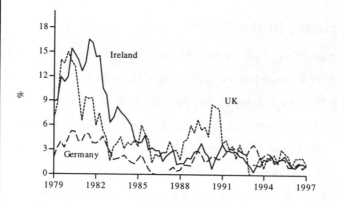

Interest rates in Ireland, UK and Germany
1979-97

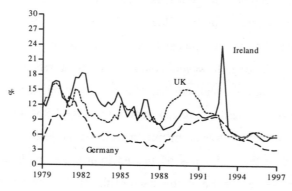

Irish pound real exchange rate
1979-97

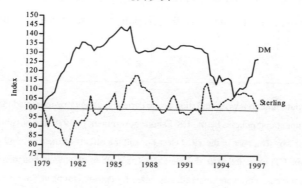

Note:

One of the witnesses to the Banking Commission (1934-38) claimed that there were only two catastrophes that Ireland had been spared, earthquakes and an exchange rate. We got an exchange rate with sterling in March 1979. Five years later, on the morning of 19 July 1984, an earthquake measuring 5.4 on the Richter scale was recorded in Dublin!

Ireland has remained a member of the narrow band ERM from 1979 until the bands were widened to ±15 per cent in summer 1993. The UK did eventually join the ERM in October 1990 but left in September 1992.

Let us now review how Ireland fared as a participant in the narrow band ERM.

Inflation

The upper diagram in Figure 22.4 shows Irish, UK and German inflation (based on the consumer price index) in the years following the launch of the EMS. The initial experience was at variance with the predictions based on the PPP model. Instead of a rapid convergence of Irish inflation to German levels, the divergence between the two rates widened. In 1980 Irish inflation was 10.25 per cent higher than the German rate. Even more disappointing was the fact that a significant gap opened up between Irish and UK inflation in the early 1980s. Britain was having more success in curbing inflation outside the ERM than Ireland in it. After 1982 the Irish rate of inflation fell and the gap between Irish and German inflation gradually narrowed. However, it was not until the third quarter of 1990, more than ten years after joining the system, that Irish inflation finally fell to the German level. In terms of Figure 22.3 it is clear that adjustment followed path B and not path A.

Interest rates

The centre diagram in Figure 22.4 shows that the behaviour of nominal interest rates following our entry into the ERM was similar to that of inflation. Convergence of Irish interest rates to the German rates occurred only after 1988. In line with the discussion of uncovered interest rate parity (UIP) in Chapter 18, the relatively high Irish interest rates reflected the market's belief that the Irish pound was overvalued and would be devalued. However, more detailed analysis shows that in fact the differential between German and Irish interest rates more than compensated for the fall in the value of the Irish pound over time. A German buying Irish government bonds over the period 1979-92 would have enjoyed a higher rate of return *in German marks* than she would have obtained from putting her money in German bonds. Over the entire period 1979-92 she would have earned 40 per cent more in Irish than in German bonds. This over-compensation for the depreciation of the currency is known as *excess returns*.[6]

The real exchange rate

The lower diagram in Figure 22.4 shows the real exchange rate of the Irish pound against the DM and sterling since the launch of the EMS. Table 22.1 shows the real

6. See Patrick Honohan and Charles Conroy, *Irish Interest Rate Fluctuations in the European Monetary System*, Dublin: The Economic and Social Research Institute, 1994.

exchange rate against selected currencies in 1979 and 1986 (which was when the Irish pound real exchange rate peaked). It can be seen that there was a significant real appreciation of the Irish pound against all the ERM currencies, the most pronounced being the 58 per cent rise relative to the Belgian franc. Inflation was much higher in Ireland than in Germany over this period, and the DM/IR£ real exchange rate appreciated by almost 40 per cent despite the 30 per cent fall in the nominal exchange rate.

If the EMS policy had been a success, Irish inflation would have converged to the lower German rate and there would have been little or no appreciation of the real exchange rate. If strict PPP holds, the real exchange rate remains constant. But the evidence shows that it does not, in the short run at least.

The sterling/Irish pound real exchange rate fell between the start of the EMS and the middle of 1981. This was followed by a long period, from 1981 to mid-1986, when the real exchange rate rose significantly. After the devaluation of 1986 and the fall in Irish inflation relative to the UK, competitiveness with Britain improved markedly, as is shown by the fall in the real exchange rate. This helped the recovery in the economy in the second half of the 1980s.[7]

Table 22.1

Change in the Irish pound real exchange rate relative to selected currencies

	1979	1986
Belgium	100	158
Netherlands	100	147
Germany	100	140
Denmark	100	147
France	100	136
US	100	100
Japan	100	147
UK	100	113
Italy	100	109
Weighted average	100	119

Source: Derived using consumer prices obtained from the OECD, *Main Economic Indicators,* and nominal exchange rates obtained from the Central Bank of Ireland, *Quarterly Bulletin.*

Wages

It quickly became apparent that joining the ERM had little or no effect on workers' wage demands. Quite the opposite: the expansionary fiscal policy in 1978 fuelled workers' expectations and led to an increase in wage demands. As the Central Bank of

---

7. Evidence on the effect of the rise in the real exchange rate on the economy is given in A. Leddin, "An Analysis of the Irish Unemployment Problem in the Context of EMS Membership", University of Limerick, January 1991.

Ireland commented in April 1979:

> *"The industrial relations situation does not appear to have adjusted yet to the changed circumstances implicit in our adherence to the EMS. There have been several pay claims in excess of 20 per cent and some union leaders have suggested that 15 per cent would be an appropriate minimum. Such high settlements do not recommend themselves in a situation where price inflation seems likely to decelerate well into single figures fairly quickly."* [8]

Obviously the social partners did not share the Central Bank's view of the speed with which inflation would fall.

The yield curve

Further evidence of the failure of membership of the ERM to bestow low interest rates and inflation is provided by the behaviour of the *yield curve* over the period since 1979. Box 22.1 explains what is meant by the yield curve and why it indicates the future direction of both interest rates and inflation.

In Ireland, over the period 1979-88, the yield curve was, with the exception of three quarters, either flat or positively sloped. Thus the market expected interest rates either to remain unchanged or to rise. This indicates that investors did not believe that a sharp disinflation would follow from entry into the ERM. Only after 1988 did long rates fall below short rates. This was a clear indication that investors were at last revising their expectations of nominal interest rates (and inflation) downwards.

Capital flight

A further indicator of the public's confidence in the government's management of the economy is provided by the flow of private capital into or out of the country. Anticipation of higher inflation and a loss of confidence in the currency will lead to a movement of funds out of the country, i.e, *capital flight*. To minimise these flows the government imposed exchange controls on the movement of funds between Ireland and the UK following our entry into the EMS. (They already existed between Ireland and the rest of the world.) However, such measures are never watertight.

---

8. McCarthy, op. cit., p. 119.

Box 22.1

The yield curve

The yield on bonds of different maturities varies. Short-dated bonds, such as exchequer bills which are redeemable within three months, may not have the same yield as medium or long-dated securities that do not mature for five or ten years. If investors expect interest rates to rise, bonds with long maturities will tend to have higher yields than bonds with short maturities. A graph showing yields on the vertical axis and maturities (from short to long) on the horizontal axis is called the *yield curve*. The yield curve reflects the *term structure* of interest rates. If longer-dated securities have higher yields than short-dated ones, the yield curve will be positively sloped. This is the normal situation, because there is always some risk that the rate of inflation will rise over the longer run.

Consider, for example, the yields on a range of Irish government stock in 1997 and 1998.

Irish government securities' yields: % per annum

Maturity	Yield November 1997	Yield October 1998
6 month	8.33	10.95
1 year	8.81	10.30
5 years	8.68	9.63
10 years	7.97	9.20
20 years	7.62	8.73

In 1997 the yield curve had an inverted U shape: the yield on a one-year bond was higher than that on a six-month bond, but yields on higher maturities were lower. In 1998 yields were lower the longer the maturity, that is, the yield curve was inverted or negatively sloped at all maturities.

The slope of the yield curve provides information on the public's expectations about interest rates. Interest rates are, in turn, related to the inflation rate via the Fisher equation (see Chapter 10). If inflation is expected to rise then this will lead to higher interest rates and vice versa. Hence, if the EMS policy were credible, the expectation of lower interest and inflation rates should have led to a negatively sloped yield curve.

The residual in the balance of payments reflects unrecorded flows across the foreign exchanges and tends to be dominated by illicit private capital flows. This residual rose to nearly £1 billion (equivalent to 6 per cent of GNP) in 1986, probably largely due to capital flight as investors contravened the exchange controls and moved money out of Ireland. This reflected a loss of confidence in the currency and a lack of credibility in the government's commitment to holding its value in the ERM.

Following the devaluation of the Irish pound in the ERM in 1986, and as a determination to restore order to the public finances became evident, capital flight subsided. By the end of the decade there was a net unexplained *inflow* across the foreign exchange. As exchange controls were relaxed in the 1990s there was no rush to move money out of Ireland. This indicates the importance of the stance of fiscal policy, rather than membership of the EMS, in restoring confidence in the Irish economy among the financial community.

Summary The record shows that the switch of exchange rate regime from the sterling link to the ERM in 1979 did not immediately establish a credible hard currency peg for the Irish pound. Markets did not accept that we were really committed to hold a fixed exchange rate with the DM. Our willingness to use successive realignments to allow the value of the Irish pound to fall, and our decision to devalue in 1983 and again in 1986, undermined the credibility of our commitment to the hard currency peg. Our entry to the ERM had little impact on wage bargaining behaviour or on the conduct of fiscal policy. Markets were right to be sceptical. Only after the stance of fiscal policy altered in the mid-1980s, and wage moderation was established (partly by a soaring unemployment rate), did we begin to reap the benefits that had been promised when we joined the ERM in 1979. We discuss the factors that undermined our credibility in the ERM in more detail in the following section.

Note:

When we joined the ERM in 1979 the exchange rate between the Irish pound and the DM was IR£1=DM3.75. By the time we joined the EMU in 1999 it had fallen to IR£1=DM2.48.

22.5 Why Ireland did not Initially Benefit from the ERM

Several factors contributed to the disparity between the expected benefits of membership of the EMS and the outcome during the first half of the 1980s.

Fiscal and monetary policy The failure of participation in the ERM to deliver the hoped-for benefits in terms of reduced inflation and interest rates until the second half of the 1980s was due above all to the inconsistency between the fiscal and monetary policies pursued in Ireland during the years 1979-82 and the declared intention of pegging the currency to the DM.

In particular, the level of borrowing and the growth of debt during this period were incompatible with the goal of maintaining a fixed exchange rate with the low inflation countries of Europe. Debt and debt service continued to rise relative to GNP until 1986, when there was concern that Ireland's international credit rating was deteriorating. If Ireland could not continue to borrow abroad, or could only do so at penal interest rates, the external reserves would have been rapidly depleted and maintaining the exchange rate within the ERM would have become impossible. These uncertainties undermined any credibility the government might have otherwise gained by participation in the EMS.

Exchange rate policy in the EMS During the early years of the EMS there were frequent currency realignments, usually involving a revaluation of the DM and a devaluation of the French franc and other weak currencies. Irish policy during these years was to "go through the middle" at realignments. But while our nominal exchange rate remained very stable against the average of the narrow-band EMS currencies until 1983, there was a significant fall in the value of the Irish pound relative to the DM, which was the strongest currency in the group. Furthermore, the Irish pound was subsequently devalued on three occasions, in 1983, 1986 and 1993. As we show below, these devaluations illustrated the continued importance of the sterling exchange rate to Ireland, despite our participation in the ERM. Thus we had not a complete switch from a sterling to a DM peg and hence could not expect to enjoy the benefits predicted on doing so.

Assessment

The evidence does not support the view that EMS entry conferred a credibility bonus on Irish economic policy in the period up to 1986. Ireland's inflation rate did not converge rapidly to the German inflation rate. The Irish pound/EMS real exchange rate rose and remained above its 1979 level. The yield curve continued to suggest that inflation would accelerate. There was evidence of large-scale capital flight. Only after a very large rise in unemployment did inflationary pressures moderate. None of these developments was consistent with the existence of a credibility bonus as a consequence of having joined the ERM.

Dornbusch summed up the situation neatly as follows:

> *"A policy that uses a fixed exchange rate to disinflate and at the same time requires fiscal consolidation can easily run into difficulties. The fixed exchange rate policy stands in the way of a gain in competitiveness and in fact easily becomes a policy of overvaluation. The overvalued currency then needs to be defended by high real*

504

interest rates. The combination of budget cutting, high real interest rates and an overly strong currency creates unemployment on each score. There is no offsetting crowding-in mechanism unless money wages are strongly flexible downwards or productivity growth is high. Neither was the case in Ireland and hence the country is locked into a high unemployment and high debt trap."[9]

It is worth bearing in mind that outside the ERM, Ireland might have experienced much greater difficulty in curbing inflation. By breaking the link with sterling in 1979 we avoided the massive rise in the real exchange rate that would have occurred if we had retained this link. The rise in our real exchange rate after 1979 was much more modest than it would have been had the sterling link been maintained. It seems clear, however, that the PPP model, which was the one underpinning our decision to participate in the ERM, may not have been appropriate for short-run policy analysis in Ireland. But even with the benefit of hindsight, it is not clear that a better option was open to us in 1979 than joining the ERM.

22.6 Belated Benefits of ERM: 1986-92

As explained in Chapter 2, there was a major improvement in the performance of the Irish economy after 1987. This was in part due to the effect of significant government spending cuts leading to increased confidence and an expansion in private spending – the so called expansionary fiscal contraction.[10] However, this explanation tends to ignore the contribution of other factors to the change in performance during these years. The main source of higher growth in 1987 and 1988 was the increase in net exports. Faster growth in world trade was the main reason for the growth of Irish exports, but the fall in the real exchange rate should also be taken into account. Between 1979 and 1986 the real trade-weighted exchange rate index appreciated by 18.9 per cent. In contrast, between 1986 and 1989 it depreciated by 9.9 per cent. This was due to the devaluation of the Irish pound in August 1986 and the convergence of the Irish inflation rate with the German rate. The competitive gain that followed the devaluation allowed Ireland to capitalise on the recovery in the world economy.

---

9. Rudiger Dornbusch, "Credibility, Debt and Unemployment: Ireland's Failed Stabilization", *Economic Policy*, April 1989, pp 174-209.

10. See Giuseppe Bertola and Allan Drazen, "Trigger Points and Budget Cuts: Explaining the Effects of Fiscal Austerity", *The American Economic Review*, March 1993, pp 11-26.

Another influence on the real growth rate was the real interest rate. Between 1981 and 1986 the real interest rate rose from − 8.3 per cent to +10.0 per cent, but between 1986 and 1989 it declined by 5.4 per cent. This coincided with a modest recovery in investment.

It is widely believed that the stabilisation of the exchange rate in the ERM after 1986 contributed to the fall in interest rates. A study of the behaviour of Irish interest rates over the period 1986-92 showed that while there was a tendency for the Irish-German differential to narrow following the stabilisation of the Irish pound/DM exchange rate after 1987, this was conditional on the level of the Irish pound relative to sterling.[11] This consideration was to have enormous consequences during the currency crisis of 1992-93 to which we now turn.

22.7 The Irish Pound and the Crisis of 1992-93

The most dramatic episode in recent Irish economic history centred on the turmoil in the world currency markets that started in September 1992.[12] Potentially important lessons for how Ireland will fare in the EMU may be learned from this episode.

Exchange rate policy in the UK   Between 1986 to 1989 the Chancellor of the Exchequer, Nigel Lawson, adopted the policy of sterling "shadowing" the DM. Sterling was pegged unofficially in the range STG£1 = DM2.94 to DM3.00.[13] This exchange rate eventually proved unsustainable due to the excessive monetary expansion that Mr Lawson permitted, and by December 1989 sterling had fallen to DM2.80. This depreciation led to pressure for sterling to formally join the ERM. Mrs Thatcher remained entrenched in her view, and stated at the Madrid Summit in June 1989, that sterling would participate "only when the time is right". In this she was supported by her unofficial economic adviser, Professor Alan Walters. Disagreement on this issue eventually led to Lawson's resignation in October 1989. But Mrs Thatcher finally

---

11. Brendan Walsh, "Credibility, Interest Rates and the ERM: The Irish Experience", *Oxford Bulletin of Economics and Statistics*, November 1993, pp 439-52.

12. For further material on the currency crisis, see Brendan Walsh, "Irish Exchange Rate Policy in the Aftermath of the Currency Crisis", *The Irish Banking Review*, Autumn 1993, pp 3-12.

13. According to Mrs Thatcher's autobiography, this policy was pursued unknown to her. Apparently it was not until Treasury officials highlighted the stability of the sterling/DM exchange rate that she confronted Lawson about this policy.

brought sterling into the ERM, albeit only into the wide (± 6 per cent) band on 8 October 1990. She argued that this would add credibility to the fight against inflation and she urged unions to accept modest wage increases in order to maintain UK price competitiveness. (This proved to be one of her last important decisions as Prime Minister. She resigned on 22 November 1990.)

Between 1990 and 1992 the British experience in the ERM was favourable. Inflation fell from 10.8 per cent in October 1990 to 4.3 per cent in August 1992, and short-term interest rates fell from 15 per cent to 10.2 per cent. It seemed that Britain had got the preconditions for participation in the ERM right and the anticipated benefits materialised quickly.

In Chapter 17 we explained how German unification led to higher German interest rates. This increase in interest rates was transmitted to other European countries at the beginning of the 1990s. The conflict between the tight German monetary policy and the needs of the rest of Europe caused tension in the ERM. Moreover, speculators noticed that Britain appeared to have entered the ERM at too high an exchange rate. In late summer 1992 the conviction grew that the sterling/DM central rate was unsustainable. Massive amounts of sterling were dumped on the foreign exchanges. Despite large-scale, but short-lived, intervention by the Bank of England, the speculators won and sterling's membership of the ERM was suspended on 16 September. Sterling depreciated by 15 per cent and interest rates in London fell from 15 per cent to 8 per cent. These developments had a profound effect on Irish money markets. With the UK outside the ERM, the Irish situation in the EMS was once again anomalous. But now the problem was compounded by the sudden massive depreciation of sterling that left the Irish pound overvalued.

The currency crisis

From the decision to join in 1979, the exchange rate against sterling had been the Achilles heel of Ireland's commitment to the ERM. For example, in March 1983 the weakness of sterling prompted a 3 per cent devaluation of the Irish pound. The same set of circumstances recurred in August 1986, when the Irish pound rose from STG£0.79 in February 1985 to STG£0.95 in July 1986. An 8 per cent devaluation of the Irish pound – the largest of any currency in the ERM up to then – restored competitiveness. This devaluation was reluctantly undertaken by the Irish authorities as

507

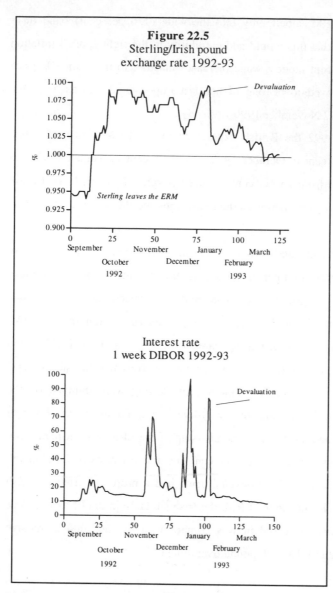

Figure 22.5
Sterling/Irish pound
exchange rate 1992-93

Devaluation

Sterling leaves the ERM

September October November December January February March
1992 1993

Interest rate
1 week DIBOR 1992-93

Devaluation

September October November December January February March
1992 1993

a means of reconciling our participation in the ERM with the non-participation of our main trading partner, Britain.

Following the 1983 and 1986 devaluations, foreign exchange markets formed the view that the Irish pound was likely to be devalued when sterling was weak. When sterling devalued in September 1992, funds flowed out of Ireland in anticipation of a devaluation of the Irish pound. The upper diagram in Figure 22.5 shows that the Irish pound rose from Stg£0.94 to well over parity. (It hit Stg£1.105 on 6 October 1992 – the highest rate ever recorded.) Despite this severe *misalignment*, the government decided on this occasion to try to resist a devaluation.

It is estimated that well over a billion pounds flowed out of Irish financial markets in a few days in September 1992. The Central Bank's external reserves fell from £3.05 billion at the end of August to £1.07 billion at the end of September, despite additional foreign borrowing. Short-term interest rates were raised to unprecedented heights to defend the currency from speculative attacks. The lower diagram in Figure 22.5 shows that inter-bank interest rates peaked at 97 per cent on 11 January 1993. Mortgage and bank commercial interest rates were increased by 3 per cent. Central

Bank lending to the money market increased from £74 million at the end of August to £1.8 billion at the end of September. Without this support, interest rates would have been much higher. The Central Bank was also required to enforce exchange controls to prevent further speculation. Overnight interest rates on the Euro-Irish pound market rose to 1,000 per cent. The combination of an overvalued currency and penal interest rates was seriously damaging the Irish economy.

In a statement issued in January 1993, on the weekend before the devaluation, the government argued that a devaluation would be inappropriate on the grounds that:

- The currency was not overvalued. As evidence of this they pointed to the surplus on the trade account of the balance of payments.

- Speculators could not be allowed to destroy the ERM which was regarded as the stepping stone to EMU.

- It was the government's desire to break our dependence on the UK and become a hard core EMS country.

- Devaluation was ineffective as it resulted in only a short-term competitive gain. It was argued that the increase in import prices brought about by a devaluation would feed into the economy and push up domestic costs and prices. If these increases were equivalent to the devaluation, then the competitive gain from the devaluation would be short term and quickly erode. In terms of the real exchange rate, the fall in the nominal exchange rate (e) would be offset by an increase in P_{irl} and the real exchange rate would return to its previous level.

- The foreign debt of £12 billion would increase as a result of the devaluation. Because the debt is denominated in foreign currencies, a 10 per cent devaluation would add £1.2 billion to its Irish pound value. This would increase the debt/GNP ratio and move us away from the Maastricht criteria for participation in EMU.[14]

To compensate for the loss of competitiveness caused by the sharp appreciation relative to sterling after September 1992, a "Market Development Fund" was launched which paid £50 per job per week to firms affected by the devaluation of sterling.

The government received support for its policy from many quarters. The Irish

---

14. This argument ignored the fact that the value of the external debt *denominated in foreign exchange* is unaffected by the exchange rate of the Irish pound. Furthermore, a devaluation raises the capacity of the economy to earn foreign exchange by increasing its net exports, which is the source from which the external debt has to be serviced. On this point, see Patrick Honohan, "Costing the Delay in Devaluing, 1992-93", *The Irish Banking Review*, Spring 1994, pp 3-15.

Congress of Trade Unions, for example, presented the Minister for Finance with a list of names of banks and stockbrokers believed to be engaging in speculation, and referred to their actions as sabotage and unpatriotic. Bishops joined in the denunciation of the speculators. Editorial writers warmed to the theme:

"It is the duty of a sovereign government to defend its currency as it would its national territory. It is the final determinant of a nation's wealth. It represents the accumulated value of its industry, its productiveness, its labour. It is a statement of a country's worth, its reliability, its intrinsic economic soundness . . . The long-term consequences of devaluation would be little short of catastrophic for the economy. Ireland would be consigned to the outer ring of monetary union, its currency most likely linked to the anaemic pound sterling. High inflation would be introduced once again. And none of this would guarantee even the short-term palliative of lower interest rates." (*The Irish Times*, 9 January 1993)

During the last weekend of January 1993, following a renewed weakness of sterling, the authorities realised the game was up, and requested permission from the finance ministers of the other European Union countries to devalue. (This was done by telephone – from a European perspective the event was not significant enough to warrant a meeting!) This permission was granted and the pound was devalued by 10 per cent on 30 January. This was the largest unilateral devaluation ever of a currency in the ERM.

In the aftermath of the devaluation, Irish politicians blamed our European partners, and the German authorities in particular, for their half-hearted support for the Irish pound during the crisis. Clearly, the Bundesbank could have intervened on a scale that would have beaten off the speculators, but they did not regard the level of the Irish pound in the ERM as sustainable in view of the depreciation of sterling.

As can be seen from Figure 22.5, in the months after the devaluation the decline in Irish interest rates was dramatic. The fear that we would suffer a long-lasting penalty in the form of a risk premium due to the possibility of further devaluations proved unfounded. The size of the devaluation was sufficient to restore our competitive position *vis-à-vis* the UK and convince the markets that the Irish pound might appreciate in the medium term. Money flowed back into the country and confidence in the economy was restored.[15] There was no resurgence in inflation, and for several years

---

15. For a detailed study of how the devaluation affected expectations, see Leonardo Bartolini, "Devaluation

510

after the event we enjoyed a competitive gain.

22.8 Was there an Alternative to Devaluation?

There *was* an alternative to devaluation. To understand what it entailed, consider Figure 22.6 which shows the familiar AS/AD diagram. Suppose the economy is initially at a point such as A with a price level of P_1 and an output level of GNP_1. The effect of an appreciation against sterling is to move the economy to a point such as B. This is because the loss of competitiveness reduces Irish exports and increases imports, thereby shifting the AD curve down to the left.

At the point B real wages have increased because inflation has fallen while the nominal wage has remained unchanged. If trade unions were to accept a *cut* in the nominal wage so as to restore the original real wage, this would be reflected in the diagram as a shift of the AS curve down to the right (not shown) and equilibrium would be established at the point C. At the point C real output is restored and inflation has fallen. Workers are not any worse off because there has been no fall in real wages. It follows, therefore, that the distance between points B and C measures the output gap brought about by the increase in real wages. The smaller the rise in real wages, the smaller will be the output gap.

A cut in nominal wages has several advantages over the devaluation option.

- First, the original level of output and employment is restored at a lower level of inflation. The fall in inflation should equal the sterling devaluation and the competitive position of the Irish economy is restored.

- Second, and most important, the adverse effects of devaluation on the foreign debt is avoided.

- Third, the social partners would be seen to have responded to the sterling devaluation in a positive and effective way without resorting to an EMS realignment, and this would help restore confidence in the Irish economy. Capital

---

and Competitiveness in a Small Open Economy: Ireland 1987-1993", International Monetary Fund, Research Department, WP/93/82, Washington, D.C., November 1993. Bortolini concludes that the devaluation exceeded investors' expectations and the loss of competitiveness since the pre-crisis period. "This 'excess' devaluation, coupled with the following appreciation of sterling . . . seems to largely explain the prompt market acceptance of the new band." The semi-official interpretation of why the devaluation was so successful is that markets were impressed by the determination of the authorities to hold out for as long as they did – an interpretation without support in theory or evidence!

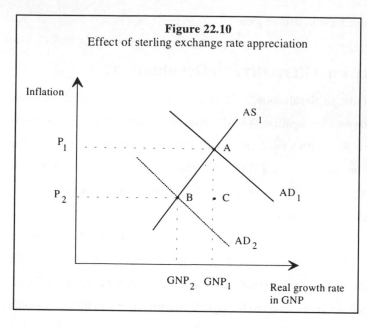

Figure 22.10
Effect of sterling exchange rate appreciation

would be expected to flow into the economy and interest rates to decline.

One of the obstacles to this policy response was that the *Programme for Economic and Social Progress* (PESP) was in place in 1992. The trade unions, who supported the strong exchange rate policy, none the less indicated that they would not renegotiate this agreement. The refusal of the trade unions to renegotiate PESP, even though inflation was falling due to the sudden appreciation of the currency, showed a lack of realism – if nothing worse – at a time when major job losses were threatened.

22.9 Lessons from the Sterling Crisis

The sterling crisis illustrates how damaging the combination of a fixed exchange rate and rigid wages can be for an economy. If the exchange rate is fixed, nominal wages must be flexible so as to accommodate external shocks. A rise in the exchange rate has to be accommodated by a fall in nominal wages. National wage agreements, such as *Partnership 2000*, are not consistent with this requirement.

The experience of 1992-93 shows that the PPP theory was a bad guide to the short-run behaviour of the economy. If PPP had held in the short run, Irish costs and wages would have fallen as our exchange rate rose in the second half of 1992. As we have seen this did not happen. While the required adjustment might have occurred in the "long run", by then large segments of Irish industry would have been shut down and unemployment would have soared. A rigid application of PPP theory also lay behind the dire predictions that if we devalued in 1992 the result would be no more than a wave of inflation that would rapidly erode the competitive gain. In fact, in the wake of the move to a *de facto* floating exchange rate in mid-1993 our understanding of the causes of Irish inflation has lessened. Inflation remained low throughout the 1990s despite the fall in the value of the currency. The evidence from the aftermath of the 1986 and 1992 devaluations of the Irish pound shows that it is possible to use the exchange rate to restore a loss in competitiveness. By joining EMU we have renounced this instrument of economic policy.

Ireland's experience in the ERM raises questions about how we shall fare as a member of the EMU. We have seen the dangers of pegging our currency to a group of currencies that does not include our most important trading partner, Britain. In 1983, 1986 and 1993 sterling weakness triggered speculative attacks on the Irish pound. The market perceived that the rise in the Irish pound relative to sterling was unsustainable. This remained the case after the return to *de facto* floating in 1993.

Inflation rates are now much more uniform across Europe than in 1987, when the previous attempt to stabilise our exchange rate relative to the DM was launched. However, the Irish economy is still not immune from the pressures that would arise if we had a fixed exchange rate against the main continental currencies and sterling were suddenly to depreciate. Thus, the fundamental dilemma posed by the reluctance of sterling to join the proposed EMU and our eagerness to do so remains.

22.10 Irish Exchange Rate Policy After the 1992-93 Crisis

Germany's continued insistence that domestic policy considerations (such as maintaining price stability in the face of the fiscal expansion that followed German unification) took precedence over European considerations resulted in further turmoil on the foreign exchanges in the summer of 1993. This time the speculators targeted the French franc, the Danish krona and the Belgian franc. After large-scale intervention by European central banks it was finally decided to widen the ERM bands from ± 2.25 per cent to ± 15 per cent for currencies except the German mark and Dutch guilder. This effectively meant that EU currencies were floating and that the ERM had ceased to exist in all but name.

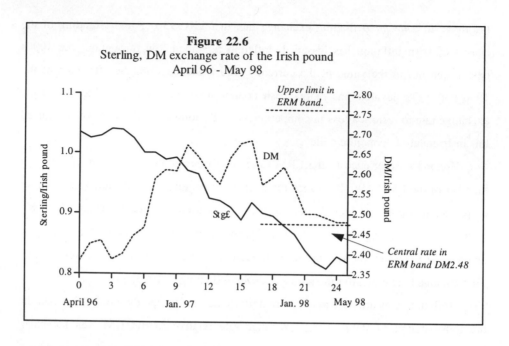

Figure 22.6
Sterling, DM exchange rate of the Irish pound
April 96 - May 98

Note:

It is important to note, however, that there was no change in the exchange rate between the French franc and the German mark throughout this period. In fact, although the franc came under heavy selling pressure on several occasions during the 1992-93 crisis the central rate remained DM1 = FF 3.35, the level that was adopted at the beginning of 1987. The market rate between these currencies at times dipped below the intervention level but by and large remained within the ± 2.25 per cent fluctuation margin. Thus for over ten years the two key currencies in the ERM have been kept within a target zone. This is the most significant development in the recent monetary history of Europe.

Following the turbulence of mid-1993 markets stabilised, but there was renewed instability early in 1995, with the Italian lira coming under attack and undergoing a 6 per cent devaluation in the ERM. During 1997 the dollar and sterling rose significantly on the foreign exchanges relative to the DM as money flowed in from the crisis-ridden economies in Asia. Thus, the launch of EMU has been preceded by further turbulence on foreign exchange markets.

It is instructive to consider how Irish exchange rate policy was conducted after 1993. Bear in mind that the pillar on which policy had been based since 1979 – the narrow band ERM – had collapsed. For the first time ever, the Irish currency was in effect floating, without a meaningful peg to another currency or basket of currencies. What was remarkable about the period 1993-1998 was how successfully the economy performed in the new environment. As we have documented in Chapters 1 and 2, this was the period when the "Celtic tiger" economy emerged. Inflation remained extraordinarily low, the real growth rate soared and unemployment fell steadily. Fears that we would suffer from the devaluation of 1993 or from the difficulty of coping with a floating exchange rate proved groundless. What accounts for the success of Irish exchange rate policy over these years?

After the widening of the ERM bands in mid-1993, the Central Bank of Ireland appeared to follow a policy of trying to stabilise the *effective* exchange rate index (see Chapter 15), that is, a weighted average of the value of the Irish pound relative to its main trading partners. In practice this involved playing off the strength of sterling against the weakness of the German mark. The Central Bank, in effect, attempted to find a middle ground by allowing the Irish pound to rise against the DM and simultaneously fall against sterling.

Figure 22.6 shows the trend in the DM and sterling exchange rates from April 1996 to May 1998 (when the exchange rates of currencies participating in the single currency area were locked). It can be seen that up to August 1997, the Irish pound drifted down against sterling and strengthened against the DM. The effective exchange rate was quite stable over this period. However, after August 1997, the DM exchange rate was allowed to drift down towards the ERM central rate of DM2.41. While this depreciation conferred a competitive advantage on the Irish economy ahead of entry to EMU, it gave rise to the fear that inflation would accelerate. This fear led to a 3 per cent revaluation of the Irish pound's central rate to DM2.48 in March 1998. This was the last adjustment of the Irish pound's value in the ERM. With the launch of EMU in 1999, the trade-off between the strength of sterling and the weakness of the DM, so successfully pursued by the Central Bank in the run-up to EMU entry, will no longer be an option.

22.11 Conclusion

In this chapter we have examined the Irish experience in the EMS in the light of our earlier discussion of macroeconomic policy in an open economy. The topics discussed included:

- Inflation and the exchange rate prior to EMS entry
- The anticipated benefits from EMS entry
- The concept of a credibility bonus

- Evidence from inflation differentials, the real exchange rate and the yield curve on the credibility of the EMS policy
- The reasons why Ireland's commitment to the ERM lacked credibility until 1987
- The currency crisis of 1992-93 and the government response
- Irish exchange policy after the 1992-93 crisis.

Chapter 23

The European Central Bank and Economic Policy in EMU

23.1 Introduction

Agreement was reached at the European summit meeting in Brussels in May 1998 that eleven countries will move to the final stage (Stage III) of the European EMU[1] on 1 January 1999. The countries that will join EMU in the first wave are Austria, Belgium, France, Finland, Germany, Ireland, Italy, Luxembourg, the Netherlands, Spain and Portugal. The United Kingdom, Sweden and Denmark have opted to remain outside EMU for the time being. Greece was not deemed eligible, although it hopes to join in three years' time.

The launch of Stage III of EMU marks a new departure of untold importance in European economic policy. The countries that are joining EMU – which we shall refer to collectively as "the Euro-zone" – will surrender their powers to make independent monetary policies to the new European Central Bank (ECB). Situated on Kaiserstrasse in Frankfurt some three miles away from the Bundesbank (the German Central Bank), the ECB will formulate policy in the interest of the Euro-zone as a whole. National currencies will be replaced by the euro.

This unprecedented experiment in supranational economic policy co-ordination is the subject of the present chapter. First we outline the design of the ECB. We discuss the goal of price stability, which will be its primary objective. We then discuss how monetary, fiscal and exchange rate policies will operate in the Euro-zone. In an Appendix we explore some technicalities as to how the ECB will influence conditions in money markets.

---

1. In the rest of the chapter we follow the usual convention and use EMU to refer to the European Economic and Monetary Union.

Table 23.1

Executive board of ECB

Wim Duisenberg (62), President	Dutch	Economist, IMF governor, former president of the EMI.
Christian Noyer (47), Vice-president	French	Civil servant in French finance ministry.
Otmar Issing (62)	German	Chief economist at Bundesbank.
Sirkka Hamalainen (58)	Finnish	Governor of Finnish Central Bank.
Eugenio Domingo Solans (52)	Spanish	Academic economist and member of council of Spanish Central Bank.
Tommaso Padoa Schioppa (57)	Italian	Economist, Italian Central Bank and former member of Delors committee.

23.2 The Design of the ECB

The Maastricht Treaty provided for the establishment of the European Monetary Institute (EMI). This was founded in January 1994 as a precursor ("John the Baptist") of a fully fledged European Central Bank. The national central banks of the EU contributed ECU 615 million to the EMI and the income from this is used to finance its running costs. In 1997, the EMI had 295 staff members mostly recruited from the EU central banks. In July 1998, the EMI was replaced by the ECB. It will remain relatively small, however, relying on national central banks to perform such functions as bank supervision, etc.

Note:

The Treaty on European Union was agreed in December 1991 and signed on 7 February 1992 in Maastricht. It entered into force on 1 November 1993. This Treaty is normally referred to as the Maastricht Treaty and it contains the statutes establishing the European Monetary Institute and the European System of Central Banks. The euro will become "a currency in its own right" in January 1999. Until they are phased out in the year 2002 national currencies (the Irish pound, French franc, German mark and so on) will technically be units of the euro based on the "conversion rates" announced in May 1998. The conversion rates at which the Irish pound will be locked to the euro are: Belgian franc 51.22, German mark 2.483, Spanish peseta 211.3, French franc 8.329, Italian lira 2,459, Dutch guilder 2.798, Portuguese escudo 254.6, Austrian schilling 17.47, Finnish markka 7.550. (The Irish pound will be the only national currency to be worth more than one euro.) The task of issuing euro notes and coins, of overseeing the conversion from national units of account into their euro equivalents, will be the responsibility of the ECB, working together with national central banks.

The new *European System of Central Banks* (ESCB) will consist of the *European Central Bank* (ECB) and the national central banks of the Euro-zone countries (Box

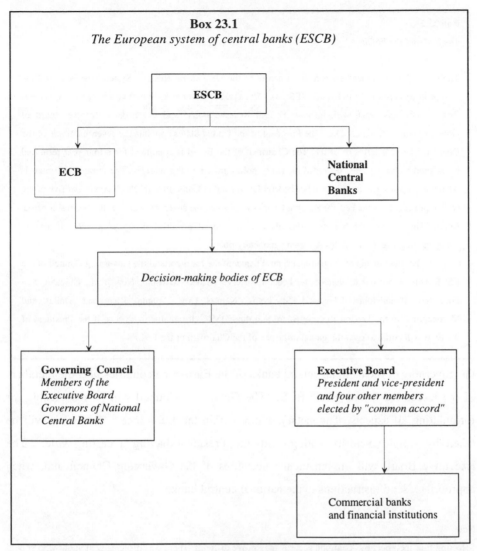

Box 23.1
The European system of central banks (ESCB)

ESCB

ECB

National
Central
Banks

Decision-making bodies of ECB

Governing Council
*Members of the
Executive Board
Governors of National
Central Banks*

Executive Board
*President and vice-president
and four other members
elected by "common accord"*

Commercial banks
and financial institutions

23.1). The ECB will be managed by an *Executive Board,* comprising the President and Vice-president of the ECB and four other members, appointed by "common accord" by the heads of the Euro-zone states for an eight year non-renewable term. Table 23.1 gives a brief profile of the people who were appointed to the executive board at the summit meeting in Brussels in May 1998. Note that Jean Claude Trichet (55), the Governor of the French Central Bank, is the president-elect and is not on the board because re-appointment is not permitted under the ECB's statutes.

The Executive Board will be responsible for the day-to-day implementation of monetary policy and giving instructions to the national central banks. The most important decision-making body of the ECB will be the *Governing Council,* comprising

There are close parallels between the structure of the US Federal Reserve System (the Fed) and the European System of Central Banks (ESCB). The Federal Reserve System consists of twelve Federal Reserve Districts (each with its own Federal Reserve Bank) and the Federal Reserve Board of Governors in Washington, D.C. The President of the United States appoints the seven members of the Board for 14 year terms of office. The Chairman of the Board is appointed for a four year term and considered to be the most powerful monetary policy maker in the world. (The current chairman is Alan Greenspan.) The twelve-member Federal Open Market Committee (FOMC) comprises five of the twelve presidents of the Federal Reserve District Banks and the seven members of the Federal Reserve Board. This Committee has been described as the "most powerful group of private citizens in America" because it formulates America's monetary policy.

The relationship of the national central banks of the Euro-zone to the Governing Council of the ESCB will be similar to that of the Federal Reserve Districts (Boston, New York, Chicago, San Francisco, Philadelphia, Cleveland, St. Louis, Kansas City, Atlanta, Richmond, Dallas and Minneapolis) to the Federal Reserve Board and the FOMC. It remains to be seen if the President of the ECB will come to rival the global influence of the Chairman of the Fed.

the governors of the national central banks of the Euro-zone countries *plus* the members of the Executive Board of the ECB. The Governing Council will be responsible for formulating all aspects of monetary policy within the Euro-zone. Decisions will be taken by simple majority voting, with the President having a casting vote. The Executive Board will implement the decisions of the Governing Council and, when appropriate, send instructions to the national central banks.

Note:

Selecting four members by "common accord" may prove difficult. There was disagreement about who should be the president of the ECB. The Germans favoured the Dutch former finance minister, Willem Duisenberg, (who was the President of the EMI in 1997/98) but the French put forward their own central banker Jean Claude Trichet. Over an eleven hour lunch at the Brussels summit in May 1998, a compromise deal was reached. Mr Willem Duisenberg was appointed president but only after he announced that he would not serve his full eight year term. However, he insisted that when he goes will depend on himself. He will be replaced by the French Central Bank Governor Jean Claude Trichet.

The Maastricht Treaty lays down the responsibilities of the ECB as follows:

- Its primary responsibility is *to maintain price stability*.

- Without prejudice to price stability, it will also support "the general economic policies in the Community" so as to contribute to realising the Community's objectives, which include "sustainable and non-inflationary growth, a high degree of convergence of economic performance, a high level of employment and social protection, the raising of the standard of living and quality of life, and economic and social cohesion."

- It will be independent of national central banks, national governments, and all other bodies in formulating policy: "Neither the ECB, nor a national central bank, nor any member of their decision-making bodies shall seek or take advice from Community institutions or bodies, from any Government of a Member State or from any other body."

- It may not lend to any Community institution or government.

- It is likely that the ECB will be concerned with one overriding objective, price stability. The commitment to promoting the general economic policies of the Community is too vague to be of much significance.

23.3 Establishing the ECB's Anti-inflation Reputation

The ECB is a new institution, managing a new currency. It will have to establish a reputation for being hard nosed and committed to fighting inflation. The Maastricht Treaty contains several provisions that make the ECB extremely independent from political interference. In fact, its independence will be even greater than that of the Bundesbank and the Fed. The Bundesbank is ultimately subject to the German parliament and the Fed to the US Congress, but the ECB cannot be interfered with by national parliaments or by the European Parliament. It would require a revision of the Maastricht Treaty to alter the powers of the ECB and this would have to be ratified by referendum in all the EU member states.

Central bank independence from political pressure is seen as essential for the attainment of low inflation. Figure 23.1 shows the relationship between central bank independence and inflation for a sample of countries. A clear inverse relationship is evident indicating that the greater the independence of the central bank, the lower the inflation rate. The Bundesbank and the Swiss Central Bank are reckoned to be very independent of political influences and to have delivered low inflation, whereas the Bank of England, for example, in the past had little independence and as a result Britain

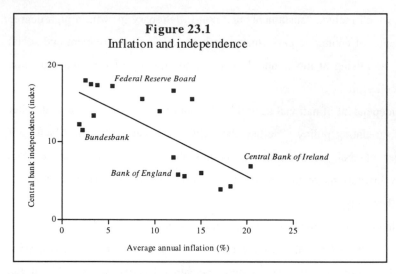

Figure 23.1
Inflation and independence

Central bank independence (index)

Federal Reserve Board

Bundesbank

Central Bank of Ireland

Bank of England

Average annual inflation (%)

suffered a relatively high inflation rate.[2] However, in 1997 the new Labour government in Britain increased the independence of the Bank of England.

Inflation bias and time inconsistency

The rationale for central bank independence may be seen by considering the problems of *inflation bias* and *time inconsistency*. To understand these problems we need to recall the Phillips curve analysis outlined in Chapter 13. We saw there that monetary policy has no long-run effect on the real economy. A monetary expansion will increase the price level but will have no effect on real variables such as the growth rate and the rate of unemployment. In the short run, however, a surprise expansionary monetary policy could be used to boost output and employment at the expense of higher inflation. (If the monetary expansion is anticipated, it will not affect output even in the short run.)

Figure 23.2 illustrates this point. An expansionary monetary policy moves the economy along the short-run Phillips curve (SRPC) from point A to B. Unemployment falls, output rises, and inflation increases. However, the reduction in unemployment is only temporary. As soon as inflation expectations adjust to the higher level of actual inflation, the SRPC shifts up. In the long run the economy returns to C. The situation depicted by C compares unfavourably with that in the initial point, A. Inflation has risen from zero to 12 per cent and unemployment is back to the natural rate.

The problem is that politicians may try to get re-elected by exploiting the movement along the SRPC. They may try to curry favour with voters by pushing unemployment below the natural rate even if this means a hike in inflation. If policy

---

2. For a discussion of this issue, see Paul De Grauwe, *The Economics of Monetary Integration,* Third Edition, 1997, Oxford University Press, Chapter 8.

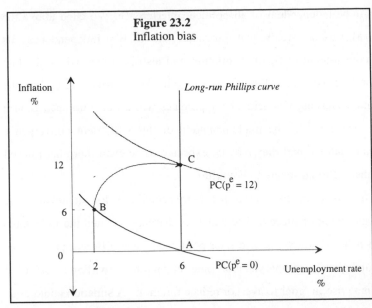

Figure 23.2
Inflation bias

Politicians tend to be inconsistent over time in their commitment to curbing inflation. On assuming office it makes sense for them to declare that they are committed to price stability, but when the next election is in the offing it is no longer optimal to adhere to this commitment. This is the problem of *time inconsistency*.[3]

makers are subservient to politicians they will be obliged to engineer the desired surprise inflation. This tendency to end up with a positive rate of inflation, instead of price stability, is referred to as *inflation bias*.

Ensuring the ECB's independence

The existence of inflation bias and the time inconsistency problem is a reason for *institutionalising* central bank independence. Most of the countries joining EMU believe that handing control of monetary policy to the ECB will increase their anti-inflation commitment. This is part of the rationale for abandoning independent national monetary policies and adopting the single currency. (In the case of Germany, however, this rationale does not apply because initially at least the ECB will not enjoy anti-inflation credentials as strong as the Bundesbank's.)[4] For this hope to be realised, the

---

3. Parents face the same dilemma when trying to motivate a child to study while in college. They may warn their son or daughter "if you don't do well in your mid-terms, we'll take you out of college" but when the student reports a bad mark in the mid-term it is no longer the best strategy for the parents to withdraw the student. "One last chance to improve" seems more humane. But wily children anticipate this and consequently their parents' original threats lack conviction.

4. This explains why the EMU project is not popular with the German public. It also raises the question why German politicians are so committed to EMU. One explanation is that it will allow Germany to shed the

ECB must be seen to be independent of all political interference. We cited above the provisions of the Maastricht Treaty that guarantee the ECB's independence. Its independence and commitment to fighting inflation will also be enhanced by the fact that *hard-nosed* men (and women) will be appointed to its decision-making bodies, the Executive Board and Governing Council. The appointees will all be European central bankers who have presided over the implementation of the Maastricht convergence criteria in their own countries[5] and they may be expected to be even more hard nosed when moved from their national sphere to Frankfurt.

However, while independence is a necessary condition for achieving low inflation it is not a guarantee of success. The countries that have created the ECB have different social and political structures, and their politicians have different preferences concerning price stability and unemployment. Some may not be as willing as others to allow unemployment to rise in order to avert or reduce inflation. A situation could arise in which the Governing Council wished to prevent a rise in inflation after an adverse supply-side shock. The resultant increase in unemployment would be extremely unpopular and would be blamed on the ECB. Politicians in member states may find a faceless international bank in Frankfurt a suitable target for their rhetoric when the economic going gets tough. It remains to be seen if the independence of the ECB would survive this sort of crisis.

The Maastricht convergence criteria offer no long-run guarantee that low inflation will be maintained. Because eleven member states managed to get inflation down to a low level in 1997 does not mean that the austerity that produced this result will be maintained indefinitely. It is for this reason that the Germans have insisted on the ratification of the Stability Pact, designed to prevent a return to loose fiscal policies once EMU is launched. (We discuss the details below.) Furthermore, we have noted that the Maastricht Treaty precludes the ECB and national central banks from financing government deficits.

---

burden of being the economy that sets European monetary policy. Other, political, motivations have also been suggested.

5. But there was an element of fudge in the application of the Maastricht criteria to many of the countries that will join EMU in 1999 and the central bankers acquiesced in this.

Accountability

The ECB will have enormous powers but it will not be directly accountable to elected politicians or the public. Under the Maastricht Treaty the ECB is required to present an Annual Report on its activities to the European Parliament, the Council of Ministers, and the Commission. The Parliament may decide to hold a debate on this Report, but it has no powers to sanction the members of the ECB's Governing Council. These limits on the accountability of the ECB could add to the feeling of "democratic deficit" that already exists in many of the EU countries. This is part of the reason why the British, Danes and Swedes have decided not to join EMU in the first wave.

As a response to these concerns, the ECB is planning to improve accountability and transparency with the regular publication of inflation reports. These reports will outline inflation targets and both explain and assess monetary policy.

23.4 What is Meant by Price Stability?

The ECB will be concerned above all else with maintaining "price stability" and preserving the value of the new currency, the euro. This objective is not as straight-forward as it might appear to be. First, there is the problem of accurately measuring the "true" rate of inflation with conventional indices such as the Irish Consumer Price Index or the EU Harmonised Index of Prices. The Boskin Commission in the US reported in 1996 that indices of this sort tend to overestimate the "true" rate of inflation by 1 to 2 per cent a year. Recent research in Germany arrived at a similar conclusion regarding their measure of inflation. This overstatement is due to the failure to allow for shifting patterns of expenditure, for improvements in the quality of consumer goods, and for the growing importance of shopping at discount retail outlets and in sales. For example, the price of a personal computer in 1998 is much the same as it was in 1988. A price index would therefore suggest no change in its price over the decade and a zero inflation rate for this item. However, the power of computers has increased a thousand-fold since 1988. In this sense the quality of the machine has improved dramatically. The price of a *constant quality* computer (assuming it were still available) would have fallen dramatically. Conventional price indexes do not take improvements in quality fully into account and therefore overestimate inflation. This is a problem that exists at the national level, but it will assume greater significance when the ECB tries to define a price stability target.

Table 23.2	
Inflation rates in the Euro-zone, January 1998	
	%
Austria	1.1
Belgium	0.5
Finland	1.8
France	0.6
Germany	0.8
Ireland	1.2
Italy	1.9
Luxembourg	1.5
Netherlands	1.6
Portugal	1.6
Spain	1.9
Average	1.21
Source: EU Harmonised Index of Consumer Prices	

A second issue is the fact that inflation has now fallen to a very low level throughout the EU, partly as a consequence of the rise in unemployment during the 1990s, means that the ECB will have to take this exceptionally low level of inflation as the benchmark relative to which it will be judged. In recent publications the ECB has indicated that an inflation target of 0-2 per cent may be appropriate. As economic recovery gathers momentum in Europe, inflationary pressures will increase and the ECB may respond with a monetary contraction at an early stage in the cycle.

A third issue arises in relation to the definition of price stability. The ECB will target the *average* inflation rate across the Euro-zone. The Maastricht convergence criteria were designed to ensure that the 1997 rate of inflation was uniform across the countries that wanted to join in 1999. Yet despite this, significant differences in inflation persist, as may be see from Table 23.2.

The rate of inflation in Italy and Spain is more than twice the rate in France and Germany, for example. Although the absolute differential is small – about one per cent – it means that achieving zero inflation in Italy and Spain might require absolute *deflation* in Germany, France and Belgium. Alternatively, allowing a relatively high rate of inflation to persist in Italy and Spain implies that the real interest rate will be lower in these countries than in France and Germany. In the course of 1998, Irish inflation rose well above the Euro-zone average.

There is never likely to be a uniform inflation rate across the Euro-zone. Even when a single market and a single currency are established, differences in the rates of inflation of non-traded goods, changing market structures and variations in transportation costs between regions will ensure that significant national inflation differentials persist. Significant differences in inflation rates do occur between the regions of the United States. Booming countries, such as Ireland in 1998, will tend to experience higher rates of inflation than the core Euro-zone countries.

23.5 Monetary Policy in EMU

How should the ECB set about achieving its primary target of ensuring price stability? Economic theory and practice has experienced fashions and fads in this regard, with alternative approaches waxing and waning in popularity. We now review some of the key issues in this area.

Inflation targeting

The approach to monetary policy that has become fashionable in recent years is known as *inflation targeting.* [6] It consists of setting a target rate of inflation and basing policy on judgments of what is needed to achieve it. Taking account of information on trends in price indices, labour costs, exchange rates, and other relevant information, the monetary authorities must take corrective action when the signs are that inflation is tending to rise above the target range.

The principal instrument used by most central banks today to fine-tune the economy and achieve a target rate of inflation is short-term interest rates. The main channels used to set interest rates are open market operations and official rediscount rates

The ECB will rely primarily on open market operations to influence the structure of short-term interest rates in the Euro-zone. Two standing facilities (that is, lines of credit) will be available to national central banks from the ECB and the terms on which this credit is offered will influence short-term interest rates throughout the Euro-zone. Only relatively small differences will persist between countries, reflecting the status of the country's debt on money markets. [7]

An advantage of this approach is that the target is transparent and provides an anchor for the public's inflation expectations. In addition, the announcement of the target increases the accountability of the central bank and allows the public to evaluate its performance.

The inflation targeting approach has been adopted in the 1990s in Canada, New Zealand, Australia, Israel, Sweden, Finland, Spain and the United Kingdom. New

---

6. For a survey of the literature on inflation targeting, see Máiréad Devine and Daniel McCoy, "Inflation Targeting: A Review of the Issues", *Central Bank of Ireland Bulletin,* Spring 1998, pp 51-71.

7. Should a crisis of confidence arise about the future of EMU, these interest rate differentials would widen dramatically.

Zealand pioneered the approach by signing a Policy Targets Agreement in 1990, setting the target inflation rate in the range between 0 and 3 per cent and raising the possibility that the governor of the Central Bank would be fired if this target was not met.[8] The United Kingdom adopted a target of 2.5 ± 1 per cent in 1992. Similar targets were subsequently adopted by the other countries listed above, except for Israel which set a target range of 8 to 11 per cent.

The problems with the inflation targeting approach are:

- How to accurately forecast inflation. Inflation is very difficult to forecast even over a short-term horizon. There is no agreement on which economic model to base forecasts. In addition there is the problem of identifying external shocks and projecting their influence on inflation.

- Changes in short-term interest rates may have a long and variable effect on the inflation rate.

- The credibility of the ECB is also important. Just because an inflation target is announced, it does not follow that the public will immediately revise their inflation expectations. The public is aware of the difficulties in forecasting and controlling inflation and may be slow to revise expectations.

Money aggregate targeting

In Box 23.3 we reproduce from Chapter 18 some of the key relationships or theories underlying international monetary economics. Monetary targeting is based on monetarist economic theory, whose cornerstone is the quantity theory of money. If velocity (V) is constant the central bank can determine the price level by controlling the money supply. If, for example, real GNP is forecast to grow at 3 per cent a year, price stability would be achieved by allowing the quantity of money (the money supply) to increase by 3 per cent. Two things would follow from a low inflation rate in Europe. First, if Euro inflation were lower than US inflation, from the PPP equation over the long run there should be an appreciation of the euro relative to the dollar. Secondly, from the Fisher equation, low inflation leads to low nominal interest rates. But Euro interest rates could only be lower than US interest rates if it were expected that the euro will appreciate relative to the dollar in the future. In this view of things, price stability is the key to a strong currency and low nominal interest rates.

---

8. The target was missed during the 1990s. The governor was not dismissed.

Key relationships

EBR	$\equiv$	Government expenditure $-$ revenue	*Government borrowing requirement*
$M^s \times V$	$\equiv$	$P_{eu} \times$ Real GNP	*Quantity theory of money*
Δe_t	$=$	$\pi_{us} - \pi_{eu}$	*Purchasing power parity (PPP)*
i_n	$=$	$i_r + \pi^e$	*Fisher equation*
$(e^e_{t+1} - e_t)/e_t = (i_{us} - i_{eu})/(1 + i_{eu})$			*Uncovered interest rate parity (UIP)*

where

M^s	$=$	Europe's money supply
V	$=$	Velocity of circulation of money
I_r	$=$	Real interest rate
P_{eu}	$=$	Price level in Europe and π_{eu} is the inflation rate in Europe
e^e_{t+1}	$=$	Expected future exchange rate ($/euro)$
i_{us}	$=$	Nominal interest rate in US
i_n	$=$	Nominal interest rate in Ireland
i_{eu}	$=$	Nominal interest rate in Europe
e_t	$=$	Spot dollar/euro exchange rate
P_{us}	$=$	Price level in US and π_{us} is the inflation rate in US

The monetarist framework was widely adopted by central banks, including the Bank of England, the Fed and the Bundesbank, in the 1970s, but it has been widely modified, if not abandoned, since then. Disillusion with the quantity theory was due to many factors including:

- There is the difficulty of deciding on the appropriate definition of the money stock for policy purposes. Should the narrow (M1) or the broad (M3) definition be used? In the past, these two definitions of money have moved in different directions in the short run, giving conflicting signals about monetary developments.

- The assumption that the velocity of circulation, V, is constant was found wanting in the 1980s. If, for example, an increase in the money supply leads to a fall in V, then changes in the money supply will have a weak and unpredictable effect on nominal output. Financial innovation and deregulation of financial markets in the 1980s led to a breakdown of a previously stable relationship between the money supply and inflation.

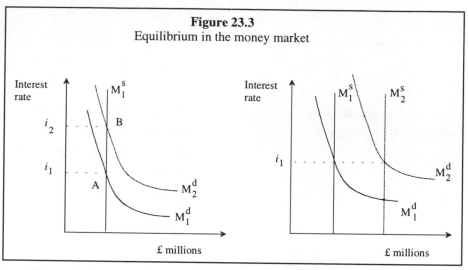

Figure 23.3
Equilibrium in the money market

None the less, the German Bundesbank has continued to rely heavily on monetary targeting and the influence of the Bundesbank on the ECB assures that this approach will continue to be used after the launch of EMU.

Difference between inflation and money supply targeting

Inflation targeting and money supply targeting are two different approaches to achieving an inflation objective. To see this, consider Figure 23.3 which shows equilibrium in the money market. Recall from Chapter 10 that the supply (M^s) and the demand (M^d) for money determines the interest rate (i). The location, or position, of the M^d curve is determined by nominal GNP. An increase in GNP shifts the M^d curve upwards and vice versa.

In the left-hand diagram, the central bank pursues a money supply target approach. This involves keeping the M^s curve constant in order to achieve an inflation target. However, because the M^d curve shifts up (due to higher GNP), the interest rate rises. Conversely, if the M^d curve moved down, interest rates would fall. Hence, if the central bank pursues a constant M^s target, it loses control over interest rates.

In the right-hand diagram, the central bank opts for a constant interest rate approach which it deems appropriate for a specific inflation objective. In this instance, the central bank varies the money supply in order to accommodate changes in the demand for money and thereby keeps interest rates constant. As the M^d curve shifts up, the central bank increases M^s and interest rates remain at i_1. In this case, the central bank loses control over the money supply.

The two approaches to achieving an inflation target are therefore independent of each other. In practice, the central bank may opt for some compromise between the two approaches. Note, however, if the demand for money is very volatile or unpredictable, the central bank's job is considerably more difficult. Considerable research has gone into determining whether or not the M^d curve is a stable function of a few variables, such as nominal GNP. If the M^d curve is unstable, it may not be possible to use either the money supply or interest rate targeting approaches to achieve an inflation objective. It is far from clear whether there will be a stable demand for money function across the EMU as a whole.

Which instruments will the ECB use?

Although we shall only be able to tell from experience, it seems likely that the ECB will use a combination of interest rates and monetary aggregate targets as instruments of monetary policy.[9]

The Maastricht Treaty gives the ECB the power to use open market operations (that is, buying and selling government bonds) to influence the level of interest rates. But it remains to be seen whether the ECB will rely as heavily on interest rates as an instrument of monetary policy as national central banks did in the days before EMU. As one author has pointed out:

"One wonders whether the current emphasis on interest rate policy will survive in [EMU], after exchange rates are locked. There will be no need for interest rate policy to defend the exchange rates within EMU. Furthermore the ECB will not have to peg the euro by intervening in foreign exchange markets, and it will thus have more control over the money supply of the euro countries as a group than the EU central banks now have over their own money supplies. Therefore, the ECB may pay close attention to the quantity of credit and may want to use a euro monetary aggregate as a proxy for it."[10]

The Council of the EMI has indicated that it favours using an inflation target for the longer-term framework and a monetary aggregate as a key policy instrument.

---

9. For a discussion of this issue, see Peter B. Kenen, *Economic and Monetary Policy in Europe,* Cambridge University Press, 1995; and Daniel Gros and Niels Thygesen, *European Monetary Integration,* Second Edition, Essex: Addison Wesley Longman, 1998, Chapter 9.

10. Kenen, op. cit., p. 61.

No approach to monetary policy can be guaranteed to deliver price stability without incurring high costs in terms of excess unemployment. It takes time for changes in interest rates or in monetary aggregates to affect the real economy, and central banks are aiming at moving targets. As the American economist Rudiger Dornbusch commented: "Shooting at a moving target in the fog is no easy task."[11] Skill and luck are required to achieve a monetary target and it remains to be seen how skilful and lucky the ECB will be after the launch of EMU.

Summary

We do not yet know how the ECB will implement its commitment to "price stability" once it assumes control of monetary policy in the Euro-zone in 1999. The transition from eleven independent national central banks to a single monetary authority (the ESCB) with an all-powerful European Central Bank and eleven subservient national central banks is fraught with risks. It is likely that the ECB will rely primarily on short-term interest rates as the instrument to achieve its inflation target. The real test of its anti-inflation credentials will come when Europe experiences an adverse shock and the ECB has to stand firm in the face of rising unemployment and mounting political criticisms of its immense power and lack of public accountability.

23.6 Fiscal Policy in EMU

In view of the constraints placed on national monetary policy by the Maastricht Treaty, it might seem that there would be greater reliance on fiscal policy as an instrument of national economic policy in EMU. But we have seen that a recurrent source of tension in the old ERM was the lack of co-ordination of national fiscal policies. If EMU is to endure, the participants must pursue consistent fiscal policies.

One possibility would be for the EU itself to conduct an active counter-cyclical fiscal policy. But the EU has no fiscal instruments designed to stabilise the economy and because of the relatively small size of the EU budget (less than 2 per cent of EU GDP) there are no EU automatic stabilisers worth talking about. Unlike the situation in federal economic structures, such as the United States, there is no significant *federal fiscalism*, that is, there is no mechanism for offsetting economic shocks by a fall in

---

11. R. Dornbusch, C. Favero and F. Giavazzi, "A Red Letter Day", CEPR Discussion Paper, No. 1804, February 1998.

taxes paid to, or a rise in transfers received from, Brussels.

In order to remove the possibility that individual Euro-zone countries would pursue divergent fiscal policies, tight constraints have been imposed as a precondition for joining. A Stability Pact[12] was agreed in Dublin in December 1996 and ratified in Amsterdam in June 1997. This pact obliges governments not to incur a fiscal deficit over 3 per cent of GDP. Over the medium term governments should aim at budgets that are "close to balanced or in surplus". This is necessary because a recession could easily add 3 per cent to the deficit through the operation of automatic stabilisers. A country that runs a deficit in excess of 3 per cent will be fined unless the deficit can be excused as "temporary" and/or "exceptional" – basically, unless the increase in the deficit is due to a fall of 2 per cent or more in GDP. (GDP has never fallen by this amount over the past three decades in Ireland.)

Given that many countries are entering EMU with fiscal deficits close to the 3 per cent ceiling, and with debt/GDP ratios above the 60 per cent set as the target in the Maastricht Treaty, their deficits could easily be pushed into the penalty zone. This could be caused by a fall in GDP of less than 2 per cent or by a rise in interest rates that added to the cost of servicing the large outstanding stock of public debt. If these eventualities arise, the EMU would be severely tested by the requirement that the offending countries be fined. Imposing these fines on countries that violate the deficit rule would cause a political crisis. How would Irish politicians react to being required to pay a fine of up to 0.5 per cent of GDP (or about £200 million) if the budget deficit were pushed above 3 per cent by a sudden drop in the economy's growth rate? On the other hand, failure to impose fines would undermine the EMU's commitment to hard-nosed anti-inflation policies. There are grounds for fearing the EMU would not survive a major shock such as the energy price increases of the late 1970s or the reunification of Germany at the end of the 1980s.

With monetary and fiscal policy severely constrained, the policy framework of EMU leaves little scope for stabilisation policy. The countries that have joined EMU have signed up to a very "classical" policy orientation, relying on the ability of the economy to adjust rapidly to shocks. This will place an enormous burden on price and wage adjustment to move the economy back to full employment in the aftermath of adverse shocks. If prices and wages in the Euro-zone countries continue to be as

---

12. Officially known as "The Pact for Stability and Growth".

inflexible, and labour as immobile, as they have in the past, the result will be protracted recession and even higher unemployment than is presently recorded in Europe. This would add considerably to political tensions between the participating countries.

23.7 Exchange Rate Policy in EMU

When the euro is launched as a currency in its own right in 1999, its initial value will be set equal to the ECU on a one-to-one basis (see Box 23.4). However, from then on the euro will be floating against the ECU and the world's other main currencies. What then will the longer-term policy of the ECB be regarding the value of the euro? To shed light on this issue we need to summarise the provisions of the Maastricht Treaty regarding exchange rate policy.

The Treaty (Article 109) divides responsibility for exchange rate policy between the Council of Ministers (which is made up of ministers from all 15 member states of the EU) and the ECB. The Council acting unanimously may conclude formal agreements linking the euro to non-Community currencies. It must consult with the ECB and try to achieve a consensus consistent with price stability, but once the Council has made an agreement the ECB will be bound by it. The Council may also promulgate less formal "general orientations" for exchange rate policy.

At first sight these provisions would appear to compromise the ECB's independence. Some European firms are in fierce competition with their American rivals on world markets (Airbus v. Boeing, for example). Politicians from the regions of Europe where these firms provide a lot of employment will lobby to have the euro at a "competitive" (i.e. low) exchange rate relative to the dollar. The EU Council of Ministers (which includes finance ministers of countries such as the United Kingdom that are not members of EMU) could decide to peg the euro to the dollar. If this happens, the ECB could lose control over monetary policy as must happen under a fixed exchange rate regime.

Note:
In our discussion of the open economy monetary model (Chapter 20) and the Mundell-Fleming model (Chapter 21) we saw that monetary policy is ineffective when the exchange rate is fixed.

But there are a number of considerations that render these concerns somewhat remote. First, a "formal agreement" of the type referred to in Article 109 implies a return to a global fixed exchange rate system similar to the post-war Bretton Woods agreement. Once the euro is launched there will be only three major, global currencies – the dollar, the euro, and the yen (in that order of importance).[13] There is little prospect of a formal agreement between the EU, the US and Japan to peg exchange rates.[14]

Second, volatility between these global currencies need be no more serious in the future than it is today between the dollar, the German mark and the yen. The monetary authorities in the US, the Euro-zone and Japan are all committed to price stability and pursuing similar monetary policies, which is a recipe for relatively stable exchange rates. This would remove the need for a formal agreement to peg the currencies in the short to medium term, while creating the preconditions for fixed exchange rates in the longer run.[15] Less formal "general orientations" – along the lines of the Plaza Agreement (1985) and the Louvre Accord (1987) – would not have much effect and are not likely to undermine the Euro-zone price stability.

A third reason for not worrying too much about the implications of EMU exchange rate policy for price stability is the fact that the Euro-zone will resemble a large and closed economy rather than the open economy described in Chapter 18. In

---

13. Because of the nth currency issue discussed in Chapter 17, there will only be *two* independent exchange rates between these *three* currencies.

14. This is the consensus view of recent commentaries on the issue: see Kenen, op. cit., p. 32.

15. This would imply a return to a global system of fixed exchange rates, akin to the gold standard of the late nineteenth century – a prospect that many would view with trepidation: see our discussion in Chapter 16 of the reasons behind the breakdown of the gold standard.

fact the Euro-zone will be a more closed economy than the US – only about 11 per cent of the Euro-zone's output is exported to non Euro-zone countries, whereas exports comprise about 16 per cent of US GDP. As a consequence, the exchange rate of the euro with non Euro-zone currencies will be less important from the perspective of price stability than the exchange rate of the US dollar is to the US monetary policy makers. An overvalued euro would impair the ability of firms in the EMU to compete with American or Asian firms on world markets. But because most of the output of the Euro-zone firms is sold within the Euro-zone, this issue will not be as vital as it was to individual countries in the pre-EMU period.

For Ireland, however, the value of the euro relative to sterling will be very important. We have a vested interest in the continuation of a hard-nosed policy by the British authorities, which will keep inflation low and sterling strong relative to the euro.

23.8 The Euro as a Global Currency

The US dollar is the most widely used currency in global commerce today. It is used outside the United States as a store of value in countries where hyperinflation has led to a distrust of the local currency ("dollarisation"). It is also widely used as a medium of exchange throughout the world. Many international contracts and the prices of most major commodities, such as oil, are specified in dollars. Finally, because of its general acceptability and good anti-inflation reputation, the dollar is the most important reserve currency held by central banks round the world as backing for their national currencies.

The emergence of the euro will provide a serious competitor to the dollar in some of its functions as a global currency. The size and economic importance of the Euro-zone guarantee this. It has been estimated that the euro could become the unit of account for up to a quarter of world trade.[16]

It is more difficult to estimate the demand for the euro as a reserve currency. At the very least it will replace the German mark and other EMU currencies, which currently account for about 22 per cent of world reserves. But the share of the euro is likely to exceed the combined share of the individual EMU currencies. By how much is difficult to predict, but it has been suggested that its share could rise to 40 per cent. However, the probability is that central banks round the world will only gradually

---

16. For a discussion of this topic, see Daniel Gros and Niels Thygesen, *European Monetary Integration,* Second Edition, Essex: Addison Wesley Longman, 1998, Chapter 9.

increase their holdings of euros to this level if the ECB delivers price stability. This will take time, so any effect of the euro on the role of the dollar will be gradual.

The demand for euros outside the Euro-zone could be met by selling off some of the surplus foreign exchange reserves of national central banks.[17] It is not envisaged that meeting this demand would place undue upward pressure on the currency in the world's foreign exchange markets.

The gradual development of the euro into a global currency would benefit the governments of the Euro-zone because they would enjoy additional seigniorage on the currency held outside the Euro-zone. At present, it is estimated that the US enjoys seigniorage equal to 0.5 per cent of GDP on the quantity of dollars held outside the US.[18] The US also finds it easy to finance current account deficits because non-residents are willing to hold dollar assets. But the willingness of other countries to hold the euro would depend on the way in which the ECB conducts its monetary policy. Just as lax monetary policy in the US in the late 1960s reduced the US dollar's acceptability as a reserve currency, any perceived laxity on the part of the ECB would reduce the demand for euros outside the Euro-zone.

23.9 Will EMU be Deflationary?

The drive to achieve the Maastricht criteria has imposed deflationary policies on Europe. Figure 23.4 shows the trend in unemployment and inflation in the EU from 1979 to 1997. An inverse relationship between the two series (as predicted by the original Phillip's curve) may be observed. As inflation fell in the 1990s, partly driven down by the desire to meet the Maastricht convergence criteria, unemployment rose. In the US, on the other hand, a looser monetary policy resulted in falling unemployment and little extra inflation.

EMU is being launched against a background of exceptionally low inflation across Europe. This low inflation has been achieved by tolerating a sharp rise in unemployment in the 1990s. It is an unfortunate feature of the European labour markets that higher unemployment will tend now to be incorporated into a higher "natural" rate of unemployment. That is, once unemployment rises in Europe, labour

---

17. Because the Euro-zone will be much less open to external trade than the individual participating countries, the ECB will require fewer reserves than the pooled reserves of the central banks that are in the ESCB.

18. *The Economist*, 11 April 1998.

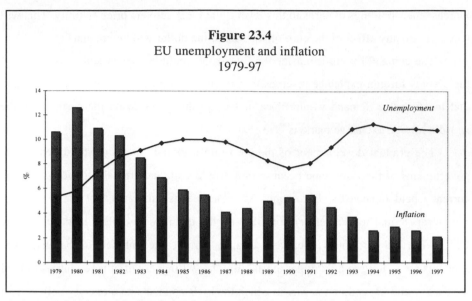

Figure 23.4
EU unemployment and inflation
1979-97

market rigidities make it difficult to bring it down. It becomes a structural problem.

When the current economic recovery in core EU economies gains momentum, inflation is likely to pick up again. The ECB will then be under pressure to prevent inflation rising above the level that prevailed at the launch of the euro. This could lead to the imposition of contractionary policies relatively early in the recovery phase of the cycle. Higher interest rates would cause severe budgetary problems in the highly indebted countries that constitute the majority in the Euro-zone, increasing the risk that they breach the Stability Pact and will be therefore forced to implement pro-cyclical corrective policies that would exacerbate the downturn.

The EMU project contains no proposals to address this issue. It is likely that the combination of the ECB's commitment to price stability and the constraints imposed by the Stability Pact could create a deflationary bias in EMU.

23.9 Conclusion

In this Chapter we discussed the framework within which economic policy will be made in the newly launched European EMU. We drew attention to the key role of the European Central Bank (ECB). Among the main points discussed were:

- The constitution and structure of the ECB
- The independence of the ECB from political pressures
- The main objective of the ECB – to maintain price stability

- The merits of money aggregate targeting and direct inflation targeting
- Fiscal policy in EMU under the Stability Pact
- The fact that there will be little room for stabilisation policy in EMU
- This will place enormous pressures on wage-price flexibility as the means of adjusting to economic shocks
- Exchange rate policy in EMU and the external value of the euro
- The risk that the EMU will have a deflationary bias.

Appendix 1

How monetary policy works

To understand how the ECB can influence interest rates and conduct monetary policy, it is necessary to study the relationship between the balance sheets of the ECB and the commercial banks and the European inter-bank money market. Figure 23.5 summarises the situation.

Inter-bank market Banks lend (supply) and borrow (demand) money from each other for periods ranging from a day to a year on the inter-bank market. This inter-bank market has no exact location. It is a market conducted through computers, telephones, fax and telex machines. The forces of supply and demand in this market determine the inter-bank interest rate (i_{ib}). The ECB exercises an important influence on the inter-bank rate through the rate at which it is willing to lend to the banks.

The inter-bank interest rate is crucially important because of its influence on all the other interest rates in the banking system. When i_{ib} changes, the commercial banks and building societies change their interest rates quickly because they are heavily dependent on the inter-bank market as a source of funds.

Minimum reserve ratio The minimum reserve ratio (referred to as the primary reserve ratio in Ireland) is a crucial link between the ECB and the commercial banks. It will be recalled from Chapter 9 that this ratio is set by a central bank and stipulates the proportion of commercial banks' liabilities or resources (deposits) that must be covered by reserves (that is, cash and deposits with the ECB). It is not yet known how the ECB will decide this ratio.

The minimum reserve ratio is equal to the required reserves (RE) divided by banks' deposits. If a bank has a deficiency of reserves, it will borrow (demand) funds on the inter-bank market. Conversely, a bank with excess reserves will supply funds to the inter-bank market and earn interest on them. There is therefore a direct link between the adequacy of the banks' reserves (their liquidity) and the supply and demand for funds on the inter-bank market. If supply exceeds demand, i_{ib} will fall and, conversely, if supply is less than demand, i_{ib} will rise. Changes in i_{ib} will spread throughout the spectrum of interest rates.

The main influences on the liquidity of the banks are:

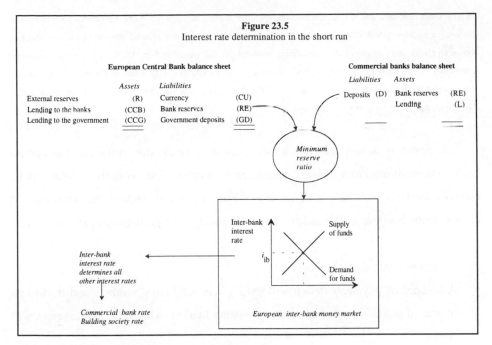

Figure 23.5
Interest rate determination in the short run

European Central Bank balance sheet

	Assets	Liabilities	
External reserves	(R)	Currency	(CU)
Lending to the banks	(CCB)	Bank reserves	(RE)
Lending to the government	(CCG)	Government deposits	(GD)

Commercial banks balance sheet

Liabilities		Assets	
Deposits	(D)	Bank reserves	(RE)
		Lending	(L)

Minimum reserve ratio

Inter-bank interest rate

i_{ib}

Supply of funds

Demand for funds

Inter-bank interest rate determines all other interest rates

Commercial bank rate
Building society rate

European inter-bank money market

- The balance of payments

- Changes in the public's holding of cash (CU)

- Bank lending

- Savings by the public

- Government borrowing.

 We now examine how these influence the money market.

The balance of payments

If the ECB pursues a fixed or "dirty floating" exchange rate policy, a balance of payments deficit or surplus is reflected in a change in the external reserves. This is because the ECB is intervening in the foreign exchange market: either buying or selling the euro. These changes in the external reserves (R) have an important influence on retail interest rates across Europe. In general, a change in the external reserves on the asset side of the ECB's balance sheet will be reflected in changes in commercial banks' reserves (RE) on the liability side. In general:

$$\downarrow R \Leftrightarrow \downarrow RE \text{ (and vice versa)}$$

Note:

To illustrate this, consider a firm in Europe importing 1 million *euro*s worth of computer parts from the US. When the importer first withdraws money from her account, deposits (D) and reserves (RE) decrease on the commercial bank balance sheet. The importer is now holding 1 million *euro*s in currency. On the ECB's

541

balance sheet, RE falls and CU increases. The importer now exchanges the domestic currency for dollars at the foreign exchange desk of the bank. The commercial bank holds only a small amount of foreign currency and is, in effect, only acting as an intermediary between the individual and the ECB. This foreign exchange transaction is reflected in the ECB balance sheet as a fall in CU (liability side) and a fall in the external reserves (R) on the asset side. Overall, on the ECB balance sheet, the fall in R is matched by an equal fall in RE (the change in CU was only temporary).

Suppose now that prior to the withdrawal of funds the banks had the correct reserves/deposit ratio to meet the minimum reserve ratio. Following the decrease in its reserves the bank will have a *deficiency* of reserves and to redress the situation will borrow from the inter-bank market. This will put upward pressure on the interest rate (i_{ib}).

Thus in general:

- A balance of payments deficit will reduce licensed banks' reserves and lead to an increased demand for funds on the inter-bank market. Domestic interest rates will rise.

- A balance of payments surplus will increase licensed banks' reserves and lead to an increase in the supply of funds on the inter-bank market and a reduction in interest rates.

As we pointed out in Chapter 15, there are numerous short-run influences on the balance of payments and therefore the level of the external reserves. Among the main influences are:

- Inflation
- Currency speculation
- Interest rates
- Real growth rates.

If, for example, speculators expect a depreciation of the dollar/euro exchange rate, capital is transferred from euros to foreign currencies in anticipation of making a capital gain. This will be reflected in the ECB's balance sheet as a fall in R and RE, and the banks will have a deficiency of reserves. The demand for funds on the inter-bank market will increase and domestic interest rates will rise.

Changes in households' cash balances

Net changes in cash balances or currency holdings (CU) by the public tend to be seasonal and reasonably predictable. For example, there is always a significant increase

542

in currency holdings in the weeks leading up to Christmas. This involves withdrawals of money from commercial banks' deposit accounts. In this case:

$$\downarrow D \text{ and } \downarrow RE \text{ (commercial banks' balance sheet)}$$

The increase in currency holdings will be reflected in:

$$\uparrow CU \text{ and } \downarrow RE \text{ (ECB's balance sheet)}$$

If the increase in CU was unexpected, and banks were maintaining only the exact ratio of reserves to deposits, they would be forced to borrow on the inter-bank market and interest rates would tend to rise. Conversely, a fall in currency holdings would tend to reduce inter-bank interest rates.

An increase in *private sector deposits*, due to a reduction in cash balances, would lead to excess reserves and the supply of funds to the inter-bank market would increase. Interest rates would tend to fall.

Government borrowing

The financing of national governments' borrowing requirements has traditionally been a major influence on the liquidity of the commercial banks. However, in the context of the restrictions placed on the countries participating in EMU, it will be much less significant in the future.

Generally, governments can borrow from:

1. The central bank
2. The commercial banks
3. Abroad
4. The non-bank public

Under the provisions in the Maastricht Treaty, the ECB and national central banks can act as agents for government but they cannot lend them money, provide credit or buy bonds directly from them. As the ECB is ruled out as a source of credit, it is possible that governments will transfer their accounts to commercial financial institutions. (Up to 1971, the Irish Government held its account with the Bank of Ireland which is a commercial bank.) Hence, borrowing from commercial banks (source 2) is likely to become much more important in the future.

If the government borrows from a *commercial bank*, the effects are similar to what happens when a firm or individual borrows. Bank lending and deposits increase. If the banks had no excess reserves, there would be a deficiency in reserves following the increase in lending to the government. This would lead to an increased demand for funds on the inter-bank market and interest rates would rise.

If a government borrows from *abroad*, it lodges the proceeds with the ECB. The result is similar to that of an increase in any other inflow across the balance of payments in that the ECB acquires additional reserves. The government, in turn, obtains additional balances with the ECB, just as it would if it borrowed directly from the bank. An internal monetary expansion will result. This type of financing is unlikely to occur under the rules of the single currency.

The most important source of funds for a government will be borrowing from the *non-bank public* by selling government securities. Purchases of government stock will lead to a fall in commercial bank deposits as money is withdrawn to pay for the stock. When the government spends the money, a large part of it will find its way back to the banks and deposits will return to their original level. In the longer term, therefore, there will be little change in bank deposits, bank reserves or interest rates.

This is why the provisions in the Maastricht Treaty are designed to constrain government borrowing to the non-bank public. Since this type of borrowing does not affect the money supply, it makes it much easier for the ECB to achieve its primary goal of price stability.

Countries that run a deficit will borrow in euros. In principle all countries will pay the same rate of interest on their debt. However, small differentials between individual countries may remain even after the launch of the EMU. These would be similar to the differentials that exist between the states of the United States, all of which borrow in US dollars, but some of which enjoy a better credit rating than others. Markets will exact higher interest rates from countries whose debt is regarded as risky – Italy may be a case in point. Another possibility is that Irish euro debt would carry a premium because of the risk that a weakness of sterling would place our commitment to EMU in question.

Appendix 2

The ECB's interest rate policy

The ECB interest rate policy will take two general forms. If the *euro* exchange rate is flexible then the ECB can influence the trend in interest rates in order to achieve a specific inflation target. On the other hand, if the ECB pursues a "dirty floating" or fixed exchange rate policy, it will pursue an interest rate sterilisation policy. Before explaining these policies, we first discuss the techniques used by the ECB to influence liquidity in Europe's money market.

ECB credit to the money market

Funds can be provided to the commercial banks through one of the following channels,

- The short-term facility (STF)
- Secured advances
- Overnight deposits.

These sources of funds comprise central bank credit to the banks (CCB). The CCB variable is shown on the asset side of the ECB's balance sheet. We do not, as yet, know what name the ECB will use in referring to the above sources of funds. Hence the short-term credit facility may, in fact, be called something else. However, the principle of operation will be the same.

The short-term facility (STF) This is similar to an individual's overdraft facility or authorisation at his bank. The commercial banks can use this facility to borrow from the ECB for a short period of time (usually seven days). Each commercial bank is given a quota which is determined by its size and participation in the inter-bank market. The banks are charged the STF interest rate on this borrowing and are penalised for frequent use of the facility by being charged a higher rate. By raising or lowering this rate, the ECB sends a signal about the direction in which it wishes interest rates to move throughout the European economy.

Secured advances Banks can also borrow from the ECB on a longer-term basis against the security of government stocks. Banks tend to avail of this facility after they have reached their short-term facility quota. The terms on which the ECB lends are related to the STF rate.

In addition to providing credit to the money market, the ECB can use the following instruments to either inject or withdraw funds:

- Foreign currency swaps
- Sale and repurchase agreements (REPOs)
- Term deposits
- Changes in the minimum reserve ratio.

We now provide a brief account of these.

Foreign currency swaps Commercial banks' holdings of foreign exchange are not included in banks' minimum reserves. If a bank has foreign exchange for use at a later date and is short of reserves, the foreign exchange can be temporarily swapped for reserves at the ECB. This facility can be used both to inject liquidity into the market (the ECB swaps euros for foreign currency) or remove liquidity (the ECB swaps foreign currency for euros).

Sale and repurchase agreements (REPOs) This facility is similar to a foreign currency swap except that government securities rather than foreign exchange are exchanged for an agreed period at the end of which the transaction is reversed. The ECB lends money to the commercial banks at a fixed rate of interest for a fixed period. Government stocks are transferred to the ECB as security, with an agreement that the banks will buy them back (repurchase) at the end of the period. This provides the banks with temporary additional reserves. Both this arrangement and foreign currency swaps are generally done at prevailing interest rates.

Term deposits The ECB may also withdraw liquidity from the inter-bank market by "quoting for funds", that is, quoting a specified interest rate for term deposits for specified periods. This instrument works only when withdrawing funds from the market, as the ECB does not keep deposits with the commercial banks and hence cannot inject liquidity by increasing these.

Changes in the minimum reserve ratio A reduction in the minimum reserve ratio increases the liquidity of the banking system; an increase in the ratio lowers it. However, it is expected that the ratio will not be changed frequently.

Influencing the trend in interest rates

The ECB can use the above-mentioned instruments to influence the *trend* in interest rates. If, for example, it forms the view that European rates have fallen too low in relation to its objective of price stability, it may wish to nudge interest rates up on the inter-bank market. If it wishes to raise interest rates, it will try to create a *liquidity shortage* by supplying the market with less liquidity than is required. It could do any, or some combination, of the following:

- Increase the STF interest rate
- Swap euros for foreign currency
- Sell government securities to the market
- Increase the interest rate on term deposits, thereby withdrawing funds from the market
- Increase the minimum reserve ratio.

These measures will force up inter-bank interest rates which, in turn, will raise interest rates across Europe. If, on the other hand, the ECB feels that a reduction in interest rates is warranted because of the possibility of *deflation* in Europe, interest rates can be lowered by doing the opposite to the above (i.e. lower the STF rate). In this way the ECB can use interest rates as an instrument to achieve its ultimate objective of price stability.

Sterilisation policy

If the ECB pursues a fixed or "dirty floating" exchange rate policy, it will have to intervene in the foreign exchange market. As mentioned earlier, changes in the external reserves will, via the commercial bank reserves, affect inter-bank interest rates. For example, an outflow of funds due to a balance of payments deficit leads to:

$$\downarrow \text{R and} \downarrow \text{RE (ECB balance sheet)}$$

The commercial banks will find themselves short of reserves (relative to the minimum reserve requirement) and this will lead to an increase in the demand for funds on the money market. Interest rates will rise. The EBC may, however, take the view that current interest rates are consistent with its inflation target and act to prevent any increase. They can do this in a variety of ways. The ECB could, for example, lend the required funds to the commercial banks (increase in CCB). The need for the banks to borrow on the inter-bank market would be avoided and interest rates would remain unchanged. That is:

$$\uparrow CCB \text{ and } \uparrow RE \text{ (ECB balance sheet)}$$

This strategy *sterilises* the effect of changes in reserves in the Euro-zone's money supply. Alternatively, the ECB could lower the minimum reserve requirement, swap euros for foreign currency or buy government stock. All of these measures would provide the funds to the market and prevent interest rates rising.

If the ECB wished to prevent interest rates falling, the minimum reserve ratio could be increased, foreign currency swapped for euros and government stock sold.

In general, the ECB will pursue the objective of *smoothing* out the fluctuations in interest rates that occur in response to changes in bank liquidity. In so far as this intervention smoothes predictable and temporary changes in interest rates, it is desirable because fluctuations in interest rates can create uncertainty and discourage investment.

Chapter 24

Will Membership of EMU be Good for Ireland?

24.1 Introduction

In the previous chapter we explained how the European Central Bank is busy planning to make the EMU work. In this chapter we explore the question of how Ireland's decision to adopt the single European currency and terminate the Irish pound will affect the economy.

We start with a discussion of the benefits of a currency union and then turn to a consideration of the costs. Our framework is the *Optimum Currency Area* (OCA) theory.[1] As its name implies, this theory was developed to assess the optimum size of an area that uses the same currency. It provides an appropriate framework for analysing the costs and benefits of a group of countries deciding to relinquish their national currencies and adopt a common currency.

EMU is an experiment without parallel in economic history. Never before has a group of sovereign, independent nations been committed to adopting a new common currency. The experiment is truly a leap in the dark. It offers the promise of considerable benefits in terms of increased efficiency and closer economic union between the countries of Europe. But it could also lead to grave adverse repercussions if the participating economies do not prove capable of adjusting to future shocks without recourse to exchange rates.

---

1. See Robert A. Mundell, "A Theory of Optimum Currency Areas", *American Economic Review,* Vol. 51 (September 1961) pp 657-65, and Masahiro Kawai, "Optimum Currency Areas", in John Eatwell, Murray Milgate and Peter Newman, *The New Palgrave: A Dictionary of Economics*, London: Macmillan, 1987, Vol. 3, pp 740-42.

The belief that adopting the euro will ensure price stability is one of the main attractions of joining EMU to countries, such as Ireland, that have suffered from high inflation in the not too distant past. However, entering EMU is not the only way in which this objective might be reached. In Box 24.1 we outline the alternative exchange rate policies that might have been adopted by the Irish authorities instead of joining EMU. It is difficult to say whether any of these would have proved more beneficial in the long run than the decision to enter EMU in the first wave. While time will eventually tell how successful EMU will be, it will never be possible to say how well Ireland would have fared had a different course of action been taken in 1998.

24.2 The Political Benefits of EMU to Ireland

On the positive side of the ledger, numerous benefits have been claimed for the adoption of a single European currency. These should be considered under two broad headings, political and economic.[2] In this section we examine the political benefits and in section 24.3 the economic benefits.

Some of the most important potential benefits from the adoption of a single European currency are political in nature. This is because it is very possible that EMU is only a prelude to a fully fledged *federal European Union*.

If a federal Europe were to emerge, then it is argued this would ensure peace in Europe. The former French President François Mitterrand is quoted as saying "Nationalism – that is war." Similarly, the German Chancellor Kohl has stated that EMU would "free Europe from war in the 21st century". While another war in Europe is inconceivable, it is clear that EMU could lead to a more effective EU foreign policy. It could be expected that Germany would play a key role in the design and implementation of such a policy. In addition, it is claimed that a single currency will increase solidarity between participants and reduce the risks of trade disputes. The EU is frequently compared to a bicycle: it must either move forward or stall, and EMU is the next logical step toward deeper integration.

The political argument that Ireland must be seen to move forward with Europe appears to be very influential in official circles. Failure to do so, it is claimed, would have serious adverse repercussions such as less favourable treatment in future allocations of structural funds and exclusion from key economic decision-making processes.

---

2. A semi-official evaluation of Ireland's EMU options was published in 1996: T. Baker, J. Fitzgerald and P. Honohan, *Economic Implications for Ireland of EMU*, The Economic and Social Research Institute, Dublin, 1996. The case against Irish membership is put by J. P. Neary and R. Thom, "Punts, Pounds and Euros", Centre for Economic Research, UCD, Dublin, October 1996, and R. Thom, "Economic and Monetary Union", Jean Monnet Lecture, UCD, November 1996. For a wide-ranging survey of the future of EMU, see David Begg, Jürgen von Hagen, Charles Wyplosz and Klaus F. Zimmerman (eds) *EMU: Prospects and Challenges for the euro*, Oxford: Blackwell Publishers, 1998.

Also by participating in EMU from its inception we shall have a voice in the formulation of European monetary policy. (The Governor of the Central Bank of Ireland will have a seat on the Governing Council of the European Central Bank.) While European monetary policy clearly will not be tailored to Irish problems, our influence will none the less be disproportionate to the size of our economy.

24.3 The Economic Benefits of EMU to Ireland

In this section we outline the main economic benefits that have been advanced for introducing a single currency in Europe.

Completing the internal market

The main economic benefit of adopting a single European currency will be the extent to which it will help complete the single, or internal, European market. There are numerous ways in which the abolition of national currencies will increase economic integration. These include:

Price transparency The use of a common currency increases the transparency of prices and costs across countries. Since all prices will be denominated in a single currency, price differentials will be immediately obvious. This should encourage arbitrage which, in turn, should lead to a convergence of prices across Europe. Using the Internet and a euro credit card, it will soon be possible to go on a virtual shopping spree across Europe. However, the single currency is not a prerequisite for this: at present there is more use of the Internet by Irish subscribers to purchase from the United States rather than from Europe. Indirect taxes are a more serious obstacle to price transparency across Europe than are national currencies, as anyone interested in buying a car in Britain or Belgium for use in Ireland will appreciate.

Reduced transaction costs A single currency eliminates exchange rate transaction costs between participating countries. In the EU Commission study, *One Market, One Money,* (1990) these costs were put at about one-half of one per cent of GDP. While the cost of converting currencies is high for small transactions, such as tourist purchases, they are smaller for larger business deals.

The more important trade is relative to GDP, the greater the savings in transaction costs from sharing a common currency with one's trading partners. The potential benefits of a common currency are therefore greater, the more open the economy. As a small and very open economy Ireland stands to gain more than most from the reduction in transaction costs that will follow from adopting the euro. The downside, however, is that the financial sector in Ireland will experience a significant fall in earnings. It has been estimated that of total foreign exchange earnings of £250 million, the annual loss of revenue could amount to £75 million if the UK stays out and £143 million if the UK enters EMU.[3] In addition, foreign exchange markets in Ireland and in other centres outside the UK and Germany could experience a significant diminution in their status following the launch of the euro.

Reduction in exchange rate uncertainty

It is argued that doing away with the risk of exchange rate fluctuations will stimulate trade and investment between countries. Uncertainty regarding exchange rate movements is seen as a deterrent to planning long-run investment across international frontiers. Plausible though this seems, the empirical research has found little evidence that floating exchange rates depress international trade and investment. Trade between Japan and the United States and Europe has grown rapidly even though their exchange rates are not pegged.[4]

However, the costs of operating a national currency are greater, the smaller the country. It does not make sense for tiny states such as Liechtenstein, Monaco and San Marino to have their own currencies, and in fact these countries use the currencies of their larger neighbours (the Swiss and French francs, and Italian lira, respectively). Luxembourg has an independent currency but it has been pegged to the Belgian franc since 1945. Ireland's smallness relative to Britain was part of the reason for maintaining the sterling link in the years after Independence. Within the EU a group of relatively small countries (Holland, Belgium, Luxembourg and Austria) have held their exchange rates very stable relative to the German mark since the mid-1980s. France is the only

---

3. Robert Hutchinson, The Financial Services Sector, page 242, in Baker, Fitzgerald and Honohan, op. cit.

4. See, for example, Paul de Grauwe, "International Trade and Economic Growth in the EMS", *European Economic Review*, Vol. 31 (1987) pp 389-98.

large country to achieve comparable stability over the same period and this has been at the expense of considerable internal tension.

Scale economies

Assuming the adoption of the euro does achieve the completion of the Single Market, and devaluations are a thing of the past within Europe, firms will make location decisions on genuine considerations of comparative costs rather than as part of a strategy of hedging against sudden currency movements. At present firms have an incentive to spread their plants around Europe to protect their profits from sudden movements in exchange rates. Following the adoption of the euro, firms will locate their plants so as to reap economies of scale, ignoring national boundaries. This could lead to an increase in regional specialisation and an efficiency gain. However, peripheral regions could suffer a decline in their share of European economic activity.

Anti-inflation reputation

Adopting a common currency should allow formerly inflation-prone countries to enjoy a stability that they were unable to attain on their own. We explained in Chapter 23 that the new European Central Bank (ECB) is designed as a clone of the German Bundesbank. In fact it is even more committed to price stability and less answerable to any political body than the German Central Bank. Adopting the euro is *in principle* irreversible and therefore more credible than an anti-inflationary commitment based only on internal rules. Borrowing an *anti-inflation reputation* is an important potential benefit of EMU for formerly inflation-prone countries.

But at the end of the 1990s most European countries had already achieved low inflation. While this was done in part under the pressure of conforming to the Maastricht criteria, it clearly is possible for independent central banks to deliver price stability. Furthermore, the ECB has yet to earn its anti-inflation credentials. In chapter 23 we outlined the problems it faces on this front.

Low interest rates

High expected inflation is one reason for high nominal interest rates. If a currency union allows a country to achieve lower inflation, nominal interest rates will fall. Under the

ERM arrangement that operated from 1979 to 1993 European currencies were pegged but adjustable. For most of the period this did not deliver low interest rates in countries like Ireland due to the perceived risk that the pound would be devalued. A single currency eliminates the risk premium associated with the halfway house of the ERM. Lower interest rates have been seen as the most important benefit to flow to Ireland from membership of EMU (see section 24.5 below). But while lower interest rates will benefit investors and borrowers, they will hurt savers. A reduction in interest rates was the last thing the Central Bank of Ireland wished for in the course of 1998. Higher interest rates would have been more appropriate to cool down the overheating economy! As a result, the Central Bank tried to postpone the EMU-induced fall in interest rates to the last moment in 1998.

24.4 The Economic Costs of EMU to Ireland

We now discuss the main costs associated with adopting the single currency.

Transition costs

Considerable effort has been devoted to designing euro notes and coins and the technical details of the transition from national currencies to the euro. This will be a very daunting task – much greater than the transition to the decimal currency in Ireland and Britain in 1971, for example. The euro will not convert exactly into units of the old national currencies. In April 1998 IR£1 = ECU1.2740 or ECU1 = IR£0.7849. The euro will be launched close to this rate in 1999 and the conversion between the national currency and the new single currency will be very awkward. It remains to be seen how retailers will handle the transition and conversion of prices.

The costs involved will have to be borne by the banking sector and by business. It has been estimated that the once-off cost to the banks of switching to the euro (spread over three years) could be as high as £130 million. This cost involves:

- Staff training (10 per cent)
- Stationary, marketing and public relations (20 per cent)
- Changes to information technology (50 per cent).[5]

---

5. Source: Robert Hutchinson, op. cit., p. 231.

This is the cost to the banking sector only. If the costs incurred by the non-bank business community are included, the total cost will be some multiple of £130 million. Furthermore, this calculation *excludes* other costs such as: adapting both the domestic and international payments system to take account of the euro, storing large volumes of euros prior to their introduction and withdrawing domestic notes and coins.

Difficulty of adjusting to asymmetric shocks

By adopting a common currency the countries relinquish the exchange rate as an instrument for adjusting to a shock that affects them differently. Such shocks are called *country-specific* or *asymmetric shocks*. In this section we examine a number of different scenarios as to how the Irish economy can adjust following an asymmetric shock.

The basic model for analytical purposes is the AD-AS framework and the labour market introduced in Chapter 12. The intersection of the AS and AD curves determines the national price level and the level of output. In the labour market, the interaction of the labour supply and demand curves determines the wage rate and employment. We use this framework to examine the relationship between Ireland and the other countries in the Euro-zone (henceforth referred to as the "rest of EMU").

Starting from the point of full employment GNP, suppose there is an adverse demand-side shock that affects Ireland more than the rest of the EMU. An example would be a slump in the demand for computers. Other countries in EMU would not be similarly affected and hence the ECB would not feel it appropriate to relax monetary policy to offset the slump. Another example would be a depreciation of sterling on the foreign exchange market (the sterling/euro exchange rate rises). As shown in Figure 24.1, the Irish AD curve would shift down to the left and the economy would move from point A to B. There will be an initial fall in the level of output and a rise in unemployment. How would the Irish economy adjust?

Devaluation A devaluation of the sterling/euro exchange rate would restore Irish competitiveness and shift the AD curve back up to its original position. The economy would quickly return to the point A and there would be little or no cost in terms of lost output and employment. However, this is not something the Irish authorities can bring

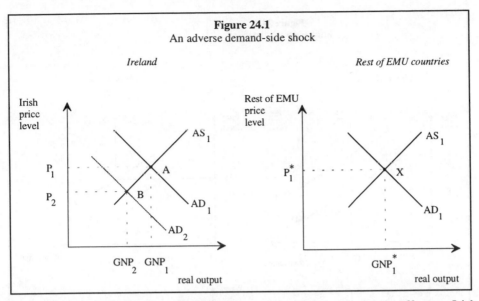

Figure 24.1
An adverse demand-side shock

Ireland   Rest of EMU countries

about. Because the fall of sterling would have a much greater adverse effect on Irish competitiveness than on that of the other EMU countries, the EMU would not see why the euro should be moved down against sterling. The ECB would not feel under any obligation to get Ireland out of its predicament.

PPP holds in the short run If purchasing power parity (PPP) holds, the fall in Irish prices relative to the rest of the world will improve domestic competitiveness for a fixed exchange rate. This will increase Irish exports and reduce imports. In Figure 24.1, the AD curve moves back to its original position and the output gap will be eliminated. The aggregate demand curve, in effect, adjusts to ensure price parity and output gaps will not persist. The costs in terms of lost output are again quite small. We reviewed the evidence relating to PPP theory in Chapter 18.

Automatic adjustment mechanism Even if PPP does not hold, there is an automatic adjustment mechanism (see Chapter 16) which will move the economy back towards equilibrium. Because of the appreciation *vis-à-vis* sterling, the Irish economy will suffer a balance of payments deficit. This will result in an outflow of money (euros) and the domestic money supply (M^s) will contract. This fall in the money supply will, via the quantity theory of money, result in a lower price level. The resulting improvement in competitiveness will eventually remove the balance of payments deficit and shift the AD

557

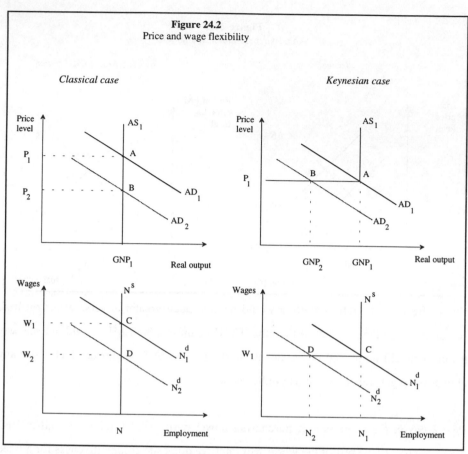

Figure 24.2
Price and wage flexibility

Classical case

Keynesian case

curve back up to the full employment level. This adjustment process will, however, take a considerable amount of time and the costs involved will be high.

Wage and price flexibility Assume once more that PPP does not hold in the short run. There is a second mechanism, which reinforces the automatic adjustment mechanism discussed above, in moving the economy back to equilibrium. Figure 24.2 illustrates two extreme classical and Keynesian outcomes. The two diagrams on the left depict the classical position where prices and wages are very flexible. In the goods market, the asymmetric shock shifts the AD curve down to the left and the price level immediately falls from P_1 to P_2. Equilibrium is re-established at the point B. In the labour market, the fall in the price level shifts the demand for labour curve downwards from N^d_1 to N^d_2. The resulting excess supply of labour causes the nominal wage fall from W_1 to W_2 and equilibrium is achieved at the point D. The fall in the price level and the nominal wage are exactly equal and, as a result, there is no change in the real wage. The overall outcome is that the initial fall in aggregate demand is offset by wage-price flexibility and output quickly returns to the full employment level.

Consider now the Keynesian case where prices and wages are assumed to be inflexible. Again the AD curve shifts down to the left. However, because the price level is rigid, the economy moves along the *horizontal* AS curve and equilibrium is established at the point B. An output gap (difference between actual GNP and full employment GNP) has now opened up. Similarly, in the labour market, because nominal wages are rigid, the economy moves along the horizontal labour supply schedule and equilibrium is established at the point D. Overall, because Irish prices and wages are inflexible, the fall in AD will cause an output gap to emerge and persist. The costs of the asymmetric shock are now very high.

It is clear from a comparison of the extreme classical and Keynesian cases that the cost associated with an adverse asymmetric shock depends on the degree of price and wage flexibility. The greater the degree of flexibility, the lower the cost in terms of lost output and employment, and vice versa.

The Keynes effect Even if prices and wages are inflexible, an output gap will not persist indefinitely. The process by which the economy reverts back to full employment GNP is known as the Keynes effect as it was first identified by J. M. Keynes in the *General Theory of Employment, Interest and Money*. Consider Figure 24.3 where the short-run AS and N^s schedules are upward sloping and the long-run schedules are vertical. Suppose, following the adverse shock, the economy is initially stuck at the point A in the goods market and X in the labour market. The rise in unemployment associated with the output gap will eventually put downward pressure on wages. This decline in wages will shift the AS schedule down from AS_1 to AS_2 and the N^s schedule from N^s_1 to N^s_2 and the economy will start to revert back to full employment GNP. Aggregate demand increases along the AD curve because the fall in the price level increases the real money supply (M^s/P) which, in turn, reduces interest rates (i). This fall in interest rates stimulates investment (I) and consumer spending (C) and aggregate demand rises. In short:

Unemployment $\rightarrow \downarrow W \rightarrow \downarrow P \rightarrow \uparrow (M^s/P) \rightarrow \downarrow i \rightarrow \uparrow$ I and C $\rightarrow \uparrow$ AD

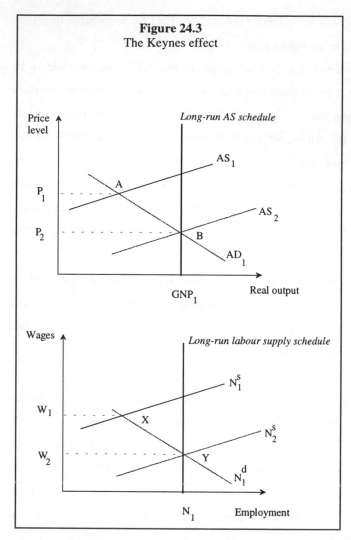

Figure 24.3
The Keynes effect

Note:

The fall in the price level will also improve competitiveness leading to an increase in net exports. This reinforces the interest rate effect described above.

Equilibrium will be achieved at the points C and Z where the output gap has been eliminated. However, this whole process could take some considerable time and the costs in terms of lost output and employment are likely to be high. Keynes, in fact, dismissed this effect as having little practical significance.

Factor mobility Faced with persistent unemployment it is likely that Irish emigration to Britain would increase – this happened on a very large scale in the 1950s and again in the 1980s. An expanding British economy could easily absorb additional Irish immigrants. Migration would help ease labour shortages in Britain and reduce unemployment in Ireland. This channel of adjustment entails personal and social costs for Ireland, however. In fact, politicians in any country have never welcomed large-scale emigration, but adopting a common currency implies accepting that it will become a more important component of the adjustment process.

The likelihood of shocks According to *optimum currency area* (OCA) theory, a currency union is more likely to be beneficial, and to endure, when there is a low risk of asymmetric shocks and when there is a high degree of price and wage flexibility. We now discuss these two issues in the context of Ireland's participation in EMU.

Some economists argue that the risk of an asymmetric shock within Europe is now minimal because the EU economies are highly integrated and structurally similar. A shock to one would be a shock to all. This reflects the growth in *inter*-industry rather than *intra*-industry trade. For example, car firms now produce the various components of cars in different countries and send them across national frontiers for final assembly (inter-industry trade). Countries have not become highly specialised in narrow branches of economic activity (intra-industry trade) but more diversified with increasingly similar industrial structures. A fall in the demand for cars would affect many European countries equally seriously.

However, this argument should not be pushed to the point of denying the possibility of future region-specific shocks. Europe experienced a major one in the early 1990s following the reunification of Germany. It is clear that a sudden strengthening of the sterling/euro exchange rate could have a very disproportionate effect on the Irish economy. Ireland experienced a massive asymmetric shock following sterling's departure from the ERM and subsequent depreciation in 1992. Our exposure to a second sterling crisis is the biggest risk of all as we join EMU without Britain. Furthermore, our heavy dependence on agriculture and a narrow range of industries such as electronic engineering, pharmaceuticals and telemarketing leave us open to further asymmetric shocks.

In the last analysis it is foolhardy to try to predict shocks – by their nature they are unforeseen and unpredictable. All we can predict with any confidence is that shocks will occur!

Price, wage flexibility and factor mobility Consider now the issue of price flexibility and factor mobility. One of the explanations commonly given for Europe's high unemployment is real wage resistance. There is little reason to believe that wage flexibility will increase dramatically following the adoption of a single currency. Although not as rigid as many continental labour markets, the Irish labour market, none the less, lacks the flexibility to avoid a serious rise in unemployment when faced with an asymmetric shock. This was demonstrated during the currency crisis of 1992-93. A three year national wage agreement was signed in 1996 (*Partnership 2000*) that contains no provisions for adjustments in the event of a shock following our entry to EMU.

With regard to factor mobility, the EU has made considerable progress towards establishing the free movement of the factors of production between the member states. However, it is still far from an integrated single market. Investment in Europe by American firms has been more important than the investment flows between European countries. Labour mobility is low by comparison with that between the regions of the United States.[6] Differences in language and culture, rigidities in housing markets and ethnic discrimination present significant barriers to the movement of labour between members states. The mobility of labour from Ireland to the UK and the US is much higher than it is within the EMU area.

Loss of fiscal autonomy

If Ireland experienced an adverse asymmetric shock, it could be compensated for rising unemployment by an increase in transfers and reduction in taxes from/to Brussels (or Frankfurt). Within federal political systems a process known as *fiscal federalism* helps regions to adjust to shocks. After an asymmetric shock the depressed regions pay less in taxes to the central government and receive more in transfer payments from it. Booming regions, on the other hand, pay more in taxes and receive less in transfer payments. These automatic stabilisers help soften the impact of regional-specific shocks.

Even the United States, with its relatively flexible labour markets and high mobility of capital and labour, relies on fiscal federalism to help dampen the effects of shocks on its regions. Similarly, in Ireland a region that suffers job losses and increased unemployment pays less in taxes and receives more in unemployment benefit and other transfer payments.

The EU is not such a federal political system. The EU budget is very small (less than 2 per cent of GDP) and there are no automatic mechanisms for transferring funds to areas that experience adverse shocks. The money paid from specific funds, notably

---

6. For evidence on this and other points discussed in this chapter, see Barry Eichengreen, "Is Europe an Optimum Currency Area?" in Borner and Grubel, eds, *The European Union after 1992: The View from Outside*, London: Macmillan, 1992.

FEOGA, the agricultural fund – does not increase in response to cyclical downturns. Nor is there any EU tax whose yield automatically falls during a recession.

The lack of automatic mechanisms for countering the effects of recessions on the regions raises a major question mark over the prospects for the success of EMU in Europe.[7] This problem could be aggravated by the operation of the proposed *Growth and Stability Pact* agreed in Dublin in December 1996. This pact obliges all participants in EMU to limit their fiscal deficits to an average of one per cent of GDP over the business cycle. If it were put into operation it could result in a *pro-cyclical* pattern of payments to the central authority rather than the *counter-cyclical* pattern that fiscal federalism ensures.

Loss of economic independence

Entry into EMU involves surrendering control over monetary and exchange rate policies. In addition, fiscal policy will be severely constrained by the stability pact. Collectively, this represents a serious loss of economic independence. A more fundamental point is that the design of EMU creates a particular type of economy in Europe. This will be a *laissez-faire* type economy, involving little bureaucracy and the minimum of policy intervention in the functioning of markets. It is based on the monetarist or neoclassical principle that, given flexible prices and wages, economies will converge to their natural rate of unemployment. Whether this type of system best suits the European economy remains to be seen.

The actual cost of surrendering monetary and exchange rate policies depends on the effectiveness of these instruments in a small open economy. Prior to EMU entry, the Irish pound was pegged to the DM within the EMS bands. This pegged or fixed exchange rate meant that Ireland could not control its money supply (see Chapter 20). In this regard, the cost of losing control over monetary policy does not seem particularly large. But what about the exchange rate? We now assess the importance of the exchange rate as a policy instrument.

---

7. Some "Eurosceptics" fear that the response will be to expand the EU's budget to include additional taxes and transfers – in other words, that EMU is inevitably a prelude to a federal Europe.

Effectiveness of the exchange rate   Generally, the exchange rate tends to be less effective as a policy instrument in open as opposed to closed economies.[8]   Therefore the costs of adopting a common currency are smaller. However, this depends crucially on the flexibility of wages and prices. It is normally the case that in a large, relatively closed economy such as the United States, devaluation increases the competitiveness of exporting sectors but has a relatively minor impact on the economy as a whole. In small open economies devaluation feeds quickly through to higher inflation and the effect on the real exchange rate tends to be quickly eroded.

Note:

Monetarists argue that the effectiveness of a devaluation depends on rigidities and money illusions that do not endure. Real adjustment requires reallocation of resources from declining industries to expanding ones. This will only be brought about by real measures such as the sectoral or regional migration of labour, education, and other supply-side interventions. Monetarists claim that these adjustments will not be achieved by a fall in the nominal exchange rate. On the other hand, the Keynesian position is that these lags and money illusions are significant and consequently the effects of devaluation can be long lived. On this issue there is no unanimity among economists, but there is evidence that in the absence of an exchange rate movement adjustment can be slow and incomplete.

However, the international evidence does not support the view that the exchange rate is an ineffective policy instrument. Belgium's commitment to a fixed exchange rate in the late 1970s led to an overvalued currency and high unemployment.[9] It has also been argued that France's commitment to the *franc fort* and maintaining a stable FF/DM exchange rate since the 1980s is part of the reason why its unemployment rate has risen to 12 per cent.

Looking further afield, failure to adjust the exchange rate was part of the reason for the Mexican crash of 1994-95 and the crisis in East Asia in 1997. It is difficult to ignore the evidence provided by these examples and to maintain that abandoning the exchange rate as a policy instrument will be virtually costless. Proponents of monetary

---

8. We reviewed the empirical evidence from the Irish economy relating to PPP theory and devaluation in Chapter 18. In the ESRI study of the implications of EMU for the Irish economy, empirical research showed that it takes prices three years and wages four years to adjust to a sterling devaluation. This would suggest that the adjustment costs are high when the economy relies on wage and price flexibility.

9. De Grauwe (Chapter 5) examines this case.

union tend to adopt an extreme monetarist position on this issue for which there is little empirical support.[10]

Our own experience during the currency crisis of 1992-93 demonstrates the difficulty of dealing with a shock (in this case the sudden depreciation of sterling) while trying to maintain a pegged exchange rate. The devaluations of 1983, 1986 and 1993 were all triggered by appreciation of the Irish pound against sterling caused by sterling's weakness against the DM. After the widening of the ERM bands in 1993, the Irish pound continued to track sterling closely.

It is clear that even after 18 years of trying to minimise it, the influence of sterling on the Irish economy remains very significant. In EMU we shall have relinquished the possibility of the type of adjustment that we regularly resorted to since the link with sterling was broken. Irish wages and prices will have to adjust to the value of the sterling/euro exchange rate which, in turn, will be set by the foreign exchange market.

Loss of unemployment/inflation trade-off

Another cost of adopting a common currency is that it prevents national governments from exploiting their short-run Phillips curves and attaining their preferred combination of inflation and unemployment. (The Phillips curve and the inflation-unemployment trade-off was discussed in Chapter 13.) Here we expand the discussion to consider two countries with different preferences concerning unemployment and inflation.

Assume there is a "hard-nosed" government in Germany that is very averse to inflation, and a "wet" government in Greece willing to tolerate higher inflation in exchange for lower unemployment. In Figure 24.4, both countries are initially at the natural rate of unemployment and experiencing 6 per cent inflation.

Germany, concerned about inflation, introduces a deflationary monetary policy and moves down the short-run Phillips curve from the point X to Y. As inflation expectations are revised downwards from 6 to 0 per cent, the short-run Phillips curve shifts down to the left and a new equilibrium is achieved at the point Z. At a cost of a temporary recession, Germany has succeeded in reducing its inflation rate.

---

10. It is ironic that Mrs Thatcher, an avowed monetarist, strongly believed that a country should have its national currency just as it had its national football team and its national anthem. On the other hand, the EU Commission takes a monetarist position on the currency question but inclines to Keynesian views on other macroeconomic issues.

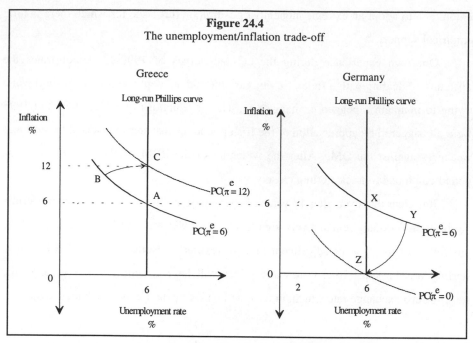

Figure 24.4
The unemployment/inflation trade-off

Greece, on the other hand, pursues a completely opposite policy. Concerned about unemployment, the government introduces an expansionary monetary policy and moves up the short-run Phillips curve from the point A to B. The fall in unemployment is, however, temporary. As inflation expectations are revised upwards, the Phillips curve shifts up to the right and a new equilibrium is established at the point C. Greece achieved a temporary reduction in unemployment but at a cost of a higher inflation rate.

The important point is that countries acting independently will arrive at different combinations of inflation and unemployment. PPP theory tells us that as a consequence of the high inflation in Greece there will be a steady depreciation of the drachma relative to the DM. This is indeed what has happened. In 1984, when Greece joined the EC (but not the EMS), the drachma/DM exchange rate was about 40:1; in 1997 it is about 160:1. High Greek inflation has inevitably led to a steady fall in the value of the drachma.

Adopting a common currency rules out this option. If Greece were to adopt the euro, the option of further depreciation would be removed. This would remove the scope for Greece to exploit the short-run Phillips curve to achieve any further temporary reduction in its unemployment rate. By adopting a common currency a country is therefore deprived of the opportunity of exploiting the short-run trade-off between inflation and unemployment.

But it may be questioned how serious a cost this is. In Germany's case, the new European Central Bank is expected to perform as well, if not better, than the Bundesbank in achieving low inflation. As long as inflation remains low in Europe, the cost to Germany of not being able to decide its own inflation/unemployment trade-off is small. Similarly, the costs may also be small for Greece. The monetarist view is that any reduction in unemployment achieved by higher inflation is very short term. In fact, it is now more widely believed that high inflation *raises* the natural rate of unemployment in the long run. Certainly the countries of Europe (such as Greece) that tolerated high inflation in the 1980s did not achieve any long-term reduction in their rate of unemployment. Surrendering a national currency and accepting the rate of inflation that follows in a monetary union may therefore entail no serious costs in terms of higher unemployment.

Loss of seigniorage

A final possible reason for wishing to retain a national currency is that governments differ in how they wish to apportion the revenue they raise between regular taxation and seigniorage (or the inflation tax).

Note:
In Box 9.1 in Chapter 9, seigniorage was explained as the process by which a government can reduce its liabilities by printing money. Briefly, money in circulation is a liability from the government's (central bank) point of view. If the government (working in conjunction with the central bank) prints money to finance its expenditure, this increases the money supply and, therefore, the inflation rate in the economy. However, an increase in inflation reduces the real value of money holdings. People who are holding money lose out while the government reduces the real value of its liabilities.

In the past, politicians in countries like Greece have relied to a greater extent on seigniorage than was the case in countries like Germany. If these two countries were to adopt a common currency they would experience a very similar rate of inflation and the inflation tax would therefore yield the same revenue in both. This could be politically difficult and an important cost for a country like Greece.

However, today the loss of seigniorage may no longer be a serious cost of adopting a common currency. The Maastricht convergence criteria were designed to ensure that the participants in EMU would achieve a uniform, low rate of inflation prior to the launch of EMU. The result is that inflation rates are now relatively low throughout the EU. Even in Greece inflation has fallen below 8 per cent, while in the rest of the EU it is generally below 3 per cent. The loss of seigniorage that a drop in inflation from 8 to 3 per cent would cause is not a serious cost and could be outweighed by the benefits of lower inflation.

24.5 Assessing the Benefits and Costs of EMU

The discussion in the previous sections suggests that it is not possible to say definitively whether a country will gain more than it will lose by adopting the euro. The best that economics can do is to set out the conditions under which the benefits are likely to be high relative to the costs.

However, in its study of the issue, the Economic and Social Research Institute did attempt to quantify the costs and benefits involved and concluded that on balance Ireland should join *even if the United Kingdom did not*. The effects on the Irish economy foreseen by the ESRI are shown in Table 24.1.

These estimates call for a number of comments. First, they refer to the *increase* in the country's growth rate due to participation in EMU. The total net effect on joining EMU in the absence of the UK is 0.4 per cent, and 1.4 per cent if the UK does go in. An increase of 0.4 or 1.4 per cent a year may seem slight, but when related to the long-run annual average growth rate of Irish GNP (approximately 3.5 per cent a year) it is very significant. An extra 0.4 per cent a year would mean the economy growing an extra 10 per cent over a 25 year period. If the "sterling in" scenario were realised, an extra 1.4 per cent per annum would amount to an extra 24 per cent after 25 years. Over the long run these potential gains are important.

Secondly, any quantified estimate of such a complex matter has to be treated with caution. The ESRI's estimates are derived from an econometric model that incorporates

Table 24.1

Benefits to Ireland of membership of EMU

The effect on the real growth rate (% per annum)

	Sterling Out	Sterling In
Gains from:		
Reduced transactions costs	0.1	0.1
Lower interest rates	1.7	1.7
Competitiveness	– 0.4	0.0
Risk of shocks	– 1.0	– 0.4
Net effect	0.4	1.4

Source: ESRI, *Economic Implications for Ireland of EMU*, Table 12.1, page 345.

a myriad of assumptions, all of which can be queried.[11] The end result is subject to a wide margin of error. The model used may include zero in the range of possible effects.

Thirdly, as we noted in Chapter 2, the Irish economy has recently been growing significantly above its long-run average growth rate, averaging over 5 per cent a year during the 1990s. Concerns have been voiced about "overheating" and the sustainability of this exceptional growth rate. It is not clear that any of the factors listed by the ESRI would increase the long-run growth potential of the economy. The biggest gain comes from a reduction in interest rates. At a sectoral level the biggest impact of this would be on the demand for houses. The construction sector is currently experiencing capacity constraints. Lower interest rates would exacerbate the risk of overheating.

Fourthly, the ESRI study lists the "risks of shocks" and a loss of competitiveness relative to sterling as the principal negative considerations. These are greater when sterling is not a member of EMU. The sectors most exposed to these risks are manufacturing sectors that export a considerable proportion of output to the UK (or compete with British firms on Irish and other markets). The study highlighted clothing, food processing and textiles as the most exposed. The potential loss of employment in these labour-intensive sectors is identified as the greatest risk attendant in Ireland's decision to participate in EMU. The evolution of the sterling/euro exchange rate will be the crucial factor for these sectors.

---

11. For a discussion of some of the estimates produced by the ESRI, see F. Barry, "The Dangers for Ireland of an EMU without the UK: Some Calibration Results", *Economic and Social Review,* 1997, Vol. 28, No. 4, pp 333-50 and the Comment in the January 1998 issue of the *Review.*

Faced with the difficulties of making a definitive judgment on the balance of costs and benefits, it has been argued that a more sensible strategy would have been to "wait and see". This is what Sweden, the UK and Denmark have decided to do. The case for postponing a decision to participate in EMU until after some initial uncertainties have been removed, and possibly until Britain declares its intention of joining, was very strong, but it was rejected. The strength of the Irish authorities' commitment to being in the first wave of members of EMU is based on political rather than economic factors. We hope that the economic costs of this political commitment will not be great.

24.6 Conclusion

In this chapter we have presented the case for and against the adoption of a common currency. Among the main benefits discussed were:

- Political benefits
- Economic benefits such as: reduced transaction costs, reduced risk, scale economies, low inflation and interest rates.
- The main costs discussed included:
- Transition costs
- Adjusting to economic shocks without the exchange rate as a policy instrument
- Acceptance of the ECB's preferences regarding the short-run inflation/unemployment trade-off.

We saw that certain preconditions make it less costly and more beneficial for a group of countries to share a common currency and relinquish the exchange rate as an instrument of economic policy. We discussed whether these preconditions were met in contemporary Europe and, in particular, whether it was wise for Ireland to be a founder member of the euro club. We concluded that it is not possible to arrive at a definitive verdict but that, as long as the United Kingdom is not a member, Irish membership entails very significant risks.

Index

credit guidelines, 193, 202

credit unions, 208, 210

CRH, 41

crowding-in, 173

crowding-out, 128–9, 232–4, 245–7

Culliton Report, 38

currency, 553–4

    forging, 181–2

    Irish development, 194–8

Currency Commission, 198, 200, 201

currency crisis, 1992-93, 360–62, 366–7, 387–92,
    467–70, 507–11, 565

    exchange rate policy after crisis, 513-15

current budget deficit, 146–7

cyclical unemployment, 10

debt accumulation, 136–8

debt crisis, 136, 170

deflation, 12, 283–6

    and EMU, 537–8

Delors Report, 393–4

Denmark, 2, 146, 366, 389, 517, 525, 569

    ERM crisis, 390

dependency culture, 318

depreciation, 85

depression, 5, 33

deregulation, 34

devaluation, 174, 503

    alternative to, 511–12

    crisis, 1992-93, 507–11

    effectiveness of, 470–71

    exchange rate policy, 484–6

    and trade balance, 486–8

diminishing returns, 29

discount rate, 193

disposable income, 99–107

dollarisation, 13–14, 358, 471, 536

Domar, Evsey, 136

Dornbusch, Rudiger, 73, 504–5, 532

double counting, 86–7

Doyle, Maurice, 393

Dublin Area Rapid Transit (DART), 143

Dublin inter-bank offer rate (DIBOR), 452

Dublin-Cork gas pipeline, 143

Duisenberg, Willem, 520

Dukes, Alan, 171

East Asia, 564

Eastern Europe, 165, 170

econometric theory, 52

Economic and Monetary Union (EMU), 126,
    174–5, 178, 274, 285, 382, 430, 532–4. *see*
    also euro

    alternatives to entry, 550

    assessing benefits and costs of, 568-70

    chronology of, 400–403

    countries in, 335n

    deflationary prospects, 537–8

    economic costs, 555–68

        adjusting to asymmetric shocks, 556-62

        loss of economic independence, 563-5

        loss of fiscal autonomy, 562–3

        loss of seigniorage, 567–8

        transition costs, 555–6

        unemployment/inflation trade-off, 565–7

    exchange rate policy, 534–6

    Ireland's future in, 513, 515, 549–70

        economic benefits, 552–5

        political benefits, 551–2

    monetary policy in, 527–32

    proposed, 391–2

    prospects for, 396–7

    role of ECB, 517–38

    run-up to, 392–6

Economic and Social Research Institute, 52, 165,
    305, 568–9

Economic Development, 159

economic planning

    1940s/1950s, 158–60

    1960s/1970s, 160–61

    1970s/1980s, 161–3

    1980s/1990s, 163–5